ENCYCLOPEDIA OF COMPUTER SCIENCE AND TECHNOLOGY

VOLUME 31

ENCYCLOPEDIA OF COMPUTER SCIENCE AND TECHNOLOGY

VOLUME 31
SUPPLEMENT 16

MARCEL DEKKER, INC.   NEW YORK • BASEL • HONG KONG

MARCEL DEKKER, INC.
270 Madison Avenue, New York, New York 10016

LIBRARY OF CONGRESS CATALOG CARD NUMBER: 74-29436
ISBN: 0-8247-2284-1

Current Printing (last digit)
10 9 8 7 6 5 4 3 2 1

PRINTED IN UNITED STATES OF AMERICA

CONTENTS OF VOLUME 31

CONTRIBUTORS TO VOLUME 31

SEBASTIAN ABECK, Ph.D. Senior Researcher, Department of Computer Science, Technical University of Munich, Munich, Germany: *Integrated Network Management*

IAN F. AKYILDIZ, Ph.D. Professor, Electrical and Computer Engineering, Georgia Institute of Technology, Atlanta, Georgia: *Gateway Performance Analysis*

PETER L. BARTLETT, Ph.D. Department of Systems Engineering, Research School of Information Sciences and Engineering, Australian National University, Canberra, Australia: *Computational Learning Theory*

BRAHIM CHAIB-DRAA Department of Computer Science, Laval University, Sainte-Foy, Québec, Canada: *Distributed Artificial Intelligence: An Overview*

KEVIN G. COLEMAN Management Consultant, National Consulting Group of CSC Consulting (a subsidiary of Computer Sciences Corporation), Waltham, Massachusetts: *Strategic Information Systems Planning*

D. VERA EDELSTEIN President, VeraQual Associates, Inc., New York, New York: *Software Engineering Standards*

MICHAEL D. GARRIS, Ph.D. Advanced Systems Division, National Institute of Standards and Technology, Gaithersburg, Maryland: *Design, Collection, and Analysis of Handwriting Sample Image Databases*

HEINZ-GERD HEGERING Professor, Department of Computer Science, University of Munich, Technical University of Munich, and Director, Leibniz Supercomputing Center, Munich, Germany: *Integrated Network Management*

STEPHEN H. KAN, Ph.D. Development Quality and Process Technology, IBM AS/400 Division, Rochester, Minnesota: *Software Quality Engineering Models*

ARTHUR M. LESK, Ph.D.   Department of Haematology, University of Cambridge Clinical School, MRC Centre, Cambridge, United Kingdom: *Computational Molecular Biology*

ROBERTO MAIOCCHI, Ph.D.   Pacific Data Images, Los Angeles, California: *Artistic Computer Graphics*

ROBERT J. MORRIS, Ph.D.   Professor of Economic and Social History, Edinburgh University, Edinburgh, Scotland: *History and Computing*

TAKASHI NAKAYAMA, Ph.D.   Associate Professor, Department of Information Science, Faculty of Science, Kanagawa University, Hiratsuka, Kanagawa, Japan: *Computer-Assisted Synthesis Planning*

WITOLD PEDRYCZ   Department of Electrical and Computer Engineering, University of Manitoba, Winnipeg, Canada: *Fuzzy Control and Fuzzy Systems*

EVAN C. RICKS   Vice President, ReZ.N8 Productions, Hollywood, California: *Artistic Computer Graphics*

MICHAEL A. SEEDS, Ph.D.   Astronomy Program, Franklin and Marshall College, Lancaster, Pennsylvania: *The Automation of Astronomical Telescopes*

BARRY G. SILVERMAN, Ph.D.   Institute of Artificial Intelligence, George Washington University, Washington, D.C.: *Expert Judgment, Human Error, and Intelligent Systems*

RENÉ WIES   Researcher, Department of Computer Science, University of Munich, Munich, Germany: *Integrated Network Management*

ENCYCLOPEDIA OF COMPUTER SCIENCE AND TECHNOLOGY

VOLUME 31

ARTISTIC COMPUTER GRAPHICS

COMPUTER GRAPHICS SYSTEMS FOR ARTISTS

Computer graphics is the creation, storage, and manipulation of models of objects and their pictures via computer. Computer graphics is the most important mechanized means of producing and reproducing images since the invention of photography and television, with the added advantage that it allows the representation of abstract synthetic objects. The applications of computer graphics range from data plotting in business, science, and technology, to cartography, design, simulation and animation, process control, and office automation. Ever since computers came into being, artists and designers have sought to use them to assist in their creative activities. To this end, the use of computing in the arts can be looked at from a number of points of view. Lansdown (1) suggested that computing can be seen as

- *A tool* in which the computer is used to help us to do things that could be done more laboriously or more slowly by hand
- *A medium* in the way that printing, oil painting, or lithography can be seen as a medium
- *A catalyst*, in other words, as a way of inspiring new creative approaches to art and design
- *An apprentice* as an assistant having enough intelligence to explore new possibilities and approaches when shown to do so

We can classify existing computer graphics systems for the computer artist as being one of four types, namely, paint systems, drafting systems, modeled systems, and user-programmed systems. In a *paint system*, the user has to make pictures in a way analogous to the ordinary process of normal drawing, by means of sketching and coloring. In a *drafting system*, a more formal technical drawing approach is required: drawings are usually assembled from instances of primitive objects (such as straight lines, arcs, rectangles, and circles) rather than sketched. In a *modeled system*, it is necessary to devise mathematical models of the items to be drawn and then ask the computer to give us views of these.

Although these three kinds of systems allow new types of imagery to be generated, the artist is somewhat at the mercy of the range of options provided by the system in use. Radically new types of imagery are possible if the artist is willing and able to program the system. With *user-programmed systems* one can create pictures either directly or indirectly to one's broad requirement or to fulfill one's aesthetic needs. With the dircet programming approach, the artist visualizes the picture he or she wants, then creates a set of algorithms and procedures to achieve it. On the other hand, the indirect programming approach implies devising the algorithms and procedures first, then seeing what pictures these can produce. Possibilities of exploring the computer as a creative partner are

1

opened up through more sophisticated programs, particularly if some approaches from artificial intelligence are adopted.

In the early stages of graphical computer art, it was primarily programmers and mathematicians who became involved in aesthetic experiments. One of the reasons was the fact that artists had little access to computer graphics systems, but there was another hurdle to be surmounted. Artists did not know how to program and were lacking the mathematical fundamentals that the first computer graphics scientists used as a base. The situation has since changed dramatically, and now an artist who is interested can find opportunities to work with a computer with graphical output. Hardware as well as software systems have been adapted for users who are not highly computer literate and these systems do not require special training. In many cases, it is possible to get acquainted with a particular system within a few hours, and the user can become familiar with the system after a few days of practice. For instance, with painting systems the user has merely to make selection decisions on the basis of a menu; after selecting the desired kind of command, color, and the like, he or she can draw directly on the screen with the light pen or on the lighting table with a cursor. It should not be overlooked, however, that compared to the formal mathematically oriented beginnings, an important element of artistic computer graphics is lost: the fact that a wealth of pictures is produced with the aid of mathematical and logical relationships that have not yet been seen by anybody and that increase our knowledge of forms and shapes considerably.

If we were to indicate some of the main reasons for using the computer in visual fine art, we would point out the increase in productivity, the exploration of new types of imagery, and the development of the computer as a more equal partner in the creative process. Computers are nowadays accessible, and they offer an artist the possibility of testing a range of ideas very rapidly within a given set of parameters. Images can be stored and retrieved almost instantaneously. This allows for the storing of an image when it is at a successful state, yet allows for further development of that source image. If a series of erroneous decisions is made during this further development, the initial stored successful image can be recalled, so that nothing has been lost physically. In addition, images can be easily transported using optical disks, floppy disks, or tapes. Finally, the structure of an image (its color, shape, size, location, density, etc.) can be manipulated in real time and certainly much faster than by any traditional physical means.

On the other hand, the artist can become obsessed, seduced, or hypnotized by the technology, and simply become an extension of it. Unless the artist is somewhat sure of the conceptual terrain to be explored, the information load can be overwhelming, especially if he or she is not sure of the purpose of using the computer. The computer generates so much information within a narrow set of parameters that it would be quite easy to stay within the narrow set of established parameters and, thus, grow neither artistically nor intellectually. In conclusion, the manner in which the artist approaches this challenging and exciting technology will determine whether the creative spirit is limited or enhanced.

INTRODUCING COMPUTERS IN THE VISUAL FINE ARTS

The use of the computer for artistic purposes is the last and decisive step toward technologizing the arts. Whereas, for instance, instruments have been used in music for a long time, their employment into the visual fine arts is much more recent. Worldwide interest in computer art was first aroused by Cybernetic Serendipity, an exhibition that took place in London in 1968. Everything that had until then appeared in the field of computer-aesthetic effort was brought together there, and all the pioneers of computer graphics were represented.

Computer graphics had become more generally known in 1965. Three mathematicians started at the same time to work systematically on the development of aesthetic computer graphics using digital computers: two Germans, Frieder Nake and Georg Ness, and the American Michael Noll. Mathematicians and scientists were aware of the graphic fascination of geometric shapes and curves derived from the observation of natural phenomena, and they first tried to use the computer for aesthetic experiments. In addition, they were among the very few who knew how to program and who had the mathematical fundamentals that were required to make the computer work. The discovery of beauty in fields outside traditional art implied an active engagement with aesthetic concepts and values. In fact, many images from mathematics and science were misinterpreted as art. An artist cannot just copy science and pass it off as art; an idea must be assimilated, understood, and transformed, otherwise, the result can be merely a bad simulacrum of science. Just using good design techniques and color selections does not automatically transform images into art.

Considering computer graphics' origins in engineering and its affiliation with science and industry, it should be no surprise that much of its imagery has evolved from the concerns of engineers, scientists, and industrialists. This also explains why computer imagery is often the visual result of either the process of problem solving or the illustration of a technique. It is, indeed, in the field of graphics and graphics design, and not in the more classical visual arts, in which the use of digital computers has achieved success. Computer graphics systems are widely and routinely used to produce slides for graphic presentation in the corporate world. The world of commercial television and advertising has increasingly turned to computer graphics, and the design of textiles and wallpaper is facilitated by computer graphics.

There is, in fact, a great difference between design and art; designers are essentially concerned with communicating ideas, whereas artists aim to generate meanings. So, if the computer has succeeded in becoming an essential tool for designers, it is in its use as a serious artistic medium in the visual arts that it has not yet achieved its anticipated potential. The lack of an adequate understanding of the characteristics of the tool as a medium for artistic creation explains the success of paint box programs, drawing programs, and illustration software. Through such programs, previous forms of artistic practice are maintained, though sometimes at a qualitative level far below that of traditional tools and media. The computer does not necessarily help the artist to bring out his or her art more freely; actually quite often what is produced on the computer can be generated more easily, quickly, and cheaply with a pencil or other traditional means. Too often images are celebrated and justified just because they are done with the computer, yet in the art world, technical criteria have traditionally been a secondary issue at best. Evidences of technical advances comprised a significant proportion of earlier computer art shows, with the improved revisions showing up each year. But whatever an artist can do using traditional means will not become more valuable once it is computer generated. It is in the realm of what was not possible before that one can see the assets of artistic involvement with technology.

The question arising from computer art is not the replacement of the conventional methods of artistic creation with electronics or a machine. Rather, it makes sense to use every possible means to extend the range of artistic expression. The art of every age has used the means of its time to give form to artistic innovation, but the demands of a new medium have to be understood in terms of previous forms of artistic expression before the medium can be freely utilized by the artist and properly appreciated by the viewer.

For instance, historians and critics proposed that early nineteenth-century photographers emulated painting style with the camera. In order to establish photography as a fine art, some artists started to exploit the camera for its unique qualities and create pure photographs that did not resemble painterly styles. Pure photography employs the camera for what it does best: capturing a slice of the real world from the personal viewpoint of the artist. Such an approach divorced photography from painting by 1920, and the artists' personal styles and photography's pure form of expression emerged.

Just as photography had to confront painting before it could take up a distinct space in the spectrum of the visual arts, computer pictures have to relate to photography, performance, painting, and sculpture before they can establish their own unique ground. Given the amazing evolution of computer technology in the last few years and the wide range of applications in which they have been employed, it is, in fact, quite difficult to define what pure computer art would be. What makes the computer unique as a tool for artistic purposes is not its computational power, but the fact that it is an uncommitted machine for which one can provide one's own definition.

Computer art is sometimes like *photography* in the sense that there is one original program which can produce pictures on any number of runs, as there is a photographic negative and many prints. But when a program incorporates randomness, the output of one run is so different from another that the minor variations of photographic prints are insignificant by comparison.

Perhaps computer art is better compared to *painting*, for in the case of painting there is one image whose copies are reproductions of little intrinsic value. Yet it would be hard to identify in computer art an equivalent of the unique artifact produced by the painter's brush. The image on the screen of the computer is not unique; it appears any time the program is run. In addition, the program is repeatable; that is, it can be copied and run on any other compatible computer. The speed of execution is another factor differentiating computer art from painting and from conventional forms of art in general. A program may generate dozens of images in a few minutes, whereas, for example, a painter, as prolific as he or she may be, needs several years to work on a theme.

Analogous to *sculpture*, computer imagery can represent objects in a three-dimensional world. But if traditional sculpture is subject to the laws of nature and to the characteristics of the material being employed, computer graphics allows the artist to create objects in a synthetic world in which such limitations are challenged. Furthermore, manual skills are no longer a precondition for engaging in sculpture. This eliminates that close connection between the creating hand and the material, which is considered to be so important by some artists. The act of artistic creativity shifts from the manual to those areas that can be described as cerebral.

Although still in its infancy, interactive computer art has close ties with the *happenings* of the early 1960s in its attempt to involve the audience. When participation becomes the subject of the aesthetic work, the viewer's critical faculties are given new responsibilities. The viewers are, indeed, no longer just judging the finished work of the artist; their own actions complete the piece. Thus, within the framework of the artist's exhibit, the participants also become creators. Given the integrative power of the technology and the possibilities to combine sound, movement, and images, environments can be conceived in which each participant can interact with the computer according to a whole network of unique possibilities.

By looking at which works of artistic significance have been produced so far, it is clear that the exploitation of the peculiar characteristics of the medium is the key to success. In fact, art does not reflect how powerful technology is, but how powerfully it serves the artist's artistic means. The need for the disappearance of the technology, for its invisibility, has to be put in the perspective of the why of art, as opposed to the how and even the what. In general, when the computer is visible, we are given an indication that the technology is not yet appropriately assimilated into the activity supported.

Often-cited successful computer artists include Harold Cohen, Myron Krueger, William Latham, John Pearson, Larry Cuba, and Yoichiro Kawaguchi, to mention a few. Their works are the result of a common fundamental premise: all of the artists have devoted a great deal of time and effort to learn how to use computers and have utilized concepts inherent in and inspired by computing. They have developed their own programs and methodologies so that the resulting images and environments they have created bear the stamp of the author. By learning a programming language, these artists had the chance of supplying the direction from their own work, rather than following the trends of the marketplace. Analogously to how musicians, writers, and filmmakers know the languages of their respective arts, so computer artists need to be aware of the concepts, methodologies, and consequences of computing.

New skills are then required of computer artists. The traditional romantic view of artists as illogical, intuitive, and impulsive, in contrast to that of programmers as constrained, logical, and precise, reflecting the separation between art and science in our society, needs to be overcome. Artists have to be programmers themselves so they need not depend on scientists to provide the software tools that realize these aesthetics needs; the essence of computer art should be a balance of psyche and technical, of right- and left-brain expressions.

In this view, computer art does not merely encourage the bringing together of the two cultures—the technical and the artistic—but also promotes the investigation of general processes of cognition. For instance, one can start wondering whether the concepts of beauty and creativity can be programmed. Beauty is a very ill-defined notion involving qualities such as learning, emotional responses, memory, and a sense of self. Many features of human intellectual behavior have now been successfully emulated by means of programs, mainly modeling rational aspects of our minds. Achievements in game playing, natural language understanding, and problem solving are the striking evidence that computers can be programmed to show a certain degree of intelligence. We are, thus, tempted to believe that once some significant features involved in art perception and creation have been formalized, we could have computers developing original thoughts and works of art.

But there appears to be at least one major difference between, for instance, playing chess and making art. When we are playing chess, we have a clear and unambiguous criterion by which to assess strategies: the good strategies win and the poor ones lose. By contrast, and even though we suspect the existence of artists' goals, we generally suppose that art making is goal-directed in the same sense that game playing is and, consequently, the notions of winning and losing cannot provide performance criteria. Indeed, there would be a problem even if we chose to consider art making as goal-oriented. What would we want a program to generate? Lines, shapes, colors? A work of art is more than just the sum of its formal parts.

A program involved in making art needs to emulate the full range of actions of a human intelligence and a human cognitive system, not merely simulate the output of an intelligence and a cognitive system. Programmers of such amazing programs must specify something similar to the symbols in our brain and their triggering patterns, which are responsible for the creation of works of art. And who should get credit when a program comes up with an idea that has not been explicitly implemented in the code? The human will certainly get credit for having invented the program but not for having had the ideas produced by the program inside his or her own head. In such cases, the human can be referred to as the "meta-author"—that is, the author of the author of the result—and the program as the author.

The same problem of authorship and of the definition of the role of the artist arises when the interactive and dynamic potential of the computer is exploited by the artist. Whereas static images do not relate to the individual viewer, the potential for the computer to sense the viewer's state of being and change the imagery accordingly has started to be explored with the so-called virtual reality environments. Virtual reality is a type of interactive simulation that allows the participant to be inside an artificial environment. In the most well-known scenarios, the effect of being there can be achieved by wearing a headset that displays the synthetic environment through tiny TVs (one for each eye) and that provides sound cues. Hand motion is tracked via a data glove. Real hand motions trigger actions in the virtual space; virtual objects may be handled, or a pointing finger can be used to propel oneself about. More sophisticated environments allow the viewer to go into the virtual reality and meet other people and have interactions with them. The amazing aspect of virtual reality environments is that not only does the computerized world become like another reality, but at the same time it offers an infinity of possibilities that we do not have in the physical world. For instance, in the physical world one cannot suddenly turn a building into a flower—it's just impossible—but in the virtual world one can.

Regarding the issue of authorship, in virtual reality environments the notion of viewers is replaced with that of participant, and the author/consumer dichotomy with a model of collaborative co-creation. The collaborative model suggests that what is designed is a dynamic environment with predispositions and potentialities, and an essential element in the authorship of experience is a dynamic participant who changes the world by being in it.

In conclusion, the use of the computer for artistic purposes brings various issues to the foreground, including the definition of a computer graphics aesthetics, the relationship with traditional art forms, the role of the computer artist, and the exploration of new artistic expressions. Within such a context, in searching for significant computer art we should ask whether the artwork could have been made without the use of a computer and whether it takes advantage of the unique new capabilities made possible by computers.

OFF-THE-SHELF COMPUTER SYSTEMS FOR ARTISTS

As well discussed in the Introduction, there are three kinds of the off-the-shelf computer systems for the artist: paint systems, drafting systems, and modeled systems. Each system implies a different approach to the production of images. In the case of paint systems, an artist needs to describe the appearance of the image itself directly to the computer. A model of the image to be represented exists in the head of the creator and an attempt is made to reproduce it externally. The information about the drawing in a paint system is held by the computer simply as a collection of pixels; the machine has no understanding of what real-life entities these pixels represent.

In the case of drafting systems, the model of what has to be depicted also resides in the user's head, but a small part of it is transferred to the computer so that the machine is able to know something of the structure of the things it is asked to represent. For example, in making an architect's drawing, a drafting system would allow the user to group information together about external walls, doors, or windows, enabling these to be manipulated, erased, or given different or like styles as a whole. In the modeled system approach, the computer is given detailed models of the objects that it is to be asked to represent. Especially where 3D objects are involved, these models not only cover the geometry of the objects but also details of texture, material composition, and so on. In addition, models incorporating lighting and shading might be involved. The effect of including these models is to enable the computer itself to produce the images. If the object to be depicted is three-dimensional, a representation of it on a modeled system is simply a computer rendering of one particular view; on the other hand, each new view of an object or a paint system requires the use of to manually redraw the scene.

In summary, the modes of the actual objects that have to be depicted in both point and drafting systems exist in the minds of the users and it is up to them to make sure that they translate these into two-dimensional images in an unambiguous way. This is exactly what they have to do in the pencil and paper case. In a modeled graphic system, on the other hand, it is expected that the users provide the computer with mathematical models of the objects they wish to depict and that the system itself produces the desired views. This is quite a different approach and it affords a range of possibilities that straightforward drawing cannot emulate. Modeled systems diminish the need for high-quality unusual drawing skills, although visual literacy and artistic imagination are still essential.

Whereas drafting systems and modeled systems have been used mainly for design purposes, paint systems have been largely employed by computer artists in the creation of their art. This is probably due to the fact that paint systems do not require a high computer literacy to be used and that they are the closest to the traditional approach to making images. For this reason, in this section we will focus on the description of the main features provided by the paint systems available on the market.

Paint Systems (by Evan C. Ricks)

Paint systems can be defined as a combination of software and hardware used as a visual medium, with an emphasis on the analogue of traditional painting with brush, palette, and support. Such a definition can be broadly embellished and, in fact, such is the case with the many existing variations. The word *system* is used here to indicate that in at least some cases the hardware is dedicated. The interactive input (brush) is through a pointing device, usually either a mouse or a pen/tablet, with the latter being preferred for its more expressive nature and pressure sensitivity. Administrative and auxiliary input is usually through a keyboard. Interactive output (support) is by color monitor(s) of various resolutions.

The application of color (paint) to pixels on the screen in an interactive manner is the primary directive of any paint system. The bit depth of the frame buffer should be sufficient to represent blended colors, although this is not always the case in less sophisticated systems. To be useful there must be a way to store and retrieve works; therefore, if we adhere to the above definition, a minimal paint system consists of a computational section, archival storage, input device, frame buffer, output device, and program. This assemblage of items also describes almost any computer. This discussion will, therefore, focus on the unique attribute, the paint program.

Graphics systems have been around since the early 1960s in various forms. The first was the famous "sketchpad" system of Ivan Sutherland. In this system, a light pen was used to interactively draw shapes on the screen. These shapes were very geometric and were of one color only. Although sketchpad almost fit the definition of a paint system, it lacked any brushlike capability. It was, in fact, more the root of the computer graphic tree, which happened to work more like modern drawing programs than modern painting programs.

It was not until the 1970s that full-color frame buffers and computers fast enough to change hundreds of pixels during a frame update became available. The first systems would interactively place various sized circles on the screen in the chosen color. This would allow a stroke to be made, although with rough edges. Any new placement of color simply overwrote what was previously there.

Following the advice of graphic designers who saw potential in these crude devices, improvements such as a matte were added. One of the challenges became to make a stroke similar to an airbrush. This was accompanied by the use of special-purpose hardware that allowed for smooth application and blending of colors.

It is difficult, if not impossible, to categorize computer art under the heading of any other art form. It is equally hard to place paint systems within any other media sphere. They are unique and are becoming accepted as such. Due to their developmental roots from outside traditional fine art, the first to use and accept paint systems were programmers and experimental video artists. These artists simply had an exciting new medium. The first stand-alone systems were developed for the video industry. Paint systems could be used to quickly create a beautiful graphic for television promotions or show openings. This is still the case. The popularity of paint and type layout programs on personal computers is also currently revamping the print industry.

The addition of the computer into the realm of art creation gives rise to an expansive range of input filtering. At the lower end of this spectrum is a simple translation of input device x, y motion to cursor motion on the screen. At the other end is the abstracted stroke, which together with pressure and acceleration, can be used to more sensitivity control a stroke or effect. Unlike the experienced oil painter who was taken years to learn to use subtle brush techniques and materials to master an effect, the electronic artist has the opportunity of using a higher-level tool, one more forgiving. Only those characteristics the artist chooses are utilized or modified. Watercolor and charcoal become different settings in the world of stroke, pressure, color, texture, and the like. A multidimensional media space exists in which the artist can freely wander.

Most paint programs now used consist of dozens of features with countless variations representing thousands of lines of code. Fortunately, these systems have existed long enough for a common structure to have evolved that can more easily be described. One of the more important considerations in the design of a good paint system is that it be efficient to use. For this reason most systems allow all user input to come from the same input device as is used for painting. Another point of efficiency is in the quick selection of brush stroke type, color, size, density, and so forth. These parameters are frequently modified. As the image itself is viewed on the color monitor, how does one modify those parameters? Several solutions have been found to be useful. You can choose to use the entire screen to paint on while the parameters are modifiable on a separate monitor. On a one-monitor system, the parameters can be either toggled off and on as an overlay or placed at the periphery. Most systems have some sort of menu for the many selections and modes.

One can divide the functionality of the common paint system, both dedicated and stand-alone program, into basic sections, which might exist as menus, sections of the screen, or separate modules:

Canvas. This is a common name for the screen representation of the image. On those systems dedicated to video, the canvas resolution is often fixed. Most systems allow for the specification of an image of arbitrary size. Tools for zooming and panning are provided. This is especially necessary when the image is specified larger than the canvas. Multiple images may reside in memory simultaneously for convenience. In addition to the color channels (usually red, green, and blue; RGB), another channel called alpha becomes part of the image and may be stored with it or as a separate entity. The alpha channel is written at the same time as the RGB is modified and indicates opacity. A new image, therefore, starts off with the alpha channel zeroed. If a visible stroke is applied, the alpha channel is modified at the same time. This becomes useful for matting this painted image over another with correct blended edges. Another channel is the matte. The graphic art analog for this channel is the frisket, used to protect parts of the image not needing modification for the current operation. Finally, the canvas usually has optional overlays such as grids and rulers for alignments and measures.

File input/output. This is for the reading and writing of image files. Due to the large size of most images, some form of compression is often used. Most systems read and write several types of image formats. Different vendors all have their preferred formats. On many systems a browse mode is offered to visually select from a page of reduced images.

Brush type. As it defines the type of mark or stroke one leaves on the canvas, the brush type is one of the most important aspects of any paint system. Round and square are commonly used to make hard-edged marks, whereas the airbrush is designed to behave like its namesake. The size of the brush may be either chosen from a predefined list or variably scale. Other types may be chalk, charcoal, or pastel. The list may be quite extensive. In addition to these rather static shapes may be the ability to change the brush in size or quality during a stroke. This topic is of interest to many researchers and has vast potential.

Color selection. Most systems offer the choice of many different color selection modes. For selecting a starting palette there is usually some kind of slider system arranged around one or many color spaces, the most common being red–green–blue and hue–saturation–value. One is readily converted to the other, so both of these are usually offered. Cyan–magenta–yellow is commonly found in print-oriented systems. A color may be deposited in a square repository for future use or immediately used on the canvas. There may also be a special canvas in which color can be mixed so an entire range is saved for use. Also, there are often special blending bars used by placing a color at either end. The program then creates a smooth gradation between the two.

Graphics. A graphics section includes tools for creating geometric shapes and typography. Rectangles and ellipses that are outlines, filled, or both, seem a minimal requirement. Filling these shapes, or indeed any shape, is standard in a paint system. The filling can be solid or graded, of the same quality as the brush type, and fill a shape defined by color, matte, color gradient, and the like. Line segments, connected lines, and curves are also found in the graphics section. These may also have the various parameters found above. Most systems have some level of typographic support. Some are very complete although this is more the domain of graphic layout. The ability to cut a section of the canvas and paste it in another place in the same or another canvas is a very useful capability. This is where the alpha channel is very handy. When pasted back in place, the matting is handled correctly.

Image processing. The more sophisticated systems may have integrated image processing to offer simulations of effects usually seen only in specific media. These include watercolor blending, oil brush effects, oil impasto, and pointillism. The most interesting of the effects are often those never before seen in any other medium.

With the current generation of paint systems, the artist has tools for almost any problem. The advancements needed are not only those that add capability in terms of effects but those that add more range at the front and back of the procress. Unless the image is to be used only digitally, it is output in some fashion, often to print. Output devices currently have trouble creating heavy textural effects or translucent qualities found in other media.

Because this medium is essentially virtual, there is always room to increase the interactive control evidenced in other media. This control derives from the unlimited variety in the real world, which must then be modeled digitally. To have as a goal the replication of reality is a dubious one. However, hundreds of years of experimentation with wet media have yielded a certain amount of common wisdom regarding technique.

A paint system, like any software, is endlessly upgradable in terms of capability and user-friendliness. This is perhaps its greatest advantage over other visual media. The enhancements come not from the experience of one master, but are distilled from hundreds of artists and researchers. The paint system is above all just another way to create an image.

USER-PROGRAMMED SYSTEMS

In the Introduction we distinguished between direct and indirect user-programmed systems. These two approaches are quite different, both in their conception and in their outcomes. In the first case, artists are using the computer as a tool to make drawings that might be difficult or tedious to produce otherwise. In the second case, the computer is more or less an intelligent apprentice that helps the artist conceive and execute an idea; the focus is not just on the result but also on the processes employed to get it. In practice, artists often use a combination of these two approaches, with the indirect technique favored by those who like to create families of related pictures. In either case, one needs to create programs that produce drawings from instructions rather than from the types of actions that are used in paint systems.

In this section we review some of the main techniques used by computer artists to create new types of imagery that we classify in mathematics-based generative techniques and artificial intelligence techniques. An extensive discussion of such techniques can be found in the works of Lansdown (2) and Maiocchi (3), respectively.

Mathematics-Based Generative Techniques

Mathematically conceived figuration is relatively accessible to mechanized production. Such forms are exceedingly ancient; among them are the ornaments whose geometric slopes, repetitions, and symmetry follow rules that can be mathematically formulated. Other milestones in the evolution toward the mathematization of art are all attempts to express aesthetic structures in mathematical form. Considerations of this kind led the Greeks to find a theory of harmony; in the plastic arts, Leonard da Vinci, Leon Battista Alberti, and Albrecht Dürer were pioneers of similar efforts, and the line leads through Piet Mondrian, le Corbusier, and Victor Vasarely to the adherents of exact aesthetics. The constructivists and the members of the Stijl movement used relatively simple mathematical relations such as proportions; gradually other rules were introduced, like those of permutation. The aim of many supporters of constructivist tendencies—a rejection of the personal element, a crystal-clear objective presentation, the maximum precision—can be realized by the computer to a hitherto unparalleled degree. A further essential advantage is, of course, the considerable saving of time afforded by the machine.

But the computer does not merely lead to a reduction of labor; it also opens up entirely new prospects. Mathematical curves of a higher order are for many reasons aesthetically more pleasing than straight lines and circles which the constructivists realized with rulers and compasses (i.e., with the aid of tools) and which they frequently used in their work as pictorial elements. Single curves of a higher order can be drawn by hand with certain effort, but it is practically impossible to combine many different, perhaps successively modified curves to complex formations. It is only through this kind of co-ordination, superimposition, or symmetrical relation that we obtain that wealth of coordinated relations that are the starting points of the perceptual processes.

Perhaps the oldest form of generative technique in computer graphics is that of directly plotting two-dimensional mathematical functions such as combinations of the circular functions, sine and cosine, with progressively changing values of parameters. Indeed, long before computers existed, mechanical devices were frequently used to make drawings of a similar sort. For instance, in 1857 the French mathematician Jules-Antoine Lissajous studied the types of curves that could be drawn by a swinging pendulum that dripped a line of fine sand as it swung. Curves defined by the formulas

$$x = a* \sin(m*A + b), \qquad y = c* \sin(n*A + d)$$

with varying values of A, a, b, c, and d are now known as Lissajous figures in his honor (Fig. 1). Because of its long history we would call direct plotting of two-dimensional mathematical functions the classical technique. Its employment often gives rise to reasonably interesting images, especially when some imagination is applied to the choice of functions and values of parameters. But the fact that drawing of the Lissajous form can be so easily produced as well as our overfamiliarity with the type of imagery generated has reduced its popularity in computer art.

A variation on the classical technique is when the function, often a point function, used is not plotted directly, but is in some sense interpreted, and the result of the interpretation is plotted. The interpretation can be as simple as a change of color in a point plot, the color depending on the absolute position, the value of the function, or a simple count of points plotted. These methods are really mappings of three-dimensional functions into two dimensions of geometrical space and one of color space.

A whole new family of generative techniques arises when two-dimensional recursive functions are employed. In these, successive values of X and Y are calculated from previous values. Thus, these functions are of the generic form

FIGURE 1 A Lissajous figure (2). Reprinted with permission of the publisher.

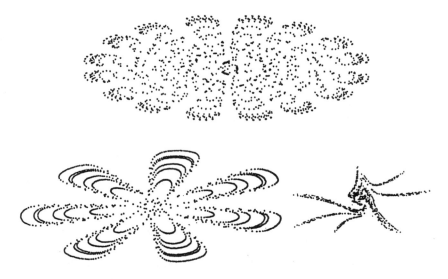

FIGURE 2 Three versions of a Gumowski function (2). Reprinted with permission of the publisher.

$$X_{n+1} = f(X_n, Y_n), \qquad Y_{n+1} = g(X_n, Y_n).$$

Gumowsky and Mira (4) proposed a pair of functions

$$X_{n+1} = h(Y_n) + f(X_n), \qquad Y_{n+1} = -X_n + f(X_{n+1}),$$

where

$$f(X) = c*X + 2*X^2 *(1 - c)/(1 + x^2), \qquad h(Y) = d*(1 + a + b*y^2)*y.$$

In these formulas, *d* acts somewhat is a scaling factor, and by varying the value of this and the other parameters *a*, *b*, and *c*, great differences in the output can result (Fig. 2). Just as the classical functions producing Lissajous figures describe the action of some physical occurrence such as the path traced by a compound swinging pendulum, so the recursive functions that give rise to this type of picture often describe the action of a physical phenomenon such as turbulence in water and air.

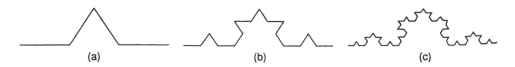

FIGURE 3   Construction of the von Koch snowflake (43). Reprinted with permission of the publisher.

A growing body of theory is developing to explain and simplify the physics and mathematics involved, going under the name of *chaos theory*. There are many phenomena that, to all appearances are quite chaotic, but that actually have an underlying basis of fairly simple mathematics that can sometimes be expressed in terms of Mandelbrot's theory of *fractals* (5,6). Their basic idea derives from the same source as the so-called monster or dragon curves created by mathematicians of the late nineteenth and early twentieth century. Two-dimensional monster curves were invented by these pioneers to illustrate special mathematical principles such as recursion and self-similarity, in which parts of the curve exactly resemble other parts but to a smaller scale. As an example of the concept of self-similarity we will consider the von Koch snowflake of Figure 3 and the process of generating it. Starting with a line segment with a bump on it, we replace each segment of the line by a figure exactly like the original line. If this process is repeated infinitely, the result is said to be *self-similar*: the entire object is similar (i.e., can be translated, rotated, and scaled) to a subportion of itself.

The work was done by these pioneering mathematicians in the belief that they were creating shapes of an entirely artificial nature having nothing whatever to do with the real world, in which Euclidean geometry held sway. Mandelbrot's major contribution was to show that far from having a counterpart in the physical world, the principle of proportional self-similarity embodied in these shapes was absolutely at the heart of the formation of all sorts of natural objects: trees, leaves, coastlines, mountains, and much more. The natural geometry, therefore, was not Euclidean but fractal. Because of this insight, the use of fractals is now universal in making images of such objects, and Mandelbrot's idea is used in most new algorithms for modeling natural forms, although sometimes in ways that do not strictly conform to his rigorous mathematical definition of fractal.

The two most famous fractal objects deserve mention here: the Julia–Fatou set and the Mandelbrot set. These objects are generated from the study of the rule $X \rightarrow X^2 + c$. There X is a complex number, $x = a + b*i$. If a complex number has modulus < 1, then squaring it repeatedly makes it go toward zero. If it has modulus > 1, repeated squaring makes it grow larger and larger. Numbers with modulus 1 still have modulus 1 after repeated squarings. Thus, some complex numbers fall toward zero when they are repeatedly squared, some fall toward infinity, and some do neither, this last group forming the boundary between the numbers attracted to zero and those attracted to infinity.

Suppose we repeatedly apply the mapping $X \rightarrow X^2 + c$ to each complex number X for some nonzero value of c, such as $c = -0.12375 + 0.056805*i$; some complex numbers will be attracted to infinity, some will be attracted to finite numbers, and some will go toward neither. Drawing the set of points that go toward neither, we get the Julia–Fatou set shown in Figure 4a. With an analogous process we can draw the Julia–Fatou set for $c = -0.012 + 0.74*i$ (Fig. 4b). Note that the region in Figure 4b is not as well connected as is that in Figure 4a. The shape of the Julia–Fatou set evidently depends on

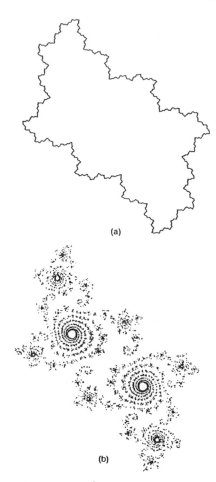

FIGURE 4   Examples of Julia–Fatou sets (43). Reprinted with permission of the publisher.

the value of the number c. If we compute the Julia sets for all possible values of c and color point c black when the Julia–Fatou set is connected and white when it is not, we get the object shown in Figure 5, which is known as the Mandelbrot set. Note that the Mandelbrot set is self-similar in that around the edge of the large disk in the set there are several smaller sets, each looking a great deal like the large one scaled down. Mandelbrot's two books (7,8), an article by Fournier, Fussel, and Carpenter (9), an excellent exposition by Voss (10), and a beautiful book by Peitgen and Richter (11) are among the prime sources for the graphical work on fractals. The latter book also gives explicit directions for generating many spectacular images on Mandelbrot and Julia–Fatou sets.

Artificial Intelligence

Computer art represents an historical breakthrough in computer applications. For the first time, computers have become involved in an activity that had previously been exclusive to the domain of humans: the act of creation. Since the mid sixties, the computer has been largely used as a tool for producing art, and programs have been written to assist artists perform various tasks during the process of making art. The question arises, "Can

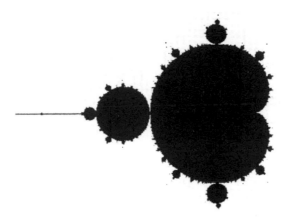

FIGURE 5   The Mandelbrot set (43). Reprinted with permission of the publisher.

computers themselves be creative?'' The short answer is no. But this answer does not do justice to the situation. If we reword the question to "Can properly programmed computers themselves produce works that simulate those made be creative people?'' then the answer must surely be yes. In order to properly program them, however, we must have, and computers must be given, a model of creativity.

The employment of random number generators has been the first technique used with the purpose of generating many different images from one program, introducing change with the selection of certain parameters to define, for instance, location, type, or size of a graphic element. Random numbers served to break the predictability of the computer, but simulated creativity is a very limited way. Random numbers have also been used in relation to aesthetic rules derived from an analysis of traditional paintings.

For example, the mathematician and computer scientist Michael Noll took a Mondrian painting, *Composition with Lines*, an abstract, geometric study with seemingly random elements, and from it he extracted some statistics concerning the patterns (12). Given those statistics, he programmed the computer to generate numerous pseudo-Mondrian paintings having the same or different values of these randomness-governing parameters (Fig. 6). He then showed the results to naive viewers. The reactions were interesting in that more people preferred one of the pseudo-Mondrians (Fig. 6a) to the genuine Mondrian (Fig. 6b).

This quite amusing fact proves that a computer can certainly be programmed to imitate mathematically capturable stylistic aspects of a given work. Randomness is actually an indispensable ingredient of creative acts, but human creativity does not simply rely on such arbitrary sources. The essence of any artistic act is not just a selection of particular values of certain parameters; rather it is in the balancing of a myriad of intangible and mostly unconscious mental forces, a judgmental act that results in many conceptual choices that eventually add up to a measurable work of art. What is important is the making of a work of art and not just the object itself.

Regarding works of art as models created by artists to represent chosen aspects of the real world, in a simplified and selective manner, the implementation of an autonomous program producing art implies the investigation of the cognitive process of representation of the artist, the understanding of his or her model, and the simulation of the artist's representational acts. In other words, an autonomous art-making program has to

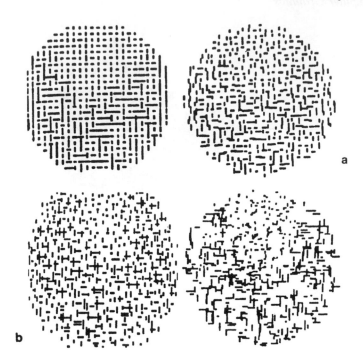

FIGURE 6   One genuine Mondrian and three computer imitations (44). Reprinted with permission of the publisher.

exercise something very like "human intelligence." Research in artificial intelligence (AI) has been founded on the dogma that "mental activities are information processing," (13) more specifically that the manipulation of symbols (representational data structures) by suitable computer programs is no more and no less than what minds do. Many features of human behavior have now been successfully emulated by means of programs, mainly modeling rational aspects of our minds. Achievements in game playing, natural language understanding, and problem solving are the striking evidence that computers can be programmed to emulate thinking. But much of our conscious intellectual life is based on intuitions and emotions that are less appropriately considered under a logical regimen, and AI and disciplines such as cognitive psychology have actually begun to increasingly overlap in the attempt to bridge the gap of the rational/emotional dichotomy.

   Because art making and viewing are processes in which typically rational and mechanical aspects interact with aesthetic and cognitive criteria, adopting the AI paradigm to the study of such processes seems particularly appropriate. There are two areas in which AI techniques have been applied in dealing with art: perception and creation. *Perception* is concerned with the experience resulting from the confrontation with an object or a scene. Perceptive machines maintain a description of the object in its structural terms (e.g., its geometry) and a description of its aesthetic relevance. *Creation* is concerned with the representation of the intentions, intuitions, and skills of an artist. Perceptual and generative processes are actually linked in that they both look at the syntactic and semantic qualities of a work of art. *Syntactic properties* reside unambiguously inside the object under consideration. Examples of syntactic properties of art are the chord sequence of a piece of music, or some geometric patterns of an abstract painting. Syntactic properties are localizable on the surface level of a piece, and, once defined, are easily described through a computer program. On the other hand, *semantic properties* depend on some sort of inner meaning housed in the piece itself and raise mental mechanisms that cannot be consciously described. Different levels of interpretation can be established in every person, depending on the circumstances that pull out different meanings, provoke different connections with previously memorized experiences, and generally evaluate all deep aspects differently.

So far in the artistic computer graphics literature several successful perceptive machines have been developed in the attempt to give a description of an art object in its structural terms; conversely, very few knowledgeable machines concerned with the representation of the intentions and intuitions of an artist have been presented. For computers to act as humans, models of perception, memory, learning, and other mental categories are required. In addition, both to understand and produce aesthetic objects one has to take into account the cultural environment in which the artwork is produced and how the artist is influenced by it, the intended meaning of the piece of art, and the definition of new forms of aesthetics. The issues raised by the research on AI and art are broad and deep, and the need for new programs involving art and science is evident.(14)

The most successful and actually unique example of a creative machine has been proposed by Harold Cohen with his AARON, a knowledge-based program designed to investigate the cognitive principles underlying visual representation. Under continuous development for 15 years, AARON is now able to make "freehand" drawings of people in gardenlike settings (15). Cohen's work will be presented in the next section of this article. The remainder of this subsection is dedicated to a brief overview of some relevant studies on art perception and understanding that look mainly at the syntactic properties of works of art.

Arrangements and Deformations

In the West, making abstract drawings by means of pattern repetition has not traditionally been thought of as art; craft, perhaps, but not art. This is in contrast to the East, particularly the Near East and India, where pattern making has always been looked on with as much favor as any other form of picture creation. Recently, however, both artists and designers have begun to change their attitude toward pattern as an art form. From early on, computer artists have developed pattern-making concepts. In particular, many have explored the potential of devising and repetitively manipulating modules (i.e., similar small elements that are repeated in various transformations all over a drawing). Sometimes the transformations are just the rigid geometrical ones of translation, mirroring, and rotation, or they might comprise changes, and perhaps distortions of all sorts combined with these. The repeated modules can be either separated or overlapping; if the latter, new emergent forms often arise, adding extra visual interest and complexity. Indeed, it might be considered that it is the appearance of these emergent forms, otherwise unlikely to have been produced, that is the greatest justification for this approach to picture making.

Governing the process of laying out the modules might be permutations (i.e., the systematic transformation in every possible order) or else straightforward arrangement. The elements might be placed randomly or deterministically according to some rule, both methods being eminently suitable for computer work. As discussed earlier, however, it should be noted that the initial attractive possibilities of randomness soon pall; some order is needed for us to make real sense of what we see, and the best computer pictures rarely display unconstrained randomness.

Undoubtedly one of the best proponents of the group of artists exploring the possibilities given by modification and arrangement is Manfred Mohr, who has produced all his artwork by the application of systematic rules and with the assistance of computer plotting. His preoccupation has mainly been with making paintings and sculptures from computer-generated perspective views of a cube that has been cut into sections which are rotated independently of one another to form something like a collage. An extensive review of Mohr's work will be given in the next section of this article.

An interesting work developed with the aim of studying the development of a basis for a minimal productive capability involving aesthetic judgment has been presented by Mazlack and Granger (16). In order for a machine to provide this feature, they identified three criteria:

1. Its results must not be precisely predictable.
2. It should operate within broad stylistic conventions.
3. It should reflect a change in the result due to aesthetic judgment from the external environment.

Following these criteria, their investigation focused on the development of a representation providing aesthetic control to an image-producing mechanism from the small set of simple standard patterns shown in Figure 7. The construction of the patterns was to be controlled by a representation specifying an aesthetic judgment as to the relative suitability of adjoining local patterns horizontally, vertically, diagonally, and by random selection. Weights were assigned representing aesthetic judgments on all possible basic pattern compatibilities and the effects that would be produced in the image. The initial weight assignment was modified on the basis of the observers' aesthetic reaction, finally resulting in pictures such as the one in Figure 8. The method worked in its limited domain and seems to be extensible by enlarging the initial set of patterns. Although the images do not pretend to be works of art, they reflect the beginning of an understanding of how aesthetic judgment could be represented.

Rule Systems

Since antiquity, there have been numerous attempts to characterize artistic creation as a set of rules—witness the Pythagorean rules of the golden section. In the Renaissance, such artists as Alberti and Dürer formalized rules for projective geometry and ideal proportions. Twentieth-century artists such as Kandinsky, Gabo, and Klee sought to describe formally methodologies for invoking a broad range of emotional responses. The rigor of their work led to structural techniques for the analysis of artwork. The evolution of this formal approach to art making and analysis has continued to the present. Contemporary artists and critics have used computers to assist them in their analysis of works

A   B   C   D   E   F

FIGURE 7   Basic set of standard patterns (16). Reprinted with permission of the publisher.

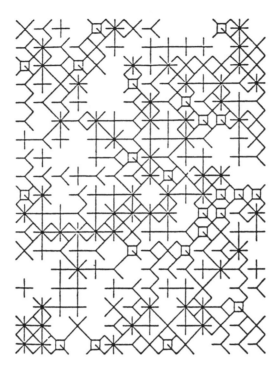

FIGURE 8 A picture generated through aesthetic control-driven pattern selection (16). Reprinted with permission of the publisher.

of art. Until recently, rules of this type could be expressed only in the form of narrative writing; with the advent of the computer, it became possible to characterize these rules finally, and the machine was then used to generate images that conformed to these rules.

One powerful technique for expressing compositional rules and facilitating the maintenance of a design rule base makes use of the so-called shape grammars. The notion of shape grammar was first developed by Stiny (17). Since then, shape grammars have been applied primarily to architectural design, but they have also been employed to characterize painting, in particular Kandinsky's Bauhaus paintings (18) and Richard Diebenkorn's paintings (19,20). A shape grammar can be defined internally as an initial shape and a set of replacement rules that operate on shapes. The repeated application of rules on the initial and intermediate shapes results in a final shape. The idea behind this approach is very interesting and provides a means of understanding the underlying structure of large classes of paintings, suggesting a computational theory of style. As a matter of fact, the formal analysis of artwork with a shape grammar is limited to its visual properties such as color, line, shape, materials, and their arrangements, the so-called plastic elements. Excluded are the extrinsic qualities of the work, that is, feelings, stories, and metaphors.

In the following we present the study of Joan and Russel Kirsh on the paintings of Richard Dieberkorn, a contemporary American painter whose work is geometric and appears to be conventionally describable and measurable. The main purpose of their work was to investigate the possibility of understanding significant work in art by means of a formal grammar.

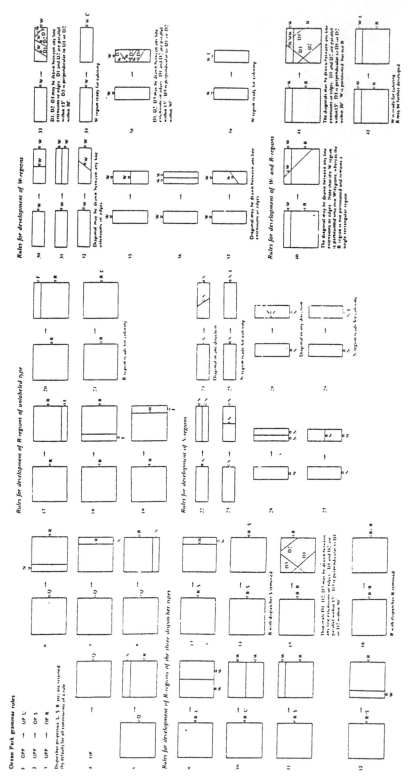

FIGURE 9 *Ocean Park* grammar rules (19). Reprinted with permission of the publisher.

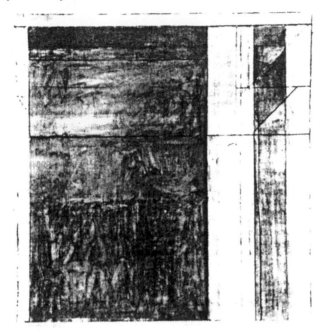

FIGURE 10 Richard Diebenkorn's *Ocean Park #111* (19). Reprinted with permission of the publisher.

Borrowing from structural linguistic terminology, they distinguished between a deep structure and a surface structure (21). The *surface structure* accounts for many of the observable properties of the finished work, including, for example, texture, variation of media, line quality, and colors and their relationships. The *deep structure* can account for the overall composition and how the work is organized in two or three dimensions. Kirsh and Kirsh (22,23) present a grammar specifying the deep structure for the paintings of Richard Diebenkorn consisting of a set of production rules in a form similar both to shape grammars and to context-dependent phrase structure grammars (Fig. 9). As in shape grammars, labels are used as control structures to regulate the applicability of the production rules. For example, in a rule such as OPP → OP/S, the dispatcher S is property added when the rule is applied and inherited in all subsequent rule applications unless specifically removed. When the dispatcher appears on the left-hand side of a rule, it serves as a condition that must be met for the rule to be applicable.

The grammar has been tested in two ways. Initially, analysis has been applied to an existing painting to determine whether or not compositional criteria used by the painter can plausibly be described by the grammar. For the analysis, the authors started with Diebenkorn's *Ocean Park #111* (Fig. 10). In Figure 11, the grammatical derivation of linear composition for the painting is shown. Then, synthesis has been used to generate compositions to determine whether or not the grammar specifies particular compositional criteria that cannot be plausibly attributed to an extension of the painter's style. A synthesis test was applied by generating a linear composition randomly from the grammar. A pseudo-Diebenkorn derived from the following sequence of rule applications is shown in Figure 12: 2, 6, 17, 17, 11, 31, 31, 30, 38, 37, 30, 31, 30, 30, 30, 32. The

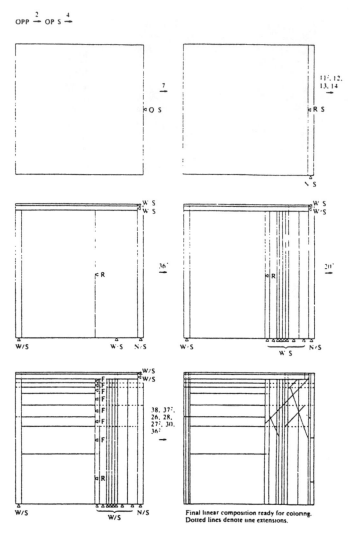

FIGURE 11   Grammatical derivation of *Ocean Park #111* (19). Reprinted with permission of the publisher.

generated structure has both a busy and an open region, as in the style of the painter. In fact, any claim that the generated pseudo-Diebenkorn could be comparable to the genuine Diebenkorns falls short in accounting for the processes that led the artist to achieve his own aesthetics and form of expression, which is the essence of a work of art.

COMPUTER ARTISTS AT WORK

In this section we review the work of some of the most innovative computer artists, those who have devoted a great deal of time and effort to learn how to use computers and have utilized concepts inherent in and inspired by computing. We start with Harold Cohen, a

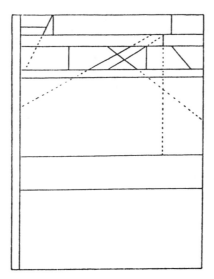

FIGURE 12 A grammar-generated Dienbenkorn-like painting (19). Reprinted with permission of the publisher.

painter who has developed a knowledge-based program designed to investigate the cognitive principles underlying visual representation. Then we introduce the work of three artists who have all employed computers to realize their sculptures, although looking at their works we can hardly say that they are all alike: John Pearson, Manfred Mohr, and William Latham. Following is Larry Cuba, who is one of the most important figures working in the tradition of so-called abstract animation. Finally, we present the work of Myron Krueger, who first started to explore the potentials of real-time interaction between humans and computers from the artistic standpoint through the creation of artificial realities.

Harold Cohen

From about 1952 until 1968 Harold Cohen built up a reputation as an abstract painter and could look forward to a rewarding career. His major concerns at the time were the use of color and the potential for meanings of marks on a surface. In 1969 he accepted a one-year visiting professorship at the University of California, San Diego, which led to a complete change in his career. In San Diego he became interested in computers as a means of carrying forward his investigation about the repertoire of decision essential to drawing and started the development of AARON, a knowledge-based program now able to make "freehand" drawings of people in gardenlike settings. The painting in Figure 13 is an example of AARON's work; more precisely, AARON has first generated the drawing by means of a plotter, and then Cohen has enlarged the drawing by projecting it on canvas.

At the outset, AARON's structure reflected Cohen's preoccupation with this puzzle: how it is that we are able to make sense of systems of marks that were generated by cultures utterly remote from our own, the cultural meaning of which we could not possibly know. He speculated that a distinction needed to be made between meanings carried by mark systems and the sense of meaningfulness generated by those systems. Meanings,

FIGURE 13   *Meeting on Gauguin's Beach*. Oil on canvas (1988). Reprinted with permission of the author.

in the sense of transmitted messages, would necessarily be less and less present as their origins become more remote from our cultural location. The sense of meaningfulness, on the other hand, must be generated through noncultural commonalities between mark-maker and markreader. Cohen concluded that he noncultural commonalities reside in the human cognitive system, which was assumed to have been essentially constant throughout human history.

The first AARON represented the attempt to identify and simulate the actions of a small set of "primitives" such as closure, insideness, repetition, and division. In its first years of existence, AARON was taught things about the human cognitive system and about drawing, but nothing about the objects of the world that were evidently evoked for viewers by its drawings (Fig. 14). The program succeeded in demonstrating the power of the cognitive system itself, devoid of world knowledge, and the degree to which visual representational systems take form and power from the cognitive system. Had the body of primitives been enlarged, AARON's drawings would have become richer and more

FIGURE 14 Hand-colored computer-generated drawing (1984). Reprinted with permission of the author.

complex. This, however, was refuted by the results obtained in the following years. Cohen started feeling that the program constituted a surprisingly powerful but fundamentally limited model of cognitive activity and that a more complex model of the principles underlying visual representation was required.

Two successive developments improved AARON's output; first, the introduction of a new procedure to the repertoire of primitives simulating the drawing skills of young children. Because all children begin drawing by scribbling and then by surrounding the scribbles with a closed line, they proclaim the drawing to represent something, so AARON started to make its final attempts at representing something. The more knowledge AARON was given about visual space, the more the entities agglomerated from its primitives took on explicit thinglike characteristics. The need to provide explicit knowledge about those things was becoming clear. Introducing object-specific knowledge was actually the next main step in AARON's history, late in 1983. Objects such as human figures, trees, and rocks were described to AARON in terms of their structure, not their appearances. For instance, an agglomeration of closed forms made in the following way—a big one in the middle, a smaller one with markings about it, approximately two appendages more or less hanging from the bottom—was called a figure, a skinny branching structure was called a tree; a big, more or less rectangular lump was a rock. Other rules were specified (e.g., rocks may be piled on each other, figures may stand on rocks but not vice versa). The first result of the introduction of knowledge of world objects is shown in Figure 15.

By any standards, AARON's knowledge of the world was still rudimentary; nevertheless, at this stage the program proved that the quality of art does not rest on how

FIGURE 15   An example of AARON's drawings during the first phase of acquisition of knowledge about world objects. Reprinted with permission of the author.

much the artist knows. The artists who knows a great deal will produce one kind of art, the artist who knows very little will produce another kind. So AARON's latest developments have been directed to increasing its knowledge about the world. In particular, knowledge bases have been specified to describe plants and human figures. Besides the obvious information about how a plant or a human figure is constructed, AARON has been taught rules governing plant's morphology and growth, and rules determining how a human figure can preserve its balance (24). Examples of AARON's current drawing abilities are shown in Figures 13 and 16. The latest version of AARON also includes knowledge of how to represent facial expressions, as documented in Figures 17–19.

In practice, AARON makes drawings of whatever it knows without requiring any further instructions for the making of a particular drawing, and indeed without possessing any mechanism through which it could take instructions. AARON is a complete and functionally independent entity capable of autonomously generating an endless succession of different drawings. The program starts each drawing with a blank sheet of paper and generates everything it needs as it goes along, building up as it proceeds an internal representation of what it is doing, which is then used in determining subsequent developments.

There is a large consensus that AARON's drawings show a high level of artistic accomplishment, but AARON does not embody any of the rules commonly believed to guide the production of art; it simply follows principles like the "find enough space" rule that governs the drawings' composition. As the author claims,

FIGURE 16 *Two Men on the Edge*. Oil on canvas (1988). Reprinted with permission of the author.

FIGURE 17 *Clarissa*. Oil on canvas (1992). Reprinted with permission of the author.

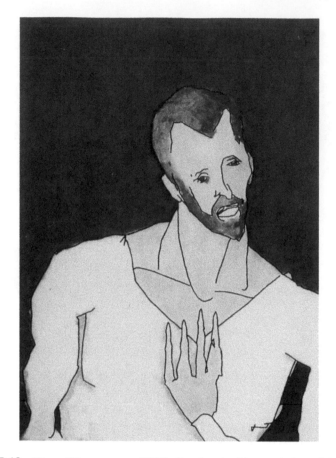

FIGURE 18   *Theo*. Oil on canvas (1992). Reprinted with permission of the author.

the aesthetics of AARON's performance can be regarded as an emergent property arising from the interactions of so many interdependent processes, the result of so many decisions in the design of the program, that it becomes meaningless to ask how much any of them is responsible for its outcome. If someone else wrote a similar program, I would expect it to exhibit a different identity and a different aesthetic.

Cohen is, indeed, AARON's source of specialized knowledge, and he also served as knowledge engineer and developer of the system; for this reason, he sees his system as an "expert's system" as opposed to an "expert system" in the usual meaning given to the latter denomination in the AI community (25). In fact, in AARON, knowledge of image-making is represented in rule form. In its first version, AARON was mainly a production system, but it also had knowledge encoded in procedural form. The kind of knowledge the program was provided was basically *procedural knowledge of representational strategies*. The controlling driver of the program consisted of a set of productions having conditions on the left-hand side and procedures on the right-hand side. The rules corresponded to cognitive primitives involved in human visual perception and representation that can be divided into the following three classes:

FIGURE 19 *Herb with Wall Hanging.* Oil on canvas (1992). Reprinted with permission of the author.

1. Distinction between figures and ground
2. Differentiation between closed and open forms
3. Differentiation between inside and outside.

The program was constructed in a hierarchical fashion. The topmost level was called artwork and was responsible for upper-level decisions such as the overall use of space in the current drawing (i.e., control of the density of information in the picture). The procedure *mapping* was a lower-level procedure in charge of the allocation of space within the drawing for each individual element (i.e., if and where an element is placed). Finally, *planning* determined what type of element to draw next.

The latest versions of AARON embed *object-specific knowledge*. Such knowledge encompasses levels of increasingly procedural and context-dependent knowledge such as the following:

1. *Declarative.* Declarative knowledge specifies the hierarchical structure of a figure (e.g., an arm has an upper arm, a forearm, and a hand; a hand has four fingers and a thumb).

2. *Functional/structural*. Functional knowledge takes its form and ranges given for a figure and has a subfigure related to its superfigure. For instance, the range of movement of a human arm from the shoulder may begin somewhere behind the back and below the waist, and end somewhere behind the back and above the head.

3. *Exemplary*. Knowledge becomes exemplary when a value for some range specified in the functional knowledge is chosen.

4. *Procedural*. Procedural knowledge is the executable code for the drawing of an element of the figure to be drawn. A detailed description of AARON's drawing mechanism can be found in Ref. 26.

With AARON, Cohen has achieved the goal of building a program that behaves as an analogue to the cognitive structures through which humans make and read visual images, and as with the human image-maker, the exercise of its representational strategies is mediated by its knowledge of what is being represented. AARON has never been given an original drawing on which to base variations, although it can be argued that the two interrelated levels of knowledge do, in fact, constitute an original of some sort. It would have to be viewed as the prototype for that class of drawings rather than as the original for a single drawing. We would need to think of it as a process description of how to go about making drawings as opposed to a formal description of what drawings should look like when they are finished; the former deals with generative principles, whereas the latter deals with appearances. This does not invalidate the notion that a program can only do what it is told to do, but it does oblige us to recognize that a program can be told to do things of a far more complex order than we might previously have suspected to be possible; that, in fact, we have not yet come within sight of any clear limit of what a program may be told to do.

John Pearson

John Pearson is a thoroughly dedicated artist who teaches and works at Oberlin College in Ohio. The use of computers for planning, particularly in sculpture, has been an intermittent practice for him. Using it truly as a medium, he, like most artists, does not use the same tool all the time. In fact, he mainly employs the computer interactively by interfacing the results achieved with it with other traditional materials. Since 1973 he has developed a love/hate relationship with the computer because it always seems to command too much of his time in learning its language, its technical attributes, and its limitations (27). Having resisted the desire to learn programming, he used software written for him in Fortran and lately rewritten in C by some of his students.

Pearson's sculptures have their genesis in plots such as those depicted in Figure 20. From these plots, the artist then builds sculptures of the kind represented in Figures 21 and 22. Examples of his most recent work, dated 1991, are given in Figures 23 and 24. The same patterns inspiring Pearson's sculptures are taken as a basis for the paintings shown in Figures 25 and 26.

In Pearson's view, technology has always been the handmaiden of the visual arts because a technical means is always necessary for the visual communication of ideas, of expression, and of the development of works of art. Without tools and without some understanding of the basic physical and chemical properties of certain elements, carving, casting, and painting could not have developed. In their attempt to strive for an understanding of truth and reality, artists have always been aware not only of the spiritual and

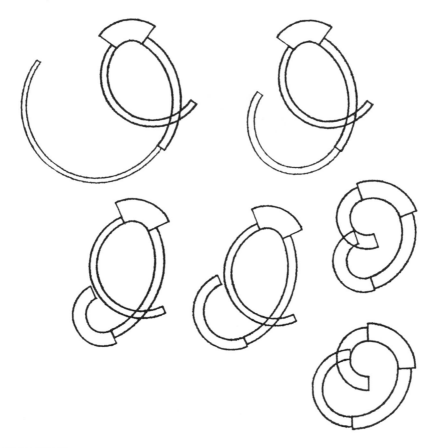

FIGURE 20   Computer-generated patterns. Reprinted with permission of the author.

intellectual climate of their times but also of the technological climate. They have embraced it, absorbed it by osmosis, and, thus, reflected it in their work or processes, or they have added to the intellectual and technological development of their times.

Given this assumption, and given that today the most powerful modes of communication are electronic, Pearson feels compelled to accept the computer as an integral part of our times and to use it to make some meaningful contribution in art. He believes that the main issues related to the use of computers for artistic purposes lie in the definition of a computer-imaging aesthetics and in how computers can be employed, like any other tool, to make art. Computers by themselves do not make art; on the other hand, the software that makes possible the attributes that then become available to the artist is where the art of computer use resides.

Not wishing to become a slave to the machine nor a slave introspectively limited to his experiences, Pearson sees the computer as on efficient tool that can clear out ideas expeditiously. In addition, it has challenged him to be much more open and adventurous by revealing that even a simple idea can be multifaceted. At a purely intuitive and subjective level, many of these facets would have been overlooked.

The program he uses for his artistic investigation generates a tremendous amount of visual information, thus creating a dilemma, or perhaps a paradox: although it seems to save time, it creates more information than can be absorbed and, thus, it seems im-

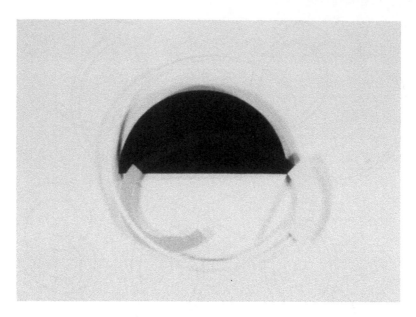

FIGURE 21   *Fresnel Proposition #34*. Acrylic on board construction (1984). Reprinted with permission of the author.

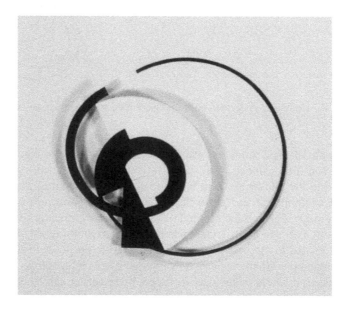

FIGURE 22   *Fresnel Proposition #38*. Acrylic on board construction (1985). Reprinted with permission of the author.

possible to keep the information under control. It can present the artist with very accurate alternatives and variations to the original image while remaining solidly embedded within the parameters of the main concept. However, although it works to generate new visual variations, it is confined to the set of parameters and cannot generate new ideas.

FIGURE 23 *Convenant #2*. Acrylic and pencil on paper (1991). Reprinted with permission of the author.

FIGURE 24 *Convenant #2SJ10*. Acrylic on canvas (1991). Reprinted with permission of the author.

FIGURE 25   *Abundance #5*. Pastel (1988). Reprinted with permission of the author.

     Pearson thinks of the computer as a useful assistant, and he intends to continue using it whenever its peculiar qualities serve his creative purposes. The artist is the decision maker, the computer the tool/servant, the means of transmitting and expressing ideas visually. The object of his work is the result of looking inward, an introspective summation of his own life experiences; it is then obvious what the role and the place of the computer are in Pearson's work.

Manfred Mohr

The origins of Manfred Mohr's work as an artist go back to the early 1960s, during which he was influenced by action painting. Also, as a jazz musician he was involved in free improvisation. Only a few years later, he disassociated himself from informal art, which seemed to him too impulsive and uncontrolled. He then turned his attention to geometry, which came to occupy more and more of a place in his vision until the spontaneous expression was finally replaced by the constructivist statement.

     The year 1969 was a turning point because it was in that year that he began to work with the computer and the plotter. Since then, several work phases have been developed but not in the sense of a progressive evolution; no phase causes or replaces another. Each

FIGURE 26   *Abundance #6*. Pastel (1988). Reprinted with permission of the author.

work phase, the development of which does not result in a single work but rather culminates in a series, is founded on a single idea, a common problem. At the same time, he is constantly searching for the "integrated artwork," a structure from which all works can be derived, a hyperstructure that one day will encompass all his works.

In the tradition of constructivism, an art direction that emphasizes rational versus spontaneous artistic expression, he took the cube as a fundamental object of investigation. The cube projected onto the two-dimensional surface is, indeed, the exclusive subject Mohr has examined and realized in his work since 1973. The 12 contour lines of the cube are selected, shifted, subdivided, titled, turned, and manifested in various other ways and shown in systematic forms (Fig. 27). Many series, however, are of a scope that can hardly be imagined, let alone mastered, so the computer has been programmed with additional selective criteria, one of which is chance. A final decision determining those lines and form arrangements—which is the result in the realization of a work of art—is for the most part still made by the artist according to his aesthetic judgment. The computer does not play any role as designer or inventor, but rather remains a calculator, and its binary limitation merely a supporting and sometimes also executing tool.

Mohr's research is concentrated on fracturing the symmetry of the cube. It is not its geometric aspect that interests him, rather the system of line relations resulting from the

FIGURE 27   An example of the Cubic Limit phase (1974). Reprinted with permission of the author.

projection of the lines. For a graphic representation of a cube, 12 straight lines are necessary (the edges of a cube), which, in an a priori arrangement, create the illusion of a three-dimensional figure. By removing the edges of the cube, one can view the gradual breakup of the three-dimensional illusion. In this way, a new system of two-dimensional signs develops, forming the basis of Mohr's generative work.

The author's algorithmic art consists of developing compositional rules that are not necessarily based on already imaginable forms, but on abstract and systematic processes. The rules are geometric (i.e., at certain points in the process, conditions have to be set for which in some cases random choices can be employed). In this way, even if the work process is rational and systematic, it is always open to surprises. In his work, Mohr leaves out the concept of spatiality; he is interested exclusively in the relation of the sign of the two-dimensional field. For this reason he has been able to extend his study to the *n*th-dimensional hypercube as well, which he drafts as a repertoire of elements for the development of signs. The idea of dimension is not understood in its physical and philosophical aspects, but only in a mathematical sense; and from the mathematical point of view, one can operate with an infinite number of dimensions.

Nevertheless, his art in not simply mathematical, but an expression of his artistic experiences; the generative process is controlled by rules that reflect his thinking and feelings. Such rules can become very complex; so in order to master them, the use of the computer becomes necessary. Only in this way it is possible to overlay as many rules as necessary without losing control.

The algorithms encoding the generative rules can be classified as combinatorial, statistical, symbolic logic, additive, and restrictive. In the *combinatorial process*, all combinatorial possibilities with the 12 edges of the cube are utilized and divided into 13 classifications. In the beginning, one line is subtracted so that new combinations can be developed with the remaining 11 lines. When two lines are omitted, there are still lines with which different structures can be created, and so forth. In all, there are 6096 (i.e., 2^{12}) signs that, as in an arbitrary artistic metalanguage, can be written down like mathematical formulas. In the *statistical process*, the lines are built up as hyperstructures in matrices using varying statistical methods. In this process, the chance factor can be used as a formative principle. In the process of *symbolic logic*, the signs are interpreted as elements of sets and manipulated graphically following the rules of set theory. In the *additive process*, signs are superimposed and joined together to create new elements and structures. These superimpositions can be built up strictly systematically, and in the end, add up to a complete cube. In the *restrictive process*, the cube is divided through its center point into halves that can be rotated independently around the common central point. A square window appears as a demarcation that separates the inside and outside from each other. During the rotation, part of the lines naturally folds inside, another part folds outside; graphically, the spatial location is translated by lines by varying width.

The working process of the artist consists of an interplay between man and machine. Mohr starts by setting up a program that he translates into a coded language and feeds into the computer. This work begins with an algorithm; he does not start with visual ideas. The machine transforms the program into signs; the artist takes samples and checks, improves, and changes them until he is satisfied with the final results. As the development of the algorithm is finished, the plotter takes over the technical realization of the program by drawing on paper or canvas.

The artist understands the computer as his partner, his aid, his assistant; it does not participate in the creation, but only in the realization. The plotter is not simply a substitute for human labor; rather, it is regarded as a variation of the act of painting. The principle of all Mohr's works is that they can be verified and rationally understood, even though at first glance they are hard to read. Often the information lies very deep and requires certain knowledge from the observer—an openness to confront complex and complicated material—yet in his drawings and paintings, which show a very high visual attraction and strong aesthetic effect, Mohr leaves more than enough room for imagination and association, without wishing to make a definite intentional claim. He leaves it to the observer to find and approach his work, whether as a pure aesthetic experience or as a cognitive experiment in rediscovering and deciphering certain processes and structures.

Three main work phases can be distinguished in Mohr's production (28,29). In the first phase, called "Cube Limit" (1973–1977), he began to work with fixed systems, the

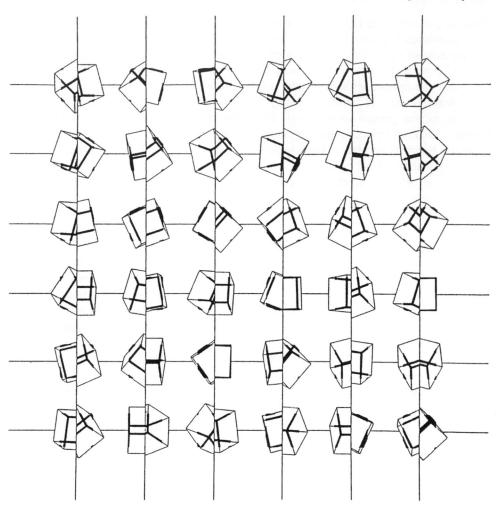

FIGURE 28   An example of the Cubic Limit phase (1977–1979). Reprinted with permission of the author.

cube and later the *n*-dimensional hypercube, which provide a repertoire of elements for developing signs. In the first part of this work phase, an alphabet of signs is created from the 12 lines of a cube. In some works, statistics and rotations are used in the algorithm to generate the images. In others, combinatorial, logical, and additive operators generate the global and local structure of the images. Figure 27 provides an example of the research. In the second part of this work phase, cubes are divided into two parts by one of the Cartesian planes. Opposite partitions of two independent rotations of the cube are thus projected into two dimensions and clipped by a square frontal window (Fig. 28).

"Divisibility," the second main work phase, which spans from 1980 to 1986, is constituted of three subphases. The cube is again used as the basic generator of signs. It is divided into four sections by a horizontal and vertical cut. Four independent rotations of the cube are projected onto corresponding quadrants created by the cut. In order to visually stabilize the structure, two diagonally opposite quadrants contain the same rotation. In the first part of this work phase, the "form-cut" is the basic structure with

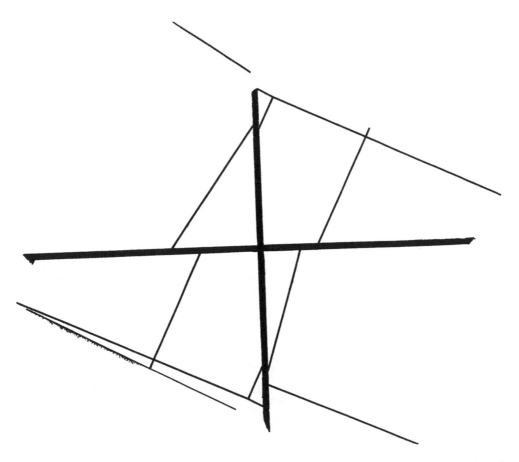

FIGURE 29   An example of the Divisibility phase (1980–1981). Reprinted with permission of the author.

which the "out-lines" form shapes and the "in-lines" create signs (Fig. 29). In the second part, a molecularlike growth is created with the form-cut as its seed. Growth results from algorithms of graph patterns deciding which out-lines of quadrants created in the preceding generation will be used to produce the form-cuts of the new generation (Fig. 30) Finally, in the third part of the second work phase, the cubes no longer appear as the principle signs. The contours of the form-cuts are seen as "shadow-form," or better, a two-dimensional visual history of the cube growth. The connecting path between the center point of the next form-cut becomes like a black growth line. Similar to the spine in a body, the growth line is here embedded in the shadow-form (Fig. 31).

In the work phase "Dimensions," the four-dimensional hypercube is the fixed structure that generates the signs. In the early work (1978–1979), the graph of the four-dimensional hypercube is the basic generator of signs. The graph is a two-dimensional representation of a hypercube indicating relationships between points, lines, squares, and cubes inherent in the structure. The global structure is generated by either selecting lines combinatorially with cubes or by searching paths between given points of the graph (Fig. 32). In the later work (1987), the four-dimensional rotation of a hypercube becomes the generator of signs and shapes. The two-dimensional projection of a hypercube at a given

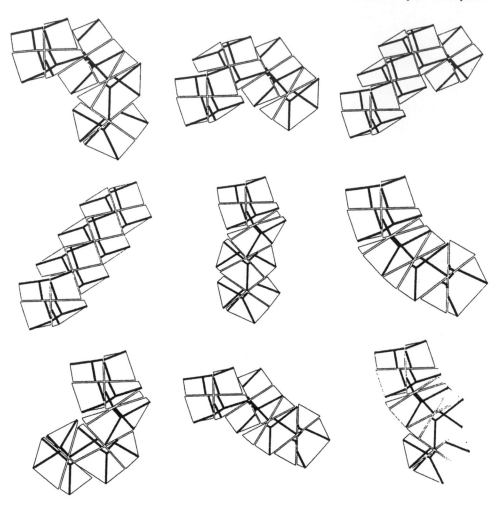

FIGURE 30   An example of the Divisibility phase (1985). Reprinted with permission of the author.

rotation is fractured into square windows related to each of its eight inherent cubes. The positioning of these cubes into front and back views, visualized by using black and gray for their representation, respectively, is an additional algorithmic element (Fig. 33).

As a final note about Mohr's work, it must be pointed out that the exclusive use of black and white as a means for sculptural design enables the artist to describe a rigorous stem of binary decisions. Because he regards his work as a linear process, color, which implies surface, would create totally different problems interfering with his intention. Only gray appears in a sense as any intermediate station apart from the dynamics of black and white.

William Latham

The work of William Latham could be described as "computer sculptures" (Fig. 34). Some may argue that sculpture has to be experienced in the round, to be touched before

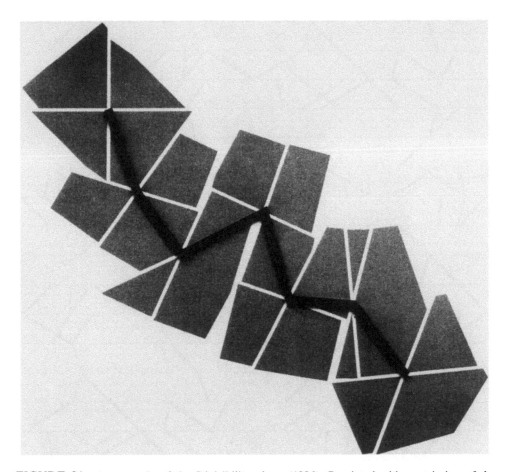

FIGURE 31   An example of the Divisibility phase (1986). Reprinted with permission of the author.

it can be so called. They might go on to say that good sculpture comes about as the artist responds to the special feeling of the chisel on stone, thumb on clay, hammer on metal, and so on. That is one form of sculpture; William Latham has shown us another.

To credit his sculptures he has been working in the computer graphics laboratory at IBM's scientific center in the United Kingdom, and all the sculptures have been created by writing computer programs while sitting at a terminal looking at a computer screen. The computer screen sits as a window looking into a three-dimensional volume of synthetic, illusory space and it is within this space that Latham makes his sculptures. Looking through this window, the sculptures appear as three-dimensional solid objects, although they do not, in fact, exist. Better yet, they exist only as data and not in physical form. What he finds interesting about working in the "computer space" is that it is a world free of such physical constraints as gravity, material resistance, and time. The computer sculptures he creates could not exist in the "real" world, for many of his sculptures float in space and are so intricate that they would be impossible to make. Yet the objects are neither paradoxical nor optical illusions. Latham shows us some parallel possible worlds in which his sculptures are real, worlds that have their own logic and con-

FIGURE 32   An example of the Dimension phase (1978). Reprinted with permission of the author.

sistency, where, indeed, most but not all the physical laws we know still hold, maybe in a slightly modified fashion.

The logic and consistency of Latham's possible worlds arises from his concept of an evolutionary approach to making sculpture. In 1984, while a student at the Royal College of Art in London, he was working with handdrawn animation and print-making. He realized that a printed image would change from its first print to the last, often to the extent that the final image was completely different from the first. Intrigued by these changes, Latham set out to document similar incremental charges in a work entitled *The Evolution of Form* (Fig. 35). At the top of the drawing are a number geometric primitives (cone, cube, sphere, cylinder, and torus) that gradually evolve into more complex forms as they are near the bottom of the drawing. The primitive shapes were altered following a list of rules he devised for ''sculptural transformation.'' The commands or rules were ''beak, bulge, scoop, union, twist'' and ''stretch.'' By carrying out these transformations

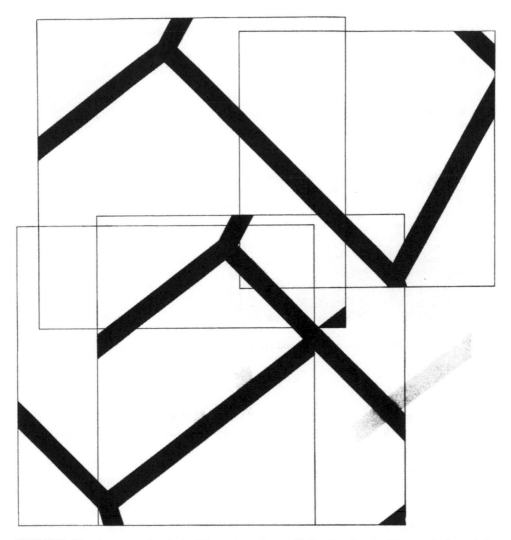

FIGURE 33 An example of the Dimension phase (1987). Reprinted with permission of the author.

repeatedly and in different sequences on a geometric form, different types of complex forms could evolve (Fig. 36).

Up to this point, Latham worked without a computer. In 1985, he produced a number of physical sculptures by selecting forms from the tree drawing and fashioning them out of plastic and wood, but he found this extremely time-consuming and creatively restricted. What really interested him was the exploration of for—and he decided than he wanted to continue working on the drawing instead of carrying out the mechanical execution of the sculptures. Looking for a faster way of making solid versions of these forms, he began to experiment with a wide variety of programs and machines. Progress was slow at first as a result of having to learn about computing, but gradually it became clearer how computers could be used for his purposes. In particular, using the Sculpture

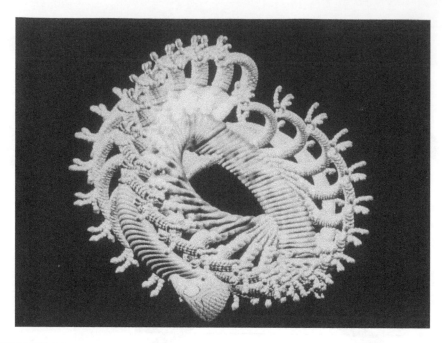

FIGURE 34   *Mutations*—branched and ribbed. Reprinted with permission of the author.

software written by Mike King of the City of London Polytechnic, he was able to simulate the sculptural transformation by manually imposing such rules on the program, as
discussed in Ref. 30.

The opportunity to further his work presented itself when IBM's scientific center
awarded him a research fellowship in 1987 to work on his evolutionary approach to sculpture using the solid modeling program IBM was developing (Winsom, the Winchester
Solid Modeler) and the interactive graphics language ESME (Extensible Solid Model Ed-
itor). At the initial stage, Latham's work consisted of creating an evolutionary program
in the ESME language and using WINDSOM to color, texture, and ray trace the image.
To create a sculpture, the evolution program was seeded with a sequence of numbers,
each defining a sculptural transformation such as the amount of twist or stretch, or the
number of primitives to be "unioned." The larger of sequence of numbers passed to the
evolution program, the greater the complexity of the form that was involved; by changing
the parameters in the sequence, the form was modified, by adding more parameters the
form evolved into a more complex state (Figures 37 and 38). His task as an artist was
then to create the high-level evolutionary program and to creatively use the program to
produce sculptures. What he had not anticipated was the variety of sculpture "types" that
could be created. Some looked like a anemones, whereas others resembled antlers,
shells, slugs, and eyes. As Latham claims, "the machine has given me freedom to explore
and create complex three dimensional forms which previously had not been accessible to
me, as they had been beyond my imagination."

In his latest work, Latham uses a new evolutionary program called Mutator developed at IBM UK by Stephan Todd, the research scientist with whom Latham collaborates

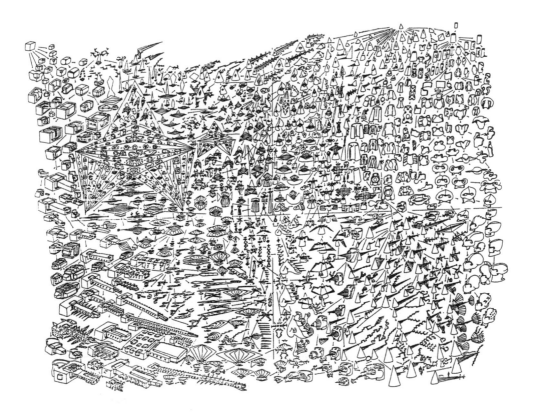

FIGURE 35   Detail of *The Evolution of Forms* (30). Reprinted with permission of the publisher.

(31,32). With this program, Latham generates an organic-appearing object as described above and selects it. The computer then randomly generates nine variations of the form. These selected or mutated offspring appear on the display. Latham then decides which offspring he will allow to survive. He chooses the most artistically pleasing offspring, which becomes the parent of the following generation. He can repeat this process through almost countless generations. In Figure 39, three generations of fractal horns are shown. The parent of each generation appears in the center of the top row. Figure 40 displays nine ray-traced mutations in which, by manipulating more primitives, the evolution of forms is more complex and unpredictable.

In practice, what Mutator does is to explore a form of three-dimensional space by generating alternative parameters. Latham's task as an artist is then to kill off the forms that are not aesthetically pleasing. The artist calls this process "evolution by aesthetics." All of Latham's work looks on the verge of turning, changing, and metamorphosing into something even more unusual and surprising. His three-dimensional sculptures always seem to be transforming into other shapes or other shape creatures.

The natural way of developing this concept is through animation, and so Latham has also produced two films, *A Sequence from the Evolution of Form* and *Mutations*, in which he illustrates the process of surreal evolutions, involving breeding the growth, with

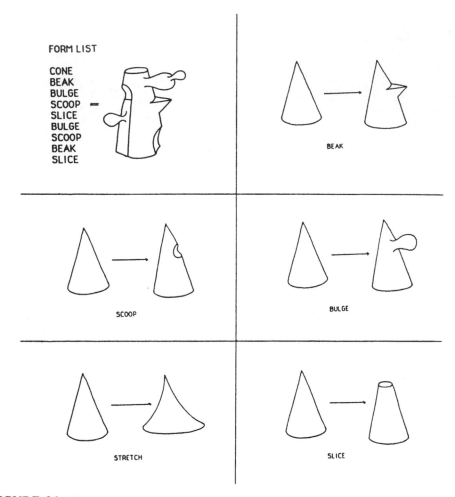

FIGURE 36   Example of complex form and relative sequence of generative commands. Reprinted with permission of the author.

many forms animating partly independently but with complex interactions. In these films the animation is controlled by a program called Director that gives the artist control of this complexity with the ease of use and expressiveness required. Director operates in three stages (33). In the first stage, the user specifies the animation required, giving the structures for the forms, the rules of animation, and the scripts to invoke them. In the second stage, Director creates and restructures this information to put it in the format required by the form and animation rules, and then invokes the procedures to implement these rules. In the final stage, Director invokes but Winsom renders the appropriate low-level recording mechanisms. In Figures 34 and 41 frames from *Mutations* are shown.

In conclusion, Latham's art is an example of successful collaboration between and an artist and a scientist; when Latham is struck with an inspiration, his collaborator has to dive into mathematics and programming to find a way of making it real. At the same time, Latham has pushed the frontiers of the science of computer modeling further, opening avenues for more conventional applications.

FIGURE 37 *Hornweb* (1989). Reprinted with permission of the author.

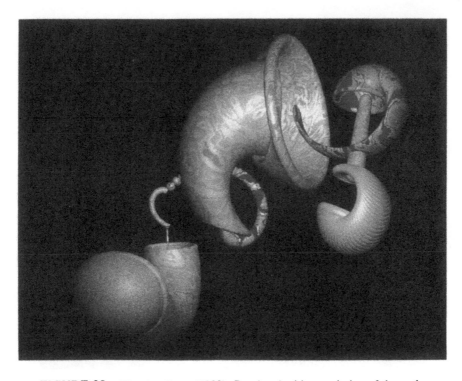

FIGURE 38 *Floating Form* (1989). Reprinted with permission of the author.

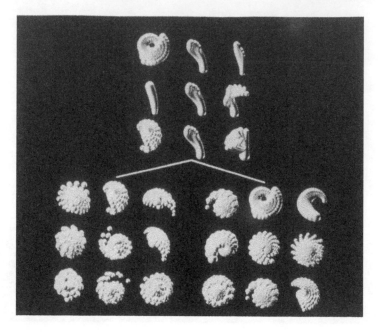

FIGURE 39   Tree of fractal horns. Reprinted with permission of the author.

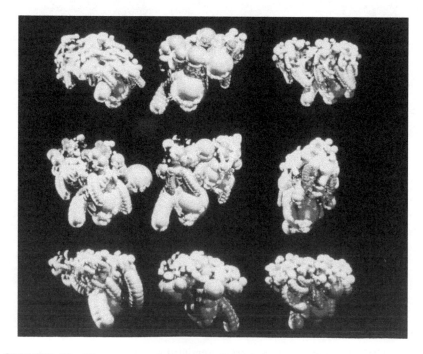

FIGURE 40   Nine ray-traced mutations. Reprinted with permission of the author.

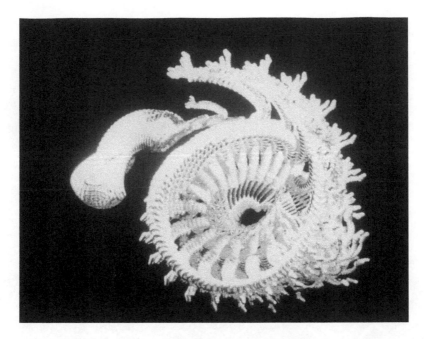

FIGURE 41   *Mutation X.* Reprinted with permission of the author.

Larry Cuba

Larry Cuba is one of the most important figures currently working in the tradition of so-called abstract animation, an approach to cinema as a purely visual experience that has intrigued different kinds of artists since the beginning of the film era (34). Unlike his predecessors, Cuba has completely bypassed the experience of making hand-generated animated films by exploring the creative use of computers to describe the underlying mathematical formula of abstract forms and to manipulate such elements to create his amazing animations.

Cuba has produced only four films in 13 years. The best known are *3/78* (1978) and *Two Space* (1979), both generated on vector systems. The imagery of these films consists of white dots on a black field (Fig. 42). In *3/78*, 16 objects, each consisting of 100 points of light, perform a series of precisely choreographed rhythmic transformations. Accompanied by the sound of a shakuhachi, the Japanese bamboo flute, the film is an exercise in the visual perception of motion and musical structure. In *Two Space*, patterns similar to the tile designs found in Islamic temples are generated by performing a set of symmetry operations (translations, rotations, and reflections) on a basic geometry figure. These exotic and complicated patterns, which are set against eighteenth-century Javanese gramelan music, are choreographed to produce a variety of illusionary effects including figure-ground reversal and afterimages of color.

In his most recent production, *Calculated Movements* (1985), Cuba has created his most complex arrangement of sequential graphic events to date. *Calculated Movements* differs from his earlier films more than they differ from one another, and the most obvious difference comes directly from the hardware that he was able to employ. *Calculated*

FIGURE 42   An image from *Two Space* (1979). Reprinted with permission of the author.

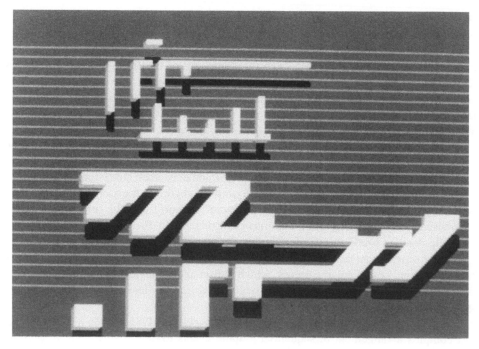

FIGURE 43   An image from *Calculated Movements* (1985). Reprinted with permission of the author.

Movements was produced at Cuba's studio in Santa Cruz on a personal computer with Tom de Fanti's Zgrass graphics language (35). The passage from a vector graphic to raster, graphic system allowed Cuba to work for the first time with solid areas and volumes rather than just dots of light. In addition, he could use four colors (i.e., white, black, light gray, and dark gray; Fig. 43).

The compositional strategy of *Calculated Movements* is more complex than in the two previous films because he was able to work in real time. In *Calculated Movements* there are five movements that alternate between two types. Each odd-numbered movement is structured as a single event about a minute long in which ribbonlike figures follow a single trajectory against a middle-gray background. Each scene represents a structural variation on this theme. In the first movement, a single ribbon appears, follows a trajectory and disappears; it is followed by another ribbon, then another, and so on, all following the same path. There are, thus, no transformations in space but a large transformation in time; that is, the figures are shifted out of phase only in time but not two dimensionally. Another option is to spread the ribbons out in a two-dimensional pattern so they can traverse the path simultaneously; so in the third movement they shifted in both time and space. In the fifth movement, they are, also shifted in time and space, but they are shorter in length, so they look more like a flock of birds following each other around.

The strategy for the even-numbered movements, in contrast, is a collection of four short events ranging from $1\frac{1}{2}$ seconds to 5 seconds, orchestrated to appear and disappear at different intervals. Each event follows the same basic structure of a trajectory, repetition of the figure, and some spatial and temporal transformation of each repetition. These events were designed using a random number generator which selected values for each parameter from within a predetermined range. Even the music score of the piece follows the same rhythmic variation of the animating; this was achieved by matching the sequence of sound events with graphics events by programming onto a sequencer the same temporal structures as the images.

To establish an appropriate content for Cuba's work we need to look at experimental animation as the design of form in motion, independent of any particular technology used to create it. The underlying problems of design in motion are universal to everyone working in this tradition, whether they use a computer or not. On the other hand, the technology is clearly important. Cuba's tool is the mathematics and the programming that depends on a computer as the medium to execute it. In his work he starts with a very ordered system and continually adds the variations that make it more and more interesting. The computer adds a new dimension to the exploration of images by discovering images that the artist might have not previsualized but that can be found starting from the original mathematical structures within the dimension of the search space. The use of mathematics in Cuba's work derives from an interest in it as a domain of thought. His goal is to use mathematics to create pictures, trying to make them affect us in the way music does. Music has an inherent mathematical structure, although no one's really clear on how or why it affects us the way it does, or what the rules are. Analogously, Cuba's artistic investigation is about the quality of the visuals that elicit an aesthetic response, the relation between the pattern that evokes that feeling and its mathematical description.

Myron Krueger

The terms *computer art* implies a novel art form based on the computer. However, most works of computer art fit into the existing tradition. They can be viewed hanging on walls, standing on pedestals, or projected as film. In a sense, they fail to exploit one of the computer's most unique features: its ability to respond in real time. The encounter between human and machine is, in fact, the focus of Myron Krueger's artistic exploration. Beginning in the late 1960s, he pioneered the development of techniques that allow the construction of "artificial realities" that the viewer can enter (36).

Krueger's work is not art in the traditional sense; instead, viewers enter an interactive space in which the interact with computer-generated visual objects or with computer-processed images of other viewers at remote locations. In this space, the rules of interaction are designed by Krueger and in his work he explores the nature of the interactions. For instance, in his most recent responsive environment, called *Videoplace*, a graphic creature called Critter perceives the viewer's movements and engages his or her video image in a whimsical interplay (Fig. 44); synthesized sound communicates the personality of the creature. This piece provides a novel experience. At the immediate level, the participant has an engaging encounter with an artificial entity; as the experience progresses, it becomes apparent that an intelligence that toys with our expectations is behind the interaction.

Although Krueger's original interest in computers was technical, his background in literature and philosophy distinguished him from his fellow students when he went to graduate school in computer science at the University of Wisconsin in 1966. At that time, he was puzzled by some of the concerns he found in the technical literature. The immediate efficiency of the computer seemed far less significant than the relationship between human and machine and the purposes to which computers were put. To him it was clear that the human was the most important component in a computer system; therefore, it followed that the human interface should be the central research problem in computer science.

Indeed, its importance transcended computer science, for the computer-human interface is a permanent part of the human condition. He observed that while humans are evolving slowly if at all, computers are the most rapidly evolving technology in history. It seemed to him that the study of the interface should focus on human qualities rather than on the transient issues of computer technology; the computer should adapt to the human rather than the human adapting to the computer. He started believing that the ultimate computer should perceive the human body, listen to the human voice, and respond through all the human senses. His goal then became to create unencumbered environmental artificial realities. *Unencumbered* means that people can experience them without wearing special instrumentation; *environmental* implies that the technology for perceiving the participant's actions is distributed throughout the environment instead of being worn.

If the responses of the computer are to be intelligent, it is imperative that its grasp of the participant's behavior be as complete as possible in real time. Computer-generated graphics and synthesizer sounds offer the most powerful and composable responses; on the other hand, participants should be able to understand how they personally elicit the responses to be engaged in the interaction. The development of these concepts has been the guiding line of Krueger's work.

In 1969 he joined a group of artists, musicians, and technologists who were working on a piece called *Glow Flow*, a computer-controlled light-sound environment that, in fact, had limited provision for responding to the people within it. The physical space was an empty rectangular room constructed within an art gallery. The display consisted of a suspension of phosphorescent particles in water pumped through four transparent tubes attached to the gallery walls. Each tube contained a different colored pigment. Because the room was dark, the lighted tubes provided the only visual reference and were arranged to distort the viewer's perception of the room, causing the room to appear wider in the center than at each end. The disorienting darkness also caused viewers to assume that the bottom tube was level with the floor. Thus, as they walked the length of the room and found the floor rising with respect to their own position, participants thought they were going downhill. This illusion was so strong that people actually leaned backward as they moved. As people's eyes grew accustomed to the low light level, they would explore the room, discovering the illusory nature of the perceived space. Although *Glow Flow* was successful visually, it was precisely the visual conception that limited its interactive potential.

The following experience, in 1970, called *Metaplay*, was a radical departure from *Glow Flow*; it integrated visual, sound, and responsive techniques in a single framework, with the goal of discovering an interactive medium. The computer was used to create a unique real-time relationship between the participants in the gallery and the artist, who was in another building. The live video image of the participant and a computer graphic image drawn by the artist were superimposed and rear-projected on a screen at the end of the gallery space. The viewer and artist both responded to what they saw on the screen. Many interactions evolved in this framework; for instance, one type of interaction derived from the artist's ability to draw graffiti on the participant's image. In another interaction, an outline could be drawn around a person and animated so that it appeared to dance to the music in the gallery.

In 1971 Krueger exhibited *Psychic Space*, which provided an experience quite different from the preceding ones. Whereas *Glow Flow* was a group event and *Metaplay* included the obtrusive interaction of the artist, *Psychic Space* was the experience of just one person with the responsive environment. *Psychic Space* employed a sensing grid on the floor of the gallery to detect the participant's movements. These movements were translated into graphically displayed sections on a large video projection screen. In this case, the responsive environment provided elaborately composed interactive relationships. In one, the participant's footsteps on the sensing floor controlled the movement of a graphic symbol within a projected graphic maze. If the participant attempted to cross a boundary illegally, the boundary could stretch elastically, the symbol could disintegrate, or the whole maze could move as if the participant's symbol were pushing it. There were approximately 40 different response modes that a participant could discover while moving through the maze. Each was designed to play with the idea of a maze and make fun of the participant's compulsion to take it seriously.

Encouraged by his work on *Psychic Space*, Krueger became determined to develop a more complex and ever-more-interactive medium. He planned to use artistic concepts of color, perception, and composition to develop a new series of interactions. These new programs eventually became *Videoplace*, his most recent piece which is still under development (37,38). The *Videoplace* system perceives one or more participants and responds to their movements in real time. Video cameras view participants standing in front of a backlighting assembly that makes it easy for the computer to distinguish their images from the background. The *Videoplace* system identifies each participant's head, arms, legs, hands, and fingers and determines their rate of movement. This analysis is performed on separate processors for each participant. Once each person's image is understood, it is analyzed with respect to the objects and creatures on the graphics screen. For instance, the computer may check to see whether a participant is touching a graphic object. Because the participant's image may be moved, scaled, or related anywhere on the screen, the relationship of the transformed image to other objects on the screen must be considered. Once each person's actions have been interpreted with respect to the graphics world, the computer must determine the consequences of these actions and initiate responses of its own. It then schedules its responses and directs subordinate processors dedicated to the generation of graphics, image transformation, and sound-to-effect responses.

Videoplace is exhibited in two modes. In one, it selects a new introduction automatically when a person enters, and it continues that interaction until all the participants have left the environment. When a new person enters, the next interaction in the sequence is triggered. In the second mode, the exhibit operates as a dialogue between two participants: one who understands and controls the system and a second naive participant who is visiting the exhibit for the first time. The knowledgeable participant is seated at the "videodesk," which operates in a manner similar to the *Videoplace* environment. The person at the desk can interact with the person in the *Videoplace* environment using the image of his or her own hands; in addition, the videodesk operator controls the selection of interactions from a menu.

The current interactions are based on a variety of themes and motivations. Some are visually interesting and provide a link to traditional aesthetics. Other interactions introduce the ingredients of artificial realities one at a time to see how people relate to each one. A final category of interactions involves a real-time dialogue between two people in different environments. The most interesting interactions are as follows:

> *Critter.* One of the most popular interactions involves a graphic creature called Critter, whose behavior is conceived and controlled in terms of states. At any given moment, Critter is in a particular state in which it attends to certain aspects of the participant's behavior and is prepared to respond in specific ways. For example, initially Critter flits about the screen just out of reach. If the participant makes a move toward it, Critter avoids contact. However, if the person is still, an emboldened Critter moves toward him or her. If the person moves away, Critter gives chase; if the participant remains still and slowly holds out his or her hand, Critter will land on it, and so on (Fig. 44).
>
> *Individual Medley* and *Body Surfacing.* These two kinds of interactions are purely visual. Each is a restricted aesthetic medium that can be composed through body movements; in fact, the participant's body becomes a means of creating art. The goal of these interactions is to communicate the pleasure of aesthetic creation; because these media are unfamiliar, dwelling as they do on dynamic images controlled by movements of the viewer's bodies, artists trained in traditional static media have no automatic advantage in creating pleasing results. Each of the *Individual Medley* interactions captures the eight most recent silhouettes of the participant and close them according to how they overlap on the screen (Fig. 45). Each method of assigning color constitutes a distinct interaction and leads to different behavior by the participants. If each new silhouette is placed on top of the others, the result suggests a political poster; if one silhouette is used as a matte, succeeding silhouettes break the person's image into a jigsaw puzzle. In the *Body Surfacing* interactions, the participant's image points continuously as it moves about the screen. The colors that are applied by the participant's body shade from one to another. The use of shading provides a sense of depth, defining interesting metallic surfaces (Fig. 46). As these surfaces are defined, colors flow along them in the direction of the participant's movement.

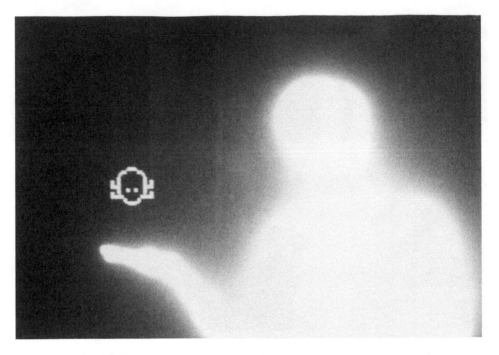

FIGURE 44   *Critter*. Reprinted with permission of the author.

Cat's Cradle. Cat's Cradle lets one play with a graphic string. A graphic curve
appears on the screen, attracted by the fingertips in the image (Fig. 47). The
curve adapts to the movements of the fingers, no matter how fast the fingers appear and disappear. The effect is exactly the same as it would be were one playing
with a real string, except that there is nothing there. More than one person can
control the curve, and more fingers create more complex shapes.

Mandala. This and other classes of interaction free the participant's image from the
constraint of gravity. For example, in *Mandala*, several copies of the participant's silhouette are arranged in a circular pattern on the screen. The left edge of
one silhouette is joined to the right edge of the adjacent one, creating a pattern
that initially appears to be abstract (Fig. 48). Movements of one limb are repeated simultaneously all around the pattern. For instance, raising an arm causes
a concentric movement from the outside to the inside of the *Mandala*. The size
of the circular pattern also changes with the participant's movements. The result
is a captivating kaleidoscopic medium.

Artwheels. In *Artwheels*, one's image rolls down a graphic string extended between
the upright forefingers of the desk operator's two hands (Fig. 49). One can
change this new shape by raising and lowering one's arms and kicking one's legs.
This motion influences the movement down the string; for instance, by shifting
the center of gravity, one can do cartwheels and control the direction of the roll.

Hanging by a Thread. In this interaction, the videodesk hand appears with a string
hanging down from the extended forefinger. The image of the *Videoplace* participant is dangling at the end of the string (Fig. 50). After a moment's investi-

FIGURE 45   *Individual Medley.* Reprinted with permission of the author.

gation, the participant wonders whether or not it is possible to swing on the string. He shifts his weight from side to side, and his image shakes a bit. Then he moves more obviously from side to side, and his image starts to swing. By synchronizing his movements with the swinging on the screen, he can pump for greater elevation.

Despite his creative, unconventional techniques, Krueger has to work more like a scientist than an artist to create the tools and technology he needs for his art. Indeed, his system achieves real-time performance through a specialized hardware and software configuration that he designed and realized. *Videoplace* hardware runs on a bus structure that allows great flexibility in the intermingling of video images, standard graphics, and the output of specialized graphics generators. Much of the programming is done in C, although each of the subordinate processors has a specialized architecture that is controlled by a unique microcode. Twelve specialized processors operate parallel to the main processor. They are told what kind of processing to perform and to do so automatically until their rules of behavior are changed.

Traditional art is created by an artist and appreciated by a viewer. In an artificial reality like those created by Krueger, the relationship between the artist and the viewer is only one of several possible relationships; the relationship of one viewer to another can also be the explicit subject of the work. In fact, an interactive exhibit augurs new relationships for artists with their audience and with their art. In its attempt to involve the audience, the artificial reality has closer ties with the happenings of the early 1960s than it does with more conventional art modes. When participation becomes the subject of the aesthetic work, the viewer's critical faculties are given new responsibilities; the viewers

FIGURE 46   *Body Surfacing*. Reprinted with permission of the author.

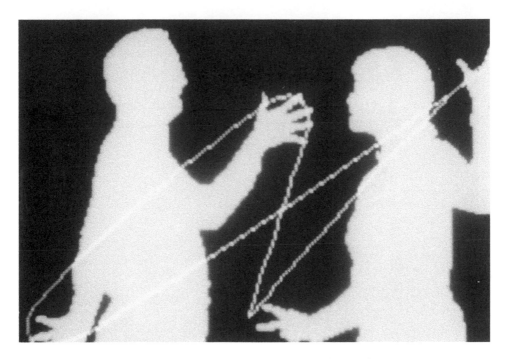

FIGURE 47   *Cat's Cradle*. Reprinted with permission of the author.

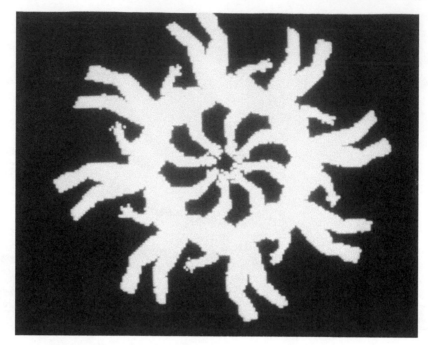

FIGURE 48 *Mandala*. Reprinted with permission of the author.

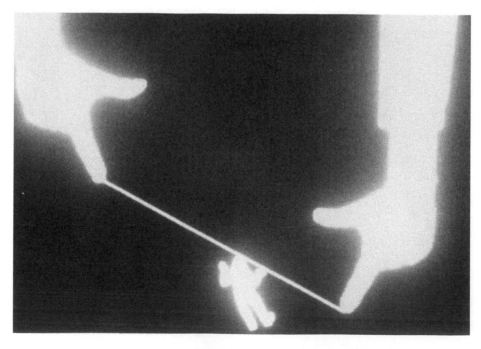

FIGURE 49 *Artwheels*. Reprinted with permission of the author.

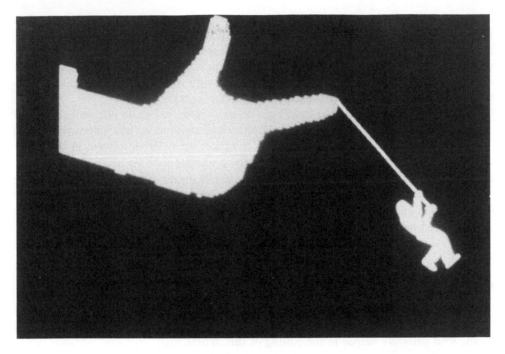

FIGURE 50 *Hanging by a Thread*. Reprinted with permission of the author.

are no longer judging the finished work of the artist—their own actions complete the piece. Thus, within the framework of the artist's exhibit, the participants also become creators.

CONCLUSION

Alan Turing looked forward to the day when computers could do such creative and imaginative things as write poetry and paint pictures. In the early 1950s, when computers had restricted capabilities, he foresaw them being used for creative tasks that even today we regard as quintessentially human (39). Although still not able to completely fulfill Turing's dream, computing has intrigued artists for nearly 30 years now.

Nowadays, many artists use computers to help them in their work and it is no longer remarkable that they do so. However, most artists who are concerned with the use of the machine employ it to realize ideas that they have devised without computer aid. Computing in this case is used as a tool for production or, perhaps, as a medium. This is by far the most popular role of computing in the arts. On the other hand, several artists have started to see computing as a catalyst to new, more exciting, and innovative work. It is, in fact, this latter use of computers in which the essence of computer art resides.

In searching for significant computer art we should ask ourselves whether the artwork could have been made without the use of a computer and whether it takes advantage of the unique new capabilities made possible by the machine. The computer's key attributes include the ability to emulate human behavior and intelligence (40); the ability to be connected to other computers over short or global distances (41); the ability to collect information through a large number of sensory modes, many of them not available directly to human sense organs; and the ability to be used in a real-time interactive interplay with humans or other input devices (42). Finally, in computer animation, the computer makes possible work that that would be practically impossible to realize by other methods, particularly in exploiting connections between sound and vision.

This implies that the artist must become more informed about different aspects of computing, algorithms, mathematics, visualization, simulation, and interactivity, and how these ideas affect our culture. But for computer art to be significant in the larger context of art history it is not enough to blindly assimilate such concepts and pass them off, untransformed, as art. Computer artists should be aware of the issues tackled by the rest of the art world and engage in genuine self-reflection. In this view, computer practices will likely not improve art practices nor aid them but will create completely different practices and lend more shape to our glowing notions of what a computer art might be.

ACKNOWLEDGMENTS

We would like to thank all the artists who have kindly contributed to the realization of this article by providing material regarding their work. A special thanks goes also to Jill Bean, who patiently helped in the editing of this article.

REFERENCES

1. J. Lansdown, "Computer Graphics: A Tool for Artist, Designer, and Amateur," in *Advances in Computer Graphics III*, Springer-Verlag, New York, 1989, pp. 147–175.
2. J. Lansdown, "Generative Techniques in Graphical Computer Art: Some Possibilities and Practices," in *Computers in Art, Design and Animation*, J. Lansdown and R. A. Earnshaw (eds.), Springer-Verlag, New York, 1989, pp. 56–79.
3. R. Maiocchi, "Can You Make a Computer Understand and Produce Art? *AI & Society*, 5, 183–201 (1991).
4. J. Gumowsky and C. Mira, "Point Sequences Generated by Two-Dimensional Recurrences," *Inform. Proc.*, 74, 851–855, 1974.
5. B. B. Mandelbrot, *Fractals: Form, Chance, and Dimension*, W. H. Freeman and Company, San Francisco, 1977.
6. B. B. Mandelbrot, *The Fractal Geometry of Nature*, W. H. Freeman and Company, San Francisco, 1982.
7. B. B. Mandelbrot, *Fractals: Form, Chance, and Dimension*, W. H. Freeman and Company, San Francisco, 1977.
8. B. B. Mandelbrot, *The Fractal Geometry of Nature*, W. H. Freeman and Company, San Francisco, 1982.
9. A. Fournier, D. Fussel, and L. Carpenter, "Computer Rendering of Stochastic Models," *CACM*, 25, 371–384 (1982).
10. R. F. Voss, "Random Fractal Forgeries," in *Fundamental Algorithms for Computer Graphics*, R. A. Earnshaw (ed.), Springer-Verlag, New York, 1985, pp. 805–835.
11. H. O. Peitgen and P. H. Richter, *The Beauty of Fractals: Images of Complex Dynamical Systems*, Springer-Verlag, New York, 1985.
12. M. Noll, "Human or Machine: A Subjective Comparison of Piet Mondrian's 'Composition with Lines' and a Computer Generated Picture," *Psych. Rec.*, 16, 1–10 (1966).

13. A. Barr, *"Artificial Intelligence: Cognition as Computation,"* in *The Study of Information: Interdisciplinary Messages*, F. Machlup and U. Mansfield, (eds.), Wiley Interscience, New York, 1983.

14. T. S. Kuhn, *The Structure of Scientific Revolutions*, University of Chicago Press, Chicago, 1970.

15. H. Cohen, "How to Draw Three People in a Botanical Garden." *Proc. AAAI* (1988).

16. L. Mazlack and M. Granger, Representing Aesthetic Judgments," in *Proc. of the International Conference on Cybernetics and Society*, Atlanta, GA, 1981.

17. G. Stiny, "Introduction to Shape and Shape Grammars," *Environ. Plan.*, B(7) 343–351 (1980).

18. R. G. Lauzzana and L. Pocock-Williams, "A Rule System for Analysis in the Visual Arts," *Leonardo*, *21*(4), 445–452 (1988).

19. J. Kirsh and R. Kirsh, "The Structure of Paintings: Formal Grammar and Design," *Environ. Plan. B: Planning and Design*, *13*, 163–176 (1986).

20. J. Kirsh and R. Kirsh, "The Anatomy of Painting Style: Description with Computer Rules." *Leonardo*, *21*(4), 437–444 (1988).

21. N. Chomsky, *Aspects of the Theory of Syntax*, MIT Press, Cambridge, MA, 1965.

22. J. Kirsh and R. Kirsh, "The Structure of Paintings: Formal Grammar and Design," *Environ. Plan. B: Planning and Design*, *13*, 163–176 (1986).

23. J. Kirsh and R. Kirsh, "The Anatomy of Painting Style: Description with Computer Rules." *Leonardo*, *21*(4), 437–444 (1988).

24. H. Cohen, "How to Draw Three People in a Botanical Garden." *Proc. AAAI* (1988).

25. H. Cohen, "Off the Shelf," The Visual Computer, *2*, 191–194 (1986).

26. H. Cohen, "What Is an Image?" in *Proc. IJCAI6*, 1979, pp. 1028–1057.

27. J. Pearson, "The Computer: Liberator or Jailor of the Creative Spirit," *Vis. Computer*, *4*(1), 19–26 (1988).

28. M. Mohr, *Fractured Symmetry: Algorithmic Works 1967–1987*, Wilhelm-Hack-Museum, Ludwigshafen au Rhein, Germany, 1987.

29. M. Mohr, *Laserglyphs*, Galerie Mueller-Roth, Stuttgart, Germany, 1992.

30. W. Latham, "Form Synth: The Rule-Based Evolutions of Complex Forms from Geometric Primitives," in *Computers in Art, Design and Animation*, J. Lansdown and R. A. Earnshaw (eds.), Springer-Verlag, New York, 1989, pp. 80–108.

31. W. Latham and S. Todd, "Sculptures in the Void," *IBM Syst. J.*, *28*(4), 682,688 (1989).

32. S. Todd and W. Latham, *Evolutionary Art and Computers*, Academic Press, New York, 1992.

33. S. Todd, W. Latham, and P. Hughes, "Computer Sculpture Design and Animation." *Vis. Computer Anim.*, *2*, 98–105 (1991).

34. R. Russett and C. Starr, *Experimental Animation: Origins of a New Art*, Da Capo, 1985.

35. T. A. DeFanti, "Language Control Structures for Easy Electronic Visualization." *BYTE*, 90–106 (November 1980).

36. M. Krueger, *Artificial Reality II*, Addison-Wesley, Reading, MA, 1991.

37. M. Krueger, "Videoplace: A Report from the Artificial Reality Laboratory." *Leonardo*, *18*(3), 145–151 (1985).

38. M. Krueger, *Artificial Reality II*, Addison-Wesley, Reading, MA, 1991.

39. A. Turing, "Computer Machinery and Intelligence." *Mind*, *59*(236), 433–460 (1950).

40. R. Maiocchi, "Can You Make a Computer Understand and Produce Art? *AI & Society*, *5*, 183–201 (1991).

41. E. Kac, "Aspects of Aesthetics of Telecommunications," in *SIGGRAPH '92 Visual Proceedings*, ACM Press, New York, 1992, pp. 47–57.

42. Ref. 36.

43. J. D. Foley, A. vanDam, S. K. Feiner, and J. F. Hughes. *Computer Graphics: Principles and Practice*. Addison-Wesley, 1990.

44. Hofstadter, D., *Metamagical Themas: Questing for the Essence of Mind and Pattern*, Bantam Books, New York, 1985.

BIBLIOGRAPHY

Alexenberg, M. (ed.), "Art with Computer." *Vis. Computer*, 4(1) (1988).

Cohen, H., B. Cohen, and P. Nii, *The First Artificial Intelligence Coloring Book*, W. Kaufmann Inc., 1984.

DeFanti, T. A. and C. A. Csuri (eds.), "Art and Animation." *IEEE CG&A*, 5(7) (1985).

Emmet, A. "Computer and Fine Arts." *Computer Graph. World*, 68–75 (October 1988).

Franke, H. *Computer-Graphics—Computer Art*, Springer-Verlag, New York, 1986.

Goodman, C., *Digital Visions: Computer and Art*, H. N. Abrams, Inc., New York, 1987.

Grimes, J., and G. Lorig, (eds.), *SIGGRAPH '92 Visual Proceedings*, ACM Press, New York, 1992.

Hofstadter, D., *Goedel, Escher, Bach: An Eternal Golden Braid*, Vintage Books, New York, 1980.

Jankel, A., and R. Morton, *Creative Computer Graphics*, Cambridge University Press, Cambridge, 1984.

Kawaguchi, Y., "A Morphological Study of the Form of Nature." *Computer Graph.*, 16(3), 223–232 (1982).

Kawaguchi, Y., "The Making of Growth, II: Morphogenesis." *IEEE CG&A* (April 1985).

Kerlow, V., (ed.), "Computers in Art and Design." *ACM* (1991).

Lansdown, J., and R. A. Earnshaw (eds.), *Computers in Art, Design and Animation*, Springer-Verlag, New York, 1989.

Linehan, T. E., (ed.), "Digital image—digital cinema." *Leonardo*, supplemental issue (1990).

Resch, M., (ed.), "Computer Art in Context." *Leonardo*, supplemental issue (1989).

Spencer, D. (chair), "Computer Art—An oxymoron? Views from the Mainstream." *Computer Graph.*, 23(5), 211–221 (1989).

Stiny, G., and Gips, J., *Shape Grammars and Their Uses*, Birkhauser, Basel, 1975.

ROBERTO MAIOCCHI
with a contribution by EVAN C. RICKS

THE AUTOMATION OF ASTRONOMICAL TELESCOPES

INTRODUCTION

Galileo probably dreamed of a clockwork that would aim his telescope automatically and record the locations of the moons of Jupiter while he slept. Any astronomer who has had to gather large amounts of observational data has daydreamed about such a robotic lackey.

To understand why astronomers are interested in the automation of telescopes, you need only imagine that you are an astronomer observing through the night. You begin in late afternoon preparing your telescope and its attached instrument, a camera, photometer, or spectrograph. After supper you begin taking calibration data, and as soon as it is dark enough, you begin collecting data. Photons from stars and galaxies stream into the telescope and funnel into your instrument. Taking a break for night-lunch about 1 A.M. seems a frivolous waste of starlight, and you work steadily through the night. At dawn, you collect more calibration data, and if you are lucky make it to bed only 12 hours after you began.

The strain of working long nights at the telescope might justify astronomers' interest in telescope automation, but there are other advantages to automation. The long nights are usually tremendously boring, and it is easy to make mistakes that will be discovered only weeks or months later when the data are reduced. Also, one night is not enough for most research projects, so an astronomer might need to observe for a number of consecutive nights. Some research projects can require months or years of nightly observations, and a human observer with human responsibilities and limitations cannot obtain such synoptic data. Thus, astronomers yearn for a robotic telescope which can observe from a distant mountaintop every night, year after year, producing dependable synoptic data.

Although astronomers have automated some parts of the observing task, most telescopes still require the presence of a human observer. In this article we discuss the true robotic telescope—a fully automated observatory that can observe night after night without the presence of a human. In fact, such fully robotic telescopes have been in operation since 1983.

THE PROBLEM

To automate an astronomical telescope we must meet two design requirements: instrument control and pointing. The first of these is straightforward, but the last is unique to astronomy.

Instrument Control

An astronomical telescope is a bit like a giant funnel gathering the faint light from a distant star and feeding it into an instrument. Whether it is a photometer, spectrograph, or camera, the instrument attached to the telescope contains a photosensitive detector, usually a photomultiplier tube or a CCD (Charged Coupled Device) camera. Control of such an instrument and the storage of data are commonplace problems in computer interfacing.

Data from an astronomical instrument are almost invariably stored as counts. Photons are counted as they arrive over a given integration time, and the automation system then reads out the accumulated counts and stores them with appropriate ancillary information such as data, time, object, filter, and so on. Data from a photomultiplier tube may amount to a single number and is easy to store, but data from a CCD camera can amount to a large mass of numbers. A CCD camera is an array of light-sensitive diodes, and the recorded image is then stored as a matrix of numbers. A 512×512 CCD image will consist of 262,144 numbers and can occupy a large part of a megabyte in memory. Thus, an automation system storing data from a CCD camera will require large amounts of memory.

Mechanical control of an instrument is straightforward. An astronomical instrument, such as a photometer, spectrograph, or camera, will include filters and other optical elements that can be moved. For example, it is standard design to place filters in a wheel driven by a stepper motor. Given a position detector on the wheel, the automation system can move the desired filter into the light path. For some elements such as lenses, mirrors, prisms, or gratings, high-precision mechanisms may be required to assure repeatability, but that is usually not the case for filters.

Pointing

The automation system must be able to point the telescope at the selected star to high precision and then center the star in the field of view so that the starlight enters the instrument. This is possible because astronomers use a coordinate system that covers the sky just as the system of latitude and longitude covers the earth. The declination (DEC) of a star is equivalent to the latitude of a city. Declination is measured north or south from the celestial equator, the line around the sky directly above the earth's equator. Right ascension (RA) is measured eastward around the sky from the vernal equinox. Thus, it is possible to specify the coordinates of a star on the sky, just as we could specify the latitude and longitude of a city on earth (1).

Pointing is confused by the rotation of the earth. If we point the telescope at a star, the eastward rotation of the earth will move the telescope eastward, and within minutes, the star will have drifted out of the field of view. Thus, astronomical telescopes need a motorized drive that moves the telescope westward to keep pace with the stars. Once pointed, the telescope will remain pointed at the proper star.

It has been common to mount a telescope using two perpendicular axes of rotation such that one axis, the polar axis, is parallel to the earth's axis of rotation. Thus, motion about the polar axis is east–west motion, and motion about the other axis, the declination axis, is north–south. Such an equatorial mounting, as it is called, simplifies pointing. Stepper motors and resolvers installed on the two axes make it possible for the control system to move the telescope from star to star.

An alternative mounting system is called an alt-azimuth system. In such a mounting, the telescope moves like a cannon; it can move in altitude perpendicular to the horizon or in azimuth parallel to the horizon. An alt-azimuth mounting is not mechanically convenient because the westward motion of the star requires that the telescope move about both axes simultaneously and at varying rates, but a control computer can quickly compute the proper rates and drive stepper motors on the axes. In addition, the field of view of a telescope on an alt-azimuth mounting will rotate as the telescope tracks across the sky. This is not a serious difficulty for photometry, but it is quite confusing for CCD imaging. Alt-azimuth mountings are generally stronger, so they have become popular for larger telescopes now that fast computers are available to convert from equatorial coordinates to alt-azimuth coordinates (2). Most astronomical telescopes are on equatorial mountings, so we will not further consider the problems unique to alt-azimuth telescopes.

Given a telescope on an equatorial mounting, the control system can point the telescope in a north–south coordinate that can be made to correspond exactly to declination, but the east–west pointing is related to the local coordinates of the telescope; that is, the resolvers tell the computer that the telescope is pointed a certain distance west of the local celestial meridian (where the local celestial meridian is a north–south line on the sky passing through the zenith). This distance measured westward from the local celestial meridian is called the hour angle (HA) of the star. If the control computer is to point the telescope at a star with known right ascension, then the computer must know the local sidereal time (LST). Local sidereal time is equal to the right ascension of a star located on the local celestial meridian, and it is simple to calculate from the current time, date, and longitude of the observatory (3). Thus, the control computer can use its internal clock and a simple algorithm to find local sidereal time. The computer can then subtract the right ascension from the local sidereal time to find the hour angle and then use the stepper motors to move the telescope to that position.

HA = LST − RA.

The hour angle of a star east of the local celestial meridian is negative.

For practical operations, we must add a final detail. The earth's axis precesses with a period of 26,000 years, and although this is a very slow motion, it does affect the coordinates of stars. Thus, when we give the declination and right ascension of a star, we must also give the date on which the star had those coordinates. Referred to as the epoch of the coordinates, these dates are listed in star catalogs as 1900.0, 1950.0, 2000.0, and so on. The telescope coordinates always have the epoch of the current date; so to point the telescope precisely, the catalog coordinates must be converted to the current epoch. For example, if the telescope is observing on the night of June 30, 1997, and using catalog coordinates from 1950.0, the control computer must use a simple algorithm (4) to transform the coordinates from 1950.0 to 1997.5. Failure to do this would probably result in the telescope failing to locate the right star.

Centering

Just pointing the telescope at a given star is not sufficient. The pointing is only as good as the internal clock in the computer, and all but the smallest telescopes are subject to flexure as they sag under their own weight. Wind loading and even the refraction of starlight passing through the earth's atmosphere can reduce the accuracy of pointing. Generally, however, pointing can be made accurate enough to place the target star in the field of view. The problem then is to move the star to the exact center of the field so that its light will enter the instrument attached to the telescope.

To assure that the light of a single star enters the instruments, astronomers use a small opening called the entrance diaphragm to isolate the image of a single star and block the light from nearby stars. Such apertures in a photometer typically include a small circle on the sky 60 to 30 arc seconds in diameter. For accurate photometry, the star must be centered in this aperture as precisely as possible. (The aperture for spectroscopy is a slit or the end of a fiber-optic cable, and these are generally much smaller than the diaphragms used in a photometer. Centering for spectroscopy is therefore, much more difficult and will be considered separately.) This problem of centering the star in the diaphragm has been solved in a number of ways.

An early solution was the squared spiral search (5). After the telescope is pointed as close to the target star as possible, the control computer begins taking a series of short integrations through the photometer, moving the telescope in a widening spiral until a star of suitable brightness is found in the diaphragm (Fig. 1).

Once the star is located, the computer must place it in the exact center of the aperture, and that can be done by making four integrations in an overlapping flower pattern (6). The computer can locate the star by determining which integrations include the star (Fig. 2). A few quick iterations will bring the star to that point where it is included in all four integrations, and the computer can then move the diaphragm to bring the star to the center. Typical times for these search and centering integrations are 1 s or less, so the process is quite rapid but is limited to stars bright enough to detect in such short integrations.

The CCD cameras provide alternative methods for the location and centering of stars. Telescope pointing is precise enough to bring the star into the field of view of a finder telescope with a wider field of view than the entrance diaphragm. A short-exposure CCD image can then be analyzed by the control computer to find the star (7), with appropriate pattern recognition if necessary (8,9), and the telescope can be moved to bring the star to the center of the aperture. CCD centering is faster and can find fainter stars better than spiral searches, but its implementation is not as simple.

The first robotic telescopes could not observe stars fainter than about an 8th magnitude (about 6.3 times fainter than the faintest stars visible to the naked eye). There are many interesting stars brighter than this limit, but there are many more that are fainter. CCD centering has allowed telescopes to observe down to the 9th magnitude or even fainter. (Each step of one magnitude is a factor of 2.5 in brightness.) However, as robotic telescopes go to fainter stars, a new problem arises. There are vastly more faint stars than

```
      7 — 8 — 9 —10
      |            |
      6   1 — 2   11
      |       |    |
  *   5 — 4 — 3   12
                   |
  17—16—15—14—13
```
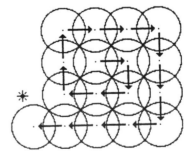

FIGURE 1   The squared spiral search allows the telescope to locate a star by making a spiral pattern of short integrations through its entrance diaphragm. Numbered integrations are shown at left; the outline of the entrance diaphragm is shown at right. In this example, the star will be found on the 18th integration.

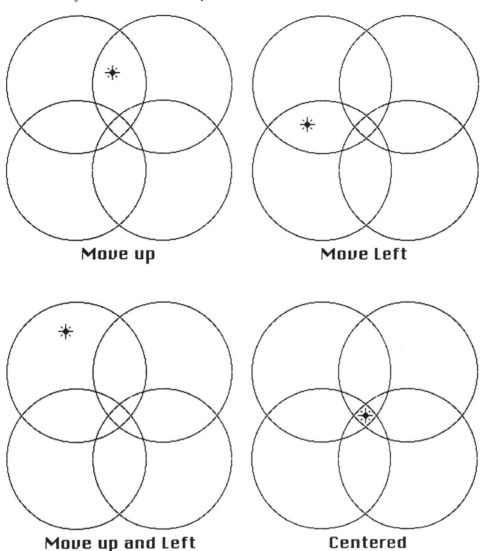

Move up   **Move Left**

Move up and Left   **Centered**

FIGURE 2 Once located, the star can be centered by making four short integrations in a flower pattern. The presence of the star in one or more integrations tells the computer how to move. The pattern is iterated until the star appears in all four integrations, at which time the computer moves the entrance diaphragm to center the star.

bright stars. Thus, a robotic telescope trying to center on an 8th magnitude star will probably find only one such star in its field of view. But if it tries to center on a 12th magnitude star, it will find many such stars in its field of view, and it will have difficulty selecting the target star. Pattern recognition might be a solution, but it is probably easier to make blind offsets from nearby bright stars. The telescope can center precisely on a nearby 8th magnitude star without ambiguity, and then calculate the exact number of stepper motor pulses needed to move to the fainter target star. For such short moves, telescope flexure and other errors are quite small.

Differential Photometry

As the final step in the definition of our problem, we can examine the procedure required for the photometry of a variable star. Procedures for spectroscopy will be slightly different, but differential photometry has been the primary task of robotic telescopes to date, and a summary of differential photometry will help us understand how instrument control, pointing, and centering can be combined to make useful astronomical observations.

Differential photometry refers to the measurement of the brightness of a target star with respect to a nearby comparison star. In practice, our target star would be a star whose brightness varies because the star is pulsating in some way or because it is part of a binary system in which two stars revolve around each other and periodically obstruct the light from their companion. Such variable stars are intrinsically interesting and many can be used to study the nature of stellar surfaces, magnetic fields, and so on. Some stars have periods of variation as short as 20 min, whereas other have periods up to 600 days. An astronomer studying such a star would like to photometer it time after time to clearly define the changes in its brightness and color. A graph of the changing brightness of the star versus time is called the light curve of the star.

Because the earth's atmosphere absorbs and scatters light, it is difficult to make absolute measurements of stellar brightness and color; rather it is common to make differential measurements by comparing the brightness of the variable star against the brightness of a nearby comparison star known to be constant. To a first approximation, any absorption and scattering due to the earth's atmosphere will affect both stars in the same amount, and, thus, the difference between their measured brightnesses will be nearly independent of the earth's atmosphere. To ensure against a comparison star that turns out to be variable itself, astronomers commonly use a second comparison star as a check star. Thus, differential photometry requires repeated measurements of three stars, the variable, comparison, and check stars.

In addition, the astronomer must also measure the brightness of the sky around the stars. The night sky is not perfectly dark, and light from the sky is included in any measurement of a star. Thus, the astronomer makes a sky measurement at a starless spot on the sky near the variable, and this sky brightness is subtracted from all star measurements during data reduction.

Although most atmospheric effects are removed in differential photometry, there are secondary effects because the variable and its comparison star are not in precisely the same position on the sky. It is possible to correct for this by determining the properties of the earth's atmosphere through the observation of a set of standard stars whose true brightnesses and colors are known (10,11). From the standard stars, the astronomer can compute constants that describe the way the earth's atmosphere dims starlight as a function of altitude above the horizon and star color. These extinction coefficients can then be used to correct the variable-star data for atmospheric extinction.

Finally, the astronomer must transform observations into a standard photometric system. Although the telescope may contain standard filters and detectors, no two filters or detectors are precisely the same. The astronomer can use the observations of standard stars to derive transformation coefficients to convert the raw observations into a standard photometric system to which all astronomers can make comparisons.

Clearly, differential photometry is an obvious target for automation. The observer, neuron or silicon, must observe three stars and a starless sky position over and over through the night, pausing only to observe certain standard stars. For longer-period stars, a single nightly set of observations of the three stars and sky position may be sufficient;

so the observer could observe many such stars once on each night. In either case, it is boring, repetitious work that can best be done by a robotic telescope.

A SHORT HISTORY

Early attempts at telescope automation took the form of observing support for a human astronomer. The human was eliminated completely only when microcomputers became fast and powerful. Thus, truly robotic telescopes are recent developments in astronomy.

Early Automated Telescopes

Many astronomical telescopes have been partially automated. It is not uncommon to find an automated photometer or spectrograph. It is also not uncommon to find a telescope interfaced with a computer so that the astronomer issues commands to the computer, and the computer then moves the telescope. A true robotic telescope, however, is one that is run without the presence of a human observer.

Two forerunners of fully robotic telescopes were designed for automated photometry. The 0.6-m telescope at Michigan State University was automated in 1972 using a Raytheon minicomputer (12). The control software was written in assembly and the computer controlled the photometer and the motion of the telescope. The telescope was not fully robotic in that a human observer was required to check the centering of stars and generally monitor operations. In a similar way, the 1.3-m telescope at Kitt Peak National Observatory was automated such that it could be run from a control room 40 miles away at the headquarters building. The program was read from punched paper tape, and once initiated, the progress of the observing was checked at 2-h intervals by a human observer. Although the telescope did eventually produce the light curve for a variable star (13), it never became fully operational because of reliability problems with the Packard-Bell 250 computer, and the telescope was eventually converted to a manual operation.

Perhaps the earliest automated telescope was developed about 1967 at the University of Wisconsin (14). Located in a modified garden shed near the main observatory, the telescope was 8 in. in diameter and was automated with resolvers on the axes of motion and a DEC PDP/8 computer containing only 4 K of RAM. The computer monitored a light sensor to detect darkness and a rain sensor to avoid opening the roof in bad weather. The telescope read star positions from punched paper tape and made photometric observations through the night. If it failed to find three stars in a row, it assumed that the sky was cloudy and shut down for a hour before trying again. The telescope operated for some years, but observed variable stars in only one special project. Normally, it observed bright standard stars and calculated constants (extinction coefficients) used to correct for the extinction in the earth's atmosphere. Thus, human observers in the main observatory measured the target stars for the night, whereas the robotic telescope supported the humans by determining the constants needed for data reduction.

In 1979, David Skillman, then a NASA computer programmer, put an automatic telescope to work observing variable stars (15). His telescope was a 12.5-in.-diam reflector run by two computers. A KIM single-board computer located on the telescope handled basic operations and communicated with an Apple computer located inside his house. Although the telescope required manual startup, it was able to continue observing the variable, the comparison star, and the sky through the night. Thus, it concentrated on a single variable star at a time and did not perform long slews across the sky. Skillman later upgraded to an automated photometer which included its own Z-80 microprocessor.

Automatic Supernova Searches

Although the study of variable stars tended to drive the development of one form of robotic telescope, the search for supernovae drove a parallel development in imaging telescopes (16).

A supernova occurs when a star explodes. From the earth, we see a new star appear in the sky and then fade over months back to invisibility. Such explosions can be caused by a massive star near the end of its life collapsing into a black hole or neutron star, or a dead star, a white dwarf, collapsing into a neutron star. In fact, astronomers probably do not know all of the situations that can trigger supernovae explosions because they are so rare—roughly one supernova per century per galaxy.

Because supernovae are so rare, we cannot wait for the eruption of supernovae in our own Milky Way galaxy. Instead, astronomers watch distant galaxies for the appearance of supernovae. If a supernova can be detected early in its rise in brightness, within a day or two of its first appearance, then astronomers around the world can study the critical early stages of its development. But with supernovae so rare, one must inspect hundreds of galaxies per night to be confident of finding a few supernovae per year. Such long-term routine surveys are difficult and exhausting for humans, but they are well suited for automation.

An early automated supernovae search was conducted at Corralitos Observatory in New Mexico in the early 1970s (17). They used a computer to move a 24-in. telescope to each galaxy and image it using an intensified television detector. The image was then presented to a human observer for comparison with a previous reference photograph, and the human had to inspect the image for the presence of a new point of light that would signal the appearance of a supernova. The frantic pace was very hard on observers and in 8 years, only 12 supernovae were found. The project was shut down due to loss of funding.

In the early 1970s, Stirling A. Colgate at the New Mexico Institute of Mining and Technology, automated a 30-in. telescope with the intention of developing a robotic supernova search. The mounting was a military surplus Nike-Ajax radar mount, and the system communicated through a 30-km microwave link with an IBM 360/44 computer on campus (18). Although the automation of the telescope was completed early, the automated acquisition and analysis of galaxy images has never been fully implemented.

As computers became less expensive and more powerful, supernova searchers turned to multiple computer systems. Carlton Pennypacker and his team (19) built a successful automated system at the University of California's Leuschner Observatory. The 30-in. telescope and 320 × 512 pixel CCD camera were controlled by two IBM personal computers and a DEC MicroVAX 3200 ran the overall system. The final configuration included dome and mirror cover automation plus an automatic weather station for a completely robotic system. During the spring of 1990, for instance, the system discovered three supernovae with no human in the observatory. The telescope was also able to photometer supernovae discovered earlier. The team is now developing a new telescope at a better site.

The automation of supernova searches is a specialized problem involving faint objects and the exact comparison of CCD frames to detect the appearance of a new star image. Much of the difficulty that astronomers have experienced in developing these robotic searches has been in the automated reduction, analysis, and comparison of CCD images. Compared to CCD imaging, photometry is much simpler and easier to automate.

The Phoenix 10 and Fairborn 10

Two related telescopes of similar size were the first to solve all of the major problems in observing many variable stars through the night without human attention. Although more sophisticated telescopes have now been built, it is worth examining the automation of these telescopes as an illustration of the basic solutions now in use. Newer telescopes will be discussed later.

Louis Boyd built an automated photometric telescope in the early 1980s that was the first to observe many variable stars through the night without human assistance. Now known as the Phoenix 10, it is a 10-in.-diam F/6 reflector with a conventional photometer using an entrance diaphragm of 60 seconds of arc (20). The mounting was designed to have a low moment of inertia and to be stiff enough to withstand 25,000 moves per night. Built entirely for robotic control, the telescope has no provision for manual operation.

Boyd describes the first control system, which used a Southwest Technical 6800-based computer and a primitive version of FORTH as "complex" and "outdated," so it was quickly replaced with a Peripheral Technology PT-69 single-board computer holding a Motorola 6809E microprocessor and all of the necessary ports, disk controller, battery-backed clock/calendar, 56K of RAM memory, and 4K of EPROM. Identical stepper motors on the right ascension and declination axes are driven by custom-made boards that use 6 V for normal motions and use 24 V for ramp-up and high-speed motions.

Part of the control system consists of an adjustable clock which sends pulses to the right ascension stepper motor to move the telescope steadily westward at the stellar rate. This, in effect, makes the sky stationary so far as the control software is concerned, and it can move the telescope from star to star without concern about the earth's rotation.

The control program was written in Microware Basic09, and it is instructive to examine how that program, called MAIN, guide the telescope through a night of observations. During the day, procedure TILDARK uses the time and date to compute the location of the sun. When the sun has set, MAIN calls STARTSCOPE, which initializes the filter wheel in the photometer and moves the telescope to a home position defined by optical limit switches. MAIN then selects a star group from a list of candidates. Each group consists of a variable star, a comparison star, and a check star plus the location for a sky measurement. MAIN then calls MOVE, which slews the telescope to the check star in the group. Although there are no shaft encoders on the telescope, the telescope is able to point at a check star to within a few minutes of arc even after a long slew. The HUNT procedure then uses the squared spiral search pattern to locate the star, and the LOCK procedure uses the flower pattern of integrations to center on the star. Integration times during HUNT and LOCK procedures are 0.2 s, so these procedures are rapid.

Good group design calls for a check star that is bright enough to be easily detected and is isolated from nearby stars that could cause confusion. Thus, the check star serves not only as a photometric check, but also as a navigation reference. With properly selected guide stars, the telescope almost never acquires the wrong star. In one 5-month period, the telescope successfully acquired 50,000 stars with zero errors.

Once the guide star is acquired, the control program photometers it through each of three filters; ultraviolet (U), blue (B), and visual (V). (These filters are selected to closely approximate the Johnson UBV photometric system.) The telescope then moves from star to star and completes a total of 33 integrations each of 10 s length in the pattern KSCVCVCVCSK, where K stands for check star, S for sky, C for comparison star, and V for variable star. The total observation takes about 9 min, after which the control program MAIN selects the next group from the observing list and begins the cycle over.

The Phoenix 10 selects stars from its list of groups using a set of criteria that can be optimized for best operation. The control program has a defined window outside of which it is not allowed to observe because it may point at nearby objects such as other telescopes or because it would be pointing near the horizon where the earth's atmosphere is less transparent. Each group is assigned a probability between 0 and 100, with 0 meaning it will never be observed and 100 meaning it will be observed every time it is selected. When the telescope is ready to move to a new group, the control program searches the list for the most westerly group that has not yet been observed that night but is still inside the observing window. This is the next group that will move out of range of the telescope, so it is appropriate to try to observe it next. A random number is then computed and compared with the probability assigned to that group. If the group passes this probability test, it is observed. If the group fails, it is skipped. Thus, the probability parameter gives the astronomer some control over the frequency with which a group will be observed.

Under normal loads of about 80 groups scattered around the sky, the telescope begins after sunset in the western sky and works eastward, reaching the eastern edge of its observing window about 2 or 3 A.M. It then repeats groups already observed and observes new groups as they rise above the eastern edge of the window (21).

On most nights, the telescope list contains groups make up of variable stars, but on certain nights, the telescope can be instructed to observe a list of standard stars. These standard star nights are then used for the determination of extinction and transformation constants needed in the data reduction. Every 3 months the data is removed from the telescope and reduced.

The Phoenix 10 began operation in October 1983. At first it required manual startup each night, but it was eventually moved from Boyd's backyard in Phoenix to the top of Mt. Hopkins south of Tucson, Arizona. There it observes from an automated observatory with motorized roof and no longer needs manual startup.

The Fairborn 10 is a close relative of the Phoenix 10, but it differs in one important way. Whereas Boyd built the Phoenix 10 from the ground up, Russell Genet, an electrical engineer living at the time in Fairborn Ohio, built the Fairborn 10 using commercial assemblies. The Fairborn 10 consists of a 10-in Mead Schmidt-Cassegrain telescope mounted on a DFM Engineering mounting controlled by two high-speed stepper motors. The first photometer was an Optec SSP-3 later replaced with an SSP-3a with a five-position filter slide driven by a stepper motor. The control computer is a PT-69 single-board microcomputer with separate high-speed stepper drivers. Genet adapted much of the software from the Phoenix 10. The first night of fully automatic operations was 19–20 September 1984, less than a year after the Phoenix 10 had begun operation. The telescope is fully documented in *Microcomputer Control of Telescopes* (22).

The Phoenix 10 and the Fairborn 10 have become known as Automatic Photometric Telescopes (APTs). Similar telescopes are now commonly referred to as APTs. New acronyms are being generated for robotic telescopes which obtain images or spectra.

The success of Genet and Boyd brought them in contact with professional astronomers who needed data on large number of stars. Douglas Hall at Vanderbilt University eventually funded Genet and Boyd in the construction of an APT to observe RS Canem Venaticorum stars—eclipsing binary stars with large spots on their surfaces. Sallie Baliunas at the Center for Astrophysics funded the construction of a 0.75-m APT for the study of spot cycles on solar-type stars. A consortium of four colleges funded construction of another 0.75-m APT to be shared among the consortium members.

Through the support of these and other astronomers, Genet and Boyd created The APT Observatory atop Mt. Hopkins south of Tucson, Arizona. The Phoenix 10 and the Fairborn 10 were moved to the new observatory and the new telescopes were built there. The APT Observatory uses a site computer to monitor weather and environmental conditions, control the roof, oversee general operations, and handle modem communications to Boyd in Phoenix. Individual computers run each of the telescopes in the observatory, which now houses seven APTs including some of the newest generation.

New Generation Robotic Telescopes

The newest robotic telescopes at the APT Observatory are innovative in three ways—optics, mounting, and control systems. The lack of a human observer simplifies the design, whereas the requirement of rapid precise movements places constraints on the design.

Two important requirements of a robotic telescope are low moment of inertia to allow rapid motion and low aerodynamic cross section to reduce deflection by wind. These and other cost factors argue for a short *f*-ratio optical system. An 0.75-m *f*/2 primary mirror has been used in a number of new generation APTs (Fig. 3), and it seems to strike the best balance between cost, aperture, and *f*-ratio (23).

The mounting used for newer APTs is specifically designed to eliminate access by a human observer and minimize the moment of inertia, aerodynamic drag, and backlash. A mounting constructed of a welded horseshoe resting on rollers at the north end of the polar axis has succeeded in keeping the telescope small. Both the right ascension and declination drives consist of stepper motor drives on steel rollers pressed against the outer edge of large steel disks. In the case of the right ascension drive, the roller drives the outer edge of the horseshoe. This has proven to be quite accurate and to have very little backlash.

The control systems for these telescopes are based on the Motorola 68000 chip and Microware OS9 operating system in either IBM machines or in clones with PC/XT slots for a common controller card. Because the CPU in such systems must be free of service interrupts, a separate hardware step generator was developed for the controller card (24). This, in fact, allows faster slews and smaller steps (microstepping) for higher-precision centering. A separate clock on the controller card generates a sidereal rate for the right ascension drive and, thus, keeps the sky stationary so far as the control system is concerned. A synchronizer assures that sidereal drive pulses do not overlap slew pulses.

Not all new generation APTs are being built at the APT Observatory. In some cases, existing telescopes are being automated for unattended operation. A good example of this is the automation of the 0.4-m telescope at Indiana University (25). That automation project uses Fortran running under VMS on a MicroVAX II and, thus, provided a different though similar set of solutions to the problems of control of a robotic telescope.

FIGURE 3   New generation automatic photometric telescopes minimize the moment of inertia and wind cross section by using a horseshoe mounting and a low profile that has no provision for human viewing. CCD cameras are used for centering and, in some cases, for data acquisition. (Courtesy AutoScope.)

THE AUTOMATIC TELESCOPE INSTRUCTION SET

The development of robotic telescopes began with individuals interfacing personal computers and homemade telescopes, but the rapid development of new generation systems has required a standardized interface between the astronomer and the automated system. This has been implemented as the Automatic Telescope Instruction Set (ATIS) (26). In general, the astronomer generates commands to the telescope in the form of ATIS instructions in an command (input) file, and the telescope control computer replies with data in the form of an ATIS output file. ATIS is specifically designed to be ASCII files, so it is independent of specific computers and languages.

The principal users of ATIS are the Principal Astronomers (PAs), the astronomers charged with supervising the operation of automatic telescopes. Users are individual astronomers who send requests for observations to the PA. The PA must assemble these requests into ATIS command files and send them to the telescope. When the data are returned from the telescope, the PA must reduce them, verify their quality, sort them by user, and distribute them to each of the users. The Phoenix 10 has been run by a human

PA since 1988, and it serves roughly 20 users. At present, a user on the Phoenix 10 need not know ATIS at all, but as more of the PA's responsibilities are automated, it may become more important for the individual user to be familiar with ATIS.

ATIS Instruction Formats

ATIS instructions can be classified into three categories. Some are specific commands that result in the telescope or instrument moving or taking some action. A few commands are information that define groups with the coordinates, brightnesses, and so on. Some ATIS instructions define parameters that the control computer uses to make group selections or otherwise oversee the operation of the telescope. Two instructions types common in output files contain the results of observations or error messages and flags.

ATIS instructions are usually two lines of ASCII text. The first line is a three-digit number that identifies the command and associated record type. The second line, an argument line, contains information presented in the proper record type. For example, instruction 105 is the move command, and it might appear in an ATIS file as

```
105
14 34 13.4 0 −4 −20
```

This would cause the telescope to move to right ascension 14 h 34 min 13.4 s, and declination −0°4′20″. A 106 command would cause the telescope to search for and center a star and might appear as

```
106
1 3 60 7.2 0.062 10
```

This would cause the telescope to use neutral density filter 1, color band 3, and a 60 arc second diaphragm to search for a star of magnitude 7.2 and color index 0.062 using a 10-s integration. In practice, different control computers might execute these two commands differently depending on the stepper motors and drivers and depending on whether the telescope used squared spiral searching or CCD centering. The advantage of ATIS is that the instructions remain the same from telescope to telescope.

ATIS Command Files

An ATIS command file contains all of the information the telescope needs to run through a single night or through many nights. It is not, however, a specific set of instructions to be executed in precise order. Such a system would often be confused by a brief period of clouds early in the night. Instead, the command file is a list of stars that could be observed, instructions as to how the telescope control computer is to select stars from the list, and instructions as to how stars are to be observed.

As in the operation of the first APTs, the basic unit of observation is a group of three stars—the variable, comparison, and check stars—and the location for a sky measurement. The astronomer begins the creation of a command file by choosing good comparison and check stars for each variable star and the position for a sky observation. The astronomer must then decide how the telescope is to select new stars from the list, and this can be done by setting probabilities, priorities, time, and date windows for each group. Finally, the astronomer must choose the filters, integration times, and sequences that the photometer is to use in observing a group.

Constructing an ATIS command file by hand could be an arduous task, but a generator program is available that simplifies the task considerably (27). The astronomer must then make the choices but can rely on the generator program to assemble the command file in its proper ASCII format.

A single command file is a general purpose file. It might specify an observing program to be used on a single night, or it might be left on the control computer for months or years. The control computer has the ability to use the command file as a resource and generate a workable sequence of observations on any night. Thus, the command computer has some of the attributes of an artificial intelligence using probabilities and priorities to make practical decisions while staying within specified ranges.

ATIS Output Files

An ATIS output file contains a great deal of information in addition to the measurements made by the telescope. Much of the information in the list of groups is passed through into the output file for purposes of reduction. For example, the coordinates of each star is repeated in the output file each time the star is observed. This adds some bulk to the output file, which can approach 200K for a single long night of photometry, but it greatly simplifies the reduction of the data. Many operational parameters and messages appear in the output file, and these can be of great help in resolving questions about telescope operation or data quality.

ATIS output files for photometric telescopes can be reduced using a number of different software packages. CREATE, written by George McCook (27), combines the generator program with a versatile reduction module. Data from the Phoenix 10 is reduced by a principal astronomer in 3-month batches using custom software (10). Other reduction software for APT data were developed by Greg Henry at Vanderbilt University. The reduction of photometric observations is a standard problem in observational astronomy and many astronomers have developed their own software.

An ATIS output file contains all of the data and echoed parameters needed for reduction except extinction and transformation coefficients. In some cases, such as the Phoenix-10, these constants are determined from entire nights dedicated to the observation of standard stars. Some of the newer telescopes include standard stars in the observing list so that extinction can be determined each night. This is more a matter of the astronomer's preference than it is a restriction of the ATIS data set.

ATIS93

ATIS has been in use since 1989, but changes in the way automatic telescopes are used have forced some modifications. In a series of meetings and e-mail conferences in late 1992, ATIS was updated to form ATIS93. The older version of ATIS is now known as ATIS89. Although ATIS93 contains many new features, it remains fully compatible with ATIS89.

Part of the need for ATIS93 is the growing interest in automatic scheduling. Principal astronomers who operate APTs have found the job sufficiently difficult that software is being developed that could automate the scheduling. The automated schedulers must be highly versatile programs capable of accepting the needs of human users and merging them to create efficient command files for the telescope. Individual users will be able to use features of ATIS93 to communicate their needs more precisely to an automatic scheduler. In the same way, the automatic scheduler will have more versatility in communicating with the telescope itself. This versatility will also support networks of astronomers using a telescope, or a single astronomer using a network of telescopes.

Another development is the falling cost of CCD cameras. Many new APTs use CCDs for centering, and CCDs are replacing single-channel photometers on newer telescopes. ATIS93 allows a command file to specify the creation of FITS files containing CCD images, and the resulting output file then contains parameters describing the operation of the camera and pointers to the appropriate FITS files. Neely and Epand have used CCD imaging with a robotic telescope at N/F Observatory since 1990 (28). The telescope, communicating over a high-speed radio link, is able to accept commands for its CCD camera to fulfill all of the functions needed for CCD photometry and return CCD images corrected for dark and flat fields and ready for reduction.

The full ATIS93 specification was published in the summer of 1993 in *Communications of International Amateur-Professional Photoelectric Photometry* (I.A.P.P.P.).

FUTURE DEVELOPMENTS

The rapid developments in computing are driving rapid changes in the nature of robotic telescopes. Some of these changes involve how such telescopes are used, whereas other developments are changing the kinds of observations that robotic telescopes can make.

Networking

Robotic telescopes are so productive that it makes sense for more than one person to use a telescope. Thus, most telescopes are administered by a Principal Astronomer who serves a number of users and balances their needs in scheduling the telescope. As automatic scheduling becomes practical, networking telescopes and computers is becoming important.

Because the earth rotates on its axis, a star remains visible from any one observatory for only 6 hours or so. A network of robotic telescopes spread around the world could follow a given star for many days without interruption. As the star moves too far west for a given telescope, that telescope could hand off to the next telescope to the west to continue the observations. For some kinds of stars and some kinds of phenomena, this kind of continuous monitoring would be very important. It does, however, raise serious questions about how telescopes and users can be networked so as not to interfere with each other. ATIS93 is a step in that direction; however, a fully implemented global network will require sophisticated scheduling if it is to serve more than a few users.

Another use of networking serves education. With a widespread network of telescopes, a teacher and a class can place a request for observations knowing that it would be forwarded to the most appropriate telescope, and it is even possible that observations could be returned to the classroom before the end of class. Given the realities of teaching, especially at the high school and college levels, it is very difficult to bring students together after school hours, but a network of telescopes could serve as a springboard for enhanced science education at many levels.

CCD Image Reduction

It has become standard in the last few years for astronomers to photometer stars by recording a CCD frame and later correcting and analyzing that frame to reveal the brightness of the stars. Although it is certainly possible for robotic telescopes to acquire CCD frames of programmed target stars and it is possible for ATIS93 to control the camera and return the frames to the users, the automated reduction of CCD frames is much more difficult.

The CCD images acquired by the telescope at the N/F Observatory (28) are partially reduced as they are recorded. In the early evening, the telescope obtains flat field exposures from the twilight sky, subtracts bias frames, and averages and normalizes the exposures all in about 30 min. Dark and bias frames are recorded periodically through the night. Each time the telescope records an exposure of a star field, the computer uses the corrected flat fields, bias, and dark frames to correct the exposure before the image is saved. The entire correction procedure takes about 15 s with a 486 computer. The images are then stored on tape, and a human at a work station extracts magnitudes at a later time.

The robotic telescope at Indiana University is even more automated. Operating without a human observer, the telescope locates star fields, records CCD images, corrects the images for flat, bias and dark frames, locates the proper stars in the image, and extracts stellar brightnesses in terms of astronomical magnitudes (25). The automation system even updates light curves each night.

Although some automated reduction has been implemented, it is not yet common. Nevertheless, as CCDs become more common and more reliable and as better software is developed to extract magnitudes, telescopes with CCD detectors will become the standard for robotic astronomy.

Spectrographic Observations

Robotic telescopes have been operating since 1983 making photometric observations. Although robotic spectrographic telescopes were discussed (29), they were implemented only recently.

Automated spectroscopy faces two problems—data storage and centering. The spectra from an astronomical spectrograph would be recorded by a CCD detector, and such images take up large amounts of memory. ATIS93 provides a way to handle such images as separate FITS files, and the falling cost of disk memory means that the storage of large numbers of images is not prohibitively expensive.

More difficult is the problem of moving a star image onto the end of the fiber-optic cable which conducts the light to the spectrograph. Although the entrance aperture of a photometer might be 60 arc seconds in diameter, the fiber optic could be as small as an arc second in diameter. Centering is clearly a problem, but it is compounded by the importance of holding the star image on the fiber over a long exposure. Active guiding is necessary to hold the star image on the end of the fiber-optic cable, but it is not practical to interrupt the light beam frequently to examine the centering as that reduces the duty time of the exposure.

Honeycutt at Indiana University as adapted a 16-in. APT to study the techniques of automated spectroscopy (30). The fiber was 12 arc seconds in diameter and was located outside the field of view of the CCD camera normally used for photometry. Guiding was accomplished by locating the stars in an acquisition field that would bring the program star onto the fiber. This proved to be a successful technique, and the telescope obtained routine H-alpha spectra of two variable stars over a 6-week trial program.

Robotic spectroscopic telescopes will become easier to develop as standards and techniques are established. ATIS93 provides the instruction set needed to control such a telescope with its CCD detector and handle the data files. The use of Indiana University spectrographic telescope shows that a star image can be placed on the end of a fiber-optic cable. AutoScope in Mesa, Arizona is currently developing a fiber-fed spectrograph specifically designed for operation with a robotic telescope.

Automation of Large Telescopes

Some very large telescopes are now beginning operation or are being built, and more are being planned. True robotic operation of these giants is unlikely in the near future, but slightly smaller, but nevertheless large telescopes are now being built for automated observation.

The largest telescopes are so valuable and observing time on them is so precious that it is unlikely that they will be fully automated in the near future. A major telescope such as the Keck 10-meter is a valuable, massive machine that moves quickly, and a simple error can damage such a telescope severely. It is economically reasonable to insist that a trained human observer be present for any observing. In addition, telescope time on these giants is so precious, that most astronomers would not like to risk their observing program to an unattended robot. An equipment failure or software glitch could shut the system down and waste a clear night. With a human in charge, such a problem might be fixed, or the observing plan might be totally rethought to make use of the observing time. Although automation of instruments and control systems are widely used on such telescopes, human supervision is not an unreasonable expense.

The true advantage of a fully robotic telescope is in gathering synoptic data night after night, month after month. The largest telescopes are not used in that synoptic mode, so true robotic operations will be limited to smaller telescopes. Nevertheless, there are large numbers of faint stars that deserve study that cannot be observed with existing robotic telescopes. Thus, new automatic telescopes with larger diameters are being built. A 1-m telescope was recently delivered to Korea, and automatic telescopes as large as 2 m are being planned.

Remote Sites

The first robotic telescopes were built in their designer's backyard, and such telescopes now operate on mountaintops many miles from the principal astronomer. But truly remote sites seem ideal for robotic telescopes.

Astronomical observations at the earth's South Pole have a tremendous advantage. Through the winter there, the sun does not rise for 6 months and the stars do not set. This allows continuous observations of Southern Hemisphere stars without interruption by daylight or the setting of the star. This can be very important for some types of stars whose periods are close to integer multiples of one day, or for stars whose variations do not repeat exactly from cycle to cycle. Winter conditions at the South Pole are severe, however, and humans cannot be expected to work at the telescope. A fully robotic telescope at the South Pole could gather a large amount of useful data on variable stars. Discussions of such a telescope focus invariably on the difficulty in making an unattended mechanism work dependably under such severe conditions.

Another site that has been proposed is the moon. Because the moon has no atmosphere and rotates slowly, it would be an ideal site for a robotic photometric telescope. Even a small-diameter telescope would be able to observe a large number of interesting variable stars. One proposal has been to send an unattended lander to the moon carrying a small robotic telescope; the alternative is to place robotic telescopes near a lunar outpost occupied by a human crew.

Space is another site where robotic telescopes could operate. Certainly some existing telescopes in space have robotic features, but these operations are much larger than envisioned by most robotic telescope enthusiasts. For example, some astronomers have discussed a small, robotic telescope in orbit interfaced to a network of users in colleges and high schools. Requests from students are merged into commands to the orbiting telescope, and observations in the form of images are returned via computer networks to the classrooms. This would be a very exciting educational tool, but it would also be expensive to create.

All of these remote sites place demands on the scheduling of the telescope, and a telescope that has both photometric, spectrographic, and imaging capabilities is especially difficult to schedule. Such future scheduling demands are being studied by a NASA/Ames team headed by Mark Drummond and Butler Hine. The development of sophisticated schedulers will allow future robotic telescopes to be not only more efficient but to be more versatile and to operate from very remote sites.

CONCLUSION

The automation of an astronomical telescope for full robotic operation is within the capability of current technology, and the rapid growth in computing speed and power is making it even easier. The locations of stars are precisely known, and the motion of the sky can be easily computed such that a telescope can be pointed accurately at a given star. Centering the star such that its light enters the instrument, operating the instrument, and recording the data are standard problems of automation that have been resolved. One of the big challenges for the future is more complex scheduling such that telescopes and users can be networked together for the most efficient data gathering.

Ultimately, telescope automation for robotic data collection must become very common. The advantages of long-term synoptic observations are too important to ignore.

REFERENCES

1. Michael A. Seeds, *Foundations of Astronomy*, Wadsworth, Belmont, CA, 1992, pp. 635–638.
2. Arne A. Henden and Ronald H. Kaitchuck, *Astronomical Photometry*, Van Nostrand Reinhold Co., New York, 1982, pp. 119–123.
3. Arne A. Henden and Ronald H. Kaitchuck, *Astronomical Photometry*, pp. 110–112.
4. Arne A. Henden and Ronald H. Kaitchuck, *Astronomical Photometry*, pp. 116–119.
5. Louis J. Boyd, Russell M. Genet, and Douglas S. Hall, *Int. Amateur-Professional Photoelectric Photometry Comm.*, *15*, 27 (1984).
6. Louis J. Boyd, Russell M. Genet, and Douglas S. Hall, *Int. Amateur-Professional Photoelectric Photometry Comm.*, p. 28.
7. Louis J. Boyd, and Russell M. Genet, in *New Generation Small Telescopes*, Donald S. Hayes, David R. Genet, and Russell M. Genet (eds.), Fairborn Press, Mesa, AZ, 1987, pp. 35–39.
8. Norman L. Markworth and John Mullikin, in *New Generation Small Telescopes*, Donald S. Hayes, David R. Genet, and Russell M. Genet (eds.), Fairborn Press, Mesa, AZ, 1987, pp. 41–49.

9. Edward J. Groth, *Astronom. J.*, *91*, 1244–1248 (1986).

10. Michael A. Seeds, in *Remote Access Automatic Telescopes*, Donald S. Hayes and Russell M. Genet (eds.), Fairborn Press, Mesa, AZ, 1989, pp. 163–167.

11. Donald S. Hayes, Russell M. Genet, and Michael A. Seeds, in *Remote Access Automatic Telescopes*, Donald S. Hayes and Russell M. Genet (eds.), Fairborn Press, Mesa, AZ, 1989, pp. 169–167.

12. Albert P. Linnell, Stephen J. Hill, and Ernest F. Brandt, *Publ. Astronom. Soc. Pacific*, *87*, 273–283 (1975).

13. Katherine I. Hudson, Hong-Yee Chiu, Stephen P. Maran, Frank E. Stuart, and Peter R. Vokac, *Astrophys. J.*, *165*, 573–580 (1971).

14. Russell M. Genet, in *The Study of Variable Stars Using Small Telescopes*, John Percy, (ed.), Cambridge University Press, New York, 1986, pp. 236–238.

15. Russell M. Genet, *The Study of Variable Stars Using Small Telescopes*, pp. 238–240.

16. Laurence A. Marschall, in *Robotic Observatories: Present and Future*, Sallie Baliunas and John Richard (eds.), Fairborn Press, Mesa, AZ, 1991, pp. 191–197.

17. J. A. Hynek, and J. R. Dunlap, in *Astronomical Observations with Television Type Sensors*, J. W. Glaspey and G. A. H. Walker (eds.), University of British Columbia, Vancouver, 1973, p. 249.

18. Stirling A. Colgate, Elliott P. Moore, and Richard Carlson, *Publ. Astronom. Soc. Pacific*, *87*, 565–575 (1975).

19. Carlton R. Pennypacker, Ned Hamilton, Deepto Chakrabarty, Heidi J. Marvin, Richard A. Muller, Saul Perlmutter, Timothy P. Sassen, Craig K. Smith, and Robert Smits, in *Advances in Robotic Telescopes*, M. A. Seeds and J. L. Richard (eds.), Fairborn Press, Mesa, AZ, 1991, pp. 17–22.

20. Louis J. Boyd, Russell M. Genet, and Douglas S. Hall, *Int. Amateur-Professional Photoelectric Photometry Comm.*, *15*, 20–32 (1984).

21. Michael A. Seeds, in *Advances in Robotic Telescopes*, M. A. Seeds and J. L. Richard (eds.), Fairborn Press, Mesa, AZ, 1991, pp. 257–262.

22. M. Trueblood and R. M. Genet, *Microcomputer Control of Telescopes*, Willmann-Bell Inc., Richmond, VA, 1985.

23. Russell M. Genet, Louis J. Boyd, and David R. Genet, in *New Generation Small Telescopes*, Donald S. Hayes, David R. Genet, and Russell M. Genet, (eds.), Fairborn Press, Mesa, AZ, 1987, pp. 27–34.

24. Russell M. Genet and Donald S. Hayes, *Robotic Observatories*, AutoScope Corp., Mesa, AZ, 1989, pp. 121–127.

25. R. K. Honeycutt and G. W. Turner, in *Robotic Telescopes in the 1990's*, A. Filippenko (ed.), Astronomical Society of the Pacific, San Francisco, 1992, pp. 77–88.

26. Russell M. Genet and Donald S. Hayes, *Robotic Observatories*, AutoScope Corp., Mesa, AZ, 1989, pp. 205–226.

27. George P. McCook, in *Advances in Robotic Telescopes*, M. A. Seeds and J. L. Richard (eds.), Fairborn Press, Mesa, AZ, 1991, pp. 263–268.

28. Bill Neely and Don Epand, *Int. Amateur-Professional Photoelectric Photometry Comm.*, *45*, 92–103 (1991).

29. Michael A. Seeds, in *New Generation Small Telescopes*, Donald S. Hayes, David R. Genet, and Russell M. Genet (eds.), Fairborn Press, Mesa, AZ, 1987, pp. 203–210.

30. R. K. Honeycutt, G. W. Turner, D. N. Vesper, J. W. Robertson, and J. C. White II, *Publ. Astronom. Soc. Pacific*, *105*, 426–431 (1993).

BIBLIOGRAPHY

Adelman, Saul J., Robert J. Dukes, and Carol J. Adelman (eds.), *Automated Telescopes for Photometry and Imaging*, Astronomical Society of the Pacific, San Francisco, 1992.

Baliunas, Sallie, and John L. Richard, (eds.), *Robotic Observatories: Present and Future*, Fairborn Press, Mesa, AZ, 1991.

Filippenko, Alex (ed.), *Robotic Telescopes in the 1990s*, Astronomical Society of the Pacific, San Francisco, 1992.

Genet, Russell M., and Donald S. Hayes, *Robotic Observatories*, AutoScope Corporation, Mesa, AZ, 1989.

Hall, D. S., and R. M. Genet, *Photoelectric Photometry of Variable Stars*, 2nd ed., Willmann-Bell, Richmond, VA, 1988.

Hall, Douglas S., Russell M. Genet, and Betty L. Thurston (eds.), *Automatic Photoelectric Telescopes*, Fairborn Press, Mesa, AZ, 1986.

Hayes, Donald S., and Russell M. Genet (eds.), *Remote Access Automatic Telescopes*, Fairborn Press, Mesa, AZ, 1989.

Hayes, Donald S., David R. Genet, and Russell M. Genet (eds.), *New Generation Small Telescopes*, Fairborn Press, Mesa, AZ, 1987.

Hayes, Donald S., and Russell M. Genet (eds.), *Automatic Small Telescopes*, Fairborn Press, Mesa, AZ, 1989.

Henden, A. A., and R. H. Kaitchuck, *Astronomical Photometry*, Van Nostrand Reinhold Co, New York, 1982.

Pennypacker, Carlton, *Hands-on Astronomy for Education*, World Scientific, Singapore, 1992.

Seeds, Michael A., and John L. Richard (eds.), *Advances in Robotic Telescopes*, Fairborn Press, Mesa, AZ, 1991.

Trueblood, M., and R. M. Genet, *Microcomputer Control of Telescopes*, Willmann-Bell, Richmond, VA, 1985.

MICHAEL A. SEEDS

COMPUTATIONAL LEARNING THEORY

The ability to learn is an essential component of intelligence. The field of computational learning theory attempts to describe the process of learning. The benefits that this theory can provide include an increased understanding of natural learning systems and tools to allow the design of machines that learn. Such machines are essential for many engineering problems. In particular, if a system is required to perform some operation that cannot be completely specified beforehand or is likely to change over time, a learning system may be essential.

As an example of a learning problem, suppose we want to install a machine in an apple-packing factory to examine apples on a conveyor belt and distinguish good apples from bad. The machine receives video images from a camera above the conveyor belt. For several truckloads of apples, an expert apple-grader labels each image as a "good apple" or "rubbish" (i.e., anything that is not a good apple). The images, together with these labels, are presented to the learning machine. From these labeled examples, we want the machine to learn to recognize good apples. It must generalize from the finite sequence of labeled images to other, unseen, images.

If we wish to build a learning machine like this, some obvious questions arise.

- Is such a machine feasible? Or is the problem impossibly difficult?
- If it is a feasible problem, how many labeled examples provide enough information for our machine to accurately classify unseen apple images?
- What is the best strategy for the machine to adopt so that it can use those labeled images to enable it to classify future images? (Such a strategy is called a learning algorithm.)
- How long will the learning process take?

These are questions about the **complexity** of the learning problem; they ask how difficult the problem is, in terms of the amount of information required and the amount of computation required. The goal of **computational learning theory** is to answer questions like these for a broad class of learning problems. To ask such questions precisely, we need to formally define the learning problem. To enable us to find answers, we make a number of assumptions which simplify the analysis.

The next section describes a particular model of learning—probably approximately correct (pac) learning. This model is not the only one possible, but it is simple and the most widely studied. The second section considers the question, "How many labeled examples are necessary for satisfactory learning within the pac framework?" The third section considers the question, "How much computation is necessary for satisfactory learning?" The section Extensions to the pac model describes more general models of learning that avoid some assumptions made by the pac learning model and allow us to study more realistic learning problems.

PROBABLY APPROXIMATELY CORRECT LEARNING

This section describes the probably approximately correct (pac) model of learning. This model is concerned with classification problems in which the examples must be divided into two classes (such as 1 and 0, or good apples and rubbish). We assume that the examples are chosen randomly. Specifically, if we define the set X of all possible examples that our learning system might see (call this set the **example space**), we assume that the examples are chosen according to a particular probability distribution on X. This distribution can be arbitrary, but it is not known to the learner. The distribution is intended to reflect the relative frequency of different examples in the real world. For the apple-grading problem, this means we assume that there is a set of possible images, and the probability distribution on this set describes the probability that particular images are presented to the machine.

We assume that the relationship between examples and their labels is a function that maps from the example space X to the set of labels $\{0, 1\}$. We call a function of this sort a **concept**. For example, we suppose that the relationship between apple images and their classifications (describing the concept "good apple") is a $\{0, 1\}$-valued function. It is this function, the **target concept**, that the learner must guess. Rather than allowing any $\{0, 1\}$-valued function, we restrict the target concept to some class of functions, the **concept class**. We can think of this class as consisting of those functions that the learner may have to learn. The learner is told the concept class but does not know which concept in the class is the target concept.

These assumptions simplify the analysis of learning but may not always be realistic. For example, the relationship between apple images and their labels may depend on an indecisive apple-grader's judgment—the grader might label the same image either way. In this case, the relationship between images and their labels is not a function. Even if the relationship were a function, it is unrealistic to assume that the learner knows the concept class. Later, we will see how these assumptions may be relaxed.

At any stage of the learning process, for some examples the learner will guess a label of 1, for others it will guess a label of 0. This defines a concept which we call an hypothesis since it is the learner's attempt to describe the target concept. The class of functions that the learner is able to compute in this way is called the **hypothesis class**. We assume that the hypothesis class contains the concept class as a subset; that is, any target concept can be computed exactly by the learner. For example, suppose that the apple-grading machine uses the training examples to adjust a number of parameters. At any stage, the machine computes a particular function that depends on the particular values of these parameters. In this case, the hypothesis class is the set of all such functions over all possible parameter settings.

Learning proceeds as follows. The learning system is presented with a number of labeled examples called the **training sample** (labeled according to the target concept). An algorithm (the **learning algorithm**) then chooses an appropriate hypothesis which is intended to be an accurate approximation to the target concept. It is unrealistic to require the learning algorithm to choose an hypothesis that is identical to the target concept since the hypothesis class might be extremely large. Instead, we aim to ensure that this hypothesis is an acceptably good approximation to the correct function.

How do we measure "acceptably good"? If t is the target concept and h is an hypothesis, the set of examples which h misclassifies is $\{x \in X : h(x) \neq t(x)\}$. If random examples in X are chosen according to the probability distribution P, the error of h [written $\mathbf{er}_P(h)$] is the probability that h misclassifies a random example:

$$\mathbf{er}_P(h) = P\{x \in X : h(x) \neq t(x)\}.$$

[Recall that a probability distribution on X is a function which maps from subsets of X to probabilities of those subsets. For example, $P\{x \in X : h(x) \neq t(x)\}$ is the probability that a random example falls in that subset of X for which h and t disagree.] We say that the hypothesis h is an accurate approximation to the target concept if the error of h is small, $\mathbf{er}_P(h) < \epsilon$ (where ϵ is a small positive number). Such an hypothesis is called "approximately correct." For example, we may require that the hypothesis classify correctly random apple images with probability at least 0.95.

It is unrealistic to require that the learning algorithm always produce an approximately correct hypothesis. It is possible (though perhaps extremely unlikely) that every training example the learner sees is quite uncharacteristic. For example, it is possible (though improbable) that all examples of good apples presented to the apple-grading machine are identical images. We cannot hope for the learning algorithm to produce an accurate hypothesis from such an unrepresentative sample. However, we would hope that our learning algorithm could produce an approximately correct hypothesis for all training samples that are not exceptional in this way. Suppose $s = (x_1, x_2, \ldots, x_m) \in X^m$ is a sequence* of m random examples, and the learning algorithm is presented with the sequence

$$((x_1, t(x_1)), (x_2, t(x_2)), \ldots, (x_m, t(x_m)))$$

of these examples labeled according to a target concept t. Suppose the algorithm produces the hypothesis $h(s, t)$ in response to this training sequence. Then the set

$$B = \{s \in X^m : \mathbf{er}_P(h(s, t)) \geq \epsilon\}$$

contains exactly those samples of length m for which the learner is misled, and produces an inaccurate hypothesis. We require that the probability of this set be small, $P^m(B) < \delta$ (where δ is a small positive number and P^m is the product probability distribution that describes the probability of sequences of m examples chosen randomly according to P); that is, the probability that the learning algorithm is presented with a misleading training sample and, therefore, does not produce an approximately correct hypothesis must be small. Because we require that the learner's hypothesis be probably approximately correct, this is known as **probably approximately correct** (or **pac**) learning.

The parameter ϵ denotes the allowable probability that the hypothesis misclassifies a random example. It describes how *accurate* the hypothesis must be. The parameter δ denotes the allowable probability that the training sample will be unrepresentative and trick the learner into choosing an inaccurate hypothesis. It describes how *confident* we are that the hypothesis is accurate. Note that accuracy is defined in terms of the probability of a set of examples, whereas confidence is defined in terms of the probability of a set of training samples (*sequences* of examples).

We require that the learner can find a probably approximately correct hypothesis for *any* probability distribution of examples, and for *any* target concept in the concept

---

*X^m is the set of all possible sequences of m examples.

class. The idea is that as we cannot know in advance what the learner's environment will be (i.e., the target concept and the distribution of examples), if the learner can cope with *any* concept in the concept class and *any* distribution, then we are guaranteed that the performance will be adequate in any environment; that is, the aim is to ensure that the learner's worst-case performance, over all distributions and concepts, is acceptable.*

Within this framework, we can ask some of the questions of the previous section more precisely:

- For what concept classes F and hypothesis classes H is pac learning feasible from a finite number of training examples?
- What is the smallest number of labeled examples that will allow a learning system to pac learn a concept in F using hypotheses in H?
- How much computation (and, therefore, time) is required to pac learn a concept in F using H?

Suppose we specify a desired accuracy ϵ and confidence δ. The smallest number of training examples sufficient for pac learning to this accuracy and confidence is called the **sample complexity** of learning. The minimum amount of computation sufficient for pac learning is called the **computational complexity** of learning. Note that both of these quantities do not depend on the particular learning algorithm; they are features of the learning problem. The sample complexity indicates how much teacher–learner interaction is necessary, and the computational complexity indicates how much work a learner needs to do. The next two sections examine sample complexity and computational complexity in some detail.

THE SAMPLE COMPLEXITY OF PAC LEARNING

To show that a particular learning algorithm is pac, we could attempt to analyze the algorithm and find bounds on the appropriate probabilities. However, this analysis is usually difficult, even for relatively simple algorithms. For this reason, it is convenient to ignore the details of specific algorithms and to investigate the learning performance of algorithms with particular properties. From this point of view, the most important class of algorithms is the class of consistent algorithms.

An hypothesis h is **consistent** with a sample $s = (x_1, x_2, \ldots, x_m)$ if it agrees with the target concept t for all examples in the sample; that is, $h(x_i) = t(x_i)$ for all examples x_i in the sample s. A consistent hypothesis is, therefore, one that "fits the facts" which the learner has seen. It is not necessarily unique, as many distinct hypotheses could be consistent with the m training examples. A **consistent algorithm** is one that always produces an hypothesis that is consistent with the training examples. It is often easy to show that an algorithm is consistent. If we can show that for a sufficiently large training sample it is likely that any consistent hypothesis is approximately correct, then any consistent algorithm is a pac-learning algorithm. This corresponds to showing that as the number of labeled training examples gets large, the set of hypotheses that are consistent with those

---

*As an alternative, the learner could aim to minimize the average misclassification probability over all environments. However, in this case we must know something about the probabilities of each possible environment (target concept and distribution of examples), which is often an unjustifiable assumption. The relationship between the worst case and average case frameworks has been examined recently [1].

examples will probably get smaller and smaller, until the only remaining consistent hypotheses are approximately correct ones.

Finite Hypothesis Classes

If the hypothesis class H is not too large, we would expect the number of consistent hypotheses in H to diminish as the number of training examples is increased. Suppose the hypothesis class H contains only a finite number of hypotheses. Let t be the target concept, and consider the set B_ϵ of hypotheses that are not approximately correct, $B_\epsilon = \{h \in H : \mathbf{er}_P(h) \geq \epsilon\}$. Suppose a consistent learning algorithm receives m random training examples, labeled according to t. For an hypothesis h in B_ϵ, the probability that h agrees with t for a random example is no more than $1 - \epsilon$. So the probability that h is consistent with t for the sequence of m random examples is no more than $(1 - \epsilon)^m$. Because this is true for a particular hypothesis h in B_ϵ, the probability that any one of these inaccurate hypotheses is consistent with m random examples is no more than $|B_\epsilon| (1 - \epsilon)^m$, where $|B_\epsilon|$ is the number of hypotheses in B_ϵ. Clearly, $|B_\epsilon|$ is no more than $|H|$, the number of hypotheses in H. So the probability that a sample of length m is consistent with an hypothesis that is not approximately correct is no more than $|H| (1 - \epsilon)^m$, and it can be shown that this quantity is less than δ if

$$m > \frac{1}{\epsilon} \left(\log|H| + \log \frac{1}{\delta} \right),$$

where log denotes the natural logarithm. This leads to

Theorem 1 *Suppose H is a finite hypothesis class, F is a concept class that is a subset of H, and ϵ and δ are the desired accuracy and confidence parameters, respectively $(0 < \epsilon, \delta < 1)$. Any consistent algorithm using H that examines more than*

$$\frac{1}{\epsilon} \left(\log|H| + \log \frac{1}{\delta} \right)$$

labeled examples is a pac-learning algorithm for F.

Example 1 Suppose the apple-grading machine uses a finite hypothesis class H, and suppose the target concept (representing "good apples") is in H. Theorem 1 shows that any consistent algorithm that sees sufficiently many labeled examples is a pac-learning algorithm in this case. The theorem also indicates how many training examples will suffice and how that number varies with the desired accuracy and confidence, and the size of the hypothesis class.

Because a consistent algorithm can pac learn from $(1/\epsilon) [\log|H| + \log(1/\delta)]$ labeled examples, this expression gives an upper bound on the sample complexity of pac learning the concept class. This indicates how much information, in the form of labeled examples, is sufficient to learn a concept in the class. To learn to greater accuracy or with higher confidence requires more examples, and the bound increases with $1/\epsilon$ and $\log(1/\delta)$, respectively. The size of the hypothesis class, $|H|$, is a measure of its representational power, and the bound increases logarithmically with the size.

The Vapnik–Chervonenkis Dimension

Unfortunately, many interesting and useful hypothesis classes are not finite; in these cases, Theorem 1 is not useful. In this section, we consider another measure of the representational power of a class of functions: the Vapnik–Chervonenkis dimension.

Suppose we have a set S of n examples, $S \subseteq X$. Because each example in S can be classified in one of two ways, there are 2^n possible ways to classify the n examples in S. Suppose we have an hypothesis class H such that for each of the 2^n classifications, there is a function in H that classifies the examples in S in that way. The hypothesis class H cannot be any more powerful with respect to the set S. In this case, we say that H **shatters** S.

The **Vapnik–Chervonenkis dimension (VC-dimension)** of an hypothesis class H [written VCdim(H)] is the size of the largest set of examples that H can shatter; that is,

$$\text{VCdim}(H) = \max \{m : H \text{ shatters some set } S \subseteq X \text{ of size } m\}.$$

If there is no largest set that H can shatter, we say that the VC-dimension of H is infinite.

Example 2 Suppose X is the real line (so an example is a single real number) and the hypothesis class contains functions of the form

$$h(x) = \begin{cases} 1 & a \leq x \leq b \\ 0 & \text{otherwise,} \end{cases}$$

where a and b are real numbers and $a \leq b$; that is, hypotheses take value 1 on the interval from a to b, and 0 elsewhere. In this case, Figure 1a shows a set of two points shattered by H. However, H cannot shatter any set of three distinct points as the classification shown in Figure 1b cannot be computed using a function in H; that is, H can shatter a set of size 2 but cannot shatter any set of size 3, so the VC-dimension of H is 2.

Example 3 Let X be the cartesian plane, $X = \mathfrak{R}^2$; an example $x \in X$ is a two-dimensional vector, $x = (x_1, x_2)$. Suppose the hypothesis class H consists of all functions of the form

$$h(x) = \begin{cases} 1 & \text{if } w_1 x_1 + w_2 x_2 - \theta \geq 0 \\ 0 & \text{otherwise,} \end{cases}$$

where w_1, w_2, and θ are real numbers. A function of this form takes the value 1 to one side of a line in the plane (the line is specified by the numbers w_1, w_2, and θ). Figure 2a

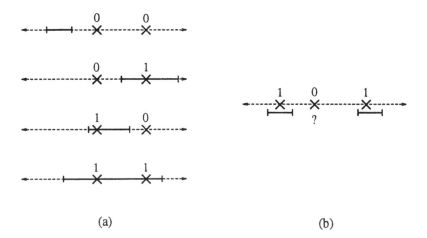

(a)   (b)

FIGURE 1   (a) Four functions in H can represent the 2^2 classifications of the two points illustrated. (b) A classification of three points that no function in H can represent.

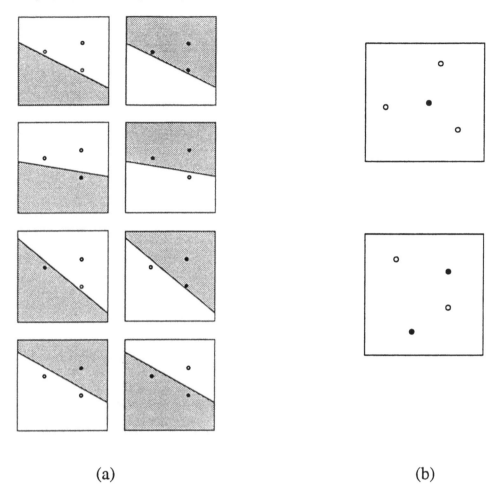

(a)   (b)

FIGURE 2   (a) Eight functions in H give all 2^3 classifications of the three points illustrated. The shaded region represents the subset of X where $h(x) = 1$. (b) Regardless of how four points are arranged, there are classifications that cannot be represented using functions in H.

shows a set of three points that are shattered by H. However, no set of four points can be shattered by H, regardless of how they are arranged. Figure 2b shows classifications of two sets of four points that cannot be computed using functions in H. Therefore, H can shatter a set of size 3 but cannot shatter any set of size 4, so the VC-dimension of H is 3.

In these examples, the hypothesis classes are particularly simple. For more complicated hypothesis classes, it is sometimes difficult to compute the VC-dimension exactly, but it is often possible to find upper and lower bounds.

The VC-dimension measures the representational power of a hypothesis class; a larger VC-dimension indicates a more complex class. We would expect that as the hypothesis class becomes more complex, the number of examples needed to distinguish approximately correct hypotheses would increase. In fact, we have the following results (proved in Refs. 2 and 3).

Theorem 2   *Suppose H is an hypothesis class with finite VC-dimension $d \geq 2$, F is a concept class that is a subset of H, and ϵ and δ are the desired accuracy and confidence parameters with $0 < \epsilon < 1/8$ and $0 < \delta < 1/100$.*

(a)   Any consistent algorithm using H that sees at least

$$\frac{1}{\epsilon(1 - \sqrt{\epsilon})} \left(\log \frac{d/(d - 1)}{\delta} + 2d \log \frac{2e}{\epsilon} \right)$$

labeled examples is a pac-learning algorithm for F.

(b)   No algorithm can pac learn H from fewer than

$$\max \left(\frac{1 - \epsilon}{\epsilon} \log \frac{1}{\delta} , \frac{d - 1}{32\epsilon} \right)$$

labeled examples. If H has infinite VC-dimension, no algorithm can pac learn H.

Theorem 2(a) indicates that the sample complexity of pac learning is no more than proportional to VCdim(H), and Theorem 2(b) indicates that it is at least proportional to VCdim(H). The sample complexity is, therefore, proportional to VCdim(H).

Note how the sample complexity depends on the confidence and accuracy parameters: it is proportional to $\log(1/\delta)$ and (within a log factor) proportional to $1/\epsilon$, as in the case of finite H.

Example 4   Suppose the apple-grading machine contains a preprocessor (that computes a fixed function) and a **two-layer neural network**. A neural network is a network of processing units that compute simple functions of their input signals (see Ref. 4). Suppose each processing unit computes a **linear threshold function** of its n inputs,

$$y = \mathcal{H} \left(\sum_{i=1}^{n} x_i w_i - \theta \right),$$

where x_i is an input to the unit, w_i is an adjustable weight, θ is the adjustable threshold, y is the output of the unit, and $\mathcal{H}$ is the threshold function

$$\mathcal{H}(\alpha) = \begin{cases} 1 & \text{if } \alpha \geq 0 \\ 0 & \text{otherwise.} \end{cases}$$

(The hypothesis class described in Example 3 contains linear threshold functions with two inputs.) A two-layer network has no path from an input to the output that passes through more than two units. In this case, the hypothesis class H is the class of functions that this network can compute. Within a log factor, the VC-dimension of H is proportional to the number of weights in the network (5,6). If we assume that the target concept is in H, the number of examples necessary and sufficient for learning is also proportional to the number of weights. Although the bounds on the constant of proportionality given by Theorem 2 are loose, the result illustrates the asymptotic behavior of the training set size.

THE COMPUTATIONAL COMPLEXITY OF PAC LEARNING

The results in the previous section indicate how many training examples provide enough information to learn a concept. In this section, we consider how difficult it is to use that information to produce an acceptable hypothesis.

The running time of an algorithm is the time it takes to process its inputs and produce an output. We define an *acceptable* running time for an algorithm in terms of its relationship to the size of the algorithm's inputs. It is clearly unacceptable for the running time of a learning algorithm to grow exponentially with the number of training examples. On the other hand, if the relationship between the size of the algorithm's inputs and its running time is described by a polynomial, that is considered acceptable performance.

Often we are interested in a number of related learning problems of different sizes but using similar hypothesis classes. For example, suppose X_n is the set of all bit strings of length n (so an example is a string of n binary digits), and the hypothesis class H_n contains functions of the form

$$h(b_1 b_2 \ldots b_n) = \begin{cases} 1 & \text{if } b_i = 1 \text{ and } b_j = 1 \\ 0 & \text{otherwise,} \end{cases}$$

where $b_1 b_2 \ldots b_n$ is a bit string, and i and j specify two of the n bits. Functions in H_n are **conjunctions** of two of the n binary variables. Suppose we have a learning algorithm for the class H_n that works for any n. It would be undesirable if the running time of this algorithm increased too rapidly as we considered larger problems (larger values of n). We can measure the size of a learning problem by the size (in binary digits) of the learning system's inputs and outputs, that is, the number of bits needed to represent the training examples and hypotheses.

We would like a learning algorithm to be efficient, in the sense that the worst-case number of operations it performs grows only polynomially with any relevant parameters. Therefore, we say that an algorithm that uses a hypothesis class H (in some set of hypothesis classes, containing hypotheses of different sizes) is an efficient pac-learning algorithm if it is a pac-learning algorithm and has a running time that increases no more than polynomially in $1/\epsilon$, $1/\delta$, the size of the representation of each example, and the size of the representation of the target function $t \in H$.

Suppose H is an hypothesis class with finite VC-dimension. The results in the previous section showed that an algorithm that finds hypotheses in H consistent with a set of training examples is a pac-learning algorithm for H. If that algorithm also has running time that is polynomial in the number of examples, the size of the representation of each example, and the size of the representation of an hypothesis in H, then it is an efficient pac-learning algorithm; that is, the existence of an efficient algorithm to find consistent hypotheses in H implies the existence of an efficient pac-learning algorithm for H. In fact, the reverse implication also applies because we can transform an efficient learning algorithm into an efficient consistent hypothesis finder (7); that is, the existence of an efficient pac-learning algorithm for H implies the existence of an efficient consistent hypothesis finder. So the problem of finding consistent hypotheses is computationally equivalent to pac learning; if one can be solved efficiently, so can the other.

To show that an hypothesis class is efficiently pac learnable, it suffices to produce a consistent hypothesis finder and show that it is efficient.

Example 5   Suppose H_n is the class of linear threshold functions with n real inputs (see Example 4). The problem of finding an hypothesis in H_n that is consistent with a particular set of training examples can be easily transformed into a linear programming problem, which can be solved using a polynomial-time algorithm (8). It can be shown that VCdim(H_n) $= n + 1$ (see Refs. 9 and 10), so this approach comprises an efficient learning algorithm for the class of linear threshold functions.

To show that an hypothesis class H is not efficiently pac learnable, it suffices to show that any algorithm that finds consistent hypotheses must be inefficient, that is, to show that the problem of finding consistent hypotheses is computationally difficult. In general, it is difficult to prove that no efficient algorithm exists to solve a particular problem (such as finding a consistent hypothesis). For this reason, we resort to comparing the difficulty of this problem to other well-studied problems. There is a large class of difficult problems, known as the NP-complete problems. An efficient algorithm to solve one of these problems can be used to construct an efficient algorithm to solve any other, so they are computationally as difficult as each other (see Ref. 11). Because many people have been trying to find efficient algorithms for these problems for many years, it is commonly assumed that no such algorithm exists. With this assumption, if we can show that the problem of finding a consistent hypothesis in H is as hard as an NP-complete problem, that implies that no polynomial-time pac-learning algorithm exists for H.

Example 6   Suppose X_n is an n-dimensional Euclidean space and H_n is the class of functions defined on X_n that can be computed by a two-layer neural network of three processing units which compute linear threshold functions (see Example 4). The VC-dimension of H_n is proportional to n, so the number of training examples necessary for learning certainly does not grow excessively quickly with the number of inputs n. However, it can be shown that any efficient algorithm that can find an hypothesis in H_n consistent with a set of training examples can be used to construct an efficient algorithm to solve an NP-complete problem (12); that is, finding a consistent hypothesis is at least as hard as an NP-complete problem, and this implies that no efficient pac-learning algorithm exists for H_n (where we have made the common assumption that an NP-complete problem cannot be solved by an efficient algorithm).

Note that the number of training examples necessary for learning is not excessive in this case (see Example 4), but the problem of using those examples to find a suitable hypothesis is computationally difficult.

EXTENSIONS TO THE PAC MODEL

The definition of probably approximately correct learning presented above makes a number of simplifying assumptions. For many learning problems, some of these assumptions are unlikely to be valid. This section describes how the pac model can be extended to relax some of the assumptions.

Learning Probabilistic Concepts

In the definition of pac learning, we assume that the relationship between examples and their labels is a (deterministic) function in a class of functions. This implies that there is a unique correct classification for every example, and the source of the labels of the training examples (the teacher) is always correct. Both situations are unlikely. Consider the apple-grading problem. It is possible that an image of a good apple and one of an apple that contains a mass of worms are identical. Therefore, the relationship between the image and the label cannot be a function. Even if the relationship were a function, it is unreasonable to expect the expert apple-grader to correctly classify every apple image.

The definition of pac learning also assumes that the learner has complete knowledge of the concept class of which the target concept is a member. It is unrealistic to expect the learner to have this much information about the target concept. For example, of what (useful) concept class is the "good apple" concept a member? For many problems, it might be reasonable to assume that the target concept is *well-approximated* by some function in a known class, but the pac-learning results presented above cannot easily be extended to this case because they rely on the fact that there will always be a hypothesis that is consistent with the training examples.

To relax these assumptions, we can model the relationship between an example $x \in X$ and its label $b \in \{0, 1\}$ as a joint distribution on the example space X and the label space $\{0, 1\}$; that is, we assume that there is a probability distribution on X that describes the relative frequency of different examples, as before, and we also assume that for each example $x \in X$, there is a certain fixed probability that x will be labeled as 1, say. We call this joint distribution a **noisy concept**.

This model of learning is more general than the pac model. It allows the teacher to make random errors and to be inconsistent in labeling hard-to-decide examples. In addition, the learner does not need to know any information about the relationship between examples and their labels, as this relationship is not required to be a function in a particular class of functions.

Within this model, the learning algorithm chooses a suitable hypothesis from some hypothesis class H, as before. However, because examples and labels are related in a probabilistic way, in general there is no "correct" hypothesis. If P is the probability distribution on $X \times \{0, 1\}$, define the **expected error** $er_P(h)$ of a hypothesis as the probability that the hypothesis is not consistent with a random labeled example,

$$\mathbf{er}_P(h) = P\{(x, b) \in X \times \{0, 1\} : h(x) \neq b\}.$$

After the learner is presented with a number of labeled examples, it should choose an hypothesis from the hypothesis class H so that its expected error is close to the smallest expected error of any hypothesis in H. This is a natural generalization of the pac model, in which the smallest error of an hypothesis in H is always zero (as the target concept is in H) and the learner must choose an hypothesis from H which has error close to zero.

In the pac model, we considered algorithms that find hypotheses that are consistent with the training examples. An analogous algorithm for noisy concepts finds an hypothesis that is consistent with the largest possible proportion of the training examples. If $s = ((x_1, b_1), (x_2, b_2), \ldots, (x_m, b_m))$ is a training sample consisting of m labeled examples, define the **empirical error** $\widehat{er}_s(h)$ **of an hypothesis** h for this training sample as the proportion of labeled examples in s with which h disagrees,

$$\widehat{er}_s(h) = \frac{\text{number of examples } x_i \text{ in } s \text{ for which } h(x_i) \neq b_i}{\text{number of examples in } s}$$

$$= \frac{1}{m}|\{i : h(x_i) \neq b_i\}| \,.$$

Now, an algorithm that chooses an hypothesis with nearly minimal empirical error will be suitable if the empirical error as an hypothesis is always close to its expected error. The following result shows that this is almost always true if the hypothesis class has finite VC-dimension and the learning algorithm sees sufficiently many training examples (13).

Theorem 3 *Suppose H is an hypothesis class with* $\text{VCdim}(H) = d$, *P is a probability distribution defined on* $X \times \{0, 1\}$, ϵ *and* δ *are the desired accuracy and confidence parameters, respectively, satisfying* $0 < \epsilon, \delta < 1$, *and* γ *is a real number satisfying* $0 < \gamma \leq 1$. *Suppose s is a sequence of m random labeled examples drawn according to P, where m is at least*

$$\frac{1}{\gamma^2 \epsilon (1 - \sqrt{\epsilon})} \left(4 \log \frac{4}{\delta} + 6d \log \frac{4}{\gamma^{2/3} \epsilon} \right).$$

Any hypothesis h in H with sufficiently small empirical error, $\hat{\text{er}}_s(h) \leq (1 - \gamma)\epsilon$ *is probably approximately correct in the sense that* $\text{er}_P(h) \leq \epsilon$ *with probability at least* $1 - \delta$.

Theorem 3 provides an upper bound on the sample complexity of the problem of learning a noisy concept. This bound is proportional to the VC-dimension d, to $\log(1/\delta)$, and (within log factors) to $1/\epsilon$ and $1/\gamma^2$. The lower bound of Theorem 2(b) also applies in this case because pac learning a function in a known function class is a special case of learning a noisy concept. Therefore, the sample complexity in this case is asymptotically proportional to the VC-dimension of the hypothesis class, as before.

Learning When the Problem Changes

The definition of pac learning assumes that the learner's environment remains constant over time. Specifically, it assumes that both the probability distribution that describes the generation of random examples and the target function that describes the relationship between examples and their labels remain the same as learning proceeds. In many situations, this assumption is a poor one. For example, in the apple-grading factory, the distribution of apple images changes slowly with time, as the apple-picking season progresses and as the weather changes. Even if we do not expect a learning problem to change a great deal with time, it is important to know how small changes would affect the sample complexity, for example.

The pac model can be extended to include variations of this kind. Of course, we need to assume that the changes occur slowly (otherwise the learning problem could be impossibly difficult). To measure the difference between two target concepts (say f and g), consider the subset S of the example space X on which the concepts disagree, $S = \{x \in X : f(x) \neq g(x)\}$. We say that a drifting concept is admissible if the probability of this difference between the target concept on subsequent examples is small—less than a positive constant Δ; that is, we assume that the target concept can change slightly between examples. It can be shown that, provided Δ is not too large (in terms of the desired accuracy and the VC-dimension of the hypothesis class), it is possible to track the changes in the target concept (14).

A similar modification can be used to study learning when the distribution of examples changes slowly over time. In this case, we measure the difference between two distributions as the largest change in the probability of a subset of the example space X. We assume that the distribution changes slightly between examples, but the difference between subsequent distributions is small (less than a positive constant, Δ). It can be shown that, provided the allowable distribution drift rate Δ is not excessive (again in terms of the desired accuracy and the VC-dimension of the hypothesis class), it is possible to track the changes in the distribution and learn the target concept (15).

In the case of noisy concepts, the relationship between examples and their labels is represented by a joint probability distribution on $X \times \{0, 1\}$. In this case, small changes in the distribution over time can correspond to simultaneous small changes in the distribution of examples and small changes in the relationship. We assume that the joint distribution changes only slightly between examples (the difference between distributions is less than Δ, say). It can be shown that, provided the allowable distribution drift rate is not excessive (in terms of the desired learning performance and the VC-dimension of the hypothesis class), a result similar to Theorem 3 holds and pac learning is still possible (15).

Although it may not always be easy to predict (or even measure) the amount by which a learning problem will change, these results describe the order-of-magnitude behavior of a learning system, as variations of this kind occur.

Learning Arbitrary-Valued Functions

In all learning problems considered so far, the aim has been to separate the examples into two classes. Often we are interested in more general learning problems. For example, in the apple-packing factory, the apple-grading machine may be required to estimate the *probability* that an image represents a "good apple." In this case, the machine is trained using a number of images labeled "good apples" or "rubbish," and from these it must estimate the appropriate probabilities. Clearly, the function to be learned (the distribution describing the probability of a good apple) takes values between 0 and 1 in this case. Alternatively, the machine may be required to sort the apple images into a number of different grades, such as "rubbish," "animal fodder," "cooking," "eating," and "connoisseur." In this case, he machine must learn an integer-valued function, where the integers represent the grade of apple. In the same factory, another learning machine might be required to estimate the volume of an apple from the video image, so the function to be learned is real valued.

These learning problems can be described by a more general model. Let X be the space of possible examples and let Y be the space of possible labels, where a label is the value associated with each training example that is provided by the teacher (for example, X might be the set of all possible apple images, and Y might be the interval $[0, 1000]$, which includes all possible apple volumes). For each example, the learning system must choose an action a from some set of possible actions A. Often, the learning system must guess the label corresponding to the example, in which case $A = Y$, but this is not the only possibility. For example, in the problem of predicting the probability that the apple image is labeled as "good," the label is always 0 or 1, but the output of the learning system (its action) is a real number between 0 and 1, so $Y = \{0, 1\}$, but A is the interval $[0, 1]$.

For many action spaces (for example, the real numbers) it is unreasonable to expect the learning system to ever produce the correct action. Instead, we define a loss function l on $Y \times A$, so that $l(y, a)$ measures the appropriateness of the action a when the label is y. We assume (as we did for learning probabilistic concepts) that there is a fixed, unknown distribution on $X \times Y$ that describes the relative frequency of different labeled examples. The learner can choose an hypothesis, a function from X to A, from a class H of such functions. The aim of learning is to choose an hypothesis so that the expected value of the loss of the actions of this hypothesis is almost always minimized; that is, with high probability the expected loss of the hypothesis must be close to the minimum over the hypothesis class H.

For example, if the learner is to estimate the volume of an apple from an apple image, X is the space of all apple images, Y is the interval [0, 1000] and so is A, and the loss function measures the distance between y and a, say $l(y, a) = (y - a)^2$. As another example, if the learner is to estimate the probability that an apple image represents a "good apple," X is the space of all apple images, Y is {0, 1}, and A is the interval [0, 1]. The loss function is again a distance between y and a, say $l(y, a) = |y - a|$, so that an hypothesis that minimizes its expected value is the hypothesis that best approximates the distribution.

Clearly, this model generalizes the pac model. The sample complexity of a learning problem in this model is the smallest number of training examples that are necessary for some algorithm to find an hypothesis with expected loss acceptably close to the minimum over the hypothesis class H. It can be shown that the sample complexity has an upper bound in terms of the desired learning performance and a quantity called the **expected covering number** of H (see Ref. 16). This quantity is a measure of how many functions are needed on average to accurately approximate any function in H over a finite sequence of random examples. The expected covering number of H depends on the joint distribution P on $X \times Y$, but for some hypothesis classes it is possible to obtain upper bounds that do not depend on P. In those cases where H is a {0, 1}-valued function, the VC-dimension provides a suitable bound.

Example 7   Suppose a learning system in the apple factory is designed to estimate the volume of apples from images. It contains a multilayer neural network of **sigmoid units**, which are processing units that compute

$$y = g\left(\sum_i x_i w_i - \theta\right)$$

where x_i is an input to the unit, w_i is an adjustable weight, θ is the adjustable threshold, y is the output of the unit, and g is the sigmoid function, $g(\alpha) = 1/(1 + e^{-\alpha})$. (These networks are popular because a simple gradient descent learning algorithm can be used to adjust the weights.) It is possible to find bounds on the expected covering number of the class of functions that particular networks of this sort can compute (see Ref. 16). The result mentioned above can be used to show that the sample complexity of learning in these networks is no more than proportional to the number of weights, as was the case for networks of linear threshold units.

CONCLUSIONS AND OPEN PROBLEMS

Computational learning theory allows us to precisely state and answer a number of important questions associated with the performance of learning systems. In particular, the amount of information that is necessary for a learning problem is known (at least asymptotically) in terms of the complexity of the learning system (the VC-dimension of its hypothesis class) and the desired performance.

However, there are many important open problems. The sample complexity bounds are not always useful in practice because the constants in these bounds are not known accurately. Tighter bounds are needed to allow a designer to accurately predict the performance of a given learning system.

The question of the computational complexity of learning is largely open. There are a number of isolated results about particular hypothesis classes, but there is no elegant characterization of what learning problems can be solved efficiently. Computational learning theory allows us to relate the difficulty of learning to the difficulty of an approximate optimization problem, so a characterization of this sort will depend on advances in complexity theory.

In this article, we assume that the learner chooses an hypothesis from a single class of hypotheses, *H*. An interesting alternative is the use of a sequence of hypothesis classes, of progressively greater complexity. In this case, the learner would choose the complexity of the hypothesis class on the basis of the training examples it has seen already (see Refs. 17 and 18). For example, some neural network training algorithms adjust the network architecture—the placement of connections and units—as well as the weights. Future advances in computational learning theory may address important questions about learning algorithms of this sort.

HISTORY AND BIBLIOGRAPHIC NOTES

The definition of probably approximately correct learning was first proposed by Valiant (19); the name "pac" was coined by Angluin (20). The fact that the VC-dimension characterizes the learnability of an hypothesis class was first shown by Blumer et al., in 1986 (in a preliminary version of Ref. 10) based on the work of Vapnik and Chervonenkis (21). Vapnik and Chervonenkis also proposed the combinatorial quantity which Haussler and Welzl named the VC-dimension (22). The sample complexity bounds in Theorem 2, due to Anthony et al. (2) and Ehrenfeucht et al. (3), slightly improve the results in Reference 10. For more information on computationally difficult problems, see the book on NP-completeness by Garey and Johnson (11). The sample complexity bound for learning noisy concepts (Theorem 3) is due to Anthony and Shawe-Taylor (13). It improves on results in Refs. 10, 17, and 21. The framework for learning arbitrary-valued functions was proposed by Haussler (16). Similar, but less general frameworks have been proposed by Kearns and Schapire (23) and Natarajan (24).

The recent books by Anthony and Biggs (25) and Natarajan (26) give a detailed coverage of the field of computational learning theory and contain extensive bibliographies. Both are very readable. The proceedings of an annual workshop on computational learning theory provide a more complete record of recent work in the field (27–31).

ACKNOWLEDGMENTS

This work was partially supported by Australian Telecommunications and Electronics Research Board. Thanks to T. Downs, R. Lister, R. Williamson and S. E. Bartlett for comments.

REFERENCES

1. D. Haussler, M. Kearns, and R. Schapire, "Bounds on the Sample Complexity of Bayesian Learning Using Information Theory and the VC Dimension," in *Proceedings of the Fourth Annual Workshop on Computational Learning Theory*, L. G. Valiant, and M. K. Warmuth (eds.), Morgan Kaufmann, San Mateo, CA, 1991, pp. 61–74.
2. M. Anthony, N. Biggs, and J. Shawe-Taylor, "The Learnability of Formal Concepts," in *Proceedings of the Third Annual Workshop of Computational Learning Theory*, Morgan Kaufmann, San Mateo, CA, 1990.
3. A. Ehrenfeucht, D. Haussler, M. Kearns, and L. Valiant, "A General Lower Bound on the Number of Examples Needed for Learning," *Inform. Comput.*, *82*, 247–261 (1989).
4. J. Hertz, A. Krogh, and R. G. Palmer, *Introduction to the Theory of Neural Computation*, Addison-Wesley, Reading MA, 1991.
5. E. B. Baum and D. Haussler, "What Size Net Gives Valid Generalization?" *Neural Comp.*, *1*, 151–160 (1989).
6. P. L. Bartlett, "Lower Bounds on the Vapnik–Chervonenkis Dimension of Multi-layer Threshold Networks," in *Proceedings of the Sixth Annual ACM Conference on Computational Learning Theory*, ACM Press, New York, 1993, pp. 144–150.
7. L. Pitt and L. G. Valiant, "Computational Limitations on Learning from Examples," *J. Assoc. Comput. Mach.*, *35*, 965–984 (1988).
8. N. Karmarkar, "A New Polynomial-time Algorithm for Linear Programming," *Combinatorica*, *4*, 373–395 (1984).
9. T. Cover, "Geometrical and Statistical Properties of Systems of Linear Inequalitites with Applications in Pattern Recognition," *IEEE Trans. Electron. Comput.*, *EC-24*, 326–334 (1965).
10. A. Blumer, A. Ehrenfeucht, D. Haussler, and M. K. Warmuth, "Learnability and the Vapnik–Chervonenkis Dimension," *J. Assoc. Comput. Mach.*, *36*, 929–965 (1989).
11. M. R. Garey and D. S. Johnson, *Computers and Intractability: A Guide to the Theory of NP-Completeness*, W. H. Freeman, New York, 1979.
12. A. L. Blum and R. L. Rivest, "Training a 3-Node Neural Network Is NP-Complete," *Neural Networks*, *5*, 117–127 (1992).
13. M. Anthony and J. Shawe-Taylor, "A Result of Vapnik with Applications," Computer Science Department, RHBNC, Technical Report CSD-TR-628, University of London, Egham, UK, 1990.
14. D. P. Helmbold and P. M. Long, "Tracking Drifting Concepts Using Random Examples," in *Proceedings of the Fourth Annual Workshop on Computational Learning Theory*, L. C. Valiant and M. K. Warmuth (eds.), Morgan Kaufmann, San Mateo, CA, 1991, pp. 13–23.
15. P. L. Bartlett, "Learning with a Slowly Changing Distribution," in *Proceedings of the Fifth Annual ACM Workshop on Computational Learning Theory*, ACM Press, New York, 1992, pp. 243–252.
16. D. Haussler, "Decision Theoretic Generalizations of the PAC Model for Neural Net and Other Learning Applications," Baskin Center for Computer Engineering and Information Sciences, UCSC-CRL-91-02, University of California, Santa Cruz, CA, 1990.
17. V. Vapnik, *Estimation of Dependencies Based on Empirical Data*, Springer-Verlag, New York, 1982.
18. N. Linial, Y. Mansour, and R. L. Rivest, "Results on Learnability and The Vapnik–Chervonenkis Dimension," *Inform. Comput.*, *90*, 33–49 (1991).
19. L. G. Valiant, "A Theory of the Learnable," *Commun. ACM*, *27*, 1134–1143 (1984).
20. D. Angluin, "Queries and Concept Learning," *Machine Learning*, *2*, 319–342 (1988).
21. V. N. Vapnik and A. Ya. Chervonenkis, "On the Uniform Convergence of Relative Frequencies of Events to Their Probabilities," *Theory Probab. Appl.*, *16*, 264–280 (1971).
22. D. Haussler and E. Welzl, "ε-Nets and Simplex Range Queries," *Discuss. Comp. Geometry*, *2*, 127–151 (1987).

23. M. J. Kearns and R. E. Schapire, "Efficient Distribution-Free Learning of Probabilistic Concepts," *Proceedings of the 31st Annual Symposium on the Foundations of Computer Science,* 1990.

24. B. K. Natarajan, "Probably Approximate Learning of Sets and Functions," *SIAM J. Comput.,* *20,* 328–351 (1991).

25. M. Anthony and N. L. Biggs, *Computational Learning Theory: An Introduction,* Cambridge University Press, New York, 1992.

26. B. K. Natarajan, *Computational Learning Theory: A Theoretical Approach,* Morgan Kaufmann, San Mateo, CA, 1991.

27. D. Haussler and L. Pitt (eds.), *Proceedings of the 1988 Workshop on Computational Learning Theory,* Morgan Kaufmann, San Mateo, CA, 1988.

28. R. Rivest, D. Haussler, and M. K. Warmuth (eds.), *Proceedings of the Second Annual Workshop on Computational Learning Theory,* Morgan Kaufmann, San Mateo, CA, 1989.

29. M. A. Fulk and J. Case (eds.), *Proceedings of the Third Annual Workshop on Computational Learning Theory,* Morgan Kaufmann, San Mateo, CA, 1990.

30. L. G. Valiant and M. K. Warmuth (eds.), *Proceedings of the Fourth Annual Workshop on Computational Learning Theory,* Morgan Kaufmann, San Mateo, CA, 1991.

31. *Proceedings of the Fifth Annual ACM Workshop on Computational Learning Theory,* ACM Press, New York, 1992.

PETER L. BARTLETT

COMPUTATIONAL MOLECULAR BIOLOGY

INTRODUCTION

A Scenario

For a fast introduction to the role of computing in molecular biology, imagine a scenario—sometime in the future—in which a new biological virus creates an epidemic of fatal disease in humans or animals. Laboratory scientists will isolate its genetic material, a molecule of DNA consisting of a long polymer of four different types of residues—their sequence is a genetic message in a four-letter alphabet. Computer software will then take over further processing and analysis.

Screening this new message against a data bank of all known genetic messages will characterize the virus and reveal its relationship with viruses previously studied (25). The analysis will continue toward the goal of developing antiviral therapies. In addition to the genome, viruses contain protein molecules which are suitable targets for interfering with viral structure or function. Proteins are also linear polymers; the sequences of their residues, called amino acids, are messages in a 20-letter alphabet. Computer software will derive the amino acid sequences of one or more viral proteins crucial to replication or assembly (1).

From the amino acid sequences, computer programs will compute the structures of these proteins (50) according to the basic principle that the amino acid sequences of proteins determine their three-dimensional structures, and, thereby, their functional properties. (This is the point at which Nature makes the leap from the one-dimensional world of genetic and protein sequences to the three-dimensional world we inhabit.) Data banks will be searched for related proteins of known structure; if any are found, the problem of structure prediction will be reduced to its "differential form"—the prediction of the effects on a structure of *changes* in sequence (40); if, as is increasingly unlikely as the corpus of known data grows larger, a protein appears genuinely new, the structure prediction must be done entirely "from scratch" (55).

Knowing the protein structure will make it possible to design therapeutic agents. Any protein will have sites on its surface crucial for function that are vulnerable to blocking—a small molecule, complementary in shape and charge distribution to such a site, will be identified or designed by a computer program to serve as an antiviral drug (50); alternatively, one or more antibodies may be designed and synthesized to neutralize the virus (50).

This scenario is based on well-established principles, and no doubt someday it will be implemented as described. The reason why we cannot apply it today against AIDS is that many of the problems are as yet unsolved. Readers may have recognized that the numbers in square brackets are **not** literature citations, but follow the convention of Knuth in indexing the difficulty of a problem! Numbers below 30 correspond to problems for which solutions already exist; those with higher numbers are themes of current research.

Finally, it should be added that competing purely experimental approaches to the problem of developing antiviral agents may well continue to be more successful than theoretical ones for many years.

The Biological Background

A biological organism is a naturally occurring self-reproducing device that effects controlled manipulations of matter, energy, and information.

The information archive—the blueprints for potential development and activity of any organism—is the genetic material, usually DNA. DNA molecules are long, *linear*, chain molecules containing a message in a four-letter alphabet (see Box I). Even for microorganisms, the message is long, typically 10^6 characters. Implicit in the structure of the DNA are mechanisms for self-replication and for translation into proteins. The double-helix, and its internal self-complementarity providing for accurate replication, are well known. Near-perfect replication is essential for stability of inheritance; but some imperfect replication—that is, mutation—is also essential, else evolution could not take place. (The genetic code is almost but not completely universal throughout life on earth. Viruses from outer space as seen in many science-fiction movies would not be at all dangerous to us if they did not share this genetic code—as well as many other biochemical similarities—as viral reproduction requires use of cellular translation machinery.)

Proteins are the molecules primarily responsible for the structure and activities of organisms. Our hair, muscle, digestive enzymes, and antibodies are all proteins. Chemically, proteins are also long, linear, chain molecules. In contrast to DNA, however, proteins contain a sequence of residues chosen from a 20-letter alphabet (see Boxes I and II). The "genetic code" is, in fact, a cipher: Successive triplets of letters from the DNA sequence specify successive single amino acids; stretches of DNA sequences encipher amino acid sequences of proteins. Typically, proteins are 200–300 amino acids long, thus requiring 600–900 letters of the DNA message to specify them. However, in most organisms, not all of the DNA enciphers amino acid sequences of proteins; some regions of the DNA sequence are devoted to control mechanisms, and many others appear to be merely "junk".

In the case of DNA, the molecules comprising the alphabet are chemically similar, and the structure of DNA is, to a first approximation, uniform. Proteins, in contrast, show a great variety of three-dimensional conformations; these are necessary to support their very diverse structural and functional roles. The 20 amino acids of the protein alphabet have diverse physicochemical properties. Therefore, even at the one-dimensional level, the amino acid sequences of proteins are characterized by individual distributions.

The amino acid sequence of a protein dictates its three-dimensional structure. For each natural amino acid sequence, there is a unique thermodynamically stable "native state" that under proper conditions is adopted spontaneously. If a purified protein is heated, or otherwise brought to conditions far from the normal physiological environment, it will "unfold" to a disordered and biologically inactive structure. (This is why our bodies contain mechanisms to maintain nearly constant internal conditions.) When normal conditions are restored, protein molecules will generally readopt the native structure, indistinguishable from the original state. Two noteworthy points: (1) This is contrary to ordinary experience: hard-boil an egg and then cool it and you do not get an native egg again; but in a suitable dilute solution the proteins would refold. (2) The fact that isolated proteins refold proves that the structure is really implicit in the amino acid sequence and not dependent on some cellular machinery, or on transient events occurring during the synthesis of the protein.

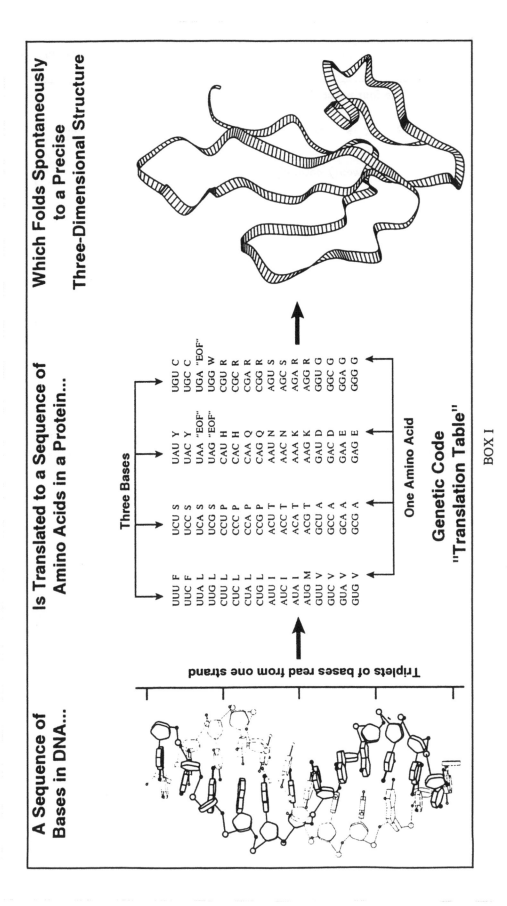

A Sequence of
Bases in DNA...

Is Translated to a Sequence of
Amino Acids in a Protein...

Which Folds Spontaneously
to a Precise
Three-Dimensional Structure

Triplets of bases read from one strand

Three Bases

UUU F	UCU S	UAU Y	UGU C
UUC F	UCC S	UAC Y	UGC C
UUA L	UCA S	UAA "EOF"	UGA "EOF"
UUG L	UCG S	UAG "EOF"	UGG W
CUU L	CCU P	CAU H	CGU R
CUC L	CCC P	CAC H	CGC R
CUA L	CCA P	CAA Q	CGA R
CUG L	CCG P	CAG Q	CGG R
AUU I	ACU T	AAU N	AGU S
AUC I	ACC T	AAC N	AGC S
AUA I	ACA T	AAA K	AGA R
AUG M	ACG T	AAG K	AGG R
GUU V	GCU A	GAU D	GGU G
GUC V	GCC A	GAC D	GGC G
GUA V	GCA A	GAA E	GGA G
GUG V	GCG A	GAG E	GGG G

One Amino Acid

Genetic Code
"Translation Table"

BOX I

The four naturally occurring nucleotides in DNA

a adenine	g guanine	t thymine	c cytosine

The twenty naturally occurring amino acids

Nonpolar-amino acids

G	glycine	A	alanine	P	proline	V	valine
I	isoleucine	L	leucine	F	phenylalanine	M	methionine

Polar amino acids

S	serine	C	cysteine	T	threonine	N	asparagine
Q	glutamine	H	histidine	Y	tyrosine	W	tryptophan

Charged amino acids

D	aspartic acid	E	glutamic acid	K	lysine	R	arginine

BOX II

The functions of proteins depend on their adopting the native three-dimensional structure; for example, the structure may create a cavity on the surface that binds a small molecule. We have the paradigm:

- DNA sequence determines protein sequence
- Protein sequence determines protein structure
- Protein structure determines protein function

Most of the organized activity of computational molecular biology has been focused on the analysis of data related to these processes, and this activity is the subject of this article. However, what this paradigm does *not* include is the higher (than the molecular) levels of structure and organization, including, for example, such questions as how tissues become specialized during development or, more generally, how environmental effects exert control over genetic events. In some simple cases of "feedback loops," it is understood at the molecular level how increasing the amount of a reactant causes an increase in the production of an enzyme that catalyzes its transformation. More complex are the "programs" of development played out during the lifetime of an organism. Although these are fascinating problems about the information flow and control within an organism and, in principle, come within the scope of our topic, their study has not yet led to substantial computational developments.

THE NATURE AND ORGANIZATION OF THE DATA

DNA Sequences

The DNA of a typical bacterium comes as a single molecule, which, if extended, would be 2 mm long. (The cell itself has a diameter of about 0.001 mm.) The DNA of higher organisms is organized into chromosomes; normal human cells contain 23 chromosome pairs. The total amount of genetic information—the sequence of nucleotides of DNA—borne by any individual is very nearly constant for all members of a species but varies widely between species.

Treating sequence data as character strings—that is, allowing 1 byte/residue—the sizes of a number of genomes are as follows (1)

Epstein–Barr virus	0.172×10^6 bytes
Bacterium (*E. coli*)	4.8×10^6 bytes
Yeast (*S. cerevisiae*)	14.4×10^6 bytes
Nematode worm (*C. elegans*)	100.0×10^6 bytes
Thale cress (*A. thaliana*)	100.0×10^6 bytes
Fruit fly (*D. melanogaster*)	165.0×10^6 bytes
Human (*H. sapiens*)	3300.0×10^6 bytes

Each of these organisms is the target of a project aimed at sequencing the total genome of at least one strain or individual. Readers will be aware of the public debate surrounding the organization and commitment of resources to the Human Genome project.

From our point of view, the complexity of the internal organization of the data is more significant than its overall size.

A single gene enciphering a particular protein molecule corresponds to a sequence of nucleotides along one or more regions of a molecule of DNA. In bacteria, the DNA sequence is collinear with the protein sequence and uninterrupted. In general, for each region of DNA that codes for protein, only one of the two strands is "read"; the other strand serves as the mechanism of replication. Therefore, the simplest object of genetic sequence information is a string of $3N$ nucleotides enciphering a string of N amino acids. Such a string, equipped with annotations, would form a typical entry in one of the genetic sequence archives.

In higher organisms, for instance, human beings, the nucleotide sequences that correspond to amino acid sequences of individual proteins are organized in a more complex manner. Frequently they appear as different segments in the genomic DNA, which must be spliced together. The term "exon" refers to a stretch of DNA that is actually *ex*pressed as protein, and "intron" to the *int*ervening regions. Many introns are very long—indeed, substantially larger than the exons. Several variations on the theme add to the complexity: In some cases, genes for different proteins may overlap, so that an exon of one gene may lie within an intron of another. Genes may be spliced together before expression in different ways in different tissues. There is cellular machinery that solves the problem of splicing together the proper segments, based on signals flanking the exons in the DNA sequences themselves.

Why are genes interrupted? In general, we do not know. In some cases, individual exons correspond to structural subunits of proteins and can be recombined in various ways to bring together different structural or functional combinations. This is a mechanism for generation of diversity. It is useful for evolution in general and finds a specialized application in our own bodies and in those of other animals for combinatorial generation of a large set of antibody molecules to provide complete coverage of the foreign molecules which must be recognized.

However, to extract the regions that code for protein from DNA sequences and regard them as independent objects is to miss important features of their context and interrelationships.

First, context. In regions of DNA that include segments coding for a protein, it is observed that outside the beginning of the coding region there are short "signal" sequences that serve as binding sites for the molecules that transcribe the DNA sequence, and other sequences that serve as a binding sites for regulatory molecules that can *block* the transcribing activity. Sometimes a series of contiguous genes code for several proteins, all under the control of the same regulatory sequence; often the proteins specified by these genes are enzymes that catalyze successive steps in an integrated sequence of reactions. One can therefore readily understand the utility of a parallel control mechanism.

Second, interrelationships. Different organisms share many types of genes and proteins, and there are differences—sometimes subtle, sometimes gross—between corresponding molecules from different sources. It is a characteristic of biological systems that objects that we observe to have a certain form arose by evolution from related objects with similar but not identical form. They must, therefore, be robust, in that they retain the freedom to tolerate some variation. We can take advantage of this robustness in our analysis: By identifying and comparing related objects, we can distinguish variable and conserved features, and thereby determine what is crucial to structure and function.

The conclusion is that to reduce genetic data to individual coding sequences—according to the paradigm proposed in the Introduction—is to disguise the very complex nature of the interrelationships among them. Robbins has expressed the situation admirably (2):

> . . . Consider the 3.3 gigabytes of a human genome as equivalent to 3.3 gigabytes of files on the mass-storage device of some computer system of unknown design. Obtaining the sequence is equivalent to obtaining an image of the contents of that mass-storage device. Understanding the sequence is equivalent to reverse engineering that unknown computer system (both the hardware and the 3.3 gigabytes of software) all the way back to a full set of design and maintenance specifications.
>
> Reverse engineering the sequence is complicated by the fact that the resulting image of the mass-storage device will not be a file-by-file copy, but rather a streaming dump of the bytes in the order they were entered into the device. Furthermore, the files are known to be fragmented. In addition, some of the device contains erased files or other garbage. Once the garbage has been recognized and discarded and the fragmented files reassembled, the reverse engineering of the codes can be undertaken with only a partial, and sometimes incorrect, understanding of the CPU on which the codes run. In fact, deducing the structure and function of the CPU is part of the project, since some of the 3.3 gigabytes are the binary specifications for the computer-assisted-manufacturing process that fabricates the CPU. In addition, one must also consider that the huge database also contains code generated from the result of literally millions of maintenance revisions performed by the worst possible set of kludge-using, spaghetti-coding, opportunistic hackers who delight in clever tricks like writing self-modifying code and relying upon undocumented systems quirks.

Protein Sequences

In principle, a database of amino acid sequences of proteins is inherent in the database of nucleotide sequences of DNA, by virtue of the genetic code. Indeed, at present, the vast majority of new protein sequence data are being determined by translation of DNA sequences rather than by direct sequencing of proteins, although historically the chemical problem of determining amino acid sequences of proteins directly was solved before the genetic code was established and before methods for determination of nucleotide sequences of DNA were developed.

Should any distinction be made between protein sequence data determined directly and those determined by translation from DNA? First, one assumes that it is possible to identify within the DNA data stream the regions that encode proteins. Pattern-recognition software has been written to accomplish this. Two types of errors are possible: A genuine protein sequence may be missed entirely, or perhaps an incomplete protein may be reported. The algorithms are generally tuned to minimize the former type of error, at the expense of reporting some sequence that may not correspond to real proteins. Conversely, some genetic sequences that "look like" genuine proteins may, in fact, be defective. The fact remains that a protein sequence derived from a DNA sequence is a hypothetical object; experiments are necessary to verify its existence.

Second, in many cases the expression of a gene produces a molecule that must be modified within a cell to make a "mature" protein that is significantly different from that suggested by translation of the gene sequence. Gene sequences provide almost—but not quite—complete information about the chemical structures of the corresponding proteins. For some applications, the missing details are quite important.

We have pointed out that not all DNA sequences code for protein. Conversely, some genes exist in multiple copies. Therefore, the actual size of the protein sequence information in an organism can only be estimated, at least until the full genomic sequence is determined. The following table gives some estimates of the number of genes in each organism of selected species:

Epstein–Barr virus	80
Bacterium (*E. coli*)	3,237
Yeast (*S. cerevisiae*)	8,000
Nematode worm (*C. elegans*)	16,000–20,000
Fruit fly (*D. melanogaster*)	15,000–25,000
Human (*H. sapiens*)	50,000–100,000

Protein Structure

Chemically, protein molecules are long polymers typically containing several thousand atoms, composed of a uniform repetitive "backbone" (or "main chain") with a particular "side chain" attached to each residue. The amino acid sequence of a protein records the sequence of side chains. Ions, small organic ligands, and even water molecules are frequently integral parts of protein structures. Biochemically, proteins play a variety of roles in life processes: there are structural proteins (for example, viral coat proteins and horny outer layer of human and animal skin); proteins that catalyze chemical reactions, the enzymes; transport and storage proteins (hemoglobin); regulatory proteins, including hormones; proteins that control genetic transcription; and antibodies and other proteins of the immune system.

The polypeptide chain folds into a space curve, the course of the chain defining a "folding pattern." The classification of the topologies of folding patterns, and integrating each newly reported structure into the scheme of things, is an important theme of current research. We find ourselves in very much the same position as the anatomists of 200 years ago who would receive a set of specimens of exotic animals and plants from expeditions of exploration.

Approximately 3000 protein structures are now known. Most were determined by X-ray crystallography, some by nuclear magnetic resonance, a few by other techniques (fiber or electron diffraction). From these we have derived our understanding both of the functions of individual proteins—for example, the chemical explanation of catalytic activity of enzymes—and of the general principles of protein structure and folding. Proteins show a great variety of folding patterns, underlying which are a number of common structural features. These include the recurrence of explicit structural paradigms—for example, regions that form helices—and common principles or features such as the dense packing of the atoms in protein interiors. [Folding may be thought of very roughly as a kind of intramolecular condensation or crystallization (3).]

The three-dimensional structures of protein molecules are determined by the one-dimensional sequences of their amino acids. Any possible folding of the main chain places different residues in proximity. The interactions of the side chains and main chain, with one another and with the solvent, determine the relative stability of the conformation. Proteins have evolved so that one folding pattern of the main chain produces a set of interactions significantly more favorable than all others. This corresponds to the native state. If we could calculate sufficiently accurately the energies and entropies of different conformations and if we could computationally examine a large enough set of possible conformations to be sure of including the correct one, it would be possible to predict protein structures from amino acid sequences on the basis of *a priori* physicochemical principles. So far, this is not possible (see the section Protein structure prediction).

We do, however, understand the general nature of the interactions between the residues. The side chains of the 20 amino acids have diverse physicochemical properties (see Box II). They vary in the following:

Size. The smallest side chain, glycine, consists of only a hydrogen atom. One of the largest, phenylalanine, contains a benzene ring.

Electric charge. Some side chains are electrically neutral; among these some consist of chemical groups related to ordinary hydrocarbons such as methane (natural gas) or benzene. Because of the thermodynamically unfavorable interaction of hydrocarbons with water, they are called "hydrophobic" residues. The congregation of hydrophobic residues in protein interiors, predicted by W. J. Kauzmann before the first protein structures were determined, is an important contribution to protein stability. This effect is analogous to the formation of droplets of oil in salad dressing.

Other side chains are polar; they participate in relatively weak attractive interactions called hydrogen bonds. Still other sidechains bear a net positive or negative charge. Charged residues of opposite sign can form attractive pairwise interactions called "salt bridges."

Shape and rigidity. The overall shape of a side chain depends on its chemical structure and on the internal degrees of freedom which many but not all side chains possess. Protein interiors are densely packed; the fitting together of the side chains is like a solved jigsaw puzzle, but because the puzzle pieces (the residues) are deformable, the folding process is more complicated than the rigid matching we know from ordinary jigsaw puzzles. These and other structural constraints on the packing go beyond the "oil drop" or "salad dressing" model that is based only on the principle that water is excluded from protein interiors.

To form the native structure, the protein must optimize the interactions between residues, subject to constraints on the space curve traced out by the main chain. Preferred

conformations of the main chain bias the folding pattern toward recurrent structural pat
terns. For instance, local regions of the chain often form helical regions, or extended regions that can interact to form sheets.

The linear polypeptide chain common to all protein structures is shown in Figure 1.
Rotation is permitted around the N–Cα and Cα–C single bonds of all residues (with one
exception: proline). The angles φ and ψ around these bonds, and ω, the angle of rotation
around the peptide bond, define the conformation of a residue. The peptide bond itself
tends to be planar, with two allowed states: $\omega \approx 180°$ (usually) and $\omega \approx 0°$ (rarely).
The sequence of ψ, φ, and ω angles of all residues in a protein defines the backbone
conformation.

The principle that two atoms cannot occupy the same space limits the values of
conformational angles to ranges of allowed values. For φ and ψ angles, the allowed
ranges tend to fall into regions defined in a Sasisekharan–Ramachandran plot: a graph in
which each residue corresponds to a point with abscissa φ and ordinate ψ (see Fig. 2).
Broken lines in the figure delimit allowed regions. The conformations of most amino acids fall into either the α_R or β regions. One of the amino acids, glycine, can occupy additional portions of the space, in particular it can form a left-handed helix: α_L. Figure 2

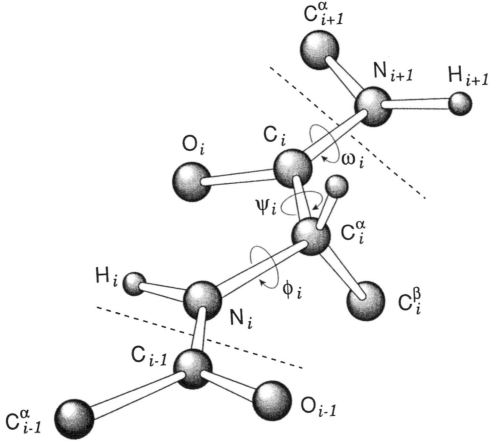

FIGURE 1   The conformation of a polypeptide chain can be specified to a rough approximation
by the values of angles of internal rotation. One residue, delimited by the broken lines, contains
three bonds that are potential axes of rotation. φ, ψ, and ω denote the settings of the corresponding angles. The conformation shown has $\phi_i = \psi_i = \omega_i = 180°$

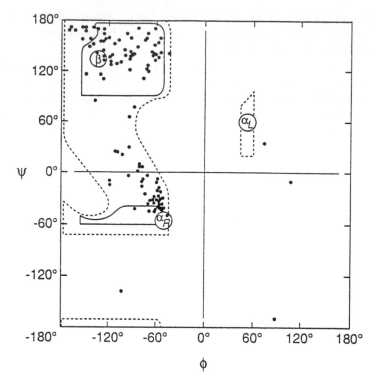

FIGURE 2   Not all values of φ, ψ, and ω are energetically allowed. Planarity constraints limit ω to two states: ω ≈ 180° (usually) and ω ≈ 0° (rarely). For the ω ≈ 180° state, only certain values of φ and ψ are allowed, the regions demarcated by solid and broken lines on this graph. Filled circles show the values of φ and ψ for the residues in a typical well-determined protein. Most but not all fall within the theoretically allowed regions.

also shows the typical distribution of residue conformations in a well-determined protein structure. Most residues fall in or near the allowed regions, but the folding forces a few into energetically unfavorable states.

The allowed regions into which the residues may fall generate standard conformations. A stretch of consecutive residues (typically 6–20 in length) in the α conformation generates an α-helix; repeating the β conformation generates an extended β-strand; two or more β-strands frequently interact to form β-sheets (see Fig. 3). Helices and sheets are "standard" or "prefabricated" structural pieces that form components of the conformations of most proteins. In some fibrous proteins, virtually all of the residues belong to one of these types of structure: wool contains α-helices, silk β-sheets. Typical globular proteins contain some helical and/or sheet regions connected by loops. In graphic representations of complex molecules requiring simplification for intelligibility, helices are often represented as cylinders and strands of sheet as large arrows (see Fig. 4).

What is important to our discussion is not the detailed definition of the parameters defining residue conformations but the "take-home lesson" that most residues are restricted to a very few discrete conformational states. This is an approximation rather than a simplification.

Figure 5 shows a few typical folding patterns of the main chain of proteins, represented by smoothed ribbons. Can the reader identify helices and sheets? Compare the

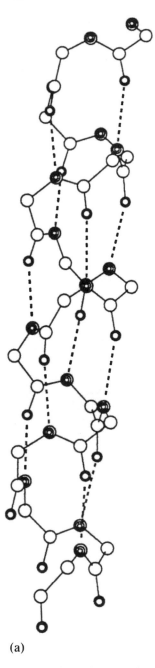

(a)

FIGURE 3 Two standard structural paradigms that recur in many protein structures: (a) the α-helix; (b) the β-sheet. These are shown in a "ball-and-stick" representation in which small circles represent individual atoms (concentric circles distinguish different atom types) and solid lines represent chemical bonds. Broken lines indicate a kind of weaker chemical interaction called a "hydrogen bond"; it is the abundance of these hydrogen bonds, together with the fact that the main chain conformations fall into the standard allowed regions (see Fig. 2) that makes these conformations of the chain stable.

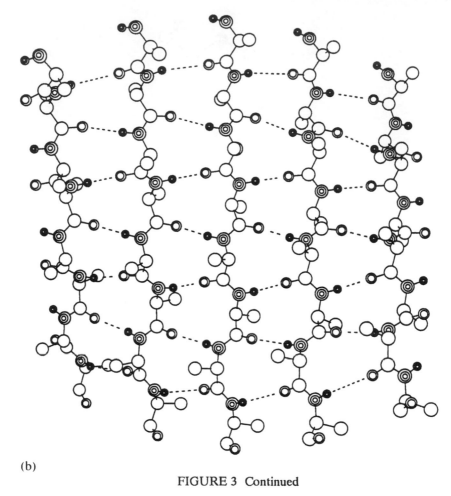

(b)

FIGURE 3 Continued

succeeding figures in which the "parsing" of the conformation is done for the reader, replacing the helices and strands of sheets with icons.

Themes and Variations: Molecular Evolution

Evolution has provided us with many examples of closely related sequences and structures. The illumination provided by comparisons among related molecules has been absolutely essential in allowing us to identify the features that are crucial to structure and function.

We now recognize that the primary events in the generation of biological diversity are the mutation, insertion, and deletion of nucleotides in DNA sequences, or the larger-scale transposition of pieces of genetic material, and that natural selection reacts to protein function as determined by protein structure. Thus, if a "wild-type" gene produces a functional protein product, a mutant gene may produce an alternative protein of equivalent function (a "neutral mutation"), or a protein that carries out the same function but with an altered rate or specificity profile, or a protein with an altered function, or a protein that does not function—or even fold—at all. Changes in the genome that alter mol-

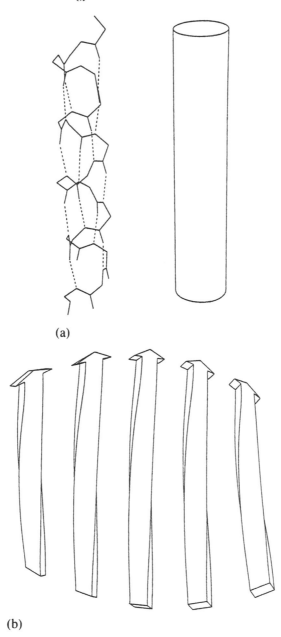

(a)

(b)

FIGURE 4   Simplified representations of recurrent structural patterns in proteins as icons. (a) Representation of the α-helix as a cylinder; (b) representation of strands of β-sheet as large arrows.

ecules involved in control of genetic activity rather than changing the sequence of the mature gene product are also very important in evolution.

Examination of homologous genes and proteins in different species has shown that evolutionary variation and divergence occur very generally at the molecular level. Proteins from related species have similar but not identical amino acid sequences. These sequences determine similar but not identical protein structures.

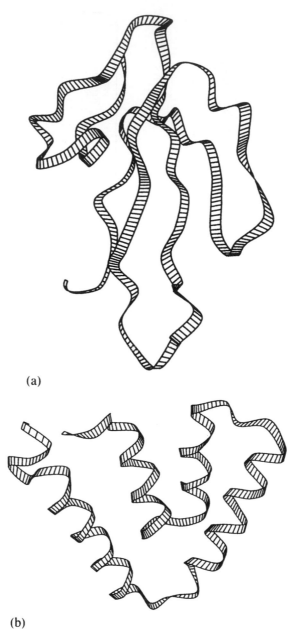

(a)

(b)

FIGURE 5   Examples of protein structures. Can you trace the chain? Can you identify helices
and sheets? (a) α-bungarotoxin; (b) uteroglobin; (c) α-amylase inhibitor; (d) photoreactive yellow
protein; (e) thioredoxin; (f) chicken triosephosphate isomerase (TIM); (g) λ repressor/DNA complex (thick lines: two protein chains, distinguished by different densities of "rungs"; thin lines: a
stretch of double helix of DNA). Needless to say, these are only a few samples from a very large
and varied set of folding patterns. To Rutherford's famous statement, "All science is either physics
or stamp collecting," the response is that the study of protein structure combines the best characteristics of both. The smooth curves in these figures were produced by "quadratic blending" (4);
fitting by splines gives similar results.

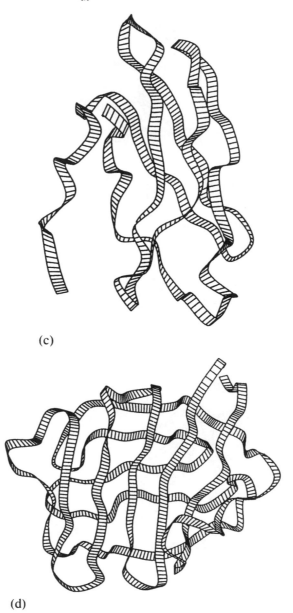

(c)

(d)

Evolutionary Changes in Protein Sequences

Globins are a class of proteins involved in oxygen and carbon dioxide transport in blood. Molecules related to hemoglobin occur in many animals, including invertebrates such as insects and worms, in plants, and even in bacteria.

Tables 1a and 1b show sets of aligned globin sequences. (Such tables are one of the fundamental types of paper objects of study by molecular biologists. At this very moment there are, around the world, probably at least 500 molecular biologists staring at similar tables.) Patterns of conservation and variation at the individual positions provide clues to the nature of the selective constraints on the molecule, more directly even than a structure itself does.

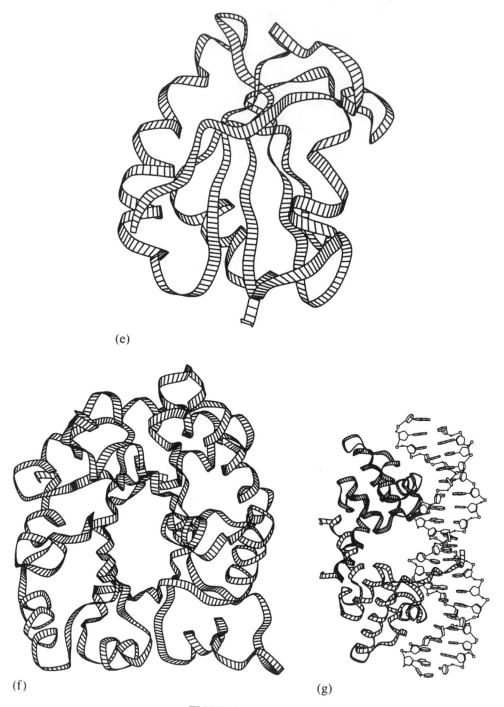

FIGURE 5 Continued

Table Ia is limited to five mammalian globins: the two related polypeptide chains (called α and β) from human and horse hemoglobin, and sperm whale myoglobin. Table Ib contains globins from much more diverse species: It includes the mammalian globins plus globins from an insect, a plant, and a bacterium.

The five mammalian globin sequences shown in Table Ia each contains approximately 140–150 residues. There are 24 positions at which the residue is conserved in all five sequences. (In the line below the tabulation, uppercase letters indicate residues that are conserved in all five sequences, and lowercase letters indicate residues that are conserved in all but sperm whale myoglobin.) Other positions show changes only among residues with very similar properties: For example, position 3 contains only serine or threonine (both of these are classified as polar side chains) (see Box II for abbreviations). Position 119 contains only valine, isoleucine, or leucine: These are all hydrocarbon side chains of moderate size. However, other positions contain residues showing very wide variations in side chain size and polarity; for example, position 32 contains glutamic acid (negatively charged), glycine (uncharged, tiny volume), or isoleucine (uncharged, medium sized).

These many similarities leave no doubt that the sequences are related. Moreover, on the basis of the patterns of residue conservation and change at different positions, there is a very obvious hierarchical classification. Position 32, for example, contains glutamic acid in the human and horse α chains, glycine in the human and horse β chains, and isoleucine in myoglobin. The reader can easily identify other such positions. These show that the α chains are more similar to each other than to the β chains or to myoglobin, the β chains are more similar to each other than to the α chains or to myoglobin, but the α and β chains are more similar to each other than either is to myoglobin. Given another mammalian globin sequence, the reader would easily be able to identify it as a hemoglobin α-chain, a hemoglobin β-chain, or a myoglobin.

The reader may also note as a feature of the patterns of conservation that several pairs of conserved residues are separated by 3, 4, or 7 in the sequence. This is an indication that they are in α-helices. The reason is that the α-helix has a periodicity of 3.6 residues per turn; therefore, these conserved residues appear on the same face of the helix (see Fig. 3a). We may infer that this face is involved in an important and conserved structural interaction. Note that this inference is available only through the comparison of related sequences.

The sequences in Table Ib include the same five mammalian globins, and additional homologues from an insect, a plant, and a bacterium. These are much more diverse—the bacterial globin is the most distant from the others—and, indeed, only four positions are conserved in all eight sequences. (In the line below this tabulation, uppercase letters indicate residues that are conserved in all eight sequences.)

It is possible to construct "evolutionary trees" from tabulations of related sequences (5, 6). Phylogenies derived from different families of proteins from the same range of species are generally mutually consistent, and also consistent in branching order with phylogenetic trees based on classical taxonomic methods. Of course, it is essential to choose functionally equivalent proteins; for example, an attempt to derive mammalian phylogenetic relationships from globin sequences would obviously have to be based on hemoglobin α chains taken by themselves or hemoglobin β chains taken by themselves or myoglobin chains taken by themselves but could not be carried out by mixing α chains from some species with β chains from others.

TABLE 1a

```
                                 10        20        30        40        50        60        70        80
                                  .         .         .         .         .         .         .         .
Human Haemoglobin α chain   VLSPADKTNVKAAWGKVGA--HAGEYGAEALERMFLSFPTTKTYFPHF-DLS------HGSAQVKGHGKKVADALTNAVAH·
Horse Haemoglobin α chain   VLSAADKTNVKAAWSKVGG--HAGEYGAEALERMFLGFPTTKTYFPHF-DLS------HGSAQVKAHGKKVGDALTLAVGH
Human Haemoglobin β chain   VHLTPEEKSAVTALWGKV---NVDEVGGEALGRLLVVYPWTQRFFESFGDLSTPDAVMGNPKVKAHGKKVLGAFSDGLAH
Horse Haemoglobin α chain   VQLSGEEKAAVLALWDKV----NEEEVGGEALGRLLVVYPWTQRFFDSFGDLSNPGAVMGNPKVKAHGKKVLHSFGEGVHH
Sperm whale myoglobin       VLSEGEWQLVLHVWAKVEA-DVAGHGQDILIRLFKSHPETLEKFDRFKHLKTEAEMKASEDLKKHGVTVLTALGAILKK

                              k  v   W KV        G eaL R         P   F   dLs         vK HGkkv         H


                                 90        100       110       120       130       140       150       160
                                  .         .         .         .         .         .         .         .
Human Haemoglobin α chain   V-----D-DMPNALSALSDLHAHKLRVDPVNFKLLSHCLLVTLAAHLP-A-EFTPAVHASLDKFLASVSTVLTSKYR·
Horse Haemoglobin α chain   L-----D-DLPGALSNLSDLHAHKLRVDPVNFKLLSHCLLSTLAVHLP-N-DFTPAVHASLDKFLSSVSTVLTSKYR
Human Haemoglobin β chain   L-----D-NLKGTFATLSELHCDKLHVDPENFRLLGNVLVCVLAHHFG-K-EFTPPVQAAYQKVVAGVANALAHKYH
Horse Haemoglobin β chain   L-----D-NLKGTFAALSELHCDKLHVDPENFRLLGNVLVVVLARHFG-K-DFTPELQASYQKVVAGVANALAHKYH
Sperm whale myoglobin       ------KGHHEAELKPLAQSHATKHKIPIKYLEFISEAIIHVLHSRHP-G-DFGADAQGAMNKALELFRKDIAAKYKELGYQG

                              d     Ls LH  Kl vd nf ll    l    La h   Ftp  a  K   v  l  KY
```

TABLE 1b

	10	20	30	40	50	60	70	80

```
                                        10        20        30        40        50        60        70        80
                                        .         .         .         .         .         .         .         .
Human Haemoglobin α chain          VLSPADKTNVKAAWGKVGA-HAGEYGAEALERMFLSFPTTKTYFPHF-DLS-------HGSAQVKGHGKKVADALTNAVAH
Horse Haemoglobin α chain          VLSAADKTNVKAAWSKVGG-HAGEYGAEALERMFLGFPTTKTYFPHF-DLS-------HGSAQVKAHGKKVGDALTLAVGH
Human Haemoglobin β chain          VHLTPEEKSAVTALWGKV------NVDEVGGEALGRLLVVYPWTQRFFESFGDLSTPDAVMGNPKVKAHGKKVLGAFSDGLAH
Horse Haemoglobin β chain          VQLSGEEKAAVLALWDKV------NEEVGGEALGRLLVVYPWTQRFFDSFGDLSNPGAVMGNPKVKAHGKKVLHSFGEGVHH
Sperm whale myoglobin              VLSEGEWQLVLHVWAKVEA-DVAGHGQDILIRLFKSHPETLEKFDRFKHLKTEAEMKASEDLKKHGVTVLTALGAILKK
Chironomus erythrocruorin          LSADQISTVQASFDKVKG-------DPVGILYAVFKADPSIMAKFTQFAG-KDLESIKGTAPFETHANRIVGFFSKIIGE
Lupin leghaemoglobin               GALTESQAALVKSSWEEFNA-NIPKHTHRFFILVLEIAPAAKDLFS-FLK-GTSEVPQNNPELQAHAGKVFKLVYEAAIQ
Bacterial globin (Vitroscilla sp.) MLDQQTINIIKATVPVLKEHGVTITTTFYKNLFAKHPEVRPLFD-M------GRQESLEQPKALAMTVLAAAQN
                                                                          P         F
```

```
                                        90        100       110       120       130       140       150       160
                                        .         .         .         .         .         .         .         .
Human Haemoglobin α chain          V------D-DMPNALSALSDLHAHKLRVDPVNFKLLSHCLLVTLAAHLP-A-EFTPAVHASLDKFLASVSTVLTSKYR
Horse Haemoglobin α chain          L------D-DLPGALSNLSDLHAHKLRVDPVNFKLLSHCLLSTLAVHLP-N-DFTPAVHASLDKFLSSVSTVLTSKYR
Human Haemoglobin β chain          L------D-NLKGTFATLSELHCDKLHVDPENFRLLGNVLVCVLAHHFG-K-EFTPPVQAAYQKVVAGVANALAHKYH
Horse Haemoglobin β chain          L------D-NLKGTFAALSELHCDKLHVDPENFRLLGNVLVVLARHFG-K-DFTPELQASYQKVVAGVANALAHKYH
Sperm whale myoglobin              -----KGHHEAELKPLAQSHATKHKIPIKYLEFISEAIIHVLHSRHP-G-DFGADAQGAMNKALELFRKDIAAKYKELGYQG
Chironomus erythrocruorin          L-P—NIEADVNTFVASHKPRG-VTHDQLNNFRAGFVSYMKAHT------DFAGAEAAWGATLDTFFGMIFSKM
Lupin leghaemoglobin               LEVTGVVVSDATLKNLGSVHVSKG-VADAHFPVVKEAILKTIKEVVG-A-KWSEELNSAWTIAYDELAIVIKKEMDDAA
Bacterial globin (Vitroscilla sp.) I—ENLPAILPAVKKIAVKHCQAG-VAAAHYPIVGQELLGAIKEVLGDAA—TDDILDAMGKAYGVIADVFIQVEADLYAQAVE
                                        H
```

Variation in Selective Constraints in Protein Molecules

Residues in proteins that are subject to strict functional constraints or that play crucial structural roles can accommodate mutations less easily than other residues. This point is seen in the aligned sequences of mammalian proinsulins. The hormone insulin is synthesized as a single polypeptide chain, from which the central portion (called the C-peptide) is excised and discarded, leaving the A and B chains. The C-peptide sequences, which do not appear in the mature functional hormone, show much higher variability than the A and B chains, which make up the active molecule:

```
B chain sequences
    Man          FVNQHLCGSHLVEALYLVCGERGFFYTPKT
    Pig          FVNQHLCGSHLVEALYLVCGERGFFYTPKA
    Cow          FVNQHLCGSHLVEALYLVCGERGFFYTPKA
    Guinea pig   FVSRHLCGSNLVETLYSVCQDDGFFYIPKD
    Rat          FVKQHLCGPHLVEALYLVCGERGFFYTPKS

C-peptide sequences
    Man          RREAEDLQVGQVELGGGPGAGSLQPLALEGSLQKR
    Pig          RREAENPQAGAVELGGG--LGGLQALALEGPPQKR
    Cow          RREVEGPQVGALELAGGPGAGGL------EGPPQKR
    Guinea pig   RRELEDPQVEQTELGMGLGAGGLQPL--QGALQXX
    Rat          RREVEDPQVPQLELGGGPEAGDLQTLALEVARQKR

A chain sequences
    Man          GIVEQCCTSICSLYQLENYCN
    Pig          GIVEQCCTSICSLYQLENYCN
    Cow          GIVEQCCASVCSLYQLENYCN
    Guinea pig   GIVDQCCTGTCTRHQLQSYCN
    Rat          GIVDQCCTSICSLYQLENYCN
```

Evolution of Protein Structures

Included in the approximately 2000 protein structures now known are several families in which the molecules maintain the same basic folding pattern over ranges of sequence similarity from near-identity down to below 20% conservation. In both closely and distantly related proteins the general response to mutation is structural change. It is the ability of protein structures to accommodate mutations in nonfunctional residues that permits a large amount of apparently nonadaptive change to occur. But the maintenance of function in widely divergent sequences requires the integration of the response to mutations over all or at least a large portion of the molecule.

Natural variations in families of homologous proteins that retain a common function reveal how the structures accommodate changes in amino acid sequence. Surface residues not involved in functions are usually free to mutate. Loops on the surface can often accommodate changes by local refolding. Buried residues can change size. Mutations that change the volumes of buried residues generally do not change the conformations of individual helices or sheets but produce distortions of their spatial assembly. The nature of the forces that stabilize protein structures sets general limitations on these conformational changes; other constraints derived from function vary from case to case.

Families of related proteins tend to retain similar folding patterns. If one examines sets of related proteins (see, e.g., Figs. 6 and 7), it is clear that although the general folding pattern is preserved, there are distortions which increase as the amino acid sequences progressively diverge. These distortions are not uniformly distributed throughout the structure. Indeed, in any family of proteins, a core of the structure retains the same qualitative fold, and other parts of the structure change conformation radically. To illustrate this idea of the common core of two structures, consider the letters B and R. Considered as structures, they have a common core which corresponds to the letter P. Outside the common core, they differ: At the bottom right B has a loop and R has a diagonal stroke.

Figure 6, showing the enzymes actinidin and papain, illustrates two structures that are quite closely related. The sequences of these molecules have 49% residue identity in the core. The common core consists of almost the entire structure except for small loop regions on the surface. The structural deviation is very small: the Cα atoms of the residues of the core can be superposed to within an average deviation of 0.77 Å.

Figure 7, showing plastocyanin and azurin, two copper-binding proteins involved in electron transport, illustrates two distantly related proteins. Less than 20% of residues are conserved. In this case, the common core is limited to less than 50% of the structure. It is clear that the long loop at the left has entirely refolded. (Ignore the fact that this region contains a helix in each molecule; these helices are independent). Nevertheless, the selective constraint on function has preserved the geometry of the copperbinding site.

Systematic studies of the structural differences between pairs of related proteins have defined a quantitative relationship between the divergence of the amino acid sequences of the core of a family of and the divergence of structure. As the sequence diverges, there are progressively increasing distortions in the main chain conformation, and the fraction of the residues in the core decreases. Until the fraction of identical residues in the sequence drops below about 40–50%, these effects are relatively modest: Almost all the structure remains in the core, and the deformation of the main chain atoms are on the average no more than 1.0 Å. Actinidin and papain illustrate this regime. With increasing sequence divergence, some regions refold entirely, reducing the size of the core, and the distortions of the residues remaining within the core increase in magnitude. Plastocyanin and azurin illustrate this effect.

A quantitative correlation between the divergence of sequence and structure applies to all families of proteins (7, 8). Figure 8 shows results from comparing pairs of homologous proteins from many related families. Each point corresponds to a pair of proteins. This graph shows the changes in structure of the core, expressed as the root-mean-square deviation of the main chain atoms after optimal superposition, plotted against the sequence divergence: the percentage of conserved amino acids of the core after optimal alignment. (The points corresponding to 100% residue identity are proteins for which the structure was determined in two or more crystal environments, and the deviations show that crystal packing forces can modify slightly the conformation of the proteins.) Figure 9 shows the changes in the fraction of residues in the core as a function of sequence divergence. The fraction of residues in the cores of distantly related proteins can vary widely: In some cases the fraction of residues in the core remains high; in others, it can drop to below 50% of the structure.

In addition to illustrating the kinds of approaches to data analysis that are practiced by molecular biologists, this section was intended to demonstrate the importance of searching for relationships among different items of data, and the futility of trying to study them one by one.

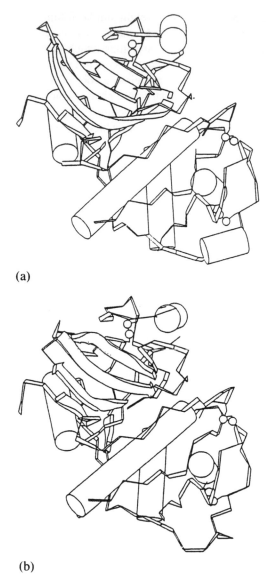

(a)

(b)

FIGURE 6   Two closely-related proteins: (a) actinidin; (b) papain. The amino acid sequences of
these molecules have about 50% identical residues.

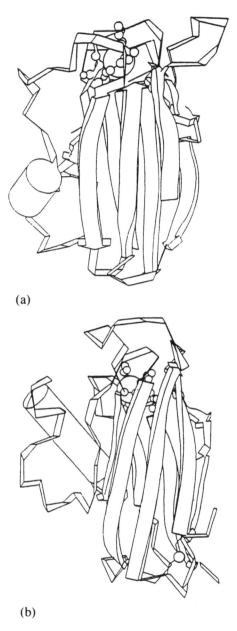

(a)

(b)

FIGURE 7 Two distantly related proteins: (a) poplar leaf plastocyanin; (b) *A. denitrificans* azurin. A copper ion is bound near the top of each of these structures. In this case, the double β-sheet portion of these molecules retains the same fold, but the long loop at the left changes its conformation completely.

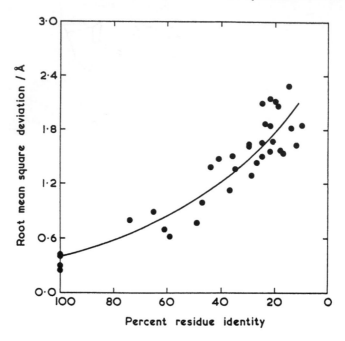

FIGURE 8   The relationship between the divergence of the amino acid sequence of the core of proteins and the divergence of the main chain conformation.

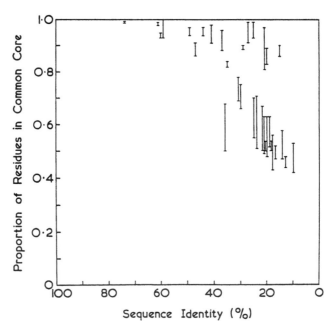

FIGURE 9   The relationship between the divergence of the amino acid sequence of the core of proteins and the relative size of the core.

DATA BANKS

Although our knowledge of sequence and structure data is very far from complete, it is nevertheless of quite respectable size and growing rapidly. Many scientists are working to generate the data or to carry out research projects analyzing the results; a very large number of people occupy themselves with discussions of what we should be doing with the data; and a few are actually archiving and distributing it. There is even some overlap among these groups. Archiving and distribution are carried out by particular data banking organizations.

DNA Sequence Data Banks

Nucleic acid sequences are collected by a tripartite association: GenBank^{TM} in the United States, with scientists at Los Alamos National Laboratory and Intelligenetics, Inc., under the umbrella of the National Center for Biotechnology Information; the EMBL Data Library at the European Molecular Biology Laboratory in Heidelberg, Federal Republic of Germany; and the DNA Data Bank of Japan, at the National Institute of Genetics, in Mishima. These groups collaborate in harvesting data from published journals and in sharing the results. To an increasing extent, the data banks are receiving data in computer-readable form directly from scientists. The data are annotated, checked, and converted to standard formats, and then exchanged among the data banks and distributed.

A sample DNA sequence entry from the EMBL data library, including annotations as well as sequence data, is the gene for bovine pancreatic trypsin inhibitor (see Box II for abbreviations):

```
ID    BTBPTIG    standard; DNA; MAM; 3998 BP.
XX
AC    X03365; K00966;
XX
DT    18-NOV-1986 (Rel. 10, Created)
DT    20-MAY-1992 (Rel. 31, Last updated, Version 3)
XX
DE    Bovine pancreatic trypsin inhibitor (BPTI) gene
XX
KW    Alu-like repetitive sequence; protease inhibitor;
KW    trypsin inhibitor.
XX
OS    Bos taurus (cattle)
OC    Eukaryota; Animalia; Metazoa; Chordata; Vertebrata; Mammalia;
OC    Theria; Eutheria; Artiodactyla; Ruminantia; Pecora; Bovidae.
XX
RN    [1]
RP    1-3998
RA    Kingston I.B., Anderson S.;
RT    "Sequences encoding two trypsin inhibitors occur in strikingly
RT    similar genomic environments";
RL    Biochem. J. 233:443-450(1986).
XX
RN    [2]
RA    Anderson S., Kingston I.B.;
RT    "Isolation of a genomic clone for bovine pancreatic trypsin
RT    inhibitor by using a unique-sequence synthetic dna probe";
RL    Proc. Natl. Acad. Sci. U.S.A. 80:6838-6842(1983).
XX
```

```
DR    SWISS-PROT; P00974; BPT1\_BOVIN.
XX
CC    Data kindly reviewed (08-DEC-1987) by Kingston I.B.
XX
FH    Key             Location/Qualifiers
FH
FT    misc\_feature    795..800
FT                    /note="pot. polyA signal"
FT    misc\_feature    835..839
FT                    /note="pot. polyA signal"
FT    repeat\_region   837..847
FT                    /note="direct repeat"
FT    misc\_feature    930..945
FT                    /note="sequence homologous to Alu-like
FT                    consensus seq."
FT    repeat\_region   1035..1045
FT                    /note="direct repeat"
FT    misc\_feature    2456..2461
FT                    /note="pot. splice signal"
FT    CDS             2470..2736
FT                    /note="put. precursor"
FT    misc\_feature    2488..2489
FT                    /note="pot. intron/exon splice junction"
FT    misc\_feature    2506..2507
FT                    /note="pot. intron/exon splice junction"
FT    CDS             2512..2685
FT                    /note="trypsin inhibitor (aa 1-58)"
FT    misc\_feature    2698..2699
FT                    /note="pot. exon/intron splice junction"
FT    misc\_feature    3690..3695
FT                    /note="pot. polyA signal"
FT    misc\_feature    3729..3733
FT                    /note="pot. polyA signal"
XX
SQ    Sequence 3998 BP; 1053 A; 902 C; 892 G; 1151 T; 0 other;
      aattctgata atgcagagaa ctggtaagga gttctgattg ttctgcttga ttaaatgggt
      tgtaacagga tagtgtcttg tcctgatcct agcattcata tggtgtgtgt tctggggcaa
      gtcatctgca gtttcttcac ctgaacaggg ggaccaggtt acatgagttt cttaaaagat
      taccagtcat gagtatgaag agtttacact ttcctgatca atgacgtcca tttcccatca
      aaatatttta gtccaaaaga ctcatctatc taatgtagat cattttctca ccaccccctct
      aaaaaattta tctttcagat atgatcattt ctctattatg aaattaatca gagagttgag
      tgacagctga gtgtcttccc tccaaaggca actgcaggaa gagcaagaaa tgcaatactt
      ttctatgagt ttgctcgtgg ggccaagact gcttttttcca ggctggtaca atagtaatca
      aatctcaaag atattcttct ttcctcctgg ccagactatt attttatttt cctatcaaga
      tatagaaagt tagaagtaga ctcataatta tataggcagg cctcatcatc aaatagacta
      acaagaattt tattttatct gcctttttcaa tgactgtgca cttggcatga ggatgaaatg
      ggagatttat tcccttgata aatattcatg aaatacttat gcttttttgtc cctaaaaagc
      atatttcttg atataggaaa acagctgtaa acaaaaggta gtaaaataat atgccttcta
      agagggatac agacaataaa gacggggggcg gattcctata ccaggtcatg atgagtgtca
      tgaggaaggt gagttatggg gttcaggatg ctgtagagga tcagggaaac cctctgtgat
      gaggagacat taagcagaag ctgccaaaaa ggagcctggt gtgtttgagc agcagccagg
      accaggtgg ctggagctga gtgggtgagg ggagggggagt ggaaggggat gaagcagaga
      ggccatgggg gcaggtcatg aggaaccttc taggacttta taaggataaa aatttgactc
      tgagagagct gggaaaccac tgagggactg gtcgttggaa caacgagata ggactggagt


         ... 39 lines deleted ...


      attgattcaa cctccaatcc ctctcccctt cctgagatgt ggatacaatg aaagaagtag
      gaatgaaaat tcccacaccc aactcaggca gttgtttccc ctgacaactt atccccattc
      ttggctttgc ttgaggcttt acaaaaactca tctccctcac atgataaagg actcccctttt
      gctctcatct cttaggaaat tccaatgttt taggagctct gtggcaggaa tgggatgcag
      accaagttaa tatttctttt ataagtcaca gtatcaatat ttcctcaata ttctattatt
```

```
agtggattgt gttgtttgca actaagaacc ttaacccata ggttccatgg aaacggtggt
ctttctcatt ttatgcagat gggtgggcag ctctccatca cctctcctca gactcagccc
taccaagtag aaggagccaa ccccttacac tgacatctac ctcttatggc cgtgccagtg
tacatgaaaa actggatgag agacacctca acaagaaaac ttttgtcctt cacttcttgg
gccaggtcaa actttggggt gtgttatttc cctgaatt
```

Protein Sequence Data Banks

Protein sequences are collected by another triple partnership. For many years, the group at the National Biomedical Research Foundation in Washington, D.C. maintained the major computer-readable archive of protein sequence data. In addition to collecting, annotating, and distributing sequences, this group has developed a powerful information retrieval system integrated with the data in the Protein Identification Resource (PIR). Allied with the NBRF group are the Martinsried Institute for Protein Sequences at the Max-Planck-Institute of Biochemistry in Munich, and the Protein Information Database JIPID in Noda, Japan.

The format of the entry for the amino acid sequence of the protein, bovine pancreatic trypsin inhibitor, in the PIR database, follows (see Box II for abbreviations):

TIB0

Basic protease inhibitor precursor—Bovine (fragment)

Species: Bos primigenius taurus (cattle)

Accession: A01205

Anderson, S., and Kingston, I. B., Proc. Natl. Acad. Sci. U.S.A. 80, 6838–6842, 1983 (Sequence translated from the DNA sequence)

Kassell, B., and Laskowski, M., Biochem. Biophys. Res. Commun. 20, 463–468, 1965 (Sequence of residues 15–72 and disulfide bonds)

Anderer, F. A., and Hornle, S., J. Biol. Chem. 241, 1568–1572, 1966 (Sequence of residues 15–72 and disulfide bonds)

Chauvet, J., and Acher, R., Bull. Soc. Chim. Biol. 49, 985–1000, 1967 (Sequence of residues 15–72 and disulfide bonds)

Dlouha, V., Pospisilova, D., Meloun, B., and Sorm, F., Collect. Czech. Chem. Commun. 33, 1363–1365, 1968 (Sequence of residues 15–72)

Huber, R., Kukla, D., Ruhlmann, A., Epp, O., and Formanek, H., Naturwissenschaften 57, 389–392, 1970 (X-ray crystallography of basic protease inhibitor, 2.5 angstroms)

DNA sequence analysis suggests that the basic protease inhibitor (residues 15–72) is encoded within an exon of a gene coding for a larger polypeptide. The inhibitor would be released from this larger protein by proteolytic cleavage.

Basic protease inhibitor is an intracellular polypeptide found in many tissues. It inhibits trypsin, kallikrein, chymotrypsin, and plasmin.

Superfamily: basic proteinase inhibitor

Keywords: serine protease inhibitor

Residues	Feature
15–72	Protein: basic protease inhibitor ⟨MAT⟩
29	Inhibitory site: Lys
16–69, 28–52, 44–65	Disulfide bonds:

```
                                        Number of residues = 89
            5        10       15       20       25       30
   1/P S L F N R D P P I P A A Q R P D F C L E P P Y T G P C K A
  31 R I I R Y F Y N A K A G L C Q T F V Y G G C R A K R N N F K
  61 S A E D C M R T C G G A I G P W G K T G G R A E G E G K G/
```

Macromolecular Structure Data Banks

The archive of three-dimensional structures of biological macromolecules is the Protein Data Bank at Brookhaven National Laboratory in New York. It collects the results of structure determinations—primarily by X-ray crystal structure analysis and nuclear magnetic resonance spectroscopy, but with a soupçon of structures determined by neutron diffraction and other techniques, plus some hypothetical structures created by modeling. Despite its name, the Protein Data Bank contains structures of biological macromolecules of all types, including nucleic acid and carbohydrate structures as well as proteins.

The Cambridge Crystallographic Data Centre in Cambridge maintains a database of small molecular structures determined by X-ray crystallography, with some overlap in coverage with the Protein Data Bank. This information is extremely useful in studies of the conformations of the component units of biological macromolecules and for investigations of macromolecule-ligand interactions.

One of the Protein Data Bank entries for the structure of bovine pancreatic trypsin inhibitor is as follows (in part):

```
HEADER     PROTEINASE INHIBITOR (TRYPSIN)           27-SEP-82   4PTI     4PTI    3
COMPND     TRYPSIN INHIBITOR                                             4PTI    4
SOURCE     BOVINE (BOS $TAURUS) PANCREAS                                 4PTIE   1
AUTHOR     R.HUBER,D.KUKLA,A.RUEHLMANN,O.EPP,H.FORMANEK,J.DEISENHOFER,    4PTI    6
AUTHOR   2 W.STEIGEMANN                                                  4PTI    7
REVDAT   6    16-APR-87 4PTIE    1         SOURCE REMARK                  4PTIE   2
REVDAT   5    31-MAY-84 4PTID    1         REMARK                        4PTID   1
REVDAT   4    23-FEB-84 4PTIC    1         JRNL                          4PTIC   1
REVDAT   3    31-JAN-84 4PTIB    1         REMARK                        4PTIB   1
REVDAT   2    30-SEP-83 4PTIA    1         REVDAT                        4PTIA   1
REVDAT   1    18-JAN-83 4PTI     0                                       4PTIA   2
SPRSDE      18-JAN-83 4PTI        3PTI                                   4PTIA   3
JRNL         AUTH   M.MARQUART,J.WALTER,J.DEISENHOFER,W.BODE,R.HUBER     4PTI    8
JRNL         TITL   THE GEOMETRY OF THE REACTIVE SITE AND OF THE         4PTI    9
JRNL         TITL 2 PEPTIDE GROUPS IN TRYPSIN, TRYPSINOGEN AND ITS       4PTI   10
JRNL         TITL 3 COMPLEXES WITH INHIBITORS                           4PTI   11
```

```
JRNL       REF   ACTA CRYSTALLOGR.,SECT.B      V. 39    480 1983       4PTIC  2
JRNL       REFN  ASTM ASBSDK  DK ISSN 0108-7681                 622    4PTIC  3
REMARK  1                                                              4PTI  14
REMARK  1 REFERENCE 1                                                  4PTIE  3
REMARK  1   AUTH   A.WLODAWER,J.DEISENHOFER,R.HUBER                     4PTIE  4
REMARK  1   TITL   COMPARISON OF TWO HIGHLY REFINED STRUCTURES OF       4PTIE  5
REMARK  1   TITL 2 BOVINE PANCREATIC TRYPSIN INHIBITOR                  4PTIE  6
REMARK  1   REF    J.MOL.BIOL.                  V. 193    145 1987      4PTIE  7
REMARK  1   REFN   ASTM JMOBAK  UK ISSN 0022-2836              070      4PTIE  8
REMARK  1 REFERENCE 2                                                  4PTIE  9
REMARK  1   AUTH   J.DEISENHOFER,W.STEIGEMANN                           4PTI  16
REMARK  1   TITL   CRYSTALLOGRAPHIC REFINEMENT OF THE STRUCTURE OF      4PTI  17
REMARK  1   TITL 2 BOVINE PANCREATIC TRYPSIN INHIBITOR AT              4PTI  18
REMARK  1   TITL 3 1.5 ANGSTROMS RESOLUTION                            4PTI  19
REMARK  1   REF    ACTA CRYSTALLOGR.,SECT.B      V. 31    238 1975      4PTI  20
REMARK  1   REFN   ASTM ACBCAR  DK ISSN 0567-7408              107      4PTI  21
REMARK  1 REFERENCE 3                                                  4PTIE 10
REMARK  1   AUTH   J.DEISENHOFER,W.STEIGEMANN                           4PTI  23
REMARK  1   TITL   THE MODEL OF THE BASIC PANCREATIC TRYPSIN           4PTI  24
REMARK  1   TITL 2 INHIBITOR REFINED AT 1.5 ANGSTROMS RESOLUTION       4PTI  25
REMARK  1   REF    BAYER SYMP.                  V.  5    484 1974       4PTI  26
REMARK  1   REFN   ASTM BAYSAH  GE ISSN 0067-4672              927      4PTI  27
REMARK  1 REFERENCE 4                                                  4PTIE 11
REMARK  1   AUTH   R.HUBER,D.KUKLA,A.RUEHLMANN,W.STEIGEMANN             4PTI  29
REMARK  1   TITL   PANCREATIC TRYPSIN INHIBITOR (KUNITZ).              4PTI  30
REMARK  1   TITL 2 PART I. STRUCTURE AND FUNCTION                      4PTI  31
REMARK  1   REF    COLD SPRING HARBOR SYMP.      V. 36    141 1972      4PTI  32
REMARK  1   REF  2 QUANT.BIOL.                                          4PTI  33
REMARK  1   REFN   ASTM CSHSAZ  US ISSN 0091-7451              421      4PTID  2
REMARK  1 REFERENCE 5                                                  4PTIE 12
REMARK  1   AUTH   A.RUEHLMANN,H.J.SCHRAMM,D.KUKLA,R.HUBER              4PTI  36
REMARK  1   TITL   PANCREATIC TRYPSIN INHIBITOR (KUNITZ).              4PTI  37
REMARK  1   TITL 2 PART /II$. COMPLEXES WITH PROTEINASES               4PTI  38
REMARK  1   REF    COLD SPRING HARBOR SYMP.      V. 36    148 1972      4PTI  39
REMARK  1   REF  2 QUANT.BIOL.                                          4PTI  40
REMARK  1   REFN   ASTM CSHSAZ  US ISSN 0091-7451              421      4PTID  3
REMARK  1 REFERENCE 6                                                  4PTIE 13
REMARK  1   AUTH   R.HUBER,D.KUKLA,A.RUEHLMANN,O.EPP,H.FORMANEK         4PTI  43
REMARK  1   TITL   THE BASIC TRYPSIN INHIBITOR OF BOVINE PANCREAS.     4PTI  44
REMARK  1   TITL 2 I. STRUCTURE ANALYSIS AND CONFORMATION OF THE       4PTI  45
REMARK  1   TITL 3 POLYPEPTIDE CHAIN                                    4PTI  46
REMARK  1   REF    NATURWISSENSCHAFTEN          V. 57    389 1970       4PTIB  2
REMARK  1   REFN   ASTM NATWAY   GW ISSN 0028-1042             049      4PTI  48
REMARK  1 REFERENCE 7                                                  4PTIE 14
REMARK  1   EDIT   M.O.DAYHOFF                                          4PTI  50
REMARK  1   REF    ATLAS OF PROTEIN SEQUENCE    V.  5     88 1973       4PTI  51
REMARK  1   REF  2 AND STRUCTURE,SUPPLEMENT 1                           4PTI  52
REMARK  1   PUBL   NATIONAL BIOMEDICAL RESEARCH FOUNDATION,            4PTI  53
REMARK  1   PUBL 2 SILVER SPRING,MD.                                    4PTI  54
REMARK  1   REFN              ISBN 0-912466-04-9               435      4PTI  55
REMARK  2                                                              4PTI  56
REMARK  2 RESOLUTION. 1.5 ANGSTROMS.                                    4PTI  57
REMARK  3                                                              4PTI  58
REMARK  3 REFINEMENT. J. DEISENHOFER*S VERSION OF THE JACK AND          4PTI  59
REMARK  3 LEVITT REFINEMENT PROCEDURE COMBINING CRYSTALLOGRAPHIC AND    4PTI  60
REMARK  3 ENERGY REFINEMENT. (A.JACK,M.LEVITT, ACTA CRYSTALLOGR.,       4PTI  61
REMARK  3 A34, 931-935, 1978).  THE R-VALUE FOR REFLECTIONS WITHIN      4PTI  62
REMARK  3 THE SHELL 1.5 TO 7.0 ANGSTROMS AND WITH                       4PTI  63
REMARK  3 2*(ABS(FO)-ABS(FC))/(ABS(FO)+ABS(FC)) LESS THAN 1.2 IS        4PTI  64
REMARK  3 0.162.                                                       4PTI  65
REMARK  4                                                              4PTI  66
REMARK  4 COORDINATES FOR 60 WATER MOLECULES ARE GIVEN FOLLOWING THE    4PTI  67
REMARK  4 MAIN BODY OF THE PROTEIN.  THE NOMENCLATURE OF THE WATER      4PTI  68
REMARK  4 MOLECULES IS THAT OF THE DEPOSITORS.                          4PTI  69
```

```
REMARK   5                                                           4PTIA   4
REMARK   5 CORRECTION. INSERT REVDAT RECORDS. 30-SEP-83.             4PTIA   5
REMARK   6                                                           4PTIB   3
REMARK   6 CORRECTION. CORRECT JOURNAL NAME FOR REFERENCE 5.         4PTIB   4
REMARK   6  31-JAN-84.                                               4PTIB   5
REMARK   7                                                           4PTIC   4
REMARK   7 CORRECTION. UPDATE JRNL REFERENCE TO REFLECT PUBLICATION. 4PTIC   5
REMARK   7  23-FEB-84.                                               4PTIC   6
REMARK   8                                                           4PTID   4
REMARK   8 CORRECTION. CORRECT ISSN FOR REFERENCES 3 AND 4.          4PTID   5
REMARK   8  31-MAY-84.                                               4PTID   6
REMARK   9                                                           4PTIE  15
REMARK   9 CORRECTION. INSERT NEW PUBLICATION AS REFERENCE 1 AND     4PTIE  16
REMARK   9 RENUMBER THE OTHERS.  CORRECT SOURCE RECORD.  16-APR-87.  4PTIE  17
SEQRES   1    58  ARG PRO ASP PHE CYS LEU GLU PRO PRO TYR THR GLY PRO 4PTI  70
SEQRES   2    58  CYS LYS ALA ARG ILE ILE ARG TYR PHE TYR ASN ALA LYS 4PTI  71
SEQRES   3    58  ALA GLY LEU CYS GLN THR PHE VAL TYR GLY GLY CYS ARG 4PTI  72
SEQRES   4    58  ALA LYS ARG ASN ASN PHE LYS SER ALA GLU ASP CYS MET 4PTI  73
SEQRES   5    58  ARG THR CYS GLY GLY ALA                            4PTI  74
FORMUL   2  HOH   *60(H2 01)                                         4PTI  75
HELIX    1  H1 SER     47  GLY     56  1                             4PTI  76
SHEET    1  S1 2 ALA    16  ALA    25  0                             4PTI  77
SHEET    2  S1 2 GLY    28  GLY    36 -1                             4PTI  78
SSBOND   1 CYS      5    CYS     55                                  4PTI  79
SSBOND   2 CYS     14    CYS     38                                  4PTI  80
SSBOND   3 CYS     30    CYS     51                                  4PTI  81
CRYST1   43.100   22.900   48.600  90.00   90.00   90.00 P 21 21 21   4 4PTI  82
ORIGX1      1.000000  0.000000  0.000000        0.00000              4PTI  83
ORIGX2      0.000000  1.000000  0.000000        0.00000              4PTI  84
ORIGX3      0.000000  0.000000  1.000000        0.00000              4PTI  85
SCALE1       .023202  0.000000  0.000000        0.00000              4PTI  86
SCALE2      0.000000   .043668  0.000000        0.00000              4PTI  87
SCALE3      0.000000  0.000000   .020576        0.00000              4PTI  88
ATOM     1  N   ARG   1      26.465  27.452  -2.490  1.00 25.18      4PTI  89
ATOM     2  CA  ARG   1      25.497  26.862  -1.573  1.00 17.63      4PTI  90
ATOM     3  C   ARG   1      26.193  26.179   -.437  1.00 17.26      4PTI  91
ATOM     4  O   ARG   1      27.270  25.549   -.624  1.00 21.07      4PTI  92
ATOM     5  CB  ARG   1      24.583  25.804  -2.239  1.00 23.27      4PTI  93
ATOM     6  CG  ARG   1      25.091  24.375  -2.409  1.00 13.42      4PTI  94
ATOM     7  CD  ARG   1      24.019  23.428  -2.996  1.00 17.32      4PTI  95
ATOM     8  NE  ARG   1      23.591  24.028  -4.287  1.00 17.90      4PTI  96
ATOM     9  CZ  ARG   1      24.299  23.972  -5.389  1.00 19.71      4PTI  97
ATOM    10  NH1 ARG   1      25.432  23.261  -5.440  1.00 24.10      4PTI  98
ATOM    11  NH2 ARG   1      23.721  24.373  -6.467  1.00 14.01      4PTI  99
ATOM    12  N   PRO   2      25.667  26.396    .708  1.00 10.92      4PTI 100
ATOM    13  CA  PRO   2      26.222  25.760   1.891  1.00  9.21      4PTI 101
ATOM    14  C   PRO   2      26.207  24.242   1.830  1.00 12.15      4PTI 102
ATOM    15  O   PRO   2      25.400  23.576   1.139  1.00 14.46      4PTI 103
ATOM    16  CB  PRO   2      25.260  26.207   3.033  1.00 13.09      4PTI 104
ATOM    17  CG  PRO   2      24.512  27.428   2.493  1.00 11.42      4PTI 105
ATOM    18  CD  PRO   2      24.606  27.382    .978  1.00 11.88      4PTI 106
ATOM    19  N   ASP   3      27.170  23.634   2.462  1.00 18.23      4PTI 107
ATOM    20  CA  ASP   3      27.284  22.163   2.498  1.00 10.58      4PTI 108
ATOM    21  C   ASP   3      26.043  21.506   3.085  1.00 15.62      4PTI 109
ATOM    22  O   ASP   3      25.752  20.350   2.705  1.00 12.96      4PTI 110
ATOM    23  CB  ASP   3      28.425  21.747   3.461  1.00 18.87      4PTI 111
ATOM    24  CG  ASP   3      29.791  21.886   2.787  1.00 34.90      4PTI 112
ATOM    25  OD1 ASP   3      29.875  22.104   1.543  1.00 26.81      4PTI 113
ATOM    26  OD2 ASP   3      30.806  21.501   3.431  1.00 30.82      4PTI 114

    ... Coordinates of residues 4 through 56 omitted ...

ATOM   445  N   GLY  57      22.225  28.050  -5.113  1.00 26.24      4PTI 533
ATOM   446  CA  GLY  57      23.639  28.131  -5.505  1.00 28.53      4PTI 534
```

```
ATOM     447  C   GLY    57       23.887  29.393  -6.316  1.00 40.53      4PTI 535
ATOM     448  0   GLY    57       22.949  30.065  -6.822  1.00 37.75      4PTI 536
ATOM     449  N   ALA    58       25.146  29.681  -6.493  1.00 46.21      4PTI 537
ATOM     450  CA  ALA    58       25.617  30.840  -7.256  1.00 45.05      4PTI 538
ATOM     451  C   ALA    58       25.248  30.735  -8.729  1.00 46.90      4PTI 539
ATOM     452  0   ALA    58       24.962  31.791  -9.369  1.00 39.78      4PTI 540
ATOM     453  CB  ALA    58       27.160  30.980  -7.146  1.00 50.07      4PTI 541
ATOM     454  OXT ALA    58       24.919  29.594  -9.172  1.00 43.54      4PTI 542
TER      455      ALA    58                                               4PTI 543
HETATM   456  0   HOH   101       14.483  32.405  -3.949  1.00 16.73      4PTI 544
HETATM   457  0   HOH   102        5.350  14.061  18.456  1.00 25.35      4PTI 545
HETATM   458  0   HOH   103       18.785  30.833  -6.010  1.00 30.52      4PTI 546

     ... Coordinates of water molecules 104-158 omitted ...

HETATM   513  0   HOH   158       14.316  11.539  10.919  1.00 38.96      4PTI 601
HETATM   514  0   HOH   159        7.638  32.125   3.901  1.00 38.78      4PTI 602
HETATM   515  0   HOH   160       26.847  17.783   3.473  1.00 38.42      4PTI 603
CONECT    43   42  440                                                    4PTI 604
CONECT   110  109  302                                                    4PTI 605
CONECT   242  241  408                                                    4PTI 606
CONECT   302  110  301                                                    4PTI 607
CONECT   408  242  407                                                    4PTI 608
CONECT   440   43  439                                                    4PTI 609
MASTER        76    0    0    1    2    0    0    6  514    1    6    5 4PTIE 18
END                                                                      4PTI 611
```

Derived Data Banks

The displayed examples of entries make evident that the databases are designed as archives, requiring information management tools to permit their effective use. There are many derived databases, of nucleic acid and protein sequences or even of all the information contained in all these archives, reformatted, in some cases extended or reannotated, and equipped with informational retrieval software.

For sequences, an important example is SWISS-PROT, created by A. Bairoch at the University of Geneva in collaboration with the EMBL Data Library (9). Numerous others are available (see Ref. 10). A group at Birkbeck College, London and Leeds University has put together a relational database as an "integrated data resource of protein sequences and structures." This contains not only sequences and structures but information derived from them, such as the conformational angles, or surface accessibility of each residue (11).

Data Distribution and "Social" Aspects

In the past, most of the data banks distributed their contents on magnetic tape, floppy disk, or CD-ROM, emitting successive releases in "burst mode" at standard intervals, typically 3 months apart. Computer networks now provide an alternative mode of data distribution (as well as for submission of data) by making archives available via ftp, or through wide-area information retrieval procedures, or by establishing Netserver facilities which respond to queries sent in via electronic mail by returning requested items, catalogs, or "help" information as a reply.

That archival database projects are serving as a kind of lens through which anyone in the user community can inspect all data generated by the source community is not new. It is the perceived importance of complete and—as near as possible—*instantaneous* transmission of the data that has created certain novel aspects, with the data banks also transmitting certain social forces between various groups both within and outside the scientific community.

Those who generate data are under pressure to deposit them in the data banks. This is enforced by a policy adopted by many journals to make submission to the appropriate data bank of results reported in an article a condition for publication. Actual or potential commercial value of the data has created a motive for keeping data confidential, as well as legal problems with respect to patents and copyrights which are currently unsolved.

The staff of the archival projects are under pressure to (a) distribute the data instantaneously and (b) maintain careful quality control over data contents and format, and annotations. (Usually the annotations are written at the data bank.) These goals are contradictory, and some data banks are releasing, as a separate category and on a *"caveat emptor"* basis, raw data that have not been checked and/or annotated. After suitable processing, these data mature to join the archives of annotated checked entries. There is consensus that quality control is necessary, otherwise archives would degenerate into bulletin boards.

Anyone who has followed the entire history of these projects cannot help being impressed by their growth from small, low-profile, and ill-funded projects carried out by a few dedicated individuals to a multinational heavy industry the components of which are subject to political takeovers and the scientific equivalent of leveraged buyouts.

USER INTERFACES TO DATA BANKS

The state of information retrieval systems in molecular biology is undergoing rapid change. This is partly a result of the great increase in the sheer amount of data available, and partly the result of advances in computing equipment that have made available very powerful systems capable of supporting high-capacity information storage capacity and transfer rates, demanding calculations, and complex real-time graphics. It is partly the result of a better definition of the roles in the partnership between the program system and the scientist; but it is also the result of our beginning to understand somewhat better the kinds of questions we want to ask. For example, until recently the one-dimensional world of sequence calculations and the three-dimensional world of structure calculations remained aloof from each other; now it is recognized that it is essential to bring both sets of data to bear on problems together. As another example, until recently, many people would work on a single protein structure or family of structures in isolation. Now we recognize the importance of free and common access to all available proteins because we can recognize structural themes common to a wide variety of structures.

Sequences

Programs and derived databases of nucleic acid and protein sequences contain facilities for a very wide variety of information retrieval and analysis operations. Categories of these operations include the following:

1. Retrieval of sequences from the database. Sequences can be "called up" either on the basis of features of the annotations or by patterns found within the sequences themselves

2. Sequence comparison. This is not a facility; it is a heavy industry! It will be discussed in the next section.
3. Translation of DNA sequences to protein sequences.
4. Simple types of structure prediction; for example, statistical methods for predicting the secondary structure of proteins from sequences alone, including hydrophobicity profiles—from which the positions of loops can be identified as minima in the hydrophobicity profile—and hydrophobic cluster analysis, from which helices can be identified from the periodicity of the hydrophobicity (compare the comments in connection with Table 1a).
5. Pattern recognition. It is possible to search for all sequences containing a pattern or combination of patterns, expressed as probabilities for finding certain sets of residues at consecutive positions. In DNA sequences, these may be recognition sites for enzymes such as those responsible for splicing together interrupted genes. In proteins, short and localized patterns sometimes identify molecules that share a common function even if there is no obvious overall relationship between their sequences. A. Bairoch has collected such a set of protein "signatures" in a database called PROSITE (12). Klingler and Brutlag have generalized the representation of patterns to sets of joint or conditional probabilities for finding sets of residues at two or more positions (13).

Structures: Molecular Graphics

Computer systems that support research and the development of applications in molecular biology and biotechnology must provide graphic displays of molecular structures, embedded in more general program systems providing facilities for database management and numerical calculations. The problems are too difficult and the database too large for even a powerful display system alone to be adequate. (In other words, being allowed to "look but not touch" is entirely unsatisfactory.) Programs must provide an integrated framework for making effective use of the separate and complementary skills of the members of a triple partnership: a powerful "number cruncher," a display device, and a scientist. The relative strengths and weaknesses of these three components, and the nature and capacity of the links between them, constrain the architecture of the program systems.

A fundamental theme of molecular graphics is the problem of making intelligible depictions of very complicated systems. To achieve this, a variety of representations have been devised, including those based on classical molecular models—collections of spheres, ball-and-stick models—and those based on artists' drawings: smoothed curves showing the course of a chain in space and a variety of simplifying "icons" representing recurring structural patterns such as cylinders representing helical regions (see Fig. 4). Not only is it necessary to be able to produce each of these representations individually, but one must be able to mix them freely in a picture. It is often necessary to "fine-tune" the level of detail, to show part of a large molecule in great detail but to include a simplified representation of its structural context.

Modern CAD techniques of solid modeling and rendering have been applied to molecular graphics. Real-time rotation and kinetic control over simulated objects are becoming possible for larger and larger systems as the power of workstations increases, and software is being developed to take advantage of these facilities. Typical applications of molecular graphics include (1) interactive fitting of a model to the noisy and fuzzy image of the molecule that arises initially from the measurements in solving protein structures by X-ray crystallography, (2) classifying and comparing the "folding patterns" of proteins, (3) analyzing changes between closely related structures, and (4) design and modeling of new structures.

The problems that molecular graphics can help us solve arise from the size, complexity, and variety of the systems we want to examine. Recall that a typical protein structure contains approximately 3000 atoms arranged with a well-defined spatial organization. The first thing we wish to do is to look at such an object in an intelligible way. The two classical types of molecular models, the representation of every atom by a sphere and the representation of every chemical bond by a line segment, are entirely inadequate for structures so large. If what we want to do is to be able to follow the course of the chain in three dimensions, a representation of a space curve following the backbone is something that does make sense to a molecular biologist (see examples in Fig. 5), particularly if additional aids to three-dimensional perception are available, such as stereo and real-time rotation.

But simplification is too simple an answer.

First, to show such a space-curve representation a lot of information has been lost. Second, we not only want to be able to look at a structure but we also want to be able to address a variety of architectural questions. We want to be able to tinker with a molecule—to ask, for example, what will be the effect on the structure of the replacement of one or more of the side chains, which can occur either through natural mutation or laboratory synthesis. We may want to design grafts of part of one protein structure into a different, unrelated protein structure—for example, the transfer of the combining site from a rat antibody to a human antibody for therapeutic purposes. These would be typical computer exercises in the field of biotechnology.

What has proved necessary has been to create a variety of representations of different degrees of simplification and to allow the user to construct a picture showing different parts of molecules in different degrees of detail. The recurring structural patterns of helices and sheets are often represented by simplified "icons": the α-helix as a cylinder and strands of sheet as long extended arrows (see Fig. 4). Showing an entire protein with combinations of these simplified representations makes it possible to analyze and interpret the structural relations between different elements of the folding pattern. For example, Figure 10 shows the enzyme phosphofructokinase, illustrating how strands form sheets by lateral assembly and interaction, and helices are packed against both surfaces of the sheets. The topology of this structure forms binding pockets for a small molecules that bind to it; these are shown in the "literal" one sphere per atom representation. In fact, this picture shows an enzyme in the process of catalyzing a reaction: a transfer of a phosphate group from ATP to fructose-6-phosphate (F6P). The reader will recognize that to show such a large structure in a completely detailed representation—one sphere for each atom or one line segment for each chemical bond between two atoms—would result in complete loss of intelligibility.

Each representation of a protein or nucleic acid conveys to the viewer a different aspect of its structure: Line drawings give the bones, space-filling models the flesh, and schematic diagrams the *gestalt* of the design. No single representation is adequate for all purposes, but the combination of several is more powerful than the total of all taken separately. For example, Figure 11 shows the structure of insulin, the hormone required by patients suffering from diabetes. The focus, in this figure, is on the local environment and the general structural content of one of the zinc ions in the structure. We need to see the

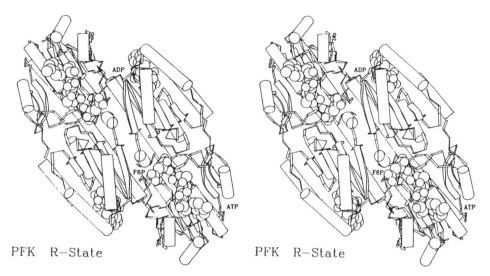

PFK R-State   PFK R-State

FIGURE 10   Intelligible pictures of very large molecules require simplified representations. This figure shows the enzyme phosphofructokinase (PFK), a large protein that contains both helices and strands of sheet. Small molecules, represented in detail by a sphere at the position of each atom, bind to the protein. ATP (adenosine triphosphate) is being induced to transfer a phosphate group to F6P (fructose-6-phosphate) by binding them at adjacent sites ("nothing propinqs like propinquity"). Another small molecule, ADP (adenosine diphosphate), is involved in the control of the activity of this molecule.

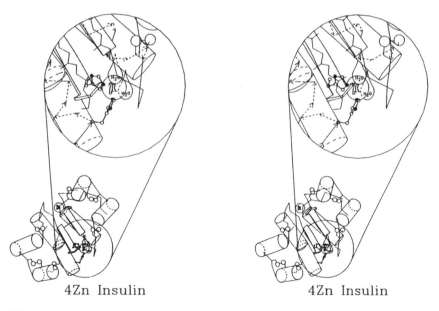

4Zn Insulin   4Zn Insulin

FIGURE 11   The off-axial zinc binding site of insulin, the hormone involved in the regulation of blood glucose levels. Cylinders represent α-helices, large arrows represent strands of a β-sheet, spheres represent zinc ions, and droplets represent water molecules. The region around one of the zinc ions is "blown up." This shows, in the one picture, *both* the details of the important site of interest and its relationship to the structure as a whole.

details of the residues interacting with the zinc, but we also need to see how the site of zinc binding fits into the structure as a whole. To show the whole structure in detail would be unintelligible. The solution presented in this figure is to show the region immediately surrounding the zinc ion in detail (the ligands are shown in the "literal" ball-and-stick representation in which each atom is a small ball and each chemical bond a line segment) and the rest of the structure in the simplified helix $\leftrightarrow$ cylinder, strand of β-sheet $\leftrightarrow$ arrow representation. The region around the zinc is "blown up" to permit simultaneous examination of the binding site and its structural context.

Representing structures visible on the surface of a protein is hard enough; showing the very important features of protein interiors is more difficult still! It is an important principle of protein structure that the interiors of proteins are densely packed. Several techniques have been developed to represent and study this. A representation that is particularly effective on the screen of a device capable of color and real-time rotation is a smoothed surface, spattered with dots, showing the topography of the exterior of the molecule or of an interior interface (Fig. 12).

Interactive Graphics

In practice, user interfaces provide facilities for interacting with a picture. Many programs make it possible to design and alter pictures, to select and label atoms, to choose different colors for different regions or atom types, to "clip" portions of three-dimensional space (for example, to display only the portion of a structure within a sphere around an atom in order to show the neighbors with which it interacts), or to translate and reorient the current viewpoint. Enhancements of perception of spatial relationships within a large molecule are achieved by perspective, stereo, depth cueing, interactive real-time shifts in clipping planes, and the kinetic depth effect upon viewing an object in a simulated state of rotation. Many of these are standard elementary operations provided for in hardware or systems software in modern workstations.

An essential feature of the user interface is the ability to control and record the orientation of an object or set of objects being displayed. The two principal problems are (1) how to specify numerically the orientation displayed and (2) how to communicate the orientation desired to the computer. (A rigid three-dimensional object has three rotational degrees of freedom, and a mouse appears to have one component too few.) There are a number of textbook treatments of translation, rotation, and perspective in terms of matrix algebra and homogeneous coordinates (e.g., Ref. 14 for a general analysis of rotations and Ref. 4 or 15 for applications to computer graphics). Here we describe an alternative approach to recording and altering the orientation based on quaternions (16). To rotate an object under interactive control, it is possible to simulate a "tracker-ball" with the mouse; quaternions can be applied to this also. Formulas collected here show how the two tasks can be managed effectively in an integrated scheme (see also Ref. 17).

To specify the orientation of an object in three-dimensional space, or equivalently to specify a rotation from a fixed original position, three parameters are required; for example, three Eulerian angles. An alternative parameterization of rotations is a quaternion: a combination of a three-vector λ and a scalar σ such that $\lambda \cdot \lambda + \sigma \cdot \sigma = 1$. The correspondence between a quaternion λ, σ and a rotation in three-space by an angle θ around an axis with direction cosines l, m, and n is: $\lambda = (l \sin(\theta/2), m \sin(\theta/2), n \sin(\theta/2))$, $\sigma = \cos(\theta/2)$. The identity is $\lambda = (0, 0, 0)$, $\sigma = 1.0$. The inverse of λ, σ is $-\lambda$, σ.

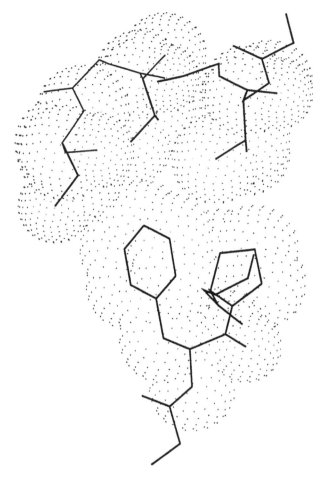

FIGURE 12 A spattered-surface diagram showing the interaction between two domains of an immunoglobulin. Residues from the two domains are distinguished by different densities of dots. Use of different colors would permit easier distinction between these sets of residues.

Given a quaternion λ, σ, the unit vector along the rotation axis, $\hat{\mathbf{n}}$, and the angle of rotation, θ, can be derived as

$$\hat{\mathbf{n}} = \frac{\lambda}{\sqrt{\lambda \cdot \lambda}},$$

$$\sin\frac{\theta}{2} = \hat{\mathbf{n}} \cdot \lambda = \sqrt{\lambda \cdot \lambda},$$

and

$$\theta = 2 \arctan(\sqrt{\lambda \cdot \lambda}/\sigma).$$

There are two equivalent solutions depending on the choice of sign of the square root.

Application to a set of points of a rotation expressed as a quaternion can be derived from the vector formula $\mathbf{r} \rightarrow \mathbf{r} - (\mathbf{r} \times \hat{\mathbf{n}} \sin\theta) + [(\mathbf{r} \times \hat{\mathbf{n}}) \times \hat{\mathbf{n}}](1 - \cos\theta)$, where

$\hat{\mathbf{n}} = (l, m, n)$ is a unit vector along the axis of rotation. In terms of the corresponding quaternion (λ, σ),

$$\mathbf{r} \rightarrow \mathbf{r} - 2\sigma(\mathbf{r} \times \lambda) + 2[(\mathbf{r} \times \lambda) \times \lambda].$$

(Note that $2\sigma\lambda = 2 \sin(\theta/2) \cos(\theta/2)\hat{\mathbf{n}} = \sin\theta\hat{\mathbf{n}}$ and $2 \mid \lambda \mid^2 = 2\lambda \cdot \lambda = 2\sin^2(\theta/2) = 1 - \cos\theta$.) Expanding the vector triple product, this is equivalent to

$$\mathbf{r} \rightarrow (2\sigma^2 - 1)\mathbf{r} + 2(\lambda \cdot \mathbf{r})\lambda - 2\sigma(\mathbf{r} \times \lambda).$$

The resultant of successive rotations can be expressed as follows: If $R_1 = (\lambda_1, \sigma_1)$ and $R_2 = (\lambda_2, \sigma_2)$, then the quaternion (λ, σ) expressing the rotation $R = R_2 R_1$ (R_1 followed by R_2) is

$$\lambda = \lambda_1\sigma_2 + \lambda_2\sigma_1 + \lambda_2 \times \lambda_1, \qquad \sigma = \sigma_1\sigma_2 - \lambda_2 \cdot \lambda_1.$$

Thus, if the user of a program specifies a sequence of rotations, it is easy to accumulate their resultant and to apply the result to a set of points.

It is possible, although often unnecessary, to express the elements of the corresponding familiar 3×3 rotation matrix in terms of the elements of $\lambda = (\lambda, \mu, \nu)$ and σ:

$$\mathbf{R} = \begin{pmatrix} (\lambda^2 - \mu^2 - \nu^2 + \sigma^2) & 2(\lambda\mu - \nu\sigma) & 2(\nu\lambda + \mu\sigma) \\ 2(\lambda\mu + \nu\sigma) & (-\lambda^2 + \mu^2 - \nu^2 + \sigma^2) & 2(\mu\nu - \lambda\sigma) \\ 2(\nu\lambda - \mu\sigma) & 2(\mu\nu + \lambda\sigma) & (-\lambda^2 - \mu^2 + \nu^2 + \sigma^2) \end{pmatrix}.$$

Alternatively, it may be desired to represent a rotation in terms of Eulerian angles (i.e., as the product of three rotations around the axes of the coordinate frame). This can be done without constructing the rotation matrix, through a useful device for decomposing a quaternion into a rotation parallel to a given axis and another around an axis in the plane perpendicular to the first axis.

The rotation $\mathbf{R}(\hat{\mathbf{n}}, \theta)$ around an axis in the direction of the unit vector $\hat{\mathbf{n}}$ by an angle θ corresponds to the quaternion $\hat{\mathbf{n}} \sin(\theta/2), \cos(\theta/2)$. Given any direction, specified by the unit vector $\hat{\mathbf{m}}$, we want to find the decomposition

$$\mathbf{R}(\hat{\mathbf{n}}, \theta) = \mathbf{R}(\hat{\mathbf{m}}, \phi)\mathbf{R}(\hat{\mathbf{k}}, \psi),$$

where we must determine the axis $\hat{\mathbf{k}} \perp \hat{\mathbf{m}}$ and the angles ϕ and ψ.

Equivalently,

$$\mathbf{R}(\hat{\mathbf{k}}, \psi) = \mathbf{R}(\hat{\mathbf{m}}, -\phi)\mathbf{R}(\hat{\mathbf{n}}, \theta).$$

The quaternions that correspond to these rotations are

$$\mathbf{R}(\hat{\mathbf{k}}, \psi) = \lambda \sin \frac{\psi}{2}, \cos \frac{\psi}{2},$$

$$\mathbf{R}(\hat{\mathbf{m}}, -\phi) = -\hat{\mathbf{m}} \sin \frac{\phi}{2}, \cos \frac{\phi}{2},$$

$$\mathbf{R}(\hat{\mathbf{n}}, \theta) = \hat{\mathbf{n}} \sin \frac{\theta}{2}, \cos \frac{\theta}{2}.$$

Then

$$\hat{\mathbf{k}} \sin \frac{\psi}{2} = -\hat{\mathbf{m}} \sin \frac{\phi}{2} \cos \frac{\theta}{2} + \hat{\mathbf{n}} \sin \frac{\theta}{2} \cos \frac{\phi}{2} - \hat{\mathbf{m}} \times \hat{\mathbf{n}} \sin \frac{\theta}{2} \sin \frac{\phi}{2}, \qquad (*)$$

$$\cos \frac{\psi}{2} = \cos \frac{\theta}{2} \cos \frac{\phi}{2} - \hat{\mathbf{m}} \cdot \hat{\mathbf{n}} \sin \frac{\theta}{2} \sin \frac{\phi}{2}. \qquad (*)$$

We want

$$\hat{\mathbf{m}} \cdot \hat{\mathbf{k}} \sin \frac{\psi}{2} = 0,$$

that is

$$\hat{\mathbf{m}} \cdot \hat{\mathbf{k}} \sin \frac{\psi}{2} = -\hat{\mathbf{m}} \cdot \hat{\mathbf{m}} \sin \frac{\phi}{2} \cos \frac{\theta}{2}$$

$$+ \hat{\mathbf{m}} \cdot \hat{\mathbf{n}} \sin \frac{\theta}{2} \cos \frac{\phi}{2} - \hat{\mathbf{m}} \cdot (\hat{\mathbf{m}} \times \hat{\mathbf{n}}) = 0.$$

But $\hat{\mathbf{m}} \cdot \hat{\mathbf{m}} = 1$ and $\hat{\mathbf{m}} \cdot (\hat{\mathbf{m}} \times \hat{\mathbf{n}}) = 0$; therefore,

$$\sin(\phi/2) \cos(\theta/2) = \hat{\mathbf{m}} \cdot \hat{\mathbf{n}} \sin(\theta/2) \cos(\phi/2), \text{ or}$$

$$\frac{\phi}{2} = \arctan\left(\hat{\mathbf{m}} \cdot \hat{\mathbf{n}} \tan \frac{\theta}{2} \right),$$

from which we can compute

$$\cos \frac{\phi}{2} = \frac{\cos(\theta/2)}{\sqrt{\cos^2(\theta/2) + (\hat{\mathbf{m}} \cdot \hat{\mathbf{n}})^2 \sin(\theta/2)}} \quad \text{and}$$

$$\sin \frac{\phi}{2} = \frac{(\hat{\mathbf{m}} \cdot \hat{\mathbf{n}}) \sin(\theta/2)}{\sqrt{\cos^2(\theta/2) + (\hat{\mathbf{m}} \cdot \hat{\mathbf{n}})^2 \sin(\theta/2)}}$$

and $\hat{\mathbf{k}}$ and ψ can be computed from Eqs. (∗); for instance,

$$\sin \frac{\psi}{2} = [1 - (\hat{\mathbf{m}} \cdot \hat{\mathbf{n}})]^{1/2} \sin \frac{\theta}{2}.$$

To derive Eulerian angles, that is, to decompose any rotation $\mathbf{R}(\hat{\mathbf{n}}, \theta)$ into a product of three rotations around unit vectors $\hat{\mathbf{x}}, \hat{\mathbf{y}}, \hat{\mathbf{z}}$ along the coordinate axes, first apply the decomposition just derived using $\hat{\mathbf{m}} = \hat{\mathbf{x}}$ to give

$$\mathbf{R}(\hat{\mathbf{n}}, \theta) = \mathbf{R}(\hat{\mathbf{x}}, \phi)\mathbf{R}(\hat{\mathbf{k}}, \psi),$$

where $\hat{\mathbf{k}}$ is in the *y-z* plane. But $\mathbf{R}(\hat{\mathbf{k}}, \psi)$ can be written as the product $\mathbf{R}(\hat{\mathbf{k}}, \psi) = \mathbf{R}(\hat{\mathbf{x}}, -\alpha)\mathbf{R}(\hat{\mathbf{x}}, \phi)\mathbf{R}(\hat{\mathbf{x}}, \alpha)$, where $\mathbf{R}(\hat{\mathbf{x}}, \alpha)$ is the rotation around $\hat{\mathbf{x}}$ that takes $\hat{\mathbf{k}}$ into $\hat{\mathbf{y}}$. The result is

$$\mathbf{R}(\hat{\mathbf{n}}, \theta) = \mathbf{R}(\hat{\mathbf{x}}, \phi - \alpha)\mathbf{R}(\hat{\mathbf{y}}, \psi)\mathbf{R}(\hat{\mathbf{x}}, \alpha).$$

There are 12 different possible sets of Eulerian angles corresponding to products of rotations around different successions of axes. (All combinations are allowed with the proviso that the same axis cannot be chosen twice in succession. Therefore, there are $3 \times 2 \times 2$ possibilities.) To convert from the $\hat{\mathbf{x}} - \hat{\mathbf{y}} - \hat{\mathbf{x}}$ choice to, for example, the $\hat{\mathbf{x}} - \hat{\mathbf{y}} - \hat{\mathbf{z}}$ choice, use the identity $\mathbf{R}(\hat{\mathbf{x}}, \alpha) = \mathbf{R}(\hat{\mathbf{y}}, -\frac{\pi}{2})\mathbf{R}(\hat{\mathbf{z}}, \alpha)\mathbf{R}(\hat{\mathbf{y}}, \frac{\pi}{2})$. Apply the $\hat{\mathbf{x}} - \hat{\mathbf{y}} - \hat{\mathbf{x}}$ decomposition to

$$\mathbf{R}' = \mathbf{R}\,\mathbf{R}\left(\hat{\mathbf{y}}, \frac{\pi}{2}\right) = \mathbf{R}(\hat{\mathbf{x}}, \phi - \alpha)\mathbf{R}(\hat{\mathbf{y}}, \psi)\mathbf{R}(\hat{\mathbf{x}}, \phi)$$

$$= \mathbf{R}(\hat{\mathbf{x}}, \phi - \alpha)\mathbf{R}(\hat{\mathbf{y}}, \psi)\mathbf{R}\left(\hat{\mathbf{y}}, -\frac{\pi}{2}\right)\mathbf{R}(\hat{\mathbf{z}}, \phi)\mathbf{R}\left(\hat{\mathbf{y}}, \frac{\pi}{2}\right)$$

to give

$$\mathbf{R} = \mathbf{R}(\hat{\mathbf{x}}, \phi - \alpha)\mathbf{R}\left(\hat{\mathbf{y}}, \psi - \frac{\pi}{2}\right)\mathbf{R}(\hat{\mathbf{z}}, \phi).$$

Of course, the angles ϕ, α, and ψ take on different values in the $\hat{\mathbf{x}} - \hat{\mathbf{y}} - \hat{\mathbf{x}}$ and $\hat{\mathbf{x}} - \hat{\mathbf{y}} - \hat{\mathbf{z}}$ decompositions. [If $\mathbf{R}$ corresponds to the quaternion $(\lambda_1, \lambda_2, \lambda_3)$, σ, $\mathbf{R}\,\mathbf{R}(\hat{\mathbf{y}}, \pi/2)$ corresponds to the quaternion $(1/\sqrt{2})(\lambda_1 - \lambda_3, \lambda_2 + \sigma, \lambda_1 + \lambda_3)$, $(1/\sqrt{2})(\sigma - \lambda_2)$.]

Next, consider how the rotations may be specified interactively. A useful way to rotate a displayed object, if only a mouse is available, is by simulating a tracker ball (17).

Imagine that the field of the mouse is a plane cutting through a sphere of unit radius; it can be the equatorial plane but need not be. Given two successive positions of the mouse—click on an initial point, drag to the final point—project these positions up to the surface of the sphere and consider the vectors $\mathbf{v}$ and $\mathbf{w}$ from the center of the sphere to these projected points on the surface of the sphere. The calculation of $\mathbf{v}$ and $\mathbf{w}$ requires two "hypotenuse" operations, which can, if necessary, be carried out without any square root computation (18–20). Imagine that this manipulation is to have the effect of rotating the tracker ball to bring $\mathbf{v}$ to the position of $\mathbf{w}$ and to induce a corresponding effect on the orientation of the displayed object.

The axis of this rotation is in the direction $\mathbf{v} \times \mathbf{w}$. In fact, given that $\mathbf{v}$ and $\mathbf{w}$ are unit vectors, $\mathbf{v} \times \mathbf{w} = \hat{\mathbf{n}} \sin \theta$, where $\hat{\mathbf{n}} = (l, m, n)$ is a unit vector along the axis of rotation, and $\mathbf{v} \cdot \mathbf{w} = \cos \theta$. Then $\mathbf{v} \times \mathbf{w}$, $\mathbf{v} \cdot \mathbf{w}$ is the quaternion $\hat{\mathbf{n}} \sin \theta$, $\cos \theta$; this specifies the correct direction but a rotation angle twice too large. In fact, using this directly to specify the orientation provides a perfectly acceptable user interface; one easily gets used to the difference in scale. Nevertheless, if at the expense of a third hypotenuse evaluation we construct the normalized vector $\mathbf{u} = (\mathbf{v} + \mathbf{w})/|\mathbf{v} + \mathbf{w}|$, then $\mathbf{v} \times \mathbf{u}$, $\mathbf{v} \cdot \mathbf{u}$ is exactly the quaternion desired: $\hat{\mathbf{n}} \sin(\theta/2)$, $\cos(\theta/2)$.

The entire rotation operation, including the interactive specification of the magnitude and direction of the rotation, and the application of the operation to a set of points requires no more than three hypotenuse operations and no evaluations of trignometric or inverse trigonometric functions.

Although this approach provides a perfectly feasible user interface for interactive rotation of a displayed object, other peripheral input devices are available and useful. Dials and joysticks have been used for a long time to control rotations around x, y, and z axes. No discussion of interaction would be complete without mentioning the Spaceball,[TM] a desktop handheld device that has six degrees of freedom—three translational and three rotational—programmable to give full manual control over an object.

ANALYSIS OF THE DATA

Databases support an active program of research. Many operations carried out on databases seek to identify a set of sequences or structures from the databases on the basis of specified features or characteristics or on the basis of similarity to a probe sequence or structure. The most common typical query is, "I have determined a new sequence, or structure; what is there in the data banks that is like it?" Once a set of sequences, or structures, that are similar to a probe object or that share some other common feature are fished out of the appropriate data banks, the next step is to identify their common features. We shall examine methods for doing this

The reader might like to keep in mind the variety of possible combinations of database searches:

- Given a sequence or fragment of a sequence, find sequences in the database that are similar to it. This is, in fact, a string-matching problem (possibly with mismatches allowed) and is the subject of an extensive literature (see, e.g., Ref. 21).
- Given a structure or fragment of a structure, find structures in the database that are similar to it. This is the extension of the string-matching problem to three dimensions.
- Given a sequence of a protein of unknown structure, find *structures* in the database that adopt similar three-dimensional structures. One is tempted to "cheat"—look in the sequence data banks for proteins with sequences similar to the probe sequence: For if two proteins have sufficiently similar sequences, they will have similar structures. However, the converse is not true, and one can hope to create more powerful search techniques that will find proteins of similar structure even among sequences that have diverged beyond the point where they can be recognized as similar.
- Given a protein structure, find *sequences* in the data bank that correspond to similar structures. Again, one can cheat by using the structure to probe a structure data bank, but this can give only limited success because there are so many more sequences known than structures. It is, therefore, desirable to have a method that can pick out the structure from the sequence.

The first two of these problems can be expressed in purely mathematical terms and, in fact, are similar to problems that arise in other fields.

Sequences

Measures of Sequence Similarity; Sequence Alignment

Given two character strings, two measures of the distance between them are

1. The *Hamming* distance, defined between two strings of equal length, is the number of positions with mismatching characters.
2. The *Levenshtein*, or edit distance, between two strings of not necessarily equal length is the minimal number of "edit operations" required to change one string into the other, where an edit operation is a deletion, insertion, or alteration of a single character in either sequence.

An *alignment* of two strings A_i, $i = 1, \ldots, N$, and B_j, $j = 1, \ldots, M$ is a correspondence or matching between substrings. For instance, if

$$A = g\ c\ t\ g\ a\ a\ c \quad \text{and} \quad B = c\ t\ a\ t\ a\ a\ t\ c,$$

then two possible alignments are

```
g c t g a - a - - c
- c t - a t a a t c
```

and

```
g c t g - a a - c
- c t a t a a t c
```

A given sequence of edit operations induces a unique alignment but not vice versa.

In general, several different sequences of edit operations may convert one string into the other in the same number of steps, but they may induce different alignments. In applications to molecular biology, we may regard certain changes as more likely to have occurred naturally than others. For example, the deletion of a succession of contiguous bases or amino acids is a more probable event than the independent deletion of the same number of bases or amino acids at noncontiguous positions in the sequences. Or, amino acid substitutions are likely to be conservative: The replacement of one amino acid by another with similar size or physiochemical properties is more likely than its replacement by another amino acid with less similar properties. Therefore, we may wish to assign variable weights to different edit operations. Algorithms may then determine not minimal edit distances but optimal alignments. Depending on the weighting scheme, the optimal alignment may or may not correspond to the minimal number of edit operations required to interconvert the strings. Moreover, the optimal alignment may be consistent with more than one sequence of edit operations.

It should also be emphasized that although a sequence of edit operations derived from an optimal alignment may correspond to an actual evolutionary pathway, it is impossible to prove that it does. The larger the edit distance, the larger the number of reasonable evolutionary pathways.

"Dot Plots"

A pictorial representation of relationships between two sequences is afforded by the "dot plot," a Boolean matrix indicating the similarity between all ordered pairs of characters from the two sequences. The i,jth element is represented by a dot if residue i from the first sequence is similar (by some criterion) to residue j from the second. Figure 13 shows a dot plot relating the α chain of human hemoglobin and sperm whale myoglobin. Stretches of similar residues show up as diagonals. Displacement of the diagonals occurs when there is an insertion or deletion. If two sequences are sufficiently closely related, the alignment can be read directly off the dot plot; in any case, the plot provides a quick overview of the nature of the relationship between the sequences. In the case of the two globins shown in Figure 13, the set of segments near the main diagonal are picking up homologous helices in the structures. (Suppose a sequence contained internal repeats: What would be the appearance of a dot plot of this sequence against itself?)

The dot plot gives a synopsis of the information contained in alignment tables such as Tables 1a and 1b but is limited to a pair of sequences.

Calculation of Optimal Alignments

A formal statement of the problem is as follows:

Given two character strings, possibly of unequal length, $A = a_1 a_2 \ldots a_n$ and $B = b_1 b_2 \ldots b_m$, where each a_i and b_j is a member of an alphabet set $\mathcal{A}$, consider sequences of edit operations that convert A and B to a common sequence. Individual edit operations include:

Substitution of b_j for a_i—represented as (a_i, b_j)
Deletion of a_i from sequence A—represented as (a_i, ϕ)
Deletion of b_j from sequence B—represented as (ϕ, b_j)

If we extend the alphabet set to include the character ϕ: $\mathcal{A}^+ = \mathcal{A} \cup \{\phi\}$, a sequence of edit operations is a set of ordered pairs (x,y) with $x, y \in \mathcal{A}^+$.

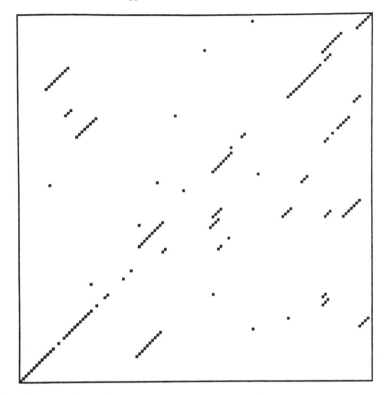

FIGURE 13   A "dot plot" in which the positions filled represent the relation between the amino acid sequences of human haemoglobin (α chain) and sperm whale myoglobin.

A *cost function d* is defined on edit operations:

$d(a_i, b_j)$ = cost of a mutation,

$d(a_i, \phi)$ or $d(\phi, b_j)$ = cost of a deletion or insertion.

Define the minimum weighted distance between sequences A and B as

$$D(A, B) = \min_{A \to B} \sum d(x, y),$$

where $x, y \in \mathcal{A}^+$ and the minimum is taken over all sequences of edit operations that convert A and B into a common sequence. If $d(x, y)$ is a metric on $\mathcal{A}^+$, $D(A, B)$ is a metric on the set of strings of characters from $\mathcal{A}^+$.

The problem is to find $D(A, B)$ and one or more of the alignments that correspond to it.

An algorithm that solves this problem in $\mathcal{O}(mn)$ time has been known for a long time (22–24). It entered molecular biology in a seminal paper by Needleman and Wunsch (22). An explanation of the method is as follows: We will create a matrix $M(i, j)$, $i = 0, \ldots, n: j = 0, \ldots m$, such that such that $M(i,j)$ is the distance between the strings that consist of the first i characters of A and the first j characters of B. Then $M(n, m)$ will be the required distance $D(A, B)$. The algorithm computes $M(i,j)$ by an inductive process. The value of $M(i, j)$ corresponds to the conversion of the initial subsequences $A_i = a_1a_2 \ldots a_i$ and $B_j = b_1b_2 \ldots b_j$ into a common sequence by L edit operations S_k, $k = 1, \ldots, L$, which can, without loss of generality, be considered to be applied in increasing order of position in the strings. Consider undoing the last of these edit operations. The resulting truncated sequence of edit operations, S_k, $k = 1, \ldots, L - 1$, is a sequence of edit operations for converting a substring of A_i and a substring of B_j into a common result. What is more, it must be an *optimal* sequence of edit operations for these substrings, for if some other sequence S_k' were a lower-cost sequence of operations for the substrings, then S_k' followed by S_L would be a lower-cost sequence of operations than S_k for converting A_i to B_j. Therefore, there should be a recursive method for calculating elements $M(i, j)$.

To see what the method involves, recognize the correspondence between individual edit operations and steps between adjacent squares in the matrix. Thus,

$(i - 1, j - 1) \rightarrow (i, j)$ corresponds to the substitution $a_i \rightarrow b_j$
$(i - 1, j) \rightarrow (i, j)$ corresponds to the deletion of a_i from A
$(i, j - 1 \rightarrow (i, j)$ corresponds to the insertion of b_j into A at position i

Sequences of edit operations correspond to stepwise paths through the matrix

$$(i_0, j_0) = (0, 0) \rightarrow (i_1, j_1) \rightarrow \cdots (n, m),$$

where $0 \leq i_{k+1} - i_k \leq 1$ (for $0 \leq k \leq n - 1$), $0 \leq j_{k+1} - j_k \leq 1$ (for $0 \leq k \leq m - 1$). Considering the possible sequences of edit operations and the corresponding paths through the matrix, the predecessor of an optimal string of edit operations leading from $(0, 0)$ to (i, j), where $i, j > 0$, must be an optimal sequence of edit operations leading to one of the cells $(i - 1, j)$, $(i - 1, j - 1)$, or $(i, j - 1)$, and, correspondingly, $M(i, j)$ must depend only on the values of $M(i - 1, j)$, $M(i - 1, j - 1)$, and $M(i, j - 1)$ (together, of course, with the parameterization specified by the cost function d).

Based on these considerations, the algorithm is as follows:

Compute the $(m + 1) \times (n + 1)$ matrix M by the initialization conditions on the top row and left column,

$$M(i, 0) = \sum_{k=0}^{i} d(a_k, \phi),$$

$$M(0, j) = \sum_{k=0}^{j} d(\phi, b_k),$$

and the recurrence

$$M(i,j) = \min\{M(i - 1, j) + d(a_i, \phi), M(i - 1, j - 1) + d(a_i, b_j),$$
$$M(i, j - 1) + d(\phi, b_j)\}$$

for $i = 1, \ldots, n; j = 1, \ldots, m$. For each cell record not only the value $M(i, j)$ but alas a pointer back to (one of) the cell(s) $(i - 1, j)$, $(i - 1, j - 1)$, or $(i, j - 1)$ selected by the minimization operation. Note that more than one predecessor may give the same value.

When the calculations are complete, $M(n, m)$ is the optimal distance $D(A, B)$. An alignment corresponding to the sequence of edit operations recorded by the pointers can be recovered by tracing a path back through the matrix from (m, n) to $(0, 0)$. This alignment corresponding to the minimal distance $D(A, B) = M(n, m)$ may not be unique.

For some applications, we may need only the value of $D(A, B)$ but not an alignment; if so, it is not necessary to save the pointers. Alternatively, we may wish to compute *all* alignments consistent with the minimal edit distance; if so, we must save multiple pointers whenever more than one predecessor of cell (i, j) gives the same value.

Several features of this algorithm are noteworthy.

- It produces a *global* optimum. It is of the greatest significance that we have a method on which we can rely not to get trapped in local minima. Sydney Brenner has commented that "the problem with biology is that it has no harmonic oscillator" (i.e., a problem, relevant to many important phenomena, that has a simple and exact solution). In the alignment algorithm—and also in a basic algorithm for three-dimensional structural superposition that we shall discuss later—we have problems that have exact, reliable solutions. Later we shall see how it is possible to take advantage of this situation by recasting other problems in the form of alignment optimizations.

- That was the good news. On the other hand, although it is possible to compute optimal alignments, the interpretation of the results is not so straightforward. First, the results do depend on the cost function d. Parameters in its definition include costs for substitutions and the relative weighting of substitution, and gap initiation and extension. For nucleic acids, a constant mismatch penalty is generally used. For proteins, until recently a substitution cost matrix derived by M. O. Dayhoff and co-workers in 1977, from a statistical analysis of mutation patterns in the relatively few protein sequences then known, has been used almost universally. Recently, several investigators have proposed new substitution cost matrices. Indeed, it is felt that different matrices are appropriate in different ranges of the overall distance between the two protein sequences. The question of gap penalties is an ongoing debate.

- The fact that the minimal distance does not, in general, correspond to a *unique* optimal alignment leaves a residual ambiguity in the result. Ideally, one would like to infer an evolutionary pathway, or a hypothetical common ancestor, from a set of alignments. This is not possible partly because of the nonuniqueness of the computed results and partly because evolution may not have effected genetic transformations by means of minimal sequences of edit operations.

- There are a number of generalizations of the basic algorithm to solve related problems (25):

  —Find the optimal matches of a relatively short pattern $A = a_1a_2 \ldots a_n$ in a long sequence $B = b_1b_2 \ldots b_m$ with $n \ll m$ (no gap penalty in the regions of B that precede and follow the region matched by A).

  —Extend the cost calculation to permit distinction between contiguous and noncontiguous gap insertion. To reflect the idea that the excision of several contiguous residues may represent a single evolutionary event, the cost of k consecutive deletions should be less than the sum of the costs of k single deletions. A special case is that of a linear gap penalty $\alpha + \beta(k - 1)$, where k is the number of consecutive deletions, α represents a cost of gap initiation and β is the cost of gap extension. For linear gap penalties, the execution time of the modified algorithm is still $\mathcal{O}(mn)$. Algorithms requiring space $\mathcal{O}(n)$ are known.

—Optimal joint alignments of more than two sequences is an extremely important generalization to be discussed in the next section.

The running time of the programs based on these algorithms is fast enough for convenient pairwise alignment of a relatively small set of sequences (less than 100, say) but not yet fast enough to make it convenient to "run the whole data bank against itself," or even for routine screening of a newly determined sequence against the entire data bank, on generally available equipment. The complete optimal alignment of all pairs of protein sequences has, in fact, recently been carried out (26), but the amount of computer time required (405 days of CPU time on workstations) does not, in my opinion, contradict the previous statement. Database screening programs using the full dynamic programming algorithm have been implemented on a massively parallel MasPar MP1104 (27) and the Thinking Machines CM2 (28).

When a scientist determines a new gene sequence, it is routine to screen it against the databases for similarity to known sequences. Approximate algorithms are commonly used, based on lookup tables. (These algorithms can detect close relationships well but are inferior to the exact ones in picking up very distant relationships; they do give satisfactory performance in the many cases in which the probe sequence is fairly similar to a sequence in the data bank and are, therefore, worth trying first). Given an integer k, the programs determine all instances of each k-tuple of residues in the probe sequence that occur in any sequence in the database. A candidate sequence is a sequence in the data bank containing a large number of matching k-tuples, with equivalent spacing in probe and candidate sequences. For a selected set of candidate sequences, approximate optimal alignment calculations are carried out, with the restriction that the paths through the matrix considered be restricted to bands around the diagonals containing the many matching k-tuples. There are several variations on this theme.

For finding *exact* matches of short patterns in all the sequences in the data bank, algorithms based on finite-state machines have been applied, which run in time $\mathcal{O}(m)$, where m is the length of the pattern.

Multiple Sequence Alignment

A table containing a joint alignment of many related sequences contains far more useful information than an alignment of a single pair of sequences. The basic reason for this is that one can examine the extent of variation at individual positions, which is an important guide to the structural or functional role of different regions of the sequence. We have already seen some examples of this in the subsection Themes and variations: molecular evolution.

There are numerous algorithms for multiple sequence alignment. [See Ref. 29 for a recent review; however, this does not mention the important work of Vingron (30) and Hausler et al. (31).]

Important classes of methods include:

1. Generalization of the dynamic programming algorithm for pairwise alignment. No more than about eight sequences of typical size can be treated in a reasonable amount of time.

2. If a phylogenetic tree is available, it is possible to attempt to reconstruct ancestral sequences at nodes of the tree and to align the input sequences to these ancestral ones.

3. Several methods are based on iterating pairwise alignments; the general idea is to align closely related pairs of sequences first, and then to combine them by aligning *sets* of aligned sequences to each other. This entails generalization of the cost function for edit operations, from a function on a *single* pair of characters from the alphabet set, to a pair of *sets* of characters from the alphabet set. One obvious way to do this is to take the minimal distance between the subsets (the minimum distance between any character from one set to any character of the other).

4. Vingron has developed an ingenious method for comparing and reconciling the dot plots calculated from all pairs of sequences from a set. A partial or complete multiple sequence alignment may be derived from the computed filtered set of mutually compatible dot plots, provided that the sequences are really sufficiently closely related to determine such an alignment.

5. A recent and very impressive result is the application of a Hidden Markov Model to the alignment of 625 globin sequences. The method involves an automatic iterative refinement of a probabilistic model.

It should be emphasized that there is a close connection between multiple sequence alignment and the extraction of common patterns that characterize a family of sequences. Given an alignment, the variability at any position and the covariation at any sets of positions may be measured, and patterns of conservation observed can be used to define patterns. Conversely, patterns may be used to "seed" alignments and to search databases for other related sequences.

Structures

Given a newly determined protein structure, how do we characterize its folding pattern, and compare it with other structures known previously?

An initial approach is to look at the conformations of successive regions along the main chain. In most cases, we will find regions that form helices or strands of sheet. The determination of the limits within the sequence of these helical and strand regions, on the basis of the pattern of hydrogen bonding between main chain atoms, defines the "secondary structure" of the protein. Looking in three dimensions, usually the helices and strands will span the protein so that their termini are at the protein surface. The "loop" regions that join successive elements of secondary structure usually lie on the protein surface. Geometric aspects of the packing of the atoms are also important, and programs exist to calculate the solvent-accessible surface area of each atom or residue (quantitatively distinguishing buried and surface residues) and atomic volumes via a Voronoi polyhedron approach (to identify the quality of internal packing and to pick up any "holes"). (See Ref. 32 for a general review and Ref. 33 for a review of applications to protein structure). This much can be thought of as an initial step in "blocking out" or "parsing" the nature of the folding pattern.

The next step is to analyze the interactions between the helices and strands of sheet. Strands are assembled into one or more sheets by lateral hydrogen-bonding interactions (see Fig. 3b). Helices and sheets are packed together at interfaces to form a dense interior: Holes larger than atoms are rare in protein interiors.

It is the network of interactions between elements of secondary structure—the pairs of helices and sheets that make contact and the relative geometry of the contacting structures—that defines the "folding pattern." The folding pattern may be represented by a matrix or tableau in which the helices and strands of sheet are listed on the diagonal in order of appearance in the chain; off-diagonal elements are blank if the corresponding helices and/or strands are not in contact, and they contain a symbol $\|$, $\uparrow\downarrow$, $\mathcal{L}$, or $\mathcal{R}$ specifying the relative geometry of secondary structural elements in contact (see Fig. 14). Using such tableaux it is possible to determine the maximal substructures of two given proteins that contain a common folding pattern.

This tableau (Fig. 14) appears to represent the appropriate degree of abstraction of what we understand, qualitatively, by the topology of protein folding patterns. A few proteins do not contain helices or sheets and would not fit this scheme without generalizing it to contain additional sets of standard substructures [as, for example, in the work of Unger et al. (34) who extracted all eight-residue regions from proteins and clustered their structure, finding 60 classes].

Other approaches to structure comparison and substructure matching for protein main chains make explicit use of conformational angles or the atomic coordinates:

1. By determining the angles of internal rotation defining the conformation of each residue, the main chain conformation of a protein may be written as a *one-dimensional* sequence of residue conformations. The algorithms for determining minimal distances and optimal alignments of strings may be applied directly to these sequences of conformations (35,36).

2. Each residue may be characterized by the distances between a point within the residue to corresponding points in other nearby residues in the sequence. This is another way to reduce the conformation to a one-dimensional sequence of objects. In this case, the objects are sets of distances. Nevertheless, it is possible to define a metric on the objects and to apply the dynamic programming algorithms (37,38).

3. The next method is, in some sense, the three-dimensional analogue of parts of sequence-comparison algorithms that search for matching k-tuples. Given ordered sets of atoms from k consecutive residues in each of two proteins, algorithms exist to find the deviation from the congruence of the point sets. (These algorithms are discussed next). It is possible to identify all well-fitting subsets of k consecutive residues from the two proteins (typically, $k = 6-8$), and combine them to determine maximal well-fitting substructures (39,40).

Superposition of Structures

As in the case of sequences, a fundamental question in analyzing structures is to devise and compute a measure of similarity. If two structures are represented by point sets

$$p_i = (x_i, y_i, z_i), \quad i = 1, \dots, N,$$

and

$$q_j = (x'_j, y'_j, z'_j), \quad j = 1, \dots, M,$$

we can anticipate using familiar geometric quantities to define a metric.

A fundamental distinction arises, depending on whether we take the correspondence between atoms as given. If we do, that is, $p_i \leftrightarrow q_i$, then N must equal M, and we

Protein Folding Pattern

(A) Order of helices and strands of sheet:
$\beta_1 \, \beta_2 \, \beta_3 \, \alpha_1 \, \ldots$

(B) Contact map of: interactions
relative directions

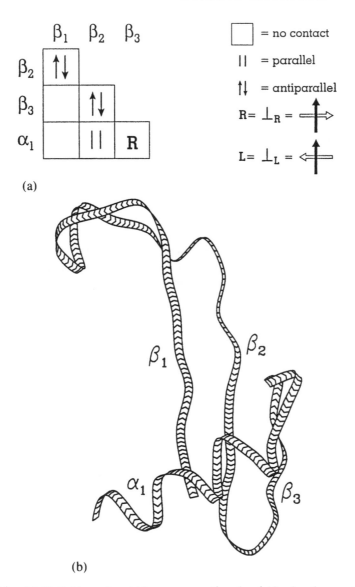

(a)

(b)

FIGURE 14   (a) Definition of a tableau representing the fold of a fragment the protein *Streptomyces* subtilisin inhibitor. (b) Structure of the fragment.

seek a measure of the differences $\|p_i - q_i\|$ after optimal superposition. If not, we must determine a set of correspondences $p_{i(k)} \leftrightarrow q_{j(k)}$, $k = 1, \ldots, K \leq N, M$ and then measure the differences $\|p_{i(k)} - q_{j(k)}\|$ after optimal superposition. In many situations, the structure of the molecule provides or at least constrains the correspondence.

It may be useful to contrast three related problems that arise in computational chemistry:

1. Similarity of two sets of atoms with known correspondences $p_i \leftrightarrow q_i$, $i = 1, \ldots, N$. The analogue, for sequences, is the Hamming distance: mismatches only.

2. Similarity of two sets of atoms with unknown correspondences, but for which the molecular structure—specifically the linear order of the residues—restricts the range of the correspondence. In the case of proteins we are restricted to correspondences in which we retain the order along the chain

    $$p_{i(k)} \leftrightarrow q_{j(k)}, \quad k = 1, \ldots, K \leq N, M,$$

    with the constraint that $k_1 > k_2 \Rightarrow i(k_1) > i(k_2)$ and $j(k_1) > j(k_2)$. This can be thought of as corresponding to the Levenshtein distance, or to sequence alignment with gaps.

3. Similarities between two sets of atoms with unknown correspondence, with no restrictions on the correspondence

    $$p_{i(k)} \leftrightarrow q_{j(k)}$$

    This problem arises in the following important case: Suppose two (or more) molecules have similar biological effects, such as a common pharmacological activity. It is often the case that the structures share a common constellation of a relatively small subset of their atoms that is responsible for the biological activity, called a *pharmacophore*. The problem is to identify it: To do so, it is useful to be able to find the maximal subsets of atoms from the two molecules that have a similar structure (See, e.g., Refs. 41 and 42).

The most general approach to these problems is based on a purely geometric closed solution of Problem 1, the case of fixed correspondence $p_i \leftrightarrow q_i$. Even if two structures are exactly congruent, the atoms may not be at the same positions in space, because the coordinate systems in which they are expressed are independent. However, it is well known that the most general motion of a rigid body can be expressed as a rotation plus a translation. Therefore, a measure of similarly of two ordered sets of points is the root-mean-square deviation $\Delta/\sqrt{N}$ after optimal superposition where Δ is defined by:

$$\Delta^2 = \min_{\mathbf{R}, \mathbf{t}} \left\{ \sum_{i=1}^{N} \|\mathbf{R}p_i + \mathbf{t} - q_i\| \right\},$$

where $\mathbf{R}$ is a proper rotation matrix (det $\mathbf{R} = 1$) and $\mathbf{t}$ is a translation vector.

It is easy to show that the optimum is achieved when the mean positions (colloquially, the "centers of gravity") of the two sets coincide. This determines the relative translation $\mathbf{t}$. The problem of determining the rotation is known as the "Orthogonal Procrustes Problem" (43).

A solution can be based on the polar or singular value decomposition of the correlation matrix

$$\mathbf{A}_{ij} = \sum_{k=1}^{N} (p_k)_i (q_k)_j.$$

$(p_k)_i$ is the ith component of the three-vector p_k. Because

$$\min \sum_i (p_i - \mathbf{R}q_i) \cdot (p_i - \mathbf{R}q_i) = \sum_i |p_i|^2 + \sum_i |\mathbf{R}q_i|^2 - 2\sum_i p_i \cdot \mathbf{R}q_i$$

$$= \sum_i |p_i|^2 + \sum_i |q_i|^2 - 2 \operatorname{Tr}(\mathbf{RA})$$

$(|\mathbf{R}q_i|^2 = |q_i|^2$ because of the orthogonality of $\mathbf{R}$),

finding the minimum of $\Sigma_i(p_i - \mathbf{R}q_i) \cdot (p_i - \mathbf{R}q_i)$ is equivalent to finding the rotation matrix $\mathbf{R}$ that gives the maximum of $\operatorname{Tr} \mathbf{RA}$.

Using the singular value decomposition to express $\mathbf{A} = \mathbf{UDV}$, where $\mathbf{D}$ is diagonal, $D_i \geq 0$, and $\mathbf{U}$ and $\mathbf{V}$ are orthogonal:

$$\operatorname{Tr} \mathbf{RA} = \operatorname{Tr} \mathbf{RUDV} = \operatorname{Tr} \mathbf{VRUD} = \operatorname{Tr} \mathbf{R'D},$$

where $\mathbf{R'} = \mathbf{VRU}$ is another orthogonal matrix. This has the maximum value $\operatorname{Tr} \mathbf{D}$ when $\mathbf{R'} = 1$, that is, $\mathbf{R} = \mathbf{V}^T\mathbf{U}$, provided $\det \mathbf{V}^T\mathbf{U} = 1$; and then $\operatorname{Tr} \mathbf{RA} = \sigma_1 + \sigma_2 + \sigma_3$, where the σ_i are the singular values of A. The alternative case, $\det \mathbf{V}^T\mathbf{U} = -1$, corresponds to the superposition of one point set onto the mirror image of the other. For some objects, for instance, a pair of gloves, this gives a better fit than any real translation or rotation. However, for our application, we must insist on a superposition possible in real three-dimensional space. If $\det \mathbf{V}^T\mathbf{U} = -1$, $\max \operatorname{Tr} \mathbf{RA} = \Sigma \sigma_i - 2 \min\{\sigma_1,\sigma_2,\sigma_3\}$ (discussed in Ref. 44 but not in Ref. 43).

Higham has pointed out that a polar decomposition of $\mathbf{A}$

$$\mathbf{A} = \mathbf{SH},$$

where $\mathbf{S}$ is orthogonal and $\mathbf{H}$ is Hermitian and positive semidefinite, is sufficient to solve the Orthogonal Procrustes Problem because $\mathbf{H}$ from the polar decomposition and $\mathbf{D}$ from the singular value decomposition are related by a similarity transformation and have the same trace (45).

Other approaches to rigid-body superposition take explicit advantage of the fact that the problem is three dimensional to solve the normal equations by determining the eigenvalues of $\mathbf{A}^T\mathbf{A}$ in closed form by solving a cubic equation (46,47). It is necessary to check that the optimal solution retains the handedness of the structures. Another way to take advantage of the three dimensionality is to introduce an explicit representation of the matrix specifying a rotation by θ around an axis in the direction of the unit vector $\hat{\mathbf{n}} = (l, m, n)$:

$$\mathbf{R} = 1 + \sin\theta N + (1 - \cos\theta)N^2,$$

where

$$N = \begin{pmatrix} 0 & n & -m \\ -n & 0 & l \\ m & -l & 0 \end{pmatrix}.$$

It follows from this representation that for any rotation of an angle θ around an axis $\hat{n} = (l, m, n)$,

$$\text{Tr}(\mathbf{RA}) = \text{Tr } \mathbf{A} + \text{Tr}(\mathbf{NA}) \sin \theta + [\text{Tr } \mathbf{A} - \text{Tr}(\mathbf{N}^2\mathbf{A})] \cos \theta$$

and, therefore, that

$$\max_\theta \text{Tr}(\mathbf{RA}) = \text{Tr } \mathbf{A} + \{[\text{Tr}(\mathbf{NA})]^2 + [\text{Tr } \mathbf{A} - \text{Tr}(\mathbf{N}^2\mathbf{A})]^2\}^{1/2}. \qquad (**)$$

Thus, given an axis of rotation, the calculation of the optimal angle of rotation is immediate (48–50). This equation provides an upper bound to the fit of two structures that will be useful when many comparisons have to be made, as in database searching.

Another approach that avoids entirely the problem of reversal of handedness is to use the quaternion expression of rotations, as discussed in the subsection Structures: molecular graphics. The optimum root-mean-square deviation is equal to the smallest eigenvalue of a 4×4 matrix (51,52).

These are only a few of a very large number of approaches to the problem of rigid-body superposition, which the author has often thought of as "the problem that would not die." For individual superposition calculations, all these methods are accurate and fast. It is for problems that require a very large number of superposition calculations (for example, comparing large numbers of subsets of two structures, or probing a structure data base with a molecule or fragment) that questions of the speed of different approaches and their suitability to be vectorized or parallelized arise.

One useful way to speed up calculations in which many superposition calculations are required is to calculate matrices of nearest-neighbor distances and use these to screen for potential matches [(53); cf. (54)]. Another is to apply formulas for lower bounds to Δ. (Recall that Δ is the root-mean-square deviation after optimal superposition).

First, the typical experimental accuracy in the coordinates implies that we need to compute $\Delta/\sqrt{N}$ to only two or three significant figures. If we are using an iterative procedure for computing eigenvalues or singular values of a matrix, Gershgorin bounds can often provide useful termination criteria based on the desired accuracy of the result. Second, in screening a data bank, it is often satisfactory to treat the following problem: Given a probe structure, determine all regions in proteins of known structure that match the probe structure within a root-mean-square deviation $\Delta \leq M$, where M is a prespecified threshold. A cheap-to-compute lower bound to Δ, even if not a sharp one, would permit avoiding many explicit determinations of Δ.

There are two sources of lower bounds. First, consider the determination of Δ from the singular value decomposition of the correlation matrix $\mathbf{A}$:

$$\Delta^2 = \sum |p_i|^2 + \sum |q_i|^2 - 2 \sum \sigma_i + [1 + \det \mathbf{V}^T\mathbf{U}] \min \sigma_i,$$

where the singular value decomposition of $\mathbf{A}$ is $\mathbf{V} \cdot \text{diag } \sigma_i \cdot \mathbf{U}$, $\sigma_i \geq 0$.

An iterative procedure for computing the singular value decomposition, such as that of Kogbetliantz (see, e.g., Ref. 55), produces a succession of transformed matrices $\mathbf{A}_n$, which have the same singular values as A, but with a steady reduction in the magnitudes of the off-diagonal elements. At any step,

$$\Delta^2 \leq \sum |p_i|^2 + \sum |q_i|^2 - 2 \text{ Tr } \mathbf{A}_n = \Delta_n^2.$$

But the Gershgorin theorems imply that if

$$Q = \sum_{i \neq j} |\mathbf{A}_{ij}|,$$

then

$$\sum \sigma_i \leq \mathrm{Tr}\, \mathbf{A}_n - \tfrac{1}{2} \sum_{i \neq j} |\mathbf{A}_{ij}| = \mathrm{Tr}\, A - \tfrac{1}{2} Q,$$

and it can be shown using equation (**) that

$$\Delta_n^2 - Q \leq \Delta^2 \leq \Delta_n^2.$$

Either a threshold on the desired precision or an absolute threshold on the magnitude of Δ provides a stopping criterion for an iterative procedure such as that of Kogbetliantz.

If an upper bound to the magnitude of Δ is imposed, that is, cases of interest are restricted to $\Delta \leq M$, then the Schwartz inequality can be applied at the time of calculation of the correlation matrix $\mathbf{A}$. To decide quickly whether the two sets of atoms, p_i and q_i, can be superposed with $\Delta \leq M$, first translate each set to its "center of gravity"; then, using the Schwartz inequality and the fact that for an orthogonal matrix $\mathbf{R}$, $|\mathbf{R}q_i| = |q_i|$, observe that

$$\Delta^2 = \sum_i |p_i - \mathbf{R}q_i|^2$$

$$= \sum_i [\,|p_i|^2 + |q_i|^2 - 2p_i \cdot \mathbf{R}q_i]$$

$$\geq \sum_i [\,|p_i|^2 + |q_i|^2 - 2|p_i||\mathbf{R}q_i|\,]$$

$$= \sum_i [\,|p_i|^2 + |q_i|^2 - 2|p_i||q_i|\,]$$

$$= \sum_i (|p_i| - |q_i|)^2$$

giving a lower bound to Δ that is independent of R. This inequality provides the basis for speeding up database screening calculations. For every prospective match, accumulate successive terms in this expression for the lower bound. If for any i the partial sum exceeds the square of the desired threshold, abandon consideration of this potential match immediately (56).

Rigid-Body Motions as "Screw" Motions

The most general motion of a rigid body is a rotation plus a translation. For optimal superposition of two structures, the translation is determined by the requirement that the mean positions of the point sets (colloquially, the "centers of gravity," although the mass differences between atoms are generally ignored) must coincide, and the rotation is determined by techniques just described. This produces a transformation of the form

$$p_i - \bar{p} = \mathbf{R}(q_i - \bar{q}),$$

where $\bar{p}$ and $\bar{q}$ are the mean positions of the point sets p_i and q_i, respectively, or, alternatively,

$$p_i = \mathbf{R}q_i + \mathbf{T},$$

where $\mathbf{T} = \bar{p} - \mathbf{R}\bar{q}$.

In analyzing conformational changes—for instance, movements in which one part of a molecule rotates with respect to another—an origin at the center of gravity is often not the appropriate choice. Consider comparing a door in open and closed states: One would naturally describe the motion as a rotation around a line through the hinges rather than as a rotation around the center of gravity plus a translation. In such cases, it is useful to apply the fact that by a suitable choice of origin any rigid-body motion can be described as a "screw" motion: a rotation together with a translation parallel to the axis of rotation. To see this, consider a change to an origin at a in the previous equation:

$$p_i - a = \mathbf{R}(q_i - a) + \mathbf{t}$$

which is equivalent to

$$p_i = \mathbf{R}q_i + a - \mathbf{R}a + \mathbf{t},$$

giving

$$\mathbf{T} = a - \mathbf{R}a + \mathbf{t}.$$

A change of origin changes the translation but not the rotation.

Given a transformation in the form $p_i = \mathbf{R}q_i + \mathbf{T}$, decompose $\mathbf{T}$ into components parallel and perpendicular to a unit vector along the axis of the rotation, $\hat{\mathbf{n}}$:

$$\mathbf{T}_{\parallel} = \mathbf{t}_{\parallel} = [\hat{\mathbf{n}} \cdot \mathbf{T}]\hat{\mathbf{n}},$$
$$\mathbf{T}_{\perp} = a - \mathbf{R}a + \mathbf{t}_{\perp}.$$

This shows that by a change of origin we cannot alter the parallel component of $\mathbf{T}$ but can reduce the perpendicular component to zero, provided we can solve the equation $a - \mathbf{R}a = \mathbf{T}_{\perp}$ for a. Because $a - \mathbf{R}a$ is unaffected by adding to a any vector parallel to $\hat{\mathbf{n}}$, we can without loss of generality assume $a \perp \hat{\mathbf{n}}$. To solve $a - \mathbf{R}a = \mathbf{T}_{\perp}$ for a, note that $a + \mathbf{R}a$, $\hat{\mathbf{n}}$, and $a - \mathbf{R}a = \mathbf{T}_{\perp}$ are mutually perpendicular:

$$a \perp \hat{\mathbf{n}}, \mathbf{R}a \perp \hat{\mathbf{n}} \Rightarrow a \pm \mathbf{R}a \perp \hat{\mathbf{n}}$$

and

$$(a + \mathbf{R}a) \cdot (a - \mathbf{R}a) = a \cdot a - \mathbf{R}a \cdot \mathbf{R}a = |a|^2 - |\mathbf{R}a|^2 = 0.$$

Therefore,

$$a + \mathbf{R}a = |a + \mathbf{R}a| \frac{\hat{\mathbf{n}} \times \mathbf{T}_{\perp}}{|\mathbf{T}_{\perp}|} = \frac{|a + \mathbf{R}a|}{|a - \mathbf{R}a|} \hat{\mathbf{n}} \times \mathbf{T}_{\perp}.$$

But if $\mathbf{R}$ is a rotation by θ,

$$|a \pm \mathbf{R}a|^2 = |a|^2[2 \pm 2 \cos \theta] = |a|^2[2 \mp 1 \pm \operatorname{Tr} \mathbf{R}].$$

We then have

$$a - \mathbf{R}a = \mathbf{T}_\perp,$$

$$a + \mathbf{R}a = \frac{|a + \mathbf{R}a|}{|a - \mathbf{R}a|}\hat{\mathbf{n}} \times \mathbf{T}_\perp = \sqrt{\frac{1 + \mathrm{Tr}\ \mathbf{R}}{3 - \mathrm{Tr}\ \mathbf{R}}}\ \hat{\mathbf{n}} \times \mathbf{T}_\perp,$$

and

$$a = \frac{1}{2}\mathbf{T}_\perp + \frac{1}{2}\sqrt{\frac{1 + \mathrm{Tr}\ \mathbf{R}}{3 - \mathrm{Tr}\ \mathbf{R}}}\ \hat{\mathbf{n}} \times \mathbf{T}_\perp.$$

The choice of origin at a given by the preceding equation converts an arbitrary rigid-body motion $p_i = \mathbf{R}q_i + \mathbf{T}$ to the screw motion

$$p_i - a = \mathbf{R}(q_i - a) + [\hat{\mathbf{n}} \cdot \mathbf{T}]\hat{\mathbf{n}}.$$

In analysis of conformational changes in proteins, this is useful for two reasons:

(a) In cases in which the motion is a pure rotation (for instance, a door opening and closing on hinges) or nearly a pure rotation, this is revealed by the vanishing or the small value of the translation. In fact, for all descriptions of a rigid-body motion in the form $p_i - a = \mathbf{R}(q_i - a) + \mathbf{t}$, the choice of a to express the motion as a screw gives a translation $\mathbf{t}$ that has minimal length.

(b) The choice of origin identifies points in the structure through which the axis passes. In the case of the door, the position of the axis would show where the hinges were. In proteins, the positions of the hinges are usually not obvious.

Multiple Superposition

There is often a need to superpose many different sets of coordinates. For example, in the determination of protein structure by NMR spectroscopy, the data leave the coordinates highly underdetermined, and the usual result is a set of more or less divergent structures all of which are equally satisfactory in terms of consistency with the experimental data and with basic structural principles. Several methods have been proposed including approaches that combine pairwise superpositions and others that solve the general multiple-structure problem exactly (57–60).

Database Searching

Screening structural databases for fragments of proteins has illuminated the range of conformations of short regions observed and has led to a number of useful applications.
1.   Probing databases with short *consecutive* segments from proteins has shown that the main chain conformations of short regions tend to recur in well-refined protein structures. It has been estimated that all eight-residue regions of main chain are similar in conformation to one of a set of about 60 structures, and all five-residue regions of main chain in well-determined proteins are similar in conformation to one of a set of about 150 structures. The latter result suggests that each residue can have about $150^{1/5} = 2.75$ conformational states per residue; this is quite reasonable given the Sasisekharan–Ramachandran plot (see the section on The nature and organization of data). The fact that eight-residue regions have fewer conformations than would occur if all residue conformations were independent is expected because the chain must avoid intersecting itself.

Probing databases with short regions picks up both homologous regions—that is, regions from related structures—and also examples where regions with similar conformations have entirely different structural contexts and interactions in different proteins. Comparisons among these regions reveals the nature of the determinants of their conformations: For example, a certain type of loop may require certain hydrogen-bonding interactions, but different proteins can provide these interactions in a number of different ways, and the loop can occur in a number of different structural contexts (61).

2. Probing databases with *two* short regions separated by a gap of fixed length can answer the question, How many ways are there for a polypeptide chain to bridge a gap between two "stumps"? This is useful both to analyze the observed repertoire of loops and to assist in model building.

Jones and Thirup built this facility into their software (it has since been widely copied) using a matrix of interatomic distances as a filter to identify candidate matches [(53); cf. (54)].

Sequences and Structures

We have seen that searching a sequence database for a probe sequence and searching a structure data base with a probe structure are problems that can be formulated in precise mathematical terms, and for which solutions are known. The "mixed" problems—probing a sequence database with a structure, or a structure database with a sequence—are less straightforward. They require a method for evaluating the compatibility of a given sequence with a given folding pattern. With this in hand, it is possible to organize the calculation in either direction.

If the essence of a known structure can be abstracted in such a way that the properties of positions in the structure can be related to general characteristics of the amino acids rather than to the particular sequence, then sequences that share these abstract properties might be expected to adopt similar structures.

The approach of Bowie, Lüthy, and Eisenberg has been to classify the *environments* of each position in known protein structures—rather than any particular sequence of residues that occupies these environments—in a way that can be linked to a set of preferences of the 20 amino acids for these structural contexts (62,63).

Given a protein structure, Bowie, Lüthy, and Eisenberg classify the environment of each amino acid side chain according to three separate categories:

1. Its main chain hydrogen-bonding interactions, that is, its secondary structure
2. The extent to which it is on the inside or the outside of the protein structure
3. The polar/nonpolar nature of its environment

The secondary structure may be one of three possibilities: helix, sheet, or loop. A side chain is considered buried if the accessible surface area is less than 40 Å^2, partially buried if the accessible surface area is between 40 and 114 Å^2, and exposed if the accessible surface area is greater than 114 Å^2. The fraction of side chain area covered by polar atoms is measured. The authors define six classes on the basis of accessibility and polarity of surroundings; side chains in each of these six classes may be in any of the three types of secondary structures, giving a total of 18 classes.

Assigning each side chain to one of 18 categories means that it is possible to write a coded description of a protein structure as a message in an alphabet of 18 letters. Bowie, Lüthy, and Eisenberg call this a "3D structure profile." In this way, algorithms developed for sequence searches can be applied to "sequences" of encoded structures. For example, one could try to align two distantly related sequences by aligning their 3D structure profiles rather than their amino acid sequences.

Next, how can one relate the encoded structure to the corpus of known sequences and structures? It is clear that some amino acids will be unhappy in certain kinds of sites; for example, a charged side chain would not be buried in an entirely nonpolar environment. Other preferences are not so clear-cut, but Bowie, Lüthy, and Eisenberg have derived a preference table from a statistical survey of a library of well-refined protein structures.

Suppose now that we are a given a sequence and want to evaluate the likelihood that it takes up, say, the globin fold. From the 3D structure profile of the known sperm whale myoglobin structure, we know the environment class of each position of the sequence. Consider a particular alignment of the unknown sequence with sperm whale myoglobin, and suppose that the residue in the unknown sequence that corresponds to the first residue of myoglobin is phenylalanine. The environment class in the 3D structure profile of the first residue of sperm whale myoglobin is: Exposed, no secondary structure. One can score the probability of finding phenylalanine in this structural environment class from the table of preferences of particular amino acids for this class. (The fact that the first residue of the sperm whale myoglobin sequence is actually valine is not used, and, in fact, that information is not directly accessible to the algorithm. Sperm whale myoglobin is represented only by the sequence of environment classes of its residues, and the preference table is averaged over proteins with many different folding patterns.) Extension of this calculation to all positions and to all possible alignments (not allowing gaps within regions of secondary structure) gives a score that measures how well the given unknown sequence fits the sperm whale myoglobin profile.

A particular advantage of this method is that it can be automated, with a new sequence being scored against every 3D profile in the library of known folds in essentially the same way as a new sequence is routinely screened against a library of known sequences.

Use of 3D Profiles to Assess the Quality of Structures

The 3D profile derived from a structure depends only very indirectly on the amino acid sequence. It is, therefore, meaningful to ask not only whether other amino acid sequences are compatible with the given fold but also whether the score of the 3D profile for its own sequence is a measure of the compatibility of the sequence with the structure. Naturally, if real sequences did not generally appear to be compatible with their own structures, one would be forced to conclude that a useful method for examining the relationship between sequence and structure had not been achieved. However, Bowie, Lüthy, and Eisenberg have shown that when a sequence does not match the structure into which it is alleged to fold, there is likely to have been an error in the structure determination.

From the computational point of view, this method translates protein structures into one-dimensional probe objects (or probeable objects) that do not explicitly retain either the sequence or structure of the molecules from which they were derived. A more complicated approach is the idea of "threading a sequence through a structure," developed by Finkelstein and Reva (64), Scharf and Sander (65), and Jones, Taylor, and Thornton (66). Given a protein structure, retain only the backbone and determine how a given sequence might best fit into it. To do this, it is necessary to determine the optimal alignment of the residues of the sequence with positions along the chain in the three-dimensional structure. For any possible alignment, several approaches have been suggested for evaluating the energy in ways such that dynamic programming algorithms can be applied. This is an active area of current research.

PROTEIN STRUCTURE PREDICTION

The observation that each protein folds spontaneously into a unique three-dimensional native conformation implies that nature has an algorithm for predicting protein structure from amino acid sequence. As discussed in previous sections, our attempts to understand this algorithm are based partly on general physical principles and partly on generalizations from observations on known amino acid sequences and protein structures. A proof of our understanding would be the ability to reproduce the algorithm in a computer program which could predict protein structure from amino acid sequence.

For many years there have been attempts to predict protein structure from basic physical principles alone. These methods attempt to reproduce as accurately as possible the interatomic interactions in proteins to define an "energy" associated with any conformation. The parameters that define the interaction are general and transferrable, applying equally to all proteins (in fact, to all molecules containing the same types of atoms). This reduces the problem of protein structure prediction to the task of finding a global minimum of this conformational energy function. So far, this approach has not succeeded, partly because of the inadequacy of the energy function and partly because the minimization algorithms tend to get trapped in local minima.

With the recent great increase in the sizes of the databases of amino acid sequences and protein structures, much attention has been paid to developing empirical methods for "knowledge-based" predictions. For example, if two proteins are closely related, it is possible to model either from the other; using as a guide the observed features of molecular evolution described in the section The nature and organization of data. In this case, one is focusing on the question of how *changes* in the amino acid sequence are reflected in *changes* in the structure; this is the "differential form" of the prediction problem.

More generally, we are coming closer and closer to saturating with known structures the set of possible folds (67). Methods such as those discussed in the preceding section are being developed to test whether a given amino acid sequence is likely to form a folding pattern similar to that of a known protein. We may wish to distinguish between empirical *identification* of a known protein structure and prediction of a fold from the sequence without explicit application of known data.

Presumably, once we have a complete set of folds and sequences, and powerful methods for relating them, empirical methods will provide pragmatic solutions of many problems. What will be the effect of this on attempts to predict protein structure *a priori*? The intellectual appeal of the problem will still be there—nature folds proteins without searching databases. But it is unlikely that the problem will continue to command interest of the same intensity if a pragmatic solution has been found.

However, there is a paradox: The methods being developed for identifying folding patterns in sequences are more than "curve fitting" or "black box" solutions of the problem. They are experiments that explore and expose the essential features of amino acid sequences that determine protein structures. When they succeed, we will have a far sounder basis for understanding sequence-structure relationships than we do now. It may be that *a posteriori* understanding will make *a priori* prediction possible.

Nonempirical Methods of Protein Structure Prediction: Conformational Energy Calculations

A protein is a collection of atoms whose interactions create a unique state of maximum stability. Find it, that's all!

The computational difficulties in this approach arise because (a) the model of the interatomic interactions is not complete or exact and (b) even if the model were exact, we face an optimization problem in a large number of variables, involving nonlinearities in the objective function and constraints.

The interactions between atoms in a molecule can be divided into the following:

(a) Primary chemical bonds—strong interactions between atoms that must be close together in space. These are regarded as a fixed set of interactions that are not broken or formed when the conformation of a protein changes but are equally consistent with a large number of conformations.

(b) Weaker interactions that depend on the conformation of the chain. These can be significant in some conformations and not in others—they affect sets of atoms that are brought into proximity by different folds of the chain.

The conformation of a protein can be specified by giving the list of atoms in the structure, their coordinates, and the set of primary chemical bonds between them (this can be "read off," with only slight ambiguity, from the amino acid sequence). Terms used in the evaluations of the energy of a conformation typically include (68):

- Bond stretching: $\Sigma_{\text{bonds}} K_r (r - r_0)^2$. Here r_0 is the equilibrium interatomic separation and K_r is the force constant for stretching the bond. r_0 and K_r depend on the type of chemical bond.

- Bond angle bend: $\Sigma_{\text{angles}} K_\theta (\theta - \theta_0)^2$. For any atom i that is chemically bonded to two other atoms j and k (or more), the angle $i - j - k$ has and equilibrium value θ_0 and a force constant for bending K_θ.

- Torsion: $\Sigma_{\text{dihedrals}} \frac{1}{2} V_n [1 + \cos n\phi]$. For any four connected atoms, i bonded to j bonded to k bonded to l, the energy barrier to rotation of atom l with respect to atom i around the j–k bond as rotation axis is given by a periodic potential. V_n is the height of the barrier to internal rotation; n barriers are encountered during the full a 360° rotation.

- Van der Waals interactions: $\Sigma_i \Sigma_{j<i} (A_{ij} R_{ij}^{-12} - B_{ij} R_{ij}^{-6})$. For each pair of nonbonded atoms i and j, the first term accounts for a short-range repulsion and the second term for a long-range attraction between them. The parameters A and B depend on atom type.

- Hydrogen bond: $\Sigma_i \Sigma_{j<i} (C_{ij} R_{ij}^{-12} - D_{ij} R_{ij}^{-10})$. The hydrogen bond is an weak chemical/electrostatic interaction between two polar atoms. Its strength depends on distance—accounted for in the form of this potential—and also on the bond angle.

- Electrostatic: $\Sigma_i \Sigma_{j<i} Q_i Q_j / (\epsilon R_{ij})$. Q_i and Q_j are the effective charges on the atoms, R_{ij} is the distance between them, and ϵ is the dielectric "constant." This formula applies only approximately to media that are not infinite and isotropic, including proteins!

Other terms penalize deviations from planarity of certain groups, or enforce chirality (handedness) at certain centers.

There are numerous sets of conformational energy potentials of this or closely related forms, and a great deal of effort has gone into the tuning of parameter sets. The energy of a conformation is computed by summing these terms over all appropriate sets of interacting atoms.

Attempts to predict the conformation of a protein by minimization of the conformational energy have, so far, not provided a method for predicting the protein structure from amino acid sequence. Part of the problem is that the models are incomplete. In particular, a very important component that is absent is a way to represent the interaction between the protein and the solvent. There are several tests of the models, which are necessary but not sufficient conditions for success. One is to take the "right answer"— an experimentally determined protein structure as a starting conformation–and minimize the energy starting from there. In general, most energy functions produce a minimized conformation that is about 1 Å (root-mean-square deviation) away from the starting model. This can be thought of as a measure of the "resolution" of the force field. Another test has been to take deliberately misfolded proteins and minimize their conformational energies to see whether the energy value of the local minimum in the vicinity of the correct fold is significantly lower than that of the local minimum in the vicinity of an incorrect fold. In such tests, it has been found that there are multiple local minima that cannot be confidently distinguished from the correct one on the basis of the method for evaluating the conformational energy.

To overcome both the problems of getting trapped in local minima and of the absence of a good model for protein–solvent interactions, molecular dynamics models have been developed, in which the protein plus explicit solvent molecules are treated—via the force field—by classical Newtonian mechanics. It is true that this permits exploration of a much larger sector of phase space. What has been found is that molecular dynamics, if supplemented by experimental data, can be an extremely powerful component of structure determinations by both X-ray crystallography and nuclear magnetic resonance. However, as an method of *a priori* structure prediction, it still has not succeeded. However, these are calculations that are extremely CPU intensive and here, perhaps more than anywhere else in this field, advances deriving from the increased "brute force" power of processors will have an effect (69).

How is molecular dynamics integrated into the process of structure determination? For any conformation, one can measure the consistency of the model with the experimental data. In the case of crystallography, the experimental data are absolute values of the Fourier coefficients of the electron density of the molecule. In the case of nuclear magnetic resonance, the experimental data provide constraints on the distances between certain pairs of residues. But in both X-ray crystallography and nuclear magnetic resonance, the experimental data underdetermine the protein structure. To solve a structure, one must seek a set of coordinates that minimizes a combination of the deviation from the constraints imposed by experimental data and the conformational energy. Molecular dynamics is extremely useful in determining such coordinate sets: The dynamics provides adequate coverage of conformation space, and the bias derived from the experimental data channels the calculation toward the correct structure and permits its identification when it has been found.

Modeling by Homology

Model-building by homology is a useful technique when one wants to predict the structure of a target protein of known sequence that is related to another protein of known sequence *and* structure. If the two proteins are closely related, the known protein structure will form the basis for a model of the target. Although the quality of the model will depend on the degree of similarity of the sequences, it is possible to specify this quality before experimental testing (see Figs. 7 and 8). In consequence, knowing how good a model is necessary for the intended application permits an intelligent prediction of the probable success of the exercise.

The steps in the procedure are as follows:

1. Align the amino acid sequences of the two proteins. It will generally be observed that insertions and deletions lie in the loop regions between helices and sheets, especially if the relation between the sequences is close.
2. Determine main chain segments to represent the loops, by database searching for the regions subject to insertions and deletions. Stitching these regions into the main chain of the known protein creates a model for the complete main chain of the target protein.
3. Replace the side chains of residues that have been mutated. For residues that have not mutated, retain the side chain conformation. For residues that have mutated, keep the same side chain conformational angles as far as possible.
4. Examine the model—both by eye and by programs—to detect any serious collisions between atoms. Relieve these collisions, as far as possible, by manual manipulations.
5. Refine the model by limited energy minimization. The role of this step is to fix up the exact geometrical relationships at places where regions of main chain have been joined together, and to allow the side chains to wriggle around a bit to place themselves in comfortable positions. The effect is really only cosmetic—energy refinement will not fix serious errors in such a model.

In a sense, this procedure produces "what you get for free" in that it defines the model of the protein of unknown structure by making minimal changes to its known relative. Unfortunately, it is not easy to make substantial improvements. A rule of thumb (referring again to Figs. 7 and 8) is that if the two sequences have at least 40–50% identical amino acids in an optimal alignment of their sequences, the procedure described will produce a model of sufficient accuracy to be useful for many applications. If the sequences are more distantly related, neither the procedure described nor any other currently available will produce a generally useful model of the target protein from the structure of its relative.

Methods Based on Distribution of Variability in Aligned Sequences

A method of prediction of protein folding patterns based on analysis of a table of aligned sequences has recently achieved a remarkable success, and in the author's opinion this work will be regarded as a major breakthrough. Benner and Gerloff successfully predicted the fold of the catalytic domain of protein kinase C—in advance of the determination of its structure (70,71).

Their approach is based on analysis of a table of aligned homologous sequences, assumed to share a folding pattern; but, in contrast with methods based on homology to a known structure, they operate *without* prior knowledge of this common conformation.

A sketch of the procedure follows:

The first step is to distinguish buried from surface residues, deriving this information from the patterns of variability of the residues. The crucial novel idea is the correlation of the variabilities at given positions with the overall deviation of the sequences. Given a table of aligned homologous sequences, consider two positions, at neither of which the residues are absolutely conserved. Suppose that at the first position, the residue is not conserved even in particular pairs of sequences which, in terms of their overall similarity, are very closely related. Suppose that at the second position, the residues are variable but change only between pairs of sequences that are very distantly related. The first residue is likely to be on the surface, and the second is likely to be buried.

From this surface/buried map, they derive the positions of the helices and sheets. This is based on patterns of hydrophobicity and surface exposure (see the discussion of Tables Ia and Ib).

By further analysis of correlated patterns of variations, derive which residues are near each other in space. From this, the general topology can be inferred; for example, the order and relative directions of the strands of a sheet, or determining the side of a sheet against which a helix packs. To identify neighboring residues, appeal is again made to the aligned sequences. Positions of neighboring residues are recognized by "covariation"—that is, pairs of positions that show similar patterns of conservation in subsets of the sequences. Suppose that for each subset of sequences in which the amino acid at a certain position is conserved, there is a strong tendency for the amino acid at a second position to be conserved also, but, *vice versa*, when the residue at the first position changes the residue at the second position changes also; these residues are likely to be neighbors.

The result is what might be called a $2\frac{1}{2}$-dimensional structure. It indicates the elements of secondary structures and their interactions but not, in general, their detailed spatial relationships. A set of coordinates is not produced.

The most important quality of the method is that it works. The prediction of the catalytic domain of cAMP-dependent protein kinase was a "blind" test in which the prediction was published before the structure was announced. The fold was a new one; therefore, getting it right is more impressive than an exercise that identified a known pattern, because all the predicted structural details were *independent*.

Unlike other successful structure predictions which have depended on *ad hoc* properties of certain structures, it is a general method. Benner and Gerloff claim, in general tests on known structures, 90% accuracy in distinguishing surface from buried residues and identification of 90% of secondary structure elements, with an overall 70% accuracy of secondary structure prediction in a residue-by-residue basis.

CONCLUSIONS

How can we extrapolate from our current situation to the computational molecular biology of the medium-term or distant future? Clearly, data collection will proceed and continue to accelerate; computing facilities of increasing power will be applied to the storage, distribution, and analysis of the results; and improved algorithms will be devised to understand them. Applications to scenarios such as that in the Introduction will be more feasible, and mature from the domain of "blue-sky" research to standard industrial practice. Some of the higher levels of biological information transfer to which we have already alluded—notably the programs of genetic development during the lifetime of individuals, and the activities of the human mind—will be included in the processes we can describe quantitatively and analyze at the level of molecules and their interactions.

One threshold will be reached when our knowledge of sequences and structures becomes more nearly complete, in the sense that a fairly dense subset of the available data from contemporary living forms has been collected. (Of course, there is no question of being able to know everything.) This will be recognized operationally when a random dip into the pot of a genome, or the isolation of a new protein structure, is far more likely to turn up something already known, rather than, as now, more likely to uncover something new.

Nature is, after all, a system of unlimited possibilities but finite choices. Some of these choices are necessary ones in that no alternative would "work"; many others are accidental. Debates in molecular biology often include the accusation: "You haven't discovered any general principle, you're just doing archeology." It is, indeed, hard to distinguish the necessary from the coincidental, but in the past it has been comprehensive knowledge that has made progress on this front possible. A test of whether we have derived general principles, that is already being accepted as a challenge to some extent, is whether we can modify life forms or even design novel ones. This is already being done, albeit in a rudimentary way, with artificial protein structures.

In Michaelangelo's frescoes on the ceiling of the Sistine Chapel, the serpent offering Eve the fruit of the tree of knowledge is represented with its legs coiled around the tree in the form of a double helix. We can hope that the temptation to knowledge embodied in our analysis of another double helix will have more fortunate consequences.

ACKNOWLEDGMENTS

The author thanks M. E. Lesk, G. Mitcheson, A. Pastore, A. Tramontano, and G. Vriend for comments on the manuscript, and the Key Kendall Foundation for generous support. Spaceball is the registered trademark of Spaceball Technology.

REFERENCES

1. J. Hodgson, *Bio/Technology*, *10*, 760–763 (1992).
2. R. J. Robbins, *IEEE Eng. Med. Biol.*, *11*, 25–34 (1992).
3. F. M. Richards, *Sci. Am. 264*, 54–63 (1991).
4. D. F. Rogers and J. A. Adams, *Mathematical Elements for Computer Graphics*, 2nd ed., Mc-Graw–Hill Book Co., New York, 1990.
5. J. Felsenstein, *Ann. Rev. Genetics*, *22*, 521–565 (1988).
6. D. L. Swofford and G. J. Olsen, "Phylogeny Reconstruction," in *Molecular Systematics*, D. M. Hillis, and C. Moritz (eds.), Sinauer, Sunderland, MA, 1990.
7. A. M. Lesk and C. Chothia, *Phil. Trans. Roy. London*, *317*, 345–356 (1986).
8. C. Chothia and A. M. Lesk, *EMBO J.*, *5*, 823–826 (1986).
9. A. Bairoch and B. Boeckmann, *Nucleic Acids Res.*, *20*, (suppl.), 2019–2022 (1992).
10. A. Lesk (ed.), *Computational Molecular Biology: Sources and Methods of Sequence Analysis*, Oxford University Press, Oxford, 1988.
11. S. A. Islam and M. J. E. Sternberg, *Protein Eng.*, *2*, 432–442 (1989).
12. A. Bairoch, *Nucleic Acids Res. 20* (suppl.), 2013–2018 (1992).
13. T. M. Klinger and D. L. Brutlag, manuscript in preparation.
14. J. D. Foley, A. Van Dam, S. Feiner, and J. Hughes, *Computer Graphics: Principles and Practice*, Addison-Wesley, Reading, MA, 1990.
15. L. C. Biederharn and J. D. Louck, *Angular Momentum in Quantum Physics: Theory and Applications*, Addison-Wesley, London, 1981.

16. S. L. Altmann, *Rotations, Quaternions and Double Groups*, Clarendon Press, Oxford, 1986.
17. A. Glassner (ed.), *Graphics Gems*, Academic Press, New York, 1990.
18. W. M. Kahan, "Interval Arithmetic Options in the Proposed IEEE Floating Point Arithmetic Standard," in *Interval Mathematics 1980*, K. L. E. Nickel (ed.), Academic Press, New York, 1980, pp. 99–128.
19. C. Moler and D. Morrison, *IBM J. Res. Devel.*, *27*, 577–581 (1983).
20. A. A. Dubrulle, *IBM J. Res. Devel.*, *27*, 577–581 (1983).
21. Z. Galil and R. Giancarlo, *J. Complexity*, *4*, 33–72 (1988).
22. S. B. Needleman and C. D. Wunsch, *J. Mol. Biol.*, *48*, 443–453 (1970).
23. D. Sankoff and J. B. Kruskal (eds.), *Time Warps, String Edits, and Macromolecules: The Theory and Practice of Sequence Comparison*. Addison-Wesley, Reading, MA, 1983.
24. G. M. Landau, "String Matching in Erroneous Input," Ph.D. thesis, Department of Computer Science, Tel-Aviv University, Tel-Aviv, 1986.
25. E. C. Tyler, M. R. Horton, and P. R. Krause, *Comp. Biomed. Res.*, *24*, 72–96 (1991).
26. G. H. Gonnet, M. A. Cohen, and S. A. Benner, *Science*, *256*, 1443–1445 (1992).
27. D. L. Brutlag, J. -P. Dautricourt, R. Diaz, J. Fier, B. Moxon, and R. Stamm, Comp. and Chem., *17*, 203–207 (1993).
28. R. Jones. *Int. J. Supercomputer Appl.*, *6*, 138–146 (1992).
29. S. C. Chan, A. K. C. Wong, D. K. Y. Chiu, *Bull. Math. Biol.*, *54*, 563–598 (1992).
30. M. Vingron, "Multiple Sequence Alignment and Applications in Molecular Biology," Thesis, Naturwissenschaftlich-mathematischen Gesamtfakultät der Ruprecht-Karls-Universität, Heidelberg (1991).
31. D. Haussler, A. Krogh, S. Mian, and K. Sjölander, "Protein Modeling Using Hidden Markov Models," C.I.S. Technical Report UCSC-CRL-92-93, University of California at Santa Cruz, 1992.
32. F. Aurenhammer, *ACM Comp. Surveys*, *23*, 345–405 (1991).
33. F. M. Richards, *Methods Enzymol.*, *115*, 440–464 (1985).
34. R. Unger, D. Harel, S. Wherland, and J. L. Sussman, *Proteins: Structure, Function, Genetics*, *5*, 355–373 (1989).
35. M. Levine, D. Stuart, and J. Williams, *Acta Crystallogr.*, *A40*, 600–610 (1984).
36. M. E. Karpen, P. L. de Haseth, and K. E. Neet, *Proteins: Structure, Function, Genetics*, *6*, 155–167 (1989).
37. M. N. Liebman, C. A. Venanzi, and H. Weinstein, *Biopolymers*, *24*, 1721–1758 (1985).
38. W. R. Taylor, and C. A. Orengo, *J. Mol. Biol.*, *208*, 1–22 (1989).
39. G. Vriend and C. Sander, *Proteins: Structure, Function, Genetics*, *11*, 52–58 (1991).
40. N. N. Alexandrov, K. Takahashi, and N. Gō, *J. Mol. Biol.*, *225*, 5–9 (1992).
41. P. Dean, *Molecular Foundations of Drug–Receptor Interaction*, Cambridge University Press, Cambridge, 1987.
42. I. Kolossváry and W. C. Guida, *J. Chem. Inform. Computer Sci.*, *32*, 191–199 (1992).
43. G. Golub and C. van Loan, *Matrix Computations*, 2nd ed., Johns Hopkins Press, Baltimore, 1989.
44. G. Golub and C. Reinsch, "Singular Value Decomposition and Least Squares Solutions," in *Handbook for Automatic Computation II. Linear Algebra*, J. H. Wilkinson and C. Reinsch (eds.), Springer-Verlag, New York, 1971.
45. N. Higham, *SIAM J. Sci. Stat. Comp.*, *7*, 1160–1174 (1986).
46. W. Kabsch, *Acta Crystallogr.*, *A32*, 922–923 (1976).
47. W. Kabsch, *Acta Crystallogr.*, *A34*, 827–828 (1978).
48. A. D. McLachlan, *Acta Crystallogr.*, *A28*, 656–657 (1972).
49. A. D. McLachlan, *Acta Crystallogr.*, *A38*, 871–873 (1982).
50. A. M. Lesk, *Acta Crystallogr.*, *A42* 110–113 (1986).
51. S. K. Kearsley, *Acta Crystallogr.*, *A45*, 208–210 (1989).
52. R. Diamond, *Acta Crystallogr.*, *A44*, 211–216 (1988).

53. T. A. Jones and S. Thirup, *EMBO J.*, *5*, 819–822 (1986).
54. A. M. Lesk, *Comm. Assoc. Comp. Mach.*, *22*, 219–224 (1979).
55. J. P. Charlier, M. Vanbegin, P. Van Dooren, *Numer. Math.*, *52*, 279–300 (1988).
56. A. Tramontano and A. M. Lesk, *Proteins: Structure, Function, Genetics*, *13*, 231–245 (1992).
57. P. R. Gerber and K. Müller, *Acta Crystallogr.*, *A43* 426–428 (1987).
58. S. K. Kearsley, *J. Comp. Chem.*, *11*, 1187–1192 (1990).
59. A. Shapiro, J. D. Botha, A. Pastore, and A. M. Lesk, *Acta Crystallogr.*, *A48* 11–14 (1992).
60. R. Diamond, *Protein Science*, *1*, 1279–1287 (1992).
61. A. Tramontano, C. Chothia, and A. M. Lesk, *Proteins: Structure, Function, Genetics*, *6*, 382–394 (1989).
62. J. B. Bowie, R. Lüthy, and D. Eisenberg, *Science*, *253*, 164–170 (1991).
63. R. Lüthy, J. U. Bowie, and D. Eisenberg, *Nature*, *356*, 83–85 (1992).
64. A. V. Finkelstein and B. A. Reva, *Nature*, *351*, 497–499 (1991).
65. M. Scharf and C. Sander, *J. Mol. Biol.*, in press.
66. D. T. Jones, W. R. Taylor, and J. M. Thornton, *Nature*, *358*, 86–89 (1992).
67. C. Chothia, *Nature*, *357*, 543–544 (1992).
68. G. M. Maggiora, B. Mao, K. C. Chou, and S. L. Narasimhan, *Theoretical and Empirical Approaches to Protein–Structure Prediction and Analysis*, in: Methods of Biochemical Analysis Vol. 35, 1991, pp. 1–60.
69. C. L. Brooks, III, W. S. Young, and D. J. Tobias, *Int. J. Supercomputer Appl.*, *5*, 98–112 (1991).
70. S. A. Benner, *Adv. Enz. Regulation*, *28* 219–236 (1989).
71. S. A. Benner and D. Gerloff, *Adv. Enz. Regulation*, *31*, 121–181 (1991).

BIBLIOGRAPHY

Bishop, M. J., and C. J. Rawlings, *Nucleic Acid and Protein Sequence Analysis: A Practical Approach*, IRL Press, Oxford, 1987.

Brändén, C.- I., and J. Tooze, *Introduction to Protein Structure*, Garland, New York, 1991.

Crippen, G. M., and T. F. Havel, *Distance Geometry and Molecular Conformation*, John Wiley and Sons, New York, 1988.

Frenkel, K. A., "The Human Genome Project and Informatics," *Comm. ACM*, *34*, 41–51 (1991).

Lander, E. S., R. Langridge, and D. M. Saccocio, "Computing in Molecular Biology: Mapping and Interpreting Biological Information," *IEEE Computer*, *24*(11), 6–13 (1991).

Lesk, A. M., "Proteina ex Machina [The Architecture of Proteins]," *KOS I*(6), 113–131 (1984).

Lesk, A. M., *Protein Architecture: A Practical Approach*. IRL Press, Oxford, 1991.

Maggiora, G. M., B. Mao, K. C. Chou, and S. L. Narasimhan, *Theoretical and Empirical Approaches to Protein-Structure Prediction and Analysis*. In: Methods of Biochemical Analysis Vol. 35, 1991, pp. 1–60.

Robbins, R. J., *IEEE Eng. Med. Biol.*, *11*, 25–34 (1992).

Rosenfeld, I., E. Ziff., and B. Van Loan, *DNA for Beginners*, W.W. Norton, New York, 1983.

Sankoff, D., and J. B. Kruskal (eds.), *Time Warps, String Edits, and Macromolecules: The Theory and Practice of Sequence Comparison*, Addison-Wesley, Reading, MA, 1983.

ARTHUR M. LESK

COMPUTER-ASSISTED SYNTHESIS PLANNING

INTRODUCTION

Computer-assisted synthesis planning means organic synthesis simulation or design using computer programs which predict starting materials and synthetic pathways for a given target molecule; that is, systems of this kind have an inference mechanism of backward search in a strict sense of the term "synthesis planning." However, they often have a forward search mechanism which predicts products from a given starting material; so both types of systems are described in this article. The first computer-assisted synthesis planning system, was initiated in 1967 by E. J. Corey at Harvard University, known as OCCS (Organic Chemical Simulation of Synthesis), and has continued to be developed as LHASA (Logic and Heuristics Applied to Synthetic Analysis) (1). Currently, a number of synthesis planning systems have been developed and are in limited practical use. They are classified into four categories according to the approaches employed: ruled based, case based, logic oriented, and integrated systems of two or more approaches. The former two are often classified as empirical knowledge or known-data-oriented approach, though the reasoning schemes of the two are different. In any case, a synthesis planning system is a kind of expert system which consists of database/knowledge base and an inference engine. Therefore, the representation and acquisition of data/knowledge are central issues for these systems. Particularly, knowledge acquisition becomes a bottleneck in the case of an empirical knowledge-oriented approach like other fields of expert system application. In the following section, the representation scheme of data/knowledge and corresponding inference mechanism for each approach are described in terms of specific systems so far reported.

LHASA

The first of synthesis planning systems began with this approach, which includes LHASA, SECS (Simulation and Evaluation of Chemical Synthesis) (2,3), SYNCHEM2 (4), and so on. The central ideas of these are the same, so the framework of this approach is described based on LHASA (5,6).

Process of Synthesis Planning

LHASA is a kind of rule-based system which searches precursors backward (retrospectively) from a give target molecule (goal). The rules are called "transforms" in LHASA. The basic process of synthesis planning is as follows:

1. Input target structure: Graphical user interface is supported for chemical structure input.
2. Perceive structural features: Structural features from the viewpoint of reactivity, such as functional groups and ring systems, are recognized and extracted.
3. Setup strategy: Synthesis strategy is set up based on the recognized structural features. This process together with the next step depends largely on users (organic chemists) of LHASA.
4. Select a transform: Actually a transform to be applied is selected by the user. Transforms are categorized according to their characters, and the selection of a transform of some category determines the behavior of the successive inference.
5. Apply the transform: The selected transform is applied to the target structure to generate precursors. If available starting materials are found among the precursors, the search process ends successfully. Otherwise, set up one of the most favorable precursors as a next target structure, and return to Step 2.

At the application and generation stage (Step 5), the applicability and relevance of the transform to the target is evaluated (corresponding to the evaluation of scope and limitations). The result of the evaluation is expressed in terms of increment/decrement of rating value. The rating value corresponds to a certainty factor in usual expert systems. Inference paths as a whole make a tree with a root being the target molecule, called retrosynthetic tree. A retrosynthesic tree results in combinatorial explosion easily, so controlling the growth of the tree is one of the key problems of practical use. The basic ideas employed for building the system of this approach are described below.

Representation of Chemical Structures

A chemical structure has to be represented in the form that atomic connectivity can be manipulated in order to analyze a target structure and perform structural transformation. A chemical structure is considered to be a graph whose nodes and edges corresponds to atoms and bonds. It is represented internally in the form of a table whose entries contain attributes of constituent atoms. This table is called a connection table, which is almost equivalent to an adjacency matrix of a graph. Variations of a connection table arise from the employed attributes of an atom. A typical example of the attributes are as follows: atom number (node identifier, this is a key attribute), atomic symbol, the number of adjacent atoms, a list of adjacent atom numbers, the number of attached hydrogen atoms, stereochemistry, and so on. Stereochemistry such as geometrical isomerism (*cis–trans* isomerism), optical isomerism (chirality), and so on plays an important role in chemical reactions, though it is not always fully implemented in a connection table.

A chemical structure is given a unique code as its identifier which is generated cannonically from a connection table. Every precursor generated successively from a target structure has to be checked to verify whether it is identical to an available known material or the other precursor already generated. This check is performed as a comparison between the two cannonical codes of chemical structures. Actually, this is a well-known graph isomorphism problem. In fact, a number of coding methods have been presented so far, although Chemical Abstracts Service employed the Morgan method (7). Some of the synthesis planning systems also use their own coding system as well as a modified Morgan code.

Representation of Reaction Data

Reaction data, which are a fact data or an instance, are not utilized explicitly in rule-based synthesis planning systems which mainly make use of a transform knowledge base (retrospective synthesis rules). However reaction data are not only central to the system of other approaches but are also important as source information of transforms. Reaction data are described in terms of their transformation from a reactant to a product with reaction conditions. Specifically, structural transformation is represented as graph data, whereas reaction conditions are represented as text data. Structural transformation necessitates a consideration from the standpoint of the representation method. It consists of structural (graph) data of a reactant and a product between which the correspondence of atoms has to be preserved. The perception and representation of the correspondence of atoms between the two structures is essential to reaction data. Only independent structural data of a reactant and a product without correspondence information are meaningless for the prediction of products or precursors. It is also an important factor for automatic acquisition of reaction knowledge (transforms) from reaction database. Further, various views are introduced to database search by categorizing constituent atoms according to their contribution to the reaction.

Transforms

Reaction data are fact data derived from the real world where the real chemical reaction occurs, and the data describes the forward transformation from a reactant to a product. On the other hand, retrosynthesis, which is the objective of the synthesis planning system, infers successive precursors backward from a target to available starting materials by using "transforms." A transform represents a backward transformation of structures from a product to a reactant. Specifically, a transform is a collection of knowledge about backward transformation with various scopes and limitations giving constraints for transform application. A collection of transforms makes a knowledge base of production rules. A sufficient quantity of transforms would make it possible to infer precursors successively from any given target to available starting materials.

A transform is written in an English-like chemical language CHMTRN in LHASA. It has been developed so that a synthetic chemist can edit a transform easily. A transform in the form of CHMTRN is compiled into a form that can be read by the inference engine of LHASA. A sample description written in CHMTRN is shown in Figure 1. A transform comprises four sections: The first is a header part which contains preliminary information like an identifier of the transform, a structural diagram of retrosynthetic transformation, and so on. Key functional goups and a default rating value are also specified. The structural information specified here is called "retron." The transform is applied to the target if the retron is found in the target. Rating is a scalar value (certainty factor) which indicates the relevancy or favorability of the transform application. The second section is qualifiers or modifiers which give descriptions of scope and limitations. Qualifiers are a collection of queries that specify structural contexts and associated rating modifications or transform elimination. A qualifier is described in the form of IF–THEN expression, where the IF part contains the structural context and the THEN part is for the associated rating increment/decrement. The increment/decrement of a rating value is determined by the organic chemist who writes the transform, that is, the rating is based on his/her empirical knowledge. This may become a critical problem for transform-based systems. Building a knowledge base with a uniform quality of transforms over a

```
       TRANSFORM 117
       NAME MICHAEL ADDITION OF HETERO NUCLEOPHILE
...HET-C-C-W => HET-H + C=C-W
       ...MARCH 585; HOUSE 596; B+P 468
       ...ORG. RXNS. VOL.5, 79-135 (1949)
       ...BULL. SOC. CHEM. FR. 254,325 (1962)
       ...PATH 2 BONDS
       RATING 50      ...Old rating 40
       GROUP*1 MUST BE KETONE OR CYANO OR ESTER OR ACID
          OR LACTONE OR AMIDE*3 OR AMIDE*2 OR AMIDE*1
          OR LACTAM OR VINYLW OR ALDEHYDE
       GROUP*2 MUST BE ETHER OR AMINE*1 OR AMINE*2 OR AMINE*3
          OR SULFIDE OR THIOL
       STUDENT
       REMOVES*STEREO CARBON2*1 ATOM*2
       BROKEN*BONDS BOND2*1

       ...
       KILL IF NO HYDROGEN ON ATOM*2
              ...REQUIRED FOR REACTION
       KILL IF MULTIPLE BOND ON ATOM*2 OFFPATH OR: ON ATOM*3 OFFPATH
              ...WOULD PRODUCE ALLENIC PRECURSOR
       IF BOND2*1 IS NOT IN A RING OF SIZE 5 THROUGH 7  &
          THEN KILL IF BOND2*1 IS IN A RING
       SUBTRACT 15 IF LEAVING GROUP ON ATOM*3
              ...POSSIBLE ELIMINATION
       ADD 15 IF ANOTHER WITHDRAWING BOND ON ATOM*2
              ...EASIER ADDITION
       SUBTRACT 15 FOR EACH WITHDRAWING BOND ON ATOM*3
              ...UNDESIRED MICHAEL POSSIBLE
       SUBTRACT 10 IF ATOM*3 IS A TERTIARY*CENTER
       IF NOT OLEFIN ON BOND*2 THEN KILL IF ATOM*2 IS NOT ENOLIZABLE
              ...STABLE ENOL PROVIDES DRIVING FORCE
       IF SECOND GROUP IS ETHER THEN CONDITIONS NaOR
       IF SECOND GROUP IS AMINE THEN CONDITIONS RNH2
       IF SECOND GROUP IS SULFIDE OR: THIOL THEN  &
          CONDITIONS NaSR

       ....
          BREAK BOND2*1
          JOIN ATOM*2 AND ATOM*3
       ....
```

FIGURE 1   A sample transform entry from the LHASA knowledge base. (Reprinted with permission from Ref. 6.)

wide range of organic chemistry is very difficult, as each rating value depends entirely on individual writers of the transform. The third section describes reaction conditions which are used to evaluate functional group interference when the transform is applied. A cross-reference table which describes the reactivity of functional groups to the reagent library is prepared to support the evaluation. Further, functional groups are categorized into several generic classes which are given generalized notations. The final section specifies a mechanism which describes the operations, like BREAK BOND2*1, for transforming the target structure to the precursor one. These four sections are delimited by isolated dotted lines in Figure 1.

Strategies and Knowledge-Base Structurization

A collection of transforms makes up the central part of the knowledge base in LHASA. An appropriate transform should be selected from the knowledge base to generate successive precursors from a given target. The opportunistic application of transforms results in combinatorial explosion easily, so a kind of control mechanism for selecting a transform is needed. There are two aspects in the solution of transform selection: strategies and structurization of the knowledge base. Five types of strategies are prepared in LHASA, and the knowledge base is structurized according to the types of strategies. A strategy is selected based on the extracted feature of the target, although the selection itself is performed by the user (a chemist). Once a strategy is set up, the corresponding access path is focused on the subdivision of the entire knowledge base. The knowledge base is characterized by two factors: the power and the function of transforms. The power gives the degree of the simplification realized by the transform, whereas the function means the transformational effects on the target structure such as connection, disconnection, rearrangement, interchange, transposition, removal, addition, inversion, and so on. These functions give a variety of search views to the knowledge base. Correspondingly, transforms are organized according to these attributes to enable actual access from any of these views. The five types of strategies are transform-based strategies, structure-goal strategies, topological strategies, stereochemical strategies, and functional-group-oriented strategies.

Transforms are organized to accept these types of strategies. Transform-based strategies need some powerful simplifying transforms. These transforms, called key transforms, correspond to powerful synthetic "reactions" reliably used. So, often the application of a key transform is specified as a strategic goal. This is called a "transform" goal or a "T-goal," and plays an important role in the long-range search. When some key transform is selected as a T-goal, the corresponding retron is searched for in the target. Usually, the retron required for the key transform will not be present in its entirety, and so a multistep look-ahead process is needed for the application of the transform. Further, there may be several potential locations in the target for the retron, so all the possible mappings between the retron and the target have to be examined. Structure-goal, or S-goal, strategies may be used if a structure of a potential starting material or retron-containing substructures could be identified, where a bidirectional search technique can be used. However, this does not always correspond to the structurization of transforms. Topological strategies utilize mainly ring-oriented transforms which disconnect particular bonds in ring systems, then lead to major skeletal simplification of the target. These particular bonds, called strategic bonds, may appear in ring systems or as connectors to appendages at rings, functional groups, or chiral centers. The heuristic criteria for recognizing strategic bonds are prepared as empirical knowledge. Similarly, strategic rings that should be disassembled or be preserved intact during retrosynthesis may be recognized. Sterospecific transforms are prepared to treat stereochemistry. Stereospecific transforms operate on the target to remove stereocenters. Functional-group-based transforms are used for functional-group-oriented strategy. This type of transform performs functional group modifications such as interconversion, addition, or removal. These are not simplifying transforms but are used to adjust the target to the retron of the other key transform to be applied. They are also used to reduce the reactivity of the target to reagents, where one refers to the functional groups/reagent cross-reference table.

An example of an LHASA session is shown in Figures 2 and 3. Figure 2a shows the screen for target structure input, and Figure 2b shows the menu for the user to specify structural perception, strategy selection, and so on. Figure 3a shows the result of the transform application, where a double arrow indicates retrosynthesis, whereas a single arrow indicates forward synthesis. Figure 3b displays a retrosynthesic tree, in which precursors are indicated by numbered nodes.

It is said that LHASA is most prospective among many computer-assisted synthesis planning systems (8); however, some tough problems remain for the future. For instance,

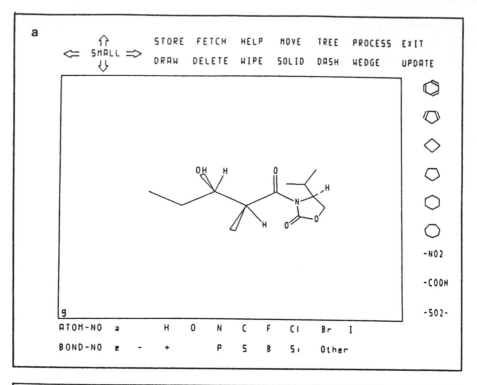

FIGURE 2   LHASA session: (a) Structure input screen. (b) Menu for tactics selection. (Reprinted with permission from Ref. 6.)

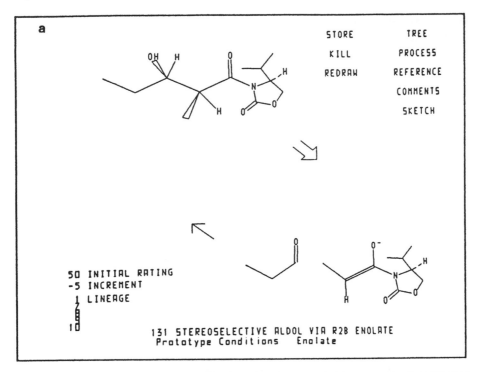

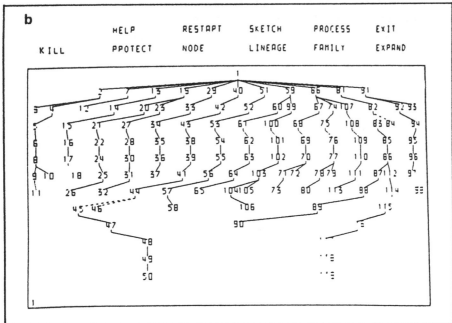

FIGURE 3   (a) LHASA precursor display. (b) LHASA retrosynthetic tree display. (Reprinted with permission from Ref. 6.)

automatic strategy selection and knowledge acquisition are of vital importance for the practical use of the system. In fact, two consortia of chemical and pharmaceutical companies are involved in the task of building a knowledge base: LHASA UK in the United Kingdom and CASAG in the United States. A similar consortium of Swiss and German phamaceutical companies, named CASP, is also active to build a knowledge (transform) base, which is an offshoot of SECS.

EROS

EROS (Elaboration of Reactions for Organic Synthesis) (9,10) is a logic-oriented deductive rule-based system which works in both forward synthesis and retrosynthesis. Here logic-oriented means that the system generates precursors/products by mechanistic applications of a small number of elementary reaction rules, called "formal reaction schemes," rather than by the application of rules (transforms) derived from known reactions. Because the application of the formal reaction schemes needs no structural contexts, combinatorial explosion may take place very quickly. Therefore, various evaluation methods are prepared to control precursor/product generation.

Formal Reaction Scheme

The basic formal reaction scheme in EROS is breaking two bonds and making two bonds, shown in Figure 4. These two bonds may be contained in two different molecules in a reaction system. Because a majority of organic reactions, like addition, rearrangement, elimination, substitution, or various electrocyclic reactions, follows this scheme, EROS employs the formal reaction scheme as a main rule for mechanistic inference. In other words, EROS is founded on a mathematical model of constitutional chemistry. Molecular structures and chemical reactions are represented as follows in the model.

A molecular structure is captured as a graph with a set of atoms and bonds between the atoms represented by a set of nodes and edges. Further, the sum of free and binding

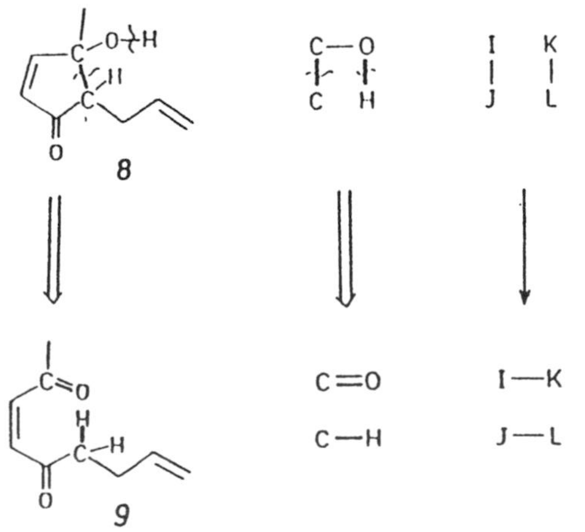

FIGURE 4   EROS basic formal reaction scheme. (Reprinted with permission from Ref. 10.)

electrons is taken to be constant. This graph is represented by a so-called "BE-matrix" (bond and electron matrix), which corresponds to an adjacency matrix. The off-diagonal values of a BE-matrix give the bond orders between the two respective atoms, and the diagonal elements represents the number of free electrons on the corresponding atoms.

A chemical reaction is represented by two matrices, one for a reactant and the other for a product. However, the essential part of the reaction is the substructure that changes between the two molecules. This is represented by the difference matrix between the two matrices, called the "R-matrix" (reaction matrix). Let B and E denote the BE-matrices of a reactant and a product, respectively, and let R be an R-matrix. Then $R = E - B$. R-matrices are considered to represent the redistribution of bonds and electrons in a reaction. These bond and electron shiftings can be formulated and categorized into several classes. The most central class is the one shown already in Figure 4. If R is added to B, then E is gained $(B + R = E)$. On the other hand, if R is subtracted from E, and B is obtained $(E - R = B)$. Thus, the bidirectional search of synthesis paths (forward and backward synthesis) is possible using the formal reaction schemes. In Figure 4, an abstract form of breaking/making bond rearrangement process is shown at the rightmost as atoms I, J, K, and L. This abstract form of reaction is the formal reaction scheme. Other types of formal schemes are shown in Figure 5. These are all the rules used in EROS, which does not need known reaction data or empirical knowledge for inference. It can generate precursors/products mechanistically and exhaustively by the application of these formal reaction schemes from a given target/starting material. The rules applied are elementary, so it can generate novel reactions as well as known reactions, which is difficult for systems using known data or transforms. Further, it is free from building and maintaining a database/knowledge base. However, it has a disadvantage due to the approach of a simple rule base. A combinatorial explosion occurs quickly because the number of possible reaction sites can become very large. Further, most of the resulted precursors/products could be meaningless. Thus, the evaluation methods for chemically feasible application of rules become very important for EROS.

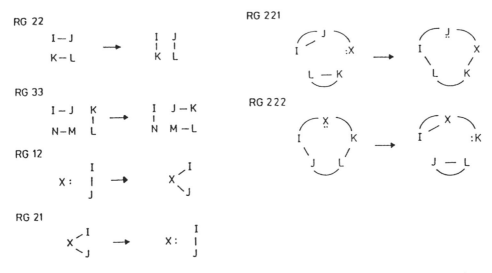

FIGURE 5 Formal reaction schemes contained in EROS. (Reprinted with permission from Ref. 10.)

Evaluations

Many factors participate in the evaluation process. The classification of evaluations, which is categorized according to objects and views, is shown in Figure 6. It shows that an evaluation method corresponds to the combination of objects (molecule, reaction, or overall synthesis) and views (physicochemical, economic, strategies, toxic, etc.). These different types of evaluation methods are used independently in EROS, so it can treat different types of problems such as those of laboratory scales, biological systems, or industrial processes. Each evaluation method is based on the respective chemistry model, which is classified as physicochemical or statistical. The following describes how physicochemical effects are quantified as evaluation models. The cause of combinatorial explosion in synthesis reasoning is the presence of multiple reaction sites in a molecular structure to which the rules are applied. It would be convenient if a certain "reactivity" value were assigned to each bond of a molecule because the application of the rules could be strictly controled by the order of the reactivity value. However, there are no known general methods available for this objective. One of the goals of the EROS project is to develop such models to give a kind of reactivity values quantitatively. Some of the measures are heats of reaction, bond dissociation energies, partial atomic charges, inductive and resonance effects, polarizability, and so on.

1. Heats of reaction: Give the enthalpy part of the overall thermodynamic expression of chemical reactions. The calculation of the enthalpy is based on the so-called additivity scheme. In this case, the sum of parameters assigned to relevant substructures in the molecule give the total enthalpy:

$$\Delta H_r = \sum \Delta H_f^{\circ} \text{ (product)} - \sum \Delta H_f^{\circ} \text{ (reactant)}.$$

This is the model for heats of reaction. The substructure contributions parameterized are from 1,2-interactions (bonds) and 1,3-interactions not involving hydrogen atoms.

2. Bond dissociation energies (BDE): This is calculated as the enthalpy entailed in homolysis of a bond:

$$A - B \rightarrow A\cdot + B\cdot,$$
$$BDE(AB) = \Delta H_r.$$

This is the model of BDE, and a procedure is prepared for the calculation, which includes effects of ring strain, aromatic delocalization energies, and so on. The estimation of heats of reaction and BDE gives an indication of feasibility of homolytic processes.

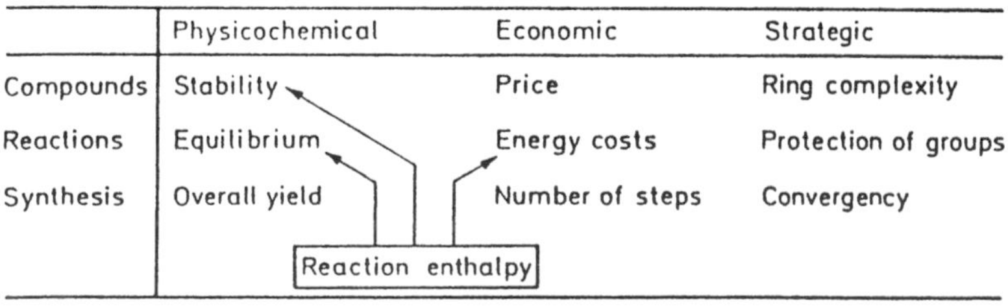

	Physicochemical	Economic	Strategic
Compounds	Stability	Price	Ring complexity
Reactions	Equilibrium	Energy costs	Protection of groups
Synthesis	Overall yield	Number of steps	Convergency
	Reaction enthalpy		

FIGURE 6   Classification of evaluations. (Reprinted with permission from Ref. 10.)

3. Electronic effects: Give a model for heterolytic processes. The basic model is shown in Figure 7, where partial atomic charge (q), electronegativity (χ), and polarizability (α) calculated for each atom in a molecule together reflect the particular molecular environment into which the atom is embedded. These electronic parameters are considered to give the reactivity of a bond (i.e., a pair of atoms). The types of electronic effects are partial atomic charge, inductive effect, resonance effect, polarizability effect, hyperconjugation, and frontier molecular orbital approach.

4. Statistical model: The electronic effects listed above are used as individual physicochemical parameters, and each calculation method gives the corresponding model. However, some kinds of property are not always fully modeled only by a single parameter; that is, there are properties that need a combination of several parameters (called multiparameter). For instance, proton affinity (PA) of hetero-substituted amine is expressed as

$$PA(amine) = 343.0 - 27.9\,\overline{\chi}_{12} + 2.99\alpha_d$$

which is calculated by two factors $\overline{\chi}_{12}$ ($= 0.5\,(\overline{\chi}_1 + 0.25\,\overline{\chi}_2)$) and α_d. Similarly, it is shown that PAs of alcohol, ether, thiol, and thioether are also calculated by the two parameters $\overline{\chi}_{12}$ and $2.99\alpha_d$. In addition, the gas-phase acidity of alcohol is shown to be modeled with the two parameters. It is reported that the combination of three factors, conductive effects, polarizability, and hyperconjugation, gives the expression of protonation reaction of ketones and aldehydes. Furthermore, the multiparameter is extended to add resonance stabilization effects of hetero-substituents and unsaturated substituents.

5. General model: The multiparameter statistical models have a limitation for direct use for EROS, which necessitates statistical treatment for each case. Thus, a general model of chemical reactivity is devised to give a unified measurement of evaluation. The general model is intended to derive a single evaluation function which takes a domain of any combination of parameters. Thus, a function-quantifying chemical reactivity is defined in the reactivity space of parameters as the probability of bond breaking (P) that is obtained by applying logistic regression analysis (LoRA):

$$P = 1/(1 + e^{-f}),$$
$$f = c_0 + c_1x_1 + c_2x_2 + \cdots c_nx_n,$$

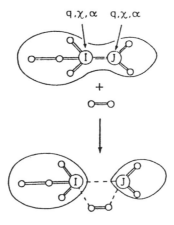

FIGURE 7   Basic mode of reactivity in EROS. (Reprinted with permission from Ref. 10.)

where x_i represent the relevant parameters. The coefficients c_i are determined so as to fit P as close as possible to the initial value P_0. The initial probability P_0 is given as a binary classification value (breakable/nonbreakable, represented by 1/0, respectively), and the calculated probability P is a continuous one; that is, the evaluation function that gives the reactivity quantitatively from qualitative value (breakable/nonbreakable) is obtained. The actual procedure for obtaining the function is as follows: (1) assign a set of selected bonds 1/0 value as breakable/nonbreakable for a set of molecules (a training set); (2) input these binary data with their calculated physicochemical property values such as BDE, Δq, Δx, α_d, and so on; (3) determine the optimal functions f and P by LoRA. The calculated function f is called the reactivity function. Although the reactivity function obtained this way has a general characteristic; some reactivity features are omitted from consideration. Heuristic rules are supported in EROS to treat such cases (the hydrogen atom and its proton at a special position, and reaction conditions are typical examples).

SYNGEN

SYNGEN (Synthesis Generation) (11,12) is also a logic-oriented synthesis planning system which, like EROS, performs inference both in forward and retrosynthetic directions. It generates products/precursors mechanistically by applying a small number of elementary reaction rules (unit reaction) rather than resorting to known reaction data or transforms. Here, also, combinatorial explosion becomes a serious problem. The criterion employed in SYNGEN to select optimal paths in synthetic tree is economy, that is, the shortest and most cost-effective synthetic paths are searched.

Representation of Chemical Structures and Reactions

A chemical structure is represented by a graph in SYNGEN. The adjacency matrix is coded uniquely by using its own algorithm, where the skeleton and functionality are treated separately (13). The skeleton of a graph is represented by the upper half of the adjacency matrix, and the functionality is represented as an added row to the matrix which contains attributes of constituent atoms of the skeleton. This added functionality row is used for atom ordering when double bonds and/or heteroatoms are included in the structure. A kind of generalized property is introduced as an attribute of carbon atoms. Assuming that the skeleton of a molecule is constituted by carbon atoms, carbon atoms are categorized into the following four types according to the connectivity of the atom with its attched atoms:

H: hydrogen atom attached
R: another carbon atom attached with a σ-bond
Π: another carbon atom attached with a π-bond
Z: electronegative hetero (N, O, S, X) attatched with a σ- or π-bond

The number of each type of attachment is denoted by h, σ, π, and z, respectively (they sum up to 4). A functional group on a carbon is represented by a string of two digits, $z\pi$ ($z = 0\text{--}4$, $\pi = 0\text{--}2$). A $z\pi$-list is defined as a list of $z\pi$ values of each carbon which is ordered according to atom numbering. The oxidation state (x) is also defined as $x = z - h$ for each carbon. This enables the change of a reaction state of a reaction to be calculated easily. Reaction is described as the exchange of attributes HRΠZ of carbon atoms that participate to the reaction. This exchange of attributes is called a "unit reaction." The unit reaction is represented by two letters, the first one for bond making and the second for bond breaking. There are 16 possible unit reactions on any one carbon. The representation scheme of chemical structures and reactions are shown in Figure 8, where 16 formal unit reactions are indicated which correspond to conventional reaction categories such as oxidation, reduction, and so on. It also shows that, for instance, there are three unit reactions, RH, RZ, RΠ, for the construction reaction, which are counterparts of fragmentation HR, ZR, ΠR, respectively. The unit reactions that are sought by SYNGEN are these construction (bond making) reactions. The reactions that make bonds can be represented as the change of functionality on the two carbon atoms that participate that bond-making reaction. Each side of the functionality change on the two carbon atoms is called a "half-reaction." All the reactions are represented by the combinations of two half-reactions, nucleophilic and electrophilic ones. The reaction site of a half-reaction ranges over three consecutive carbons, labeled α, β, and γ from the bond constructed as shown in Figure 9. Half-reactions that are possible within the ranges are also listed below the carbons in Figure 9. All the bond constructions are realized through the combination of half-reactions of each side of the bond. For instance, the change of the π-bond to the σ-bond of β-carbon in Michael addition is represented as HΠ. The bond construction accompanies an update of the zπ-list.

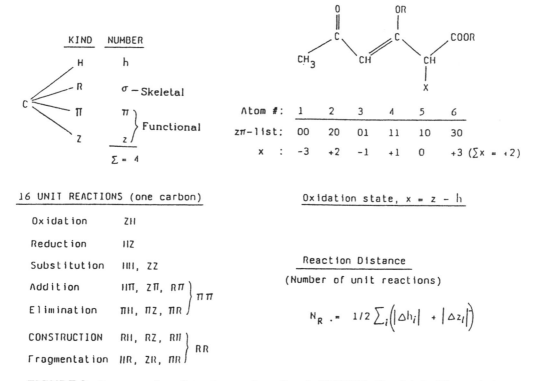

FIGURE 8 Representation of structures and reactions in SYNGEN. (Reprinted with permission from Ref. 11.)

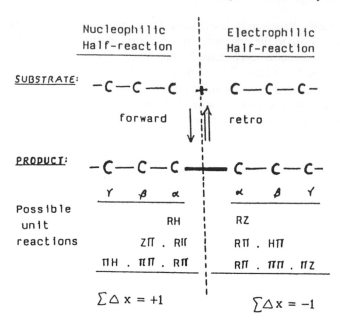

FIGURE 9   Generalized form of construction reactions in SYNGEN. (Reprinted with permission from Ref. 11.)

Half-Reactions

As mentioned earlier, rules for forward/retrosynthesis are represented in terms of half-reactions in SYNGEN. It generates products/precursors by mechanistic application of half-reactions to a starting material/target, not resorting to a database or knowledge base. The construction half-reactions, like RH, RZ, RΠ, described above are called basic half-reactions. These basic half-reactions bring about two shortcomings due to the simplicity.

First, there is a type of construction, called a composite construction, that cannot be simulated by the basic half-reactions. A composite construction is composed of a basic unit reaction coupled with a refunctionalization unit reaction in its original position. This lack of expressiveness of rules is caused by excessive generalization of reactions. In order to treat this shortcoming, the basic half-reactions are subdivided in terms of the functionality level ($z + \pi$) of α-carbon, which means specialization of abstract (basic) half-reactions. This specialization results in the 25 half-reactions shown in Figure 10. Sixteen of those half-reactions in groups I, II, and III are nucleophilic, and 9 half-reactions in group IV are electrophilic, which give 114 full construction reactions. (Although $16 \times 9 = 144$ reactions are possible combinatorially, 30 reactions are rejected chemically.) These are the contents of the SYNGEN rule base. Each half-reaction is given a label of two letters: the first for the functionality level ($z + \pi$) of α-carbon, the second for the span of carbon (1–3) which indicates the range of reaction site (α β γ). (Several exceptions are applied to the definition of the two letters.) The half-reactions shown in Figure 10 correspond well to the conventional categories of reactions.

Second, many chemically meaningless products/precursors are generated by the simple application of half-reactions. Therefore, the mechanistic test facility is supported in SYNGEN for evaluation. This is explained in the subsection Evaluation.

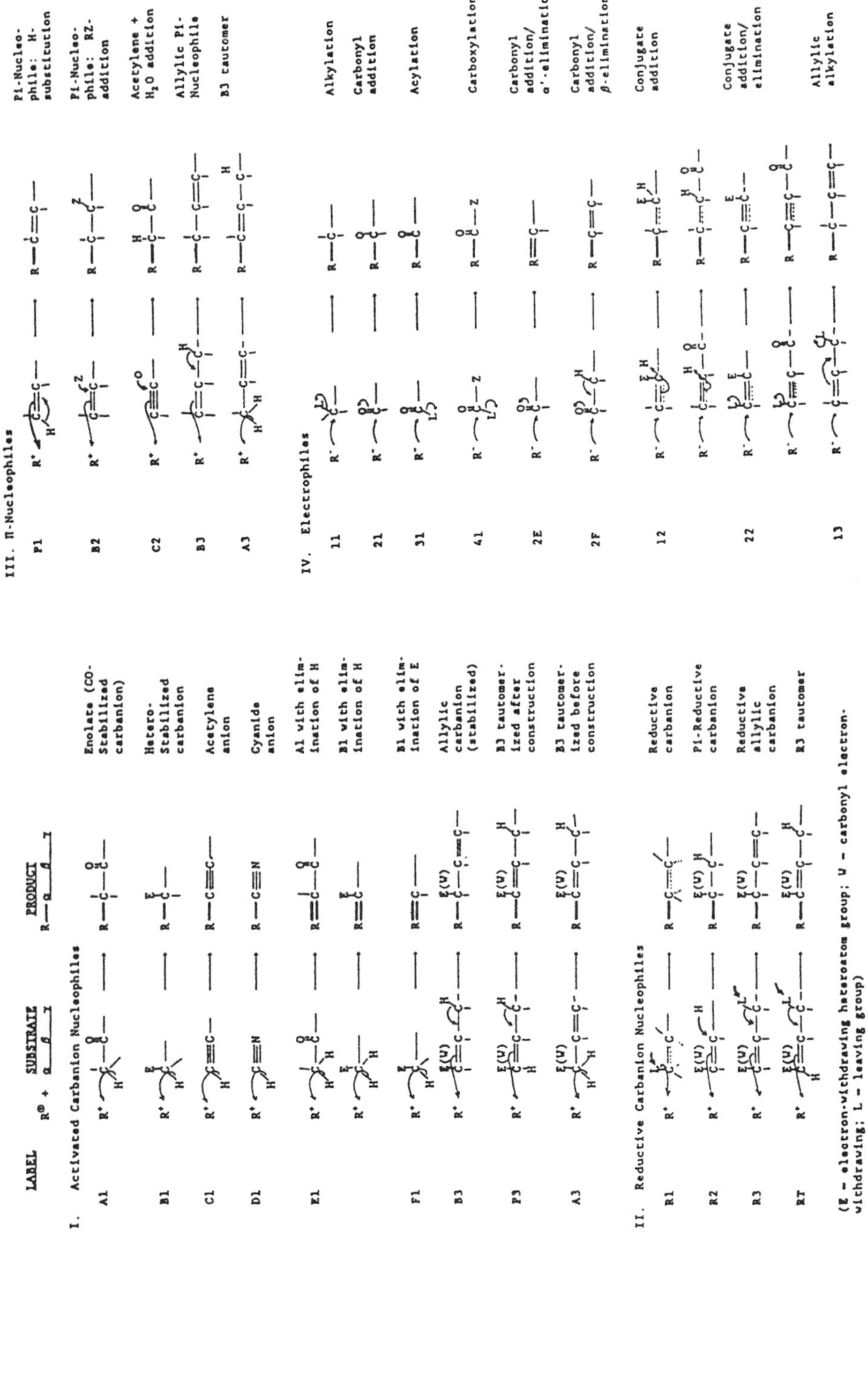

FIGURE 10 Half-reactions used in SYNGEN. (Reprinted with permission from Ref. 12.)

Planning Procedure

The procedure of synthetic planning by SYNGEN is as follows:

1.   Partition a target structure into four substructures. First, a target is divided into two substructures, then each of the substructures is divided into two. The broken bonds in this partition process make a "bondset." This process is performed so that divided parts become the members of available materials (6000 materials are cataloged in SYN-GEN). In other words, a bondset which gives four available materials is searched, where the number of bonds in the bondset is maximally six. The bonds in the bondset are ordered.

2.   The functionality of a target structure is defined as a $z\pi$-list of three atoms from the bond in question. The $z\pi$-list of a precursor is obtained by adding the $\Delta z\pi$-list of each half-reaction to the $z\pi$-list of the target, where the condition $z + \pi \leq 4 - \sigma$ is required, and the pair of half-reactions that are applied to each side of the bond has to be composed of one nucleophilic and one electrophilic half-reaction. This process allows the precursors generated by isohypic bond construction to be defined in terms of the $z\pi$-list. (Each half-reaction has its own $\Delta z\pi$-list expressed as an attribute vector, which works as a reaction operator to a reaction site.)

3.   The bond in question is set to the bondset bond of the next order. Then procedure 2 is applied recursively to the resulting substructures including the obtained precursors. When these processes are completed for all the bondset bonds, four starting materials have been reached. If the four materials are found in the SYNGEN catalog of 6000 compounds, the synthetic paths just found are concluded as successful.

Evaluation

A simple application of half-reactions to a target results in a number of meaningless precursors. The reasons are twofold: First, there are cases in which some activating functional groups are required to exist but not to change themselves during the construction. Functional groups of this kind are not described in half-reactions. Second, synthetic paths can be deviated by the presence of some functional groups. In short, the effects of the surrounding substructures of a reaction site have to be taken into account. This can be checked to some extent by introducing a rough model of the reaction mechanism. This evaluation method is realized in SNYGEN by incorporating a procedure, called a "mechanism test," for each half-reaction. The mechanism tests consist of two kinds: "require" and "reject." The "require" is a test with respect to required topological situation of surroundings, like the presence of functional groups of the first type mentioned above; the "reject" is a test about the presence of unfavorable functional groups or interfering side effects. It is too rough to generalize electronegative heteroatoms altogether into Z to realize these mechanism tests. Thus, the mechanistic function, called "z-function," is defined as the subclass of Z in addition to the kind of attached atom (N, O, S, X). The value of z-functions are E for electron withdrawing, O for electron donating, L for electron leaving, and W for electron withdrawing with a multiple bond (e.g., $C=O$, $C=N$). When a heteroatom is a member of a skeleton, a $\Delta z\pi$-list of half-reactions is treated similar to a carbon atom, but z-functions are differently utilized.

A site of a half-reaction is remodeled so that the skeleton consists of four atoms which are labeled α, β, β', and γ. β'-carbon is a branching atom from α-carbon, which represents the surrounding substructure; γ is any carbon attached to β. As shown in Table 1, a checklist is prepared for four constituent atoms of a half-reaction site to indicate required (R) or reject (X). The generation of meaningless precursors are suppressed by

TABLE 1 Mechanism Test Checklist

no π	α							β							γ							β'						
	S	N	O	L	E	O	W	S	N	O	L	E	O	W	S	N	O	L	E	O	W	S	N	O	L	E	O	W
A1	R	R	R	—	—	—	X	R	—	—	X	—	—	R	—	—	—	—	—	—	—	R	—	—	X	—	—	R
B1	X	X	X	X	R	X	X	—	—	—	X	—	—	—	—	—	—	—	—	—	—	—	—	—	X	—	—	—
D1	X	R	R	—	R	—	R	—	X	—	—	—	—	—	—	—	—	—	—	—	—	—	—	—	—	—	—	—
R1	—	—	—	—	—	—	X	—	X	—	X	—	—	—	—	—	—	—	—	—	—	—	X	—	X	—	—	—
11	X	X	X	X	X	X	X	X	X	X	—	—	—	—	—	—	—	—	—	—	—	—	X	X	—	—	—	—
21	—	—	—	—	R	—	X	—	—	—	—	—	—	—	—	—	—	—	—	—	—	X	—	X	—	—	—	—
31	—	X	—	R	R	R	R	—	—	—	—	—	—	—	—	—	—	—	—	—	—	—	—	—	—	—	—	—
41	X	—	—	R	X	R	R	X	X	X	—	X	R	X	X	X	—	—	—	—	—	—	X	—	—	—	—	—
B2	X	X	X	X	X	X	X	X	X	X	R	X	R	R	R	R	X	—	—	—	X	X	X	X	—	—	—	R
B2H	X	X	X	X	X	X	X	X	X	X	R	X	X	R	R	R	R	—	X	—	X	X	X	X	—	—	—	X
C2	X	R	R	X	—	X	X	X	X	X	X	X	X	R	—	—	—	—	—	—	X	—	X	X	X	—	—	X
R2	X	—	—	X	—	X	X	X	X	X	X	X	—	X	X	X	—	X	—	—	X	X	—	X	—	—	—	—
12	X	X	R	—	—	—	X	X	R	X	—	R	X	X	X	X	X	—	—	—	—	X	—	X	—	—	—	—
12H	X	X	X	X	R	X	X	X	X	R	X	X	X	X	X	X	X	—	—	—	X	X	—	X	—	—	—	—
12C	X	X	X	X	X	X	X	X	X	X	X	—	—	X	—	X	X	—	—	—	R	X	—	X	—	—	—	—
π(αα')																												
E1	—	R	—	R	R	—	X	—	—	—	X	—	—	R	—	—	—	—	—	—	—	—	—	—	X	—	—	R
F1	X	X	X	—	—	X	X	—	—	—	X	—	—	—	—	—	—	—	—	—	—	—	—	—	X	—	—	—
2E	X	X	X	X	X	X	X	X	X	X	—	—	—	—	—	—	—	—	—	—	—	X	X	X	—	—	—	—
π(αβ)																												
P1	X	X	X	X	—	X	X	X	X	X	X	X	X	X	X	X	—	—	—	—	X	X	X	X	X	—	—	—
P1H	X	X	X	X	X	X	X	X	X	X	—	—	—	X	—	—	—	—	—	—	—	X	X	X	X	—	—	—
R1	X	X	X	—	—	—	X	X	X	X	X	X	—	X	X	X	X	X	—	—	X	—	X	—	X	—	—	—
R2	X	X	X	X	R	X	X	X	X	X	X	X	—	X	—	—	X	X	—	—	X	—	X	X	—	—	—	R
B2	X	X	X	—	—	X	X	X	X	X	R	X	R	X	—	—	—	—	X	X	X	X	X	X	—	—	—	—
12	X	X	X	X	X	X	X	X	X	X	X	R	X	X	X	X	X	X	X	X	R	—	—	—	—	—	—	X
12H	X	R	X	X	X	X	X	X	X	X	X	X	X	X	X	X	X	X	—	—	—	—	—	—	—	—	—	—
12C	X	—	R	X	X	—	X	X	R	X	X	—	X	X	X	X	—	X	—	—	—	—	—	—	X	X	—	X
22	X	R	—	—	—	X	X	X	—	R	—	R	X	X	—	—	X	X	—	—	R	—	X	X	X	X	—	X
2F	X	—	R	X	X	X	X	X	R	R	—	—	X	X	R	R	—	X	X	—	—	X	X	X	—	X	—	—
P3	X	X	—	R	R	X	X	X	—	X	X	X	—	X	X	X	X	R	X	X	R	X	X	X	X	—	—	R
A3	X	X	R	R	R	X	X	X	R	R	—	—	—	X	X	R	—	R	X	—	—	—	X	X	—	X	—	R
A3C	X	X	—	R	R	X	X	X	—	X	X	X	X	X	X	R	X	R	X	—	X	—	X	X	X	—	—	—
RT	X	X	X	—	—	X	X	X	X	X	X	X	—	X	X	R	X	R	X	—	X	—	X	X	—	—	—	R
π(βγ)																												
B3	X	X	X	X	X	X	X	X	X	X	—	X	—	X	X	R	—	—	X	—	X	X	X	X	—	—	—	X
B3H	X	R	R	R	R	—	X	X	X	X	—	X	—	X	R	R	—	X	X	—	X	R	X	X	X	—	—	R
R3	X	R	R	—	R	—	X	X	X	X	—	X	—	X	R	R	—	—	X	—	X	X	X	X	X	—	—	R
A1H	X	X	X	X	X	X	X	X	X	X	—	—	—	X	R	R	X	X	X	X	X	X	—	—	X	—	—	X
13	X	—	X	—	X	—	X	X	—	X	—	—	—	X	X	X	—	—	—	—	X	—	X	—	—	—	—	—

Source: Reprinted with permission from Ref. 12.

looking up this table before applying half-reactions. This model of a half-reaction suggests the importance of the representation level of reaction rules.

SYNTREX

This is a database-oriented (or case-based) synthesis planning system, which utilizes instances of reaction data for reasoning precursors/products rather than abstract reaction rules (14). Synthesis planning in SYNTREX is carried out by searching similar instances automatically to fit the target. This automatic fitting mechanism is not yet incorporated in SYNTREX but is performed through the interaction with the user.

Representation of Reactions

Reaction data are composed of summary data and a reaction scheme. The former is string (text) data, containing reaction conditions, reagent name, catalyst, solvent, and so on; the latter is represented in the form of a reaction connection table. A reaction connection table is a compacted form of connection tables of a reactant and a product, in which the correspondence of atoms between the two is preserved, and the description of an atom that does not change connectivity through the reaction is unified to a single common entry.

Structural information is classified and represented so as to allow a variety of search views:

1. Atoms: Atoms in a reactant and a product are classified according to the extent of their contribution to the reaction. The most central is called reacting atoms (i.e., reaction center), which are defined strictly as atoms that are present in both a reactant and a product and that changed adjacency. The next classes are for added atoms in a product and for eliminated atoms in a reactant. The last class is for atoms whose adjacency is unchanged through the reaction.

2. Rings: A ring is represented by an attribute list which consists of ring size, the number of heteroatoms, the number of oxygen, the number of sulfur, the number of nitrogen, path length between heteroatoms (1,2 and 1,3), and type of ring system (single, spiro, fused, bridged, composite of these, aromatic). However, it is not a cannonical representation sufficient for practical use. Rings represented by these attributes are then classified according to the relationship to reacting atoms: rings reconstructed (broken, expanded, contracted, newly constructed, reconstructed to the same size); rings whose constituency is unchanged through the reaction but contain reacting atoms; rings that do not contain reacting atoms, and are present in both a reactant and a product. This classification is applied to a reactant and a product, respectively.

3. Functional groups: In SYTREX, a functional group is defined rather mechanically as a substructure which consists of a heteroatom and its adjacent atoms. A larger functional group is represented by the combination of the primitive representation. These functional groups are classified according to the relationship to reacting atoms the same way as rings. However, the definition of reacting atoms is extended so that eliminated/added atoms are included, which allows one to take into account the contribution of surrounding atoms of functional groups to the reaction.

4. Reaction sites. A reaction site consists of reacting atoms and their adjacent eliminated/added atoms. Because both functional groups and a reaction site consist of central (hetero/reacting) atoms and their adjacent atoms, their codes are obtained easily

by ordering attribute lists of atoms. These codes of rings, functional groups, and reaction sites are used as index files for the reaction database.

Retrieval and Planning

The procedure for reaction retrieval and planning is as follows:

1.   Give a reaction scheme as a query; that is, both the structures of a reactant and a product are input, preserving the correspondence of atoms between the two.

2.   Extract structural features of the query from the viewpoint of reaction sites, functional groups, and rings, respectively. They are coded for index search.

3.   Set up a retrieval mode to either the product condition, or the precursor condition or the reaction condition. Either forward synthesis or retrosynthesis can be done interactively according to the mode. When forward search is required, the precursor mode is specified and the product part of the query is ignored; so the reactant part ignored for retrosynthesis. When the both a reactant and a product are specified to be searched, the retrieval instance would give the remaining reaction data, that is, reaction condition. In any case, the retrieval is performed with respect to the whole structure. Thus, the synthetic paths searched by SYNTREX is the sequence of reaction instances from the database.

4.   Set up retrieval level. When the query is a new target that has not yet been synthesized, or a new synthesis path is desired, the query for the whole structure explained above is issued in vain because, apparently, the query structure itself or the synthesis path (i.e., reaction data) does not exist in the database in its entirety. In order to circumvent this problem, a kind of abstract query structure has to be accepted by the system. The retrieval level concerning functional groups, rings, and reaction sites is introduced for this purpose. This give a partial matching mechanism for structure search in the database, where the query substructure is set up, layered starting with the reacting atoms. The most generalized query is composed of reacting atoms only, and the search is done for reaction data that have these reacting atoms. The larger the query substructure becomes, the more specialized is the search. The partial matching mechanism mentioned above allows, to some extent, the similarity-based search of reaction data, which cannot be realized by exact matching of a whole structure. The retrieval levels are specified for reaction sites, functional groups, and rings. For reaction sites, there are four levels of matching: null structure which means that the matching is not attempted for reaction sites, atom type, atom type with bond multiplicity, and a whole site. For functional groups, there are two levels: one for functional groups that contains reacting atoms, and the other for those that do not contain reacting atoms. For rings, eight levels can be specified by the combination of two kind of views. One of the views specifies whether the ring contains reacting atoms or not, which give two cases. Another specifies one of the four attributes of a ring: ring size, type of ring systems, aromaticity, and a full code of the ring.

SYNTREX allows a user to specify a variety of views for reaction search as described above. Particularly, the focusing mechanism for controlling the range of a query substructure is essential, which allows an inductive synthesis planning feature by searching similar instances of reaction data. In other words, it realizes the synthesis planning system based on case-based reasoning, though the search strategy has to be set up by the user. As the query specification is totally committed to the user, the interactive session of SYNTREX is critical for practical use of the system. This is actually a highly intelligent process which is expected to be incorporated in the future, as LHASA's automatic strategy selection.

PROSPECT

Computer-assisted synthesis planning system has a long history of development. At the first stage, it was called a simulation system or organic synthesis, and is now called an expert system. In fact, it is an expert system as long as it works as if an organic chemist does the synthesis design, in spite of the variation of implementations. On the other hand, the variation of the approaches suggests the difficulty of realizing a robust system. A number of computer-assisted synthesis planning systems is reported, and actually under development, involving database/knowledge-base building. However, all of these are still under development or prototypical, although they are claimed prospective (6). The major problems are the same as those difficulties that are common to the field of artificial intelligence; combinatorial explosion, knowledge acquisition, incomplete knowledge and data, similarity perception, intuition, and so on. Particularly, chemical reactions are very diverse and complex. For instance, the number of compounds reported so far exceeds 10 million. As a matter of fact, synthesis planning is a difficult problem even for organic chemists due to the large size of the compound space. Thus, the development of computer-assisted synthesis planning systems is strongly desired in spite of its difficulties.

REFERENCES

1. Corey and W. Todd Wipke, "Computer-Assisted Design of Complex Organic Syntheses," *Science*, *166*, 178–192 (1969).
2. W. T. Wipke, H. Braun, G. Smith, F. Choplin, and W. Sieber, "SECS—Simulation and Evaluation of Chemical Synthesis: Strategy and Planning," in *Computer-Assisted Organic Synthesis*, ACS Symposium Series 61, W. T. Wipke and W. J. Howe (eds.), American Chemical Society, Washington, DC, 1977, pp. 97–127.
3. W. T. Wipke, Glenn I. Ouchi, and S. Krishnan, "Simulation and Evaluation of Chemical Synthesis—SECS: An Application of Artificial Intelligence Techniques," *Artificial Intelligence*, *11*, 173–193 (1978).
4. H. L. Gelernter, A. F. Sanders, D. L. Larsen, K. K. Agarwal, R. H. Boivie, G. A. Spritzer, and J. E. Searleman, "Empirical Exploration of SYNCHEM," *Science*, *197*, 1041–1049 (1977).
5. David A. Pensak and E. J. Corey, LHASA—Logic and Heuristics Applied to Synthetic Analysis," in *Computer-Assisted Organic Synthesis*, ACS Symposium Series 61, W. T. Wipke and W. J. Howe (eds.), American Chemical Society Washington, DC, 1977, pp. 1–32.
6. E. J. Corey, Alan K. Long, and Stewart D. Rubenstein, "Computer-Assisted Analysis in Organic Synthesis," *Science*, *228*, 408–418 (1985).
7. H. L. Morgan, "The Generation of a Unique Machine Description for Chemical Structures—A Technique Developed at Chemical Abstracts Service," *J. Chem. Doc.*, *5*, 107–113 (1965).
8. Thomas V. Lee, "Expert Systems in Synthesis Planning: a User's View of the LHASA Program," *Chemometrics Intelligent Lab. Syst.*, *2*, 259–272 (1987).
9. Johann Gasteiger and Clemens Jochum, "EROS A Computer Program for Generating Sequences of Reactions," *Topics Current Chem.*, *74*, 93–126 (1978).
10. Johann Gasteiger, Michael G. Hutchings, Bernt Christoph, Leopold Gann, Christian Hiller, Peter Low, Mario Marsili, Heinz Saller, and Kazumi Yuki, "A New Treatment of Chemical Reactivity: Development of EROS, and Expert System for Reaction Prediction and Synthesis Design," *Topics Current Chem.*, *137*, 19–73 (1987).
11. James B. Hendrickson, Zmira Bernstein, Todd M. Miller, Camden Parks, and A. Glenn Toczko. "New Directions in the SYNGEN Program for Synthesis Design," *in Expert System*

Applications in Chemistry, ACS Symposium Series 408, B. A. Hohne and T. H. Pierce (eds.), American Chemical Society, Washington, DC, 1989, pp. 62–81.
12. James B. Hendrickson and A. Glenn Toczko, "SYNGEN Program for Synthesis Design: Basic Computing Techniques," *J. Chem. Inform. Comput. Sci.*, *29*, 137–145 (1989).
13. James B. Hendrickson and A. Glenn Toczko, "Unique Numbering and Cataloguing of Molecular Structures," *J. Chem. Inform. Comput. Sci.*, *23*, 171–177 (1983).
14. Ikutoshi Matsuura, "Development of PC-SYNTREX, A CAD System for Organic Synthetic Route, Based on Reaction Database (in Japanese)," *Mol. Design*, 7, 2–31 (1986).

TAKASHI NAKAYAMA

DESIGN, COLLECTION, AND ANALYSIS OF HANDWRITING SAMPLE IMAGE DATABASES

INTRODUCTION

A handwriting sample image database is comprised of two major types of data (images and reference classifications). The images represent a specific application where a computer is used to automatically convert the pixel data in the image into ASCII data for further computer processing. In the case of automated character recognition, these images include credit card slips, checks, insurance claims, tax forms, and so on. These types of systems greatly reduce the amount of human labor required to enter information into computer databases.

Handwriting sample image databases also contain reference classifications for use in training and testing recognition systems. In May 1992, the First Census Optical Character Reconsign Systems Conference was hosted by the National Institute of Standards and Technology (NIST) under the sponsorship of the Bureau of the Census (1). At this conference, 47 different character recognition systems were evaluated as to how well they could classify images of individual characters including digits and uppercase and lowercase letters. Of the 47 systems, 23 achieved error rates between 3% and 5% on digits. These performance levels are sufficient for the technology to be economically advantageous and these systems appear to be approaching near-human performance. System developers agree that improving the performance of these systems will require an enormous amount of effort and an enormous increase in the number of images used to train these systems. This is why handwriting sample image databases are so important, and without reference classifications assigned to each image in the database, these types of system evaluations and future system improvements are not possible.

The next section discusses the design and collection of *NIST Special Database 1*. The third section describes the production of segmented character databases *NIST Special Database 3* and *NIST Special Database 7*. A method for machine-assisted labeling of segmented character images is presented. The fourth section introduces a method for measuring the complexity of large collections of handwriting.

DESIGN AND COLLECTION OF *NIST SPECIAL DATABASE 1*

In 1988, the Image Recognition Group at NIST undertook a project sponsored by the Bureau of the Census to design and collect a large database of handprinted characters. The database was designed to be used in training and testing high-speed high-throughput character recognition engines. *NIST Special Database 1* (SD1) (2) contains 2100 full-page images of handwriting samples printed by 2100 different writers geographically distributed across the United States with a sampling roughly proportional to population density. The writers used in this collection were permanent Census field representatives experienced in filling out forms.

Database Content

Each of the 2100 pages in the database is an image of a structured form filled in by a unique writer. A field template specifying the number of entry fields, their size, and location was used. An image of one of the blank forms used in the database is shown in Figure 1. The form is comprised of 3 identification boxes, 28 numeral boxes, 2 alphabetic boxes, and 1 unconstrained text paragraph box. This structured form layout provides a total character count of over 1,000,000 characters in the database; about 300,000 numerals and 700,000 alphabetic characters. In addition to the primary form images, 33 isolated subimages of the boxes on each primary page, excluding the name field, are included, accounting for 71,400 individual images in the entire database. With an individual form image requiring approximately 1 MB of memory, the total image database, in uncompressed form, occupies approximately 3 GB of mass storage. Therefore, the images are 2-dimensionally compressed in accordance with CCITT Group 4 (3,4), reducing the overall size of the database to under 700 MB.

Handwriting Sample Form Layout

Figure 2 displays an actual form from the database. Each entry field on this form is represented as a box. The writers in the database have been made anonymous by blacking out the name field. The string of machine-printed information above each box instructed the writer what to print in the box. The instructions on the form requested that the writer print within the box the information provided above each box. Assuming the writer followed the directions and correctly completed the form, each box is self-referenced. This method of collection reduces the overall cost incurred by eliminating the need for transcribing the printed samples by hand. The instructions do not specify what writing implement should be used. Therefore, the database contains a random assortment of pencils and pens resulting in handwriting samples varying in width, contrast, and color.

Careful planning went into the design of this form. The form strategy applied was developed to ensure successful data capture based on current forms processing techniques. Every field is consistently defined as a bold box explicitly defining the location and spatial extent of each field. The single-line boxes are 7 mm in height, giving writers ample room to fit entire characters within the box. This served to minimally constrain the writer's print but more importantly aids the automated field isolation within a recognition system. By using a consistent field demarcation such as a rectangular box, a single software or hardware solution can be implemented to locate every field on the form. The boxes on this form are maximally spaced in an attempt to minimize crowding and clutter. The more cluttered a form layout, the more difficult it becomes for a computer to locate and identify fields, thereby increasing the potential for recognition failures. This implies a trade-off between minimizing the amount of paper handled by increasing the amount of data entered on each page versus lower recognition rates due to increased clutter and increased recognition confusion.

Ignoring the first three identification boxes shown in Figure 2, as one scans down the form, there is a progression of increasing recognition difficulty. The first series of boxes are comprised of digits only, followed by boxes comprised of alphabetic characters.

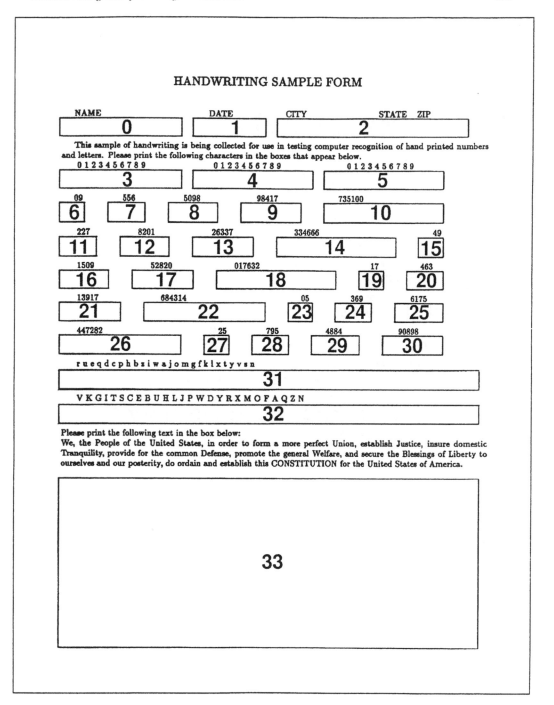

FIGURE 1 The Handwriting Sample Form is comprised of 34 indexed entry field boxes.

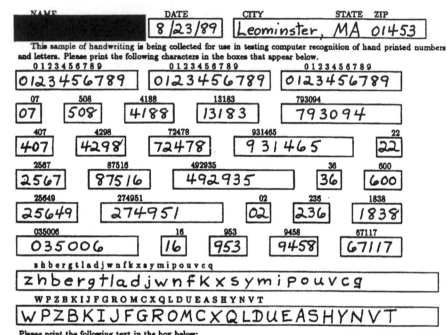

HANDWRITING SAMPLE FORM

NAME   DATE   CITY   STATE   ZIP

8/23/89   Leominster, MA 01453

This sample of handwriting is being collected for use in testing computer recognition of hand printed numbers and letters. Please print the following characters in the boxes that appear below.

0 1 2 3 4 5 6 7 8 9   0 1 2 3 4 5 6 7 8 9   0 1 2 3 4 5 6 7 8 9
0123456789   0123456789   0123456789

07   508   4188   13183   793094
07   508   4188   13183   793094

407   4298   72478   931465   22
407   4298   72478   931465   22

2567   87516   492935   36   600
2567   87516   492935   36   600

25649   274951   02   236   1838
25649   274951   02   236   1838

035006   16   953   9458   67117
035006   16   953   9458   67117

z h b e r g t l a d j w n f k x s y m i p o u v c q
zhbergtladjwnfkxsymipouvcg

W P Z B K I J F G R O M C X Q L D U E A S H Y N V T
WPZBKIJFGROMCXQLDUEASHYNVT

Please print the following text in the box below:
We, the People of the United States, in order to form a more perfect Union, establish Justice, insure domestic Tranquility, provide for the common Defense, promote the general Welfare, and secure the Blessings of Liberty to ourselves and our posterity, do ordain and establish this CONSTITUTION for the United States of America.

We, the People of the United States, in order to form a more perfect Union, establish Justice, insure domestic Tranquility, provide for the common Defense, promote the general Welfare, and secure the Blessings of Liberty to ourselves and our posterity, do ordain and establish this CON- STITUTION for the United States of America.

FIGURE 2   A completed form containing very legible and neat handprint.

There are only 10 unique classes of digits, 0 through 9, versus 26 possible classes of the alphabetic characters, A through Z. The reduced size of possible classes makes the recognition of numeric character fields easier than the recognition of alphabetic fields which, in turn, are easier to recognize than alphanumeric fields. There also is a progression down the form of increased character segmentation difficulty. The segmentation of lowercase characters is challenging because extenders on the characters, g, j, p, q, and y, often extend beyond the bottom of the box. The Constitution box, the last box on the form, pushes the outer limits of current segmentation and recognition technology due to the handwriting being unconstrained; no specific line breaks designated, no form lines to guide the writer left to right, no form lines to constrain the height of the characters, and so on.

There are 50 variations of the form layout in the database. As stated above, a single field template was used so that all 2100 forms contain the same number of boxes, each of the same size and relative location. The variations are realized in the information provided above each box. Every form requested that the writer print the sequence of digits, 0 through 9, three times in boxes 3, 4, and 5. Depending on the form variation, the digits in boxes 6 through 30 vary; however, the number of digits in each box remain fixed. The variations in forms provide 50 different random orders of the lowercase alphabet and 50 different random orders of the uppercase alphabet across the 2100 forms.

Database Acquisition

The 50 form variations were tightly specified using a typesetting software package and printed on a laser printer. The 50 templates were then massively reproduced with a photocopier. From copies of the original 50 variations, 3520 blank forms were mailed to 12 regional offices within the Bureau of the Census. There, the forms were filled out by Census field representatives and returned via business return envelopes. This process greatly reduced administrative and mailing overhead expenses while providing a sampling roughly proportional to geographic population distributions within the United States. Figure 3 illustrates the 12 different census regions.

Out of 3520 forms mailed to regional offices, 2100 completed forms were returned in time to be included in the database. The number of forms mailed to each regional office and the number of completed forms included in the database from that region are listed in Figure 4. Region 0 represents forms in which the field containing city, state, and zip code was left empty. From August 1989 through October 1989, the forms received at NIST were sequentially indexed, sorted by region, logged, and digitized. Figure 5 lists the information recorded in the Historical Log provided with the database. Included is the form identification index, the form variation type (1 of 50), the date received and processed at NIST, the assumed writing implement used in completing the form, the color of the implement's ink or lead, and a subjective quality rating.

IHead Image File Format

Image file formats and effective data compression and decompression are critical to the usefulness of these types of databases. Each page returned was digitized in binary form at 12 pixels per millimeter [300 dots per inch (dpi)], 2-dimensionally compressed using CCITT Group 4, and temporarily archived onto computer magnetic mass storage. Once all forms were digitized, the images were mastered and replicated onto ISO-9660 formatted CD-ROM discs for permanent archiving and distribution.

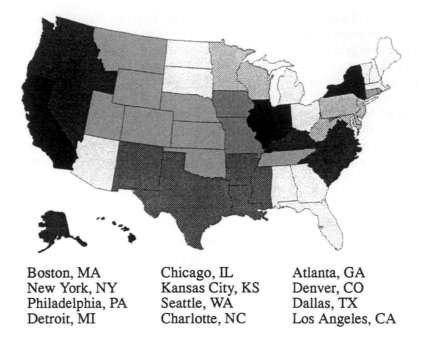

Boston, MA   Chicago, IL   Atlanta, GA
New York, NY   Kansas City, KS   Denver, CO
Philadelphia, PA   Seattle, WA   Dallas, TX
Detroit, MI   Charlotte, NC   Los Angeles, CA

FIGURE 3   The Bureau of the Census' geographical regions within the United States.

In this application, a raster image is a digital encoding of light reflected from discrete points on a scanned form. The 2-dimensional area of the form is divided into discrete locations according to the resolution of a specific grid. Each cell of this grid is represented by a single bit value 0 or 1 called a pixel; 0 represents a cell predominantly white, 1 represents a cell predominately black. This 2-dimensional sampling grid is then stored as a 1-dimensional vector of pixel values in raster order; left to right, top to bottom.

After digitization, certain attributes of an image are required to correctly interpret the 1-dimensional pixel data as a 2-dimensional image. Examples of such attributes are

Region	Office	# Mailed	# In SD1
0	Anonymous	0	12
1	Boston	310	152
2	New York	250	51
3	Philadelphia	350	196
4	Detroit	250	158
5	Chicago	220	126
6	Kansas City	240	152
7	Seattle	270	121
8	Charlotte	350	188
9	Atlanta	300	232
10	Dallas	350	241
11	Denver	400	250
12	Los Angeles	230	221
		3520	2100

FIGURE 4   Forms mailed to each region and included in *NIST Special Database 1*.

```
REGIONAL OFFICE 1
NAME: BOSTON, MASS
          OFFICE CODE NO.: 2100
          MAILED: 310 pieces
```

	INDEX	TMPLT	DATE RECEIVED	WRITING TOOLS	COLOR	QUALITY RATING
1)	0817	40	08-29-1989	PENCIL	BLACK	MEDIUM
2)	0818	03	08-29-1989	BALL POINT	BLACK	LIGHT
3)	0819	13	08-29-1989	PENCIL	BLACK	LIGHT
4)	0852	40	08-29-1989	FELT TIP PEN	BLACK	MEDIUM
5)	0855	46	08-29-1989	PENCIL	BLACK	LIGHT
6)	0869	20	08-29-1989	PENCIL	BLACK	LIGHT
7)	0872	30	08-29-1989	BALL POINT	BLACK	MEDIUM
8)	0874	26	08-29-1989	BALL POINT	BLUE	LIGHT
9)	0889	48	08-29-1989	BALL POINT	BLACK	LIGHT
10)	0891	44	08-29-1989	PENCIL	BLACK	DARK
11)	0892	23	08-29-1989	PENCIL	BLACK	MEDIUM
12)	0895	48	08-29-1989	PENCIL	BLACK	LIGHT
13)	0896	44	08-29-1989	PENCIL	BLACK	MEDIUM
14)	0897	19	08-29-1989	FELT TIP PEN	BLACK	DARK

FIGURE 5   A portion of the Historical Log provided in *NIST Special Database 1*.

the pixel width and pixel height of the image. These attributes are stored in a machine-readable header prefixed to the raster bit stream. A program that manipulates the raster data of an image is able to first read the header containing these attributes and determine the proper interpretation of the data that follows it.

NIST has designed, implemented, and distributed images based on this paradigm. A header format named IHead has been developed for use as an image interchange format. Numerous image formats exist; some are widely supported on small personal computers, others supported on larger workstations; most are proprietary formats, few are public domain. IHead is an attempt to design an open image format which can be universally implemented across heterogeneous computer architectures and environments. IHead has been successfully ported and tested on several systems including UNIX workstations and servers, DOS personal computers, and VMS mainframes. Both documentation and source code for the IHead format are publicly available. IHead has been designed with an extensive set of attributes in order to (1) adequately represent both binary and gray level images, (2) represent images captured from different scanners and cameras, (3) and satisfy the image requirements of diversified applications, including but not limited to image archival/retrieval, character recognition, and fingerprint classification.

The IHead structure definition written in the C programming language is listed in Figure 6; Figure 7 lists the header values from an IHead file corresponding to these structure members. This header information belongs to the isolated box image displayed in Figure 8. Referencing the structure members listed in Figure 6, the first attribute field of IHead is the identification field, **id**. This field uniquely identifies the image file, typically by a file name. The identification field in this example not only contains the image's file name but also the reference string the writer was instructed to print in the box. The reference string is delimited by double quotes. This convention enables an image

```
/***********************************************************
      File Name: IHead.h
      Package:  NIST Internal Image Header
      Author:   Michael D. Garris
      Date:     2/08/90
 **********************************************************/
/* Defines used by the ihead structure */
#define IHDR_SIZE      288      /* len of hdr record (always even bytes) */
#define SHORT_CHARS    8        /* # of ASCII chars to represent a short */
#define BUFSIZE        80       /* default buffer size */
#define DATELEN        26       /* character length of data string */

typedef struct ihead{
   char id[BUFSIZE];                    /* identification/comment field */
   char created[DATELEN];               /* date created */
   char width[SHORT_CHARS];             /* pixel width of image */
   char height[SHORT_CHARS];            /* pixel height of image */
   char depth[SHORT_CHARS];             /* bits per pixel */
   char density[SHORT_CHARS];           /* pixels per inch */
   char compress[SHORT_CHARS];          /* compression code */
   char complen[SHORT_CHARS];           /* compressed data length */
   char align[SHORT_CHARS];             /* scanline multiple: 8|16|32 */
   char unitsize[SHORT_CHARS];          /* bit size of image memory units */
   char sigbit;                         /* 0->sigbit first | 1->sigbit last */
   char byte_order;                     /* 0->highlow | 1->lowhigh*/
   char pix_offset[SHORT_CHARS];        /* pixel column offset */
   char whitepix[SHORT_CHARS];          /* intensity of white pixel */
   char issigned;                       /* 0->unsigned data | 1->signed data */
   char rm_cm;                          /* 0->row maj | 1->column maj */
   char tb_bt;                          /* 0->top2bottom | 1->bottom2top */
   char lr_rl;                          /* 0->left2right | 1->right2left */
   char parent[BUFSIZE];                /* parent image file */
   char par_x[SHORT_CHARS];             /* from x pixel in parent */
   char par_y[SHORT_CHARS];             /* from y pixel in parent */
}IHEAD;
```

FIGURE 6   The IHead C programming language structure definition.

recognition system's hypothesized answers to be automatically scored against the actual characters printed in the box.

The attribute field, **created**, is the date on which the image was captured or digitized. The next three fields hold the image's pixel **width**, **height**, and **depth**. A binary image has a pixel depth of 1, whereas a gray-scale image containing 256 possible shades of gray has a pixel depth of 8. The attribute field, **density**, contains the scan resolution of the image; in this case, 12 pixels per millimeter (300 dpi). The next two fields deal with compression.

In the IHead format, images may be compressed with virtually any algorithm. Whether the image is compressed or not, the IHead is always uncompressed. This enables header interpretation and manipulation without the overhead of decompression. The **compress** field is an integer flag that signifies which compression technique, if any, has been applied to the raster image data following the header. If the compression code is zero, then the image data is not compressed, and the data dimensions, width, height, an depth, are sufficient to load the image into main memory. However, if the compression code is nonzero, then the **complen** field must be used in addition to the image's pixel dimensions. For example, the image described in Figure 7 has a compression code of 2. By convention, this signifies that CCITT Group 4 compression has been applied to the image data prior to file creation. To load the compressed image data into main memory, the value in **complen** is used to load the compressed block of data into main memory. Once the compressed image data has been loaded into memory, CCITT Group 4 decompression can be used to produce an image which has the pixel dimensions consistent with those stored in its header. A compression ratio of 20 to 1 was achieved using CCITT Group 4 compression on the full-page images in SD1.

The attribute field, **align**, stores the alignment boundary to which scan lines of pixels are padded. Pixel values of binary images are stored 8 pixels (or bits) to a byte. Most images, however, are not an even multiple of 8 pixels in width. To minimize the overhead of ending a previous scan line and beginning the next scan line within the same byte, a number of padded pixels are provided to extend the previous scan line to an even-byte boundary. Some digitizers extend this padding of pixels out to an even multiple of 8 pixels; other digitizers extend this padding of pixels out to an even multiple of 16 pixels. This field stores the image's pixel alignment value used in padding out the ends of raster scan lines.

The next three attribute fields identify binary interchanging issues among heterogeneous computer architectures and displays. The **unitsize** field specifies how many contiguous pixel values are bundled into a single unit by the digitizer. The **sigbit** field specifies the order in which bits of significance are stored within each unit; most significant bit first or least significant bit first. The last of these three fields is the **byte_order** field. If **unitsize** is a multiple of bytes, then this field specifies the order in which bytes occur within the unit. Given these three attributes, binary incompatibilities across computer hardware and binary format assumptions within application software can be identified and effectively dealt with.

The **pix_offset** attribute defines a pixel displacement from the left edge of the raster image data to where a particular image's significant image information begins. The **whitepix** attribute defines the value assigned to the color white. For example, the binary image described in Figure 7 is black text on a white background and the value of the white pixels is 0. This field is particularly useful to image display routines. The **issigned** field is required to specify whether the units of an image are signed or unsigned. This attribute determines whether an image with a pixel depth of 8 should have pixels values interpreted in the range of -128 to $+127$, or 0 to 255. The orientation of the raster scan may also vary among different digitizers. The attribute field, **rm_cm**, specifies whether the digitizer captured the image in row-major order or column-major order. Whether the scan lines of an image were accumulated from top to bottom or bottom to top is specified by the field **tb_bt**, and whether left to right, or right to left, is specified by the field **rl_lr**.

The final attributes in IHead provide a single historical link from the current image to its parent image, the one from which the current image was derived or extracted. In Figure 7, the **parent** field contains the full path name to the image from which the image displayed in Figure 8 was extracted. The **par_x** and **par_y** fields contain the origin, upper-left-hand corner pixel coordinate, from where the extraction took place from the parent image. These fields provide an historical thread through successive generations of images and subimages. We believe that the IHead image format contains the minimal amount of ancillary information required to successfully manage binary and gray-scale images.

IMAGE FILE HEADER

Identity	: box_03.pct "0123456789"
Header Size	: 288 (bytes)
Date Created	: Thu Jan 4 17:34:21 1990
Width	: 656 (pixels)
Height	: 135 (pixels)
Bits per Pixel	: 1
Resolution	: 300 (ppi)
Compression	: 2 (code)
Compress Length	: 874 (bytes)
Scan Alignment	: 16 (bits)
Image Data Unit	: 16 (bits)
Byte Order	: High-Low
MSBit	: First
Column Offset	: 0 (pixels)
White Pixel	: 0
Data Units	: Unsigned
Scan Order	: Row Major,
	Top to Bottom,
	Left to Right
Parent	: hsf_0/f0000_14/f0000_14.pct
X Origin	: 192 (pixels)
Y Origin	: 732 (pixels)

FIGURE 7   The IHead values for the isolated box image displayed in Figure 8.

Database Examples

SD1 embodies a wide range of handwriting styles. The completed forms in this database illustrate the difficulty in recognizing handprinted characters with a computer. Frequently, even humans cannot positively identify characters without confirming their best guesses against the font information printed on the forms above each box. A quick scan of these handwriting samples shows great variation in size, slant, contrast, spacing, shape, the random interchanging of uppercase and lowercase, and the random switching between print and cursive script. In this section, a select set of handwriting samples from the database are shown in an attempt to illustrate to the reader the extreme variation in handwriting existing between different writers.

Compare the handprint in Figure 2 to the sample shown in Figure 9. If all handprint were of the style and quality shown in Figure 2, the challenge of recognizing handprint would no longer exist. The quality of handprint in Figure 9 is dramatically lower. Especially notice how the quality of the writing degrades from left to right, top to bottom, within the Constitution box. The characters in the top left corner of this box are well

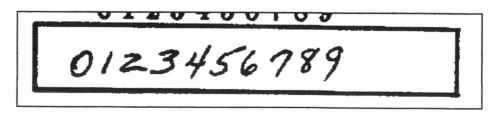

FIGURE 8   An IHead image of an isolated box from *NIST Special Database 1*.

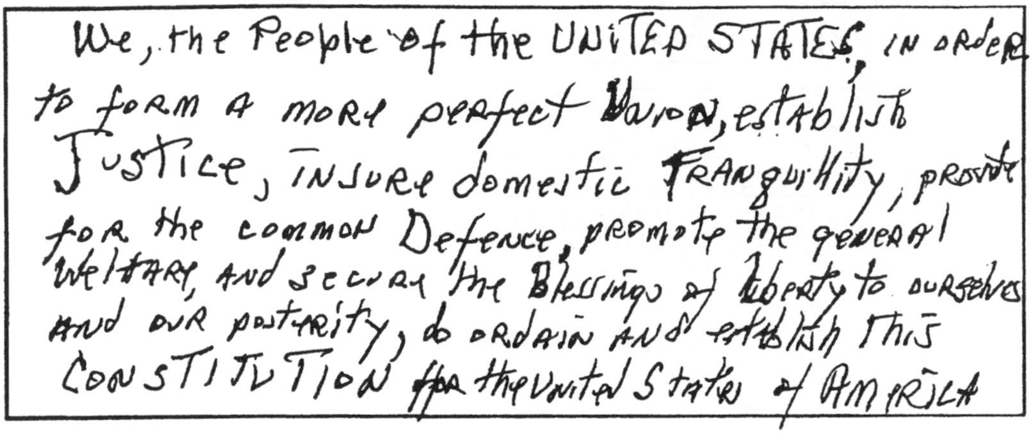
We, the People of the UNITED STATES, in order
to form a more perfect Union, establish
Justice, insure domestic Tranquility, provide
for the common Defence, promote the general
Welfare, and secure the Blessings of Liberty to ourselves
and our posterity, do ordain and establish this
CONSTITUTION for the United States of AMERICA

FIGURE 9 Handprint which is not very legible.

spaced both horizontally and vertically and appear reasonably legible. As the writer became cramped for space at the end of lines and toward the bottom of the box, the restriction of space visibly impacted the neatness and readability of the person's writing.

Figure 10 shows an example of a person's handprint written with a pronounced slant. It is interesting to note how the slant of characters from this writer varies. The characters printed in the digit boxes contain substantial slant, but when the person printed within the unconstrained Constitution box, the slant is even more pronounced. It is curious how the slant is almost completely missing from the characters printed in the two alphabetic boxes.

The average size of characters between writers also greatly varies. Figure 11 contains a sample of handprint which is relatively tall. If this person wrote any taller, the characters would not remain within the boxes. Note how the writer's lowercase extenders on the g, y, q, p, and j all extend well below the bottom of the lowercase alphabet box. In contrast to tall print, Figure 12 shows a portion of a form containing extremely small handprinted characters. Here the writer's handprint is almost the same size as the machine-printed information on the form.

In this database, the writers were not told what writing implement should be used to fill in the form. Therefore, the forms in this database represent different hardness of pencils, different colored ink pens, and different pen tips. A static scanner setting was used to digitize all the forms in the database regardless of the contrast between a form's background and the handprinted information it contains. The result is a database of images varying greatly in image quality or contrast. An example of a box completed using a hard-lead pencil is shown in Figure 13. The characters in this image are barely readable, some are not. Note how the individual characters are breaking up. Most character recognition systems would have significant problems reading this image. On the other hand, Figure 14 shows a section of a form which was completed using a broad felt-tipped pen. In this image, the pen strokes are extremely wide, causing most interior holes in characters to be closed. Note how difficult it is to distinguish 3's from 8's.

It has been observed that writers frequently make no distinction when printing lowercase and uppercase letters. Also, writers tend to randomly mix handprint with cursive script. Figure 15 shows a section of a form completed by a writer who printed nearly

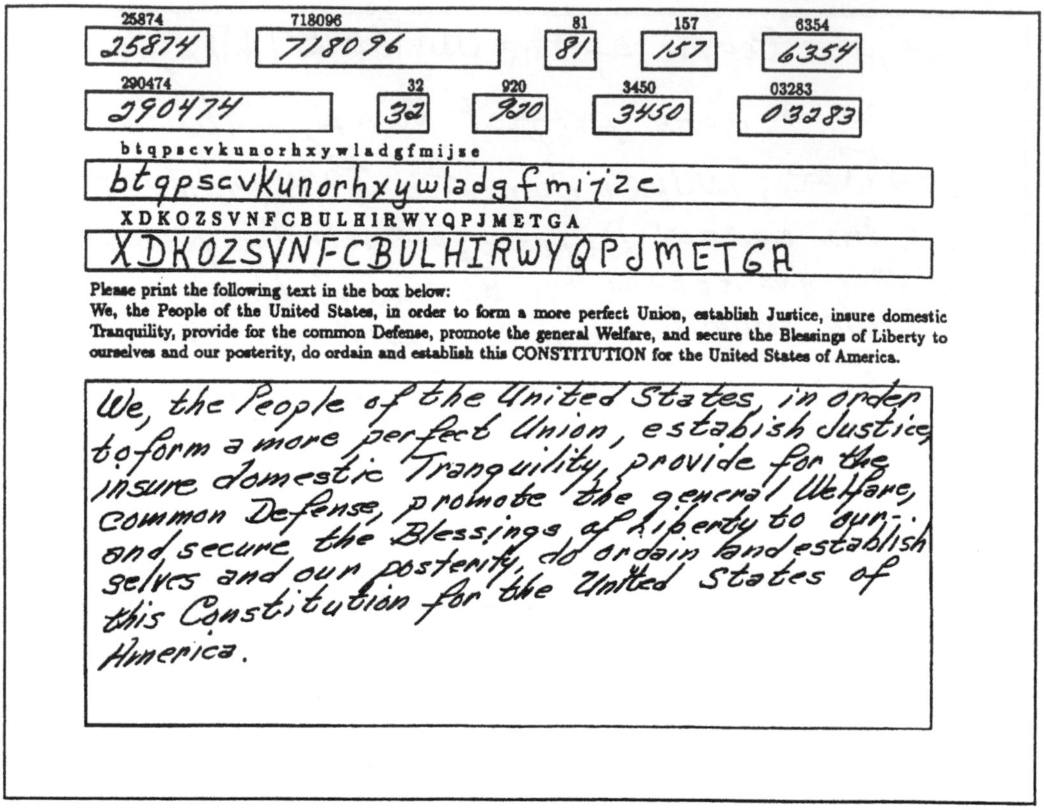

FIGURE 10   Handprint written with a pronounced slant.

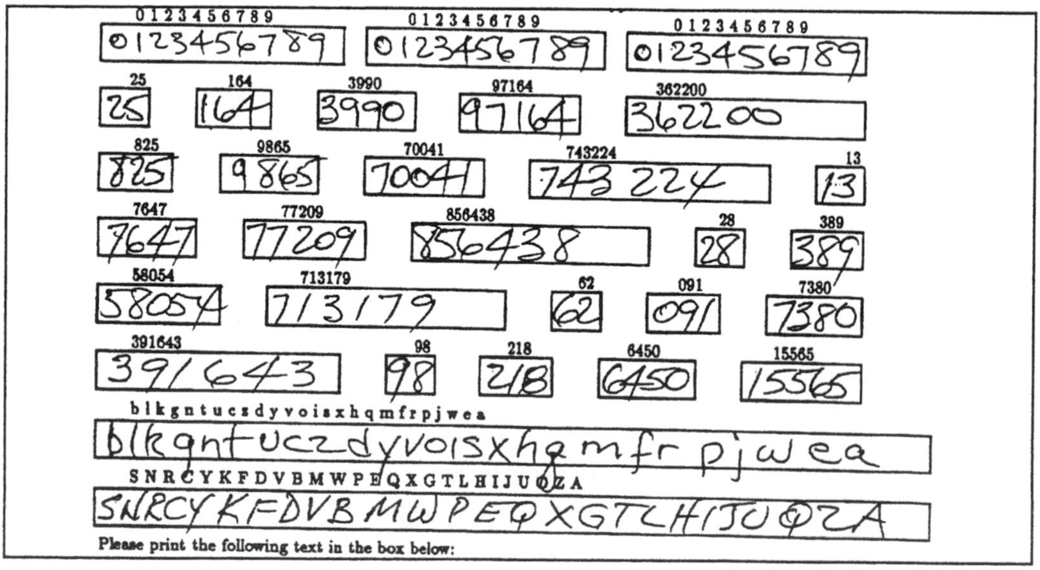

FIGURE 11   Handprint which is very tall.

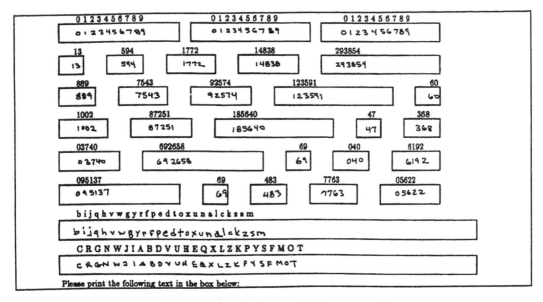

FIGURE 12   Handprint which is very small.

every lowercase letter in the lowercase alphabetic box the same way as the uppercase letters were printed. Note how the writer of this form printed within the alphabetic boxes but switched completely to cursive script when filling in the Constitution box. In Figure 16, the two boxes illustrate a writing style in which the writer printed all characters in the lowercase alphabetic box as cursive and filled in the upper case alphabetic box with printed letters. A robust recognition system must account for these inconsistencies.

Measurements Acquired During Processing

Robust document recognition systems detect and account for form rotation within an image. NIST has developed a model recognition system based on the forms in SD1 (5). This hybrid system combines traditional image processing, biologically motivated image

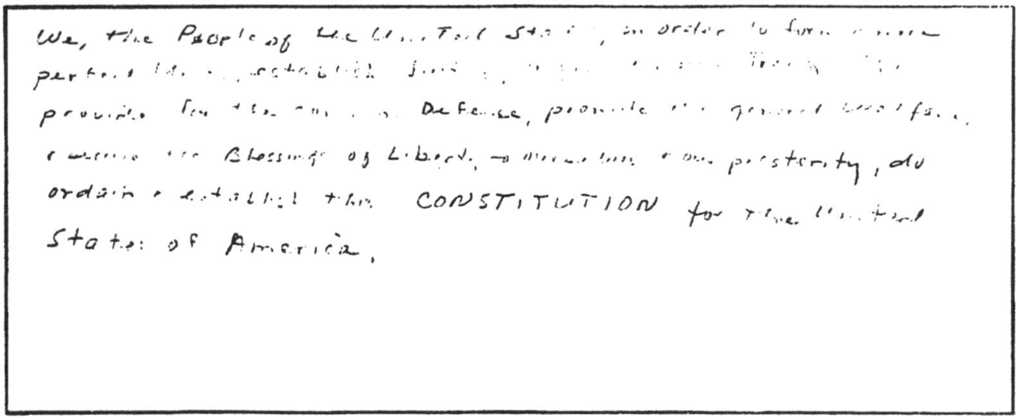

FIGURE 13   Digitized handprint which was printed very lightly with a hard-lead pencil.

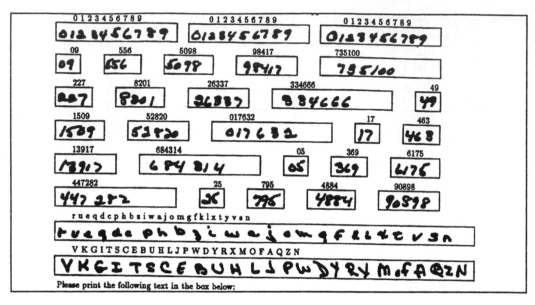

FIGURE 14   Digitized handprint which was printed with a broad felt-tipped pen.

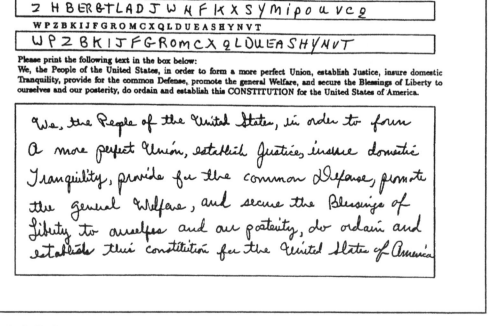

FIGURE 15   Example of printing lowercase letters as uppercase and switching to cursive script.

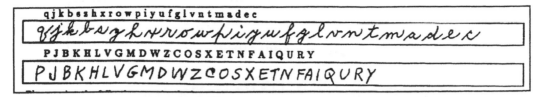

FIGURE 16   Example of writing all lowercase letters in cursive.

filtering, and neural networks on a massively parallel machine. One component in this system identifies form rotation and normalizes the image appropriately. The database contains images of forms rotated between +1.45° and −2.23° with an average of 0.3°.

This rotation was introduced at two different points in time. First, the original 50 form variants were reproduced using a photocopier. This introduced small rotational variations in the pages produced by the photocopier. The second source of rotational noise was introduced during the scanning of the completed forms. Note that despite the tight controls NIST placed on the printing, reproducing, and scanning of these forms, significant rotational noise exists in the database. Figure 17 shows an image from the database of a form with substantial rotational noise.

PRODUCTION OF SEGMENTED CHARACTER IMAGE DATABASES

As stated earlier, SD1 was collected to be used in training and testing high-speed high-throughput character recognition engines. Character classifiers typically recognize one individual character at a time, so in order to train and test these classifiers a subset of the more than 1,000,000 characters contained in SD1 had to be segmented into individual images and assigned reference classifications. This section discusses the creation of two segmented character image databases, *NIST Special Database 3* (SD3) (6) and *NIST Special Database 7* (SD7) (7).

Creation of *NIST Special Database 3*

The 2100 form images contained in SD1 are included in SD3. The digit and uppercase and lowercase fields on each form were segmented into isolated character images with each resulting image automatically assigned a character classification. Each segmented image from a field was assigned a consecutive character from the field's associated reference string. Using this technique, each image is assigned its correct reference classification, assuming there are no errors incurred during segmentation.

Unfortunately, the segmenter used was only about 80% accurate, frequently merging and splitting characters. Therefore, the classification assignments from the reference string often became unsynchronized with the actual images. This caused many images to be labeled incorrectly. Each referenced image was manually checked by a human, discarding the image when segmentation errors were detected and correcting the character image's classification when recognition errors were detected. Every referenced character image in this database has been manually checked and verified at two independent times, each time by a different person. This checking process took approximately 6 months to complete. As a result, SD3 contains 313,389 referenced character images.

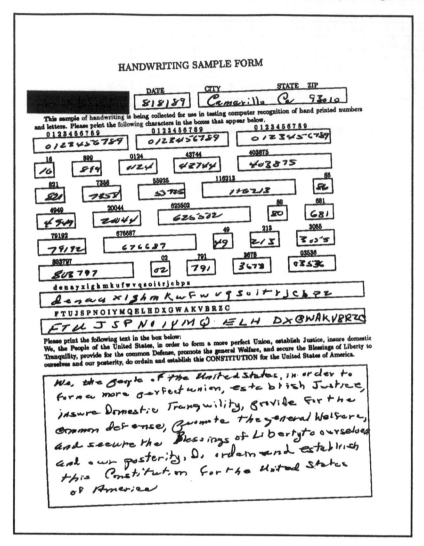

FIGURE 17   An image of a form from the database containing substantial rotational noise.

Multiple Image Set (MIS) File Format

Based on experience gained from creating and manipulating large on-line image databases, NIST has developed a number of diversified file formats. One such file format has been developed to manage large volumes of segmented character images. Storing character images in individual files has proven to be very inefficient, especially when manipulating databases containing hundreds of thousands of characters. Devoting a separate file node for each character image creates enormous file system overhead, and unreasonably large directory tables must be allocated. Rarely are experiments conducted on only a single-character image in isolation. Rather, most experiments require a large sample of characters. Experience has shown that the gathering of a large sample of characters from a file system where the images have been stored in individual files greatly burdens the computer's disk controller. This results in slow experiment loading times as well as limiting the access of other applications to data stored on the same storage device.

In addition to creating large directory tables, storing segmented character images in individual files results in sparse usage of the storage device. This sparseness is even more exaggerated when the images are compressed. For example, segmented character images in SD3 have been centered within a 128 × 128 binary pixel image. The resulting image size is 2344 bytes, 296 bytes for the IHead header and 2048 bytes of image data. These files when CCITT Group 4 compressed average 360 bytes in size, 296 bytes for the IHead header and only 64 bytes of compressed image data. Storing these compressed image files onto CD-ROM for example, which uses a 2048 block size, would be extremely wasteful. Only 18% of each block containing image data would be used.

In light of these observations, NIST has developed a Multiple Image Set (MIS) file format. The MIS format allows multiple images of homogeneous dimensions and depth to be stored in one file. MIS is a simple extension or encapsulation of the IHead format described previously. It can be seen in Figure 18 that the IHead structure is included as a member within the MIS definition.

An MIS file contains one or more individual images stacked vertically within the same contiguous raster memory, the last scanline of the previous image concatenated to the first scanline of the next image. The individual images that are concatenated together are referred to as MIS *entries*. The resulting contiguous raster memory is referred to as the MIS *memory*. The MIS memory containing one or more entries of uniform width, height, and depth is stored using the IHead header format. The IHead attribute fields are sufficient to describe the MIS memory. The IHead structure's **width** attribute specifies the width of the MIS memory, and likewise the IHead structure's **height** attribute specifies the height of the MIS memory. In this way, the MIS memory can be stored just like any normal raster image, including possible compression.

Due to the uniform dimensions of MIS entries, the IHead structure's **width** attribute also specifies the width of the entries in the MIS memory. What is lacking from the original IHead definition is the uniform height of the MIS entries and the number of MIS entries in the MIS memory. Realize that given the uniform height of the MIS entries, the number of entries in the MIS memory can be computed by dividing the entry height into the total MIS memory height. The interpretation of two of the IHead attribute fields, **par_x** and **par_y**, changes when the IHead header is being used to describe an MIS memory. The **par_x** field is used to hold the uniform width of the MIS entries, and the **par_y** field is used to hold the uniform height of the MIS entries. In other words, **width** and **height** represent MIS memory width and MIS memory height, respectively, whereas **par_x** and **par_y** represent MIS entry width and MIS entry height, respectively. Using this convention, an MIS file is treated like an IHead file.

Figure 18 lists the MIS structure definition written in the C programming language. The structure contains an IHead structure, **head**, and an MIS memory, *data*. In addition, there are six other attribute fields which hide the details of the IHead interpretation from application programs that manipulate MIS memories. The MIS attributes **misw** and **mish** specify the width and height, respectively, of the MIS memory. These values are the same as the **width** and **height** attributes contained in the IHead structure pointed to by **head**. The MIS attributes **entw** and **enth** specify the uniform width and height, respectively, of the MIS entries. These values are the same as the **par_x** and **par_y** attributes contained in the IHead structure pointed to by **head**. The MIS attribute **ent_alloc** specifies how many MIS entries of dimension **entw** and **enth** have been allocated to the MIS memory **data**. The MIS attribute **ent_num** specifies how many entries out of the possible number allocated are currently and contiguously contained in the MIS memory **data**.

```
/***********************************************************
        Filename: Mis.h
        Author: Michael D. Garris
        Date: 7/18/90
************************************************************/
typedef struct misstruct{
    IHEAD *head;
    unsigned char *data;
    int misw;
    int mish;
    int entw;
    int enth;
    int ent_num;
    int ent_alloc;
} MIS;
```

FIGURE 18   The MIS C programming language structure definition.

Checking the results of segmenting the digit, uppercase, and lowercase fields from the 2100 full-page form images produced 313,389 referenced character images in SD3. Each segmented character was centered and stored into a separate 128 × 128 binary pixel memory preserving the original size and density of the character. The characters segmented from each form image were then organized into three different MIS files containing character images segmented from the digit fields, uppercase fields, and lowercase fields. An example of an MIS memory is displayed in Figure 19.

There is a potential for 6300 MIS files in the database, 2100 forms times the 3 character groups. Due to segmentation errors, the database actually contains 6166 MIS files including 23,125 digits, 44,951 uppercase letters, and 45,313 lowercase letters. A statistical log is provided with SD3 which lists all those forms missing one or more of the three MIS file groups. Every MIS file in the database has been compressed using CCITT Group 4, and the database is approximately 135 MB in size. Uncompressed, the database would require approximately 2.75 GB of storage.

Character Classification (CLS) File Format

For each segmented character image in SD3 there is an associated character classification which has been assigned and manually checked. Punctuation characters are often interpreted by disk operating systems and shells as special characters; so a character-naming convention has been developed at NIST which avoids these ambiguities. The classification value stored for each character image is the hexadecimal representation of the character's ASCII value. For example, an image of a handprinted 2 is assigned the class 32, a lowercase z is assigned the class 7a, and a handprinted semicolon (;) is assigned the class 3b.

These classifications are stored in Character Classification (CLS) files and correspond one-to-one to the entries in an associated MIS file in the database. Figure 19 displays an MIS memory along with its associated CLS file. The CLS file is an ASCII file with the first line containing the number of classifications values listed in the file, one value per successive line. Each ASCII text line is terminated with the linefeed character,

MIS Memory

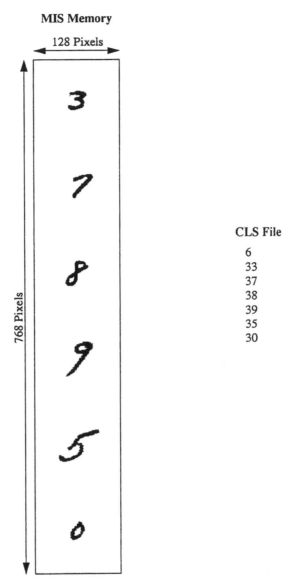

128 Pixels

768 Pixels

CLS File

6
33
37
38
39
35
30

FIGURE 19 MIS memory and CLS file examples.

0x0A. Every MIS file in SD3 has an associated CLS file, and for each entry in a MIS file, there is a corresponding classification value in the CLS file. Figure 20 lists the frequency with which each digit and letter occurs within SD3.

Creation of *NIST Special Database 7*

Upon the creation of SD3, a conference for comparing the performance of various handprint character recognition systems was proposed. It was determined that SD3 would be distributed to conference participants for use in training and initial testing of their character classifiers. Details of the conference are recorded in Reference 1.

	Digits		Uppers		Lowers
0	22,971	A	1,649	a	1,738
1	24,772	B	1,691	b	1,766
2	22,131	C	1,732	c	1,794
3	23,172	D	1,712	d	1,748
4	21,549	E	1,759	e	1,769
5	19,545	F	1,756	f	1,608
6	22,128	G	1,707	g	1,740
7	23,209	H	1,677	h	1,791
8	22,029	I	2,102	i	1,838
9	21,619	J	1,633	j	1,446
		K	1,662	k	1,740
		L	1,830	l	2,021
		M	1,716	m	1,731
		N	1,732	n	1,777
		O	1,774	o	1,800
		P	1,723	p	1,589
		Q	1,664	q	1,554
		R	1,707	r	1,738
		S	1,755	s	1,776
		T	1,559	t	1,692
		U	1,763	u	1,827
		V	1,749	v	1,777
		W	1,705	w	1,765
		X	1,785	x	1,861
		Y	1,631	y	1,614
		Z	1,778	z	1,814

FIGURE 20   Frequency distribution of digits and letters in SD3.

Because all of SD3 was used as training data, a new segmented character database was required to test the systems entered in the conference. Blank handwriting sample forms like the ones used in SD1 were distributed to high school math and science students. From the set of filled out forms, 500 were selected for use in creating SD7. In association with the conference, this database is also referred to as *NIST Test Data 1* (TD1).

Machine-Assisted Reference Classifications

To test the character classifiers submitted to the conference, referenced character images had to be produced from the 500 forms. The 6 months required to produce SD3 was too long and demanded too much manual effort to meet the proposed schedule for the conference. Therefore, a new method for creating reference character images was proposed.

Within this same period of time, the Image Recognition Group as NIST completed the development of a massively parallel model recognition system (5). The system was designed to automatically process the Handwriting Sample Forms in SD1, reading the handprinted information contained in the digit and alphabetic fields. The system locates the entry field boxes on the form, segments the handprint within each field, and uses a neural network classifier to assign character classifications to each of the segmented images. Segmented character images along with their recognized classifications are stored as output from the model recognition system. At that time, the system was 94% accurate across all of SD1 with no rejections when reading digits, and less than 80% accurate when reading uppercase and lowercase letters. These performance statistics were computed by using the NIST Scoring Package, *NIST Special Software 1* (SS1) (8,9) which applies the methods described in Reference 10.

A database production method was proposed that uses the results of the model recognition system to initially assign classifications to segmented character images. The details of this machine-assisted method are documented in Reference 11. The recognition system computes a confidence value for each character classification made. Based on the confidence value, a classification is labeled by the recognition system as accepted if the confidence is sufficiently high, otherwise the classification is labeled as rejected.

The segmented images whose classifications were accepted by the system are sorted by class and visually checked by a human. This phase, known as the *checking pass*, is very efficient, as up to 1024 characters images allegedly belonging to the same class are displayed simultaneously on a computer screen. In this way, any images containing segmentation errors or not belonging to the class being displayed are quickly located and flagged. The remaining images not flagged, along with their verified classifications, are stored as part of the database. The checking pass quickly incorporates the correctly segmented and correctly classified character images into the database.

A second phase, known as the *correcting pass*, is more labor intense. Here, images containing segmentation errors are separated from images that are correctly segmented but have been assigned an incorrect classification. The images containing segmentation errors are discarded, whereas the remaining images are reclassified by the human. The correcting pass is initiated by collecting all the images initially rejected by the recognition system and any images flagged during the checking pass and sorting them all by class. During the correcting pass, the images are displayed one at a time along with the image's currently assigned classification. The human is asked to verify that the current image is properly segmented. If the image is deemed to contain segmentation errors, it is discarded. If the image is properly segmented, the human is asked to verify that the current classification is correct. If the classification is deemed incorrect, the human is asked to enter the correct classification. Nondiscarded images from the correcting pass are then collected into a new checking pass.

The segmented images along with their classifications oscillate between the checking and correcting passes with image/classification pairs being incorporated into the database within the checking pass and image/classification pairs being reclassified or discarded within the correcting pass. Upon several complete oscillations, the database production reaches a steady state and the process is terminated. Figure 21 illustrates the two-pass process. Using this machine-assisted labeling approach, SD7 was ready for CD-ROM mastering in 2 weeks.

Database Content

The above labeling method produced approximately 83,000 images of handprinted digits and letters, and assigned to each image a correct reference classification for testing character recognition systems. The images from each form were organized into MIS files according to groups similar to SD3. In all, about 59,000 digits and 24,000 uppercase and lowercase letters are contained in SD7. The reference classifications were organized into corresponding CLS files and are provided on a separate floppy disk. This way the images can be distributed as testing material separate from the reference classifications which are the answers to the test. In May 1992, the First Census Optical Character Recognition Systems conference was hosted at NIST and the success of this event was heavily dependent on the production of SD3 and SD7.

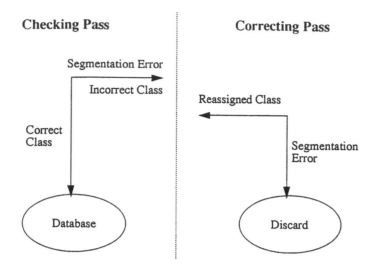

FIGURE 21   Machine-assisted reference classification labeling.

ANALYSIS OF HANDWRITING SAMPLE COMPLEXITY

As stated earlier, SD3 contains handwriting samples from regional data-takers employed by the Bureau of the Census, whereas SD7 contains handwriting samples from high school math and science students. Based on these samples, one might ask, "Are the handwriting styles within these two databases similar or are they quite diverse? Does this diversity make one database more difficult to recognize than the other? If given a choice, what combination of writers would make up the ideal training set for maximizing recognition performance across the remaining writers from both databases?" Questions like these and many more face researchers and developers of optical character recognition systems. The goal of these databases is to provide sufficiently numerous and varied training and testing images that the performance of a character classifier can be reliably measured. It is widely acknowledged within the neural network and pattern recognition communities that the robustness of a classifier depends on the generality contained within the training set. A method of cross-validation has been applied to these databases in an attempt to unlock some of the answers related to handwriting complexity (12).

In standard v-fold cross-validation, a population of segmented and referenced character images is divided into v equally sized partitions. A character classifier is tested, reserving one partition as testing data and using the remaining partitions as training data. Recognition results are accumulated as each partition is used in turn for testing, and the remaining partitions are used for training. Statistics are then computed and analyzed to assess the amount of diversity contained within a given population.

To compare diversity across two database populations, a cross-cross-validation must be conducted. Once again, each database is divided into equally sized partitions. In this case, a large number of partitions from the first database are selected as a fixed training set, whereas each partition in the second database is used, one at a time, for testing. Statistics are computed on the results from testing with each partition from the second database. Then the roles of testing and training are reversed: A large number of partitions from the second database are selected as a fixed training set, whereas each partition from the first database is used for testing. The statistics computed are used to analyze the diversity between the two databases.

A study comparing SD3 to SD7 was conducted in Reference 12. In this study, the first 500 writers from SD3 were compared against the 500 writers in SD7. The two collections of 500 writers were each divided into 10 partitions with handprinted digits from 50 different writers in each partition. A standard 10-fold cross-validation was computed for each set. Each partition of 50 SD3 writers were selected in turn and used for testing the character classifier trained with the remaining 450 SD3 writers; 10 results were accumulated. The same was done for each partition of 50 SD7 writers, testing each partition in turn against the character classifier trained with the remaining 450 SD7 writers. The results from both standard 10-fold cross-validations are entered along the main diagonal of the validation comparison matrix shown in Figure 22. The results are shown as a mean percent error with associated standard deviation.

The cross-cross-validation is shown in the off-diagonal elements of the matrix in Figure 22. Four hundred fifty SD3 writers were used to train the character classifier, and then the partitions of 50 SD7 writers, one partition at a time, were used in testing. The resulting statistics are shown in the top-right element of the matrix. In reverse, 450 SD7 writers were used to train the character classifier, and then the partitions of 50 SD3 writers, one partition at a time, were used in testing. The results of training on SD7 writers and testing with SD3 writers is shown in the bottom-left element of the matrix.

The actual percentages of error shown in the matrix are not relevant to the comparison. The same character classifier was used throughout in an attempt to gain information about the data, not to gain information about the performance of the classifier. What is important are the differences in relative magnitudes between the various cross-validation statistics. The on-diagonal elements of the validation comparison matrix show that SD7 is a more diverse digit set than is SD3. When trained and tested on partitions of itself, the SD3 tests achieved a mean error rate of only 1.7%, whereas the SD7 tests achieved a mean error rate of 3.8%. In essence, SD7 is a more complex and difficult database to recognize than is SD3. The off-diagonal elements show that SD3 used as training prototypes for SD7 is markedly inferior to SD7 used as a training set for SD3. The classifier

Mean Error ±σ	Test SD3 50 writers	Test SD7 50 writers
Train SD3 450 writers	$1.7 \times 10^{-2} \pm 0.3$	$6.8 \times 10^{-2} \pm 0.4$
Train SD7 450 writers	$3.5 \times 10^{-2} \pm 0.3$	$3.8 \times 10^{-2} \pm 0.5$

FIGURE 22   Cross-validation results comparing SD3 and SD7.

trained on SD7 and testing with SD3 achieved a mean percent error of 3.5%, whereas the classifier trained on SD3 and testing with SD7 achieved a mean percent error of 6.8%. This suggests that handprinted digits in SD7 represent a superset of the variation found in the samples contained in SD3. In other words, SD7 is a more general dataset.

CONCLUSION

Databases like *NIST Special Databases 1, 3,* and *7* are critical to advancing automated character recognition technologies. The Image Recognition Group at NIST is currently using these databases to research areas including field isolation, box detection and removal, character segmentation, and writer-independent character classification. Through the production of these databases, the First Census Optical Character Recognition Systems Conference was made possible, and practical lessons learned include issues of file formats, compression, and organization. As a result, techniques such as machine-assisted labeling of reference classifications and cross-validation studies for analyzing database complexity have been developed. These general techniques have broad application beyond character recognition. Together, these databases represent the largest publicly available collection of handprinted character images available for recognition system training and testing with copies being distributed and used around the world.

REFERENCES

1. R. A. Wilkinson, J. Geist, S. A. Janet, P. J. Grother, C. J. C. Burges, R. Creecy, B. Hammond, J. J. Hull, N. J. Larsen, T. P. Vogl, and C. L. Wilson, "The First Census Optical Character Recognition System Conference," Technical Report NISTIR 4912, National Institute of Standards and Technology, July 1992.
2. C. L. Wilson and M. D. Garris, "Handprinted Character Database," *NIST Special Database 1,* **HWDB**, April 1990.
3. Department of Defense, "Military Specification—Raster Graphics Representation in Binary Format, Requirements for, MIL-R-28002," December 1988.
4. CCITT, *Facsimile Coding Schemes and Coding Control Functions for Group 4 Facsimile Apparatus,* 1984, ITU, Geneva, Fascicle VII.3-Rec. T.6.
5. M. D. Garris, C. L. Wilson, J. L. Blue, G. T. Candela, P. J. Grother, S. A. Janet, and R. A. Wilkinson, "Massively Parallel Implementation of Character Recognition Systems," in *Conference on Character Recognition and Digitizer Technologies,* SPIE, San Jose, CA, 1992, Vol. 1661, pp. 269–280.
6. M. D. Garris and R. A. Wilkinson, "Handwritten Segmented Characters Database," Technical Report Special Database 3, **HWSC**, National Institute of Standards and Technology, February 1992.
7. R. A. Wilkinson, "Handprinted Segmented Characters Database," Technical Report Test Database 1, **TST1**, National Institute of Standards and Technology, April 1992.
8. M. D. Garris and S. A. Janet, "Scoring Package Release 1.0," Technical Report Special Software 1, **SP**, National Institute of Standards and Technology, October 1992.
9. M. D. Garris and S. A. Janet, "NIST Scoring Package User's Guide, Release 1.0," Technical Report NISTIR 4950, National Institute of Standards and Technology, October 1992.
10. M. D. Garris, "Methods for Evaluating the Performance of Systems Intended to Recognize Characters from Image Data Scanned from Forms," Technical Report NISTIR 5129, National Institute of Standards and Technology, February 1993.

11. R. A. Wilkinson, M. D. Garris, and J. Geist, ''Machine-Assisted Human Classification of Segmented Characters for OCR Testing and Training,'' in *Conference on Character Recognition Technologies*, D. P. D'Amato (ed.), SPIE, San Jose, CA, 1993, Vol. 1906, pp. 208–217.

12. P. J. Grother, ''Cross Validation Comparison of NIST OCR Databases,'' in *Conference on Character Recognition Technologies*, D. P. D'Amato (ed.), SPIE, San Jose, CA, Vol. 1906, pp. 296–307.

MICHAEL D. GARRIS

DISTRIBUTED ARTIFICIAL INTELLIGENCE: AN OVERVIEW

INTRODUCTION

For many years, research in artificial intelligence has been mostly oriented toward a single agent, with fixed knowledge and a specified goal. The agent evolves in a static environment and its main activities are gathering information, planning, and executing some plan to achieve its goal. This approach has been proven insufficient due to the inevitable presence of a number of agents in the real world. In fact, we must plan the activities of agent while keeping in mind the other agents' activities that can either help or hinder him. Hence, the scientific community is interested in Distributed Artificial Intelligence (DAI) with the goal of studying such types of interaction. DAI, a relatively new but growing body of research in Artificial Intelligence (AI), is based on a different model than traditional artificial intelligence. Indeed, the latter stipulated that an intelligent system simulates a certain form of human reasoning, knowledge, and expertise for a given task, whereas distributed artificial intelligence systems were conceived as a group of intelligent entities, called agents, that interacted by cooperation, by coexistence, or by competition.

Why DAI?

Recently, DAI has became a research topic as important as knowledge representation and learning. The interest and high regard that researchers have for DAI are shown in many ways. The first way is related to the necessity to treat distributed knowledge in applications that are geographically dispersed such as sensor networks, air-traffic control, or cooperation between robots. Another way consists in attempting to extend the man–machine cooperation with an approach based on the distributed resolution between man and machine(s). The third way is that DAI brings about a new perspective in knowledge representation and problem soving, by providing richer scientific formulations and more realistic representation in practice. Finally, from a general point of view, DAI approach sheds new light on the cognitive sciences and artificial intelligence. Certain researchers, notably Nilsson (1), believe that DAI could be crucial to our understanding of artificial intelligence. There are many arguments to support this belief. First, a system may be so complicated and contain so much knowledge that it is better to break it down into different cooperative entities in order to obtain more efficiency (i.e., modularity, flexibility, and a quicker response time). That is the case of Chang's participating machine systems (2), which facilitate simultaneous interactions between several people and several machine agents collaborating on the same task. A second argument is that work done with DAI could allow the modeling of our intuitions about the reasoning based on knowledge, action, and planning. Currently, methods exist that represents beliefs, plans, and actions for the purpose of reasoning about interactions between intelligent systems. Hence, knowing how an artificial system can reason about others should help us to better understand how this same system can reason about itself. A third argument is that methods used by an intelligent system to reason about the actions of other systems can also be used to reason with other environmentally nonintelligent dynamic processes. Without these methods it is probable that artificial intelligence would remain confined to the study of static areas. Lastly, research in DAI contributes to our understanding of the communication process using natural language. Indeed, communicative acts between intelligent systems generally are an abstraction of certain aspects of the production and comprehension of natural language, and the study of this abstraction can help to clarify certain problems studied in natural language.

An Overview of DAI Applications

Constructing a distributed solution is, in fact, often related to the nature of the problem at hand. Thus, most of the work done in the area of DAI has been aimed at sensory networks such as air-traffic control or robotic systems (3–6). The main reason is that these applications necessitate a distributed interpretation and distributed planning by means of different intelligent sensors. Planning includes not only the activities to be undertaken but also the use of material and cognitive resources to accomplish interpretation tasks to be solved; these application areas are characterized by a natural distribution of sensors and receivers in space. In other words, the sensorial data interpretation and action planning are interdependent in time and space. For example, in air-traffic control, a plan for guiding an aircraft must be coordinated with the plans of nearby aircraft to avoid collisions. This interdependence results from possible overlaps in intercepted zones. Therefore, the best way to take advantage of these overlaps in order to eliminate imprecision and uncertainty is to engage in a cooperation with the neighboring groups of sensors to evaluate and to interpret the available data.

In addition to applications involving sensory networks, researchers have also investigated the application of DAI techniques to system automation, such as flexible workshops (7), and to cooperation between expert systems in engineering (8–11). These applications are motivated by the traditional positive aspects of distributed processing systems (e.g., performance, reliability, resource sharing). Furthermore, ideas from DAI are becoming important to research fields such as distributed databases, distributed and parallel computing, computer-supported cooperative work, computer-aided design and manufacturing, concurrent engineering, and distributed decision making.

The objective of this article is to give an overview of the DAI field and survey new avenues that have emerged recently in this field. It is organized as follows. In the next section, a taxonomy of DAI is presented, divided along three main lines: the social abilities of an individual agent involved in a group of agents, the organization of agents, and the dynamics of this organization (e.g., the coherence and the coordination) through time. This is followed by a discussion on emerging concepts in DAI. The third section presents a review of recent DAI research and development. Finally, the last section presents a short summary of new directions for further DAI research.

DISTRIBUTED ARTIFICIAL INTELLIGENCE TAXONOMY

The DAI literature discusses many important concepts such as commitment (12–15); negotiation (10,16–19), cooperation, and distributed problem solving (19–21); coherence

(6,14); and understanding other agents (22). However, there is no attempt to propose a framework integrating these concepts. Our taxonomy of DAI (see Fig. 1) is a step toward remedying this problem by providing a framework which integrates most of the current concepts used in DAI. This taxonomy views DAI systems as *social systems* because they involve multiple agents and assumes that the properties of DAI systems are not derivable or representative solely on the basic of properties of their component agents. In fact, a social perspective of a group is not a new idea. For instance, Mead (23) states that

> . . . the whole (society) is prior to the part (the individual), not the part to the whole; and the part is explained in terms of the whole, not the whole in terms of the parts.

In addition, we propose a DAI taxonomy that is viewed along three dimensions: the social abilities of an individual agent, the organization of agents, and the dynamic control of this organization (see Fig. 1).

The social abilities of an individual agent include:

1. *Reasoning about others.* that is, the agent's ability to reason about the actions and plan of other agents in order to predict their behavior as well as her own behavior
2. *Assessment of a distributed situation.* that is, the agent's ability to assess her environment in order to update her model of the surrounding world and her models of other agents.

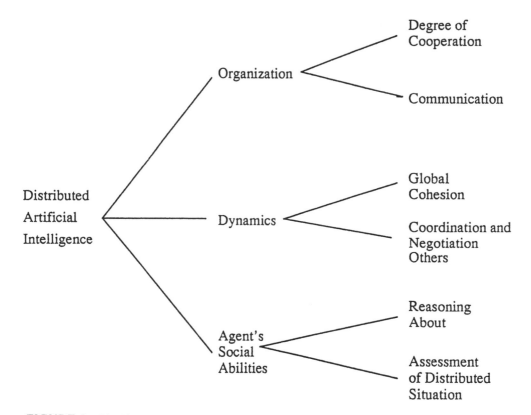

FIGURE 1   Distributed artificial intelligence taxonomy.

The agent's organization includes the *degree of cooperation* between agents and the *way of communicating* between them. Finally, the dynamic control of the agent's organization concerns the *global cohesion* of the entire group and the *coordination of agents using the negotiation process*. These three dimensions are examined in the next subsections.

The Social Abilities of an Individual Agent

As mentioned earlier, the social abilities of an agent involved in DAI comprise its abilities to reason about and to change beliefs, actions, and plans of others and to assess a distributed situation. We now detail these abilities.

Ability to Reason About, and to Change, Beliefs, Actions, and Plans of Other Agents

Multiagent systems need the ability to reason about, and to change, beliefs and actions of other agents, as well as their behavior. According to Sycara (18), this ability constitutes a necessity in multiagent negotiations.

Let us first consider the ability to reason about, and to change, beliefs and actions of other agents. Much of the research done in this area has been aimed at understanding the knowledge required to perform certain actions and how that knowledge can be acquired through communication.

Early work by McCarty and Hayes (24) argued that a planning program needs to explicitly reason about its ability to perform an action. Moore (25) took this argument one step further by emphasizing the crucial relationship between knowledge and action. Knowledge is necessary to perform actions, and new knowledge is gained as result of performing actions. Moore went on to construct a logic with *possible-worlds* semantics that allowed explicit reasoning about knowledge and action, and then considered the problem of automatically generating deductions within the logic.

In the area of reasoning about another agent's beliefs, Halpern (26) notes that most models of knowledge and belief are based on the possible-worlds model. In this model, an agent is said to know a fact if this fact is true in all worlds that he thinks are possible. Such situations are often formally described using a modal propositional logic and Kripke structures. Some of the problems that researchers have had to deal with are *logical omniscience* (agents are able to derive all valid formulas and their logical consequences) and *common knowledge* (not only does everyone know that a fact is true, but they know everyone knows, etc.).

Recently, Shoham (27) considered that role played by the concept of action in AI. He first summarizes the advantages and limitations of past approaches which take the concept to be primitive, as embodied in the situation calculus (24) and the dynamic logic (28). He also summarizes the alternative, namely, adopting a temporal framework, and points out its complementary advantages and limitations. The author then proposes a framework that retains the advantages. Specifically, Shoham proposed to start with the notion of time lines and to define the notion of action as the ability to make certain choices among sets of time lines. This framework sheds new light on the connection among time, action, knowledge, and on reasoning about the same events at different levels of detail. Shoham and Moses (29) complement this work by investigating the relation between the notion of knowledge and belief. In this context and contrary to the well-known slogan about "knowledge being true belief," the authors propose that belief should be viewed as defeasible knowledge. Specifically, they offer a definition of belief as knowledge-relative-to-assumptions and tie this definition to the notion of nonmonotonicity.

In a similar way, Galliers (30) describes strategies that allow rational agents to change their beliefs during conversational interaction. Her approach includes the following:

1. a foundation theory: Beliefs are sustained by explicit justifications and are dropped if the justifications change.
2. a coherence theory: Beliefs persist until challenged.

Lizotte and Moulin (31) extend this view to the connection between goals and beliefs. They introduce the notion of decision space where goals are bound to beliefs by preconditions and current conditions. A goal can be activated only if concurrent conditions hold and must be dropped if concurrent conditions change.

Behind the ability to reason about, and to change, beliefs and actions of other agents, intelligent agents must also reason about (and change) the behavior of others. In this respect, agents must reason about other agents' plan in order to recognize their potential actions. Many AI models of plan recognition have viewed it as a process of belief and intention ascription (32–35). Such a plan recognition model could abstractly be viewed over a space of all plans that can be constructed from the known actions and processes. Each plan constructible in this search space could be viewed as a script structure. Kautz (36) has criticized this model for its failure to provide a formal analysis of the defeasible reasoning inherent in plan recognition. In particular, Kautz notes that this model presents only a space of *possible* inferences, and little is said about why one should infer one conclusion instead of another, or what one should conclude if the situation is ambiguous. Kautz himself provides a plan recognition formalization, stated in terms of circumscription. However, his model relies on two strong assumptions.

1. The *observer*, that is, the agent performing the plan recognition, is assumed to have a complete knowledge of the domain.
2. The *actor*, which is the agent whose plan is being inferred, has a correct plan.

Pollack (37,38) has shown that these assumptions are too strong for a useful model of plan recognition, particularly in the real world. Consequently, she proposes, with her colleague Konolige (39), an alternative formalization of plan recognition, one in which it is not necessary to assume that the actor's plan is correct from the perspective of the observer but is preferred over others. This plan recognition model, which uses defeasible reasoning and direct augmentation for the ascription of belief, is actually used to support communication (40).

Assessment of Distributed Situation

An intelligent agent involved in DAI may have, at any moment, a wide variety of choices about what to believe, what knowledge can be considered as relevant, and what actions to pursue. In other words, the problem of which agent does what, and when, can be seen as the basic question of distributed artifical intelligence. To solve this problem, each individual agent (or only one agent if the control is centralized) must assess the distributed situation in which many agents evolve. Generally, the *situation assessment* involves acquiring, organizing, and evaluating information about the environment, which may either correlate well with the agent's expectations or serve to create new ones. This question may be partially answered by using planning that involves multiple agents operating in dynamic worlds.

Until recently, all work in automatic planning has been concerned with methods of representing and solving what might be called the classical planning problems. In this type of problem, the world is considered as being in one of a potentially infinite number of states. Performing an action causes the world to pass from one state to the next. In the specification of a problem, we are given a set of goals, a set of allowable action, and a description of the world's initial state. The planning system is then asked to find a sequence of actions that will transform the world from any state satisfying the initial-state description to one that satisfies the goal description. This framework has typically been used to model real-world problems that involve a single agent operating in an environment that changes only as the result of the agent's action, and otherwise remains static.

Much contemporary research, however, is concerned with broader classes of planning problems, particularly those that involve multiple agents operating in dynamic worlds. To model multiagent planning, appropriate representations for simultaneous actions and continuous processes are required, along with mechanisms for solving problems by using such representations. Hendrix (41) was one of the first to address these representational issues, having developed a system for simulating the effects of simultaneous actions in a dynamic world. More recent contributions have been made by Allen (42), Georgeff (43,44), Lansky (45), and McDermott (46–48), each of whom has used a different approach to the problem of representing actions and state-based logic, whereas McDermott prefers a logic that combines states with continuous time lines.

Generally, a multiagent plan is built to avoid the duplication of effort and inconsistent or conflicting actions. It is typically used in a multiagent environment to identify and plan around resource conflicts. In fact, research on planning for multiple agents has gone in two directions. One is the *centralized multiagent planning* where one agent has information about the other agents' activities, and the second is the *distributed multiagent planning* where planning is done in a distributed manner. In centralized multiagent planning, Georgeff (49) developed an approach where the plans of individual agents are first formed, and then some central agent collects them and analyzes them to identify potential interactions, such as conflicts between the agents over limited resources. The central agent then performs a safety analysis to determine which potential interactions could lead to conflicts. She next groups together sequences of unsafe situations to create critical plans. Finally, she communicates commands to other agents so that they avoid these critical plans. Georgeff and Lansky (43,45) and Stuart (50,51) have pursued this centralized multiagent planning approach further. More precisely, Georgeff has used alternative representations for time and events in multiagent domains, and Stuart has examined the problem if synchronizing plans were executed by different agents to avoid undesirable interactions among plans.

Cammarata et al. (52) proposed another approach to centralized multiagent planning to avoid collision in air-traffic control. In this approach, agents, that is, aircraft, negotiate to choose a coordinator that is, for example, the least constrained. Each agent then sends relevant information, and the coordinator builds a multiagent plan that specifies all of the agents' planned actions. The advantage of this centralized approach is that it avoids generating inconsistent plans. However, it may require many planning cycles to reach an acceptable solution.

Contrary to centralized planning, there is no single agent with a global view of group activities when planning is done in a distributed manner. In this case, detecting and resolving interactions between agents is much more difficult, and the general approach is to provide each agent with a planning capacity that takes into account the activities of others. In this context, the approaches developed by Lochbaum (40) and Chaib-draa (53,54) that explore the roles that particular beliefs and intentions play in collaborative activity seem promising.

Organization

In DAI, we need knowledge to create agents that can reconfigure their actions and interactions as their context changes. Historically, DAI systems have had very limited flexibility for adapting their global behavior, as they usually focused on a single aspect of the problem at hand, such as task allocation (3,6,52). Today, it is critical to develop a useful framework to make DAI systems more adaptable. This ought to be done by following some basic concepts of organization and organizational change. Therefore, it is helpful to have a better idea of what we mean by "organization." We first distinguish an organization from a structure. In a multiagent environment, a *structure* is the pattern of information and control relationships that exist between agents, and the distribution of problem-solving capabilities among them. In cooperative distributed problem solving (see the subsection Degree of cooperation) for example, a structure gives each agent a high-level view of how the group solves problems and the role each agent plays within this structure. With this view, the agents can ensure that they meet conditions that are essential to successful problem solving, including the following (55):

- *Coverage*: any necessary portion of the overall problem must be within the problem solving capabilities of at least one agent
- *Connectivity*: agents must interact in a manner that permits the covered activities to be developed and integrated into an overall solution
- *Capability*: coverage and connectivity must be achievable within the communication resource limitations, as well as the reliability specifications of the group

Generally, the structure must specify roles and relationships to meet these conditions. For example, to ensure the coverage, the structure could assign roles to agents according to their competences and knowledge for a given subproblem. The structure must then also indicate the connectivity information to the agents so that they can distribute subproblems to competent agents. This connectivity information should also allow agents with overlapping competences to avoid duplication of effort when solving the same subproblem.

An *organization* for DAI is less structured in perspective and more related to current organization theory (56,57). For example, Gasser (58) views an organization as:

> a particular set of settled and unsettled questions about beliefs and actions through which agents view other agents. Organizational change means opening and/or settling some different set of questions in a different way, giving individual agents new problems to solve and . . . a different base of assumptions about the beliefs and actions of other agents.

Clearly, an organization should not be conceived as a structural relationship among a collection of agents or as a set of externally defined limitations to their activities. In fact, the best way to define an organization is to view the concept of organization as embedded in the beliefs, intentions, and commitments of agents themselves. In other works, an organization is defined as a set of agents with mutual commitments, global commitments, mutual beliefs, and, eventually, joint intentions when these agents act together to achieve a given goal.

Evidently, notions such as beliefs, intentions, and commitments are driven by the degree of cooperation that exists between agents and by the spectrum of communication methodologies that is offered to the agent in order to exchange beliefs, intentions, and commitments. The following subsections address these two dimensions.

Degree of Cooperation

The degree of cooperation characterizes the amount of cooperation between agents that can range from fully cooperative (i.e., total cooperation) to antagonistic (20). Fully cooperative agents that are able to resolve nonindependent problems often pay a price in high communication costs. These agents may change their goals to suit the needs of other agents in order to ensure cohesion and coordination. Conversely, the antagonistic systems may not cooperate at all and may even block each others' goals. Communication costs required by these systems are generally minimal. In the middle of the spectrum lie traditional systems that lack a clearly articulated set of goals. Notice that most real systems have a weak degree of cooperation.

Total cooperation is done in the cooperative distributed problem-solving (CDPS) studies (19), where agents can work together in a loosely coupled network to solve problem that are beyond their individual capabilities. In this network, each agent is capable of resolving complex problems and can work independently, but the problems faced by the agents cannot be completed without total cooperation. Total cooperation is necessary because no single agent has sufficient knowledge and resources to solve a given problem and different agents might have the expertise to solve its different parts (i.e., subproblems). Generally, CDPS agents build cooperatively a solution to a problem by using their local knowledge and resources to individually solve subproblems, and then by integrating these subproblems solutions into an overall solution. For example, geographically separated aircraft have different perceptions because their sensors pick up different signals. Only by combining information about their views they be able to form an overall picture of aircraft movements to resolve conflicts among them. Note that CDPS is particularly useful when a distributed control becomes uncertain (59). The presence of other uncertainties such as incomplete or imprecise information, or an aggregation of information from multiple sources, makes the need for total cooperation even more crucial (60).

CDPS is also particularly useful when each agent has specific knowledge and does not have a clear idea of what he might do or what information he might exchange with others. This is the case for many realistic artificial intelligence systems which are often built from so-called cooperating experts where each expert has all the knowledge of its particular domain. In this context, Smith and Davis (61) advocate the use of cooperative frameworks that minimize communication, allow load balancing, and distribute control, while also maintaining coherent behavior. Their proposed solution, Contract-Nets, is based on negotiation mechanism discussed in the subsection Coordination and negotiation.

The fully cooperative-to-agnostic spectrum of cooperation has been surveyed by Genesereth (62) and Rosenschein (63). They note that the situation of total cooperation, known as the *benevolent agent* assumption, is accepted by most DAI researchers but that it is not always true in the real world where agents may have conflicting goals. Such conflicting goals are reflected, for example, by a set of personal meeting-scheduling agents where each agent tries to schedule a meeting at the best time for its particular owner. To study this type of interaction, Genesereth and Rosenschein define agents as entities operating under the constraints of various rationality axioms that restrict their choices in interactions.

More recently, Sycara (18) has dealt with situations where cooperative behavior cannot be assumed and resolution of ensuring conflicts is necessary. Conflict resolution is achieved through direct negotiation among interacting agents or through a third party, the Mediator.

Communication

In DAI, the possible solutions to the communication problem range between those involving no communication to those involving speech acts. The implicit solutions in previous research in DAI falls somewhere in between.

No Communication: Here the agent rationally infers other agents' plans without communicating with them. Schelling (64) and Tubbs (65) term this *tacit bargaining* and point out that it works best when agents' goals are not conflicting. To study this behavior, Genesereth (62) and Rosenschein (66) use a game-theoretic approach characterized by payoff matrices that contain agents' payoffs for each possible outcome of an interaction. This approach also assumes that agents have common knowledge of the payoff matrix associated with the interaction, an assumption that may be unrealistic when considering that agents are nonbenevolent. Recently, Rosenschein (67) has extended this approach by providing agents with a mechanism for further refining the agents' choice of rational moves. This probablistic extension represents explicitly uncertainty about other players' moves and is particularly suitable for use by a deductive engine in deciding on a move in an interaction. However, this approach, which does not use communication, presents a major difficulty: The mutual rational deduction would lead to an enormous computational cost if the situation requires several agents. Indeed, agents must rely on sophisticated local reasoning compensating the lack of communication to decide on appropriate actions and interactions.

Primitive Communication Using: In this case, communication is restricted to two fixed signals with fixed interpretations like those used by CSP (68,69). Georgeff (49) has applied this work to multiagent planning to avoid conflicts between plans involving more than one agent. Evidently, the limited number and types of signals available in this approach limit the cooperation between agents. In fact, these signals have been applied to avoid conflicts between sequential processes or to coordinate parallel activities (70), and complex actions cannot be formed as there is no syntax of signals to build up complex actions. Hence, requests, commands, and complex intentions cannot be expressed with these signals.

Plan and Information Passing: Rosenschein (66) proposed an approach where an agent A1 communicates her total plan to agent A2, and A2 communicates her total plan to A1. According to its author, this method has two severe problems. First, total plan passing is computationally expensive. Second, there is no guarantee that the resulting plan will be warranted by the recipient's knowledge base. In addition to these author's criticisms, there are other difficulties with total plan passing (71). First, the total plan passing is not guaranteed by any medium of communication. Second, the plan passing is difficult to achieve in real-world applications because there is a great deal of uncertainty about the present state of the world, as well as its future. Consequently, for real-life situations, total plans cannot be formulated in advance, and general strategies must be communicated to a recipient.

Information Exchanges Through a Blackboard: In AI, model used most often as shared global memory is the blackboard model (72–79) on which agents write messages, post partial results, and find information. It is usually partitioned into *levels* of abstraction derived from the problem at hand, and agents working at a particular level of abstraction view a corresponding level of the blackboard along with the adjacent levels. In this way, data that have been synthesized on any level can be communicated to higher levels, and higher level goals can be filtered down to drive the expectations of lower-level agents. The simplicity with which the blackboard paradigm represents the classical problem of data-driven versus goal-driven information flow is perhaps the reason why blackboard models are widely used in existing distributed artificial intelligence system.

Message Passing: Undoubtably, the work of Hewitt and his colleagues (80–83) on actor languages is an excellent representation of the message-passing application to DAI. The essential idea about actors is clearly summarized in the words of Agha and Hewitt (84) as follows:

> An actor is a computational agent which carries out its actions in response to processing a communication. The actions it may perform are:
> (1) send communication to itself or to other actors;
> (2) create more actors;
> (3) specify the *replacement behaviour*.

The "replacement behavior" describes the new "actor machine" produced after processing the communication, that is, the new state of the actor.

Note that Hewitt's intuition is fundamentally correct when he states that control of multiagent environments is best looked at in terms of communication structures. In his work, however, agents have an extremely simple structure, and the model gives no formal syntax, semantics, or pragmatics for such communication structures. Consequently, this model was rarely used as a theory of communication between complex agents. In addition, several works in DAI have used classic message passing with a protocol and a precise content (52,59,85). Indeed, from a pragmatic point of view, classical message passing offers a more abstract means of communication that shared memory like the blackboard, and its content is generally well understood. It also is easier to program than blackboard because it is more abstract (86).

High-Level Communication: Research on natural language understanding and particularly research on intentions in communication (87) are relevant to DAI research because both research areas might investigate reasoning about multiple agents with distinct and possibly contradictory intentional states such as beliefs, facts, and intentions. In natural language, examination of even simple dialogues illustrates the utility of mental states such as beliefs and intentions, and an extra-linguistic knowledge about environment. For example, to find missing phrases in a dialogue, a computer system capable of taking the role of a hearer will need to use extra-linguistic knowledge about the domain and likely intentions (i.e., plans) of the speaker. In this respect, Allen (42,88) and Litman (35) have developed a natural language system using plans and goals for understanding questions, generating helpful responses, and dealing with indirect speech acts. However, their system does not give an explicit formal theory of how complex intentional states are formed by the process of communication

Recently, Cohen and Levesque (87,89,90) developed a formal theory for taking into account intentional states in the communication process. They derive the basis of a theory of communication from a formal theory of rational interaction based on the agent's intentions and commitments. Their major result is a demonstration that not all illocutionary acts (i.e., things you can do with an utterance) need be primitive but rather can be treated as complex actions. Galliers (91) extends this theory to situations involving conflict between agents as well as cooperation. Precisely, she proposes a strategic framework which incorporates a theory of agenthood, multiagent, and rational interaction as the basis for communication. In her strategic framework, agents no longer need be or be assumed to be unoccupied and benevolent for cooperative action.

Werner (71,92) also takes an important step in this direction. He provides a general theoretical framework for designing agents with a communicative and social competence. His framework, for designing agents with a communicative and social competence, is based on the agent's cognitive states, such as knowledge and intentional states.

To summarize, research on high-level communication such as speech acts is particularly relevant to DAI research because this research area also investigates the reasoning about multiple agents. Indeed, dialogue between agents allows the generation and the interpretation of utterances which are speech actions planned to convey the information that the speaker is in particular mental states (beliefs, commitments, and intentions) which consist to induce a particular mental states in the hearer. Through an appropriate dialogue, agents can converge on shared mental plans (i.e., webs of mutual beliefs, commitments, and intentions) for how they should coordinate their activities (53,93).

Dynamics

Given an organization of agents, how does one arrive at a control for it? In other words, how does one arrive at a coherent behavior of agents and a coordination of their distributed resources? This section deals with these two issues.

Coherent Behavior

Assuming that a group of agents is cooperating to some extent, the problem is to know how to ensure that agents act coherently in making decisions or taking action, accommodating the global effects of local decisions and avoiding harmful interactions; precisely, how agents can achieve coherent behavior or global coherence. *Global coherence* means that actions of agents make sense with respect to the common goals of the entire group. Of course, the structure that is developed says something about how the group achieves coherence. For example, Kornfeld and Hewitt (82) present a team structure they term a *Scientific Community Metaphor* for cooperative distributed problem solving. This structure is based on the observation that "scientific communities are highly parallel systems." Agents are structured into loose classes that have general problem-solving goals. *Proposers* suggest possible solutions to the problem at hand. *Proponents* then collect and present evidence in favor of a proposal, whereas *skeptics* collect and present evidence to disprove this proposal. *Evaluators* examine proposals and balance the system so that more work is done on those proposals that seem to be more favorable. Note that evaluators, by controlling which proposals seem more favorable, provide *metalevel control* without altering the structure of agents.

The information communicated among agents also affects coherence. In this respect, Durfee (6) has shown that there are three major characteristics of communicated information that affect a coherent behavior: relevance, timeliness, and completeness. For a given message, *relevance* measures the amount of information that is consistent with the solution derived by the group of agents. Irrelevant messages may redirect the receiving agent into wasting its processing resources on attempts to integrate inconsistent information, so higher relevance of communicated information can result in more global coherence because this information stimulates work along the solution path. The *timeliness* of a transmitted message measures the extent to which a transmitted message will influence the current activity of the receiving agent. In this way, any transmitted information, which redirects the receiving agent to work in a more promising area, must be sent promptly. Finally, *completeness* of a message measures the fraction of a complete solution that the message represents. Completeness affects coherence by reducing the number of partially or fully redundant messages communicated between agents.

These characteristics of communicated information are affected by both the agent's social abilities (which generate the potential information that can be transmitted) and the communication policy (which decides what information should be sent, to what agents, and when). So, increased global coherence could be achieved by improving only an agent's social abilities, by improving only communication policies, or by a combination of both. In each of these cases, more coherent decisions result if an agent has a better understanding of what it has already done, what it is likely to do, and the activities and intentions of other agents.

Notice that "coherence" can also refer to how well the system behaves as a unit. In this context, the term coherence can be used in discussing properties of the total DAI system (94):

- *Satisfactory global solution*. This is the organization's ability to reach satisfactory global solution.
- *Efficiency*. This is the organization's overall efficiency is achieving global solution.
- *Capacity to reconcil disparities*. This is the organization's capacity to resolve disparities (disparities are generally due to differences between agent's representations and the affair to which the representation refer).
- *Graceful behavior in presence of failure*. This is the organization's behavior in the presence of failure.

Coordination and Negotiation

In DAI, agents should coordinate their distributed resources which might be physical (such as communication capabilities) or informational (such as information about the problem decomposition). Clearly, agents must find an *appropriate technique* for working together in harmony. This technique depends on the distribution of the shared resources and on the local autonomy of agents. Notice that autonomous agents have their own possibly disparate goals, knowledge and reasoning process including decision-making criteria. Nevertheless, they should still find ways to agree on how to coordinate themselves when coordination could help them to better achieve their goals.

Notice that coordination does not necessarily imply total cooperation because antagonists can be coordinated. This is the case, for example, for any game where generally "rules for play" permit antagonists to play together in harmony. On the other hand, coordination and coherence are partially related (94). Better coordination may lead to better coherence by avoiding "extraneous" activity such as synchronizing and aligning agents' tasks. However, good local decisions do not necessarily add up to good global behavior because good local decisions may lead to undesirable global decisions.

According to Malone (95), there are two general criteria for evaluating how well the coordination scheme itself performs: *flexibility* and *efficiency*. More precisely, Malone states that there is a trade-off between flexibility and efficiency in multiagent environments. This trade-off involves moving between, on the one hand, highly coupled structures with formalized procedures for dealing with almost all eventualities, and on the other hand, loosely coupled structures that depend on massive amounts of informal communication and mutual adjustment to adapt to rapidly changing complex environments.

Generally, researchers in DAI use the *negotiation* process to coordinate a group of agents. Unfortunately, negotiation, like other human concepts, is difficult to define. Sycara (96) for example, states that:

> the negotiation process involves identifying potential interactions either through communication or by reasoning about the current states and intentions of other agents in the system and modifying the intentions of these agents to avoid harmful interactions or create cooperative situations.

Durfee (19), another researcher in DAI, defines negotiation as

> the process of improving agreement (reducing inconsistency and uncertainty) on common viewpoints or plans through the structured exchange of relevant information.

Although these two descriptions of negotiation capture many of our intuitions about human negotiation, they are too vague to provide techniques for how to get agents to negotiate. Also, a number of very different approaches with varying techniques, but all embodying aspects of negotiation, have been developed by drawing on the rich diversity of how humans negotiate in different contexts (3,16,18,63,97). One of the most studied protocols for negotiation goes back to the human organization metaphor (3,98). The activity modeled by this protocol, termed Contract-Nets, is task sharing, where agents help each other by sharing the computation involved in the subtasks for a problem. More precisely, an agent who needs help decomposes a large problem into subproblems, announces the subproblems to the group, collects bids from agents, and awards the subproblem to the most suitable bidder. In fact, this protocol gives us the best negotiation process for dynamically decomposing problems because it is designed to support task allocation. It is also a way of providing dynamically opportunistic control for the coherence and the coordination of agents.

Discussion

We have outlined a taxonomy for distributed artificial intelligence including social abilities of an individual agent, the organization of agents, and its dynamic control through time. Social abilities of an individual agent require a sophisticated local control which includes reasoning about what other agents are doing (their goals, plans, intentions, and beliefs) and how this fits into what they know about others. Social abilities also require a distributed situation assessment which leads each agent to acquire, organize, and evaluate information about its environment where several agents interact.

Another important point in DAI concerns the organization design because, without organization, agents cannot interact in predictable ways. Notice that the organization and the organizational change must be embodied in shared information and in shared agreements between agents (i.e., the degree of cooperation). Evidently, this organization type has an evolutive control through time. Generally, this evolution must take into account the global coherence of the group and the coordination between agents. The problem of global coherence is to ensure that agents act coherently in making decisions or taking actions and accommodating the nonlocal effects of local decisions. To accomplish this, we must look for an adequate structure and an organization that allow a group of agents to obtain and maintain a global coherence. We need also to develop policies to guide agents' decisions about what information to exchange, with whom, and when, because agents (and their global coherence) are influenced by the information they receive.

The coordination is without doubt the fundamental aspect of DAI and of intelligent behavíor. An effective coordination requires a flexible structure, reasoning capabilities, and a structured exchange of relevant information.

REVIEW OF SOME RECENT DAI WORKS

In this section, some recent DAI world are reviewed; our survey article would be incomplete without it. Of course, it is by no means to be exhaustive; rather, it should augment and argument the previous sections of this article.

As mentioned earlier, DAI refers to systems in which decentralized agents interact. Within this definition, however, there is wide variability in the operational definitions of terms. "Agents" may refer to arbitrary numbers of more or less sophisticated entities. In the same way, "decentralized" may refer to the distribution of knowledge, information, control, or resources among different intelligent entities. Finally, the "interaction" of agents belongs to their degree of cooperation that range between fully cooperative systems to more or less antagonistic systems.

These alternative definitions of terms have entailed a space of DAI works. Many of which, however, may be categorized in terms of the following:

1. Social behavior of a collection of agents
2. Conflict resolution and negotiation between agents
3. Multiagent planning
4. Blackboard, architectures, tools, and languages for building DAI systems
5. Applications for DAI

In the following subsections, we review the recent work done in each category.

Social Behavior of a Collection of Agents

The social behavior of a collection of agents is a new field of DAI that researchers have investigated recently. Werner (71,92), for example, develops the foundations for the design of systems of agents that behave as a social unit or group. To develop this, Werner presents a unified theory of communication, cooperation, and social structure. More precisely, he develops a formal account of the agent's intentional states and then links the linguistic message with its effect of the planning process. This allows him to give an account of social cooperative action because the agents' intentional states are mutually modified by a communicative exchange (i.e., a conversation or a discourse). This theory of intentional states also makes possible the author's attempt to provide a unified theory of communication and social structure because the intentional states are set up by communication in conjunction with social structures in such a way that the social goal is achievable. Finally, the theory of communication and social structure was used to give a formal analysis of the Contract-Net (98) and Wittgensteinian (99).

Another contribution is Star's (100) work on the ''structure of ill-structured solutions.'' Star argues that the development of distributed artificial intelligence should be based on a social metaphor rather than on a psychological one. Then, he suggests replacing the Turing Test (101) by the ''Durkheim Test'' (102), that is, systems should be tested with respect to their ability to meet community goals. To contribute to this, Star proposes the concept of *boundary objects* derived from analyses of organizational problem solving in scientific communities and suggests that this concept would be an appropriate data structure for DAI. Boundary objects are those objects that are plastic enough to be adaptable across multiple viewpoints, yet maintain continuity of identity.

Gasser and his colleagues (103) developed a new framework for representing and using a organizational knowledge in distributed AI systems. In the authors' view, a coordination framework or organization is a particular set of settled and unsettled questions about belief and action that agents have about other agents. Organizational change means opening and/or settling some different sets of questions, giving individual agents new problems to solve and, more importantly, different assumptions about the beliefs and actions of other agents. To test these ideas, Gasser et al. have used a testbed called the Intelligent Coordination Experiment (ICE) in which two classes of agents, *red* and *blue*, may move in all directions in a rectilinear *grid*.

Bond (12) shares the same view of organization for DAI as Gasser et al. He uses the concept of *commitment* introduced by Becker (104) in sociology. In Becker's description, individual agents participate in several organizations or settings. Hence, to regard their behavior in any one setting as consistent lines of activity, we must introduce the notion of commitments consequent to the individual's participation in other settings. These commitments constrain the individual's action and can be used explicitly in negotiation between agents. Commitment appears then as a central concept for DAI that Bond attempts to formulate and to propagate it into notions of agent and organization. In this context, an organization is defined as a set agents with consistent mutual commitments. Notice that the issues of agent integrity, plans, and resources, and their representation, are also discussed in Bond's work.

Finally, Hogg and Huberman (105) present a simple and robust procedure for freezing out chaotic behavior in systems composed of interacting agents making decisions based on imperfect and delayed information. Their procedure, which generates a diverse population out of an essentially homogeneous one, is able to control chaos through a series of dynamical bifurcations into a stable fixed point.

Conflict Resolution and Negotiation Between Agents

Work in DAI has, since its earliest years, been concerned with negotiation strategies. Smith's work on Contract-Nets (98) introduced a form of simple negotiation among cooperating agents, with one agent announcing the availability of tasks and awarding them to other bidding agents. Although Smith's original work assumed some autonomy among agents, these agents willingly bid for tasks without explicit motivation. Malone refined this technique by overlaying it with a more sophisticated economic model (106) providing optimality under certain conditions.

Zlotkin and Rosenschein (107) use game-theoretic techniques in an analysis of multiagent negotiation, in a way analogous to Malone's model. By introducing the formal language of game theory, suitably modified for use in an AI context, they provide tools for designing negotiation into automated agents. Precisely, a novel, stable, negotiation protocol is introduced for the case of agents who are able to share a discrete set of tasks with one another. The case of agents who may lie to one another during the negotiation, either by hiding some of their tasks or by creating fictitious tasks, is analyzed. It is shown that under some considerations, lies are beneficial. Recently, this work has been extended to general noncooperative domains (108,109).

Sycara's work (96) also relates to negotiation which is considered to be an iterative process that involves identifying potential interactions either through communication or by reasoning about the current states and intentions of other agents, and modifying the intentions of these agents so as to avoid harmful interactions or to create cooperative situations. Sycara (110) has explored these situations using a general negotiation model that handles multiagent, multiple-issue, single or repeated encounters based on an integration of case-based reasoning and multiattribute utility theory. Her model is able to generate a proposal, or a counterproposal that narrows the agents' differences, to take into consideration changing circumstances, to reason about other agents' beliefs, and to modify other agents' beliefs. It is implemented in a computer program called the "Persuader" that resolves adversial conflicts in the domain of labor relations (96,111,112). In fact, Sycara's research extends the DAI domain, where most work deal with groups of agents pursuing common goals to include noncooperative, multiagent interactions where cooperation cannot be assumed but needs to be dynamically induced during problem solving.

Adler and colleagues (113) also explore negotiated agreements. They discuss methods of conflict detection and conflict resolution in the domain of telephone network traffic control. In this network, planning capabilities are given to agents to increase the power of their interaction without undue addition of single-agent domain knowledge. The authors discuss several conflict-resolution strategies and present initial performance results. They also argue that negotiation is inextricably bound with planning because each process needs information gained from the other to function efficiently and effectively.

Another area that requires negotiation is the resource reallocation problem which requires multiagent choices under multiple criteria. To study this, Sathi and Fox (17) propose human negotiation procedures, such as logrolling, bridging, and unlinking. This methodology, in contrast to other approaches for negotiation, uses the concept of constraint-directed negotiation, where the agent's objectives are represented via sets of constraints together with their utilities. When a conflict occurs, agents negotiate by modifying either the current solutions or the constraints until a compromise is reached. Thus, joint solutions are generated through a process of negotiation that configures or reconfigures individual offerings. This constraint-directed negotiation approach is validated for the quality of solution in comparison to expert human negotiators on a variety of negotiation problems using a partial factorial design. Results obtained with the final version of their system show that the problem-solver performs marginally better than human experts on experimental problems.

Durfee and Montgomery (85,114) propose a hierarchical protocol as a negotiation process for coordinating multiagent behavior. Precisely, their work describes how a behavior hierarchy can be used in a protocol that allows AI agents to discover and resolve interactions flexibly. Agents that initially do not know with whom they might interact use this hierarchy to exchange abstractions of their anticipated behaviors. By comparing behaviors, agents interactively investigate interactions through more focused exchanges of successively detailed information. In this way, the hierarchical protocol gives agents a richer language for coordination that they get through exchanging plans or goals. To illustrate this, the authors use a prototype implementation in a robotic environment called MICE (the Michigan Intelligent Coordination Experiment testbed).

Finally, Conry and her colleagues (97,115) developed a limited form of negotiation in task allocation. They consider a class of task allocation problems called *distributed constraint satisfaction problems*, in which a coordinated set of actions is required to achieve the goals of the network, but each agent, termed node, has only limited resources available for completing all of its assigned tasks. The combination of local resource constraints and the need for coordination of actions among nodes give rise to a complex set of global, interdependent constraints. This kind of task allocation was investigated by its authors in the long-haul transmission "backbones" of larger, more complex communication networks. In these networks, nodes tentatively choose local actions and iteratively exchange this information. Through the iterative exchange of relevant information, the nodes converge toward compatible choices or recognize that the problem is overconstrained.

Multiagent Planning

With respect to the representation of action, it is commonly argued that classical frameworks [e.g., STRIPS (116)] are not adequate for reasoning about multiagent domains (43,45). Some researchers, however, remain within the classical framework. Thus, Pednault (117) proposes a new language, called ADL, to formulate multiagent, dynamic-world problems. ADL combines the notational convenience of the STRIPS operator language with the semantics and expressive power of the situation calculus and first-order dynamic logic. From the point of view of syntax, description in ADL resemble STRIPS operators with conditional add and delete lists. This syntax permits actions to be described whose effects are highly state dependent. At the same time, it allows the frame problem (118) to be circumvented to the extent that one needs only specify what changes are made when an action is performed, not what remains unaltered. However, the semantics of ADL is drastically different from that of STRIPS. Whereas STRIPS operators define transformations on state descriptions, ADL schemas define transformations on the states themselves. Furthermore, by adopting a different semantics, ADL avoids the pitfalls of the STRIPS language that are discussed by Lifschitz (119). Notice that Pednault's approach has the central objective of saving time and engendering cooperation by means of "parallel" plans. Whereas the classical approach of planning proceeds from the idea that each of several agents has a task of his own that he performs by carrying out an appropriate sequential plan (49–51).

Katz and Rosenschein (120) also takes the STRIPS representation of actions as plan representation. Indeed, they use STRIPS representation and directed acyclic graphs (DAGs) as a plan representation particularly to present methods for the verification, generation, and execution of plans for multiple agents represented as DAGs.

Cooperation by planning also focuses on mechanisms allowing an agent, in a distributed planning system whose agents are myopic, to assess and to reason about the nonlocal impact of local decisions. Conry and her colleagues (115,121) have explored these mechanisms. They propose algorithms for determining the conflict, exclusion, and infeasibility sets associated with a plan fragment. In addition, mechanisms for propagation are devised, allowing an agent to incorporate in its local data structures the knowledge it acquires and to reason using this new knowledge. A system utilizing these mechanisms in distributed planning for service restoral in communication systems has been implemented.

The object-oriented approach also seems to have its place in works on cooperation by planning. Thus, Kamel and Sayed (122) describe an object-oriented solution to the problem of generating coordinated, concurrent actions involving multiple agents, such as robots, to transform an initial state of a given world into a desired goal state. Their solution views agents as subplanners, each of which generates a plan to solve a subproblem of the given planning problem. The problem decomposition into subproblems is performed by applying an ''object-oriented decomposition'' approach: Each agent is assigned specific objects on which to act.

Blackboards, Architectures, Tools, and Languages for Building DAI Systems

There are now a number of blackboard shells and architectures for building DAI systems. Some of these have been designed specifically for DAI applications, whereas others are more general-purpose programming tools. We review here some recent works chosen for their significance.

Hayes-Roth and her colleagues (123) proposed a DAI model which metaphorically resembles a single intelligent individual characterized by adaptability, versatility, and coherence. To support these capabilities, Hayes-Roth and her colleagues created a DAI architecture based in the blackboard control architecture, in which some of the proposed features are already implemented (73,123–125), whereas others are in earlier design stages. Their proposed DAI architecture is based on three main capabilities:

1. Perception to acquire information from the environment
2. Action to affect entities in the environment
3. Cognition to interpret perceived information, solve problems, make decisions, and plan actions.

More precisely, the proposed architecture distributes the intelligence underlying these functions among locally controlled *perception/action agents* and *reasoning agents*, under the supervision of a single *control agent*. This architecture is instanced in the guardian system for intensive-care monitoring.

Another use of the blackboard paradigm has been developed by Nii, Aiello, and Rice (126). Their work concerns two software systems, Cage (127,128) and Poligon (126) which are two blackboard systems designed to exploit multiprocessor hardware with the intent of achieving computational speedup. Cage and Poligon, the results of two subprojects of advanced architectures project at the Knowledge Systems Laboratory of Stanford University, are attempts to produce high-performance parallel blackboard systems. One the one hand, the Cage system is a conservative attempt to introduce parallelism into the existing serial blackborad architecture AGE (129). On the other hand, Poligon anticipates future development in parallel hardware architecture. It is designed to work on the next generation of distributed-memory machines using hundreds or thousands of processors. Results of experiments have shown that Cage achieves a peak speedup factor of 5.7 for 16 processors and improves to 5.9 for 32 processors and that Poligon outperforms

Cage approximately by a factor of 10. These results show that the blackboard systems using parallelism can be exploited in many critical-time applications, and particularly in real-time applications.

Silverman et al. (130) have also investigated an implementation of a blackboard model by designing a tool called the Blackboard System Generator (BSG). The ultimate research objective of BSG is to describe a theoretic version of the blackboard model that will facilitate the application of known decision technology that can help minimize team decisions that are clearly dominated in terms of global and local agent objectives functions. A number of BSG projects are underway in case-based reasoning, machine learning by discovery, and template-relevant applications (131–133).

Work also has been done in the DAI architecture area. For example, Gasser et al. (134) have worked on a flexible testbed for DAI experiment called MACE (Multi-Agent Computing Environment). MACE is an instrumented testbed for building a wide range of experimental DAI systems at different levels of granularity. Its computational units (called ''agents'') run in parallel and communicative via messages. In fact, MACE is a *distributed*, *object-oriented system* which provides the following:

1. A language for describing agents
2. Utilities for tracing and instrumentation
3. A facility for remote demons
4. A collection of system-agents which construct user-agents from descriptions

Gasser et al. have validated MACE by building a blackboard system which implements a parallel arithmetic calculator. In this system, different knowledge sources reduce subexpressions, perform simple arithmetic operations, and synthesize results.

Using an adaptable architecture for DAI systems based on message passing, Shaw et al. (135) incorporate learning methods in DAI systems. To do this, they use two mechanisms of adaptation abstracted from human organizations (a market) and natural systems (evolution) in the hope of achieving DAI systems with comparable performance and sophistication. They point out the different types of learning processes that can occur in DAI systems and discuss the impact of these processes on problem solving in DAI systems.

Application for DAI

Recently, more work has been done in the distributed expert system area using DAI techniques. Bond (12), for example, examines the cooperation of specialists with distributed knowledge, in the context of knowledge-based support for collaboration among different engineering departments in carrying out large design tasks. In reality, Bond examines the problem of collaborative reasoning, which differs from other DAI approaches and in which intelligent systems cooperatively produce an agreed design. It is however, closely related to Hewitt's organizational problem solving using the notion of microtheories (136,137).

The approach taken by Mason and Johnson (138) is also very interesting. They propose a distributed ATMS (Assumption-based Truth Maintenance System), DATMS, which is a problem-solving framework for multiagent assumption-based reasoning. It uses familiar rule-based expert system technology, as each DATMS agent is an expert system where contradiction knowledge, communication knowledge, and domain knowledge are expressed as rules. In addition, the system supports a belief revision policy that allows agents to consider multiple alternative perspectives at once.

Huhns (139) recently reviewed truth maintenance in multiagent environment. He presents an algorithm that generates local consistency for each agent and global consistency for data shared by the agents. His algorithm is shown to be complete in the sense that if a consistent state exists, the algorithm will either find it or report failure. The implications and limitations of this for cooperating agents are discussed, and several extensions are described. The algorithm has been implemented in a distributed expert system shell.

Let us examine now some other applications of DAI. An interesting practical example is the use of Contract-Nets (98) in a flexible manufacturing system by Parunak (7). His system, called YAMS (Yet Another Manufacturing System), is a factory control system for discrete manufacturing, in which the distributed control is dictated by hardware, physical factory size, and real-time response constraints. It is different from other factory control systems because it has been designed so that controllers at every level but the lowest (machine level) are similar to one another. These controllers differ primarily with respect to their knowledge bases rather than to the methods they use in accomplishing their work. The system consists of pallets that move from one manufacturing node to another along transport links. Pallets can be single parts or abstract entire steamships containing boxcars full of boxes filled with single parts. Furthermore, nodes can be individual machines or entire factories, and links can be conveyors or complex transportation networks. Control is distributed in a hierarchy that is statistically initialized but free to change through the dynamic use of negotiation.

In fact, YAMS attempts to avoid one of the problems with the negotiation metaphor: the required amount of communication bandwith. To accomplish this, it uses *audience restriction* which consists, for a node, in retaining an audience set for each class of tasks that it performs, rather than broadcasting task descriptions to everyone. To support audience restriction, Parunak has modified the Contract-Nets protocol to allow a new node in the system to be given a chance to bid on any task, and that nodes be allowed to give a *null bid* when they cannot currently perform a task but would like to "stay on mailing list" for future tasks. YAMS also uses metalevel communication between nodes to reduce scheduling anomalies that can occur if a node is not aware of what other nodes are doing.

Lane et al. (140) have also used DAI architecture for a knowledge-based vision task. More precisely, they used a hierarchical architecture with a number of interconnected processing agents termed rational cells. Different levels in this hierarchy are arranged to correspond to different levels of processing in the vision. Their approach differs from other hierarchical architecture for computer vision because of the way that mutually inconsistent and incorrect hypotheses can be represented throughout the architecture and the way these hypotheses are exchanged when cells interact. Their results confirm that. These results concern the automatic detection and the classification of objects and shadows contained in image data derived from an active sector scanning sonar system.

Signal interpretation is also an application domain for DAI techniques. For example, Dawant and Jansen (141) use an object-oriented system that is organized around a blackboard for coupling numerical and symbolic methods for signal interpretation. In this approach, morphological and contextual (e.g., spatio-temporal relationships) information about events to be detected by the system is represented in terms of frames, and a model interpreter is in charge of matching the events' attributes with data. Features needed by the model interpreter are extracted from signals by independent "specialists," which consist of a set of specific digital signal processing routines and the knowledge required to select the most appropriate one for a given task. The system has been tested on the problem of automatic electroencephalogram (EEG) interpretation and its results are promising.

Discussion

New avenues of research are emerging, filling gaps in DAI literature and practice. Particularly, new theories, both pragmatic and abstract, are coming to light. Thus, some researchers begin to develop approaches from sociology (14,100); whereas other researchers are developing new methods based on classical AI which is traditionally turned to psychology, linguistic and cognitive science (13,18,53,85,92). There are also new problem-solving architectures for DAI that have begun to complement earlier DAI architectures such as blackboards, multiagent planning, and task allocation.

Notice also that there is now a wide range of perspectives on planning in multiagent worlds, which can be organized along a spectrum from those dealing with simple mathematically characterizable agents, working in abstract constrained worlds, to experimentally useful but theoretically uncharacterized multiagent planners, and on to more qualitative models or "situated" theories of cooperative planning like those of Suchman (142), Agree (143), Levesque et al. (13), and Grosz and Sidner (93).

Works in DAI also show that researchers are beginning to carefully define their objects of analysis, and research methods using clear comparative studies, in order to strengthen the scientific basis of DAI.

Finally, it seems that it is now much easier to use careful experimental methods in DAI. This is due to many years of effort in building problem-solving architectures, distributed object-oriented languages, and programming environments.

RESEARCH ISSUES IN DAI

DAI has opened new directions in the study of intelligence, and today there are important issues for which much of the groundwork has been done and in which research is urgently needed. Essentially, these issues are as follows:

DAI methodology: Today no clear consensus has yet emerged on the central problems of DAI, and in the literature, DAI continues to speak of many important concepts such as commitment, coordination, negotiation, cooperation, distributed problem solving, and so on. Consequently, DAI needs much more discussion and debate concerning its foundations and its research methods. These discussions can be fruitful, as they refine the premises on which DAI research rests, and provide definitions of the areas in which problems can be solved. For example, Hewitt (15) recently proposed *Open Information System Semantics* as a foundation for the further development of DAI. This framework, which integrates methods from sociology with methods from concurrent systems science, might provide many suggestions and discussions to DAI researchers.

Reasoning about knowledge and action: The problems of reasoning about knowledge action and time have been recognized as issues in AI for many years. Today, DAI presents opportunities to investigate the use of knowledge by multiple agents and collective action or collective commitments and intentions that are different from actions or intentions of individual agents. DAI research must also continue to investigate the hypothesis that a base of *common knowledge* (i.e., everyone knows that a fact is true, and also knows that everyone knows, etc.) is necessary for multiagent interaction. Without this common knowledge, agents may overload their means of communication that are physically limited.

Reasoning about coherence and coordination: This issue must be viewed as a fundamental aspect of intelligent behavior. Indeed, it could be argued that we judge the in telligence of an agent by how it interacts with us: whether we can understand its goals, plans, and beliefs as embodied in its actions, whether we can communicate with it, and whether it appears to be understanding us. DAI research must then continue to study reasoning about coherence and coordination that must go into AI systems because if AI systems meet criteria for intelligence, then cooperation, coexistence, and concurrence among these systems are facilitated.

Hypothetical viewpoints and learning in DAI: Some statements of fundamental AI problems have recognized that multiple actors with different viewpoints are an important part of AI (24,116). DAI research contributes to this because it basically deals with multiple agents. More precisely, DAI offers an appealing approach to hypothetical viewpoints among several agents where each agent explores alternatives and form hypotheses, after he has investigated the viewpoints of other agents. This approach needs more attention because little work has been done. Another approach which also needs further research is learning in DAI. Indeed, learning research in DAI allows intelligent agents to build an adaptive organization and to intelligently use their structure in a flexible way.

CONCLUSION

This article has investigated an overview DAI which is a subdomain of AI. It appears that the application of AI techniques and the examination of the process of human interaction and social organization are undoubtably key contributions in the DAI area. On the one hand, AI techniques allow an individual agent to have a sophisticated local control in order to reason about its own problem solving and how this fits in with problem solving by other agents. On the other hand, the examination of the process of human interaction and social organization allows DAI designers to conceive a dynamically adaptive organization of agents.

The article also reviews some recent work done in DAI and shows how DAI research continues to reveal the complexity of group coordination and coherence. It also reflects on how DAI research brings to the forefront issues in areas such as introspecting, planning, language, and reasoning about belief. As Nilsson (1) predicted in his early implication in DAI, research in distributed artificial intelligence forces researchers to address many of the basic problems in AI.

For further reading in DAI and in cooperative distributed problem solving, see Refs. 4,5,20,85,94, and 144–150.

ACKNOWLEDGMENT

This work was supported by a NSERC-Canada grant.

REFERENCES

1. N. J. Nilsson, "Two Heads Are Better Than One," *Sigart Newsletter*, *73*, 43–43 (1980).
2. E. Chang, "Participant Systems for Cooperative Work," in *Distributed Artificial Intelligence*, (M. N. Huhns (ed.), Morgan Kaufmann Publishers, Los Altos, CA, 1987, pp. 311–339.

3. R. Davis and R. G. Smith, "Negotiations as a Metaphor for Distributed Problem Solving," *Artificial Intelligence*, *20*, 63–109 (1983).

4. M. Fehling (ed.), "Report on Third Annual Workshop on Distributed Artificial Intelligence," *Sigart Newsletter*, *84*, 3–12 (1980).

5. R. G. Smith (ed.), "Report on the 1984 Workshop on Distributed ai," *AI Magazine*, 234–243 (1985).

6. E. H. Durfee, V. R. Lesser, and D. D. Corkill, "Coherent Cooperation Among Communicating Problem Solvers," *IEEE Trans. Computers*, *C-36*(11), 1275–1291 (1987).

7. H. V. D. Parunak, "Manufacturing Experience with the Contract-Net," in *Distributed Artificial Intelligence*, M. N. Huhns (ed.), Morgan Kaufmann Publishers, Los Altos, CA, 1987, pp. 285–310.

8. A. H. Bond, "The Cooperation of Experts in Engineering Design," in *Distributed Artificial Intelligence, Vol. 2*, L. Gasser and M. N. Huhns (eds.), Morgan Kaufmann Publishers, Los Altos, CA, 1989, pp. 463–484.

9. V. R. Lesser, J. Pavlin, and E. Durfee, "Approximate Processing in Real-Time Problem Solving," *AI Magazine*, *9*(1), 49–61 (1988).

10. M. Klein, "Supporting Conflict Resolution in Cooperative Design Systems," *IEEE Trans. Syst. Man. Cybern.*, *SMC-21*, 1379–1390 (1991).

11. S. Sycara, S. Roth, N. Sadeh, and M. Fox, "Distributed Constraint Heuristic Search," *IEEE Trans. Syst. Man Cybern.*, *21*(5), 1446–1461 (1991).

12. A. H. Bond, "A Computational Model for Organization of Cooperating Intelligent Agents," in *Proceedings of the Conference on Office Information Systems*, Cambridge MA, 1990, pp. 21–30.

13. H. J. Levesque, P. R. Cohen, and J. H. T. Nunes, "On Acting Together," in *Proceedings of the 8th National Conference on Artificial Intelligence*, Boston, 1990, pp. 94–99.

14. L. Gasser, "Social Conceptions of Knowledge and Action: DAI Foundations and Open Systems Semantics," *Artificial Intelligence*, *47*, 107–138 (1991).

15. C. Hewitt, "Open Information Systems Semantics for Distributed Artificial Intelligence," *Artificial Intelligence*, *47*, 79–106 (1991).

16. A. Sathi, "Cooperation Through Constraint Directed Negotiation: Study of Resource Reallocation Problems," Ph.D. thesis, Graduate School of Industrial Administration, Carnegie-Mellon University, 1988.

17. A. Sathi and M. S. Fox, "Constraint-Directed Negotiation of Resource Reallocations," in *Distributed Artificial Intelligence, Vol. 2*, L. Gasser and M. N. Huhns (eds.), Morgan Kaufmann Publishers, Los Altos, CA, 1989, pp. 129–162.

18. K. R. Sycara, "Multiagent Compromise via Negotiation," in *Distributed Artificial Intelligence, Vol. 2*, L. Gasser and M. N. Huhns (eds.), Morgan Kaufmann Publishers, Los Altos, CA, 1989, pp. 119–137.

19. E. H. Durfee, V. R. Lesser, and D. D. Corkill, "Trends in Cooperative Distributed Problem Solving" *IEEE Trans. Knowledge Data Eng.*, KDE-1(1), 63–83 (1989).

20. K. S. Decker, "Distributed Problem-Solving Techniques: A Survey," *IEEE Trans. Syst. Man Cybern.*, *SMC-17*(5), 729–740 (1987).

21. K. S. Decker, E. H. Durfee, and V. R. Lesser, "Evaluating Research in Cooperative Distributed Problem Solving, in *Distributed Artificial Intelligence, Vol. 2*, L. Gasser and M. N. Huhns (eds.), Morgan Kaufmann Publishers, Los Altos, CA, 1989, pp. 485–519.

22. S. P. Robertson, W. Zachary, and J. B. Black, (eds.), *Cognition, Computing, and Cooperation*, Ablex Publishing, Norwood, NJ, 1990.

23. G. H. Mead, *Mind, Self, and Society*, University of Chicago Press, Chicago, 1934.

24. J. McCarty and P. Hayes, "Some Philosophical Problems from the Standpoint of Artificial Intelligence," in *Machine Intelligence, Vol. 4*, B. Meltzer and D. Mitchie (eds.), Edinburgh University Press, Edinburgh, 1969, pp. 463–502.

25. R. C. Moore, "Reasoning about Knowledge and Action," Technical Note 191, Artificial Intelligence Center, SRI International, Menlo Park, CA, 1980.

26. J. Y. Halpern, (ed.), *Theoretical Aspects of Reasoning about Knowledge: Proceedings of the 1986 Conference*, Morgan Kaufmann Publishers, Los Altos, CA, 1986.

27. Y. Shoham, "Time for Action: On the Relation Between Time, Knowledge and Action," in *Proceedings of the 11th International Joint Conference on Artificial Intelligence*, Detroit, MI, 1989, pp. 954–959.

28. V. R. Pratt, "Semantic Considerations on Floyd-Hoare Logic," *Proceedings of the 17th FOCS, IEEE*, 1976, pp. 109–121.

29. Y. Shoham, "Beliefs as Defeasible Knowledge," in *Proceedings of the 11th International Joint Conference on Artificial Intelligence*, Detroit, MI, 1989, pp. 1168–1173.

30. J. R. Galliers, "Modeling Autonomous Belief Revision in Dialogue," in *Decentralized Artificial Intelligence 2: Preceedings of the Second European Workshop on Autonomous Agents in a Multi-Agents World*, Y. Demazeau and J.-P. Muller (eds.), 1991.

31. M. Lizotte and B. Moulin, "A Planning System Which Implements the Actem Concept," *Knowledge-based Systems*, 2(4), 210–218 (1989).

32. C. F. Schmidt, N. S. Sridharan, and J. L. Goodson, "The Plan Recognition Problem: An Intersection of Artificial Intelligence and Psychology," *Artificial Intelligence*, 10(1), 45–83 (1978).

33. J. F. Allen, "Recognizing Intentions from Natural Language Utterances," in *Computational Models of Discourse*, M. Brady and R. C. Berwick (eds.), MIT Press, Cambridge, MA, 1983.

34. C. L. Sidner, "Plan Parsing for Intended Response Recognition in Discourse," *Computational Intelligence*, 1(1), 1–10 (1985).

35. D. J. Litman and J. F. Allen, "Discourse Processing and Commonsense Plans," in *Intentions in Communication*, P. Cohen et al. (eds.), MIT Press, Cambridge, MA, 1990, pp. 365–388.

36. H. A. Kaultz, "A Circumscriptive Theory of Plan Recognition," in *Intentions in Communication*, P. Cohen et al. (ed.), MIT Press, Cambridge, MA, 1990.

37. M. E. Pollack, "A Model of Plan Inference that Distinguishes Between the Beliefs of Actors and Observers," in *Reasoning About Actions and Plans: Proceedings of the 1986 Workshop*, M. P. Georgeff and A. L. Lansky (eds.), Morgan Kaufmann Publishers, Los Altos, CA, 1987, pp. 279–295.

38. M. E. Pollack, "Plans as Complex Mental Attitudes," in *Intentions in Communication*, P. Cohen et al., (ed.), MIT Press, Cambridge, MA, 1990, pp. 77–103.

39. K. Konolige and M. E. Pollak, "Ascribing Plans to Agents: Preliminary Report," in *Proceedings of the 11th International Joint Conference on Artificial Intelligence*, Detroit, MI, 1989, pp. 924–930.

40. K. E. Lochbaum, B. J. Grosz, and C. L. Sidner, "Models of Plans to Support Communication: An Initial Report," in *Proceedings of the 8th National Conference on Artificial Intelligence*, Boston, pp. 485–490.

41. G. G. Hendrix, "Modeling Simultaneous Actions and Continuous Processes," *Artificial Intelligence*, 4, 143–180 (1973).

42. J. F. Allen and C. R. Perrault, "Analyzing Intention in Utterances," *Artificial Intelligence*, 15, 143–180 (1980).

43. M. Georgeff, "The Representation of Events in Multiagent Domains," in *Proceedings of the 5th National Conference on Artificial Intelligence*, Philadelphia, 1986, pp. 70–75.

44. M. Georgeff, "Actions, Process and Causality," in *Reasoning About Actions and Plans: Preceedings of the 1986 Workshop*, M. P. Georgeff and A. L. Lansky, (eds.), Morgan Kaufmann Publishers, Los Altos, CA, 1987, pp. 99–122.

45. A. L. Lansky, "A Representation of Parallel Activity Based on Events, Structure and Causality," in M. P. Georgeff and A. L. Lansky (eds.), *Reasoning About Actions and Plans: Proceedings of the 1986 Workshop*, Morgan Kaufmann Publishers, Los Altos, CA, 1987, pp. 123–159.

46. D. McDermott, "A Temporal Logic for Reasoning about Processes and Plans," *Cognitive Sci.*, *6*, 105–155 (1982).

47. D. McDermott, "Generalizing Problem Reduction: A Logical Analysis," in *Proceedings of the 8th International Conference on Artificial Intelligence*, Karlsruhe, West Germany, 1983, pp. 230–308.

48. D. McDermott, "Reasoning about Plans," in *Formal Theories of the Commonsense Worlds*, J. R. Hobbs and R. C. Moore (eds.), Ablex Publishing, Norwood, NJ, 1985.

49. M. Georgeff, "Communication and Interaction in Multi-Agent Planning," in *Proceedings of the 8th International Joint Conference on Artificial Intelligence*, Karlsruhe, Germany, 1983, pp. 125–129.

50. C. Stuart, "An Implementation of a Multi-Agent Plan Synchronizer," in *Proceedings of the 9th International Joint Conference on Artificial Intelligence*, Los Angeles, CA, 1985, pp. 1031–1033.

51. C. Stuart, "Branching Regular Expressions and Multi-Agent Plan," in *Reasoning About Actions and Plans: Proceedings of the 1986 Workshop*, M. P. Georgeff and A. Lansky (eds.), Morgan Kaufmann Publishers, Los Altos, CA, 1987, pp. 161–187.

52. S. Cammarata, D. McArthur, and R. Steeb, "Strategies of Cooperation in Distributed Problem Solving," in *Proceedings of the 8th International Joint Conference on Artificial Intelligence*, Karlsruhe, Germany, 1983, pp. 767–770.

53. B. Chaib-draa, "Plans in Natural Language Dialogues," *Knowledge-Based Systems*, *6* (1993).

54. B. Chaib-draa and P. Millot, "A framework for Cooperative Work: An Approach Based on the Intentionality," *Artif. Intell. Eng.*, *5*(4), 199–205 (1990).

55. D. D. Corkill and V. R. Lesser, "The Use of Meta-Level Control for Coordination in a Distributed Problem Solving Network," in *Proceedings of the 8th International Joint Conference on Artificial Intelligence*, Karlsruhe, Germany, 1983, pp. 748–756.

56. D. Maines (ed.), *Urban Life*, 1984; special issue on negotiated order theory.

57. A. Strauss, *Negotiations: Varieties, Processes, Contexts and Social Order*, Jossey-Bass, San Francisco, 1978.

58. L. Gasser, "The Integration of Computing and Routine Work," *ACM Trans. Office Inform. Syst.*, *4*(3), 205–225 (1986).

59. V. R. Lesser and D. D. Corkill, "Functionally-Accurate, Cooperative Distributed Systems," *IEEE Trans. Syst. Man Cybern.*, *SMC-11*(1), 81–96 (1981).

60. P. P. Bonissone, "Plausible Reasoning: Coping with Uncertainty in Expert Systems," in *Encyclopedia of Artificial Intelligence*, C. S. Shapiro (ed.), Wiley, New York, 1986.

61. R. G. Smith and R. Davis, "Framework for Cooperation in Distributed Problem Solving," *IEEE Trans. Syst. Man Cybern.*, *SMC-11*(1), 61–70 (1981).

62. M. R. Genesereth, M. L. Ginsberg, and J. S. Rosenschein, "Cooperation without Communication," in *Proceedings of the 5th National Conference on Artificial Intelligence*, Philadelphia, 1986, pp. 51–57.

63. J. S. Rosenschein and M. R. Genesereth, "Deals Among Rational Agents," in *Proceedings of 9th International Joint Conference on Artificial Intelligence*, Los Angeles, 1985, pp. 91–99.

64. T. C. Schelling (eds.), *The Strategy of Conflict*, Harvard University Press, Cambridge, MA, 1960.

65. S. L. Tubbs (ed.), *A System Approach to Small Group Interaction*, 2nd ed., Addison-Wesley, Reading, MA, 1984.

66. J. S. Rosenschein, "Rational Interaction: Cooperating Among Intelligent Agents," Ph.D. thesis, Computer Science Department, Stanford University, 1986.

67. J. S. Rosenschein and J. S. Breese, "Communication-free Interactions among Rational Agents," in *Distributed Artificial Intelligence*, *Vol. 2*, L. Gasser and M. N. Huhns (eds.), Morgan Kaufmann Publishers, Los Altos, CA, 1989, pp. 99–118.

68. E. W. Dijkstra, "Cooperation Sequential Process," in *Programming Languages*, F. Genuys (ed.), Academic Press, New York, 1968.
69. C. A. R. Hoare, "Communicating Sequential Processes," *Commun. ACM, 21,* 666–677 (1978).
70. T. Lozano-Perez, "Robot-programming," *Proc. IEEE, 71*(7), 821–841 (1983).
71. E. Werner, "Cooperating Agents: An Unified Theory of Communication and Social Structure, in *Distributed Artificial Intelligence, Vol. 2*, L. Gasser and M. N. Huhns (eds.), Morgan Kaufmann Publishers, Los Altos, CA, 1989, pp. 3–36.
72. R. E. Cullingford, "Integrating Knowledge Sources for Computer Understanding Tasks," *IEEE Trans. Syst. Man Cybern., SMC-11*(1), 52–60 (1981).
73. B. Hayes-Roth, "A Blackboard Architecture for Control," *Artificial Intelligence, 26*(3), 251–321 (1985).
74. S. Y. Harmon, W. A. Aviles, and D. W. Gage, "A Technique for Coordinating Autonomous Robots," in *Proceedings of the IEEE International Conference on Robotics and Automation*, San Francisco, 1986, pp. 2029–2034.
75. H. P. Nii, "Blackboard Systems: The Blackboard Model of Problem Solving and the Evolution of Blackboard Architectures (Part I)," *AI Magazine*, 38–53 (1986).
76. H. P. Nii, "Blackboard Systems: Blackboard Application Systems, Blackboard Systems from a Knowledge Engineering Perspective (Part II)," *AI Magazine*, 82–106 (1986).
77. D.D. Corkill, K.P. Gallaghen, and K.E. Murray, "Gbb: A Generic Blackboard Development System," in *Proceedings of the 5th Naitonal Conference on Artificial Intelligence*, Philadelphia, 1986, pp. 1008–1014.
78. B. Chaib-draa and P. Millot, "Architecture pour les systèmes d'intelligence artificielle distribuèe," in *Proceedings of the IEEE compint 1987*, Montréal, CND, 1987, pp. 64–69.
79. H. Laasri, B. Maitre, and J. P. Haton, "Organization, cooperation et exploitation des connaissances dans les architectures de blackboard: Atome," in *Proceedings of the 8th International Workshop on Expert Systems and their Applications*, Avignon, France, 1988, pp. 371–390.
80. C. Hewitt, "Viewing Control Structures on Patterns of Passing Messages," *Artificial Intelligence, 8,* 323–364 (1977).
81. C. Hewitt and B. Kornfeld, "Message Passing Semantics," *Sigart Newsletter, 73,* 48–48 (1980).
82. W. A. Kornfeld and C. Hewitt, "The Scientific Community Metaphor," *IEEE Trans. Syst. Man Cybern. SMC-11*(1), 24–33 (1981).
83. W. Clinger, "Foundations of Actors' Semantics," Technical Report No. 633, MIT Artificial Intelligence Laboratory, Cambridge, MA, 1981.
84. G. Agha and C. Hewitt, "Concurrent Programming Using Actors," in *Object-Oriented Concurrent Programming*, Y. Yonezawa and M. Tokoro (eds.), MIT Press, Cambridge, MA, 1988.
85. E. H. Durfee and T. A. Montgomery, "A Hierarchical Protocol for Coordination Multiagent Behavior," in *Proceedings of the 8th National Conference on Artificial Intelligence*, Boston, 1990, pp. 86–93.
86. T. J. Leblanc, "Shared Memory Versus Message-Passing in Tightly-Coupled Multiprocessors: A Case Study," Tech. Report Butterfily Project Report 3, University of Rochester Computer Science Department, Rochester, NY, 1986.
87. P. R. Cohen and H. J. Levesque, "Intention Is Choice with Commitment," *Artificial Intelligence, 42,* 213–261 (1990).
88. J. F. Allen, *Natural Language Understanding*, Benjamin/Cummings Publishing, Menlo Park, CA, 1986.
89. P. R. Cohen and H. Levesque, "Persistence, Intention and Commitment," in *Reasoning About Actions and Plans: Preceedings of the 1986 Workshop*, P. M. Georgeff and A. L. Lansky (eds.), Morgan Kaufmann Publishers, Los Altos, CA, 1986, pp. 297–340.

90. P. R. Cohen and H. J. Levesque, "Rational Interaction as the Basis for Communication," Report No. CSLI-87-89, SRI international, Menlo Park, CA, 1987.

91. J. R. Galliers, "A Strategic Framework for Multi-Agent Dialogue," in *Proceedings of the 8th European Conference on Artificial Intelligence*, Munich, 1988, pp. 415–420.

92. E. Werner, "An Unified View of Information, Intention and Ability," in *Decentralized Artificial Intelligence 2: Proceedings of the Second European Workshop on Autonomous Agents in a Multi-Agents World*, Y. Demazeau and J. P. Muller (eds.), Elsevier Science Pub./North-Holland, Amsterdam, 1991.

93. B. Grosz and C. Sidner, "Plans for Discourse," in *Intentions in Communication*, P. Cohen et al. (ed.), MIT Press, Cambridge, MA, 1990, pp. 417–444.

94. A. H. Bond, and L. Glasser, *Readings in Distributed Artificial Intelligence*, Morgan Kaufmann Publishers, Los Altos, CA 1988.

95. T. W. Malone, "Organizing Information Processing Systems: Parallels Between Human Organizations and Computer Systems," in *Cognition, Computing, and Copperation*, S. P. Robertson, W. Zachary, and J. B. Black (eds.), Norwood, NJ, 1990.

96. K. Sycara, "Resolving Goal Conflicts via Negotiation," in *Proceedings of the 7th National Conference on Artificial Intelligence*, St Paul, MI, 1988, pp. 245–250.

97. S. E. Conry, R. A. Meyer, and V. R. Lesser, "Multistage Negotiation in Distributed Planning," in *Readings in Distributed Artificial Intelligence*, A. Bond and L. Gasser (eds.), Morgan Kaufmann Publishers, Los Altos, CA, 1988, pp. 367–386.

98. R. G. Smith, "The Contract-Net Protocol: High-Level Communication and Control in a Distributed Problem Solver," *IEEE Trans. Computers*, C-29(12), 1104–1113 (1980).

99. L. Wittgenstein, *Philosophical Investigations*, Basil Blackwell, Oxford, 1953.

100. S. L. Star, "The Structure of Ill-Structured Solutions: Boundary Objects and Heterogeneous Distributed Problem Solving," in *Distributed Artificial Intelligence, Vol. 2*, L. Gasser and M. N. Huhns (eds.), Morgan Kaufmann Publishers, Los Altos, CA, 1980, pp. 37–54.

101. A. Turing, "Computing Machinery and Intelligence," *Mind*, 59, 433–460 (1950).

102. E. Durkheim, *The Rules of Sociological Method*, Free Press, New York, 1983.

103. L. Gasser, N. F. Roquette, R. W. Hill, and J. Lieb, "Representing and Using Organization Knowledge in Distributed ai Systems," in *Distributed Artificial Intelligence, Vol. 2*, L. Gasser and M. N. Huhns (eds.), Morgan Kaufmann Publishers, Los Altos, CA, 1989, p. 520.

104. H. S. Decker, "Notes on the Concept of Commitment," *Amer. J. Sociol.*, 66, 32–40 (1960).

105. T. Hogg and B. A. Huberman, "Controlling Chaos in Distributed Systems," *IEEE Trans. Syst. Man Cybern.*, SMC-21(5), 1446–1461 (1991).

106. T. W. Malone, R. E. Fikers, and M. T. Howard, "Enterprise: A Market-Like Task Scheduler for Distributed Computing Environments," in *Ecology of Computation*, B. A. Huberman (ed.), North-Holland, Amsterdam, 1988.

107. G. Zlotkin and J. S. Rosenschein, "Negotiation and Task Sharing among Autonomous Agents in Cooperative Domains," in *Proceedings of the 11th International Joint Conference on Artificial Intelligence*, Detroit, MI, 1989, pp. 912–917.

108. G. Zlotkin and J. S. Rosenschein, "Negotiation and Conflict Resolution in Noncooperative Domain," in *Proceedings of the 8th National Conference on Artificial Intelligence*, Boston, MA, 1990, pp. 100–105.

109. G. Zlotkin, "Cooperation and Conflit Resolution via Negotiation among Autonomous Agents in Noncooperative Domains," *IEEE Trans. Syst. Man Cybern.*, SMC-21(5), 1317–1332 (1991).

110. K. R. Sycara, "Argumentation: Planning Other Agent's Plans," in *Proceedings of the 11th International Joint Conference on Artificial Intelligence*, Detroit, MI, 1989, pp. 517–523.

111. K. Sycara, "Resolving Adversarial Conflicts: An Approach Integrating Case-Based and Analytic Methods," Ph.D. thesis, School of Information and Computer Science, Georgia Institute of Technology, Atlanta, GA, 1987.

112. K. Sycara, "Utility Theory in Conflict Resolution," *Ann. Oper. Res. 12*, 65–84 (1988).
113. M. R. Alder, A. B. Davis, R. Weihmayer, and R. W. Worrest, "Conflict-Resolution Strategies for Nonhierarchical Distributed Agents," in *Distributed Artificial Intelligence, Vol. 2*, L. Gasser and M. N. Huhns (eds.), Morgan Kaufmann Publishers, Los Altos, CA, 1989, pp. 139–161.
114. E. H. Durfee and T. A. Montgomery, "Coordination in Distribution Search in a Hierarchical Behavioral Space," *IEEE Trans. Syst. Man Cybern.*, SMC-21(5), 1363–1378 (1991).
115. R. P. Pope, S. E. Conry, and R. A. Meyer, "Distributing the Planning Process in a Dynamic Environment," in *Proceedings of the 11 International Workshop on Distributed Artificial Intelligence*, Glen Arbor, MI, 1992, pp. 317–331.
116. R. E. Fikes and N. J. Nilsson, "Strips: A New Approach to the Application of Theorem Proving to Problem Solving," *Artificial Intelligence, 2*, 189–208 (1971).
117. E. F. D. Pednault, "Formulating Multiagent Dynamic World Problems in the Classical Planning Framework," in *Reasoning About Actions and Plans: Proceedings of the 1986 Workshop*, M. P. Georgeff and A. L. Lansky (eds.), Morgan Kaufmann Publishers, Los Altos, CA, 1987, pp. 47–82.
118. P. Hayes, "The Frame Problem and Related Problems in Artificial Intelligence," in *Artificial and Human Thinking*, A. Elithorn and D. Jones (eds.), Jossey-Bass, San Francisco, 1973.
119. V. Lifschitz, "On the Semantics of Strips," in *Reasoning About Actions and Plans: Proceedings of the 1986 Workshop*, M. P. Georgeff and A. L. Lansky (eds.), Morgan Kaufmann Publishers, Los Altos, CA, 1987, pp. 1–9.
120. M. J. Katz and J. S. Rosenschein, "Plans for Multiple Agents," in *Distributed Artificial Intelligence, Vol. 2*, L. Gasser and M. N. Huhns (eds.), Morgan Kaufmann Publishers, Los Altos, CA, 1989, pp. 147–228.
121. S. E. Conry, R. A. Meyer, and R. P. Pope, "Mechanisms for Assessing Non-Local Impact of Local Decision in Distributed Planning," in *Distributed Artificial Intelligence, Vol. 2*, L. Gasser and M. N. Huhns (eds.), Morgan Kaufmann Publishers, Los Altos, CA, 1989, pp. 245–258.
122. M. Kamel and A. Sayed, "An Object-Oriented Multiple Agent Planning System," in *Distributed Artificial Intelligence, Vol. 2*, L. Gasser and M. N. Huhns (eds.), Morgan Kaufmann Publishers, Los Altos, CA, 1989, pp. 259–290.
123. B. Hayes-Roth, M. Hewett, R. Washington, and A. Seive, "Distributing Intelligence Within an Individual," *Distributed Artificial Intelligence, Vol. 2*, L. Gasser and M. N. Huhns (eds.), Morgan Kaufmann Publishers, Los Altos, CA, 1989, pp. 385–412.
124. B. Hayes-Roth, "A Multi-Processor Interrupt-Driven Architecture for Adaptive Intelligent Systems," Technical Report KSL-87-31, Stanford University, 1987.
125. B. Hayes-Roth, "Dynamic Control Planning in Adaptive Intelligent Systems," in *Proceedings of DARPA Knowledge-Based Planning Workshop*, 1987.
126. H. P. Nii, N. Aiello, and J. Rice, "Experiments on Cage and Poligon: Measuring the Performance of Parallel Blackboard Systems," in *Distributed Artificial Intelligence, Vol. 2*, L. Gasser and M. N. Huhns (eds.), Morgan Kaufmann Publishers, Los Altos, CA, 1989, pp. 319–383.
127. N. Aiello, "User-Directed Control of Parallelism: The Cage System," Technical Report KSL-86-31, Knowledge Systems, Computer Science Department, Stanford University, 1986.
128. J. Rice, "A System for Parallel Problem Solving," Technical Report KSL-86-19, Knowledge Systems Laboratory, Computer Science Department, Stanford University, 1986.
129. H. P. Nii, and N. Aiello, "Age: A Knowledge-Based Program for Building Knowledge-Based Programs," in *Proceedings of the 6th International Joint Conference on Artificial Intelligence*, Tokyo, 1979, pp. 645–655.
130. B. G. Silverman, "Distributed Inference and Fusion Algorithms for Real-Time Control of Satellite Ground Systems," *IEEE Trans. Syst. Man Cybern.*, SMC-17(2), 230–239 (1987).

131. B. G. Silverman, "Facility Advisor: A Distributed Expert System Testbed for Spacecraft Ground Facilities," in *Expert Systems in Government Symposium, Proceedings of the IEEE, CS Order No. 738*, IEEE Press, New York, 1986, pp. 23–32.

132. J. Simkol, G. Wenig, and B. G. Silverman, "Jams: A Computer Aided Electronic Warfare Vulnerability Assessment (CA-EWVA) *Technique*," in *Symposium Aerospace Applications of AI*, 1986.

133. G. W. Garret, "NASA Selects Small Business Proposals," *NASA News*, 1986.

134. L. Gasser, C. Braganza, and N. Herman, "Mace: A Flexible Testbed for Distributed ai Research," in *Distributed Artificial Intelligence*, M. N. Huhns (ed.), Morgan Kaufmann Publishers, Los Altos, CA, 1987, pp. 119–152.

135. M. J. Shaw and A. B. Whinston, "Applying Distributed Artificial Intelligence to Flexible Manufacturing," in *Advanced Information Technologies for Industrial Material Flow System*, X. X. Moody and Q. Q. Nof (eds.), Springer-Verlag, New York, 1989, pp. 81–93.

136. C. Hewitt and P. De Jong, "Analyzing the Roles of Descriptions and Actions in Open Systems," in *Proceedings of the 3rd National Conferences on Artificial Intelligence*, Washington, DC, 1983.

137. C. Hewitt, "Offices Are Open Systems," *ACM Trans. Office Inform. Syst.*, 4(3), 270–287 (1986).

138. C. L. Mason and R. R. Johnson, "Datms: A Framework for Distributed Assumption Based Reasoning," in *Distributed Artificial Intelligence, Vol. 2*, L. Gasser and M. N. Huhns (eds.), Morgan Kaufmann Publishers, Los Altos, CA, 1989, pp. 293–317.

139. M. N. Huhns and D. M. Bridgland, "Multiagent Truth Maintenance," *IEEE Trans. Syst. Man Cybern.*, SMC-21(5), 1437–1445 (1991).

140. D. M. Lane, M. J. Chantler, E. W. Robertson, and A. G. McFadzean, "A Distributed Problem Solving Architecture for Knowledge Based Vision,"in *Distributed Artificial Intelligence, Vol. 2*, L. Gasser and M. N. Huhns (eds.), Morgan Kaufmann Publishers, Los Altos, CA, 1989, pp. 433–462.

141. B. M. Dawant and B. H. Jansen, "Coupling Numerical and Symbolic Methods for Signal Interpretation," *IEEE Trans. Syst. Man Cybern.*, SMC-21(1), 115–133 (1991).

142. L. Suchman (ed.), *Plans and Situated Actions: The Problem of Human–Machine Communication*, Cambridge University Press, New York, 1987.

143. P. Agree, "The Dynamic Structure of Everyday Life," Ph.D. thesis, Department of Computer Science, MIT, 1988.

144. R. Davis (ed.), Report on the Workshop on Distributed ai. *Sigart Newsletter*, 73, 42–52 (1980).

145. R. Davis (ed.), Report on the Second Workshop on Distributed ai. *Sigart Newsletter*, 80, 13–23 (1982).

146. G. M. P. O'Hare, "New Directions in Distributed Artificial Intelligence," in *Proceedings of the 2nd International Expert Systems Conference*, London, 1986, pp. 137–148.

147. M. N. Huhns (ed.), *Distributed Artificial Intelligence*, Morgan Kaufmann Publishers, Los Altos, CA, 1989.

148. J. F. Ferber and M. Ghallab, "Problématiques des univers multi-agents intelligents," in *Proceedings of Actes des Journes Nationales IA PROC-Greco*, Toulouse, 1988, pp. 295–320.

149. L. E. C. Hern, "On Distributed Artificial Intelligence," *Knowledge Eng. Rev.*, 3(1), 21–57 (1988).

150. L. Gasser and M. Huhns (ed.), *Distributed Artificial Intelligence, Vol. 2*, Morgan Kaufmann Publishers, Los Altos, CA, 1989.

BRAHIM CHAIB-DRAA

EXPERT JUDGMENT, HUMAN ERROR, AND INTELLIGENT SYSTEMS

INTRODUCTION

This article surveys the issues confronting how knowledge-based systems could reduce the errors of experts and other proficient task performers engaged in real-world tasks. Many have concluded that biased judgment and human error are the principal causes of major industrial catastrophes, transportation accidents, medical misdiagnoses, forecasting failures, and the like. The interesting issues examined here include: Why do errors occur? How should we model error processes? What are the most promising routes to error detection and mitigation? What should the role for knowledge-based systems be?

Of particular interest are ways currently being taken to overcome the many research problems confronting the following topic areas.

Better Psychological Models of Errors and Biases

- Models of fallible expert reasoning and judgment (e.g., skill–rule–knowledge levels, recognition primed decision making, bounded rationality, confirmation bias). How can models be more predictive?
- More precise/formal models of human error (slips, lapses, accidents, group errors, phenologies, etc.)
- Reducing biases and errors in real-world safety-critical complex systems
- Making decision analysis methods more cognitively natural and domain knowledge enriched (embedding decision models in knowledge bases, embedding rules in behavioral decision models, etc.)

Improved Ways to Integrate AI and HCI into Error/Bias Repair Tasks

- Getting expert critiquing systems, expert advisors, tutors, and so on to "say the right thing at the right time"
- Designing more naturalistic knowledge-based human–computer interactions (e.g., managing trouble, handling misunderstanding, discussive versus directive explanations, persuasiveness, user modeling)
- Exploring multimedia and other usability enhancing factors (e.g., hypermedia, "ecological interfaces," interaction devices, I/F evaluations). Recovering when users fail to understand a correction
- Strengths/weaknesses of deep text generation, plan formulation, user modeling, and intention sharing
- Computer-supported cooperative work, theories for augmenting collaboration, cooperative explanations

This article examines these topics by summarizing recent work from psychology, judgment and decision making, human–computer interaction, and artificial intelligence.

BACKGROUND

Several workshops in the past have addressed aspects of the problem of having knowledge-based systems reduce the consequences of proficient humans' errors. For example, the judgment and decision-making community (J/DM) has a large literature on the interaction of human error models and reparative procedures. The Cambridge University Press, among others, includes several proceedings of this type of workshop. The results show, among other things, that the J/DM community relies on decision analytic methods, rather than on knowledge-based systems, for reparative procedures. One workshop which attempted to plant some seeds to shift J/DM away from strictly decision analytic procedures was the 1986 NATO workshop on "Expert Judgment and Expert Systems" (1).

From a different perspective, the safety critical technology community has a long-standing interest in human error and how intelligent systems can help in its mitigation. For example, the 1986 NATO research workshop on "Intelligent Decision Support in Process Environments" typifies the blending of psychological models and intelligent decision support that is of interest here (2).

Finally, much of interest has happened (and continues to unfold) on a tool level in the field of knowledge-based human–computer interaction. For example, important elements of the literature include notes from meetings such as the AAAI '90 research workshop on "Knowledge Based Human Computer Cooperation" (3).

Most important to this article is a research workshop held in Vienna in 1992 which bears the same title as the title of this article; see Reference 4. The Vienna workshop was an attempt to revisit the waterfront of issues confronting knowledge-based mitigation of proficient practitioners' errors, to build bridges between diverse communities, and to see what progress various researchers had (or had not) been making. "Air time" was allotted for presentations from researchers who had built actual systems, who had run relevant experiments, and/or who offered a well-founded viewpoint. Twenty researchers participated in the workshop including 12 researchers from 8 European countries and 8 researchers from across the United States. There were also several observers, one from as far away as Japan. Most of the participants had not previously met one other, or heard the subtleties of their respective views. This set the stage for useful discussion and "bridge-building." What follows was presented, in an early version, to the participants as a workshop wrap-up talk, and in written draft. This write-up includes their reviews and comments.

WHAT SHOULD BE REPLACED: THE HUMAN, THE TECHNOLOGY, OR NEITHER?

Any time researchers working in the error mitigation field get together, there is generally some discussion of the three pathways to consider. Let me briefly summarize these three paths to mitigation. First, in some situations human error can be eliminated via automation. A current example of this is receptionists and telephone operators being replaced by voice mail. Some people feel the automation route is the most reliable, yet many do not subscribe to this view. For one thing, automation is costly. For example, consider the domain of aircraft carriers in the U.S. Navy. On each sea tour, it seems that a few seamen lose their lives through carelessness, accident, and error (e.g., falling off the side, getting sucked into engines, crashing into the ship, etc.). Yet, the Navy does not have the funds, or know-how, to automate all these jobs. Even in the far simpler voice mail example it seems that how to automate is not obvious. In fact, users may exhibit increased errors and reduced performance in telephone usage as a result of voice mail. A related concern is that software itself can never be guaranteed to be error-free (e.g., witness recent near-nationwide telecommunication system crashes). Finally, there are innumerable situations that are too ill-structured for automation. Humans must be kept in the task performance loop. For these and related reasons, this survey will omit the option of replacing humans with software.

The second error mitigation pathway is to redesign organizations, procedures, technology, and so forth so they reduce humans' propensity to err. The MacIntosh "look and feel" drove this point home to society, and other electronic-based industries (VCRs, televisions, cameras, etc.) are finally beginning to change their digital displays to a more "intuitive" error-reducing approach as well. From an organizational design perspective, it seems that aircraft carriers are a superb model of error reduction through the interface flexibility afforded different teams of sailors performing diverse, but interrelated tasks.

The Human Computer Interaction (HCI) community appears to place the highest priority on this overall "redesign" pathway. As but one of many possible examples, under the sponsorship of BellCORE, Huguenard and Lerch (5) are researching a human error modeling approach to the (re)design of voice mail menus. The conventional wisdom in voice mail is to use short menus with many layers, so as to avoid humans forgetting what is on a given layer of the menu. By simulating working memory (via a mixed production system/connectionist approach) and running verification experiments, Lerch and Huguenard showed that conventional menus promote navigational errors, errors in traversing the menu due to forgetting higher-level choices. Their results so far seem to indicate that broad but shallow menus may be better. Further research is warranted on the impact of alternative menu designs, simulations of diverse human working memory capacities, and so on. The research thus far is content-free; that is, it ignores ambiguity in the content of the menu selections.

A vast number of equally excellent redesign projects are documented in the HCI literature. As another example, there have been initial attempts to develop "ecological interfaces," screens that display information at the level at which its cognitively useful; see Rasmussen (6). Unecological interfaces load up the screen with graphics and direct manipulation objects that might be faithful domain metaphors, but that do not directly improve the nature of problem solving itself (as will be discussed later). There is work in progress about the nature of groups and how inappropriate corporate culture can foster error. Improved group culture might be one of the major underresearched areas that could greatly reduce human error, particularly in safety critical situations; see Ref. 7.

In the end, it is difficult to disagree with the HCI view that it is important to diagnose the errors due to poor design and to use "after-the-fact" redesign to minimize error reoccurrence wherever possible. It would be foolish, for example, to build an expert system to help people set the clock on their VCR when, through simple VCR design fixes, it could be made intuitively obvious how to set it. Where it is not possible to eliminate all sources of human error through after-the-fact redesign, or where designs are already locked in, AI solutions may be fruitful in helping to mitigate the consequences of human errors; that is, in some situations after-the-fact diagnosis and redesign may be too late. This brings up the third and final pathway to human error mitigation, that of using knowledge-based systems to help humans detect and recover from their errors.

The third pathway assumes that complex human–computer systems might better be designed around the expectation of human errors. The philosophy here is that the problem is not the errors themselves but the consequences of leaving the errors unattended. This third path of having the machine help humans recognize and recover from their errors is the major focus of most of the rest of this survey.

There is a research gap in the HCI community; that is, there is such an overriding focus on the redesign of items so they will be ''error-free,'' that the HCI community is currently placing almost no attention on error recovery issues and research. Yet organizational designs, procedures, technology, and so on will never entirely eliminate human error. A draft set of research challenges for the HCI community is included in a later section A shopping list of HCI challenges.

BEHAVIORAL AND COGNITIVE PSYCHOLOGY: A ROLE FOR EACH

The human error research community divides generally into two groups: those working on errors related to human action (behavior) and those working on errors related to human judgment (cognition). Judgments often are precursors to actions, but researchers tend to focus on the two as separate tasks. The similarities between the action and judgment error research communities are that they share three top-level goals: (1) both are trying to develop taxonomies of error types; (2) both are trying to overcome the general lack of models of human error (and error recovery) processes; and (3) both are interested in getting machines to help detect and repair the errors.

The differences between the two communities, on the one hand, are that *actions* take place in time under dynamic circumstances such as flying a plane, driving a car, or controlling a power plant. People who act are usually not experts, in the expert system sense. Rather they are proficient performers, competent practitioners, and professionals. Human action researchers generally assume their subjects made the correct judgments about what schema to activate. It is the slips, lapses, and other real-time schema execution errors that interest these researchers.

Judgments, on the other hand, are usually studied in static environments without strict time limitations. Also, researchers who study judgments often are interested in heuristics and cognitive processes used up to and including the point of deciding what course of action to pursue. They focus on systematic tendencies, or reproducible cognitive biases arising from these heuristics. These researchers ignore the action stage or assume the action schemas will be executed as planned.

Having pointed out these differences, there are many instances of overlap. For example, chess players are experts, but what they do is not characterized as judgment, but rather situation assessment planning, and so on. They and certain other categories of professionals (e.g., doctors, trial lawyers, etc.) execute schemas that might variously be studied by both communities. Conversely, action researchers increasingly are coming to see recurring patterns in some of the accidental schema execution slips and lapses of process operators. Many apparently accidental execution errors, in fact, may be due to systematic biases of heuristics used during action-based ''judgments.''

Despite any gray areas, the differences in action versus judgment focus translate into real differences in how the two communities investigate the three goals they have in common. In terms of the first goal, action-oriented researchers tend to focus on the "automaticity" errors, such as the various types of slips and lapses that can occur when executing a proper schema. This line of investigation began with Norman's (8) seminal work on the subject. Since then, researchers increasingly are trying to create computer implementable versions of automaticity theory. For example, Hollnagel (9) is developing a rigorous, consistent, and machine-implementable phenology of erroneous actions. Phenotypes are the manifestations of erroneous actions (behavioral view), as opposed to genotypes which include the causes (cognitive processes). Hollnagel's work is largely based on timing (e.g., premature start, omission, delayed ending) and sequence (e.g., jump forward, jump backward, reversal) errors. Its value lies in the fact that the taxonomy only includes errors that can be observed (e.g., loss of attention is a cause not an observable phenotype), and so the taxonomy can be machine implemented.

By way of contrast, Silverman (10) is developing a taxonomy of genotypes (causes) of judgment errors. Although there are probably a million pages of published literature on judgment biases, almost none of this is machine implementable; see Ref. 11. Silverman, Donnell, and Bailley (12) explain a feasible, yet time- and effort-intensive procedure that they and their colleagues are pursuing to try and make headway in developing judgment-related genotypes. Due to the large scope of the undertaking, rather than tackle specific classes of error (e.g., time based), their approach is to examine all the types of error that arise in a given class of task (e.g., information acquisition, forecasting, decision making under uncertainty). There is a similar lack of machine-implementable taxonomies in both communities; however, this obstacle is likely to be eliminated sooner for the action community.

The behavioral versus cognitive psychology distinctions carry into the second goal of how the two communities develop models of error and error-recovery processes. The behaviorists build situational, rather than mental, models. They find mental models too slow and inaccurate for error monitoring in real-time safety-critical systems. Mental models and models of intentionality are too coarse-grained and lead to unacceptably high rates of false alarms. Moreover, the closer the system gets to a hazard, the less important is the operator's mental state and the more important it becomes to focus on avoiding the hazard. Situational or engineering models are useful here, as they can infer accurately whether observable action streams hold errors that may jeopardize the safety of the system.

All is not a bed of roses with situational models though. For example, Greenberg (13) points out that a lot of context information is required before inserting machine actions into the operator's action stream. Related to this is the Gibsonian idea of affordances (a chair "affords" sitting) and the machine-generated conclusion that affordances missed are errors. Greenberg contends that affordances are too low level. More useful are linguistic/semantic techniques à la Winograd. Instead of affordances, Greenberg favors tracking commitments not fulfilled. Greenberg's research with error-monitoring systems shows often that there is user resistance to suggestions of affordances missed and/or of active remediation; also consult the related work of Rouse and Morris (14). Simply allowing users the ability to authorize/deauthorize the machine-suggested action is insufficient. Among other things, more research is needed to show that machine-generated remedies are reliable and sometimes crucial. For example, as Booth (15) suggests, a

Boeing 737-400 flight management system demanded the complete attention of the co-pilot throughout the Kegworth air disaster. At no time did it offer suggestions to help avert or diminish the crisis.

Mental modeling, in turn, is proving useful to the both the HCI/redesign and the judgment errors communities. Huguenard and Lerch (5) was an example of the value of cognitive models to the redesign community. Johnson et al. (16) provide a lucid example for the judgment errors community. Johnson studied why expert accountants at major accounting houses are so poor at detecting fraudulent bookkeeping at firms and banks intending to deceive investors and auditors. By building cognitive models of their heuristics and biases, Johnson was able to replicate and explain the fraud detection (judgment) errors to which accountants succumb. We will say more about Johnson's work shortly.

Given the importance of cognitive modeling to so many researchers, it is increasingly important for cognitive modelers to develop computer-implementable versions of their models. An interesting development in this regard is Fox et al.'s (17) discussion of a specification language they have been developing to help cognitive modelers make their models more precise. Consider the example of how SOAR is a cognitive model that one can study by either reading a textbook theory that may or may not be faithful to the actual computational model, or by studying the full 30,000 lines of SOAR source code. Using their tool, Fox et al. reduced the actual code to a very few pages of cognitive model specs. These specs are themselves rules. Researchers can run these rules to exercise the model and to study consequences of different model assumptions. The error community will more rapidly harness the cognitive research literature and results, as more psychologists develop similar computational level specs for other cognitive models.

The third and last shared goal of the action and judgment error communities concerns implementations of systems on the machine. The works mentioned up to this point by Greenberg, Hollnagel, Lerch, Silverman, and others include descriptions of and lessons learned from systems in various stages of being fielded.

NEEDED: A THEORY OF CONTEXT

One issue that keeps arising in human error studies is that of context. Expertise in one context may be an error in another, and vice versa. For example, Moustakis et al. (18) offer a nice case study of a medical domain where the theoretically correct expertise was being contradicted in practice. It turned out that patients from remote villages, who were unlikely to continue medication and office visits, were being recommended for immediate out-patient surgical correction of their problem. The local doctors were seeing to their patients needs in the context of the care delivery system rather than as recommended by a theoretically correct textbook approach.

Ford and Agnew (19) offers three types of experts: (1) "Socially selected" experts, those who have some sort of societal recognition or perception of expertise by their blind-faith followers. Con artists, quacks, sincere-but-misguideds, and others often are Type 1 experts. (2) Type 2 experts are socially selected, but they also possess "personally constructed" expertise that comes from functioning and practicing with their degree, title, job, and so on. These experts, through (possibly fallible) experience, have constructed a "rational " domain model that allows them to make functional decisions that their local constituents value and find difficult to make themselves. The doctors in Moustakis' case study fall into this category, as do other professionals such as lawyers, accountants, coaches, teachers, and others who also must keep passing some domain-relevant performance tests. (3) Finally, " reality relevant" experts are able to pass all of the above tests plus the scrutiny of scientific society. Type 3 experts include major theoreticians of a given discipline. Most experts exist at the middle level, and a very few reach the highest level. At all three levels, however, expertise is located in the expert-in-context; that is, experts exist in social niches dependent on social validation (Moustakis' doctors' rules are wrong for metropolises). Also, expertise is subject to a relatively short half-life. The duration of the half-life grows longer as one progresses up the three rungs of the expertise ladder. Conversely, the fallibility frequency of the expert decreases as the ladder is ascended. However, at each level, expertise remains at the mercy of a variety of meta-selectors.

Virtually all participants agreed on the need for AI to have a better handle on the context problem, yet they disagreed on what was needed. There were two basic "camps," the engineers and the scientists. The engineers felt it was best to work toward a simple "theory of context," one they could immediately implement. This group offered various proposals, For example, Siklossy (20) suggested all expert systems should contain a meta-frame used to describe the limits of their knowledge and the extent of their ignorance. Siklossy coined the term "ignorance representation" and indicated that such a frame could help an expert system with such problems as advising its users when it was being used out of context. The meta-frame is an admittedly weak implementation that would be unable to handle unexpected situations and would leave a number of context issues unresolved.

The scientists' camp felt only a full-blown theory of context would allow knowledge-based systems (KBSs) and their designers to handle the problem properly. Such a theory would allow a KBS to be socially "aware." It would help the KBS to know what knowledge and tools to use, when, and for whom. Further, this theory would permit the KBS to handle communication difficulties and other types of trouble. Although a laudable long-term research goal, developing a full context theory involves solving the complete AI problem as well as having an accepted theory of human cognition and group behavior. Although research is needed to overcome the overall context obstacle, pragmatic solutions also are needed. The latter could provide significant benefits in the near term.

BUG THEORY MAY WORK AFTER ALL

In this section we further discuss the work of Johnson et al. (16), mentioned earlier, who explain how they are successfully applying bug theory to error detection. Van Lehn (21) documented the theory of bugs in problem solving and applied it to student learning situations. The errors that students make in a learning task are the "bugs," and an enumeration of these errors is the "bug theory" of that domain. Many researchers have concluded that bug theory is limited because in even seemingly simple domains, there is an explosion of possible bugs. For example, in the domain of learning subtraction, school children's bug catalogs are vast and innumerable.

Van Lehn explains that impasses arise during problem solving that are generally overcome through two main types of repairs: generalizations and integrations of procedural knowledge. Inappropriate generalizations and integrations create bugs in the procedural knowledge used to solve the problem. Bug theory is, thus, a theory of error that is potentially useful to the judgment or cognition community, although it is irrelevant for the action-oriented errors (slips, lapses) community. If subjects tend to repeat bugs under similar circumstances, then the idea of a bug is the computer science jargon for what psychologists refer to as a judgment or cognitive bias.

Johnson's contribution to bug theory comes from demonstrating its usefulness in professional domains. Johnson's results support the position that bug explosions appear unlikely in professional settings. Due to the nature of professions, there appear to be only a few bugs that predominate; that is, Johnson's empirical findings seem to show that in sophisticated professional domains (i.e., accounting, medicine), the bugs one finds in practice are limited to a very few repeated procedural errors. A half dozen bugs often accounts for 60–90% of all professionals' errors. This is because, unlike open domains such as learning, professions may be highly constrained to a few heuristics everyone already follows. This finding is consistent with the judgment and decision-making community's results concerning cognitive bias in judgment. What is interesting here is that Johnson's findings (1) provide a bridge between the two sets of concepts (bugs and biases) and (2) open the door to a new (noneducational) use for bug theory. This general significance of the use of the term bugs, rather than biases, is that it may help computer scientists better understand the task of designing expert critiquing systems to help humans repair their buggy procedures in decision support applications.

IMPROVING EXPERT CRITIQUING SYSTEMS

Expert critiquing systems are a form of expert systems useful for expert support settings. They take as input both the statement of the problem and the user's proposed solution. Their output is a critique of the human's solution, and many critics include a set of repair suggestions. Critics are thus, an error-checking software that have been built for applications as diverse as medicine (22), engineering design (23), programming (24), and document generation (25) among many others; for a more thorough review, see Ref. 26. Expert critic technology is also found in grammar and style checkers available in many word processing packages.

Expert critiquing systems already are a viable, commercially successful technology. Yet they often fail to say the right thing at the right time, intrude when users do not want them, and too often appear to be situation-insensitive automatons. Let us now review how several researchers are addressing these and related challenges. This is a nonexhaustive sample that is illustrative of the types of work currently being pursued at a variety of research centers.

Greenberg (13), referred to earlier, explains his use of Assessment nets (Anets) to constantly monitor the distance of the system to a hazard state. Anets are organized in order of situation severity and are constantly monitored to anticipate the most hazardous consequences of a human operator's actions. If a hazard is approached, the Anet triggers the appropriate remedy suggestion. Anets can incorporate factors such as the human operator's intentions, beliefs, cognitive workload, level of fatigue, and so on, but research to date has omitted these. For his system to work in real time, Greenberg feels it is necessary to forego the "differential analysis" step that critics often undertake. This is the step where the critic compares the user's solution, intentions, mental state, and so on to the normative ideal. Instead, Greenberg's critics are streamlined to react only when system hazards appear imminent.

Silverman (25), in contrast, presents an example of the opposite idea. Here, the computer evaluates the human's choice of mental model for a task, determines if that model is suboptimal, and attempts to shift the human to a more normative mental model. Silverman is unconcerned with mathematical formulations of models, but focuses instead on the use of normative heuristics and cues. Silverman (25) includes an actual working example for a forecasting task in the U.S. Army. Here the critics test for several commonly occurring bugs or biases related to nonregressive models. If these biases are present, the critic sends the user through a step-by-step procedure that causes them to realize the value of a regression approach to the forecast. No one actually performs a regression, but the result is that the users adopt a more normative solution to the problem. A concern about Silverman's use of critics is it appears to rely on bias theory to help detect errors. Yet bias theory has a history of nonrelevance to real-world tasks. However, an increasing amount of recent empirical evidence, like the army forecaster and accounting fraud examples, indicates that professionals may, indeed, succomb to common judgment biases with regularity. The use of published bias theory helps critic designers get started (it is a generative bug theory), but they must adapt and extend those theories for the particular application.

Hagglund (27) gives an overview of several critic research efforts his group has been doing to improve the quality of a critic's textual dialogue. For example, his student, in work by Harrius (28) presents some research on dynamic text generation for a criticism using rhetorical structure theory (RST) and other methods of linguistics. In particular, once the differential analyzer identifies an error, the critique builder selects a schema from a library of aggregate schemas of argument structures. The aggregate schemas are descriptions of how to construct the argumentation. For example, an aggregate schema for "disagree" presents a negative statement and motivates it with support. RST indicates the nucleus and satellite pieces of text for any given element of an aggregate schema. With the help of a user model (what the user knows already), Toulmin forms, and the RST are used to instantiate the aggregate schema with actual text relevant to the current situation. At the end of a given criticism, the user model is updated. Research to date has progressed along the lines of studying human-to-human criticism in a real-world domain to isolate the relevant rhetorical structures, relations, and schemas. The goal of the research is to develop high-quality machine texts. The goal does not include two-sided human–computer discussions, which would be a valuable result as well.

DO EXPLANATION KBs EMPOWER USER?

Expert critics evolved out of the desire to improve user acceptance of KBSs in decision support settings. Ford et al. (29) suggest an alternative paradigm for improving KBS acceptance and user support. In the explanation approach of most expert systems, the user is a relatively passive receiver of information (e.g., unwinded rule stacks, canned text, or graphs). The central idea of participatory explanation is to put the users in an environment where they can actively explore the domain model and construct their own explanations.

To implement this concept, Ford has created the NUclear Cardiology Expert System (NUCES). In NUCES, when a user requests an explanation, the performance environment is interrupted, and the user is switched into the context-sensitive explanation subsystem. From there, users freely browse among a wealth of KB development and support objects (e.g., audio, video, documents, images, repertory grids, concept maps, rules, etc.) Users end their browsing when they have constructed an adequate explanation from the available information. The system is about a year from fielding, but medical doctors are already using it on a trial basis. The participatory nature of the explanation subsystem apparently helps the doctors feel they are in control.

Discussants at the workshop noted that this approach to explanation must be expensive and raised several questions about the cost–benefit ratio. In particular, where does the explanation model come from, and is it not expensive to build? One discussant observed that in many expert systems the explanation function is rarely consulted once the users come to trust its results—so why invest so heavily in that side of the effort? Other participants expressed doubts that doctors would take (or even have) the time to browse the domain model when acquiring an explanation. Finally, there was some discussion supporting and rebutting the phenomenon that "the more explanation an expert system gives, the less users trust the system."

Although he could not yet present economic justification to his approach, Ford, of course, had considered all this. He felt the problem with traditional expert systems' explanations was casting the user in the passive role. The explanation material that users browse is no more than the same material the knowledge engineers collect and sort through when acquiring the KB. Ford organized this material with the help of the Integrated CONstructivist Knowledge Acquisition Tool (ICONKAT).

A SHOPPING LIST OF HCI CHALLENGES

An international HCI panel consisting of Peter Johnson and Sotiris Papantonopoulos, co-chairs, and Paul Booth, Frances Brazier, Mark Maybury, Pat Patterson, and John Rosbottom presented and discussed the following issues in HCI and multimedia at the Vienna research workshop. They are reproduced here to stimulate further discussion.

1. Before he retired, Jens Rasmussen (6) published a provocative proposal for "ecological interfaces" that reduce human error by making the invisible visible in safety-critical situations. This proposal suggests that in safety-critical situations, most interfaces fail to present information in units that are cognitively natural to problem solving and error mitigation. Errors arise, in part, because human users must cognitively map screen information into the units needed to solve the problems.

2. Explanation need not be text. From an error reduction viewpoint, this raises questions about what is the optimum mix of media, audio, video, and so on.

3. One of the features of direct manipulation is the availability of immediate fine-grained semantic feedback about the consequences of the user's actions. In real-time systems the time delays are so large that this style of interaction may be inappropriate. What should be done about the lag between the command and the effect on the "world" in terms of feedback to the user?

4. The theory of minimalism [e.g., John Carroll's (30) Nurnberg Funnel] suggests that computers (a) be concise with the ability to elaborate (e.g., via hypertext), (b) support guided exploration, and (c) offer error recognition and recovery abilities. Very little has been learned to date about how to do the last of these items; that is, it is often taken for granted that error recognition and recovery will be built into any good interface. So, few guidelines have emerged, and many systems overlook this feature. What can be done to reverse this situation and what have we learned already?

5. Much trouble and many misunderstandings could be mitigated if the computer could just recognize and react to the human's intentions on goals. Yet, interfaces that adapt to individual differences and personal objectives have been disappointing. More effective user models and adaptive interfaces appear unlikely in the near term.

6. There seems to be no good cognitive models of core activities such as browsing, searching, controlling, fault finding, and so on. Although these activities underlie much of the interaction required between people and complex systems, there is little advice available about the way the user interface should support these core activities. What are the prospects for better cognitive models of core activities that would lead to prescriptive guidance for interface designs?

7. It seems that part of the error problem is the lack of any understanding of how to predict the way a system is going to behave when a person is interacting with it. There is a need for case histories of known design errors and discussion of how the error(s) could have been predicted.

CONCLUSIONS AND NEXT STEPS

In summary, it seems that the field of "knowledge-based mitigation of proficient practitioners' errors" is still immature. The past few years since several predecessor workshops has witnessed a blossoming of many new lines of investigation, but these have yet to bear much fruit in practice. Although, in mid-1980s workshops researchers were merely proposing new lines of investigation, in 1992 many researchers are able to discuss real results from working knowledge-based systems and from actual field experiments. We have a better idea of where the true obstacles lie and of what has not proved to be helpful. There are a number of laboratory prototypes and about-to-be-fielded systems that promise to yield still further insights in the near term.

It will be vital for this community to maintain interdisciplinary links and to reconvene from time to time, particularly as major breakthroughs might be just around the corner. It would also be useful for certain research communities to expand the range of what they normally do. A few examples are as follows:

1. Psychologists should attempt to produce computer-implementable cognitive model specs.

2. HCI researchers should consider ways to add active error mitigation into their designs.

3. Critic builders should more aggressively pursue both taxonomies/mental models of professional judgment bugs and linguistic/rhetorical approaches to improving criticism texts.

4. For surface credibility purposes, the automaticity error (slips, lapses) field needs to attain and document several application successes, particularly in real-time hazard avoidance.

These and other extracommunity research efforts would lead to a test of an integrated set of the latest psychological, AI, and HCI suggestions, and advance the error mitigation field significantly.

REFERENCES

1. J. Mumpower et al. (eds.), *Expert Systems and Expert Judgment*, NATO Workshop Series, Springer-Verlag, Berlin, 1987.
2. E. Hollnagel, G. Mancini, and D. D. Woods (eds.), *Intelligent Decision Support in Process Environments*, Springer-Verlag, Berlin, 1986.
3. G. Fischer et al. (eds.), *Research Workshop on Knowledge Based Human Computer Cooperation*, Menlo Park, 1990.
4. B. G. Silverman (ed.), *Research Workshop on Expert Judgment, Human Error, and Intelligent Systems*, European Conference on Artificial Intelligence, Vienna, 1992.
5. B. R. Huguenard and F. J. Lerch, "PBI Designer: A Design Tool for Predicting Working Memory Failure in Phone-Based Interaction," in *Research Workshop on Expert Judgment, Human Error, and Intelligent Systems*, B. G. Silverman (ed.), European Conference on Artificial Intelligence, Vienna, 1992, pp. 94–112.
6. J. Rasmussen, "The Design of Ecological Interfaces," Risoe National Lab. Tech. Report, Copenhagen, 1989.
7. J. Reason, *Human Error*, Cambridge University Press, New York, 1990.
8. D. A. Norman, "Categorization of Action Slips," *Psychol. Rev.*, *88*, 1–5 (1982).
9. E. Hollnagel, "The Phenotype of Erroneous Actions," *Int. J. Man–Machine Studies*, 1992.
10. B. G. Silverman, "Expert Critics: Operationalizing the Judgment/Decisionmaking Literature as a Theory of "Bugs" and Repair Strategies," *Knowledge Acquisition*, *3*, 175–214 (1991).
11. D. Kahneman, P. Slovic, and A. Tversky, *Judgment Under Uncertainty: Heuristics and Biases*, Cambridge University Press, Cambridge, 1982.
12. B. G. Silverman, M. L. Donnell, and D. Bailley, "Toward the Implementation of Cognitive Bias Theory: A Methodology and a Rule Base," *Int. J. Man–Machine Studies)*, 1992.
13. A. Greenberg, "Monitoring for Hazard in Complex Systems," in *Research Workshop on Expert Judgment, Human Error, and Intelligent Systems*, B. G. Silverman (ed.), European Conference on Artificial Intelligence, Vienna, 1992, pp. 169–186.
14. W. B. Rouse and N. M. Morris, "Conceptual Design of a Human Error Intolerant Interface for Complex Engineering Systems," *Automatica*, *23*, 231–235 (1987).
15. P. A. Booth and R. W. Paulson, "Errors and Failures," in *Research Workshop on Expert Judgment, Human Error, and Intelligent Systems*, B. G. Silverman (ed.), European Conference on Artificial Intelligence, Vienna, 1992, pp. 156–168.
16. P. E. Johnson, S. Grazioli, K. Jamal, and I. A. Zualkerman, "Success and Failure in Expert Reasoning," *Organizational Behav. Human Decision Processes*, 1992.
17. J. Fox, et al., "Building Computational Models of Cognition," in *Research Workshop on Expert Judgment, Human Error, and Intelligent Systems*, B. G. Silverman (ed.), European Conference on Artificial Intelligence, Vienna, 1992, pp. 87–93.
18. V. Moustakis, G. Potamias, et al., "Bias Identification Using Inductive Learning Techniques: A Medical Case Study," in *Research Workshop on Expert Judgment, Human Error, and Intelligent Systems*, B. G. Silverman (ed.), European Conference on Artificial Intelligence, Vienna, 1992, pp. 113–123.
19. K. M. Ford and N. M. Agnew, "Expertise: Socially Situated, Personally Constructed, and 'Reality' Relevant," in *Research Workshop on Expert Judgment, Human Error, and Intelligent Systems*, B. G. Silverman (ed.), European Conference on Artificial Intelligence, Vienna, 1992, pp. 79–86.
20. L. Siklossy, "Representing Ignorance, or Knowing What We Do Not Know," in *Research Workshop on Expert Judgment, Human Error, and Intelligent Systems*, B. G. Silverman (ed.), European Conference on Artificial Intelligence, Vienna, 1992, pp. 47–56.
21. K. Van Lehn, *Mind Bugs: The Origins of Procedural Misconceptions*, MIT Press, Cambridge, MA, 1990.
22. P. L. Miller, "ATTENDING: Critiquing a Physician's Management Plan," *IEEE Trans. PAMI*, *PAMI-5*, 449–461 (1983).

23. R. L. Spickelmier and A. R. Newton, "Critic: A Knowledge-Based Program for Critiquing Circuit Designs," in *Proc. of the 1988 IEEE International Conf. on Computer Design: VLSI in Computers and Processors*, IEEE Computer Society Press, New York, 1988, pp. 324–327.

24. G. Fischer, "A Critic for Lisp," *Proc. 10th International Joint Conf. on Artificial Intelligence, Los Altos*, Morgan Kaufman, San Mateo, CA, 1987, pp. 177–184.

25. B. G. Silverman, "Criticism Based Knowledge Acquisition for Document Generation," *Innovative Appl. Artificial Intelligence*, AAAI Press, New York, 1991, pp. 291–319.

26. B. G. Silverman, *Critiquing Human Error: A Knowledge Based Human–Computer Collaboration Approach*, Academic Press, London, 1992.

27. S. Hagglund, "Expert Critiquing as a Paradigm for Giving Consultative Advice," in *Research Workshop on Expert Judgment, Human Error, and Intelligent Systems*, B. G. Silverman (ed.), European Conference on Artificial Intelligence, Vienna, 1992, pp. 124–130.

28. J. Harrius, "AREST, a System for Deep Generation of a Critique Using Aggregate Schemas," in *Research Workshop on Expert Judgment, Human Error, and Intelligent Systems*, B. G. Silverman (ed.), European Conference on Artificial Intelligence, Vienna, 1992, pp. 131–145.

29. K. M. Ford, A. J. Canas, and J. Adams-Weber, "Explanation as a Knowledge Acquisition Issue," in *Research Workshop on Expert Judgment, Human Error, and Intelligent Systems*, B. G. Silverman (ed.), European Conference on Artificial Intelligence, Vienna, 1992, pp. 146–155.

30. J. M. Carroll, *The Nurnberg Funnel: Designing Minimalist Instruction for Practical Computer Skill*, MIT Press, Cambridge, MA, 1990.

BARRY G. SILVERMAN

FUZZY CONTROL AND FUZZY SYSTEMS

INTRODUCTION

Uncertainty and complexity become intrinsic constituents one is faced with when dealing with real-life problems. Human reasoning involves some general categories in which individual objects are ill-structured with imprecisely defined boundaries. Our abilities to carry out reasoning processes in the presence of incomplete and/or uncertain information are eminent. A vast number of tasks ranging from almost trivial in our human sense (like driving a car, recognizing objects, avoiding obstacles) to complex ones (such as managing manufacturing processes, scheduling, designing, etc.) still constitute a continuous challenge for computer algorithms.

The reasoning process of humans and those traditionally implemented at the level of computers are realized at the two essentially disjoint conceptual platforms. The first one handles all pieces of information at a linguistic level in a symboliclike fashion. The specific representation can be and usually is adjusted according to the problem at hand. The underlying concept on which all the computer algorithms are based is that they almost exclusively process a rigid and extremely nonmodifiable numerical information. To stimulate any further progress, one should look carefully at possible ways of narrowing the existing gap. A certain visible alternative lies in the realm of soft computing. In its very essence, this paradigm of computations encapsulates diverse faculties including fuzzy sets, neurocomputations, genetic algorithms and genetic programming, to name just a few. The main objectives one strives to achieve pertain to

- processing linguistic form of information, coping with complete and heterogeneous character of available knowledge
- producing user-friendly computing environment (both in terms of its significant customization that attempts to meet the needs of an individual user and in the sense of its increased interpretation capabilities)

Our objective is to introduce the fundamentals of fuzzy models and fuzzy modeling as well as discuss some of their applications in fuzzy control. The intent of the overall discussion will be to look at fuzzy models from a more general point of view and develop a general methodology of their construction with some systematic studies on its algorithmic side.

The development of fuzzy models initiated by Zadeh's classic paper on fuzzy systems [1] has been rapid. The diversity of the models entwines now fuzzy relational structures, fuzzy regression, "local" fuzzy models [2–12], to refer to some of the classes available nowadays. The applications are directed mainly toward analysis and interpretation of numerical and "soft" data, including those constituting classic benchmarks found in standard regression analysis.

What is lacking is a general methodology of fuzzy modeling that could provide a global and unified look at the existing variety of fuzzy models. In particular, this methodology should address such general issues as the nature of processing fuzzy information and in the formation of linkages between the processing part of the fuzzy models and their environment.

The material of this article is organized into sections. We will depart from studying a notion of the fuzzy model. (Note: The term "fuzzy system" which is frequently used nowadays can be treated as a synonym of the fuzzy model used here. From the methodological point of view, the use of the latter is more appropriate though). We will highlight the role of fuzzy modeling with the realization of the principle of incompatibility. The fuzzy models will be looked at as conceptual structures with the three clearly distinguished functional blocks of input and output interfaces and a processing block situated between them. These will be studied thoroughly with respect their concepts as well as computational details, see the second and fifth sections. The processing procedures will be mainly concentrated on fuzzy neural networks (third). The networks of this category are built with the aid of basic logic-based neurons. Several categories of the neurons will be investigated, followed by a discussion of their role in complete networks. Afterward we will study control problems in this framework. It will also be revealed how their solutions can be aggregated into a single structure of a fuzzy controller (sixth section). There, the fuzzy controller will be realized as another fuzzy neural network.

FUZZY SYSTEMS AND THEIR MODELING—TOWARD REALIZATION OF THE PRINCIPLE OF INCOMPATIBILITY

The fundamental idea of fuzzy models and fuzzy modeling is to model systems at a level of linguistic labels. The role of fuzzy modeling is to look at the system from a certain suitable "distance" by ensuring a proper cognitive perspective. The cognitive perspective is formed with the use of fuzzy sets. In a limit case, the models of this class can be utilized to represent relationships among variables at a numerical (pointwise) level. The fuzzy partition constructed in this way can be adjusted separately to meet specific requirements of the modeling task. Some details can then be selectively hidden and will not increase the unnecessary computational burden associated with the model building.* If more details should be captured, one can formulate another more detailed fuzzy partition and redesign the fuzzy model. The fuzzy models developed in this way concur with the principle of incompatibility formulated by Zadeh (15); a similar formulation can be found in Ref. 16. This principle states that any activity of model building calls for a judicious and justifiable trade-off between significance (relevance) and precision as the two conflicting objectives have to be sustained within the same model. It should be stressed that one should sacrifice (to a certain degree) precision to reach an acceptable level of generality. This necessary trade-off is achieved by admitting a relevant level of specificity of the cognitive perspective. Overall, the properties of the frame of cognition applied to modeling are inherited and become built into the models.

---

*In a so-called qualitative modeling, all relationships are defined among symbolic quantities, cf. (13); the extension including linguistic variables is reported in (14).

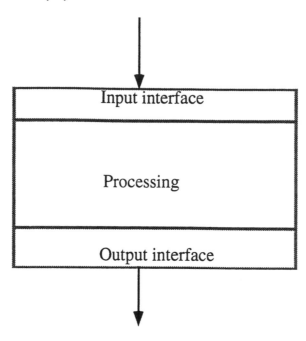

FIGURE 1   Functional blocks of the fuzzy model.

Fuzzy models can be envisioned congruously as a class of modeling structures with three clearly distinguished functional blocks (5,17); see also Figure 1.

- **Input interface** Its role is to transform (internalize) the input information into an appropriate format to be processed by the model (3). The input interface realizes processes of knowledge representation by transforming all available data into coherent pieces of information. Different linguistic labels contributing toward fuzzy partitions can generate quite different internal formats of the data.
- **Processing block** At this level, all computations are carried out for the quantities produced by the input interface. The main objective at this stage is to reveal logical relationships among fuzzy sets of the fuzzy partitions defined for the input and output variables of the fuzzy model, cf. (5,6,18).
- **Output interface** The results obtained at the processing level are retransformed from the internal quantities of the model into some other formats including numerical (pointwise) quantities as required by the environment of the model.

In the following sections we will discuss these functional blocks in great detail. The discussion will be concentrated intentionally on single-input–single-output fuzzy models. The extension to fuzzy models with many inputs is straightforward.

FRAME OF COGNITION AS AN INPUT INTERFACE

The role of the input interface is to convert any input datum coming from the environment into an internal format acceptable by the fuzzy model at its processing level. This goal is accomplished by expressing the input information in terms of basic information granules modeled by fuzzy sets. First, we will formally introduce the notion of the cognitive perspective arising out of these granules, comment on the variability of information granularity to be encapsulated there, and highlight its primordial features. Second, we will discuss a way in which the input information can be translated within the cognitive perspective. We will comment on diversity of types of information that could be handled efficiently there.

The knowledge about the system as well as the perspective from which one is interested to take a look are articulated with the aid of linguistic labels. They constitute generic pieces of knowledge that are deemed by the user to be essential in describing and understanding the functioning of the system. The linguistic labels modeled by fuzzy sets (19) play the role of elastic constraints defined over a universe of discourse, distinguishing its elements that are viewed with the highest degrees of compatibility with the specified linguistic term. The linguistic labels are also referred to as information granules, cf. (20). When considered together, these information granules constitute a frame of cognition (fuzzy partition) (18,21). Being more formal, the family of fuzzy sets

$$\mathcal{A} = A_1, A_2 \cdots , A_n,$$

where $A_i : \mathbf{X} \to [0, 1]$, constitutes a frame of cognition $\mathcal{A}$ if the following properties are satisfied:

- $\mathcal{A}$ "covers" universe $\mathbf{X}$: each element of the universe is assigned to at least one granule with a nonzero degree of membership. This leads to the requirement

$$\underset{x}{\forall} \, \underset{i}{\exists} \, A_i(x) > 0.$$

  This coverage property warrants that any piece of information defined in $\mathbf{X}$ could be properly represented (described) in terms of A_i's.
- The elements of $\mathcal{A}$ are unimodal and normal fuzzy sets (i.e., they are defined through unimodal membership functions with the highest membership values equal to 1). This allows us to distinguish several regions of $\mathbf{X}$ (one for each A_i) that are highly compatible with the labels.

The frame of cognition can be constructed either experimentally or it could involve some algorithmic enhancements applied to the process of elicitation of membership functions. In the first instance, the linguistic labels are specified by studying the problem and recognizing basic relevant information granules. In this way, the subjective evaluation of the membership functions completed by the user/developer of the model becomes a key factor. It is the user/developer who provides relevant membership functions of the variables of the system and in this manner creates his own individual cognitive perspective. In this regard, the standard methods of membership function estimation discussed, for example, in Refs. 5 and 22, can be utilized. The second approach, which could be helpful when some records of numerical data are available, relies on a suitable utilization of fuzzy clustering techniques. Fuzzy clustering techniques (23) can be helpful in discovering and visualizing the structures in the data set. With the aid of clustering algorithms, the elements of the data set become structured into a number of groups (clusters) according to the values of a predefined proximity measure used to express similarities among the data points. The number of clusters is also defined in advance so that the derived clusters correspond directly to the linguistic labels of the frame of cognition. Based on that, the algorithm generates grades of membership of the elements of the data set in the given clusters. If necessary, these grades of belongingness can be also converted into an analytical form of the final membership functions in $\mathcal{A}$

The frame of cognition is characterized by several essential features:

Specificity of the frame of cognition. The frame of cognition $\mathcal{A}'$ is more specific than $\mathcal{A}$ if all the elements of $\mathcal{A}'$ are more specific than the elements of $\mathcal{A}$. The specificity measure can be defined in the same sense as introduced in Ref. 24, cf. also (25,26).

Let us consider the following frame consisting of three information granules,

$\mathcal{A}$ = {Negative, Zero, Positive}.

This frame is less specific than the frame

$\mathcal{A}'$ = {Negative Large, Negative Medium, Negative Small, Zero, Positive Small, Positive Medium, Positive Large};

see also Figure 2. It is noticeable that in the second frame the variable takes on more levels of the linguistic quantification. The partition $\mathcal{A}'$ is less general than the previous one or, equivalently, the information granularity of $\mathcal{A}'$ is finer than that conveyed by $\mathcal{A}$.

Information hiding of the frame of cognition refers to the individual elements of $\mathcal{A}$. This quality states that some elements of **X** can be made equivalent associating them with the same level of membership (equal, for instance, 1.0). From the perspective of membership values, all these elements return the same value. Maintaining abstraction through information hiding plays a primordial role in information reduction that otherwise had to be processed in a numerical manner. The lower the number of linguistic labels, the less detailed is the model emerging. Subsequently such a model calls for lower computational demands associated with its development. An obvious relationship holds: The lower the

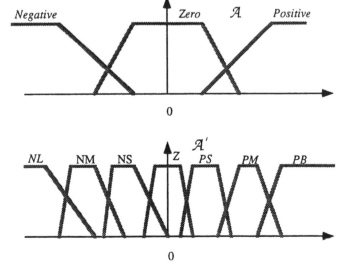

FIGURE 2 Examples of fuzzy partitions with different levels of specificity.

membership level, the more significant is the level of information hiding. Furthermore, referring to Figure 2, we can learn that fuzzy sets with higher specificity result in their weaker abilities of information hiding. Note additionally that set theory realizes information hiding at a single level, whereas fuzzy sets could perform information hiding at many levels, depending on selection of successive λ-cuts.

For the fixed number of labels, the information hiding can be additionally accomplished by enhancing regions of $\mathbf{X}$ that are associated with the higher grades of membership. For instance, the operation of contrast intensification (15) applied to fuzzy set amplifies "high" membership values (greater than 0.5) and suppresses those which have already been viewed as quite insignificant.

Robustness   The frame $\mathcal{A}$ exhibits an interesting property of robustness. It arises as a straightforward corollary of smooth transitions in membership functions of fuzzy sets and allows us to tolerate imprecision of the input information. To illustrate this phenomenon, let us consider the input numerical datum $x \in \mathbf{R}$ which after being exposed to noises is received as x' and, as such, is mapped onto the frame $\mathcal{A}$. This mapping is realized by taking membership values of A_i's at x, say $A_1(x), A_2(x), \ldots, A_c(x)$ and describes the levels of activation of A_1, $A_2, \ldots, A_c \in \mathcal{A}$. On the other hand, the noisy version of x induces $A_1(x')$, $A_2(x'), \ldots, A_n(x')$. The lower the difference between the corresponding membership values $A_1(x)$ and $A_1(x')$, the higher the robustness (noise immunity) of the frame. The sum of absolute differences taken over all the labels,

$$r(x) = |A_1(x) - A_1(x')| + |A_2(x) - A_2(x')| + \cdots + |A_c(x) - A_c(x')|,$$

will serve as a suitable indicator of robustness of $\mathcal{A}$. Subsequently, the global measure of robustness of the frame can be built by completing standard averaging of $r(x)$ over the universe of discourse, say

$$\int_x r(x)\, dx.$$

(We assume that this integral does make sense.)

It is also obvious that the above expression could attain low values, as x and x' can generate relatively similar values of the membership function (for relatively low amplitudes of disturbances). In the case of sets, the lack of continuity in the membership values of $A_i(x)$ and $A_i(x')$ could result in very distinct membership values even for some very close values of x and x', say

$$x \approx x' \quad \text{but } A_i(x) = 0 \text{ and } A_i(x') = 1.$$

For more computational details on the robustness problem, refer to Ref. 27.

The fuzzy partition essentially carries out a transformation of the input datum (despite its character) and converts it into a series of degrees of compatibility with the linguistic labels in the frame. We can write this down schematically as

$$A \rightarrow \mathcal{A} \rightarrow [0, 1]^c$$

or, equivalently,

input information →frame of cognition→ x,

where A can be a single numerical quantity, viz $A \in \mathbf{R}$, set $A \in \mathcal{P}(\mathbf{X})$, or fuzzy set $A \in \mathcal{F}(\mathbf{X})$; here $\mathcal{P}(\cdot)$ and $\mathcal{F}(\cdot)$ are used to denote families of sets or fuzzy sets.

It is worth noting the following:

(i) This transformation generates a homogeneous form of information (viz, elements of the n-dimensional unit hypercube) that is furnished into the processing block of the fuzzy model.

(ii) The input information can be uniquely expressed in terms of linguistic labels. The converse statement is not true; knowing the representatives of the input information at the level of the information granules of $\mathcal{A}$, one cannot reconstruct it in a unique manner. This phenomenon is due to the level of generality inserted by fuzzy sets.

The determination of the compatibility degrees for A and the elements of A constitute another issue. We will concentrate on the use of possibility measures, although some other alternatives such as equality indices (28) are available as well. This choice is motivated mainly by a profound utilizing of possibility measures throughout various constructs of fuzzy sets including fuzzy controllers and various schemes of reasoning as well as their clear interpretation capabilities; cf. (29,30). Let us recall that the possibility measure of A taken with respect to A_i, $\mathrm{Poss}(A \mid A_i)$ or simply $\pi(A \mid A_i)$, is computed as

$$\mathrm{Poss}(A \mid A_i) = \sup_{x \in \mathbf{X}} [\ \min(A(x), A_i(x))].$$

(This formula is quite often generalized by considering some t-norm instead of the minimum operator.) When considering all elements of $\mathcal{A}$, A is converted into $\mathbf{x}$ as

$$\mathbf{x} = [\mathrm{Poss}(A \mid A_i)\ \ \mathrm{Poss}(A \mid A_2)\ \ \ldots\ \ \mathrm{Poss}(A \mid A_i)\ \ \ldots \mathrm{Poss}(A \mid A_n)].$$

For a pointwise (numerical) input information given as a single numerical quantity x_0, $A = \{x_0\}$, the computations are reduced and vector $\mathbf{x}$ includes

$$\mathbf{x} = [A_1(x_0)\ \ A_2(x_0)\ \ \ldots\ \ A_n(x_0)].$$

For interval-valued information $A = [x_1, x_2]$, the resulting vector $\mathbf{x}$ is expressed as

$$\mathbf{x} = [\sup_{x \in [x_1, x_2]} A_1(x)\ \sup_{x \in [x_1, x_2]} A_2(x)\ \cdots\ \sup_{x \in [x_1, x_2]} A_n(x)].$$

The character of this input information results in higher values of all the entries of $\mathbf{x}$. Apparently,

$$\sup_{x \in [x_1, x_2]} A_i(x) \geq A_i(x_0)$$

for any $x_0 \in [x_1, x_2]$. In a limit situation formed by $A = \mathbf{X}$, the vector of possibilities has all its entries equal to 1. This implies a total lack of specificity.

The selection of the information granules of $\mathcal{A}$ is influenced by the level of information granularity to be accepted by the input interface. If the granularity of $\mathcal{A}$ is too high with respect to the fuzzy data being used afterward, this will result in a simultaneous activation of several labels. This, of course, will not be beneficial—later we will comment on this phenomenon in the context of the sampling properties of $\mathcal{A}$. The problem of compatibility of information granularity for A and $\mathcal{A}$ has been discussed in Ref. 31. This will become visible again in discussions on the development of the output interface.

Let us consider fuzzy set A being one of the elements of the fuzzy partition. The pieces of input information $X_1, X_2, \ldots, X_K$ "activate" A to some degrees equal to the possibility values $\pi_k = \text{Poss}(X_k \mid A)$, $k = 1,2, \ldots, K$. Now we will look at the following problem:

Given the collection of X_k's and the corresponding π_k's, determine A.

As the problem stands, one can treat the X_k's as a stream of sampling signals being used to sample the unknown object A and returning π_k's as the results of this sampling. We will be interested in analyzing the abilities of different families of X_k's to capture (reconstruct) A.

The solution to the problem can be obtained easily after translating it into an equivalent task residing within the domain of fuzzy relational equations (2). First, observe that the sampling conditions can be read as

$$\pi_k = \text{Poss}(X_k \mid A) = \sup_{x \in \mathbf{X}} [X_k(x) \wedge A(x)],$$

$k = 1,2, \ldots, K$. For A treated as an unknown fuzzy set for π_k and X_k provided, they are nothing but a collection of fuzzy relational equations

$$\pi_k = X_k \circ A.$$

The maximal solution to a single equation in this family is provided by

$$\hat{A}_k = X_k \, \alpha \, \pi_k.$$

This is a result of a maximal reconstruction of A (reconstruction set) $\wedge A_k$) based on X_k and π_k where the corresponding membership function equals

$$\hat{A}_k(x) = \begin{cases} 1 & \text{if } X_k(x) \leq \pi_k \\ \pi_k & \text{if } X_k(x) > \pi_k. \end{cases}$$

For the entire collection of the sampling conditions (assuming that the solution set is non-empty, namely, the sampling results are consisting) we obtain a better estimate of A that is provided as an intersection of successive $\hat{A}_k$'s.

$$\hat{A}(x) = \min_{k=1, 2, \ldots, K} \hat{A}_k(x).$$

Furthermore, $A \subset \hat{A}$.

The results of reconstruction carried out for a certain family of X_k's viewed as interval-type data are displayed in Figure 3.

Obviously,

- For coarser X_k's, their ability to reconstruct A diminishes rapidly; the reconstructed fuzzy set tends reveals a very rough shape of A.
- When the number of intervals increases, assuming that they still cover the whole universe, the reconstruction set approaches A. In the limit case, viz., for a pointwise information distributed densely over the entire universe, the produced reconstruction becomes ideal. In contrast to this pointwise sampling, too coarse pieces of knowledge (broad intervals) used previously do not allow for any successful reconstruction of A.

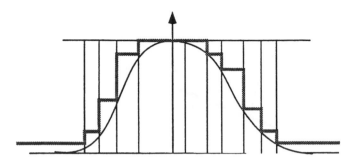

FIGURE 3   Reconstruction results for a given family of sampling intervals.

(iii)   The matching method considered at this point will have a profound effect on the operations realized by the output interface: A reconstruction procedure involved there should yield the results complementary to those produced by the input interface.

FUZZY RELATIONAL CALCULUS AND FUZZY NEUROCOMPUTATIONS

We will concentrate on a broad class of fuzzy models emerging as fuzzy relational structures They originated as single-level computational structures and have been exploited as fuzzy relational equations. cf. (2,32). Then they evolved toward multilevel structures that could be viewed as fuzzy neural networks. We will study both of them, proceeding first with the fundamentals and a concise discussion of the underlying theory. The learning procedures applicable to the fuzzy neural networks will be discussed later.

Fuzzy Relational Equations

The models based on relational calculus capture links between the linguistic labels of the fuzzy partitions and express them in terms of fuzzy relations. The statements about the system's variables read as

there exists a relationship between elements of $\mathscr{A}$ and $\mathscr{B}'$

or, equivalently,

$\mathscr{A}$ and $\mathscr{B}$ are related.

One can look at this as a collection of constraints

$\mathscr{A} \ R \ \mathscr{B}$

Fuzzy sets, fuzzy relations, and the calculus of these objects are put together into a form of fuzzy relational equations. These equations originally developed outside fuzzy sets as a branch of relational calculus and applied vigorously to problems or operations research, cf. (33) were afterward reformulated and generalized in Refs. 32 and 34. Some interesting links between them and ideas of multivalued logic have been underlined in Ref. 32.

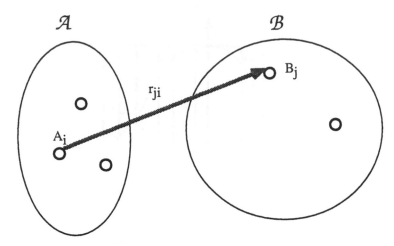

FIGURE 4   Single-level relational structure as a directed graph.

Since then, many theoretical results have been obtained and a detailed methodology of their use followed by a series of specific applications has been formulated (6–8,35).

The main classes of relational structures (and subsequently fuzzy relational equations) are summarized below. Fuzzy set $\mathbf{y}$ results from combining $\mathbf{x}$ and R as

$$\mathbf{y} = \mathbf{x} \circ R,$$

where, as before, $\mathbf{x}$ and $\mathbf{y}$ stand for vectors summarizing the levels of activation of $\mathcal{A}$ and $\mathcal{B}$, respectively, whereas a fuzzy relation $R \in [0, 1]^{n \times m}$ is used to summarize dependencies between the labels. For example, $r_{ji} = R(A_i, B_j)$ expresses a strength of dependency reported between A_i and B_j; see Figure 4.

The composition operator "$\circ$" involves triangular norms (t- and s-norms) (36). This yields

$$y_j = S_{i=1}^{n} [x_i \, t \, r_{ji}],$$

$j = 1, 2, \ldots, m$. The well-known max-min composition (15) arises as a particular case within this class of the relational structures.

The relational structure can be treated as a relational equation with the two generic problems formulated accordingly:

(i) $\mathbf{x}$ and $\mathbf{y}$ are given. Determine R.
(ii) $\mathbf{y}$ and R are given. Determine $\mathbf{x}$.

For the max-min as well as the max-t composition, the analytical solutions are available. Furthermore, one can show that an nonempty family of solutions usually contains more than a single solution. The extremal (maximal) solutions to these equations are determined with the use of the residuation operation (ϕ-operator), cf. (2,4).

The fundamental results about the solutions are then concisely summarized:

For (i): If the family of solutions $\mathcal{R} = \{R \mid \mathbf{y} = \mathbf{x} \circ R\}$ is nonempty, then its maximal element $\hat{R} = \max \mathcal{R}$, is determined through the ϕ-operation applied pointwise to $\mathbf{x}$ and $\mathbf{y}$;

$$\hat{R} = \mathbf{x} \phi \mathbf{y},$$

that is,

$$\hat{r}_{ji} = x_i \phi y_j$$

with the residuation operation defined as

$$a \phi b = \sup\{c \in [0, 1] \mid a \ t \ c \le b\}.$$

For (ii): Assuming that the family of solution $\mathscr{X} = \{\mathbf{x} \mid \mathbf{y} = \mathbf{x} \circ R\}$ is nonempty, its maximal element is calculated as

$$\hat{\mathbf{x}} = R \phi \mathbf{y}$$

or

$$\hat{x}_i = \min_{j=1, 2, \ldots, m} (r_{ji} \phi y_j).$$

The dual class of the fuzzy relational equations involves the *t-s* composition. Now

$$\mathbf{y} = \mathbf{x} \Delta R,$$
$$y_j = T^n_{i=1} (x_i \ s \ r_{ji}),$$

$$j = 1, 2, \ldots, m.$$

Again the two more specialized families of the composition operators include min-max and min-*s* aggregation. The analytical solutions are available in these two cases. The character of the results is dual to those reported previously. Briefly speaking, the obtained solutions are minimal in the family of solutions:

For (i),

$$\check{R} = \mathbf{x} \beta \mathbf{y}, \qquad r_{ji} = x_i \beta y_j;$$

For (ii),

$$\check{\mathbf{x}} = R \beta \mathbf{y}, \qquad \check{x}_i = \max_j [r_{ji} \beta y_j],$$

where the definition of the β-operator includes the *s*-norm in the equation

$$a \beta b = \inf\{c \in [0, 1] \mid a \ s \ c \ge b\}.$$

The theory also provides us with the solutions to the families of fuzzy relational equations; cf. (2,5). These solutions are computed either by taking the intersection or union of the extremal solutions to the individual equations.

The max-*t* and min-*s* relational structures are examples of single-level computational architectures: treating $\mathbf{x}$ as a vector of inputs; $\mathbf{y}$ is calculated through the distributed structure of the fuzzy relation. In the next subsection, we will look at their generalizations that lead toward multilevel structures. We will be referring to them as fuzzy neural networks, whereas the logic-based character of processing realized there will be strongly supported by the nature of the logic-processing units. Each will be designed as a single-level relational structure, including the max-*t* or min-*s* composition operation.

Fuzzy Neural Networks

By the class of fuzzy neural networks we mean highly distributed and parallel computing structures heavily employing logical operations existing in the theory of fuzzy sets. As opposed to the standard neural networks, the architectures arising within this framework are usually strongly heterogeneous. This feature is achieved by incorporating neurons of different logical characteristics. The studies on these models have been initiated in Ref. 13 and 37; refer also to some application-oriented considerations (17,31,38–41).

First we will discuss two basic types of neurons (aggregative and reference) and afterward concentrate on the logical processor constituting a generic architecture of the fuzzy neural networks. In sequel learning, algorithms will be studied.

Aggregative Logic-Based Neurons

The logic-based neurons aggregate input signals, $x_1, x_2, \ldots, x_n \in [0, 1]$ using some basic logic operations. The two basic logical connectives (AND and OR) are utilized to construct the so-called AND and OR neurons:
AND neuron:

$$y = (x_1 \text{ OR } w_1) \text{ AND } (x_2 \text{ OR } w_2) \text{ AND } \ldots \text{ AND } (x_n \text{ OR } w_n);$$

OR neuron:

$$y = (x_1 \text{ AND } w_1) \text{ OR } (x_2 \text{ AND } w_2) \text{ OR } \ldots \text{ OR } (x_n \text{ AND } w_n),$$

$w_i \in [0, 1]$, $i = 1, 2, \ldots ,n$. We will adopt a vector notation $y = \text{AND}(\mathbf{x}; \mathbf{w})$ and $y = \text{OR}(\mathbf{x}; \mathbf{w})$, respectively.

The role of weights (connections) w_i is to enhance or eliminate influence of x_i's on the output y. We have the following:

- The lower value of w_i, the more evident is the influence of x_i on y (AND neuron).
- Higher values of w_i enhance the importance of x_i (OR neuron).

The AND (OR) neuron can be enhanced functionally in two different ways:

By incorporating complements of its input signals, $\bar{x}_i = 1 - x_i$. This allows us to realize inhibitory performance of the neural while still maintaining coding of the connecting within the unit interval. By choosing appropriate values of the connections in the neuron, one can easily achieve its inhibitory or excitatory behavior.

The second modification involves the inclusion of a nonlinear transformation following the neuron. Its role is to modify (calibrate) the obtained grades of membership while the logical properties of the neuron are left intact. The standard two-parametric sigmoid function can serve as one of the possible instances, say

$$z = \left[1 + \exp\left(\frac{-(y - m)^2}{\alpha} \right) \right]^{-1}.$$

The parameters $m \in [0, 1]$ and $\alpha > 0$ are adjusted to come up with an appropriate calibration. By straightforward inspection one can verify that the AND neuron is realized as a single-level max-t relational structure. The dual structure is based on the relational structure with the min-s composition.

Referential Logic-Based Neurons

In comparison to the AND, OR, and OR/AND neuron-realizing operations of the aggregative character, the class of neurons discussed now accomplishes reference computations. The main idea is that the input signals are not directly aggregated as happened with the aggregative neuron; rather they are analyzed first (e.g., compared) with respect to the given reference point. The results of this analysis (including matching, inclusion, difference, dominance) are afterward summarized in the aggregative part of the neuron in the manner described earlier. In general, one can write down the reference operator as

$$y = OR(REF(\mathbf{x}; \textbf{reference\_point}), \mathbf{w})$$

(disjunctive form of aggregation) or

$$y = AND(REF(\mathbf{x}; \textbf{reference\_point}), \mathbf{w})$$

(conjunctive form of aggregation), where $REF(\cdot)$ stands for the reference operation carried out with respect to the provided point of reference.

Depending on the reference operation, the functional behavior of the neuron is described accordingly:

(i) MATCH neuron:

$$y = MATCH(\mathbf{x}; \mathbf{r}, \mathbf{w})$$

or, equivalently,

$$y = S_{i=1}^{n} [w_i \, t \, (x_i \equiv r_i)],$$

where $\mathbf{r} \in [0, 1]^n$ denotes a reference point defined in the unit hypercube. The matching operator will be defined as (28)

$$a \equiv b = \tfrac{1}{2}[(a \phi b) \wedge (b \phi a) + (\bar{a} \phi \bar{b}) \char94 (\bar{b} \phi \bar{a})],$$

where $\wedge$ denotes minimum, $a, b \in [0, 1]$. To emphasize the referential character of processing, one can rewrite the above formulas of the neurons as

$$y = OR(\mathbf{x} \equiv \mathbf{r}; \mathbf{w}),$$
$$y = AND(\mathbf{x} \equiv \mathbf{r}; \mathbf{w}).$$

The use of the OR neuron indicates an "optimistic" (disjunctive) character of the final aggregation. The pessimistic form of this aggregation can be realized by using the AND operation.

(ii) Difference neuron: The neuron combines degrees to which $\mathbf{x}$ is different from the given reference point $\mathbf{g} = [g_1, g_2, \ldots, g_n]$. The output is interpreted as a global level of difference observed between the inputs and the reference point,

$$y = DIFFER(\mathbf{x}; \mathbf{w}, \mathbf{g}),$$

that is,

$$y = S_{i=1}^{n} [w_i \, t \, (x_i \equiv | \, g_i)],$$

where the difference operator $|\equiv$ is taken as a complement of the matching operator,

$$a \mid \equiv b = 1 - a \equiv b.$$

As before, the referential character of processing is underlined by noting that

$$\text{DIFFER}(\mathbf{x}; \mathbf{w}, \mathbf{g}) = \text{OR } (\mathbf{x} \equiv \mid \mathbf{g}; \mathbf{w}).$$

(iii) The inclusion neuron summarizes the degrees of inclusion to which $\mathbf{x}$ is included in the reference point $\mathbf{f}$,

$$y = \text{INCL}(\mathbf{x}; \mathbf{w}, \mathbf{f}),$$
$$y = S_{i=1}^{n} [w_i \ t \ (x_i \rightarrow f_i)],$$

The relationship of inclusion is expressed in the sense of the pseudocomplement operation (implication). Due to the properties of the ϕ-operator one obtains:

- If $a < b$, then $a \phi b = 1$.
- If $a < b' < b$, then $a \phi b' \le a \phi b$;

$a, b, b' \in [0, 1]$, namely, the output of the neuron becomes a monotonic function of the satisfaction of the inclusion property.

(iv) The dominance neuron expresses a relationship dual to that carried out by the inclusion neuron,

$$y = \text{DOM}(\mathbf{x}; \mathbf{w}, \mathbf{h}),$$

where $\mathbf{h}$ stands for a reference point. In other words, the dominance relationship generates the degrees to which $\mathbf{x}$ dominates $\mathbf{h}$. The coordinatewise notation of the neuron reads as

$$y = S_{i=1}^{n} [w_i \ t \ (h_i \rightarrow x_i)].$$

Logical Processors as Basic Processing Units

The AND and OR neurons can be put together to form a so-called logic processors (LP). Roughly speaking, the aim of the LPs is to approximate any function with the use of logic-based neurons. This form of approximation reveals logical characteristics of the approximated function (or a collection of experimental data). Essentially, we will discriminate among the following topologies of the logic processors:

The first topology realizes approximation via a sum of products (min-terms) of the input variables. We will refer to this realization of the LP as a Sum of Min-terms (SOM). The network includes three layers. The input layer consists of $2n$ nodes and includes both x_i's as well as their complements $(\bar{x}_i)$. The hidden layer includes p AND nodes. The output layer is built with a single OR node.

- the hidden layer forms p min-terms z_j,

$$z_j = T_{i=1}^{2n} \ (w_{ij} \ s \ x_1'), \quad j = 1, 2, \ldots, p,$$

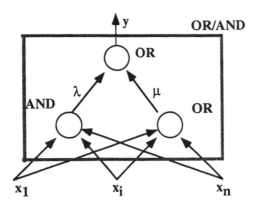

FIGURE 5   Architecture of OR/AND neuron.

where **x′** is an extended vector of the $2n$ inputs, including complemented values of all x_i's,

$$\mathbf{x'} = [x_1 \quad x_2 \quad \ldots x_n \quad \bar{x}_1 \quad \bar{x}_2 \quad \ldots \quad \bar{x}_n].$$

- Output layer. The min-terms are combined by taking the OR operation on z_j's:

$$y = S^p_{j=1} \, (v_j \, t \, z_j).$$

The dual structure of the logical processor computes y by considering a product of min-terms and combining the results of the hidden layer by ANDing them. We will refer to this structure as a product of max-terms (POM). Its formal model is given accordingly:

- Hidden layer:

$$z_j = S^{2n}_{i=1} \, (w_{ij} \, t \, x'_i), \quad j = 1, 2, \ldots ,p,$$

- Output layer:

$$y = T^p_{j=1} \, (v_j \, s \, z_j).$$

It is legitimate to study more advanced logic-based neurons sharing some properties of pure AND and OR neurons. We will refer to them as (mixed) OR/AND neurons. As a matter of fact, these computing units are formed by putting both AND and OR neurons in a single structure; see Figure 5.

By modifying the connections (λ and μ), one can achieve a balance between the AND and OR properties induced by the neurons situated at the lower level of the structure. From the input–output point of view, the derived characteristics place the neuron between the pure AND and OR neurons; the limits are achieved by setting λ to 0 and μ to 1 or vice versa.

Learning

The basic learning procedures applied to the network are mainly of a parametric nature and deal with a series of suitable adjustments of the weights (connections) of the network. The supervised learning is carried out on the basis of the learning set of input–output patterns $(\mathbf{x}_k, y_k)$, $k = 1, 2, \ldots, N$, and is driven by a specified performance index Q. Usually Q is given as the sum of squared errors (MSE criterion) measuring distances between y_k's and the values at the output of the network while driven by $\mathbf{x}_k$, say $N(\mathbf{x}_k)$,

$$Q = \sum_{k=1}^{N} (y_k - N(\mathbf{x}_k))^2,$$

where $N(\cdot)$ stands for a general notation of the output of the network obtained for $\mathbf{x}_k$. The adjustments of the connections are made following a standard Newton-like method. The abbreviated form of the scheme follows:

$$(\text{connections})_{\text{new}} = (\text{connections}) - \alpha \frac{\partial Q}{\partial (\text{connections})};$$

α specifies a rate of learning. This rate implies a suitable speed of learning. Too high values of α could result in oscillations in learning; too small values could cause a very slow learning.

The general learning formula can be applied to different networks upon specification of all details (such as triangular norms and the topology of the network).

In the logic processor, the size of the hidden layer p determines its representation capabilities, that is, uniquely specifies a number of the generalized min-terms (max-terms) of the hidden layer that are used to approximate the data (function). The determination of the size p is out of the stream of the parametric learning. Its choice should be guided by the obtained values of the performance index Q. Two basic strategies are worth pursuing in this regard:

(i) **Successive expansions** The values of Q are used to guide a growth of the network. Starting from some small values of p we successively increase the size of the hidden layer. This process is terminated once Q, viewed as a function of p, tends to stabilize.

(ii) **Successive reductions** Starting from a large number of nodes in the hidden layer, it is successively reduced up to a point at which the values of the performance index Q increase significantly.

The logical approximation between the hypercubes can be accomplished either by combining m logic processors or building a logic processor with many outputs. In the first option, the processors are learned separately, whereas the training of the second architecture is worked out for all the outputs at a same time. As far as these two architectures are concerned, the collection of the individual processors is superior with respect to an overall modularity and easiness of further expansions and additional training. The m-output logic processor is more economical in hardware implementation.

In addition to standard gradient-oriented organization methods, one can also consider the use of genetic algorithms (42). The ideas exploited there are of particular interest because of the coding efficiency one can obtain for these networks (all the connections take on values within the same unit interval) and an ability of cope with local minima of the performance index. (This occurs in particular, for the max-min and min-max composition operation applied in the neurons.)

OUTPUT INTERFACE

The processing block of the fuzzy model returns a vector of degrees matching the elements of the fuzzy partition specified for the output variable. These results can undergo various transformations depending on the character of this interpretation. As before, let us consider $\mathcal{B}$ to be the fuzzy partition.

1. **Linguistic interpretation** In this mode, **y** is translated directly into a series of statements

B_j is y_j,

> $j = 1, 2, \ldots, m$. The maximal coordinate of **y** selects the corresponding element of $\mathcal{B}$ as the linguistic characterization. Obviously, the generation of this quite rough characterization does not require any computational effort.

2. **Interpretation via a reconstruction problem** In this interpretation mode, one converts **y** into another fuzzy set that is built on the elements of $\mathcal{B}$ Its construction depends directly on the way in which the input interface has been set up. For the possibility-based computations, one looks at transforming B_j into another fuzzy set $\hat{B}_j$ to which the condition

$y_j = \mathrm{Poss}(\hat{B}_j \mid B_j)$

> is conformed. Treating the above formula as a fuzzy relational equations to be solved with respect to $\hat{B}_j$, we derive (see the subsection and Refs. 2 and 4) the following:

> - The solution set $\{\hat{B}_j \mid y_j = \mathrm{Poss}(\hat{B}_j \mid B_j)\}$ is always nonempty (observe that the elements of $\mathcal{B}$ are normal fuzzy sets).
> - The maximal element of the solution set is computed as

$\check{B}_j(y) = B_j(y) \; \alpha \; y_j.$

> Solving the reconstruction problem for all the elements of $\mathcal{B}$, the final result is taken as the intersection of $\hat{B}_j$'s (this aggregation complies with the basic findings of the theory),

$$\hat{B} = \bigcap_{j=1}^{m} \hat{B}_j.$$

> An illustration of the reconstruction problem for several selected forms of **y** are summarized in Figure 6. Note that the reconstruction results depend heavily on the levels of activation of **y**. For a single label being activated to the highest degree, the result becomes an interval centered around this fuzzy set. The width of this interval depends directly on the granularity of the fuzzy partition, cf. Figures 6a–6b. For $\mathbf{y} = [\epsilon \; 1 \; \epsilon]$, these nonzero activation levels of the remaining labels contribute to the broader interval of the reconstructed fuzzy set.

3. **Numerical representation** provided by the output interface converts **y** into a single numerical representative. Let us consider $b_1, b_2, \ldots, b_m$ as being numerical representatives (prototypes) of the corresponding labels in $\mathcal{B}$. Those could be, for instance, modal or mean values associated with the membership functions. The numerical representative $\hat{y}$ of **y** is then determined as a weighted sum,

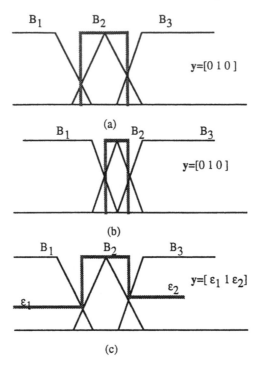

FIGURE 6   Reconstruction problem in the output interface for various levels of granularity of $\mathcal{B}$ and various y's.

$$\hat{y} = \frac{\displaystyle\sum_{i=1}^{m} b_i\, y_i}{\displaystyle\sum_{i=1}^{m} y_i}\, .$$

It should be stressed that this set-to-number transformation is associated with inevitable loses of information. The reconstruction is not ideal in the sense that when one takes a numerical value $\hat{y} \in \mathbf{R}$, transforms it via $\mathcal{B}$, and reconstructs it as shown above, the derived result will not exactly match $\hat{y}$. The difference between these two values can be viewed as a reconstruction error. It has been found in Ref. 31 that the reconstruction error depends on the granularity of $\mathcal{B}$—the higher the granularity, the lower the reconstruction error. In some sense, this finding concurs with the observation made with respect to the previous construct in which higher specificity induced narrow intervals.

The construction of the fuzzy model and its optimization as outlined in the third section is guided by the performance index expressed in terms of the elements of $\mathcal{A}$ and $\mathcal{B}$. The ultimate goal was to approximate within these universes and come up with the best mapping at the level of the linguistic terms. This, of course, does not guarantee that the transformation from the level of the granules in $\mathcal{B}$ into the numerical quantities has been optimized in any way. If the main thrust of the fuzzy model is to follow a collection of numerical data points rather than their representations in $\mathcal{B}$, one should formulate another performance index embracing this modified approximation request. This, in turn, calls for optimization of the logic processor driven by the distance function defined in the output space. One can also augment the expression for $\hat{y}$ by adding some parameters to be adjusted or admitting a polynomial form of b_i's. Then the learning procedure should involve both the parameters of the network and the output interface.

CONTROL IN FUZZY MODELS

We will consider control problems in fuzzy dynamical systems. We will be concerned especially with a first-order dynamical model described as

$$\mathbf{x}(k+1) = \mathrm{FM}(\mathbf{u}(k),\ \mathbf{x}(k),\ \mathcal{W}),$$

where $\mathcal{W}$ is used to summarize all the connections of the logic processor, and $\mathbf{u}(k)$, $\mathbf{x}(k)$, and $\mathbf{x}(k+1)$ denote the degrees of activation of the linguistic labels in $\mathcal{U}$ and $\mathcal{X}$ in successive time instances.

In general, one can consider control activity as aiming at a maximal satisfaction of goals and constraints specified in the system. These objectives are defined as elements in the corresponding fuzzy partitions. Let the goal defined in $\mathcal{B}$ be equal to $\mathbf{g}$ and the constraint given in $\mathcal{A}$ be expressed as $\mathbf{c}$. For the dynamical fuzzy model the control task reads as the following vector optimization problem:

$$\mathrm{Max}_{\mathbf{u}(k)}\ \mathcal{F}_1(\mathbf{g},\ \mathbf{x}(k+1)),$$
$$\mathrm{Max}_{\mathbf{u}(k)}\ \mathcal{F}_2(\mathbf{c},\ \mathbf{u}(k)),$$

where $\mathcal{F}_1$ and $\mathcal{F}_2$ are predicates describing relationships to be satisfied by the objectives. For instance, one can treat these predicates as basic matching operations realizing a pointwise comparison (matching) of the corresponding elements of $\mathcal{X}$ and $\mathcal{U}$. By this pointwise matching type of operation we mean a class of transformations such that $\mathcal{F}(\mathbf{a},\mathbf{b}) = 1$ if $\mathbf{a} = \mathbf{b}$, where $\mathbf{a}$ and $\mathbf{b}$ are elements of the same unit hypercube. Generally, the objectives $\mathbf{g}$ and $\mathbf{c}$ could be functions of time and depend explicitly on the current state variable.

The optimization problem will be handled utilizing an architecture visualized in Figure 7.

Based on the character of determination of the fuzzy control, two modes of operation will be distinguished:

On-line computations of fuzzy control Within this version of computations, we generate control $\mathbf{u}$ which maximizes the above performance index for a given state $\mathbf{x}(k)$ provided. The fuzzy model (FM) serves as a standard predictor determining outcomes [namely $\mathbf{x}(k+1)$] produced by $\mathbf{u}(k)$. The functional blocks $\mathcal{F}_1$ and $\mathcal{F}_2$ return degrees of satisfaction of the objectives. We are looking for the global satisfaction of these objectives achieved at all the elements of $\mathcal{X} \times \mathcal{U}$. The array shown in Figure 7 summarizes the individual levels of satisfaction of the objectives. The value t_j specifies a degree to which the ith and the jth coordinate of the constraint and the goal are satisfied. The degree is computed by AND-ing the values of the pointwise matching produced by $\mathcal{F}_1$ and $\mathcal{F}_2$. This aggregation complies with a common practice of decision making in a fuzzy en-

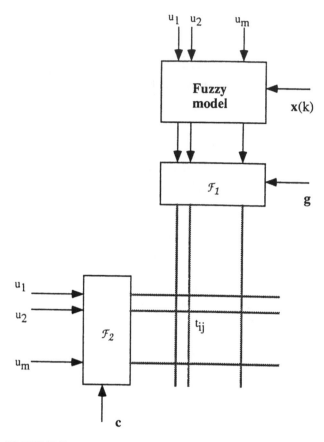

FIGURE 7   Architecture of the optimization of fuzzy control.

vironment, cf. (43). The vector optimization problem is then replaced by its scalar version taking on the form

$$\text{Max}_{\mathbf{u}(k)} \ T,$$

where

$$T = \sum_{i,j}^{n,m} t_{ij},$$

The control $\mathbf{u}(k)$ is valid only for the given $\mathbf{x}(k)$. Any new $\mathbf{x}(k)$'s require a complete repetition of all the computations.

Off-line computations of fuzzy control   The calculations of the fuzzy control can be completed off-line and their results encapsulated into a new structure. We will refer to it as a fuzzy controller. The synthesis of the controller will rely on a collection of training points (control situations) encountered in this structure. The idea behind this is to come up with some optimized scenarios including $\mathbf{x}(k)$ and the corresponding $\mathbf{u}(k)$; we will also collect the values of T, say $T(l)$, associated with each pair of the training set. At the second step, one downloads these data

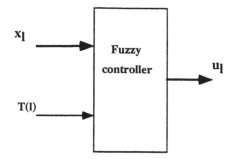

FIGURE 8   Block diagram of a fuzzy controller.

onto the structure of the fuzzy controller. The architecture of the fuzzy controller (FC) itself is formed with the aid of an *m*-output logic processor; see Figure 8.

Within its training, the controller maps the elements of the training set through a series of modifications of the connections of its logic neurons. The performance index which guides these adjustments is taken as a weighted sum of distances between **u**'s and the control actions produced by the FC,

$$\sum_{\mathbf{x}_1 \in \Xi} T(l)(u_1 - \mathrm{FC}(\mathbf{x}_1, \textbf{connections}))^2.$$

The weighting factor $T(l)$ discriminates between various elements of the training set such that the weak candidates [namely, those with low values of $T(l)$] will not be allowed to have a significant impact on the resulting fuzzy controller.

The selection of the training set Ξ deserves some attention. First, the samples should cover a broad variety of control situations [namely, $\mathbf{x}(k)$ should be distributed evenly across $\mathscr{X}$. Second, one should strive to include many successful cases, that is, those with high values of $T(l)$'s. Bearing this in mind, the following guidance criteria should be envisioned:

1. Inclusion of Boolean data. The generation of the optimal control set is carried out via direct enumeration: Apply $\mathbf{x}_1$ and search through all Boolean-type $\mathbf{u}_s$'s, selecting the one that yields the highest value of T. The data set derived in this manner is quite exhaustive and distributed evenly across the state space. It might not cover most of the optimal options though.
2. The further extension of the data set relies on generation of states $\mathbf{x}_1$ and optimizing $\mathbf{u}_1$ using some standard optimization techniques or Genetic Algorithms.

CONCLUSIONS

We have investigated fuzzy sets as a formalism capable of representing and processing uncertainty visible in many systems, particularly those where a factor of human interaction with the environment plays a central role. The methodology of fuzzy sets in developing fuzzy models has been discussed in depth. A particular emphasis put on distinguishing between the linguistic (conceptual) and numerical (real-world) levels makes it possible to comprehend the role of fuzzy sets in developing fuzzy models. The models discussed in this article have been arranged according to their levels of structural dependencies. By considering an amount of initial knowledge available about the system to be modeled, one can select the most suitable class of models. Subsequently, the straightforward adjustment of the cognitive perspective (that is easily accomplished by changing a number as well as a form of the corresponding fuzzy sets allows the fuzzy models to be customized to meet the requirements of the individual user. The flexibility of these customized models achieved in this way is significant. Fuzzy sets realize sub-symbolic computations; thus, the linguistic terms can be either treated as pure symbols or could include membership functions reflecting the semantics residing within the terms. This feature is of a special value in constructing links between the architectures of Artificial Intelligence (such as knowledge-based systems) and those purely numerical structures like neural networks.

ACKNOWLEDGMENT

Support from the National Sciences and Engineering Research Council of Canada and MICRONET is fully acknowledged.

REFERENCES

1. L. A. Zadeh, "Fuzzy Sets and Systems," *Proc. Symp. Syst. Theory*, Polytechnic Institute, Brooklyn, NY, 1965, pp. 29–37.
2. A. Di Nola, S. Sessa, W. Pedrycz, and E. Sanchez, *Fuzzy Relational Equations and Their Applications in Knowledge Engineering*, Kluwer/Academic Press, Dordrecht, 1989.
3. B. Heshmaty and A. Kandel, "Fuzzy Linear Repression and Its Application to Forecasting in Uncertain Environment," *15*, 159–191 (1985).
4. W. Pedrycz, "On Generalized Fuzzy Relational Equations and Their Applications," *J. Math. Anal. Appl.*, *107*, 520–536 (1985).
5. W. Pedrycz, *Fuzzy Control and Fuzzy Systems*, Research Studies Press/J. Wiley, Taunton/New York, 1989 (2nd extended edition, 1993).
6. W. Pedrycz, "Fuzzy Systems: Analysis and Synthesis. From Theory to Applications," *Int. J. Gen. Syst.*, *17*, 139–156 (1990).
7. W. Pedrycz, "Processing in Relational Structures: Fuzzy Relational Equations," *Fuzzy Sets Syst.*, *40*, 77–106 (1990).
8. W. Pedrycz, "Fuzzy Modelling: Fundamentals, Construction and Evaluation," *Fuzzy Sets Syst.*, *41*, 1–15 (1991).
9. D. A. Savic and W. Pedrycz, "Evaluation of Fuzzy Linear Regression Models," *Fuzzy Sets Syst.*, *39*, 51–63 (1991).
10. T. Takagi and M. Sugeno, "Fuzzy Identification of Systems and the Applications to Modelling and Control," *IEEE Trans. Syst. Man and Cybern.*, *SMC-15*, 116–132 (1985).
11. H. Tanaka, S. Uejima, and K. Asai, "Linear Repression Analysis with Fuzzy Model," *IEEE Trans. Syst. Man Cybern.*, 903–907 (1982).
12. H. Tanaka, "Fuzzy Data Analysis by Possibilistic Linear Models," *Fuzzy Sets Syst.*, *24*, 363–375 (1987).
13. J. De Kleer and J. S. Brown, "A Qualitative Physics Based on Confluence," *Artificial Intelligence*, *24*, 7–83 (1984).

14. B. D'Ambrosio, *Qualitative Process Theory Using Linguistic Variables*, Springer-Verlag, New York, 1989.

15. L. A. Zadeh, "Outline of a New Approach to Analysis of Complex Systems and Decision Processes," *IEEE Trans. Syst. Man Cybern.*, SMC-1, 28–44 (1973).

16. Ch. J. Puccia and R. Levins, *Qualitative Modeling of Complex Systems*, Harvard University Press, Cambridge, MA, 1985.

17. W. Pedrycz, T. Takagi, and K. Hirota, "Fuzzy Associative Memories: Concepts, Architectures and Algorithms," in *Proc. Int. Engineering Symp.*, Yokohama, 13–15 Nov. 1991, Vol. I, pp. 163–174.

18. W. Pedrycz, "Fuzzy Set Framework for Development of a Perception Perspective," *Fuzzy Sets Syst.*, *37*, 123–137 (1990).

19. L. A. Zadeh, "PRUF—A Meaning Representation Language for Natural Language," *Int. J. Man–Machine Studies*, *10*, 395–346 (1978).

20. L. A. Zadeh, "Fuzzy Sets and Information Granularity," in *Advances in Fuzzy Set Theory and Applications*, M. M. Gupta, R. K. Ragade, and R. R. Yager (eds.), North-Holland, Amsterdam, 1979, pp. 3–18.

21. W. Pedrycz, "Selected Issues of Frame of Knowledge Representation Realized by Means of Linguistic Labels, *Int. J. Intelligent Syst.*, *7*, 155–170 (1992).

22. I. B. Turksen, "Measurement of Membership and Their Acquisition," *Fuzzy Sets Syst.*, *40*, 5–38 (1991).

23. J. C. Bezdek, *Pattern Recognition with Fuzzy Objective Function Algorithms*, Plenum Press, New York, 1981.

24. R. R. Yager, "On Measuring Specificity," Technical Report, Iona College, New Rochelle, NY, 1990.

25. R. R. Yager, "On a Hierarchical Structure for Fuzzy Modeling and Control," Technical Report MII-1213-E, Iona College, New Rochelle, NY, 1992.

26. A. Ramer and R. R. Yager, "Analysis of Specificity of Fuzzy Sets," in *Proc. IEEE Int. Conf. on Fuzzy Systems*, San Diego, 8–12 March, 1992.

27. W. Pedrycz, N. Yubazaki, M. Otani, and K. Hirota, "Robustness and Sensitivity in Fuzzy Computational Structures," *Proc. IFSA '91*, Brussels, vol.: Computer, Management and Systems Science, pp. 197–200.

28. W. Pedrycz, "Direct and Inverse Problem in Comparison Fuzzy Data," *Fuzzy Sets Syst.*, *34*, 223–236 (1990).

29. D. Dubois and H. Prade, *Possibility Theory—An Approach to Computerized Processing of Uncertainty*, Plenum Press, New York, 1988.

30. L. A. Zadeh, "Fuzzy Sets as a Basis for a Theory of Possibility," *Fuzzy Sets Syst.*, *1*, 3–28 (1978).

31. W. Pedrycz, "Hierarchical Fuzzy Modelling for Heterogeneous Information Processing," in *Neural Networks and Soft Computing*, R. R. Yager and L. A. Zadeh (eds.), to appear.

32. E. Sanchez, "Resolution of Composite Fuzzy Relation Equations," *Inform. Control*, *34*, 38–48 (1976).

33. S. Rudeanu, *Boolean Functions and Equations*, North-Holland, Amsterdam, 1974.

34. R. S. Ledley, *Digital Computer and Control Engineering*, McGraw-Hill, New York, 1965.

35. W. Pedrycz, "Relational Structures in Fuzzy Sets and Neurocomputations," *Proc. Int. Conf on Fuzzy Logic and Neural Networks*, Iizuka, 20–24, 1990, pp. 235–238.

36. K. Menger, "Statistical Metric Spaces," *Proc. Nat. Acad. Sci.*, USA, *28*, 535–537 (1942).

37. K. Hirota and W. Pedrycz, "Fuzzy Logic Neural Networks: Design and Computations," *Int. Joint Conf. on Neural Networks*, Singapore, 18–21 November 1991, pp. 152–157.

38. W. Pedrycz, "Neurocomputations in Relational Systems," *IEEE Trans. Pattern Anal. Mach. Intelligence*, PAMI-13, 289–296 (1991).

39. W. Pedrycz, "Referential Scheme of Fuzzy Decision-Making and Its Neural Network Structure," *IEEE Trans. Syst. Man Cybern.*, 1593–1604 (1991).

40.   W. Pedrycz, "Fuzzy Neural Networks with Reference Neurons as Pattern Classifiers, *IEEE Trans. Neural Networks*, 770–775 (1992).
41.   A. F. Rocha, *Neural Nets: A Theory for Brain and Machine*, Lecture Notes in Artificial Intelligence Vol. 638, Springer-Verlag, Heidelberg, 1992.
42.   L. Davis (ed.), *Handbook of Genetic Algorithms*, Van Nostrand Reinhold, New York, 1991.
43.   R. E. Bellman and L. A. Zadeh, "Decision Making in a Fuzzy Environment," *Manag. Sci.*, *17*, 8141–8164 (1970).
44.   L. A. Zadeh, "Toward a Theory of Fuzzy Systems," in *Aspects of Network and System Theory* R. E. Kalman and N. De Claris (eds.), 1971, pp. 469–490.

WITOLD PEDRYCZ

GATEWAY PERFORMANCE ANALYSIS

INTRODUCTION

The interfaces between local-, metropolitan-, and wide-area networks are referred to as gateways. They perform necessary protocol conversions, implement flow-control algorithms, and route packets over the long-haul network. Additionally, gateways act as a buffer between networks with different transmission rates. Due to recent technological advances, the paradigm of slow long-distance communications has changed. The task of a gateway is more difficult when communication has to be maintained between networks with different transmission capabilities, for example, Ethernet-type networks exchanging data with high-speed networks such as FDDI or DQDB. On the other hand, the imbalance of fast local transmission rates and slow long-distance transmission rates may be reversed, for example, a metropolitan-area network backbone with a capacity greatly exceeding the transmission rates of the local area networks connected to the backbone. In the near future, it is expected that several communications systems from different generations will coexist. Internetwork design must consider the implications of network components with varying transmission speeds; failure to do so would result in the system suffering a decrease in throughput due to link congestion and packet loss caused by overflow of gateway buffers.

Few performance studies of gateways in interconnected networks have been done so far. Exley and Merakos (1,2) studied two interconnected broadcast networks by simulation and obtained stability conditions for the network load. They compute values for packet delays under different network access strategies. Lazar and Robertazzi (3) investigate flow-control issues using a queueing model of two interconnected networks. Ben-Michael and Rom (4) studied two Aloha networks connected via a gateway. By assuming unbounded buffer capacities of gateways, they derive analytical formulas for throughput and queueing delay. Varakulsiripunth et al. (5) analyze a special flow-control policy which constrains the amount of traffic accepted. They consider the finite buffer space of the gateways and obtain blocking probabilities. Heath (6) simulates high-speed local-area networks and demonstrates the importance of performance decrease due to finite buffer capacity stations. Cheng and Robertazzi (7) gave an overview of recent studies on performance analysis of interconnected networks.

In this article, we present analytical solutions to demonstrate the effects of finite buffers of gateways and network access units on the performance of the network. The article is organized as follows: In the next section, we describe the system model. In the third section, we develop a queueing model. Numerical examples are given in the fourth section. We demonstrate how the performance of the network is affected if certain parameters are varied. Conclusions are given in the last section.

SYSTEM DESCRIPTION

We consider networks with several local area, metropolitan-area, and wide-area networks connected by a long-haul network. The subnetworks are connected to a wide-area network by gateways as shown in Figure 1.

In the network, there is communication either between hosts of each subnetwork or between hosts of different subnetworks. Hosts in the same subnetwork communicate with each other using a shared broadcast channel. The channel is accessed by hosts via an interface called a network access unit. Based on communication protocols considered in this study, only one packet is allowed to be sent on the channel at a time. If a host wants to transmit a packet to another host in the same subnetwork, it forwards the packet to its network access unit. The access protocol of the subnetwork decides which packet will be transmitted on the channel next. All packets in network access units of the hosts can be regarded as waiting in a global queue for accessing the channel. Although physically still residing at the hosts, these packets belong logically to the broadcast channel. Once a packet obtains access to the channel, it is immediately transmitted to the destination host if source and destination hosts belong to the same subnetwork. If they do not belong to the same subnetwork, the packet is put into the network access unit and the channel sends the packet to the gateway of the source subnetwork. The gateway then transmits the packet to the gateway of the destination subnetwork which forwards the packet to the appropriate host through its broadcast channel. The packet, in obtaining access to the broadcast channel, may compete with local traffic packets.

If a gateway has a buffer capacity for storing only a limited number of packets for transmission on the wide-area network, it is possible that the storage capacity will be exhausted. In this case, no more packets are allowed to be forwarded to the gateway because of the buffer overflow problem. All hosts wanting to transmit internetwork packets using this gateway must wait until space becomes available in the buffer of the gateway. This type of situation occurs if the transmission rate of the subnetworks is much higher than the transmission rate of the internetwork. High-speed local networks are a representative example where the high speed of the subnetwork may cause buffer overflows at the gateways. A low transmission rate for internetwork traffic such as in packet-switched satellite networks has the same effect.

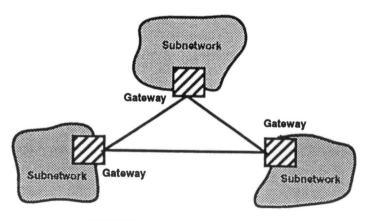

FIGURE 1   Interconnected network.

MODELING

The model of the interconnected network consists of M subnetworks. Each subnetwork contains a station for the broadcast channel and a fixed number of host stations. Each subnetwork has a gateway station which is composed of an input queue GW_{in} and an output queue GW_{out} as shown in Figure 2. All host stations in the subnetwork put their packets to the buffer of the appropriate channel which represents the broadcast channel of subnetwork. From the channel, the packets are routed to either one of the host stations or to the appropriate gateway GW_{out}. A station of type GW_{in} transmits all its output to the appropriate channel. Internetwork connections are established by routing from a station GW_{out} to one or more other stations GW'_{in}.

The complete model of the interconnected network has N total number of stations where N is composed of $N = R + M + 2G$, where R is the total number of hosts in the subnetwork, M is the total number of channels, and G is the total number of gateways. The load of the interconnected network is determined by the fixed number of packets traversing the network at a time and is denoted by K. In our model, packets are routed with fixed probabilities. The service time of all stations is exponentially distributed. The scheduling discipline of all stations is FCFS. All stations may have a finite buffer size denoted by B. The host stations are assumed to have no buffer constraints. Buffer overflows are handled as follows: A packet in any station is not allowed to leave if the destination station is full, that is, the number of packets in the destination station is equal to its buffer capacity. In this case, the packet is blocked in the current station until a packet in the destination station is transmitted and a buffer space becomes available. The complete queueing model of the interconnected network is given in Figure 3.

Here, we assume that the buffer size of the gateways is limited ($B_{GW_{in}}$; $B_{GW_{out}} \leq K$). A gateway does not accept packets if its buffer is full. Hence, packets which are ready for transmission to a full station have to remain in the current station until a space becomes available in the full destination buffer, thus keeping the server of the current station idle. We refer to this phenomenon as a *blocking event*. Because the gateway has one queue for incoming traffic (GW_{in}), as well as for outgoing traffic (GW_{out}), a full buffer in the gateway may cause blocking at one or more remote gateways GW'_{out} or at the local channel.

Because we are primarily interested in studying the performance of interconnected subnetworks due to gateway buffer constraints, we introduce an approach which allows a separate analysis of subnetwork and internetwork traffic. The analysis of the suggested network configurations will be carried out in two steps. First, we analyze the performance of each subnetwork independently using the mean value analysis algorithm (8). Second, we obtain the overall performance of the interconnected network by analyzing

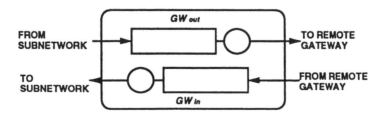

FIGURE 2   Queueing model of a gateway.

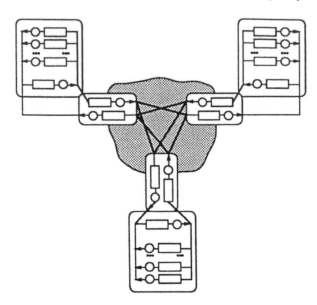

FIGURE 3   Queueing model of the interconnected network.

internetwork communications. In the internetwork analysis, blockings may occur due to
the finite capacity buffers of the gateways. Because blocking causes interdependencies
between the stations, analytical methods such as mean value analysis (8) cannot be applied for internetwork analysis in the second step. In recent years, we have developed
some exact and approximate analytical solutions for this type of queueing models where
blockings may occur (9–12). We analyze the internetwork model by the method given in
Ref. 10. This hierarchical solution approach not only has the advantage of separating the
analysis for different types of traffic, that is, local and internetwork traffic, but also reduces the computational complexity of the analysis and allows us to analyze internetwork
traffic under different workloads without redoing the computations for the entire network.

EXPERIMENTS

In the first experiment, we analyzed a network model given in Figure 4. Here, we considered an interconnection of two homogeneous subnetworks. Each subnetwork has only
three hosts connected to it. The service time of the channel is set to $1/\mu_{CH} = \frac{1}{3}$ msec.
The service time of the channel includes the time spent in the network access unit. Assuming a packet length of 1000 bytes/packet, the service time of the channel corresponds
to a network with a maximum transmission rate of 3 Mbit/sec. The buffer capacity of the
channel stations is assumed to be $B_{CH} = 3$. The ratio of subnetwork traffic and internetwork traffic is set to 3.7 and shows heavy internetwork activity. The service time of
the gateway stations is assumed to be $1/\mu_{GW_{in}} = 1/\mu_{GW_{out}} = 1$ and the service time for
the hosts is assumed to be the same for all three stations, that is, $1/\mu_H = 3$. The transition
probabilities are given in Table 1.

We varied the input parameters such as the total number of packets in the network
and demonstrated the effect of buffer capacity of the stations on the performance of the
network as shown in Figure 5.

TABLE 1   Transition Probabilities

P_{ij}	CH	H	$GW_{j.in}$	GW_{out}
H	1	0	0	0
CH	0	0.1	0	0.7
GW_{in}	1	0	0	0
GW_{out}	0	0	1	0

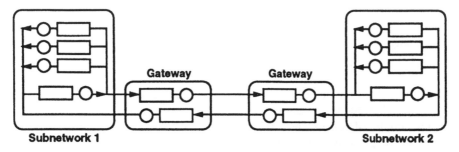

FIGURE 4   Interconnection of subnetworks.

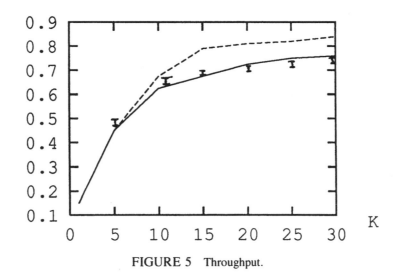

FIGURE 5   Throughput.

Approximate results are compared with the confidence intervals of simulations. Simulations were performed on an IBM 4381 using the RESQ simulation package (13) with confidence intervals set to 95%. The confidence intervals in the figure are denoted by " | ." It can be observed that the throughput decreases in the finite buffer case. This is explained by the increased occurrence of blocking events for networks under heavy load.

In the second experiment, three subnetworks are connected to each other via gateways. The number of hosts in each subnetwork is set to 10. Including the channel and the gateway stations, the entire queueing network has $N = 39$ stations. Our goal for this example is, starting from a set of parameters, to show how the performance of the network changes if certain parameters are changed. We varied the parameters of the stations of one particular subnetwork. The parameters for the network are given in Table 2.

TABLE 2   Buffer Sizes and Service Times

B_{CH}	10
$B_{GW_{in}}$, $B_{GW_{out}}$	2
$1/\mu_{CH}$	⅓ ms
$1/\mu_{GW_{in}}$, $1/\mu_{GW_{out}}$	2ms
$1/\mu_H$	3 ms

Transition probabilities are given in Table 3.

Throughput results are given in Figure 6. The dashed line shows throughput values of the corresponding infinite capacity gateway network.

Now assume that subnetwork 1 is improved in such a way that the maximum transmission rate is increased to $\mu_{CH_1} = 40\text{ms}^{-1}$ All other parameters remain unchanged. It can be observed in Figure 7 that the total throughput of the network remains also unchanged.

In the following, we investigate which parameters of subnetwork 1 must be changed to achieve improved performance. In addition to the faster channel, we increase the service rate of the gateway belonging to subnetwork $\mu_{GW_{1,in}} = \mu_{GW_{1,out}} = 2 \text{ ms}^{-1}$. Clearly, the throughput values can be improved as demonstrated in Figure 8.

Another way to improve the performance is to increase the buffer space of the gateway connected to subnetwork. We assume the buffer size of the gateway to be $B_{GW_{1,j}} = 5$ for $j = in, out$. Figure 9 plots the throughput values.

TABLE 3   Transition Probabilities

P_{ij}	CH	H	$GW_{j,in}$	GW_{out}
H	1	0	0	0
CH	0	0.07	0	0.3
GW_{in}	1	0	0	0
GW_{out}	0	0	0.5	0

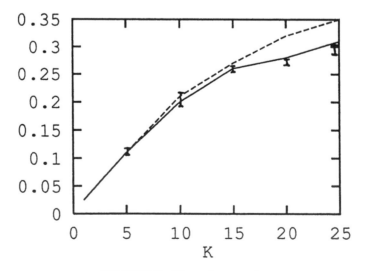

FIGURE 6   Throughput results.

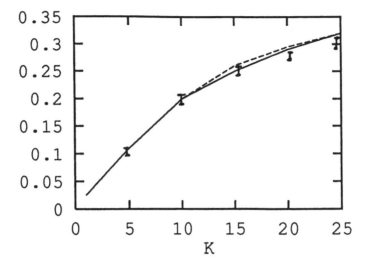

FIGURE 7 Throughput results.

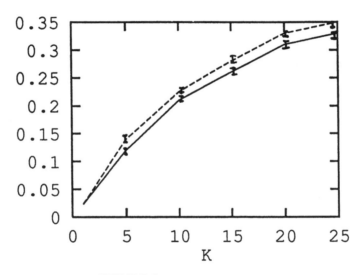

FIGURE 8 Throughput results.

It can be observed that an increase of the gateway buffer size does not improve the performance as the reduced service time of the gateway.

CONCLUSIONS

In this study, we investigated the performance degradation of interconnected computer networks due to finite storage space of the involved stations by developing queueing network model. Through experiments, we demonstrated the performance differences of the various network configurations. Due to the topology of interconnected subnetworks, the performance of internetwork traffic was shown to be sensitive to variations of the pa-

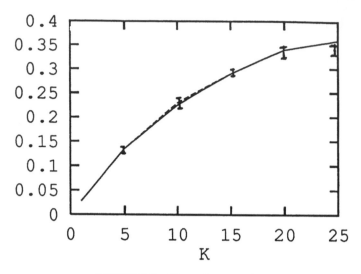

FIGURE 9   Throughput results.

rameters of gateway stations. An improvement of the transmission rate in a subnetwork was ineffective for internetwork communication unless the parameters of the gateway stations were improved at the same time.

REFERENCES

1. Exley,G., and L. Merakos, "Packet Delay Characteristics in Interconnected Random Access Networks," *Proc. GLOBECOM '86*, Houston, 1986, pp. 455–459.
2. Exley, G., and L. Merakos, "Throughput-Delay Performance of Interconnected CSMA Local Area Networks," *IEEE J. Selected Areas Commun.*, SAC-5, (9), 1380–1390 (1987).
3. Lazar, A. A., and T. G. Robertazzi, "Optimal Flow Control of Networks Interconnected via Gateways," *Proc. 19th Annual Conf. Information Science Systems*, Baltimore, March 1985, pp. 263–268.
4. Ben-Michael, S., and R. Rom, "Gatewaying Two Aloha Networks," *Proc. INFOCOM '86*, Miami, 1986, pp. 30–33.
5. Varakulsiripunth, R., N. Shiratori, and S. Noguchi, "Congestion Control Policy on Internetwork Gateway," *Proc. ICCC '86*, P. Kuhn (ed.), North-Holland, Amsterdam, 1986, pp. 659–664.
6. Heath, J. R., "Analysis of Gateway Congestion in Interconnected High-Speed Local Networks," *IEEE Trans. Commun.*, 36 (8), 986–989 (1988).
7. Cheng, Y.-C, and T. G. Robertazzi, "Annotated Bibliography of Local Communication System Interconnection," *IEEE J. Selected Areas Commun.*, SAC-5 (9), 1492–1499 (1987).
8. Reiser, M., and S. S. Lavenberg, "Mean Value Analysis of Closed Multichain Queueing Networks," *J. ACM*, 27 (2), 313–322 (1980).
9. Akyildiz, I. F., "Mean Value Analysis for Blocking Queueing Networks," *IEEE Trans. Software Eng.*, SE-14 (4), 418–429 (1988).
10. Akyildiz, I. F., "Product Form Approximations for Queueing Networks with Multiple Servers and Blocking," *IEEE Trans. Comp.*, C-15(1), 99–114 (1989).
11. Akyildiz, I. F., and J. Liebeherr, "Application of Norton's Theorem on Queueing Networks with Finite Capacities," *Proc. INFOCOM '89*, Ottawa, Canada, April 1989, pp. 914–923.

12. Akyildiz, I. F., and J. Liebeherr, "Gateway Performance Analysis in Interconnected Networks," *Computer Commun. J.*, *14* (1), 15–26 (1991).

13. Sauer, C. H., E. A. MacNair, and J. F. Kurose, *The Research Queueing Package Version 2*, IBM Thomas J. Watson Research Center, Yorktown Heights, NY, 10598.

14. Baskett, F., K. M. Chandy, R. R. Muntz, and G. Palacios, "Open, Closed and Mixed Network of Queues with Different Classes of Customers," *J. ACM*, *22*, (2), 248–260 (1975).

15. Chandy, K. M., U. Herzog, and L. Woo, "Parametric Analysis of Queueing Network Models," *IBM J. Res. Devel.*, *19* (1), 43–49 (1975).

IAN F. AKYILDIZ

HISTORY AND COMPUTING

Computers began to take an important place in historian's work in the 1960s. At that time, computers were best at "number crunching"; hence, it was natural that historians used them for tasks which involved relatively complex and repetitive calculations, often following developments in other social sciences, notably econometrics and demography. Early use involved a number of topics in economic history. These included the nature and timing of economic growth and a detailed examination of the contribution of various forms of technological progress to output and productivity. From the start, the impact of computing on historians took on a dual role. At one level, this impact gave rise to an increasingly technical discussion, not only on the nature of software and hardware but also on the specification of variables for total factor productivity calculations and for a variety of regression equations. Historians using computers also showed an ability to challenge, often in very disturbing ways, some of the features of the historical assumptions and practices which were central to a number of national and cultural traditions.

An early target was one of the cultural heroes of U.S. expansion and nation-building, the steam locomotive railway. Fogel in a detailed analysis suggested that the contribution was limited (1). His conclusion depend on the formalization of a technique that remains central to much econometric analysis of historical development, the "counterfactual." He did not ask what did the steam locomotive railway contribute to the United States economy, but what did it contribute that would not otherwise have been provided. The answer in the 1890s was very little, perhaps 5% of gross national product because of the potential of the canal and navigable waterway system. The British did much better. Railways in 1865 were found to have boosted national income by around 10%. The potential of water transport was much less and the contribution made to the carrying of coal much more significant (2). The impact of computer-based history was not always identified with one book and in some areas took several years to emerge. Over the 1960s and 1970s, the British industrial revolution was gradually smoothed away by a variety of studies of growth, demography, and socio-economic structure (3,4). The notion of a short "revolutionary" period of change and innovation which initiated economic development, W. W. Rostow's "take-off," was replaced by an account of a long process of cumulative change. Despite its demanding technical base, the historian's use of the computer could become intensely political. The debate raised by Fogel's study of slavery was not so much caused by the detail or direction of the results but by the discussion of an issue which was central to United States political and civic morality in terms of quantifiable measures of demography, welfare, and productivity (5).

By the 1970s, historians were beginning to use a number of the developing high-level languages and a variety of analytical packages, notably SPSS (Statistical Package for the Social Sciences). Historians were able to create larger data sets and to handle information as strings of characters without having to reduce the information to numerical codes. This was the start of the era of nominal list processing. Historians rapidly identified a series of documents which provided information on individuals in a semi-standardized form. Census records, voting lists, and property tax registers were central to this work. Populations could be reconstructed and their characteristics analyzed on a scale that had previously been impossible within the time budget of most historians. The studies which emerged from this period, and many took over a decade to come to fruition, again had a tendency to go for questions which were central to the assumptions which western society has about itself. In the United States, list processing had an early concern with issues of social mobility. When these were compared with studies made of European cities, the land of opportunity had only a small edge which seemed to be identified with the greater upward mobility of unskilled labor (6). A large database constructed from census and other records for the city of Philadelphia produced results which questioned the ability of American society to act as a "melting pot." Housing and job markets provided major structural barriers to the assimilation of blacks, of the Irish, and of other immigrant groups (7). Western society has long cherished a notion of the extended family which was destroyed by the impact of industrialization. This myth melted away under the harsh gaze of list processing and family and household analysis. The nuclear family had a long history, notably in Britain, whereas Europe showed a considerable variety of complex household structures (8). The techniques of family and household reconstitution revealed new sets of relationships between economic change and family structure. Proto industrialization theory linked changes in age of marriage and increased birth rates with the availability of proletarianized wage labor. Political historians began to study the voting registers of 18th and 19th century England and explore the meaning of "party." The easy association of key developments in British politics with the growth of social class identity was brought into question as the voting habits and political gains associated with events like the passing of the Reform Act of 1832 or the growth of urban representative government were seen to be related as much to religious identity and to client relationships with landlords as to social class or status, whereas the computer-based study of the 18th century English electorate replaced the notion of a small, servile, and corrupt electorate with a picture of lively dialogue between a powerful elite and an electorate capable of independent challenge if their expectations were not met. "Party," rather than religion or social class, was the means of mediating this negotiation (9,10). By the 1980s, it was not just the self-image of British and U.S. society which was under pressure from list processing. Australia has long cherished a love–hate relationship with myths based on the early use of the Australian colonies as convict settlements. Analysis of shipping lists has shown that these "convicts" were drawn from a wide range of British society. Indeed, the occupation characteristics of the "convicts" were very like those which attract maximum points for those applying for landed immigrant status in modern Australia (11).*

In the past decade, there has been a qualitative and quantitative revolution in the relationship between history and computing. Historians now first encounter the machine when they are doing the "easy" things, namely, word processing and then may be drawn into some database work and a little graphical and statistical presentational work. This has been the direct result of two changes in computing technology. First, the machines

---

*I owe insights into Australian history to Hamish Maxwell Stewart. As an example of the importance of computer usage for many history doctoral students see his *The Bushrangers and the Convict System of Van Diemen's Land, 1803–1846*, Ph.D, Edinburgh, 1990.

have become more user-friendly. They are cheaper and the learning curves are dramatically reduced. We are no longer faced with a choice between powerful but often unwieldy packages like SPSS and the writing of dedicated software in a chosen high-level language. The list processing begun in the 1970s is now much easier with the advent of database technologies. Second, data storage and data access has become both cheaper and faster. Historians typically seek to handle large quantities of data in a relatively free format and in the 1970s were often frustrated by space constraints. Thus, the changes of the late 1980s have brought a wide range of new opportunities. There are four aspects of this that need emphasis:

1. The machine enables historians to handle much larger quantities of information than ever before.
2. The machine demands much greater rigor and consistency in handling data if the results are to be meaningful; hence, social science methodology is more important than ever to historians.
3. The machine has recently made available a range of attractive presentational facilities both passive and interactive which have important implications for teaching and research. Indeed the impact on teaching is only just beginning to be fully investigated.
4. The machine presents opportunities for the creation, exchange, and use of information which is only just beginning to be explored by historians.

ORGANIZATION AND MEETINGS

In the United States, the intellectual activity of computer-using historians tended to be organized around groups like the Social Science History Association and the journal *Historical Methods*. Europe developed a more specific organization. The Association for History and Computing was formed in March 1986 after a meeting organized in Westfield College, London by Peter Denley and Deian Hopkin. This meeting and a subsequent meeting in 1987 had the excitement and turmoil of a bazaar. Their success was due not only to the numbers who came and the variety of applications which presenters found for computing in history but also for the manner in which the machine drew together individuals from the full range of those who were "doing history." The educational world was represented from primary school to university; papers ranged from Greek cities in the 1st century to 20th century politics (12,13). The Association grew rapidly from its initial European base. A close alliance was formed with Quantum and the Centre for Historical Research at Cologne University where the third conference of the Association was held in 1988. The leading papers showed the increased interest in teaching history with computers, database work, and the use of images and graphics (14,15). Quantum and the Centre at Cologne had a long-standing interest in social science history and, hence, were a natural focus for the scholarly discussion of historians use of computers, especially in the German-speaking world. The conferences of 1989 and 1990 were held under French direction at Bordeaux and Montpellier. Specific publications are emerging from these meetings (16), but attention should also be drawn to *Histoire et Mésure*, which is the leading French-language academic journal in this field. The French branch of the Association for History and Computing also publishes its own newsletter, *Memoire Vive*, edited by Caroline Bourlet and Jean Marc Wolff. Any list of publications will be out of date before this entry is printed but they now include *Cahier VGI* (Vereniging voor Geschiedenis en ilnformatica), published by the Dutch Association, and the *Newsletter/Bulletin of the Canadian Committee on History and Computing*.

DATABASE WORK

From the very beginning of their association with usable computer technology, historians have anticipated making major gains by the ability to manipulate large amounts of information from "Particular Instance Papers." Such documents arose typically from the confrontation of an individual, a property, or a group with an institution, often the state; the census, a tax document, a welfare claim, a court record, even entries in an account book produced semistandardized information which clearly could yield a rigorous scientific increase in understanding society and economy in the past if processed consistently and in quantity. Such information was linked with that from other series of papers and with other listings, themselves often the result of "particular instances" in the past like poll books and membership lists. In Britain, demographic studies, family history, and political history were first to gain from this. The result for historians has been the creation of a number of substantial databases.

The manuscript census of 1851 has been an object of research since the counter sorter which preceded computer use by historians of social and family structure. It was the first census manuscript of a quality which enabled historians to identify households and families with some confidence (17–19). The National Sample from the 1851 Census of Great Britain was created between 1972 and 1988 under the direction of Professor Michael Anderson of Edinburgh University. It is a 2% systematic cluster sample (drawn by selecting every 50th ennumeration book or settlement). It was stratified according to general settlement types (urban, village, rural, institutional, etc.). The sample produced 980 data clusters which included over 400,000 persons. The structure of the initial data input was a complete and uncoded replication of the original document, in accordance with the best practice developed in the 1970s which separated coding from data input. The project has also created a series of public data formats with associated coding directories and software to ease the preparation of the data for modern database management systems. This data set is now deposited with the ESRC data archive in Essex University. Results from this project have already taken their place in the vast literature on family and household structure in Britain (20). Several lessons must be drawn from this project. The creation of high-quality data sets requires considerable resources and a long lead time. Confident utilization of such data sets requires the application of social science methodology and concepts in a careful and rigorous manner.

Given the richness of Scandinavian sources, it is not surprising that some of the most important database projects derive from that area. The Stockholm Historical Database (SHD) is one of the most impressive. This project is a division of the City Archives of Stockholm. The project is based on the Roteman Archives. This was a listing begun in 1878 in an attempt by the government authorities to keep track of a rapidly expanding population and reflected contemporary concern over housing, sanitation, water supply, health, schooling, and crime. The Registers themselves have around nine million entries. However, the unit of organization was the unit of real property in the city, thus tracing the life cycle of any individual entails substantial searching and reorganization of information. Once this linking has been done, information is available on time and place of birth and death, name, title or profession, civil status, sex, family and household relationships, church registration, migration, education, military service, poor relief, medical care, and prison service as well as details of property and address, but, more important, a full record will give short- and long-term changes in these variables (21). Given the attention paid to life-cycle change in modern social science history analysis, the importance of such a source is clear. This potential has been explored in a recent publication. The article on prostitution is one example of the contribution which this source is making to important historical debates. The SHD now contains some 1.5 million entries from the Roteman, principally from the Old Town area. These are being linked to 80,000 entries from the criminal records and to some 14,000 records from the 1901 census. Because of the long-term nature of this project, care has been taken to ensure that the data archive is independent of specific hardware and software.

Despite its potential, the creators of this database have felt that its potential is not utilized as much as it should be. Several steps have been taken to remedy this. One officer of the project is now dedicated to information and research contacts. The SHD now produces its own newsletter, *Backspace*, which gives background information on specific areas of the data.* In a new series, called "Fiche and Chips," the SHD provides specially tailored data sets which are suitable for teaching and as an introduction for those who are not familiar with the source.† Although much of this material is produced in English, language does remain a barrier to widespread research use. Here the production of files which translate both variable and value names into English should be mentioned. The presentation of another smaller project by Jan Oldervoll has been greatly enhanced by the ability to switch on-screen information from Norwegian to English and back with great rapidity, thus keeping faith with the original document and easing access to the information (23). The demographic database at Umea University has generated a database for earlier in the century derived from the church registers of seven selected rural parishes in Sweden between 1749 and 1890 (24). This data has already increased understanding of migration patterns in early modern society and modified views on the relationship between rural and urban areas (25).

The linking together of data from a variety of sources has become an important feature of many projects. The BERNHIST project has linked together area data for the canton of Berne with the aim of providing a public access database for public, educational, and research use. Recent results have traced patterns of agricultural modernization in Switzerland and have linked agricultural fortunes and climatic change over the 19th century (26). The methodological issues raised by linking "chains" of records for individuals is discussed in the first of the Research Studies published by the Association for History and Computing (27). Another project, based on the Regensburg archive in Germany, has recently extended its ambitions to include objects and images. The variety of new inputting devices, notably scanners of differing qualities and prices, has brought such projects within the grasp of historians in the past two or three years (28).

Many historians have come to see relational database management systems (RDBMS) as more source orientated and, hence, able to serve a wider range of historians' needs. This is reflected in the work done by Dan Greenstein for the History of the University of Oxford project. A collective biography (prosopography) of the members of a

---

Backspace, (No. 1), 1990, contains an introduction to the Parish of Maria, 1878–1926.

†The files currently available are on emigrants, 1878–1926, and on the families and people of Cepheus (a block in the old town), 1878–1926.

major elite educational institution during the 20th century will illuminate not only the history of the university in its relationships with British society but contribute to many other themes of recent British history. Basic information was collected on all 130,000 members of the university between 1900 and 1970. More substantial information was gathered by record search for 6500 at Oxford between 1900 and 1935 and by a survey questionnaire for those who attended after 1939. Like many massive and multisourced projects, the "tables" of the RDBMS represent not only individual sources but also information required for coding. This coding information, say, for occupations or schools, may itself be source derived or theoretically based. This project displays a feature which has become increasingly common for historians. Various facilities, both hardware and software, are chained together at appropriate parts of a project. One application rarely serves inputting, manipulation, and output as SPSS often did in the 1970s. In the Oxford case, INGRES provided the RDBMS and produced output which was analyzed by SAS in a standard flatfile format. Also worthy of note is the success in using an optical scanner, the Kurzweil Data Entry Machine, during the initial stages of data capture to take the 130,000 members from the printed lists of university matriculants and examinees (29).

The databases mentioned so far have been large and often complex, but the structure of the data has been given by the source itself in a fairly direct manner. Many historical sources contain standardizable information but in a nonstandardized or semistandardized form. Legal documents such as property deeds and wills are characteristic of this. Before the historian can use the computer's ability to manipulate large quantities of information, he or she must impose a structure on the data in a far more active manner than the projects already mentioned. In many medieval sources, the lack of specified date and topographical information only adds to problems. The DEEDS project, led by Michael Gervers, is based at University of Toronto. At its center is the Cartulary of the Order of the Hospital of St. John of Jerusalem in England which contained 967 entries from around 1120 A.D. and, in the process, a vast amount of information on the economy and society of Essex in England where the order held large amounts of property. The county was rich in surviving charters and property documents such as the Feet of Fines. Two features of this project are of general interest. First, a variety of different software environments was chosen for each stage of data manipulation. Data capture used KEDIT, a text-editing package. The structuring of the data was done through ORACLE 5.1B, a powerful relational database management system, used in this case on a PC 386-33. Statistical analysis used SAS, whereas topographical information was processed using PC-GIMMS and a digitized map of Essex. This connectivity among different software environments, and often hardware environments, has become an increasing feature of historians' use of computers in the last few years. Second, the power and flexibility of the relational database form enabled the researchers to organize their information around the concept of three "sentences": person-to-person relationships; property-to-property relationships; and person and property relationships. This and the associated coding schemes (also provided as database tables) enabled the data set to be interrogated through the ORACLE SQL facility to provide the raw material for statistical or topographical analysis. In the course of this processing, the analysis of dated information regarding names enabled the undated information to be dated with increasing accuracy (30).

Computer-aided analysis of text has traditionally been the preserve of literary and linguistic studies. It is likely that text analysis will have increasing importance for historians in the next decade. The increasing quality and reducing cost of scanner-based text inputting together with the historian's interest in more rigorous discourse analysis is likely to be the basis of this trend. Biblical scholars have the longest experience of text analysis in an historical context. Recent work on the New Testament by David Mealand at New College in Edinburgh has located the Acts of the Apostles much more firmly in the context of contemporary Greek literary culture as much as in the Semitic and popular traditions which have attracted most attention in recent decades. His work and that of other scholars has been made possible by the encoding of the majority of Greek literary texts from Homer to A.D. 600 by the Irvine Institute at the University of California. The *Thesaurus Linguae Graecae* is now available on CD-ROM (31). Such projects benefit, of course, from the relatively small universe of texts with which such historians are concerned. Text analysis work on the recent past will of necessity have a much more specific database. Characteristic of this is work by Philippe Dautrey, which enables the various versions of Les Déclarations des Droits by the French Assembly since 1789 to be analyzed in both a research and a teaching context. Text searching enables a wide variety of themes to be followed through from 1798 to 1948 (32).

The handling, analysis, and linking of large amounts of data raised a variety of technical and methodological issues. Many of these were discussed since the midseventies, notably in *Historical Methods*. Many of these concerns have been brought together in the work of Manfred Thaller undertaken since 1978 at the Max Planck Institut für Geschichte in Göttingen. The aim of this ambitious project has been to create and maintain an Historical Workstation, by which they mean a computer environment specifically designed for the needs of historians. The current versions of the software are all written in C but have become increasingly hardware independent. Central to the project is a database management system Kleio. This is not (yet, at least) a user-friendly system, but it does have great flexibility which enables the DBMS to respond to the structure of the historical source in a manner which is often difficult even with the most powerful commercial systems. Recent meetings in Europe have often led to fierce arguments between those who use commercial, "off the shelf" software and those who advocate "bespoke" purpose-written software. No session is complete without accusations that someone is "re-inventing the wheel." Even for those who will not necessarily use Kleio, Thaller's work has enabled historians to identify many specific needs which the commercial providers are unlikely to serve. Calendar dates on a huge variety of systems, different currency and measurement systems, and name-matching problems that will not be solved in the traditional SOUNDEX codes of the airline booking system are some obvious examples. An integrated interface to some form of desktop publishing or word processing system and to statistical software has been a requirement from the 1970s (33). More recent work has included procedures for the easy transfer of data from one system to another, work on images and on text processing and analysis. The DBMS and the philosophy behind it remain the central part of this system.

The list processing which now dominates historical computing has brought with it a series of new methodological issues for historians. Two will be dealt with here. As historians began to deal with the huge quantities of data which the computer enabled them to handle, they faced the problems of codification and standardization common to all social science enquiry. This was especially acute in the case of occupational titles. It is now accepted that the best practice involves entering occupational information and, indeed, all information exactly as it appears in the original document. It was rapidly realized that the historians faced problems additional to those of social science practice. Occupational titles are and were value loaded and the practice of the past concealed meanings. Titles favored full-time paid occupations concentrated on one area of production. This tended to hide women's work and the multiple occupations and income sources common in the past. Other dangers of anachronism emerged from the changing structure of production in the past, especially the imperfect division between production and retailing. Then there were titles which had migrated in meaning such as clerk and surgeon. Two sorts of solutions have emerged. Some have adapted codes devised in the past such as that of Charles Booth. Others have adapted to principles of current coding schemes to past situations. All have found the need for multidimensional codes to cope with the vast amount of information contained in any given title (34–36).

Nominal record linkage has been central to historians' use of computers since the late 1960s (37–39). It has now been applied to a wide range of documents in the study of demographic, family, community, and political history. The basic principles of this work were outlined by Winchester in the early 1970s (40). Nominal entries were selected from a document or group of documents in such a way that they were closely associated in time or space. If those entries were associated with names that were the same or similar, then there was a strong case for claiming that the information in these entries referred to the same individual. In this way, information about the fortunes and experience of groups of individuals in the past could be created which opened up an enormous range of fields of enquiry. The environment of the 1970s dominated by high-level programming languages like FORTRAN and powerful if sometimes cumbersome analytical packages like SPSS was an environment well-suited to the search for rule-based methods of record linkage.

The basic problems were fairly rapidly identified. In any document or universe of documents, these were:

(i)   The existence of multiple common names, or in English terms: Which John Smith in list one should be linked to which John Smith in the other lists?

(ii)   The issue of spelling variations in names: In English terms, is Mr. Jack Smith the same as John Smyth, Esq.?

These problems are still with us. They are at the heart of a discussion which is beginning to merge rule-based approaches with more traditional historical intuition.

The search for an automatic rule-based method of record linkage was most active and most fully documented and discussed in the area of family reconstitution which opened up a wide range of questions in demographic and family history. The complexity and the logic of demographic events helped here. It was relatively easy to justify rules which specified that an individual's birth must precede their death, or a little more cautiously to suggest that the mother of a child must be more than 15 and less than 50 years of age. Ironically, the logic of linking was more fraught with risk in simpler documents like the parliamentary poll books. Clearly, multiple links could not be sorted out by continuities in political behavior as this would bias results in ways that were fundamental to the purpose of the inquiry. Could they be sorted out by address or by occupation? Doing this clearly creates risks of bias in favor of the geographically and economically stable. Given that recent historiography tends to emphasis continuity rather than change, there is danger in doing this. The technology and logic of record linkage equally tend to create research designs which focus on a limited area, thus directing attention to the geographically stable.

The arrival of database software platforms in the mid-1980s has turned attention away from the search for rule-based record linkage toward more intuitive procedures. Database technology made the line-by-line sorting and examination of machine-readable versions of documents much easier than the exacting and technically more demanding process of writing the code for automatic linkage, especially with data sets of a modest size. This coincided with the realization that the logic of linking the knowledge base on which a full linking procedure depended was so complex that fully automatic linkage was out of reach. For those who believe (or fear) that computers can displace the historian's judgment, the experience of nominal record linkage is a salutary lesson. Indeed, it is vital to realize that the rules themselves simply formalize judgments based on traditional historical techniques of source appraisal and the appreciation of the social, economic, administrative, and political processes involved. The application of these rules by the computer simply intensifies the impact of these judgments and, more seriously, often hides the results from further scrutiny. Any rule or set of rules exposes the historian to two types of risks:

(i) That of making a false link between entries referring to two different individuals
(ii) That of failing to make a link between an entry referring to the same individual (41).

There is no way of avoiding these risks, but they must be assessed because as they accumulate, they may bring in bias in the final population of linked individuals which then emerges as part of the "results." The bias may arise from the interaction of the logic of the documents and the historian's judgments, hence the ease with which the impact of such decisions can be hidden. Simple factors may be easily identified. For example, the historian linking a series of parliamentary poll books for one constituency may happily link Josiah Holroyd in 1832 with Josiah Holroyd in 1835 and 1837, if there is only one such entry in each list. This commonsense rule risks interacting with the very human practice of naming eldest son after father and of eldest sons moving into the business and property of father. Thus, there is a risk that persistence rates can be exaggerated. More subtle and more general effects can arise from commonsense linkage rules. By their nature, historians want to make maximum use of the information available. Now, in most groups of documents, there is more information about high-status individuals than about low-status individuals. The names of the high status tended to be more complex. Their property holding patterns and occupational or courtesy titles were more complex and more specific. Thus, in any given universe of documents, high-status individuals are more likely to be linked than others. This feature can be compounded by others. In 19th century cities, persistence rates and status were linked by both socio-economic and historical methodological considerations (42). More important record linkage is always easier for males. They own property, carry votes, and rarely change their name in early adulthood in the manner of the majority of women. Hence, record linkage has a built-in bias toward the study of the male life cycle. This makes documents like the Roteman archives of Stockholm in which women can be traced from house to house and occupation to occupation of especial value (43).

Database technology has made record linkage more widely available but paradoxically has led to a decline in the discussion of the principles and methods involved. Indeed, the growth of prosopography or collective biography has signaled a move away from mass semiautomatic rule-based record linkage.*

---

*But see the account of some of the French-based studies of medieval populations notably Jean Philippe Genet, "The PROSOP System," in *History and Computing*, P. Denley and D. Hopkin (eds.), Manchester, 1987.

DATA ARCHIVES

It should be clear from what has been said that the work of data archives is of increasing importance to historians. These organizations can supply support and management for large data sets. They can also ensure the preservation of the many smaller data sets created in the course of a wide variety of historical projects. This is necessary not only because the original researcher rarely exhausts all the possibilities of a data set, but also because the data set becomes a quasi document in its own right and future researchers need access to it to verify the results of their predecessors. Social Science Data archives have existed since the 1960s and have always given important support to historians. The ICPSR (Inter-University Consortium for Social and Political Research) founded in 1962 and based at Ann Arbor, Michigan is one of the most extensive and already includes data sets created by and for historians. In the past few years, considerable discussion has taken place in Europe concerning the special needs of historians as awareness has grown that the first generation of historical data sets is beginning to languish in file stores from which they might never emerge. The Centre for Historical Social Research at Cologne, the Netherlands Historical Data Archive at Leiden, and the ESRC Social Science Data Archive at Essex University in England have all recently initiated surveys to complement their data preservation activities.

In Southampton, Chris Woolgar has taken the traditional archivist's task of cataloguing an important archive, in this case the papers of the Duke of Wellington, and transformed this into the creation of a powerful machine-readable database which will ensure that the future historians' task of using the archive will be in some senses easier, but above all more thorough (43).

GRAPHICS AND VISUAL DATA

There can be no doubt that an area scarcely explored by historians using computer technology is that of graphical and visual presentation and analysis. Some of the projects in this area are of mouth-watering richness in terms of resources. Although this may be irritating for those who still have to argue that spending on scanners and portables is not extravagant, these massively funded projects do show glimpses of the future, and historians are already finding less expensive routes to similar ends.

The National Museum of Ethnology in Tokyo has combined with IBM Research in Tokyo to produce an image database of objects in the museum's collection. This provides not only for the efficient management of an image database, but also for an exacting retrieval of images through the matching of shapes and colors (44). Another project which owes support to state and industrial backers is the Automation Project of the General Indies Archive supported by IBM Spain and the Spanish Ministry of Culture as part of the fifth centennial of the "discovery" of America. This huge and often fragile archive was founded in 1785 to gather into one place all the documents relating to the Spanish colonization of America. The machine archive which is now being created will contain digital images of all the documents which will be embedded in a text database that will contain full descriptions of the documents. The images themselves can be accessed on high-resolution screens through software which has the capability of resolving problems of legibility due to staining, fading, and the appearance of text from the reverse side of the document. The finished product will not only be easier of access but more portable than the original archive and contribute to solving that contradiction of every archivist's life, the need to both protect and make available documents in care (45).

As centenaries have come and gone, one project with potentially one of the most important outcomes for English history has been the Domesday project directed by John Palmer in Hull. This relatively complete survey of land use and land ownership and occupation made in 1086 is by far the earliest of its kind. The Hull group has constructed a text database, so that subsequent users can impose their own interpretation of the data. This is a source where even the interpretation of simple measures of area can often be bitterly contested. The software being provided will entail not only text analysis but the creation of statistical databases and the input for some spectacular mapping output which will increase the accessibility and usability of this complex source to a wide variety of historians (46). In common with database projects in many universities, the Hull project has been one inspiration to the provision of undergraduate teaching in history which involves substantial experience with computers in an historical context (47).

Not all projects need to be on this scale. Some of the most innovative and well-established projects have taken the focus of a town or small area. Francesca Bocchi and her colleagues have used the computer to reconstruct the property and building relationships of the Italian town of Carpi using a cadastral survey of 1471–1480 which relates to the period just before the important reconstruction of the town in the 1500s. The end result was a complete video-based cadastral map recreated through CAD (Computer-Aided Design) software as well as the usual database files. This was important for data which contained complex, incomplete, and imprecise information on spatial and topographical details. CAD proved especially valuable for constructing thematic maps relating to the social status and profession of owners. The results were further secured on the accurate survey map of 1893 and the air photograph survey of 1983 (48,49).

Developments in technology and methodology mean that considerable functionality and analytical power is now available for historians who are able to make only small investments in both equipment and human capital and yet want to handle the complexity of visual and spatial material. Recent work in Scotland has employed some of these developments to examine the changing spatial relationships of credit granted to craftsmen and small businesses in Perthshire in northeast Scotland. Information from the sequestrations (a bankruptcy process under Scottish law) was organized through the ORACLE relational database. Appropriate output was then transferred to data files for the GIMMS mapping package. Interaction with this powerful package were handled through GEOLINK which provided a user-friendly mask file (50). Equally heartening for those with small budgets is the activities of art historian Michael Greenhalgh. His problem may be stated quite simply: How does one handle the graphical information that art historians must control as part of their trade, typically a slide collection of over 100,000 items which need to be accessed by date, subject, period and many other logical categories? His solution, based on the Amiga A2500AT microcomputer, was costed at $32,334 and included image capture, graphics database, and output devices (51).

TEACHING

It is clear that as costs fall and user-friendliness increases, computers will come to have a central place in history teaching (52). No one is quite sure exactly what this place should be. There are the enthusiasts and detractors of simulations and games. Some of these "games" take the student back to the real historical outcome at each decision point; others have little historical content but claim to be teaching the logic of historical situations. Equally controversial are simulations like that produced by the British publishers Longman's "Palestine 1947" which allows 1875 different combinations of policy but only four outcomes. These include World War III but not the creation of an Arab state (53). CAL (Computer-Assisted Learning) packages also have a place as traditional teaching packages for prompting and testing factual material. The most important advances have been made through source and databased teaching. Every post now brings offers of data sets prepared for teaching. Many are included in a listing made by the CTICH Centre at Glasgow University in Scotland (54). The HiDES project at Southampton University links data to packages which endeavor to mimic tutorial exchange and has recently begun to exploit multimedia applications (55).

WARNINGS AND FUTURES

The quantity and range of work being done by historians using computers has thus increased dramatically over the last 5 years or so. Some projects which have run for over a decade are now beginning to have a major impact on historical understanding. The problems and opportunities of research training and management, teaching, documentation, and method will all change under the impact of information technology. The quantity of information which historians are able to handle has increased. This demands not only greater rigor in the handling of such information but has also increased the variety of ways in which such information can be interrogated. Historical "facts" will be central to computer-driven practice, but all historians know that "facts" can never be free of the values of the context which created them or the scholars who use them. The apparent hardness and authority of computer environments make the traditional historians' tasks of source criticism and context sensitivity more vital than ever. The approach to that information in the machine will demand the imagination and judgment which writing history has always needed, together with the analytical rigor and logic which the conjunction with social science has always demanded of historians.

Despite the wealth of activity taking place, worries must remain. The most dominant arises from the characteristic data structures invited by the computer. The machine is best and most advantageous when handling standardizable information in a series of repetitive tasks. This does not mean, as some fear, that the historian's judgment has been replaced. It does mean that attention is being drawn away from the particularity of an individual time, place, or person. To some extent, the nature of database technology which selects information about defined individuals as well as groups can be used to counter this but the risk remains.

Second, the ability of the computer to handle large amounts of information and to examine more about more has increased the complexity of the results. This is providing major problems of communications for historians. Protoindustrialization was a concept created and then destroyed by computer-using historians as the variety of relationships between demographic and economic structures in the early modern period became evident. There is now simply no one-line answer. Questions about social mobility, political behavior, and the geographical segregation of social classes in 19th century industrial towns have suffered the same fate.

Linked to this is the danger inherent in much computer technology that the insights and power of computer-based history are becoming available to a privileged elite in both social and world terms. The author of this article, using disks and electronic mail, already finds it easier to communicate and share the new methods of "doing history" with colleagues in Australia, Germany, and the United States than with former students teaching in the west of Scotland. A generation ago, the published book was available to all of us.

Thus, the historian's use of computers is not only technically and intellectually demanding but also intensely creative and intensely political. The speed of change is such that any survey article like this one is almost certainly out of date before it is written. It can no longer be claimed, as was done in the 1960s, that all historians of the future will have to be computer literate, but it can be asserted that no historian will be able to work and write without taking account of the impact of the computer users among them.

REFERENCES

1. Fogel, Robert W. *Railroads and American Economic Growth*, John Hopkins Press, Baltimore, 1964.
2. Hawke, G. R., *Railways and Eonomic Growth in England and Wales, 1840–1870*, Oxford University Press, Oxford, 1970.
3. Crafts, N. F. R., *British Economic Growth During the Industrial Revolution Oxford University PressOxford 1985*.
4. Wrigley, E. A., and R. S. Scholfield, *The Population History of England, 1541–1871*, Cambridge University Press, 1981.
5. Fogel, R. W., and Stanley L. Engerman, *Time of the Cross. The Economics of American Negro Slavery*, Wildwood House, Camabridge, London, 1974.
6. Kaeble, Hartmut, "Social Mobility in American and Europe: A Comparison of Nineteenth Century Cities," *Urban History Yearbook*, 1981, pp. 24–31.
7. Hershberg, Theodore, (ed.), *Philadelphia, Work, Space, Family and Group Experience in the 19th Century*, Oxford University Press, New York, 1981.
8. Anderson, Michael, *Approaches to the History of the Western Family, 1500–1914*, Macmillan, London, 1986.
9. O'Gorman, Frank, *Voters, Patrons and Parties*, Clarendon Press, Oxford 1989.
10. Phillips, John, *Electoral Behaviour in Unreformed England 1761–1802*, Princeton University Press, Princeton, 1982.
11. Nicholas, S. (ed.), *Convict Workers: Re-interpreting Australia's Past*, Cambridge University Press, Cambridge, 1988.
12. Denley, Peter, and Deian Hopkin (eds.), *History and Computing*, Manchester, 1987.
13. Denley, Peter, Stefan Fogelvik, and Charles Harvey (eds.), *History and Computing II*, Manchester, 1989.
14. Best, Heinrich, Ekkehard Mochmann, and Manfred Thaller (eds.), *Computers in the Humanities and Social Sciences. Achievements of the 1980s. Prospects for the 1990s*, K. G. Saur, München, 1991.
15. *Historical Social Research/Historische Sozialforschung, 14* (3,4) (1989); *15* (1) (1990).
16. "*L'Ordinateur et le Métier d'Historien*," *IVe Congrès "History and Computing," Talence, 14–16 Septembre 1989, CNRS and Maison des Pays Ibériques, Bordeaux, 1990*.
17. Anderson, Michael, *Family Structure in Nineteenth Century Lancashire*, Cambridge University Press, Cambridge, 1971.
18. Armstrong, Alan, *Stability and Change in an English County Town*, Cambridge University Press, Cambridge, 1974.

19. Higgs, Edward, *Making Sense of the Census. The Manuscript Return for England and Wales, 1801–1901*, Public Record Office, London, 1989.

20. Anderson, Michael, Households, Families and Individuals Some preliminary results from the national sample from the 1851 census of Great Britain, *Continuity and Change, 3*, 421–438 (198).

21. Fogelvik, Stefan, in Studier och handlingar rörande *Stockholms Historia*, VI, Stockholm, 1989.

22. Johansson, Gunilla, in *Stockholms Historia* (1989).

23. Oldervoll, Jan, "CENSSYS—a System for Analyzing Census Type Data, *Historical Social Res., 14*, 17–22 (1989)

24. Stenflo, Gun, and Jan Sundin, "Using a Large Historical Database. An Example from the Demographic Database at Umea," in *History and Computing II*, P. Denley and D. Hopkin (eds.), Manchester, 1987.

25. Langton, John, and Göran Hoppe, "Urbanization, Social Structure and Population Circulation in Pre Industrial Times: Flows of People through Vadstena (Sweden) in the Mid Nineteenth Century," in *Work in Towns, 1850–1850*, Penelope J. Corfield and Derek Keene (eds.), Leicesten University Press, Leicester, 1990.

26. Schüle, Hannes, "Drought Stress and Forest Damages: Building a Historical Model for Drought Stress in Swiss Forestry and Agriculture," in *L'ordinatuer et le Métier d'Historien*, Bordeaux, 1990.

27. Kitts, Arno, David Doulton, and Elizabeth Reis, *The Reconstitution of Viana do Castelo*, Research Studies in History and Computing, number one, Association for History and Computing, London, 1990.

28. Callies, Bettina, and Lothar Kolmer, "A Computerized Medieval City Archive: The Project "Regensburger Bürger—und Häuserbuch," in *History and Computing II*, P. Denley, S. Fogelvik, and C. Harvey (eds.), Manchester, 1989.

29. Greenstein, Daniel I., "A Source Orientated Approach to History and Computing: The Relational Database," *Historical Social Res., 14*, 9–16 (1989).

30. Gervers, Michael, Gillian Long, and Michael McCulloch, "The DEEDS Database of Medieval Charters," *History and Computing, 2*, 1–11 (1990).

31. Mealand, David, "Computers in New Testament Research. An Interim Report," *J. Study New Testament, 33*, 97–115 (1988).

32. Dautrey, Philippe, "Les Déclarations des Droits: Une Approche Quantitative," in *Proceedings of the Fourth Congress of the Association for History and Computing*, Université de Bordeaux III, September 1989.

33. Thaller, Manfred, "The Historical Workstation Project," *Historical Social Res., 16*, 51–61 (1991).

34. Katz M., "Occupational Classification in History," *J. Interdisciplinary History, 3*, 63–68 (1972).

35. Morris, R. J., "Occupational Coding: Principles and Examples," *Historical Social Res. Historische Sozialforschung, 15*, 3–29 (1990).

36. Armstrong, W. A., "The Use of Information about Occupation," in Wrigley, E. A. (ed.), *Nineteenth Century Society*, Cambridge University Press, Cambridge, 1972, pp. 226–310.

37. Katz, M., and J. Tiller, "Record Linkage for Everyman: A Semi Automated Process," *Historical Methods Newsletter, 5*, 144–150 (1972).

38. Wrigley, E. A., and R. S. Scholfield, "Nominal Record Linkage by Computer and the Logic of Family Reconstruction," in *Identifying People in the Past*, E. A. Wrigley (ed.), Edward Arnold, London, 1973.

39. Morris, R. J., "In Search of the Urban Middle Class. Record Linkage and Methodology: Leeds, 1832," *Urban History Yearbook*, 15–20 (1976).

40. Winchester, Ian, "The Linkage of Historical Records by Man and Computer: Techniques and Problems," *J. Interdisciplinary History, 1*, 107–124 (1970).

41. Adman, Peter, Stephen Baskerville, and Katherine Beedham, "Computer Assisted Record Linkage: or How Best to Achieve the Ideal of Optimizing Links without Generating Errors," *History Computing, 4* (1) pp. 2–15 (1992).

42. Katz, Michael B., *The People of Hamilton, Canada West*, Harvard University Press, Cambridge, Mass., 1975.

43. Miller, Roger, "Cross Sectional and Longitudinal Analysis in Historical Geographical Research—Some Methodological Consideration," in *Studier och handlingar rörande. Stockholms Historia*, VI, Stockholm, 1989.

43. Woolgar, C. M., The Wellington Papers Database: An Interim Report, *J. Soc. Archivists, 9*, 1–20 (1988).

44. Hong, Jung-Hook, and Sigehara Sugita, "A Colour Image Database for an Ethnology Museum—A Multi-Window System for Electronic Cataloguing and Browsing of Ethnographic Samples on the PC, in Best et al. (eds.) *Computers in the Humanities and the Social Sciences: Achievements of the 1980s. Prospects for the 1990s*, K. G. Saur, München, 1991.

45. González, P. "Computerisation Project for the 'Archivo Genera de Indias' " in Peter Doorn et al., Data, Computers and the Past, *Cahier VG1*, 5, pp. 52–67 1992.

46. Palmer, John J. N., The Hull Domesday Database Project, *Humanistiske Data*, 2–87, 4–21 (1987).

47. Ayton, Andrew, "Computing for History Undergraduates: A Strategy for Database Integration," *Historical Social Res./Historiche Sozialforschung, 14*, 46–51 (1989).

48. Bocchi, Francesca, and Fernando Lugli, Computer Methods Used to Analyse and Reconstruct the Cadastral Map of the Town of Carpi (1472), in *History and Computing*, P. Denley and D. Hopkin (eds.), Manchester, 1987.

49. Francesca Bocchi, and others, *Il catasto di Carpi del 1472 analizzato con il computer, Storia della Città*, vol. 30. 1985.

50. Craig Young, Computer Assisted Mapping of the Credit Fields of Nineteenth Century Rural Tradesmen in Scotland, *History and Computing*, vol one, 1989, 105–111

51. Greenhalgh, Michael, "Graphical Data in Art History and the Humanities: Their Storage and Display," *History Computing, 1*, 121–134 (1989).

52. Denley, Peter, "The Computer Revolution and 'Redefining the Humanities,' " David S. Maill (ed.), *Humanities and the Computer, New Directions*, Oxford University Press Oxford, 1990.

53. Blow, Frances, " 'A Fertile Error is More Productive Than a Barren Truth': Computer Assisted Learning in History," in *History and Computing*, P. Denley and D. Hopkin (eds.), Manchester 1987.

54. Spaeth, Donald A., *A Guide to Software for Historians*, Computers in Teaching Initiative Centre for History, Glasgow, 1991.

55. Hall, Wendy, and Frank Colson, "Multimedia Teaching with Microcosm-HiDES: Viceroy Mountbatten and the Partition of India," *History Computing, 3.2*, 89–98 (1991).

BIBLIOGRAPHY

Best, Heinrich, Ekkehard Mochmann, and Manfred Thaller (eds.), *Computers in the Humanities and Social Sciences. Achievements of the 1980s. Prospects for the 1990s*, K. G. Saur, München, 1991.

Boonstra, Onno, Leen Breure, and Peter Doorn (eds.), *Historische Informatiekunde*, Verloren Hilversum, 1990.

Denley, Peter and Deian Hopkin (eds.), *History and Computing*, Manchester University Press, Manchester, 1987.

Denley, Peter, Stefan Fogelvik, and Charles Harvey (eds.), *History and Computing II*, Manchester University Press, Manchester, 1989.

Doorn, Peter, Céleste Kluts, and Ellen Leenarts (eds.), *Data Computers and the Past, Cahier VGI*, 5, Verloren, Hilversum, 1992.

Genet, Jean Philippe (ed.), *Standardisation et échange des bases de donées historiques*, C.N.R.S. Paris, 1988.

"L'Ordinateur et le Métier d'Historien," IVe Congrès "History and Computing," Talence, 14–16 Septembre 1989, CNRS and Maison des Pays Ibériques, Bordeaux, 1990.

Journals

United States: *Historical Methods, Social Science Computer Review*, and *Social Science History*
Europe: *Histoire et Mesure, Historical Social Research/Historische Sozialforschung*, and *History and Computing*.

ROBERT J. MORRIS

INTEGRATED NETWORK MANAGEMENT

REQUIREMENTS OF INTEGRATED NETWORK MANAGEMENT

Integrated network management incorporates the worldwide activities to design concepts and systems which facilitate the management of computer networks and distributed systems in a heterogeneous environment. We talk of a heterogeneous environment if the managed resources are different in their make and/or complexity. However, a formal definition of integrated network management does not exist.

The term network and system management comprises the methods and products employed for the planning, configuration, control, fault repair, and administration of computer networks and distributed systems. The aim is to develop a user-friendly economic support for network providers and users when working with the network and its components. Thus, it is the sum of all steps and actions taken to ensure an effective and efficient use of the managed resources.

The concrete **design** of a management solution depends on a number of aspects:

- The purpose of the network, derived from analyzing the applications. This includes the services which are to be provided or guaranteed and their quality. Indicators for the quality of services provided can either be quantitative (e.g., availability, reply time, throughput, utilization, fault rates) or nonquantitative (e.g., flexibility for change, data security, user interfaces).
- The characteristics of the communication, that is, the network traffic from the point of view of time and quantity which can be derived from requirement analysis.
- The physical network structure. This is given by the cabling and its topology. It is evident that a uniform and structured cable layout, as well as a simple topology (e.g., bus, star, tree, ring), eases management compared to a network of various media and of mashed structure.
- The logical structure. This is set by the existing communication architecture and the associated protocol hierarchies. This includes the aspects of subnets and linked networks.
- The distribution of providing services across the resources.
- The structural and operational organization of network users. This influences the distribution of resources for users (CPU capacity, data, programs, equipment) and the question of whether closed user groups or an open population are to be supported.
- The organization of network providers. This aspect determines the delegation of management tasks according to competence, responsibility, and jurisdiction.

The complexity of the management task depends on the complexity of the systems to be managed. This **complexity** is shaped by the following:

- The number and variety of resources to be managed. This includes data terminals (e.g., hosts, workstations, PCs, terminal), transmission devices (e.g., media, modems, multiplexers, concentrators), and switching devices (e.g., switches, branch exchanges, bridges, routers).
- The heterogeneity of systems with regard to their system software, interfaces, and protocols including their profiles and versions.
- The spatial (geographical) distribution of components.
- The number of involved organizations or authorities. Whether a single autonomous network (one provider) or a conglomerate of networks is operated plays a significant role when managing the networks.
- The degree of service integration (value-added services) and subnetwork provision.
- The types of distributed applications being supported.

Figure 1 shows an attempt in structuring the management task by outlining it in different dimensions. It illustrates that depending on the phase in the life cycle, the management functional area or the goals of management, different aspects, information, and functions are relevant for the management task.

Tackling the complex task of network and system management requires the support from modern computers. Until today, numerous different management tasks have led to a large number of stand-alone tools. A special but isolated tool exists for almost every

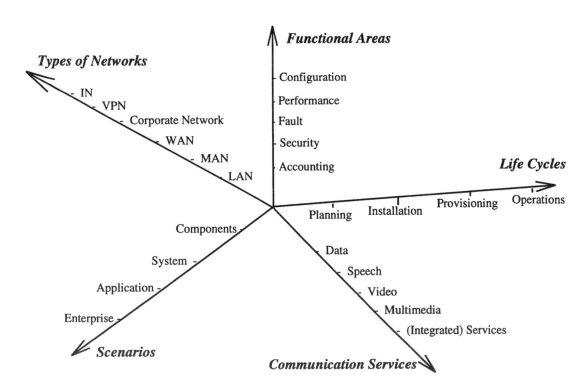

FIGURE 1   Three dimensions of the management task.

point in the three-dimensional management space. A close look at this situation concerning isolated tools helps to identify the following problems:

- The variety of user interfaces is labor-intensive and a source of error.
- The existing tools are predominantly designed for the management of components. A global view of the network is seldomly supported.
- The support for different views on one resource or a hierarchy in access rights for the functions of a tool are scarce.
- The integration of aspects of time is missing.
- The tools show insufficient functionality (lack of relevant data and evaluation thereof, lack of security, insufficient automation).

An isolated management—isolated in terms of manufacturer, functional area, views, aspects of time, and so on—is no longer feasible considering the complex, heterogeneous, highly distributed area of network and system management. The ultimate goal is an integrated network and system management which takes into account and supports the following:

- Integration of architectures, that is, types of systems and networks
- Integration of management functional areas
- Integration of organizational aspects (concept of domains)
- Common concept for a management database
- Extensive standardized concepts for network and system management
- Support of distributed applications and distributed systems
- Common programming interface and user interface

A necessary prerequisite for integrated network management is the ability of the components to be managed in a heterogeneous environment to deliver or provide commonly interpretable information across a well-defined interface. This information must be independent from the manufacturer of the component. In other words, manufacturer-independent integrated network management is only possible on the grounds of accepted standards. A framework of standards relevant for network management is called a management architecture.

SUBMODELS OF A NETWORK MANAGEMENT ARCHITECTURE

Every management architecture for integrated network management in heterogeneous environments must provide a suitable model for the following aspects (see Fig. 2):

- Description objects to be managed (information model)
- Handling of and support for organizational aspects (organizational model)
- Description of common protocols for the exchange of management information (communication model)
- Structuring of management tasks (functional model)

Information Model

The core of a management architecture consists of a database for management information and an information model describing the management information contained therein.

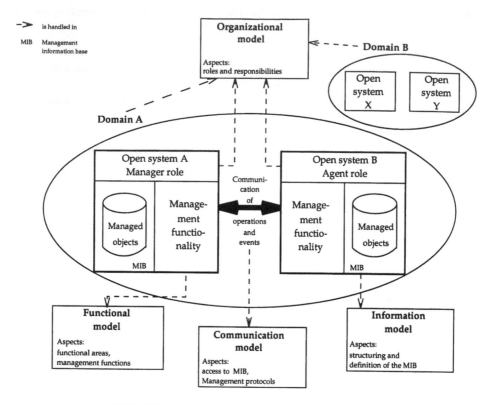

FIGURE 2   Submodels of management architecture.

The term management information combines all data and information which enable and support the operation and use of a communication network. The conceptual repository for management information is called the Management Information Base (MIB).

A managed object (MO) is some management information which, from a managerial point of view, describes resources that are to be administered and controlled. Hence, MOs are abstractions of resources. Examples of MOs are network components (hosts, terminals, modems, links, multiplexers, switches, hubs, etc.), protocol entities, logical links, services, management procedures (guidelines, rules, filters), administrative objects (domains, service personnel, locations, trouble tickets), relationships between objects, and so on.

The information model comprises all concepts for the description of management-relevant objects and information in form of MOs. The meaning of these MOs must be uniform across all systems within a cooperative distributed management environment. This requires a standardized description language for management information on the grounds of one conceptual model, without presupposing a concrete implementation of the MOs. Hence, the information model is only a conceptual scheme defining the following aspects of MOs:

- The type of MO (identification)
- The structure of the MO (i.e., its components) and its characteristics (i.e., its attributes)
- Its behavior
- The operations by which it can be manipulated (actions)
- Asynchronous events emitted by the MO (notifications)
- The relationships to other MOs
- How it can be accessed from the outside by use of management protocols

The definition of an **information model** and its application includes the following:

- The choice of a modeling paradigm (e.g., entity-relationship model, data type approach, or object orientation).
- Determining a unique syntax for describing management information.
- The ability to describe the object's behavior by use of state diagrams, operations, events, and notifications.
- The selection of managed objects, identification of object properties, and relationships between objects. The matter of concern here is which MOs in the MIB of a system are to be supported exactly.
- Mapping MOs to real resources. The access to a MIB object must always be mapped to access of the real hardware or software resource as represented by the object. Furthermore, tools are required to administer the MIB. (This aspect is not really part of the information model, but it must be taken into consideration when designing the necessary mappings.)

Organizational Model

Management systems differ in terms of their flexibility to handle the geographical distribution of its management specific components and their flexibility to allocate management objects to different domains. These characteristics determine and restrict the possible organization of network management and, hence, the adaptability of a network management system to the provision and operation of the network by its provider. The adaptability depends on the flexibility to physically distribute the components of the network management system, that is, the possible degree of distributing functions such as data gathering, data evaluation, and control. This flexibility determines, for example, whether the management is centralized or decentralized, or if a mainstream or sidestream concept is chosen. The consideration of these aspects is part of the organizational model. It defines the players and their roles within the network management architecture.

Possible approaches are a symmetrical concept, which assumes a cooperative management of systems, or a hierarchical concept in which the systems within the network are arranged in levels of management competence. The organizational model could provide for different roles (e.g., manager role, agent role, proxy agent) and even MOs with some autonomy.

The allocation of roles may not always be applied to all resources of a system as a whole but may require a number of domains to allow for different views on resources and to embed management applications in a more general management context. A domain is a logical grouping of resources for organizational purposes. If the organizational model supports the concept of domains, it must address the following issues:

- Setting up of subdomains for a variety of tasks (e.g., accounting, security, etc.)
- Allocating MOs to subdomains
- Changing roles and domains

A single system within a network may take on different roles depending on the way in which (overlapping) domains are set up. Even if the roles are predefined, it may be useful to vary the distribution of tasks of an application within the domain, depending, for example, on the "intelligence" of a component or the load on a manager. If this is to be a part of the management architecture, the preconditions for such a "Management by Delegation" (i.e., description, transport, and implementation of management functionality) must be formalized in the organizational model.

Communication Model

Network management is the control of geographically distributed resources. The exchange of management information is an inherent part thereof. The communication model of a network management architecture defines concepts for the exchange of management information among the participants (i.e., the elements of the architecture). The communication is done depending on its purpose by the following:

- Exchange of control information to act on a resource, that is, on the managed object representing the resource
- Polling information
- Events (asynchronous)

The communication model must cover the following aspects:

- Definition of communicating partners.
- Definition of communication mechanisms for the above three types of communication. This implies a specification of services and protocols for management applications as well as mechanisms to specify profiles.
- Definition of syntax and semantics of data structures used in the communication process (i.e., data-exchange formats).
- Embedding management protocols in the service and protocol architecture of the underlying communication architecture. This includes the access points/interfaces to the usual (nonmanagement) protocol entities, application processes, and local operating systems.

Functional Model

The functional model divides the overall complex task of management into management specific functional areas (e.g., configuration, accounting, fault management, etc.) and tries to specify generic management functions for these areas. The following are essential aspects when defining a functional area:

- The expected functionality to be covered by the area
- The services necessary to provide this functionality
- Management objects of interest for this area
- Possible subsets of provided functions

The use of functional areas allows not only a modular approach in developing management tools but also increases the number of management functions available to network providers. A problem of this approach is, however, the existence of overlapping functionalities between functional areas, which countervails an exact definition of the boundary of a functional area. Examples of overlaps are as follows:

- Sequences of actions. Fault management localizes a fault and requests the configuration management to replace the faulty device by reconfiguring the network

- Mutually used objects. Performance and accounting management both use identical counters in monitoring and accounting applications.

EXAMPLES OF MANUFACTURER-INDEPENDENT MANAGEMENT ARCHITECTURES

OSI Network Management

In addition to its efforts to provide a concept for an open communication of systems in a heterogeneous environment (OSI, Open System Interconnection), the ISO (International Organization for Standardization) has defined a network management architecture. The management framework (1) is an extension to the well-known OSI reference model, the seven-layer communication architecture (2).

OSI Information Model

OSI follows a strict object-oriented approach for modeling resources, that is, managed objects. Objects with common properties are grouped together in object classes. A characteristic of this approach is that an object is an instantiation of an object class which defines the properties of the object. An object class can be defined as a subclass of one or more superclasses. The properties can then be extended or restricted. If one object can be treated as an instantiation of more than one class, we talk of allomorphic behavior. Inheritance and allomorphism are characteristic of an object-oriented approach. The property of inheritance induces a natural hierarchy among classes, that is, an inheritance hierarchy.

The management information of a single system forms the management information base (MIB). The OSI standard for the structure of management information (SMI) does not allow the definition of MOs that span more than one OSI system; in other words, a global view of the network is not supported. A simple template-oriented language based on the ASN.1 macro mechanism is used to describe MOs (3).

OSI–SMI currently defines nine generic template structures: Managed Object Class, Package, Parameter, Attribute, Attribute Group, Behavior, Action, Notification, and Name Binding. The template for a managed object class marks the top of a hierarchy in which other templates are used to further specify the object class. The constituencies of a MO class definition are as follows:

- The attributes visible at the MO boundary, which characterize the properties and status of the management object. The types of attributes used depend on the object to be modeled. Types of attributes include counters, thresholds, gauges, names, timers, and more complex types. For each attribute, the permissible values and operations are specified. This, for example, allows a limitation of value ranges or the implementation of write protections. The Attribute template is used to describe these attributes. The Attribute Group template supports a grouping of attributes which can then be accessed by a single operation. The use of operations can be controlled by filters which are provided by the Common Management Information Services (CMIS).

- A set of notifications. In general, a managed object can be an abstraction of an autonomous resource which may emit asynchronous events. Notifications are a mechanism to report the occurrence of such events, which may be issued without a special request from the management side. Notifications are defined using the Notification template.
- A set of actions, which are operations used to manipulate MOs. Actions are defined using the Action template.
- The behavior of an object and parts thereof (i.e., packages) is defined in the Behavior template. The template allows the description of the MO's behavior, that is, its semantics in plain-text format. It specifies the effect of actions and operations on a managed object, the relationships and interdependencies between attributes, side effects, and so on.
- Conditional packages, which are a means to introduce a variety of properties and functions. Whether a conditional package becomes an integral part of the MO is decided during the creation of the MO. This may ease the mapping of an MO to a real resource.
- The position of the class in the inheritance hierarchy and references to super-classes.

An attribute for the identification of a managed object is a mandatory attribute in every MO class definition. The allocation of a value to this attribute, that is, the name of the MO, is done only at the time of creating the MO; in other words, when an instance of the MO class is created. As the MIB is specific for every system, it is obvious that every MO of one OSI system is linked-in somewhere in a containment hierarchy which starts at the root called SYSTEM. The containment hierarchy provides a natural naming-tree producing global unique names for MOs. This approach can also be found in the directory service X.500.

The introduction of a new MO with a locally unique name is done with the aid of the Name Binding template, resulting in a global unique name. The MIB is, thus, structured in two independent ways, that is, the inheritance hierarchy and the containment hierarchy.

It is important to emphasize that the information model only provides a framework for describing MOs. It does not specify any particular resources in form of MOs, nor does it specify parts of a MIB. The choice of which resources are to be modeled and how this is done is the work of the developer of a concrete network management system. Furthermore, the developer of a resource can have a major influence on the degree to which a resource can be modeled and, hence, may influence the content of the MIB.

With respect to the interoperability of network management systems, the creation of a MIB and the modeling of resources as MOs, it would be advantageous to use standardized MO class libraries. The reusability of class definitions is one significant advantage of an object-oriented approach. Several groups of researchers and developers are working on the definition of MO classes (e.g., ISO, OSI–NM–Forum, CCITT, ANSI, IEEE, CNMA, OIW NMSIG, Internet-IAB). However, a coordination and harmonization of the efforts is necessary.

OSI Organizational Model

The organizational model specifies roles and a possible concept for domains. [ISO 10040] supports two roles: the manager role and the agent role. OSI systems may take on both roles—even simultaneously. Specific management protocols are used for the data exchange between manager and agent. The data exchanged can be operations on MOs, results of operations, notifications from objects, and fault reports. The OSI–NM architecture supports active MOs, which are autonomous objects, that is, they issue notifications without being polled by the manager.

A concept for domains is planned but not yet specified in detail. This concept distinguishes between domains built for organizational reasons and domains based on administrative aspects. Organizational domains are groups of management objects, grouped together for the following reasons:

- Functional purposes, for example, security management, accounting management, and so on
- To allow the application of common actions (management methods, policies)
- Temporary allocation of manager or agent roles

Administrative domains are groups of MOs administered by exactly one authority. This type of domain is necessary to

- Facilitate and manipulate organizational domains
- Control measures taken within overlapping domains

OSI Communication Model

The goal of network and system management is to control the resources in a way to support the requirements of network providers. This requires the possibility to exchange information among cooperating open systems. The OSI communication model supports the following management categories for this purpose: System Management, Layer Management, and Layer Operation. These terms are further explained using Figure 3. The OSI–NM architecture does not specify how these network management categories cooperate nor does it describe how they cooperate with local management (i.e., operating systems). This makes sense from the point of view of standardization but is highly unsatisfactory for the implementer of NM systems. All the above network management categories can access the information in the MIB (4).

Systems Management: System Management covers all management aspects of cooperating systems. It consists of distributed management applications (System Management Applications, SMAs) which are made up of System Management Application Processes (SMAPs). The part of the network management application responsible for the communication is called System Management Application Entity (SMAE), which exchanges management information with SMAEs of other applications by use of suitable NM application protocols (Systems Management Protocols). This form of management communication is the normal case in the OSI–NM architecture but requires the system to support the full OSI functionality, that is, all seven layers of the protocol stack.

The OSI–NM architecture provides a well-defined mechanism to exchange management information among network management application processes. This requires the use of specially designed services, the Common Management Information Services (CMIS), and its associated management protocol called the Common Management Information Protocol (CMIP).

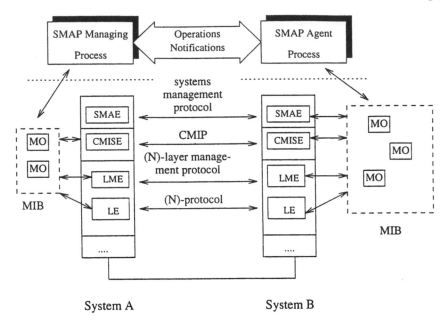

FIGURE 3   OSI communication model.

CMIS supports the access and manipulation of (distributed) MOs and allows operations on the entire information tree (containment tree) of the MIB. CMIS is a connection-oriented service. The possibility to select MOs and to transfer parameters to MOs by using CMIS/CMIP and the structure of protocol data units (CMIP–PDUs) is based on the OSI information model, showing the model's flexibility and strengths. The methods available to select MOs are of great importance. CMIS allows services to

- Specify a set of MOs relevant for the particular service as a subtree of given depth (scoping).
- Select certain objects from this set by use of filters (filtering). A filter consists of one or more clauses about the existence or the value of MO attributes. Thus, a filter is used to select objects on a basis of their attributes.

Layer Management: Layer Management deals with functions, services, and protocols which are specific for a particular layer and do not require the services of higher OSI layers. Examples for these simple management specific functions are loop-back tests (layer 1), protocols for loading software (layer 2), and exchange of routing information (layer 3).

Despite the fact that the OSI–NM architecture identifies layer management as a separate category as stated earlier, this area has been scarcely addressed. Exceptions are the definition of protocols for the exchange of routing information and the definition of libraries for layer-3 and layer-4 objects. This topic will not be discussed further; however, in connection with the introduction of LAN and MAN technologies by the Institute of Electrical and Electronics Engineers (IEEE), a number of specifications for layer management are developed in the IEEE 802.X standards. The communicating entities of layer management are called (N)-Layer Management Entities, the associated protocol (N)-Layer Management Protocol.

Layer Operation: Certain management information and functions are naturally part of the OSI-layer protocols. Examples are window size and timers, the HDLC test frame, the RESET-PDU in X.25, and protocol parameters used in connection establishment and disconnection as well as fault information. It would be advantageous if all management-relevant protocol elements were easily identified as such. This need has been recognized and is taken care of in the development of new protocols (e.g., ATM, FDDI, DQDB) and in the revision of some application protocols (e.g., X.400). There is, however, still a lot more to be done.

OSI Functional Model

Management activities can be classified in different functional areas (System Management Functional Areas, SMFAs). OSI defines five such areas:

- configuration Management: definition and naming of resources (MOs), creating and deleting MOs, setting and changing MO attributes, gathering data on status information, and guaranteeing everyday operation
- Fault Management: recognition, localization, and elimination of faults
- Performance Management: gathering statistical data and keeping a network history to improve the performance of resources
- Accounting Management: user administration, specification, and accounting of MO, utilization and consumption of resources, authorization
- Security Management: authentication, access control, key management

The construction of functional models for different management functions has led to a number of management support functions (Systems Management Functions, SMFs) which can be used by the functional areas as building blocks. The SMFs are very complex in some cases but are generic in their definition to allow flexible use. The management information which corresponds to these support functions and the functional models is defined in so-called Support Managed Objects Classes. OSI–NM has defined the following functions (5): object management function, state management function, attributes for representing relationships, alarm reporting function, event report function, log control function, security alarm reporting function, security audit trail function, objects and attributes for access control, accounting metering function, workload monitoring function, test management function, summarization function, confidence and diagnostic test categories, and scheduling function.

IEEE LAN/MAN Management

The IEEE LAN/MAN management architecture (6) uses concepts of OSI network management to a large degree, in particular the OSI information model.

Naturally, the IEEE LAN/MAN management applies to layers 1, 2a, and 2b. It is characteristic of the network components (modems, repeaters, bridges, etc.) that a full seven-layer OSI functionality is not available and that management activities are required especially when certain subfunctions are defective. Hence, the system management as favored by OSI is not applicable, and the concept of layer management must be utilized. This implies that layer-specific management protocols for LANs must be derived and that management applications must be able to take advantage of the lower LAN protocol layers. Local interfaces should be defined between LAN protocol entities and the layer management. Furthermore, the definition of LAN-specific management objects and attributes is required.

The management protocol is based on the connectionless LLC service (Type 1) in its confirmed/unconfirmed variants. The reasons for this choice are numerous: Many applications have few requirements concerning data integrity or they confirm on the level of their applications, other applications such as real-time applications cannot afford the overhead of a connection-oriented protocol.

Due to the same underlying OSI information model, both CMIS and the corresponding LAN service (LAN/MAN Management Service, LMMS) offer nearly equal functionality. Furthermore, the LAN/MAN Management Protocol (LMMP) uses the PDUs and procedures of the CMIP specification.

As a result of these similarities, CMIP and LMMP can co-exist within the same management or/and agent system, and it is easy to implement proxy agents, which act as a relay between systems based on CMIP and LMMP.

However, due to the missing protocol layers 3–6 a Convergence Protocol Entity (CPE) is needed to bridge the differences between LLC Type 1 and LMMP (Fig. 4). The CPE can recognize duplicates, data loss, and sequence errors, and it can handle the abstract syntax of management information and so on.

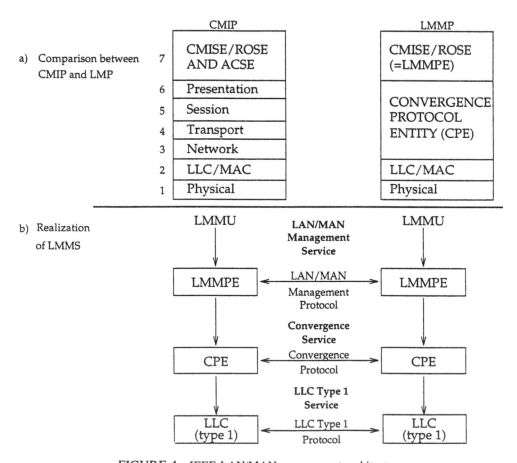

FIGURE 4   IEEE LAN/MAN management architecture.

Internet Management

The Internet management is the basis for most manufacturer-independent management solutions today. The Simple Network Management Protocol (SNMP) constitutes a central part thereof. It is developed by the Internet Activity Board (IAB). The underlying principles for these management concepts are simplicity and ease of implementation. These principles are basically the same as those applied to the communication protocols TCP/IP, or the application protocols FTP and SMTP among others (7).

The **architectural model** of Internet management, like OSI management, is based on a client–server structure. SNMP is used to transfer information between the manager and the agent. Because SNMP is an application protocol, Internet management, according to OSI terminology, belongs to the category of systems management.

Two aspects of the description of management information are covered within the **information model** of Internet management:

1. Structuring and naming realized by an Internet registration tree containing all of the Internet management information
2. Provision of a syntax based on ASN.1

Based on the Internet information model numerous object libraries, so-called Internet MIBs, have been defined (see Fig. 5).

The most important Internet MIB is MIB-II (8), which contains general object definitions applicable to every Internet resource. Objects defined in MIB-II primarily concern the functional areas of configuration management, performance management, and

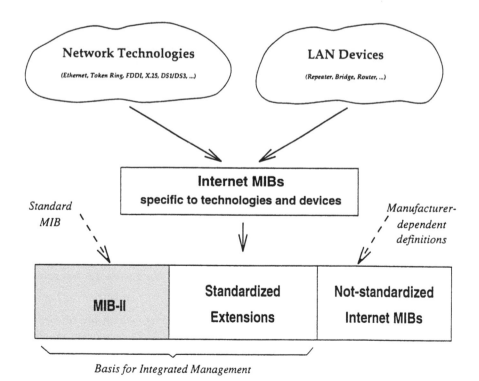

FIGURE 5   Overview of Internet MIBs.

fault management. Other Internet MIBs besides MIB-II describe standardized information necessary to manage certain communication technologies (such as Ethernet, Token Ring, FDDI, DS1/DS3) or LAN devices (such as Repeaters, Bridges, Routers). These Internet MIBs especially contribute strongly to manufacturer-independent management. The more detailed the management information is in the standardized Internet-MIBs, the fewer manufacturer-dependent MIBs are needed.

The Internet **communication model** primarily consists of the Simple Network Management Protocol (SNMP). SNMP operations enable the manager to write to or read from the MIB implemented by the agent. Additionally, a trap operation is supported which provides a simple mechanism to inform the manager asynchronously of specific events which have occurred in the agent.

An explicit **organizational model** or **functional model** does not exist so far. The only approach which covers some functional aspects is provided by the Remote Network Monitoring Management Information Base (RMON–MIB). This Internet MIB, among others, contains simple filter objects and measurement objects which represent the management functions of a protocol analyzer.

At present, an overall revision of the Internet management approach has been worked on. This revision, known as **SNMP version 2** (SNMPv2), does not touch conceptual basics of the existing approach (9). Therefore, the coexistence of SNMPv2 with existing SNMP "version 1" implementations is guaranteed. The improvements are mainly the result of practical experiences. The introduction of a new protocol feature, better handling of SNMP operational failures, and the extension of the security concept are some of the major examples.

CCITT Telecommunications Management Network (TMN)

A brief introduction to CCITT's management architecture TMN follows, especially because CCITT considers public data networks as an important aspect of management. Traditionally, PTTs (or public carriers) talk of OAM (operation, administration, and maintenance) rather than of network management.

Starting from the present situation where heterogeneous management systems are used to manage different network devices, a homogeneous management solution for heterogeneous networks is proposed. The situation of public network providers hardly differs from that of private network providers: management systems from different manufacturers with different user interfaces are used to manage only specific areas of the network. Already with the physical integration of networks and services, and especially with the emergence of intelligent networks and virtual private networks, this approach is not longer suitable.

CCITT's recommendation M.3010 (10) defines the TMN reference model. It is based on its own dedicated management network which comprises the following functional units:

- Telecommunication Network (TN): separate subnets which are offered by one carrier, for example, telephone network, ISDN, X.25 networks, mobile communication networks, teletext networks, and video conferencing networks.
- Network Element (NE), Network Element Function (NEF). This component provides the network services for subscribers to the TN. Examples are branch exchanges, switches, multiplexers, and cross-connects.

- Operating System (OS), Operating System Function (OSF): a component of TMN which processes management information in order to control the TNs. The OS is the actual management system which performs the analysis of data and global control.
- Mediation Devices (MD), Mediation Function (MF): a component of TMN which supports the transfer of management information between NE(F)s and OS(F)s. It is, thus, a management gateway. These mediators can perform the following functions: gathering and transfer of data, data processing and compressing, filtering data (''forwarding discriminator''), and identification of network devices. Furthermore, the protocol conversion is done in these components (i.e., from connection oriented to connectionless, access protocols, etc.).
- Workstation (WS), Workstation Function (WSF): a component of the TMN which provides a uniform interface for the use of the TMN by the human network manager.
- Data Communications Network (DCN), Local Communications Network (LCN), Data Communications Function (DCF): components of the TMN which support the communication between TMN components or devices.

Figure 6 illustrates the above components and shows some reference points which are interfaces between TMN entities defined by their services and protocols. Not all reference points have yet been standardized.

OSF Distributed Management Environment

The OSF is a cooperation between a number of manufacturers with the goal of meeting the growing challenge of new data processing requirements based on distributed systems, by employing the client–server concept. The project Distributed Computing Environment (DCE) was started to specify services and tools which support the creation, usage, and administration of distributed applications in heterogeneous environments. The DCE architecture is based on the following three concepts:

- The client–server concept is used to define a method to structure distributed applications.
- The Remote Procedure Call (RPC) concept offers a mechanism for direct communication between processes of a distributed application executed on different systems.
- The concept of a common database allows the handling of data in a distributed environment. For this purpose, the components of a distributed application all use a common and global virtual database.

Distributed Management Environment (DME) is the management architecture associated with DCE (11). DME is designed to cover the management of both networks and distributed systems. System management concerns the management of services such as data storage, spooling, electronic mail, information systems, user administration, and hardware and software administration, that is, the basic and essential services which are to be provided to a distributed application by the distributed set of systems, structured by applying the client–server concept. DME is naturally based on DCE services. (Note, that the term ''system management'' in the DME context has a more extensive meaning compared to ''systems management'' in the OSI network management context.)

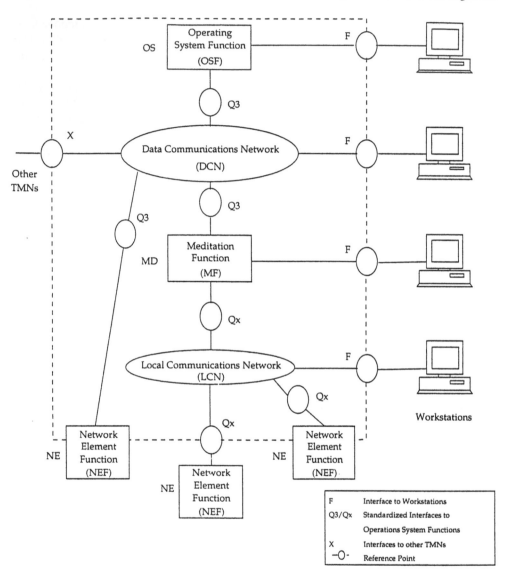

FIGURE 6   TMN reference model.

The ideas of DME form a general architecture of management platforms, that is, a common groundwork of management systems. Figure 7 show a typical structuring of a management platform.

The basic building blocks of DME are the infrastructure, the basic applications, and the development tools. The communication module of the infrastructure provides for the communication with distributed resources and with other management stations. The information administration module maintains the MIB and the operations thereon. The interface module provides mechanisms to describe management objects and to control the user interface. This includes the representation of object symbols and network maps, as well as the design of a menu with its associated functions such as editing, searching,

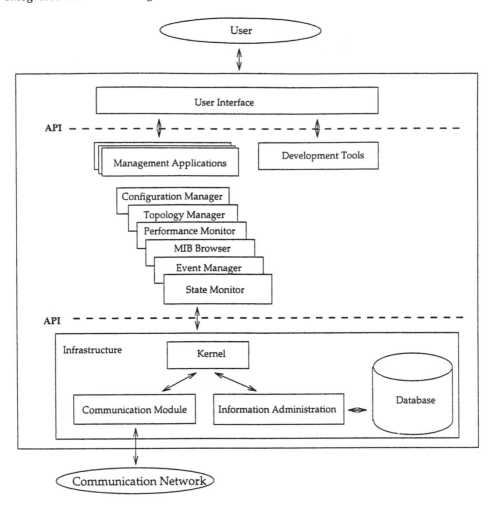

FIGURE 7 A general architecture of management platforms.

and "navigation." The basic and essential functions include status control of resources, monitoring thresholds, event handling, applications for configuration purposes, administration of topology, and performance control.

The efforts for integrating network and system management strives mainly for the transfer and application of concepts and models of network management architectures to system management. This applies in particular to the information and the communication models.

EVALUATION AND CONCLUSION

OSI Management Versus Internet Management

Comparison of OSI management and Internet management reveals different goals of these two standardizing organizations. ISO's goal is to provide a very flexible and powerful concept capable of solving management problems of nearly any complexity. Therefore, a

universal and **generic** approach is taken. In contrast, the IAB's initial goal is to provide a quick solution for the management of the Internet. As a consequence, Internet management does not intend to develop a universal but, instead, a **pragmatic** approach. The ease of implementation is one central requirement of all concepts developed by IAB. Although Internet management suffers from some obvious deficiencies, it is valuable because most practical experiences stem from the use of SNMP-based management tools. One important result from this experience is that Internet management is too simple to solve certain complex management tasks in an adequate way, for example, in the field of system management (in the DME sense) or application management.

A comparison of the submodels of both architectures follows. As Internet Management provides no explicit functional or organizational model, the investigation is restricted to the information and the communication models.

Information Model

A comparison of both information models reveals fundamental differences between ISO and IAB approaches. In OSI management, the information is modeled in an object-oriented way, whereas Internet objects are simple variables contained in a registration tree.

There are obvious advantages and disadvantages of the two information models:

- The object-oriented OSI information model is more complex and its application is more sophisticated. The use of adequate tools can reduce the complexity. Object orientation is adequate to model complex objects in a generic way. Applying the object-oriented principles such as inheritance and encapsulation in the right way, well-structured and readable object libraries can be defined. This eases the reuse of MO descriptions.
- Because the Internet information model specifies less structural rules than the OSI model, the process of defining management information is easier. A closer look at the numerous Internet MIBs reveals that the simple information model leads to confusing object libraries. One obvious deficiency is caused by the missing inheritance concept. As a result, logically related management information is completely scattered.

Communication Model

To compare both communication models, CMIP and SNMP must be compared. The most important differences are as follows:

- SNMP uses an unreliable, connectionless service, whereas CMIP is based on a reliable, connection-oriented service.
- CMIP provides more services than SNMP does. Additional CMIP services are introduced to establish and release the association, to initiate an action, or to dynamically create managed objects.
- CMIP offers a mechanism of scoping and filtering. It supports a flexible selection of information of multiple managed objects. There is no comparable mechanism in SNMP.

The kind of service a management protocol offers strongly depends on the underlying information model. The mechanism of scoping and filtering is a good example of demonstrating this influence, as scoping and filtering assumes as object-oriented information model.

Résumé

It is undisputable that both OSI management and Internet management make a valuable contribution to the goal of a manufacturer-independent management solution. The OSI concepts are strongly influenced by a top-down approach that takes into account general management requirements, whereas Internet is characterized by a bottom-up approach that focuses on basic requirements of component management.

The contribution of Internet consists in practical experiences resulting from the work with SNMP-based tools. In the medium and long term, OSI management concepts will be considered in practical management solutions for they promise a greater flexibility. Such concepts are especially the object-oriented approach to model management information or the Systems Management Functions which provide generic management functionality.

Some efforts have been taken to bring both approaches together. The goal of integrated management can only be achieved by a cooperation instead of a confrontation.

Migration

The heterogeneity of networks and systems is accompanied by a heterogeneity of applications and especially of network and system management concepts. The term migration is used to describe the movement and development away from manufacturer specific management solutions for homogeneous environments toward a global generic manufacturer-independent solution for heterogeneous environments. This migration, however, affects not only the already complex models (information, communication, organizational, and functional models) of a network management architecture but also needs to address the task of integrating different existing management systems.

Methods to achieve this are, for example, a standardization of existing management solutions, that is, the services and functionality, or a hierarchical combination of management systems in a superordinate management system.

IBM's open network management architecture (ONMA), implemented in the product NetView, is an available integration of non-SNA management systems and tools into the central management solution for SNA environments. In this approach, the organizational model was extended by a proxy agent, the communication model by a simple Vector Transport Protocol, and the functional model was enhanced by a precise structuring. However, NetView supports no object-oriented approach in its information model.

This approach already indicates the difficulties and problems encountered when integrating different manufacturer-specific solutions. There is a strong need for open management solutions. Even manufacturers of good management systems for homogeneous environments recognize this fact, as IBM's announcement of SystemView shows. Most of the existing management solutions such as DEC's EMA, SNI's TRANSVIEW, or HP's OpenView are advertised as open management solutions. However, most of these are derivatives of former manufacturer-specific management systems, where the integration of other foreign systems is generally limited. A true migration toward a manufacturer-independent network and system management concept is by far more complex than the currently developed systems. The integration of other business aspects, such as logistics or production planning as discussed in the next section, builds on an integrated network and system management solution. This emphasizes the need for the migration toward a global generic management solution for heterogeneous environments.

Application Management and Enterprise Management

Today, network management and system management are parts of the integrated management solution. In the near future, two more areas of management, application management and enterprise management, will have to be considered.

Distributed applications consist of software processes which run on distributed computer systems and which communicate using the communication network. Consequently, communication systems and computer systems provide resources which are used by distributed applications to fulfill certain tasks, for example, automation of production (computer-integrated manufacturing, CIM) or realization of distributed information systems (electronic mail systems or directory services). This is why distributed applications play a major role; they are responsible for the efficient use of network resources and system resources. The task of application management is to guarantee this requirement.

Although the importance of application management is realized, only few solutions exist today. One reason, of course, is the complexity of this area which arises from the diversity of distributed applications. The most relevant activity toward standardization in the field of distributed applications certainly is ISO's Open Distributed Processing (ODP). The goal of ODP is to provide a general framework for the development of distributed applications. This framework, therefore, must be taken into account when thinking about integrated application management. In the future, the role of ODP with respect to integrated application management might be the same as the role of the OSI reference model with respect to integrated network management. But, in contrast to the OSI reference model, ODP today is not yet stable enough to take on this role.

Enterprise Management is a new term in the field of integrated management, which takes into consideration the economical relevance of management systems in a company. **Corporate Management** is a related term. Corporate Management concentrates on the technical aspects of enterprise management, which concern the interconnection of different management systems used by a company.

The idea of enterprise management is to place the management of networks, systems, and applications into the overall enterprise context. This means that not only technical but also organizational and financial aspects are to be considered. Although this research area is quite complex, it is the only way to motivate the enterprise to invest in integrated management solutions.

Conclusion

It took a long time before standardizing organizations, research groups, and industry became aware of the relevance of integrated management. Continuously growing communication networks and the trend to open communication forces the development of adequate solutions.

An indicator of the growing importance is the great number of international symposiums and workshops on this topic. Certainly the most important state-of-the-art conference is the biannual IFIP International Symposium on Integrated Network Management (12). INTEROP, which takes place in San Jose, is the most famous event where vendors present their management products. Presently, the number of events and journals grows as well as the number of documents published by standardizing organizations. The importance of integrated network management, especially concerning the fields of system and application management, grows as

- high-speed networks and powerful workstations cater for downsizing and/or rightsizing
- telecommunication networks and data communication networks are intermingled as a result of the ever-increasing digitalization.

This development leads to terms such as multiservices, service integration, and intelligent networks, which similar to the new services of freephone and virtual private networks require integrated management. This integration concerns the overlapping aspects of networks, systems, and applications as well as the emerging and growing importance of a cooperation between networks for operating and administrative tasks. It is not surprising that due to this complexity almost all research and development is based on OSI–NM concepts.

We have shown that a number of sound concepts already exist and that the architectural concepts, especially those of the ISO and the IAB, are the most sophisticated and advanced so far developed. An open management architecture is a necessary prerequisite in providing an integrated management solution; however on our way toward this solution there are still a number of tasks to be tackled.

REFERENCES

1. ISO, *Information Processing Systems—Open Systems Interconnection—Basic Reference Model Part 4: Management Framework*, International Organization for Standardization, 1989.
2. ISO, *Information Processing Systems—Open Systems Interconnection—Basic Reference Model*, International Organization for Standardization, 1984.
3. ISO, *Information Processing—Open Systems Interconnection—Structure of Management Information, Part 1–6*, International Organization for Standardization, 1992.
4. ISO, *Information Processing Systems—Open Systems Interconnection—Systems Management Overview*, International Organization for Standardization, 1991.
5. ISO, *Information Processing Systems—Open Systems Interconnection—Systems Management, Part 1–15*, International Organization for Standardization, 1992.
6. IEEE, *LAN/MAN Management*, IEEE Press, New York, 1991.
7. J.D. Case, M. Fedor, M.L. Schoffstall, and C. Davin, "Simple Network Management Protocol (SNMP)," *RFC 1157*, IAB, 1990.
8. K. McCloghrie and Rose, M.T. (eds.), "Management Information Base for Network Management of TCP/IP-based Internets: MIB-II," *RFC 1213*, IAB, 1991.
9. J. Casek, K. McClogharie, M. Rose, S. Waldbusser, "Introduction to version 2 of the Internet-standard Network Management Framework," *RFC* 1441, IAB, 1993.
10. CCITT, *M. 3010, Principles for a Telecommunications Management Network*, ITU, Geneva, 1991.
11. Open Software Foundation, *Distributed Management Environment—Rationale*, Open Software Foundation, 1991.
12. Heinz-Gerd Hegering and Yechiam Yemini (eds.), *Third International Symposium on Integrated Network Management*, International Federation of Information Processing (IFIP), 1993.

BIBLIOGRAPHY

Black, Uyless, *Network Management Standards—The OSI, SNMP and CMOL Protocols*, McGraw-Hill, New York, 1992.

Hegering, Heinz-Gerd, and Sebastian Abeck, *Integrated Network Management and System Management*, Addison-Wesley, Reading, MA, 1994.

Rose, Marshall T., *The Simple Book*: *An Introduction to Management of TCP/IP-based Internets*. Prentice-Hall, Englewood Cliffs, NJ, 1991.

Stallings, William, SNMP, SNMPv2, and CMIP: The Practical Guide to Network Management Standards, Addison-Wesley, 1993.

Terplan, Kornel, *Communication Network Management*. Prentice-Hall, Englewood Cliffs, NJ, 1992.

HEINZ-GERD HEGERING

SEBASTIAN ABECK

RENÉ WIES

SOFTWARE ENGINEERING STANDARDS

INTRODUCTION

Software has gradually, relentlessly, assumed a pivotal role in virtually every aspect of our lives. It is directly or indirectly involved in operating, managing, or controlling businesses, transportation systems, utilities, financial transactions, and local and national defense systems. We are immersed in it at home, in our microwaves, VCRs, entertainment systems, and automobiles. Software controls almost everything, from the trivial to the critical, so that we have come to depend on its reliable functioning to support our personal, professional, and social lives, as we have other invisible technologies (e.g., electricity, radio, etc.).

Of course, dependency on software technology increases our exposure to the potential consequences of its failure. Failure of software control programs can result in consequences ranging from embarrassment to inconvenience, disruption, injury, and death. Software reliability and quality have been elusive in practice because application complexity has increased faster than the state of engineering practice.

Over the years, however, there has been a concerted effort to bring consistency and reliability to the industry, accomplished in large part of identifying and refining standard terminology, procedures, and measures. There are a great many governmental, corporate, and academic organizations actively pursuing standardization of software engineering. This article is intended to provide an overview of the basic issues involved and directions for the future. The following areas will be discussed:

- Standards definitions and concepts
- Standards and software engineering practice
- Major standards producers
- Current standards activities
- Future directions

STANDARDS DEFINITIONS AND CONCEPTS

Webster defines a standard as "a basis of comparison; a criterion; measure."

Standards are used in any discipline or endeavor to accomplish various objectives: establishment of a common and consistent communication framework; definition of a repeatable procedure; description of desired results or outcomes; and definition of measurement units. Standards codify expertise and the best of our practical experiences, so that others may benefit.

Engineering is a disciplined approach to the problem of developing new "things" to meet a set of technical requirements. It is concerned with the principles involved with planning, designing, constructing, maintaining, and managing these "things" being introduced in the context of an operational environment. Software Engineering, then, is that branch of engineering which is concerned with the application of engineering principles to the development of software "things."

STANDARDS AND SOFTWARE ENGINEERING PRACTICE

There is a lively and ongoing discussion concerning the applicability of standards to software engineering. In fact, in May 1991 the Fourth Software Engineering Standards Application Workshop featured a debate on this issue ("Are Software Standards Necessary?"). Although there were a variety of interesting counterarguments, the consensus was that standards are essential to developing a reliable, predictable, and coherent software development process.

Application to Practice

Standards provide a framework which give us universal definitions and measures. Sound engineering practices depend on this consistency. Process control and improvement are impossible without a clear definition of what we mean by "process" and "improvement."

Achieving high quality in any complex product by chance is unlikely. This is especially true for intangible products such as software. Quality software cannot be produced without quality processes, well-defined and implemented development processes which are themselves reliable and predictable. The quality built into these processes represents good engineering practice, practice captured and codified in recognized standards.

Good engineering practice suggests that process variability (randomness) be minimized. Without standards as a basis for definition, process variability cannot be determined, let alone controlled. One of the more obvious manifestations of this problem is demonstrated by the notorious inability of software developers to accurately estimate their development budget and/or schedule. Using standards to define software development processes makes process management possible.

Standardized practice enables software developers to achieve higher productivity levels. Reduced variability for the developer means that there is less guessing and rework. Consistency enables the use of powerful development tools, including CASE, which depend on predictable environments much as we rely on semantics to understand language and the placement of the controls when we drive a car. Basic consistency in practice establishes an infrastructure which serves as a springboard, minimizing the need to be concerned with underlying mechanics. Additional productivity gains come from enhanced personnel mobility between projects and reduced start-up effort because project "templates" are available. Testing does not add quality to a product; it only measures the degree of quality. Much of the "quality" in software is currently achieved through testing, an error-detection process. Therefore, standards are also essential for error prevention. With software engineering standards, the quality can be built-in from the start, instead of detecting errors at the time of testing when the cost of finding and fixing errors grows exponentially. In other words, if you do not put a quality software product into test, you will not get a quality product out. Detection involves rework, thereby reducing productivity. Good practice enables the engineer to avoid the creation of errors in the first place.

Furthermore, experts agree that lack of use of quality principles during the initial software development have an adverse impact on the costs of the entire life cycle of a software product. As much as 60% to 80% of the cost of a software product is incurred during the maintenance of a product. The main portion of this cost is most often attributable to fixing problems after a product is released to a customer/user.

Software quality is governed by process quality. By improving the process quality, you will improve the product. The process needs to be defined and measured. To do this, there is a need to use engineering management methods, that is, set targets, measure progress, and take corrective action. Steps to control the software process entails establishing management controls, setting quality standards, defining the process, measuring and evaluating, and continuously improving. Applicable standards in the software process deal with specifying requirements, evaluating results and guiding and controlling the process. Software standards are critical for facilitating control—reducing diversity, increasing visibility, and improving productivity.

Software standards also provide for flexibility by enabling people mobility from project to project, reducing start-up costs, and serve as templates for action. Process standards incorporate practices which prevent defect creation in the first place by anticipating their causes. Testing becomes more of a certification process, and detected problems are substantially reduced.

Standards enable the comparison of information from project to project. All cost and schedule estimation predictors require the same kind of information gathered from several projects. Evaluation of software development techniques and tools are best when based on project-to-project comparisons.

Finally, software standards establish the basis for continual improvements to processes and products. Improvement of any kind means that performance is known, manageable, and controlable. Standardized processes allow comparisons to be made among projects, providing valuable information on ways to make the process more effective, reliable, predictable, and productive.

Practical Implementation

Implementing standards requires vision and leadership to achieve major modifications in organizational or institutional culture and behavior. Software standards cannot be applied as a "quick fix." Successful implementation requires organizational commitment, a real understanding of true "customer" requirements, careful planning, good people management, and comprehensive training.

Standard development occurs at one or more levels (project, organization, industry, national, or international), reflecting the concerns of the originators. Project-level standards are less likely to be adaptable to multiple environments than those developed for national or international use. Implementors choose between developing their own standards or adopting those already in existence. Their operating environment often determines which of the following options is most practical:

- Development of new, independent (but possibly redundant) standards
- Modification of existing standards
- Adoption of existing standards in their entirety
- Use of standards required by a contracting agent

In most unregulated environments, standards tend to be "homegrown," prepared internally by management and/or development staff. They typically do not look for any consensus of opinion outside the work group. These local standards are useful for organizing internal work efforts but seldom address general issues of software development. Consequently, internal standards are often incomplete and so heavily influenced by the environment that application by other organizations is not practical.

Other software engineering groups utilize existing industry and/or national standards in their entirety or as reference points for their in-house standards. In many cases, these groups add detailed implementation procedures, often left out of consensual existing standards. As with the internally developed standards, practical application to other environments may be problematic due to the local tailoring.

Software contractors in certain industries must often adhere to purchaser-dictated standards. Industries with specialized concerns for safety and reliability (e.g., military, aerospace, nuclear power, transportation, etc.) also establish their own engineering standards. These industry standards tend to be fairly generic with respect to engineering procedures but are heavily influenced by issues such as mission-criticality, personnel survival, durability, and robustness.

Contractors may utilize other standards in addition to the required ones, if desired, but they are subject to regular procedure audits and must be able to demonstrate compliance based on thorough documentation. Because of their special requirements, these standards do not have wide acceptance in more conventional applications. Practical implementation outside the specific industries generally involves selection of specific parts of the standard and adaptation to local needs.

MAJOR SOFTWARE ENGINEERING STANDARDS PRODUCERS

There are dozens of organizations issuing standards relating to software engineering. Many of these are limited to particular industry associations. Others have undertaken charters at the national and international levels. Some of the most influential standards bodies, and their respective roles, are discussed below.

American National Standards Institute (ANSI)

ANSI is a standards repository, not a producer. Its role has been to adopt significant industry standards prepared by recognized industry groups. It also acts as the official U.S. representative on many international standards bodies.

Institute of Electrical and Electronics Engineers (IEEE)

The IEEE Computer Society is one of the most active software standards producers in the United States. In addition to developing standards, it serves as the technical advisor to ANSI in international activities. IEEE Technical Advisory Groups (TAGs) prepare draft standards and provide comments on standards in progress.

U.S. Department of Defense (DoD)

The Department of Defense has long been noted for its comprehensive and voluminous body of standards, covering virtually all aspects of product development, deployment, and operation. Software producers working as defense contractors must demonstrate compliance with a variety of MIL-SPEC (military specification) documents describing project planning, quality assurance, and system documentation. Generally, these standards are extremely rigorous and, as a result, have had significant influences on the definition of other software standards. Wide application in the broader software industry has been minimal.

American Society for Quality Control (ASQC)

ASQC, until recently, did not have an active software engineering component. A Software Division was introduced in 1989; its first international conference was held in June 1991. Currently, ASQC's role is that of facilitator, rather than producer, concentrating on coordination and training.

Software Engineering Institute (SEI)

SEI was established at Carnegie–Mellon University under the auspices of the Department of Defense. Although it has been active in many areas of research, one of its most notable outputs has been the Maturity Model. This model is used to assess software producer capabilities, based on the maturity of their software development practices.

International Standards Organization (ISO)

Joint Technical Committee 1 and its Subcommittee 7 (JTC1/SC7) specifically deals with the software engineering standards development. SC7's area of work is standardization of management techniques, the supporting methods and tools necessary for the development and testing of software.

The Standards Development Process

Most recognized software engineering standards are developed in a very democratic, consensual fashion, emphasizing the need to capture the best of current thinking and practice. Typically, the major standards-producing bodies follow a similar sequence of events:

1. Proposal for a suggested standard is submitted
2. Proposal is voted on by the executive committee members
3. Working Group is created to work on proposed standard
4. Working Group submits draft for members review and comment
5. Comments are addressed; revised draft submitted for approval by members
6. Members approve adoption of standard

Steps 4 and 5 may be iterated several times before agreement is reached. Depending on the organization, membership in the working group may be open to the public.

Current Standards Development Activities

The discussion of current activities will focus on two representative groups, whose participants are typically members of standards bodies associated with specific interests. From a national perspective, the Institute of Electrical and Electronics Engineers (IEEE) is recognized as the standards body for commercial and scientific interests. Internationally, the International Standards Organization (ISO) is one of the primary bodies, particularly within the European Community.

Standards Activities: IEEE

Current Activities: The IEEE Computer Society has a wide variety of projects active at the current time (see Table 1). These include revisions and/or extensions to some of these standards, as well as development of new standards. IEEE produces three basic types of documents:

TABLE 1   IEEE Current Activities

General area	Standard number		Current project/type title
Terminology	610.12-1990		Standard Glossary of Software Engineering Terminology
Life cycle	1074-1991		New Standard for Developing Software Life Cycle Processes
		P1074.1/-New	Guide for Developing Software Life Cycle Processes
Requirements	830-1983	Rev	Guide for Software Requirements Specifications
Design	1016-1987		Recommended Practice for Software Design
Descriptions		P1016.1/New	Guide to Software Design Descriptions
Testing/valida- tion and verification	1008-1987		Standard for Software Unit Testing
	1012-1987		Standard for Software Verification and Vali- dation Plans
	1028-1988		Standard for Software Reviews and Audits
		P829/Rev	Standard for Software Test Documentation
		P1044/New	Standard for Classification of Software Er- rors, Faults, and Failures
		P1059/New	Guide for Software Verification and Valida- tion Quality
Assurance	730.1-1989		Standard for Software Quality Assurance Plans
	730.2	Rev	Guide to Software Quality Assurance Planning
Configuration management	828-1990		Standard for Software Configuration Management Plans
	1042-1987		Guide to Software Configuration Management
Management information	982.1-1988		Standard Dictionary of Measures to Produce Reliable Software
	982.2-1988		Guide for the Use of 982.1
	1058.1-1987		Standard for Software Project Management Plans
		P1045/New	Standard for Software Productivity Metrics
		P1058.2/New	Guide for Software Project Management Plans
		P1061/New	Standard for a Software Quality Metrics Methodology
		P1062/New	Recommended Practice for Software Acquisition
Systems engi- neering		P1220/New	Standard for Systems Engineering Management
		P1233/New	Standard for System eEquirements Specification
Miscellaneous	1002-1987		Standard Taxonomy for Software Engineer- ing Standards

TABLE 1   (Continued)

General area	Standard number		Current project/type title
	1063-1987		Standard for Software User Documentation
			Recommended Practice for the Evaluation of
		P1209/New	CASE Tools
		P1219/New	Standard for Software Maintenance
		P1228/New	Standard for Software Safety Plans

• Standards: specification of uniform minimum conformance requirements
• Guides: explanation and clarification of Standards which do not impose any additional requirements
• Recommended practices: suggestions for use or creation of processes and/or products, based on the current state of the art

To promote consistency and more efficient utilization by practitioners, IEEE is anticipating a new numbering scheme which would associate standards, guides, and recommended practices more clearly.

To ensure that Standards remain appropriate over time, IEEE requires that each standard be reviewed every 5 years for potential revision.

IEEE Long-Range Plan: The SEI Maturity Model mentioned previously introduced a conceptual target for standards developers. The IEEE Computer Society has set a goal of establishing the standards necessary to enable practitioners to achieve a very high maturity "Level 4" of software development practices by the year 2000.

Level 4 is characterized as a "managed" development process, one that is measured and controlled. This goal is to be achieved through use or adaptation of as many appropriate national and/or international standards as possible. This effort, however, will require a high degree of coordination and "harmonization" among many different standards-producing organizations.

For years, standards developers have been concerned about rampant duplication and fragmentation resulting from the activities of many overlapping organizations. A multiorganizational group being led by the IEEE Computer Society represents a recognition that long-range planning is needed for effective standards management on an industry-wide basis. The study group's proposed mission is to promote implementation of effective standards which fit together in content and purpose. The IEEE study plan has three objectives:

• Determine User Requirements for software engineering standards
• Harmonize existing software engineering standards prepared by multiple organizations
• Strategize development of new standards in those areas not yet addressed

This approach should reduce confusion among software developers and vendors who are trying to satisfy multiple audiences. Software purchasers, users, developers, and vendors face a dilemma; it is virtually impossible to determine how to establish compliance with the "best" set of standards. Use of a common set of procedures promotes greater productivity and reliability and may also provide the first significant step toward certifiable software products.

TABLE 2   ISO/IEC JTC1 SC7 Current Activities

General area	Standard number		Current project/type title
WG 1: Symbols, charts, and diagrams	ISO 6593	7.06	Program Flow for Processing Sequential Files in Terms of Record Groups
	ISO 5806	7.08	Documentation Symbols and Conventions for Data, Program, and System Flowcharts, Program Network Charts, and System Resource Charts
	ISO 5806	7.07	Single Hit Decision Logic Table
	ISO 8790	7.16	Computer System Configuration Diagram Symbols and Conventions
		7.11	Basic Constructs for Programs and Conventions for Their Application
		7.19.01	Standard Diagrams for Software Development Methods
		7.19.02	Charting Techniques for Software Development and Maintenance
		N796	Conventions for Usage of Symbols and Icons in Software Engineering
WG 2:System software documentation	ISO TR9127	7.03.01	User Documentation and Cover Information for Consumer Software Packages
		7.18.02	Guidelines for Management of Software Documentation
		N807	Management of Information Transfer Between Life Cycle Phases
WG 4: Tools and environment		7.25	Evaluation and Selection of CASE Tools
WG 6: Evaluation and metrics		7.13	Evaluation of Software
		7.13.02	Software Quality Sub-Characteristics
		7.13.03	Software Quality Management and Rating
		7.24	Software Quality Requirements and Testing Directives
		N051	Measurement and Rating of Data Processing Performance
WG 7: Life cycle management		7.21.	Life Cycle Management
		7.26	Guide to Life Cycle Management
WG 8: Integral life cycle processes		7.23	Software Configuration Management
		7.27	Integral Life Cycle Processes
		7.27.10	Overview Document
		7.27.02	Project Management
		7.27.03	Software Quality Assurance

TABLE 2   (Continued)

General area	Standard number	Current project/type title
	7.27.04	Verification and Validation
	7.27.05	Formal Reviews and Audits
	N967	Software Maintenance
WG 9: Classification and mapping	7.20.03	Mapping of Relevant ISO Standards to Reference Model
	7.20.03.01	Mapping of Relevant SE Standards for SC7
	7.20.03.02	Mapping of Relevant SE Standards—Categorization of SW Standards
	7.22	Categorization of Software
	N982	Software Integrity Levels
WG10: Software process assessment	N986	Software Process Assessment
WG11: Description of data for software engineering	N1001	Description of Data for Software Engineering

Standards Activities: ISO

Current Activities: Joint Technical Committee 1 (JTC1) of the International Standards Organization (ISO) and the International Electrotechnical Commission (IEC) has established Subcommittee 7 (SC7) on Software Engineering Standards. SC7 has nine Working Groups (WGs) dealing with different areas of the field. Table 2 shows activities of these Working Groups.

Like IEEE, SC7 is concerned with fragmentation and duplication of effort. With the 1991 plenary meeting, the Working Groups were reorganized to implement a strategic business plan.

The emphasis for the next 3 years will be on establishing a robust and flexible foundation on which to build future standards. The initial work focuses on the definition of a common framework with a set terminology and symbology. These fundamental definitions affect software engineering and include efforts to specify a generalized model of the software engineering process: minimal documentation expectations for computerized systems; development of diagramming symbols and techniques; software life-cycle processes; software quality assurance characteristics and metrics; technical specifications, such as requirements, design, and testing.

FUTURE DIRECTIONS

People have come to have great expectations of software technology and its developers. Along with expectations of functionality, software users also anticipate predictability, reliability, and ease of use. In the process of maturing, the field of software engineering has been proceeding in many diverse directions. Quality as a factor in perceptions of competitiveness is now sharpening the focus on software engineering standards, locally, nationally, and internationally. Total Quality Management (TQM) practices will require producers at all levels to examine the reliability, not only of their products but also of the processes which create the products. Buyers are beginning to eliminate unreliable producers from their lists of "preferred vendors," contracting only with those who use TQM processes.

Software can be created by virtually anyone. Software engineering practices have emerged on an individualized basis, as opposed to other "hard" engineering disciplines facing severe physical and/or operational constraints. This has forced software engineering standards bodies to accommodate tremendously diverse professional opinions, representing individual views of the "best" practices. Over time, there has been a degree of convergence on a consistent model of the development process; however, there are still fundamental disagreements among practitioners. The future activities are centered around a systems viewpoint. There is also an attempt to make the standards robust across all types of applications (military and commercial), and common across different cultures and governing systems.

The software engineering standards will affect software markets. Besides supporting open architectures, standards are likely to establish procedural requirements and further specify certification criteria that will be used worldwide. There is an urgency for U.S. experts and industry participation in international software engineering standards development. Factors creating the urgency include EC 92, Pacific Rim economic capabilities, international software marketplace—compliance to quality/verification requirements, ISO 9000 standards, and international software factories.

Harmonization of the multiple standards and conceptual models defined by the various standards bodies will be an important step in achieving a true definition of Software Engineering. IEEE and ISO undertaking vigorous efforts to establish clear frameworks for organizing their activities. Practitioners of the mysterious and arcane art of software development, long frustrated by the lack of clear direction, may now find powerful new tools and practices at their disposal. The promise of software, long anticipated in science fiction, may finally come to fruition once this hurdle has been overcome.

BIBLIOGRAPHY

Crosby, P. B., *Quality Is Free*, McGraw–Hill, New York, 1979.

Deming, E. W., *Quality, Productivity, and Competitive Position*, MIT Technology, Cambridge, MA, 1982.

Edelstein, V., and S. Mamone, "Standard for Software Maintenance. A Framework for Managing and Executing Software Maintenance Activities", *IEEE Computer* (June 1992).

Edelstein, V., R. Fujii, C. Guerdat, and P. Sullo, *International Software Engineering Standards*, Software Engineering Auerbach Publishers, 1991.

Edelstein, V., S. Mamone, and P. Sullo, "Implementing Structure Testing Techniques in an R&D Telecommunications Organization," in *Proceedings International Conference Reliability '90 in Computer Science*, Czechoslovakia, 1990.

Edelstein, V., P. Sullo, and L. Boguchwal, "Making Software Engineering Happen in Telecommunications R&D Organization," *IEEE J-SAC*, special issue on Telecommunication Software, 1990.

IEEE, *IEEE Software Engineering Standards Collection*, IEEE, Inc., New York, 1991.

International Software Engineering Standards Application Workshp (SESAW), San Diego, May 1991, IEEE Computer Society, New York, 1991.

Mills, H. *Software Productivity*, Dorset House Publishing, New York, 1988.

Pressman, R. *Software Engineering a Practitioners Approach*, 2nd ed., McGraw–Hill, New York, 1991.

D. VERA EDELSTEIN

SOFTWARE QUALITY ENGINEERING MODELS

INTRODUCTION

In recent years, there has been an emerging trend in the software industry to use scientific methods to achieve precision in managing software projects. In progressing toward this goal, the role of software quality engineering models is pivotal. Modeling is a systematic way to describe the complex reality. The knowledge we gain from modeling can help us develop quality strategies scientifically and manage quality accordingly and appropriately.

This article summarizes major models used for software quality engineering in the software industry. Many of these models are used for estimating software reliability; some are for managing quality during the development process, and a few are complexity models that can be used by software engineers to improve their work. Where appropriate, examples of applications of some of these models in real-life development environments are also provided. These examples include cases from the development of the Application System/400 (AS/400) software system at IBM, Rochester. As the home site of the AS/400, IBM Rochester develops and manufactures the midrange computer system and was the winner of the Malcolm Baldrige National Quality Award (MBNQA) in 1990. In its software development organization, there are more than 1500 members. Therefore, examples of software quality engineering models used for the AS/400 represent applications of such models in a large scale development environment.

As pinpointed by the title, in this article we confine our discussions to models related to software quality engineering. Other models in software engineering such as those related to size and efforts, staffing, schedule and resource allocation and productivity are not included. Examples of such models include the COCOMO model (1), Putnam's resource allocation model (2), Jensen's model (3), and various studies and analyses by experts in academia and industry. In general, models about software project management in relation to the above parameters are more well known among software development practitioners, especially development managers and product managers. Models about software quality engineering, numerous in count and having emerged in the recent past, are less well known and used.

In the following sections, we cover the following topics:

- Reliability models
- Quality management models
- Complexity metrics and models
- Criteria and issues of software quality engineering models

In the Bibliography, a list of recommended readings on software metrics and models is provided.

RELIABILITY MODELS

Software reliability models are used to estimate the reliability of the software product when it is available to the customers. Such an estimate is important for two reasons: (1) as an objective statement of the quality of the product and (2) for resource planning in order to ensure continual programming and service support. The criteria variable under study is the number of defects (or defect rate normalized to lines of code) in specified time intervals (weeks, months, etc.) or the time between failures. Reliability models can be broadly classified into two categories: static models and dynamic models. A static model uses other attributes of the project or program modules to estimate the number of defects in the software. A dynamic model, usually based on statistical distributions, uses the current development defect patterns to estimate end-product reliability. A static model of software quality estimation has the following general form:

$$y = f(x_1, x_2, \ldots, x_k) + e.$$

The dependent variable y is the defect rate or the number of defects. The independent variables x_i are the attributes of the product, the project, or the process through which the product is developed. They could be size (lines of code), complexity, skill level, count of decisions, and other meaningful measurements. e is the error term (because models do not completely explain the behavior of the dependent variable.

Coefficients of the independent variables in the formula are estimated based on data from previous products. For the current product or project, the values of the independent variables are measured, then plugged into the formula to derive estimates of the dependent variable.

The static models are static in the sense that the coefficients of their parameters are predetermined by previous products. In contrast, for the dynamic models, the coefficients are estimated based on the data available from the current product at the time of modeling. From our observations and experience, static models are generally less superior than dynamic models when the unit of analysis is at the product or system level. When the unit of analysis is much more granular, such as at the program module level, the static models can be powerful. Moreover, the significance of the independent variables in relation to the defect rate can be used to derive improvement actions by the software engineer (for instance, the relationship between program complexity and defect rate). In the section on complexity metrics and models, several such relationships are described.

As the macro-level models are less useful for estimating the reliability of a software product, we will not get into the specifics here. In the following sections, we describe several major dynamic models. A common denominator of dynamic models is that they are all expressed as a function of time or its equivalent (such as development phase).

The Rayleigh Model

The Rayleigh model is a member of the family of the Weibull distribution. The Weibull distribution has been used for decades for reliability analysis in various fields of engineering, ranging from the fatigue life of deep-groove ball bearings to electron tube failures and the overflow incidence of rivers. It is one of the three known extreme-value distributions (4), and one of its marked characteristics is that the tail of its probability density function approaches zero asymptotically but never reaches it. Its cumulative distribution function (CDF) and probability density function (PDF) are

CDF:

$$F(t) = 1 - \exp\left[-\left(\tfrac{t}{c}\right)^m\right],$$

PDF:

$$f(t) = \left(\frac{m}{t}\right) \left(\frac{t}{c}\right)^m \exp\left[-\left(\tfrac{t}{c}\right)^m\right],$$

where m is the shape parameter, c is the scale parameter, and t is time.

Figure 1 shows several Weibull probability density curves with varying values of the shape parameter. The Rayleigh model is a special case of the Weibull distribution when $m = 2$. Its CDF and PDF are

CDF:

$$F(t) = 1 - \exp\left[-\left(\tfrac{t}{c}\right)^2\right],$$

PDF:

$$f(t) = \left(\frac{2}{t}\right) \left(\frac{t}{c}\right)^2 \exp\left[-\left(\tfrac{t}{c}\right)^2\right].$$

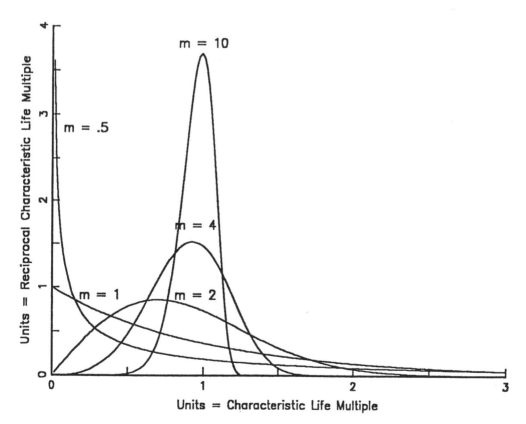

FIGURE 1   Weibull probability density.

The Rayleigh PDF first increases to a peak and then decreases at a decelerating rate. The c parameter is a function of t_m, the time at which the curve reaches its peak. By taking the derivative of $f(t)$ with respect to t, setting it to zero, and solving the equation, t_m can be obtained:

$$t_m = \frac{c}{\sqrt{2}}.$$

After t_m is estimated, the shape of the entire curve can be determined. The area below the curve up to t_m is 39.35% of the total area.

It has been empirically well established that software projects follow a life-cycle pattern described by the Rayleigh density curve (2). The basic assumption for using the Rayleigh model is that if more defects are discovered and removed in the earlier development phases, fewer will remain in later stages, which results in better quality of the system. Figure 2 shows an example of a Rayleigh curve modeling the defect removal pattern of an IBM AS/400 product in relation to the six-step development process: high-level design (I0), low-level design (I1), coding (I2), unit test (UT), component test (CT), and system test (ST). Given the defect removal pattern up through ST, the purpose is to estimate the defect rate when the product is shipped, the post-general-availability phase (PGA) in the figure. In this example the X-axis is the development phase which can be regarded as one form of logical equivalents of time. In many actual practices, the actual time units (e.g., weeks or months in the development cycle) were used (2, see examples).

Implementation of the Rayleigh model is relatively easy. If the defect rate data are reliable, the model parameters can be derived from the data by computer programs that utilize statistical functions available in many statistical software packages. After the model is defined, estimation of end-product reliability can be achieved by substitution of data values and calculation.

Our estimations of the Rayleigh model parameters are implemented by programs written in SAS which uses the nonlinear regression procedure. From the several methods in nonlinear regression, we choose the DUD method for its simplicity and efficiency (5).

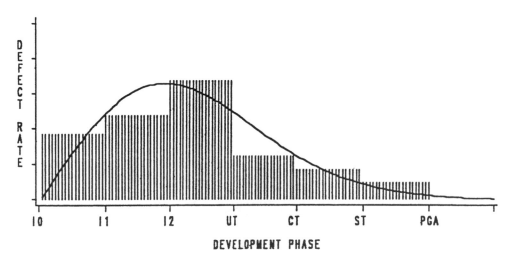

FIGURE 2   Rayleigh model.

DUD is a derivative-free algorithm for nonlinear least squares. It competes favorably with even the best derivative-based algorithms when evaluated on a number of standard test problems.

Our SAS programs estimate model parameters, produce a graph of fitted model versus actual data points on a GDDM79 graphic terminal screen (as shown in Fig. 2), perform the chi-square goodness-of-fit test, and derive estimates for the latent-error rate. The probability (p-value) of the chi-square test is also provided. If the test results indicate that the fitted model does not adequately describe the observed data ($p > .05$), a warning statement will be issued in the output. If proper graphic support is available, the colored graph on the terminal screen can be saved and plotted.

With regard to predictive validity, given the few available input data points, the chance of having satisfactory confidence intervals for the estimate (of end-product reliability) is very slim. Our strategy, therefore, is to rely on intermodel validity. Our use of other models, including the exponential model and other reliability growth models, are described in the next section. Although the confidence interval for each model estimate may not be satisfactory, if the estimates by different models are close to each other, our confidence about the estimates is strengthened. On the other hand, if the estimates from different models lie far apart, our confidence will not be strong even if the confidence interval for each single estimate is very small. Furthermore, to establish predictive validity, model estimates and actual outcomes must be compared. When applying the Rayleigh model to study the life cycle of manpower of software projects, Wiener-Ehrlich and associates (6) found that the model underestimated the manloading scores at the tail. At IBM Rochester, actual defect data after the system is shipped are available for several releases of the System/38, a predecessor system for AS/400. When comparing the Rayleigh estimates with the actual defect rates, we also found that the Rayleigh model consistently underestimated the latent-error rates. Using the Rayleigh estimates directly, therefore, will not be predictively valid. Our strategy is to adjust the Rayleigh output based on the System/38 experience. The adjustment factor is the mean difference between the Rayleigh estimates and the actual defect rates reported. The adjustment is logical, given the similar architectures of AS/400 and System/38 and the similar structural parameters in the development process, including organization, management, and work force.

The Exponential Model

The exponential model is yet another special case of the Weibull family, with the shape parameter equal to 1. It is best used for statistical processes that decline monotonically to an asymptote. Its CDF and PDF are

CDF:

$$F(t) = 1 - \exp\left[-\left(\frac{t}{c}\right)\right]$$
$$= 1 - \exp^{(-\lambda t)}$$

PDF:

$$f(t) = \frac{1}{c}\exp\left[-\left(\frac{t}{c}\right)\right]$$
$$= \lambda\,\exp^{(-\lambda t)},$$

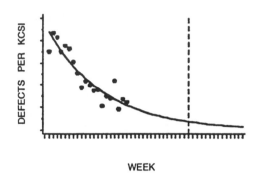

FIGURE 3   Exponential model—density distribution.

where c is the scale parameter, t is time, and $\lambda = 1/c$. When applied to software reliability, λ is referred to as the error detection rate or instantaneous failure rate.

The above formulas represent a standard distribution; specifically, the total area under the PDF curve is 1. In actual cases, the formulas are multiplied by a constant, K, the total number of defects or the total cumulative defect rate.

The exponential model is one of the better-known software reliability models and is the basis of many software reliability growth models. For many models, the assumption of the error detection process during software testing is that it follows a binomial distribution, a Poisson distribution, or a nonhomogeneous Poisson distribution. The mean value function (CDF) of these error detection processes often follows the exponential distribution. For instance, the Goel–Okumoto Nonhomogeneous Poisson Process Model (NPPM) shows a mean value function of exponential growth (7). Misra (8) used the exponential model to estimate the defect-arrival rates for the Shuttle Ground System software of the National Aeronautics and Space Administration (NASA). The software provided the flight controllers at the Johnson Space Center with processing support to exercise command and control over flight operations. Actual data from a 200-hr flight mission indicated that the model worked very well.

Figures 3 and 4 show an example of the exponential model applied to the data of one of the AS/400 software products. We modeled the weekly defect-arrival data since the start of the system test, when the development work was virtually complete. The

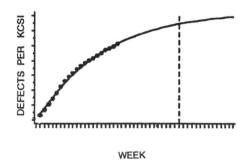

FIGURE 4   Exponential model—cumulative distribution.

system-testing stage uses customer interfaces, tests external requirements, and simulates end-user application environments. The pattern of defect arrivals during this stage, therefore, should be indicative of the latent-defect rate when the system is shipped.

Our implementation of the exponential model is also by SAS computer programs. Our defect-arrival data is calendar-time based. In other words, it is less precise than execution-time data. Ohba (9) noted that the exponential model does not work well for calendar-time data with a nonhomogeneous time distribution of testing effort. For our case, the testing effort for the AS/400 remained consistently high and homogeneous throughout the system test phase. The system is also very large (7.1 million lines of source code at the first release) and the defect rates tend to be stable even though no execution-time data are available.

In the case that the testing effort is clearly not homogeneous, models other than the exponential model should be considered. Another method is to homogenize the calendar-time units with testing effort if data are available. For instance, if data on person-hours of testing effort are available throughout the entire testing phase, the average number of person-hours in testing per week can be used as the time unit (instead of the actual calendar weeks). Adjustments of this sort can avoid artificial fluctuations in the data and can make the model work better.

Reliability Growth Models

In addition to the basic exponential growth model, there are many software reliability growth models, each having its own assumptions. In this section we briefly summarize the notable ones. The criteria variable for reliability growth models is usually the number of defects (or defect rate) for specified time intervals, or successive times between failures. A common denominator of all reliability growth models is that they are based on data from the testing phase of the software development cycle. When failures occur and defects are fixed, the software becomes more and more stable, and reliability grows over time.

Jelinski–Moranda Model

The Jelinski–Moranda (J–M) model is one of the earliest models in software reliability research (10). Its criteria variable (dependent variable) is times between failures. It assumes there are N software faults at the start of testing, that failures occur purely at random, and that all faults contribute equally to cause a failure during testing. It also assumes the fix time is negligible and that the fix is perfect for each failure that occurs. Therefore, the software product's failure rate improves by the same amount at each fix.

Littlewood Models

The Littlewood (LW) model (11) is similar to the J–M model, except it assumes that different faults have different sizes, thereby contributing unequally to failures. Faults with larger sizes tend to be detected and fixed earlier. As the number of errors is driven down with the progress in test, so is the average error size, causing a law of diminishing return in debugging. The introduction of the error size concept makes the model assumption more realistic. Littlewood also developed other models such as the Littlewood Non-homogeneous Poisson Process (LNHPP) model (12). The LNHPP model is similar to the LW model except that it assumes a continuous change in failure rate, rather than discrete jumps, when fixes take place.

Goel–Okumoto Nonhomogeneous Poisson Process Model

Whereas the criteria variable of the J–M model and the Littlewood models is times between failures, the Goel–Okumoto (G–O NHPP) model (7) is concerned with modeling the number of defects detected or failures observed in given testing intervals. It belongs to the class of fault count models. When faults or defects are removed from the system, it is expected that the observed number of failures per unit time will decrease. Here, time can be calendar time, execution time (CPU time), number of test cases run, or some other relevant measurements. The time intervals are also fixed a priori (13). The cumulative number of failures observed at time t is modeled as a Poisson process with a time-dependent failure rate. It assumes that the failure rate improves continuously in time. Its mean value function (time-dependent failure rate) follows an exponential pattern. Therefore, the G-O NHPP model is a direct application of the exponential model.

Musa–Okumoto Logarithmic Poisson Execution Time Model

Similar to the G–O model, in this model the observed number of failures by a certain time is also assumed to be a nonhomogeneous Poisson process (14). However, its mean value function is different. It attempts to consider that later fixes have a smaller effect on the software's reliability than earlier ones. The logarithmic Poisson process is considered to be superior for highly nonuniform operational user profiles, where some functions are executed much more frequently than others. Also the process modeled is the number of failures in specified execution time intervals (instead of calendar time). Musa also provides a systematic approach to convert the results to calendar time data (15). This model is used by software projects at AT&T and is being adopted by other companies as well.

The Delayed-S and Inflection-S Models

With regard to the software defect removal process, Yamada, Ohba, and Osaki (16) argued that a testing process consists of not only a defect detection process but also a defect isolation process. Because of the time needed for failure analysis, significant delay can occur between the time of the first-failure observation and the time of reporting. They offered the delayed S-shaped reliability growth model for such process, in which the observed growth curve of the cumulative number of detected defects is S-shaped. The model is based on the nonhomogeneous Poisson process and has its mean value function as follows:

$$m(t) = K\left[1 - (1 + \lambda t)\exp^{(-\lambda t)}\right],$$

where t is time, λ is the error detection rate, and K is the total number of defects or total cumulative defect rate.

In 1984, Ohba proposed another S-shaped reliability growth model—the Inflection-S model (9). The model describes a software failure detection phenomenon with a mutual dependence of detected defects. Specifically, the more failures we detect, the more undetected failures become detectable. Also based on the nonhomogeneous Poisson process, the model's mean value function is

$$I(t) = K\,\frac{1 - \exp^{(-\lambda t)}}{1 + i\exp^{(-\lambda t)}},$$

where t is time, λ is the error detection rate, i is the inflection factor, and K is the total number of defects or total cumulative defect rate.

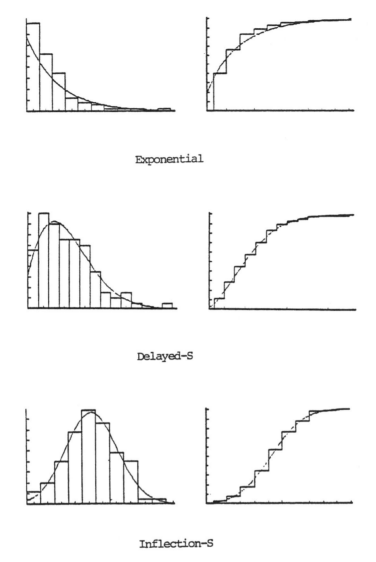

Exponential

Delayed-S

Inflection-S

FIGURE 5   Exponential, Delayed-S, and Inflection-S models.

The Delayed-S and Inflection-S models are similar to the G–O NHPP model except that they account for the learning period that testers go through as they become familiar with the software at the start of testing. The learning period is associated with the delayed or inflection patterns as described by the mean value functions. The mean value function (CDF) and the density function (PDF) curves of the two models, in comparison with the exponential model, are shown in Figure 5. The exponential model assumes that the peak of defect arrival is at the beginning of the test phase, and continues to decline thereafter; the Delayed-S model assumes a slightly delayed peak; and the Inflection-S model assumes a later and sharper peak.

The Delayed-S model and the Inflection-S model are used in software projects at IBM Japan as well as some Japanese software development companies. At IBM Rochester, we also implemented the two models via an IBM internal tool.

Most of the software reliability growth models emerged during the past 15–20 years. In addition to the ones described above, there are many others one can find in the literature, especially in *IEEE Transactions on Software Engineering*. Due to their differing assumptions and limitations, it is impossible to generalize that some models are superior to others. For a specific software project in a certain development environment, one model may be far better than others, whereas in another situation it may be worse. Goel (13) provided a good discussion on the assumptions and limitations of classes of software reliability growth models. The key assumptions for the two major classes, the times between failure models and the fault count models, are as follows:

- Times between failure models

  Independent times between failures.
  Equal probability of the exposure of each defect.
  Embedded defects are independent of each other.
  Defects are removed after each occurrence.
  No new error injection during correction, that is, the fixes are perfect.

- Fault count models

  Testing intervals are independent of each other.
  Testing during intervals is reasonably homogeneous.
  Number of defects detected during nonoverlapping intervals is independent of each other.

THE REMUS–ZILLES DEFECT REMOVAL EFFICIENCY MODEL

The models described thus far are all statistical models. Remus and Zilles derived mathematical formulas to predict the number of defects to be discovered after the product is shipped, based on the defect removal efficiency (or effectiveness) during the development process. The Remus–Zilles (R–Z) model is based on the development experiences at IBM Santa Teresa.

Assume there are two broad stages of defect detection activities:

- Those activities handled directly by the development organization (design reviews, code inspections, unit test)
- The formal machine tests handled by an independent test organization

Define:

MP = Major problems found during reviews/inspections and unit test (those handled by the implementing development group)
PTM = Errors found during formal machine test (after unit test)
μ = MP/PTM, $\mu > 1$ (Note: the higher the value of μ, the more efficiency is the front-end defect removal process)
Q = Number of errors projected for the released product

Further assuming that the defect removal efficiency is the same for reviews/inspections and formal machine test, then from a series of mathematical derivations, the following is obtained:

$$Q = \frac{PTM}{\mu - 1}$$

In other words, given the defect removal during the front end of the development process (reviews, inspections, and unit test) and the defects found (and fixed) during formal machine test prior to ship, one can estimate the number of latent defects to be shipped for the product. The above is the simplest form of the model. The model also covers a lot more, including the scenario when defect removal efficiency is different for each development step, the estimated number of defects existing at entry and at exit of a development step, the influence of bad fixes, total lifetime defects, cumulative defect removal efficiency of the development process, and defect retention. The R–M model is used by IBM Santa Teresa Development Laboratory. The predictive validity of the model, however, is yet to be verified.

SOFTWARE QUALITY MANAGEMENT MODELS

It is important to assess the quality of a software product when development work is complete. It is as important, if not more so, to monitor the quality during development. Software quality management models serve as the measuring tool. Such models must be able to provide early signs for warning or improvement so that timely improvement actions can be planned and implemented.

Any software quality management models must cover the early development phases in order to be useful. Models that are based on data collected at the end of the development process permit little time for actions, if needed. The reliability growth models, which are based on system-test data when development work is virtually complete, therefore, may not be as useful for in-process quality management as for reliability assessment. Nonetheless, the reliability growth models are useful for quality management in terms of tracking current status and determining when to end system testing for a specific, predetermined quality goal.

Unlike the reliability models which are numerous in count and with new ones emerging constantly, there are very few models for in-process quality management in the literature. In the following subsections, we describe those models we know about and use.

The Rayleigh Model

A Rayleigh model derived from a previous release or from historical data can be used to track the current pattern of defect removal of the current project under development. If the current pattern is more front-loaded than the model would predict, it is a positive sign, and vice versa. When sufficient data are available before development work is complete, parameters of the model can be reestimated, and projections of the final quality index can be made. For models based on defect removal rates of development steps (in our case, six steps), at least two data points are required for parameter estimation. Such early projections would not be reliable as compared to the final estimate at the end of the development cycle. Nonetheless, for in-process quality management, they can indicate the direction of the quality of the current release so that timely actions can be taken. For instance, if projections at the coding stage (12) indicate a poor final quality index, one feasible action is to increase focus on code inspection or code walk-through, allowing fewer defects to escape to the testing phases.

Perhaps the most famous axiom in software engineering is, "Do it right the first time." The axiom speaks to the importance of managing quality throughout the entire development process. Our interpretation of the axiom, in the context of software quality management, is threefold:

- The best scenario is to prevent error in the first place, therefore reducing the error injection in the process.
- When errors are introduced, improve the front end of the development process to remove them as much and as early as possible. Specifically, in the context of the waterfall development process, rigorous design reviews and code inspections are needed.
- If the project is beyond the design and code phases, unit test and any additional tests by the developers serve as the gatekeeper for defects that escaped the front-end process before the code is integrated into the system library. In other words, the phase of unit test or preformal test (the development phase prior to system integration) is the last chance for the do-it-right-the-first-time axiom. If high defect rates are found after integration (during formal machine testing phases), clearly the axiom is not achieved by the project.

The Rayleigh model is perfect in articulating the above points as they relate to quality management. Based on the model, more defect removal at the front end of the development process will lead to lower defect rate at the later formal machine testing phases and field defect rate. In addition, if the error injection rate is reduced, the entire area under the Rayleigh curve becomes smaller, leading to a smaller projected field defect rate. Both scenarios aim to lower the formal machine-testing defects, and hence the defects to be found by customers. The relationship between formal machine-testing defects and field defects as described by the model is congruent with the famous counterintuitive principle in software testing by Meyer (18), which basically states that the more defects found during formal testing, the more remained (to be found later). The reason for that is because at the late stage of formal testing, errors in the programs are already injected; the higher testing defects indicates that the error injection is higher, and, hence, if there is no significant improvement in testing, more defects will escape to the field.

Figure 6 and 7 illustrate the principles of early defect removal and lower error injection by the Rayleigh model, respectively. At IBM Rochester, the two principles are in fact the major directions for our improvement strategy in development quality. For each direction, actions are formulated and implemented. For instance, to facilitate early defect removal, actions implemented include focus on the design review/code inspection (DR/CI) process, deployment of moderator training (for review and inspection meeting), use of inspection checklist, use of in-process escape measurements to track the effectiveness of reviews and inspections, use of mini build to flush out defects by developers before the build of system library takes place, and many others. Plans and actions to reduce error injection include the laboratory-wide implementation of the defect prevention process, the use of powerful workstations and associated CASE tools for development, focus on communications among teams to prevent interface defects, and others. The bidirectional

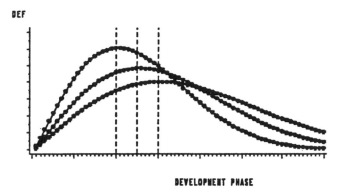

FIGURE 6   Rayleigh model—early defect removal.

quality improvement strategy is illustrated in Figure 8 by the Rayleigh model. In summary, the goal is to shift the peak of the Rayleigh curve to the left and at the same time lower it as much as possible.

The Phase-Based Defect Removal Model

The phase-based defect removal model (DRM) is based on the R–Z model discussed earlier. It is a discrete version of the Rayleigh model. Whereas the Rayleigh curve models only the pattern of defect removal, the DRM deals with both defect removal and error injection phase by phase. The DRM takes a set of error-injection rates by development phase and a set of inspection and testing-effectiveness rates as input, then models the defect removal pattern step by step. The defect injection and removal activities at each step (17) are described in Figure 9.

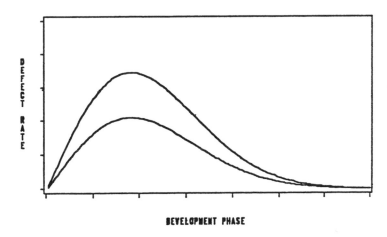

FIGURE 7   Rayleigh model—lower error injection.

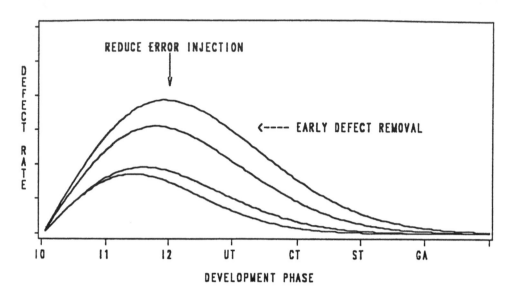

FIGURE 8   Rayleigh model—directions for development quality improvement.

The DRM takes a simplified view of Figure 9 and works like this:

Defects at the		defects escaped		defects		defects
exit of a	=	from previous	+	injected in	−	removed in
development step		step		current step		current step.

The error-injection rates and the inspection and testing effectiveness are usually based on estimates from the previous release or from historical data. If the total number of defects, or defect rate, of the system are known, the final quality index can be calculated based on the model output at the exit of the last development step. However, unlike the parametric models, the DRM cannot estimate the final quality index. It cannot do so because the total defect rate (or for that matter, the latent-defect rate when the system is shipped), the very target for estimation, is needed as input to the model. It is a tracking tool instead of a projection tool. The rationale behind this model is that if one can ensure that the defect removal pattern by step is similar to that for a previous experience, one might reasonably expect to see approximately the same quality.

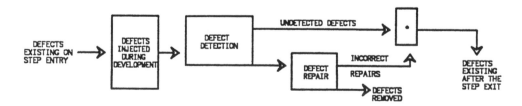

FIGURE 9   Defect injection and removal step.

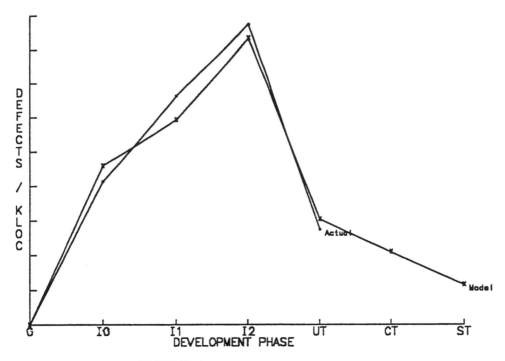

FIGURE 10   Discrete defect removal model.

The DRM is a useful management tool which can track current quality status during development (as shown in Fig. 10) and verify the final quality index that is estimated from independent methodologies such as the reliability growth models.

More importantly, the DRM can be used to evaluate the influence of inspection and testing effectiveness or error-injection rates on the final quality index. If we plan to improve the inspection effectiveness by 15% at the low-level design stage, how much can we expect to gain in system quality? If we invest in a defect prevention process and plan to reduce the error-injection rate at the coding stage by 5%, how much could we gain? Approximate answers to questions like these could be obtained through the DRM. Once the DRM is verified, one can vary the input (for instance, inspection effectiveness of a particular stage) and compute the final quality index again. Table 1 presents the percent improvement in the final quality index (QI) by improving inspection effectiveness for a software product.

TABLE 1   Percent Improvements in QI by Improvement in Inspection Effectiveness for a Product

| Inspection type | % Improv. in Insp. Effectiveness | | | |
	2%	5%	10%	15%
I0	0.0%	0.2%	0.4%	1.1%
I1	0.2%	1.1%	3.3%	4.3%
I2	1.1%	4.3%	9.8%	14.1%

Defect Rate

		Higher	Lower
	Higher	Not bad/ Good	Best Case
Inspection Effort			
	Lower	Worst Case	Unsure

In the case of two major defect removal steps in the development process, such as the scenario discussed earlier in the R–Z model (i.e., step 1: reviews/inspections/unit test; step 2: formal machine test), the R–Z model indicated that when μ is 3.5 or higher, the end-product quality will be at a desirable level (in terms of current industry standard). Note that μ is the ratio of defects removed in step 1 to defects removed in step 2. Based on experience from previous releases and the quality goal for the current release, the development team can set specific μ values as the in-process quality target.

One problem with the defect removal model is related to the assumption of the error-injection rate. Error-injection rates are estimated based on previous experience; however, one has no way of knowing how accurate they are when applied to the current release. When tracking the defect removal rates against the model, lower actual defect removal could be the result of lower error injection or poor reviews and inspections. On the other hand, higher actual defect removal could be the result of higher error injection or better reviews and inspections. At IBM Rochester, we use the review/inspection effort (hours spent on reviews/inspections per thousand lines of source code) to facilitate interpreting the defect removal model. Specifically, a matrix such as the following is used. The high–low comparisons are between actual data and the model, or between the current and previous releases of a product.

- High Effort/Low Defect Rate: an indication that design/code was cleaner before review, and yet the team spent enough effort in DR/CI (design review/code inspection)—therefore ensuring better quality.
- High Effort/High Defect Rate: an indication that error injection may be high, but higher DR/CI effort to remove the defects. If effort is significantly high, this situation may be a good scenario.
- Low Effort/Low Defect Rate: not sure whether the design and code were much cleaner, therefore less time in DR/CI was needed, or DR/CI was hastily done, hence finding less defects. In this scenario, we need to rely on the team's subjective assessment and other information for a better determination.
- Low Effort/High Defect Rate: an indication of high error injection, but DR/CI was not rigorous enough. Chances are that high defect rates will be observed at formal machine testing.

The Program Trouble Report Submodel

For the DRM (as well as for the Rayleigh model), when used for tracking quality status during development, we also use a submodel to track the Program Trouble Report (PTR) data during the machine-testing stages. The PTR is the vehicle for defect reporting and for integrating fix when the code is placed under a formal change-control process. Valid PTRs are, therefore, code defects found during machine testing. A PTR submodel is necessary because the period of formal machine testing (component test, component regression test, and system test) usually spans months, and one must ensure that the chronological pattern of defect removal is also on track. Simply put, the submodel spreads over time the number of defects that are expected to be removed during the machine-testing phases so that more precise tracking is possible. It is a function of three variables:

- Expected overall PTR rate (per thousand lines of code)
- Planned or actual lines of code integrated over time
- PTR-surfacing pattern after code is integrated

The expected overall PTR rate can be estimated from historical data. Lines-of-code integration over time is usually available in the current implementation plan. The PTR-surfacing pattern after code integration depends on both testing activities and the driver-build schedule. For instance, if a new driver is built every week, the PTR discovery/fix/integration cycle will be faster than that for biweekly or monthly drivers. Assuming similar testing efforts, if the driver-build schedule differs from the previous release, adjustment to the previous release pattern is needed. If the current release is the first release, it is more difficult to establish a base pattern. Once a base pattern is established, subsequent refinements are relatively easy. For the AS/400 system, the base pattern was estimated from System/38 data and refined several times during the development process. The pattern of the initial release of AS/400 involved a 7-month spread of PTRs after the code was integrated.

Figure 11 shows an example of the PTR submodel with actual data. The code integration changes over time during development, so the model is updated periodically. In addition to quality tracking, the model also serves as a powerful quality impact statement for any slip in code integration or testing schedule. Specifically, any delay in development and testing will skew the model to the right, and the intersection of the model line and the vertical line of the general-availability (GA) date will become higher.

The PTR Arrival/Backlog Projection Model

Near the end of the development cycle, a key question is whether the scheduled code-freeze date can be met without sacrificing quality. Will the PTR arrival and backlog decrease to the predetermined desirable levels by the code-freeze date? The PTR submodel discussed is not sufficiently precise and objective. It is a tracking tool, not a projection tool. On the other hand, the exponential model, or other reliability growth models based on system-test data, is sufficient but requires data points well into the system test. To fill this void, we developed the PTR arrival/backlog projection model based on the polynomial regression model. Specifically, a few weeks after the start of the system test (usually a couple of months before the planned code-freeze date), we modeled the PTR arrival and backlog trend based on polynomial terms of chronological time, time-lag variables, cumulative lines-of-code integrated, and other significant dichotomous variables.

This model is different from the exponential model in several aspects. First, the time frame covers all machine testing (all PTRs) after the code is integrated (component test, component regression test, and system test). The exponential model applies only to

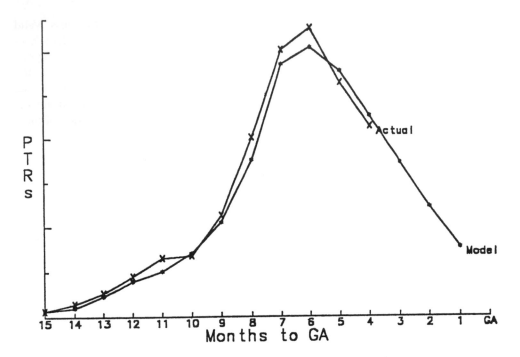

FIGURE 11   PTR submodel.

defect arrivals during the system test. Second, the data for this model are PTR arrivals and backlog, whereas the exponential model includes only valid PTRs (defects).

Figure 12 compares the PTR arrival projection model for AS/400, Release 1, with actual data points for the projection period. The model, with $R^2 = 95.6\%$, produces a projection that is accurate within a week in terms of when the PTR arrivals would decrease to the predetermined desirable level for code-freeze.

Unlike other models discussed, the PTR arrival/backlog projection model is really a modeling approach, rather than a specific model. Statistical expertise, modeling experience, and a thorough understanding of the data are necessary in order to deal with issues pertaining to model assumptions, variables specification, and final model selection. A desirable outcome often depends on the model's R-square and on the validity of the assumptions. Furthermore, it requires a fairly large number of data points and the data must pass the last inflection point of the process in order for the projections to be accurate.

Reliability Growth Models

Whereas reliability growth models are meant for reliability assessment, they are also useful for quality management at the back end of the development process. Models developed from a previous product or a previous release of the same product can be used to track the testing defects of the current product. To have significant improvement, defect arrival rate (or failure density) of the current project must fall below the model curve. Figure 13 shows an example from a product of the AS/400 system. Each data point rep-

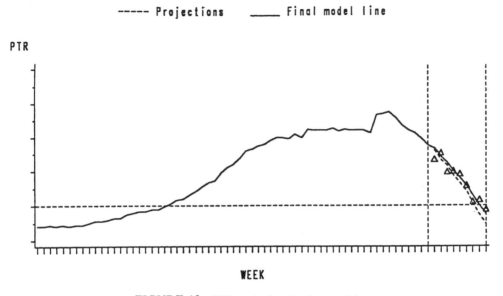

FIGURE 12   PTR arrival projection model.

resents a weekly defect arrival rate during the system-test phase. The defect-arrival patterns as denoted by the triangles and cycles represent two later releases of the same product. Compared to the baseline model curve, both new releases have witnessed significant reduction in defect rates during the system test.

When using the reliability growth models as a quality management tool, one of the advantages is that comparisons can be made when the first data points become available. If unfavorable signs are detected (for instance, defect arrivals are much higher than the model curve), timely actions can be formulated and implemented. On the other hand, for

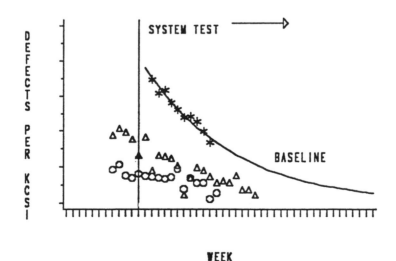

FIGURE 13   Reliability growth model for quality management.

reliability assessment and projection, a substantial amount of data has to be available for the models to be reliable. For models with an inflection point (such as the Delayed-S and Inflection-S models), there must be data available beyond the inflection point for the models to work. In a recent study by Ehrlich and associate (19), the exponential process model provides a reasonably adequate fit to the data with data of about 60% into the system test.

COMPLEXITY METRICS AND MODELS

Thus far, the reliability and quality management models we discussed are at either the project or the product level. Both categories of models tend to monitor the behavior of the product or project from an external view, without looking into the internal dynamics of design and code of the software. In this section, we describe the complexity metrics and models that articulate the relationship between design and programming and software quality. The unit of analysis is more granular, usually at the program module level. Such metrics and models tend to take an internal view and can provide clues for software engineers to improve quality in their work.

Whereas reliability models are developed and studied by researchers and software practitioners with sophisticated skills in mathematics and statistics, software complexity research is usually conducted by computer scientists. Like the reliability models, many complexity metrics and models have emerged in the recent past. In the following, several key metrics and models are described.

Lines of Code

The lines-of-code count is usually for executable statements. It is actually a count of instruction statements. The interchangeable use of the two terms apparently originated from assembler programs in which a line of code and an instruction statement are the same thing. As lines-of-code count represent the program size and complexity, it is not surprising that the more lines of code in a program, the more defects are expected. More intriguingly, researchers found that defect density (number of defects normalized to the lines of code) is also significantly related to the lines of code count. Early studies pointed to a negative relationship: The larger the module size, the smaller the defect rate. For instance, Basili and Perricone (20) examined FORTRAN modules mostly with fewer than 200 lines of code and found higher defect density in smaller modules. Shen and colleagues (21) studied software written in Pascal, PL/S, and assembly language, and they found an inverse relationship existed up to about 500 lines. Because larger modules are generally more complex, a lower defect rate is somewhat counterintuitive. Interpretation of this finding rests on the explanation of interface errors: Interface errors are more or less constant regardless of module size, and smaller modules are subject to higher error density because of a smaller denominator.

More recent studies point to a curvilinear relationship between lines of code and defect rate: Defect density decreases with size and then curves up again at the tail when the modules become very large. For instance, Withrow (22) studied modules written in Ada for a large project at Unisys and confirmed the concave relationship between defect density (during formal test and integration phases) and module size. Specifically, of a total of 362 modules with a wide range in size (from less than 63 lines to more than 1000), Withrow found the lowest defect density at the size category of about 250 lines.

Maximum Source Lines of Modules	Average Defect per Thousand Source Lines
63	1.5
100	1.4
158	0.9
251	0.5
398	1.1
630	1.9
1000	1.3
>1000	1.4

Explanation of the rising tail is readily available. When module size becomes very large, complexity increases to a level beyond a programmer's immediate span of control and total comprehension. This new finding is also consistent with previous studies in which the defect density of very large modules was not addressed.

Experience from the AS/400 development also lends support to the curvilinear model. Figure 14 shows an example. In the example, although the concave pattern is not as significant as that in Withrow's study, the rising tail is still evident.

The curvilinear model between size and defect density sheds new light in software quality engineering. It implies that there may be an optimal program size that can lead to the lowest defect rate. Such an optimum may depend on language, project, product, and environment, and apparently many more empirical investigations are needed. Nonetheless, when an empirical optimum is derived by reasonable methods (for example, based on the previous release of the same product, or based on similar product by the same development group), it can be used as a guideline for new module development.

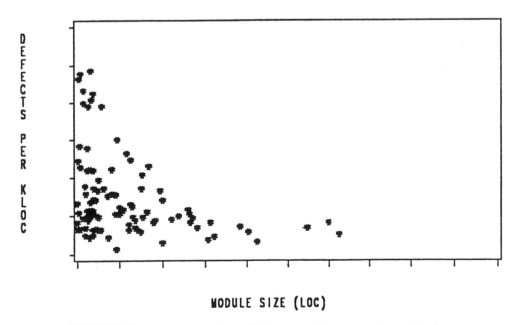

MODULE SIZE (LOC)

FIGURE 14   Curvilinear relationship between defect rate and module size.

Software Science

Halstead distinguished software science from computer science (23). The premise of software science is that any programming task consists of selecting and arranging a finite number of program "tokens," which are basic syntactic units distinguishable by a compiler. A computer program, according to software science, is considered as a collection of tokens that can be classified as either operators or operands. Based on the basic units of operators and operands, Halstead developed a system of equations predicting program size, effort, volume (number of bits required to store the program in memory), errors, and so on. The major equations include the following:

$$\text{Vocabulary } (n): \quad n = n_1 + n_2,$$
$$\text{Length } (N): \quad N = N_1 + N_2 = n_1 \log_2(n_1) + n_2 \log_2(n_2),$$
$$\text{Volume } (V): \quad V = N(\log 2)n,$$
$$\text{Level } (L): \quad L = V^*/V,$$
$$\text{Effort } (E): \quad E = V/L,$$
$$\text{Faults } (B): \quad B = V/S^*,$$

where

n_1 = number of unique operators
n_2 = number of unique operands
N_1 = total number of appearances of operators
N_2 = total number of appearances of operands
V^* = the minimum volume represented by a built-in function performing the task of the entire program
S^* = the mean number of mental discriminations (decisions) between errors (S^* is 3000 according to Halstead)

Halstead's work has made a great impact on software measurement. His work was instrumental in making metrics studies an issue among computer scientists. However, software science has become very controversial since its introduction and has been criticized from many fronts. Areas under criticism include methodology, derivations of equations, human memory models, and others. Empirical studies provided little support to the equations except for the estimation of program length. In terms of quality, the equation for B appears to be oversimplified for project management, lacks empirical support, and provides no help to software engineers.

Cyclomatic Complexity

The measurement of cyclomatic complexity by McCabe (24) was designed to indicate a program's testability and understandability (maintainability) by measuring the number of linearly independent paths through the program. To determine the paths, the program procedure is represented as a strongly connected graph with a unique entry and exit point. The general formula to compute cyclomatic complexity is

$$V(G) = e - n + 2p,$$

where $V(G)$ = cyclomatic number of G, e = number of edges, n = number of nodes, and, p = number of unconnected parts of the graph.

FIGURE 15   Simple control graph example.

As an example, Figure 15 is a control graph of a simple program that might contain two IF statements. If we count the edges, nodes, and disconnected parts of the graph, we see that $e = 8$, $n = 7$, and $p = 1$, and that $M = 8 - 7 + 2 \cdot 1 = 3$.

In order to have good testability and maintainability, McCabe recommended that no program module should exceed a cyclomatic complexity of 10. As the complexity metric is based on decisions and branches, which is consistent with the logic pattern of design and programming, it has a good appeal to software professionals. Since its inception, cyclomatic complexity has become an active area of research and practical applications. Many experts in software testing recommend use of the cyclomatic representation to ensure adequate test coverage, and the use of McCabe's complexity measure has been gaining acceptance by practitioners.

Because of its appeal to programmers and researchers, many studies have been conducted to relate McCabe's complexity measure to defect rate, and moderate to strong correlations were observed. Figure 16 shows an example from a component product of the AS/400 system. The component provides facilities for message control between users, programs, and the operating system. It has about 70 thousand lines of source code and consists of 72 program modules. The correlation coefficient between McCabe's complexity metric and defect level (number of defects during formal machine testing), .65, was statistically significant. The radiant shape of the scattergram indicated that modules with a high complexity index may or may not have high levels of defects. Perhaps the most impressive finding from Figure 16 is the blank area in the upper left-hand part of the scattergram, confirming the relationship between low defect level and programs with a low complexity index. As can be seen from the figure, there are many modules with a complexity index way beyond McCabe's recommended level of 10 (probably due to the complexity of the function the component performs).

In terms of its correlation with defect level, we must investigate one important issue: Is the effect of complexity index still significant after the source line-of-code count is taken into account? In other words, is defect level simply a function of program length, and the complexity measure just an indicator of program length? To answer this question, we did the following:

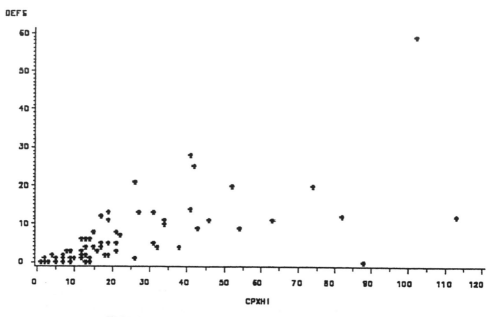

FIGURE 16   Cyclomatic complexity and defect level.

- Normalized the defect level by lines of code
- Included other relevant variables as control variables in the analysis: defect history, number of macro calls in the program, and number of changes of the program during development
- Performed a multiple regression analysis

Results of our analysis indicated that after the effects of the control variables were partialed out, the correlation between cyclomatic complexity and defect rate reduced, as one would expect. However, the correlation remained statistically significant. This finding has significant implications for software development practitioners: Complexity contributes to more defects regardless of lines of code and other variables. As the complexity index can be measured as soon as the code is ready, but the defect level will not be known until much later, one can use the complexity level as an intervenable variable to improve quality. For instance, set a specific level of McCabe's index as the upper limit for all program modules.

Structure Metrics

Lines of code, Halstead's software science, McCabe's cyclomatic complexity, and other metrics that measure module complexity implicitly assume that each program module is a separate entity. Structure metrics try to take into account the interactions between modules in a product or system and quantify such interactions. Many approaches in structure metrics have been proposed. Some good examples include invocation complexity by McClure (25), system partitioning measures by Belady and Evangelisti (26), information flow metrics by Henry and Kafura (27), and stability measures by Yau and Collofello (28). Many of these metrics and models, however, are yet to be verified by empirical data from software development projects.

Perhaps the most commonly used design structure metrics are the fan-in and fan-out metrics which are based on the ideas of coupling proposed by Yourdon and Constantine (29) and Meyers (30):

- Fan-in: a count of the number of modules that call a given module
- Fan-out: a count of the number of modules that are called by a give module

In general, modules with a large fan-in are relatively small and simple and are usually located at the lower layers in the design structure. On the other hand, modules that are large and complex are likely to have a small fan-in. Therefore, modules or components that have a large fan-in and a large fan-out may be indications of poor design. Such modules have probably not been decomposed correctly and are candidates for redesign. From the complexity and defect point of view, modules with a large fan-in are expected to have negative or insignificant correlation with defect levels, and modules with a large fan-out are expected to have a positive correlation. In the AS/400 experience, we found a positive correlation between fan-out and defect level, and no correlation between fan-in and defects. However, the standard deviations of fan-in and fan-out were quite large in our data. Therefore, our experience was inconclusive.

Henry and Kafura's structure complexity is defined as

$$C_p = (\text{fan-in} \times \text{fan-out})^2.$$

In an attempt to incorporate the module complexity and structure complexity, Henry's recent work (31) defined a hybrid form of their information-flow metric as

$$HC_p = C_{ip}(\text{fan-in} \times \text{fan-out})^2,$$

where C_{ip} is the internal complexity of procedure p, which can be measured by any module complexity metrics such as McCabe's cyclomatic complexity.

Based on various approaches to structure complexity and module complexity measures, Card and Glass (32) developed a system complexity model:

$$Ct = St + Dt,$$

where Ct = system complexity, St = structural (intermodule) complexity, and Dt = data (intramodule) complexity; relative system complexity is defined as

$$C = Ct/n,$$

where n is the number of modules in the system.

Structure complexity and data complexity are further defined as

$$S = \frac{\sum f^2(i)}{n},$$

where S = structural complexity, $f(i)$ = fan-out of module i, and n = number of modules in the system;

$$D(i) = \frac{V(i)}{f(i) + 1},$$

where $D(i)$ = data complexity of module i, $V(i)$ = I/O variables in module i, $f(i)$ = fan-out of module i;

$$D = \frac{\sum D(i)}{n},$$

where D = data (intramodule) complexity, $D(i)$ = data complexity of module i, n = number of new modules in the system.

Simply put, according to Card and Glass, system complexity is a sum of structural (intermodule) complexity and overall data (intramodule) complexity. Structural complexity is defined as the mean (per module) of squared values of fan-out. This definition is based on the findings in the literature that fan-in is not an important complexity indicator and that complexity increases as the square of connections between programs (fan-out). With regard to data (intramodule) complexity of a module, it is defined as a function which is directly dependent on the number of I/O variables and inversely dependent on the number of fan-out in the module. The rationale is that the more I/O variables in a module, the more functionality needs to be accomplished by the module; therefore, the higher internal complexity. On the other hand, more fan-out means that functionality is deferred to modules of lower levels; therefore, the internal complexity of a module is reduced. Finally, the overall data complexity is defined as the average of data complexity of all new modules. Only new modules enter into the formula because often the entire system consists of reused modules which have been designed, used, aged, and stabilized in terms of reliability and quality.

In Card and Glass's study of eight software projects, they found that the system complexity measure was significantly correlated with subjective quality assessment by a senior development manager and with development error rate. Specifically, the correlation between system complexity and development defect rate was 0.83, with complexity accounting for fully 69% of the variation in error rate. The regression formula is

Error rate $= -5.2 + 0.4$ (complexity).

In other words, each unit increase in system complexity increases the error rate by 0.4 (errors per thousand lines of code).

Card and Glass's model appears to be quite promising and has an appeal to software development practitioners. They also provided guidelines on achieving a low complexity design. When more validation studies become available, the Card and Glass's model and related methods may gain greater acceptance in the software development industry.

CRITERIA AND ISSUES OF SOFTWARE QUALITY ENGINEERING MODELING

As stated in the beginning of the article, the software reliability models are for assessing and predicting reliability of the software, the quality management models are for managing quality when the software is under development, and the complexity models are to provide principles and guidelines for software engineers in improving design and programming. As each type of model addresses a different aspect of software quality engineering, the criteria for evaluation also differ.

Criteria for Model Evaluation

For reliability models, a group of experts in 1984 (33) came up with a set of criteria for model assessment and comparison. The criteria are listed as follows by order of importance as determined by the group.

- Predictive validity: the capability of the model to predict future failure behavior or the number of defects for a specified time period from the present data on which the model is based.
- Capability: the ability of the model to estimate with satisfactory accuracy quantities needed by software managers, engineers, and users in planning and managing software development projects or controlling change in operational software systems.
- Quality of assumptions: the likelihood that the model assumptions can be met in reality, and the assumption's plausibility from the viewpoint of logical consistency and software engineering experience.
- Applicability: the model's degree of applicability across different software products (size, structure, functions, etc.).
- Simplicity: A model should be simple in three aspects: (1) simple and inexpensive to collect data, (2) simple in concept and does not require extensive mathematical background for software development practitioners to comprehend, and (3) readily implementable by computer programs.

From the software development practitioner's point of view and with recent observations of software reliability models, we contend that the most important criteria are predictive validity, simplicity, and quality of assumptions, in order of importance. Capability and applicability are less significant. As the state of the art is still maturing and striving to improve its most important purpose of predictive accuracy, extra criteria of demanding more functions (capability) for multiple environments (applicability) seems burdensome. Perhaps the accuracy of software reliability models can best be summarized as: Some models sometimes give good results, some are almost universally awful, and none can be trusted to be accurate at all time (34). A model with good predictive validity but poor capability and narrow applicability is certainly superior to one with good capability and wide applicability but very poor ability to predict.

On the other hand, simplicity should be much more important, second only to predictive validity. Experts in software reliability models are usually academicians who are well versed in mathematics and statistics. Many modeling concepts and terminologies are outside of the discipline of computer science, let alone to be comprehended and implemented by software developers in the industry. Simplicity is a key element in bridging the gap between the state of the art and the state of practice in software reliability modeling.

With regard to quality management models, we propose that timeliness of quality indications, scope of coverage of the development process, and capability be the major criteria for evaluation.

The earlier a model can detect signs of quality problems or improvements, the more time for proactive planning. Furthermore, corrections made in the early phases of the development process are much less expensive than those made at the back end. For instance, IBM Santa Teresa found that the cost of detecting and fixing a defect at design review phase, during machine test, and in the field shows a ratio of 1 : 20 : 82 (35).

Model coverage of all phases of the entire development process is important. To have a good quality end product, the quality of intermediate deliverables at each phase, as defined by the phase entry and exit criteria, is a prerequisite. Each development phase must be managed and appropriate quality actions implemented. In case a single model cannot perform the tasks adequately, the use of multiple models is recommended.

Although we contend that capability (other than predictability) is not an important criterion for software reliability models at the current state of the art, to the contrary, it is very important for management models. If capability refers to the model's ability to provide information for planning and managing software development project, that is the purpose of quality management models. For instance, given the current in-process defect injection and removal pattern, will the project be likely to achieve its quality goal? If the effectiveness of the design review process improves by certain points, what is the possible impact on end-product quality? Although quality management models may never reach the degree of accuracy and precision that reliability models have (or aim for), it is their capability to provide estimates for various in-process management questions that distinguish them as a separate category of software quality engineering models.

For complexity models, clearly explainability and applicability are the two major criteria. Explainability refers to the relationships among complexity, quality, and other programming and design parameters. Applicability refers to the degree to which the models and metrics can be applied by software engineers to improve their work in design, code, and test. As a secondary criteria to explainability, consistency between the model's measurements and the common reasoning pattern of software engineers also plays a significant role. As a case in point, McCabe's complexity metrics may appeal more to programming development professionals than Halstead's token-based software science. During design, code, and test, software engineers' line of reasoning is more in terms of decision points, branches, and paths, rather than the number of operators and operands.

Issues and Observations

Software engineering, especially software quality engineering, is a relatively new discipline. Of the three types of models we discussed, reliability models are more advanced than the other two, and quality management models are probably still in their infancy stage. It is safe to say that in spite of a good deal of progress, none of the three types of models has reached the mature stage. The need for improvement will surely intensify in the future as software is playing an increasingly critical role in the modern society. Large-scale software projects need to be developed in a much more effective way with much better quality.

Second, one can observe that the three types of models are developed and studied by different groups of professionals. Software reliability models are developed by reliability experts who were trained in mathematics, statistics, and operations research, and complexity models and metrics are studied by computer scientists. The differing originations explain why the former tends to take a black-box approach—monitoring and describing the behavior of the software from an external viewpoint—and the latter tends to take a white-box approach—looking into the internal relationships with regard to complexity. Quality management models, although still in their infancy stage, emerged from the practical needs of large-scale development projects and draw on principles and knowledge in the field of quality engineering (traditionally being practiced in manufacturing and production operations). For software quality engineering to become mature, an interdiscipline effort to combine and merge the various approaches is needed. A systematic body of knowledge in software quality engineering should encompass seamless linkages among the internal structure of design and programming, the external behavior of the software system, and the logistics and management of the development project.

From the standpoint of the software industry, perhaps the most urgent challenge is to bridge the gap between state of the art and state of practice. Better training in software engineering, in general, and modeling, in particular, needs to be incorporated into the curriculum for computer science. Some universities and colleges are taking the lead in this regard; however, much more needs to be done at a faster pace. On the other hand, this gap poses a challenge for academians in modeling research. Models, concepts, and an algorithm for implementation need to be communicated to the software development community (managers, software engineers, designers, testers, quality professionals) in their language, instead of sophisticated statistical formulas and notations.

For a software development organization to choose its models, the criteria discussed above can serve as a guideline. In addition, it is important to verify the models with historical data and establish empirical validity relative to the organization and its development process. Furthermore, a good practice is to use more than one model. For reliability assessment, cross-model reliability can be examined. In fact, recent research in reliability growth models indicated that combining the results of individual models may give more accurate predictions (36). For quality management, the multiple model approach can increase the likelihood of achieving the criteria of timeliness of indication, scope of coverage, and capability.

Finally, with regard to applying software quality engineering models in large-scale development environment, the largest obstacle is often data constraint. One basic premise for modeling is that the data quality is good. Moreover, usually the more sophisticated the model, more reliable and precise data is needed. Garbage in, garbage out: Without reliable data, the value added by modeling is limited. A broader issue of data reliability is the data tracking system for the development process. Clearly, the software development industry needs to invest resources in this area before the practice of modeling and quality engineering can take hold.

CONCLUSION

In this article we have briefly described and illustrated with examples the three types of models in software quality engineering: reliability models, quality management models, and complexity models. Criteria for model evaluation were proposed and some issues and observations as they relate to the deployment of these models in the software industry were discussed. Although the discipline of software engineering in general and software quality modeling in particular is still new, undoubtedly tremendous progress has been made in the recent past and continue at an accelerating pace.

Modeling is a systematic way to describe the complex reality in simpler terms. Because reality changes, the models must be reexamined and improved, in terms of both research and deployment. Through modeling, we gain understanding of the mechanics of how to engineer quality into the software development life cycle. Software quality models are playing an increasingly significant role in the effective development of large-scale high-quality software.

ACKNOWLEDGMENTS

Portions of this article are based on the article "Modeling and software development quality" in *IBM Systems Journal* Vol. 30, No. 3, 1991, by the author. Permission to republish was obtained from the *IBM Systems Journal*. Materials in this article will also appear in a book titled *Metrics and Models in Software Quality Engineering* by the author and will be published by the Addison-Wesley Publishing Company. I would like to thank David N. Amundson and Kathy A. Dunham of IBM Rochester for their support of the project.

REFERENCES

1. B. W. Boehm, *Software Engineering Economics*, Prentice-Hall, Englewood Cliffs, NJ, 1981.
2. L. H. Putnam, "A General Empirical Solution to the Macro Software Sizing and Estimating Problem," *IEEE Trans. Software Eng.*, *SE-4*, 345–361 (1978).
3. R. W. Jensen, "A Comparison of the Jensen and COCOMO Schedule and Cost Estimation Models," in *Proceedings of International Society of Parametric Analysis*, 1984, pp. 96–106.
4. P. A. Tobias and D. C. Trindade, *Applied Reliability*, Van Nostrand Reinhold, New York, 1986.
5. M. L. Ralston and R. I. Jennrich, "DUD, a Derivative-Free Algorithm for Nonlinear Least Squares," *Technometrics*, *20*, 7–14 (1978).
6. W. K. Wiener-Ehrlich, J. R. Hamrick, and V. F. Rupolo, "Modeling Software Behavior in Terms of a Formal Life Cycle Curve: Implications for Software Maintenance," *IEEE Trans. Software Eng.*, *SE-10*, 376–383 (1984).
7. A. L. Goel and L. Okumoto, "A Time-Dependent Error-Detection Rate Model for Software Reliability and Other Performance Measuures," *IEEE Trans. Reliability*, *R-28*, 206–211 (1979).
8. P. N. Misra, "Software Reliability Analysis," *IBM Syst. J.*, *22*, 262–270 (1983).
9. M. Ohba, "Software Reliability Analysis Models," *IBM J. Res. Develop.*, *28*, 428–443 (1984).
10. Z. Jelinski and P. Moranda. "Software Reliability Research," in *Statistical Computer Performance Evaluation*, W. Freiberger (ed.), Academic Press, New York, 1972, pp. 465–484.
11. B. Littlewood, "Stochastic Reliability-growth: A Model for Fault Removal in Computer-programs and Hardware-designs," *IEEE Trans. Reliability*, *R-30*, 313–320 (1981).
12. D. R. Miller, "Exponential Order Statistic Models of Software Reliability Growth," *IEEE Trans. Software Eng.*, *SE-12*, 12–24 (1986).
13. A. L. Goel, "Software Reliability Models: Assumptions, Limitations, and Applicability," *IEEE Trans. Software Eng.*, *SE-11*, 1411–1423 (1985).
14. J. D. Musa and K. Okumoto. "A Logarithmic Poisson Execution Time Model for Software Reliability Measurement," in *Proceedings Seventh International Conference on Software Engineering*, IEEE Computer Society Press, Los Alamitos, CA, 1985, pp. 230–238.
15. J. D. Muusa, A. Iannino, and K. Okumoto. *Software Reliability: Measurements, Prediction, Application*, McGraw-Hill, New York, 1987.
16. S. Yamada, M. Ohba, and S. Osaki, "S-Shaped Reliability Growth Modeling for Software Error Detection," *IEEE Trans. Reliability*, *R-32*, 475–478 (1983).
17. H. Remus and S. Zilles, "Prediction and Management of Program Quality," *Proceedings of the Fourth International Conference on Software Engineering*. Munich, 1979, pp. 341–350.
18. G. J. Myers, *The Art of Software Testing*, John Wiley & Sons, New York, 1979.
19. W. K. Ehrlich, S. K. Lee, and R. H. Molisani, "Applying Reliability Measurement: A Case Study," *IEEE Software*, 46–54 (March 1990).
20. V. R. Basili and B. T. Perricone, "Software Errors and Complexity: An Empirical Investigation." *Commun. ACM*, 42–52 (January 1984).
21. V. Y. Shen, T. J. Yu, S. M. Thebaut, and L. R. Paulsen, "Identifying Error-prone Software: An Empirical Study," *IEEE Trans. Software Eng.*, *SE-11*, 317–324 (1985).
22. C. Withrow, "Error Density and Size in Ada Software," *IEEE Software*, 26–30 (January 1990).

23. M. H. Halstead, *Elements of Software Science*, Elsevier/North-Holland, New York, 1977.
24. T. J. McCabe, "A Complexity Measure," *IEEE Trans. Software Eng.*, SE-2, 308–320 (1976).
25. C. L. McClure, "A Model for Program Complexity Analysis," *Proceedings IEEE Third International Conference on Software Engineering*, May 1978, pp. 149–157.
26. L. A. Belady and C. J. Evangelisti, "System Partittioning and Its Measure," *J. Systems Software*, 2, 23–39 (1981).
27. S. M. Henry and D. Kafura, "Software Structure Metrics Based on Information Flow," *IEEE Trans. Software Eng.*, SE-7, 510–518 (1981).
28. S. S. Yau and J. S. Collofello, "Some Stability Measures for Software Maintenance." *IEEE Trans. Software Eng.*, SE-6, 545–552 (1980).
29. E. Yourdon and L. L. Constantine, *Structured Design*, Prentice-Hall, Englewood Cliffs, NJ, 1979.
30. G. J. Myers, *Composite Structured Design*, Van Nostrand Reinhold, Wokingham, UK, 1978.
31. S. M. Henry and C. Selig, "Predicting Source-Code Complexity at the Design Stage," *IEEE Software*, 36–44 (March 1990).
32. D. N. Card and R. L. Glass, *Measuring Software Design Quality*, Prentice-Hall, Englewood Cliffs, NJ, 1990.
33. A. Iannino, J. D. Musa, K. Okumoto, and B. Littlewood, "Criteria for Software Reliability Model Comparisons," *IEEE Trans. Software Eng.*, SE-10, 687–691 (1984).
34. S. Brocklehurst and B. Littlewood, "New Ways to Get Accurate Reliability Measurements," *IEEE Software*, 34–42 (July 1992).
35. H. Remus, "Integrated Software Validation in the View of Inspection/Review," *Proceedings of the Symposium on Software Validation, Darmstadt, Germany*", North-Holland, Amsterdam, 1983.
36. M. R. Lyu and A. Nikora, "Applying Reliability Models More Effectively," *IEEE Software*, 43–52 (July 1992).

TRADEMARKS

The following trademarks appear in this article:

- Application System/400, trademark of International Business Machines Corporation
- AS/400, trademark of International Business Machines Corporation
- SAS, trademark of SAS Institute, Inc.

BIBLIOGRAPHY

Albrecht, A. J., and J. E. Gaffney, "Software Function, Source Lines of Code, and Development Effort Prediction: A Software Science Validation," *IEEE Trans. Software Eng.*, SE-9, 639–647 (1983).

Agresti, W. W., and W. M. Evanco, "Projecting Software Defects from Analyzing Ada Designs," *IEEE Trans. Software Eng.*, SE-18, 988–997 (1992).

Baker, A. L., and S. H. Zweben, "A Comparison of Measures of Control Flow Complexity," *IEEE Trans. Software Eng.*, SE-6, 506–512 (1980).

Basili, V. R. (ed.), *Tutorial on Models and Metrics for Software Management and Engineering*, IEEE Computer Society Press, Los Alamitos, CA, 1980.

Basili, V. R., R. W. Selby, and T. Y. Phillips, "Metric Analysis and Data Validation Across FORTRAN Projects," *IEEE Trans. Software Eng.*, SE-9, 652–663 (1983).

Brocklehurst, S., P. Y. Chan, B. Littlewood, and J. Snell, "Recalibrating Software Reliability Models," *IEEE Trans. Software Eng.*, SE-16, 458–470 (1990).

Burrill, C. W., and L. W. Ellsworth, *Quality Data Processing: The Profit Potential for the 80s*, Burrill-Ellsworth Associates, Inc., Tenafly, NJ, 1982.

Cai, K. Y., C. Y. Wen, and M. L. Zhang, "A Critical Review on Software Reliability Modeling," *Reliability Eng. System Safety*, 32, 357–371 (1991).

Chillarege, R., I. Bhandari, J. Chaar, M. Halliday, D. Moebus, B. Ray, and M.-Y. Wong, "Orthogonal Defect Classification—A Concept for In-Process Measurements," *IEEE Trans. Software Eng.*, SE-18, 943–956 (1992).

Christensen, K., G. P. Fitsos, and C. P. Smith, "A Perspective on Software Science," *IBM Syst. J.*, 4, 372–387 (1981).

Conte, S. D., H. E. Dunsmore, and V. Y. Shen, *Software Engineering Metrics and Models*, The Benjamin/Cummings Publishing Company, Menlo Park, CA, 1986.

Coulter, N. S., "Software Science and Cognitive Psychology," *IEEE Trans. Software Eng.*,, SE-9, 166–171 (1983).

Curtis, B., S. B. Sheppard, P. Milliman, M. A. Borst, and T. Love, "Measuring the Psychological Complexity of Software Maintenance Tasks with the Halstead and McCabe Metrics," *IEEE Trans. Software Eng.*, SE-5, 96–104 (1979).

Davis, J. S., and R. J. LeBlanc, "A Study of the Applicability of Complexity Measures," *IEEE Trans. Software Eng.*, SE-14, 1366–1371 (1988).

Deutsch, M. S., and R. R. Willis, *Software Quality Engineering: A Total Technical and Management Approach*, Prentice-Hall, Englewood Cliffs, NJ, 1988.

Dunn, R. H., *Software Defect Removal*, McGraw-Hill, New York, 1984.

Ebert, C., "Visualization Techniques for Analyzing and Evaluating Software Measures," *IEEE Trans. Software Eng.*, SE-18, 1029–1034 (1992).

Endes, A., "An Analysis of Errors and Their Causes in Systems Programs," *IEEE Trans. Software Eng.*, SE-7, 140–149 (1975).

Felician, L., and G. Zalateu, "Validating Halstead's Theory for Pascal Programs," *IEEE Trans. Software Eng.*, SE-15, 1630–1632 (1989).

Freiberger, W. (ed.), *Statistical Computer Performance Evaluation*, Academic Press, New York, 1972.

Gaffney, J. E., "Estimating the Number of Faults in Code," *IEEE Trans. Software Eng.*, SE-10, 459–464 (1984).

Gill, G. K., and C. F. Kemerer, "Cyclomatic Complexity Density and Software Maintenance Productivity," *IEEE Trans. Software Eng.*, SE-17, 1284–1288 (1991).

Grady, R. B., and D. L. Caswell, *Software Metrics: Establishing a Company-Wide Program*, Prentice-Hall, Englewood Cliffs, NJ, 1987.

Hall, N. R., and S. Preiser, "Combined Network Complexity Measures," *IBM J. Res. Develop.*, 28, 309–315 (1984).

Hamlet, D., "Are We Testing for True Reliability?" *IEEE Software*, 21–27 (July 1992).

Harrison, W., "An Entropy-Based Measure of Software Complexity," *IEEE Trans. Software Eng.*, SE-18, 1025–1028 (1992).

Humphrey, W. S., *Managing The Software Process*, Addison-Wesley, Reading, MA, 1989.

Ishikawa K., *Guide to Quality Control*, Asian Productivity Organization, Tokyo, 1982.

Jewell, W. S., "Bayesian Extensions to a Basic Model of Software Reliability," *IEEE Trans. Software Eng.*, SE-11 (1985).

Jones, C., *Programming Productivity*, McGraw-Hill, New York, 1986.

Jones, C., *Applied Software Measurement: Assuring Productivity and Quality*, McGraw-Hill, New York, 1991.

Jones, C., "Critical Problems in Software Measurement," Software Productivity Research (SPR), Inc., Burlington, MA, 1992.

Khoshgoftaar, T. M., J. C. Munson, B. B. Bhattacharya, and G. D. Richardson, "Predictive Modeling Techniques of Software Quality from Software Measures," *IEEE Trans. Software Eng.*, SE-18, 979–987 (1992).

Levendel, Y., "Reliability Analysis of Large Software Systems: Defect Data Modeling," *IEEE Trans. Software Eng.*, *SE-16*, 141–152 (1990).

Lipow, M., "Prediction of Software Failures," *J. Systems Software*, 71–75 (1979).

Lipow, M., "Number of Faults per Line of Code," *IEEE Trans. Software Eng.*, *SE-8*, 437–439 (1982).

Littlewood, B., "How to Measure Software Reliability and How Not to," *IEEE Trans. Reliability*, *R-28*, 103–110 (1979).

Littlewood, B., and L. Strigini, "The Risks of Software," *Scientific American*, 62–75 (November 1992).

Mourad, S., and D. Andrews, "On the Reliability of the IBM MVS/XA Operating System," *IEEE Trans. Software Eng.*, *SE-13*, 1135–1139 (1987).

Musa, J. D., A. Iannino, and K. Okumoto, *Software Reliability: Measurement, Prediction, Application*, (Professional Edition), McGraw-Hill, New York, 1990.

Pressman, R. S., *Software Engineering: A Practitioner's Approach*, 2nd ed., McGraw-Hill, New York, 1987.

Putnam, L. H. (ed.), *Software Cost Estimating and Life-Cycle Control: Getting the Software Numbers*, IEEE Computer Society, Los Alamitos, CA, 1980.

Ramamoorthy, C. V., and F. B. Bastani, "Software Reliability: Status and Perspective," *IEEE Trans. Software Eng.*, *SE-8*, 354–371 (1982).

Rombach, H. D., "Design Measurement: Some Lessons Learned," *IEEE Software*, 17–25 (March 1990).

Schneidewind, N. F., and H. Hoffmann, "An Experiment in Software Error Data Collection and Analysis," *IEEE Trans. Software Eng.*, *SE-5*, 276–286 (1979).

Schneidewind, N. F., and T. W. Keller, "Applying Reliability Models to the Space Shuttle," *IEEE Software*, 28–33 (July 1992).

Sheldon, F. T., K. M. Kavi, R. C. Tausworthe, J. T. Yu, R. Brettschneider, and W. W. Everett, "Reliability Measurement: From Theory to Practice," *IEEE Software*, 13–20 (July 1992).

Shen, V. Y., S. D. Conte, and H. E. Dunsmore, "Software Science Revisited: A Critical Analysis of the Theory and Its Empirical Support," *IEEE Trans. Software Eng.*, *SE-9*, 155–165 (1983).

Shooman, M. L., *Software Engineering: Design, Reliability and Management*, McGraw-Hill, New York, 1983.

Shooman, M. L., "Software Reliability: A Historical Perspective," *IEEE Trans. Reliability*, *R-33*, 48–55 (1984).

Smith, C. P., "A Software Science Analysis of Programming Size," *Proceedings of the ACM National Computer Conference*, October 1980, pp. 179–185.

Smith, D. J., and K. B. Wood, *Engineering Quality Software: A Review of Current Practices, Standards and Guidelines including New Methods and Development Tools*, 2nd ed., Elsevier Applied Science, New York, 1989.

Trachtenberg, M., "The Linear Software Reliability Model and Uniform Testing," *IEEE Trans. Reliability*, *R-34*, 8–16 (1985).

Yamada, S., H. Ohtera, and H. Narihisa, "Software Reliability Growth Models with Testing Effort," *IEEE Trans. Reliability*, *R-35*, 19–23 (1986).

Yu, T.-J., V. Y. Shen, and H. E. Dunsmore, "An Analysis of Several Software Defect Models," *IEEE Trans. Software Eng.*, *SE-14*, 1261–1270 (1988).

STEPHEN H. KAN

STRATEGIC INFORMATION SYSTEMS PLANNING

Competition forces organizations, both large and small, to develop strategies to defend their market position. Corporate Strategy provides the ability to compete against your rivals, often times under advantageous conditions. In the business environment of today, the adopted strategy must deal with competition on a global scale never seen before. Information technology is changing the way we conduct business. Consequently, Information Technology is becoming a prominent aspect in the formulation of corporate strategy. Proper application of technology can positively alter the competitiveness of a organization.

Strategic Information Systems Planning (SISP) is a process crucial to developing and sustaining competitive advantage. The primary objective of SISP is to maximize competitiveness through the use of information processing technology.

Technology has never before played such an important part in business and in our everyday lives. Virtually all aspects of our day-to-day activities are influenced by some form of technology. The ability to rapidly change and refocus our businesses to better address our clients' needs is crucial in the competitive marketplace of today. This ability often is attributed to use of the proper hardware and software. New data-input devices, new architecture that supports enterprise-wide databases, customer information systems, and executive information systems allow businesses to quickly respond to management's and their customer's information needs.

Supporting technologies plays an important role in achieving our information goals and objectives. Identifying emerging technologies in time to plan and prepare for their implementation is a key aspect of a successful information systems plan. Technological progress is very dynamic and must be monitored continuously. Imaging, artificial intelligence, CASE, data visualization, and alternative input devices are all areas which can and will play an important part in information systems that support tomorrow's businesses.

The remainder of the article will explain the importance of managing information technology for competitive advantage. In addition, a framework for developing a Strategic Information Systems Plan will be presented. This frame work is an excellent foundation on which to build your customized methodology for SISP.

Strategic Information Systems Planning is the marriage between business and technology. SISP should not be confused with Strategic Technology Management. Strategic Technology Management deals with the introduction of new or emerging technology into the product line specifically, such as the use of micro controllers in the design of consumer appliances. SISP is the use of information technology to support and improve business processes, operations, and decision making, Often, technology is an answer in search of a problem. However, all to often, technology is used just for the sake of using new technology. Inversely, businesses have traditionally thought of information technology as a necessary evil. They have not recognized the advantages when properly applied information technology can provide almost any business. SISP approaches technology as a means of supporting business processes or operations. SISP ensures that all data necessary to support the business goals and objectives are collected and processed and that management and the workers have all the information necessary to efficiently perform their duties. The collection, processing, and distribution of data allows the business to accurately measure, forecast the market, serve customers, and identify business changes.

Technology, when properly applied to support business, can achieve significant improvements in almost every area. The use of bar-coding devices and scanners can improve warehouse operations. The collection of sales data can allow the sales department to more accurately forecast sales and inventory requirements. Improved data collection and processing can allow information to be presented to management in a more timely and meaningful fashion. All these characteristics serve to make the business processes and overall operation more effective, efficient, and profitable.

The improvement of business performance is not the only reason for implementation of information technology. Information Technology, specifically new or recently introduced information technology, has been used to portray the organization as visionary or as being a progressive company. This serves to improve the overall image of the company. This has numerous benefits such as making the company more attractive for top performers from the ever-shrinking human resource pool. In addition, companies have improved their image by becoming more environmentally conscious. The implementation of well-designed information systems coupled with redesigned business processes can reduce the use of paper documents. Another example of environmental impact of information technology is reduced hazardous waste through improved data collection and control of industrial processes. All these examples serve to improve the image of the company which can have a positive impact on performance.

Strategic Information Systems Planning provides a mechanism by which to identify and plan for the introduction of information technology into the business operation. Businesses are quick to recognize the importance of strategic planning as it relates to business direction but have been slow to address the significant importance of information and information systems to support and assist them in achieving their strategic goals and objectives. By early identification of information technology that supports the vision of the company, planning, technical, managerial, and financial, can be conducted to lessen the repercussions felt throughout the organization.

Change is always difficult. For this reason, management must assess the impact radical change has to business processes and their information systems. The changes brought about by the redesign of their processes and systems will not only effect personnel but customers and stockholders as well. Early identification of the critical implications of change allows the company to become proactive rather than reactive. Plans can be developed to promote a shift in corporate culture, beliefs, and behavior that would impede the implementation of the new processes and systems but may effect the overall success of the redesigned business processes and supporting systems in meeting the stretch goals and objectives of the business.

ASSESSMENT

The purpose of the assessment is to build the foundation on which the strategic information systems plan will be developed. Current evaluation of where the organization is determines the baseline from which the future direction of the organization will be charted. The assessment is a dual-focus activity. This means both the business and information technology side is concurrently addressed.

The assessment of the current state of business deals with identification of the key processes and the commonality that bonds these processes together. Key executives take part in the assessment of the functional operation currently in place. Identification of important business architectural characteristics early in the assessment process tends to feed the process redesign that takes place in the reengineering phase of the SISP. Some basic characteristics of the business architecture includes specification of geographic locations, definition of roles, and responsibilities. This allows the business to establish a future direction and to refine and enhance this vision later in the process.

In recent years, MIS has been continuously challenged. Substantial changes in technology and the way we conduct business has required MIS to adapt more quickly than ever before. A comprehensive effectiveness review can benefit in a number of different ways.

Improvement in short-term decision making
Identification of new applications
Prioritization of system development projects
Improved resource allocation
Identification of operational cost-savings
Improvement in communications with the users

There are six phases in the evaluation of the effectiveness of MIS. They are as follows: organization of the review process and procedures, evaluation of MIS organization and its management, hardware and software and system configuration analysis, application effectiveness, work-flow analysis, and, finally, the analysis of data at an enterprise level. These areas serve to contribute to the overall efficiency with which MIS operates. While this analysis is being conducted, information pertaining to MIS services that may play an important role in the future is gathered. Technologies such as Electronic Data Interchange (EDI) or Electronic Funds Transfer (EFT) may be able to contribute to the companies ability to satisfy their clients.

The next activity that needs to be completed is the definition of the current marketplace direction. This identifies meaningful trends which may influence the way that business is conducted. Another key consideration that must be investigated is the direction of your customer base. Analyze how and why the current profile of the customer is changing. Detailing the current state of the business, market/customer base, and supporting information technology is the next step in this sequence of events. Additionally, the development of various models which represents the existing business, market and technology infrastructure of the organization is necessary to illustrate the current methods of operation and to validate the conceptual redesign of the business and information systems. In this assessment, current performance measures and results measures (often referred to as P & R measures) are documented for business processes. The review of information system effectiveness is required to gauge the level of service currently being provided as well as to identify areas where change is required.

Now that you have validated your beliefs about the current state, you must detail the future state of the business, market/customer base, and supporting information technology. Additionally, as in the previous step, you need to develop a model which represents the future business, market, and technology infrastructure of the organization.

Market statistics, studies, and trends are available from a number of sources. Caution must be exercised when taking this information at face value. Often, when these studies are conducted by organizations within the market or who have an interest in a rosy outlook for the market, the information is quite misleading. In this future vision, the way in which we will monitor the operation must be defined. Which indicators will be meaningful in the marketplace of tomorrow? New performance measures and result measures must be defined to reinforce the direction and objectives of the organization. These measures, if incorrect, will cause difficulty in reaching the organizational goals. The difficulties can manifest themselves in poor control, human resource issues like low job satisfaction, and the ability of the organization to identify areas for improvement as time goes on.

REENGINEERING

Business change starts with a common vision that is shared throughout the organization. This vision paints a picture of where the organization is headed and what the organization will become. The development of a strategic vision requires insight, intuition, creativity and out-of-box thinking. Additionally, the current view of overall operations developed during the assessment phase of the SISP is the base from which the strategic vision is developed. Business processes must be analyzed and adapted to meet goals set for future operations of the organization. The redesign of processes addresses those changes and modifications for both the business processes and supporting information systems.

Improvement of the existing business processes which use information technology is one of the goals of Strategic Information Systems Planning. To accomplish this, one needs to identify bottlenecks and inefficiencies that require attention. Once these areas are identified, new innovative processes based on the future vision of the market/ customer base and organization can be developed. These new processes are what may determine how competitive the organization will be in the future marketplace. Redesign of the business processes is not the only focus of the reengineering effort. Changes in job definitions, organizational structure, controls, values, beliefs and culture, and the management style and philosophy must also be evaluated. These areas must be modified to match the future vision of the organization.

The next area we must address is to identify stretch goals and objectives for the future organization. These stretch goals and objectives should focus on the business enterprise, with emphasis placed on financial benefit. Additionally, the goals need to be challenging to the organization as a whole, while being viewed as attainable by the individuals throughout the organization. The establishment of these goals will influence the performance and results measures that are set to monitor and control the business operation in the future.

The next consideration is business globalization. The world is becoming one marketplace. The next generation of business leaders will be challenged by the unique characteristics of the global market. Business globalization entails the identification of processes, functionality, and systems that will allow the organization to conduct business efficiently throughout the world. Communications, both voice and image/data, is an important part of the globalization effort. However, supporting the organization's ability to operate at a scale not seen before requires much more. Special processes that deal with restriction on trade with other countries must be identified, planned, and implemented.

These processes not only deal with the export of goods and services out of the host country but the import of these items into the receiving country.

Strict controls are necessary on items controlled by the Expert Administration Regulations because of the substantial penalties that can be imposed for noncompliance. Other considerations around mechanisms that will be used for information gathering and control must be considered and evaluated prior to completing the reengineering effort.

Now that we have painted a picture of what the organization will become, we must turn our attention to the information technology that supports us in our endeavors. Technology should not be the driving force behind the reengineering project. Business processes are the focus of a reengineering effort. Technology provides the support necessary to efficiency accomplish the execution of business processes.

Often the use of technology stimulates the design of the reengineered business processes. Identification of technologies that improve our ability to perform or better serve our customers must be leveraged in an effort to gain advantage in the marketplace. Information technology plays an important part in gaining sustainable competitive advantage. The identification of new or emerging technology that supports our new vision is the most interesting portion of the SISP. This can be accomplished by developing relationships with leaders in emerging technologies. These relationships should be established to improve the collection of accurate and timely information. The relationships are not something that you develop just while your are conducting the SISP. Rather, they are cultivated over time and reinforced by the sharing of information between both the technology vendor and the organization.

In order to support this effort, the organization must have the appropriate infrastructure in place. The infrastructure is probably the single most important factor that determines the success or failure of information systems within an organization. For this reason, careful review and evaluation of reporting structure, personnel, and budgets is imperative.

STRATEGY

The formulation of a strategy defines the path the organization will take to obtain its goals. Strategy involves forecasting technological change and preparing the organization to take full advantage of these changes. The early introduction of new technologies assists the organization in obtaining its desired position in the marketplace. Just as there are business drivers, there are fundamental technology drivers. These drivers must be identified and monitored in an ongoing fashion.

A well-formulated strategy provides opportunities to favorably affect the future course and direction of the organization. The strategy must be broad based and flexible to adapt to the ever-changing business world. Additionally, a methodology for the ongoing analysis and evaluation of emerging technologies that may impact the organization must be developed.

Defining the importance of new and emerging technologies to the organization in a way that supports the new direction and the way business is conducted is a key component in the SISP. Determine the benefit and importance of these technologies in achieving the organizational goals. Develop a short list of technologies that are new or emerging that may provide significant advantage in the short term to mid-term (3–5 years). Finally, identify technologies that may come to market in the mid-term as well as the next 5–7 years. Long-range planning for information systems does not produce significant benefits. The rapid advancement of technology that we have seen over the past 20 years has made it next to impossible to plan that far in advance.

Most organizations have not been successful at recognizing and implementing valuable new technologies. One approach is to organize a Technology Task Force (TTF). The TTF diagnoses the current technology monitoring, identifies meaningful research and developments efforts, and monitors the evolution of technologies out of R & D to mainstream business utilization.

Once the mechanism for monitoring the progress on new technologies is implemented, identification of promising technologies can take place. In order for the organization to keep in front of the power curve, organizations must be aggressive in their pursuit of new technologies. Identification of research and development that may yield significant breakthroughs requires relationships with leading research institutions and organizations.

No strategy is complete without addressing all points of the diamond. Business processes, values, beliefs and culture, reskilling, human resources, and information systems are all factored into the formulation of a strategy. One must consider the effects of the reengineering process on the existing organization. Reengineering by definition promotes radical change to the way business is currently conducted. The success of the reengineering implementation is very much dependent on the preplanning and execution of the methods used to promote the acceptance of the new processes within the organization.

UNIFICATION

The purpose of unification is to identify information processing technology that favorably affects the future course of action in terms of management information systems. This activity requires both business content experts and skilled information systems practitioners to maximize the benefits that can be achieved.

The unification is the merger of the Strategic Business Plan and the Strategic Information Systems Plan. The identification of a clear business direction and a vision of where the company will be in the future becomes the focal point of the process. In the Strategic Business Plan, the company has identified what business it wants to be in, the image the company wants to have, the products and/or services the company wants to provide, and corporate objectives and goals. These goals and objectives and the overall vision serve as the foundation on which the Strategic Information Systems Plan is developed. Each product/service, stretch goal, and objective is reviewed and information systems implications are identified.

The direction of information technology is charted and emerging technologies that may positively influence the overall goals and objectives of the company are listed. Key questions such as, ''How should the corporate information infrastructure change to support the strategic direction of the company?'' are asked. Through the resolutions of issues such as this, a high-level strategic information direction is formulated. Based on this direction, technologies which may or may not be to market at this point are reviewed and their importance determined as to their support of the new vision. A technological model is defined that identifies general information technology capabilities and relates to the functional areas within the corporation.

The development of a high-level business information model is suggested. This model provides an overview of ways in which information and data can be collected, created, processed, analyzed, and used within the business. This model may be broken down into current state and end state vision of business information. Many times, due to an incremental development approach, several intermediate state snapshots are developed. These intermediate snapshots serve as an objective for each phase of the improvement process.

Specific technical capabilities are defined and related to individual business processes. The completed view of information technology tied to the business processes serve to form a technology architecture. This architecture diagram identifies the business functions, the processes involved in each function, and the systems and technology that support each function and process. Once the proper selection of the supporting technology has taken place, priorities are assigned to each of the process/system improvements.

The prioritization is based on impact not only in financial gains but other focal areas such as customer satisfaction. Those areas that are most critical to the overall business success receive the most attention and are scheduled for the earliest development and implementation.

Technological change is difficult and often causes concern of those individuals who are affected by this change. A plan to educate the organization on new technologies is a critical success factor in positively effecting change. Technology workshops must be conducted in an effort to enlighten individuals and to improve the social significance of information technology.

Once the awareness of technology has been brought to the appropriate level, it is important for the organization to be able to identify risk and potential benefits. For this reason, analysis of cost and risk must be conducted. Detailed comparison of current operations and estimation of the potential gains of the new systems if they were to be implemented must be calculated:

Business and market dynamics
Technological advances
Corporate culture
Organizational structure
Management style

PLANNING

The planning of information system design and development is as critical as any other activity in the SISP process. This phase is designed to layout at a high level how the strategic systems which were identified in previous phases of the SISP will be implemented. The recommendation is to use an incremental approach. This approach leverages small manageable segments that can be implemented in a short period of time. The limited scope of this segmentation serves not only to reduce risk but also the small successes foster an atmosphere of achievement. The planning process must include financial planning, managerial and socio-technological planning, and human resource planning.

Develop a financial plan that will support implementation of the various segments of the project. Often, this is referred to as building the business case. Detail the cost for

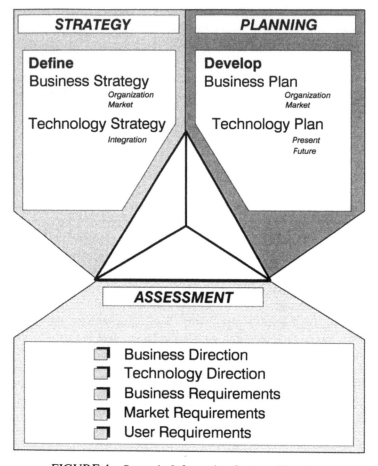

FIGURE 1   Strategic Information Systems Planning.

design, development, implementation, and support. Calculate the benefit that the organization will receive through the use of the new system and process. This calculation must include tangible and intangible benefits. Keep in mind that in strategic positioning, quick payback may not be the motivation behind the redesign.

Define the plan to implement the changes to the organization that are necessary to support the redesigns and new systems. Define a change management program that will minimize the implications of these changes. Define a communication facility to ensure timely and accurate transfer of information about the changes that will take place. Identify critical timing issues around the announcement of changes.

The implementation of new information systems, particularly those which refocus the organization or change the direction of the organization, causes a feeling of discomfort throughout the organization. Change, although inevitable, is not received well. This is a normal response. Activities must be designed that promote a shift from the old methods to the new.

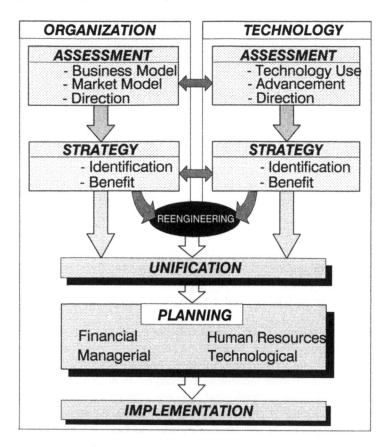

FIGURE 2 Strategic Information Systems Planning: process.

IMPLEMENTATION

This phase of the SISP deals with putting the plan into action. The project or projects are selected, staff assembled, and preparations for life cycle development and support are put in place. A development methodology should be selected or, if one exists, reviewed, and training for developers should be evaluated. Additional information regarding the overall architecture of the project as well as the hardware, networking, and software support standards are formulated and communicated. Operating principals and procedures are formulated, documented, and disseminated throughout the entire project team.

The first activity that must be done in this phase is the clear and concise definition of scope. With this clarification, operating principles and procedures can then be defined. At this point, a detailed workplan is developed, and time and resource estimates are fine-tuned.

A methodology is required to support the management of a systems development project. There are three parts to this process. They are Planning, Execution, and Control. The selection of the methodology should be based on specific needs of the organization. Influencing factors, such as human resources, budget, and systems development experience, must be weighed prior to selecting a methodology. In addition, advances in methodologies must be evaluated to determine benefit/risk. Rapid Application Development is quickly becoming one of the most popular flavors of methodologies. This is due to the shorter turn-around time in the field that other more traditional methods.

CONCLUSION

SISP is a process critical to the development of competitive advantage and long-term success. The dynamic business environment mandates modification and tuning of our business strategy, organization, and use of technology. Advances in science and technology, particularly in the area of information processing, have become a competitive weapon. Proper application of this technology provides cost reduction, improvements in quality, and increased productivity.

In this era of accelerated technological change, it becomes vital for businesses and organizations to monitor and evaluate technology on a continuing basis. SISP provides a vehicle for identifying areas for change. Additionally, it allows organizations to develop or acquire systems or technology that permits the organization to adapt to the marketplace dynamics.

The ability of businesses and organizations to compete depends on how well management prepares themselves for the future. As a matter of survival, businesses and organizations must respond to market needs faster and more accurately, improve product cost and quality, and anticipate technological changes. In order to accomplish this, companies must formulate clear technological objectives which are integrated with and support the firm's strategic goals. Strategic Information Systems Planning and the integration of new technology will allow companies to face the challenges and opportunities that lie ahead.

KEVIN G. COLEMAN